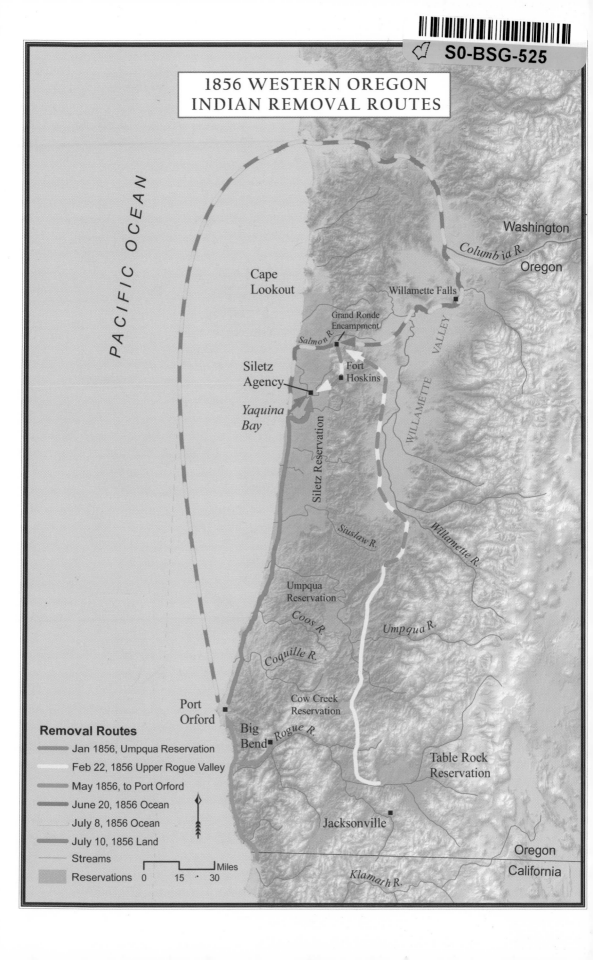

1856 WESTERN OREGON INDIAN REMOVAL ROUTES

PACIFIC OCEAN

Washington

Oregon

Columbia R.

Cape Lookout

Willamette Falls

Grand Ronde Encampment

Salmon R.

Siletz Agency

Fort Hoskins

WILLAMETTE VALLEY

Yaquina Bay

Siletz Reservation

Siuslaw R.

Willamette R.

Umpqua Reservation

Coos R.

Umpqua R.

Coquille R.

Port Orford

Cow Creek Reservation

Big Bend

Rogue R.

Table Rock Reservation

Removal Routes

Jan 1856, Umpqua Reservation
Feb 22, 1856 Upper Rogue Valley
May 1856, to Port Orford
June 20, 1856 Ocean
July 8, 1856 Ocean
July 10, 1856 Land
Streams
Reservations

0   15   30   Miles

Jacksonville

Oregon

California

Klamath R.

The People Are Dancing Again

The PEOPLE *Are* DANCING AGAIN

The History of the Siletz Tribe of Western Oregon

CHARLES WILKINSON

UNIVERSITY OF WASHINGTON PRESS

Seattle & London

UNIVERSITY OF WASHINGTON PRESS
P.O. Box 50096, Seattle, WA 98145 U.S.A.
www.washington.edu/uwpress

LIBRARY OF CONGRESS CATALOGING-IN-PUBLICATION DATA
Wilkinson, Charles F., 1941–
The people are dancing again : the history of the Siletz tribe of western Oregon /
Charles Wilkinson.
p. cm.
Includes bibliographical references and index.
ISBN 978-0-295-99066-8 (hardback : acid-free paper)
1. Siletz Indians—History.
2. Siletz Indians—Government relations.
3. Siletz Indians—Politics and government.
4. Indians of North America—Oregon—History.
5. Indians of North America—Oregon—Government relations.
6. Indians of North America—Oregon—Politics and government.
I. Title.
E99.S544W45 2010
979.5'10049794—dc22   2010022917

The paper used in this publication is acid-free and 90 percent recycled from at least 50 percent post-consumer waste. It meets the minimum requirements of American National Standard for Information Sciences—Permanence of Paper for Printed Library Materials, ANSI Z39.48-1984.∞

FRONTISPIECE: Emma John, circa 1900 (see page 44).
Photograph courtesy of the Lincoln County Historical Society.

For the Ancestors

CONTENTS

MAPS

PREFACE

I LOVE DRIVING IN THE AMERICAN WEST. ONE OF MY FAVORITE trips is from Eugene over to Siletz, which lies about six miles from the Oregon Coast. This two-hour journey, which I've made many times, is emotional and central to me beyond the saying.

After heading north to Corvallis, I take a left turn and drive due west on Route 20. As I pass through Philomath, where the agricultural Willamette Valley gives way to forest, and climb toward the low crest of the Coast Range, the old, heavy mix of land and time and human experience and right and wrong wells up and takes over. Then, at a point a few miles east of Eddyville, I pull over and park.

There, on the eastern edge of the great 1855 Siletz Treaty Reservation, I walk up an old logging road and take some time to think and feel. This border, twenty-four miles by road from the coastal town of Newport, stretched a full 105 miles north to south, beginning well south of Eugene and reaching all the way to what are now the southern suburbs of Portland. The reservation encompassed 1.1 million acres, 1,700 square miles, nearly 2 percent of Oregon, and took in the magnificent spruce, cedar, and Douglas fir forests in the Coast Range and all the salmon rivers feeding the ocean and, on the edge of the sea, the rocks and beaches and points and capes and mussels and oyster beds and seals and sea lions and seaweed and sea anemone. It all belonged to the Siletz, and they belonged to it. The treaty called it their "permanent residence." In return for that promise, skilled and tenacious warriors agreed to lay down their weapons.

Words and honor were no match for greed and shortsightedness. The United States of America prides itself on the justice it has wrought. There have

been times, though, when dispossessed peoples have been ground under—
and the breakup of the Siletz Reservation, one of the finest Indian reserves
ever created, is one of those dark and stained episodes.

I have made the drive from Eugene to Corvallis so often because I once represented the Siletz Tribe as their lawyer. Chairman Joe Lane and Vice Chairman Robert Rilatos came out to Boulder, Colorado, in early 1975 and asked
the Native American Rights Fund to represent the tribe. I was a staff attorney
with NARF at the time and had worked on the Menominee Restoration Act,
passed by Congress in 1973, which made the Menominee of Wisconsin the
first terminated tribe to be restored to full federal recognition. (*Termination*,
official federal Indian policy in the 1950s and later roundly repudiated, called
for cutting off the federal relationship, including treaty obligations, with a
number of tribes. *Restoration* is the term for statutes repealing termination
laws and reinstating those tribes.) Joe, Robert, and others at Siletz were determined to make the Siletz the second terminated tribe to achieve restoration.

NARF decided to take on the Siletz cause and assigned me to work on it.
Later that year, I joined the law faculty at the University of Oregon, where I
spent twelve especially important years of my life. As a professor, I continued
my work with the tribe.

Siletz restoration was not intrinsically controversial, but any Indian cause
faced stiff opposition in the charged atmosphere of the Northwest fish wars.
The Siletz restoration proposal became a prominent and contentious political
issue in the state, and I found myself immersed in the politics, society, and
landscape of Oregon. The experience reached to the quick of me. I came to
love the state—its coast-valley-mountains-high desert magnificence and its
progressive social and political bent. I also gave my heart to the Siletz Tribe,
among whom I made lifelong friends and gained a deep-dyed admiration for
the way they have survived their brutal history.

After passage of the two statutes necessary to achieve restoration, in 1977
and 1980, I stepped down as tribal attorney so that a practicing lawyer could deal
with the full range of tribal legal matters in a way that a working professor could
not. I kept up with people at Siletz over the years and visited a number of times.

In late 2004, out of the blue, the tribe asked me to write a tribal history.
At that moment—having just finished one book and enjoying the process of
deciding what the next one might be—I was in one of my favorite times of life.

I pondered, but not for long. This was the journey I wanted to take. I mentioned to Chairman Delores Pigsley and the Siletz Tribal Council that I would need complete freedom. I'm passionate about this subject—why else would a person invest all the years it takes to write a book?—but you don't get good history unless the author is open-minded, clear-eyed, rigorous, and above all independent. The Siletz leaders plainly understood that and easily agreed.

I hold no degree in history but I have always viewed the world through that lens. From my first law review article to the present, my scholarship has been heavily weighted with history and most of my books have been histories or heavily reliant on history. In beginning this book, I was keenly aware of the mostly unhappy terrain of tribal histories. All too often, they have been written from the point of view of the white world. That perspective is surely relevant; after all, there is no doubting the pervasive presence of non-Indians in tribal histories ever since contact with outsiders. And it is not a matter of venality: most works display genuine sympathy for the tribal peoples. Yet much of the scholarship fails to examine critically the explicit and subtle stereotypes about Indians, convey the humanity of Indian people, and present the Indian voice. Fortunately, recent scholarship, especially now that increasing numbers of Native scholars are at work, is beginning to alter this pattern.

I made up my mind to present the Siletz side as best I could, along with a full and fair rendition of non-Native accounts. The key, as I saw it, was to honor the Native voice. I and my research assistants—Gregg de Bie, Josh Tenneson, Maria Aparicio, Carrie Covington, Alison Flint, Matt Samelson, and Daniel Cordalis—conducted more than one hundred interviews, mostly with Siletz tribal members.

In my work with Indian peoples over nearly forty years, I have come to stand in awe of the accuracy and extent of their accounts of historical events. I don't mean to overstate this. There are variations among tribes as to the strength of the oral tradition. Also, tribal cultures have been assaulted by official policies of the larger society, and the passage of information by the oral tradition has been fractured in various ways and to varying degrees. Some of the information is simply inaccurate. But the larger truth is that contemporary Indians and their forebears hold a treasure trove of valuable historical information. I do not believe it is possible to write an accurate tribal history without tapping deeply into this knowledge.

Native peoples tend to pay careful attention to their own tribal and family histories. Indian tribes are place-based societies, and most have resided on their lands for millennia. They think of themselves as being part of the natural world, lodged in it, organic with it. The history of their place is part of their being.

American society, on the other hand, is so mobile. This is not to deny that some non-Indian Americans have profound attachments to place. In the American West, I know ranch and farm families who have lived on their land for five, six, or even seven generations. But most Americans are like me. I possess a pitiful amount of family history, having only the vaguest sense of my mother's parents and their lives in Michigan and of my father's parents in Atlanta.

We are suspicious, consciously and unconsciously, of oral history, where much Native history is found. We mostly leave our understanding of history to books. Tribal people, who traditionally lacked words written on pages, have a different mechanism for recording history. Certain people had the duty of receiving the oral accounts accurately and passing them on in the same fashion. In addition to those with formal responsibility, it is my experience that Indian people generally try hard to learn their own tribal histories through the accounts handed down orally.

Native oral history, like printed-page history, can be wrong. But in the course of my exposure to it, I have found the accuracy and depth of the Native accounts to be—as with good printed-page history—informative, reliable, and sometimes stunningly revelatory.

So it has been with my interviews with Siletz people and the accounts they gave to anthropologists and historians in existing printed-page sources. This tribal knowledge allows for extensive insights into early history, including life before Europeans came, the epic Rogue River War and removals of whole tribes to the Siletz Reservation, and reservation life during the chaotic years when some twenty-eight separate tribes and bands were thrown together under the iron rule of the U.S. Army and the Bureau of Indian Affairs.

I found another extraordinary source of information in the form of a new kind of scholar—the tribal historian. Robert Kentta and Bud Lane, both Siletz tribal members, grew up hearing the oral history from the elders. They also steeped themselves in the printed-page history of western Oregon as it bears upon the tribes. Further, they learned from elders the dances, songs, language, and weaving, all of which led to a still deeper understanding of the history. My knowledge of Siletz history pales in comparison with their deep, comprehensive grasp of the Siletz experience. They gave a good two thousand hours to this book, and I lack the words to express my gratitude and admiration. Tribal historians are found on other reservations, and their work, like Robert's and Bud's, is central to the modern revival of Indian tribal culture, history, and sovereignty.

❦

As my work wore on, I realized that writing a tribal history should go a step beyond interviewing tribal people, working broadly with them, and attempting to bring tribal knowledge and voice into the book. A tribe also has the right to review the manuscript and react to it. This promotes accuracy. It also allows tribal members to raise objections to portrayals and conclusions. It is up to the author to resolve any differences, but the tribe should be heard out, loud and clear.

For this book, I met first with Lane, Kentta, and Pigsley to review the first two chapters of the manuscript, which address the aboriginal experience. Professor Rebecca Dobkins, an anthropologist from Willamette University, and Marianne Keddington-Lang, my sponsoring editor at the University of Washington Press, also participated in the meeting, as did three of my research assistants. We gathered for a full day on the Oregon Coast, at the Bureau of Land Management interpretive center for the Yaquina Head Outstanding Natural Area, and went through the two chapters page by page. The session was exhilarating—a detailed, far-ranging, and fascinating discussion of aboriginal Siletz culture that strengthened the manuscript in countless ways.

For a review of the whole manuscript, I met with the Siletz Tibal Council (Lane and Kentta are both council members) in a retreat setting at the tribe's conference facility on the Coast for two-and-a-half long days. Dobkins and Keddington-Lang again participated, as did two of my research assistants. This page-by-page discussion also identified many areas that needed to be corrected or refined and, as well, drew out several new matters that needed to be explored.

The tone of those discussions with the council was especially memorable. Siletz history, like that of other tribes, comes in three broad time periods: the aboriginal times, which from the tribal perspective are positive; the period of contact with whites, from the late 1700s through the 1950s, when land rights, sovereignty, and culture were relentlessly battered; and the modern era since the 1960s, which again is a generally positive time for Indian people. Most of the pages in this book relate the middle era. The pain was palpable in the room when we worked through those manuscript chapters, which recounted the insults to Native peoples' lifeways and human rights. Still, the council members trudged on with determined professionalism, focused on getting it right no matter how wrong the march of history often was.

I am indebted to many people for their assistance with this book, and I thank them formally in the Acknowledgments. But the greatest credit by far goes to the Siletz people, from this century back to those distant ancestors whose words have been preserved in writing and in memory. My name is on this volume, but they brought to it more essential details and concepts than could ever be counted. If these pages prove to be accurate and useful history, then let it be clear that Siletz people made it so.

When I began this book, I conceived of its central purpose as being to chronicle an important swath of American history, one that encompasses events that the nation can be proud of and a much larger number of events that it cannot. As my writing went on, I found myself focusing ever more on one improbable historic fact: the tribe's survival. Given the forces levied against them, how can there be a Siletz Tribe?

John Steinbeck, in a passage I keep in front of me on my desk, spoke about the essential attributes of the human condition in his acceptance address upon receiving the Nobel Prize for Literature in 1962. He alluded to "our many grievous faults and failures." But he also urged us to "celebrate man's proven capacity for greatness of heart and spirit—for gallantry in defeat—for courage, compassion and love. In the endless war against weakness and despair, these are the bright rally-flags of hope and emulation."

For generations, Siletz people have endured conflicts on battlefields in the Upper Rogue River Valley, in the middle Rogue wilderness, and on the Coast; in recurring councils with white people anxious for Native land; in classrooms and work places; in courthouses and state houses. They continued on, with almost every encounter a losing one, in the soul-deep belief in the worth and beauty of their ancient community systems of respect and sharing; their baskets, songs, dances, and gods; and their land.

What staying power. What courage, compassion, and love. What gallantry in defeat. What greatness of heart and spirit. Ultimately, it is those qualities, and the light and inspiration they offer to all of us, that most distinguish the history of the Siletz Tribe of Indians.

The People Are Dancing Again

INTRODUCTION:
TABLE ROCKS, 2003

S ILETZ PEOPLE, SOME THREE TO FOUR HUNDRED OF THEM, CAME to the Table Rocks area in the late summer of 2003 to commemorate, not celebrate. They gathered outside modern-day Medford on the groomed grounds of Tou Velle State Park, with its mature oak and pine trees, to hear reflective speeches, socialize at a salmon bake, and, come dusk, revel in traditional dances, with dancers in full regalia. The weather matched the journal entries of the "bright, beautiful" day, a century and a half past, that drew them here.

To a person, the assembled Indians gave their thoughts and hearts to this place. They could look north across the Rogue River, large but smooth running in this level terrain, toward the imposing south face of Lower Table Rock. Four million years ago, a river of lava from the volcanic Cascade Mountains rushed into the valley. The lava hardened, but eons of river, rain, and wind ate most of it away, leaving the most distinctive formations in the Upper Rogue River Valley: Table Rocks, two flat-topped, 800-foot-tall mesas with sheer rim-rock cliffs.

The scene brought remembrance and gravity to the occasion. For Native Americans, the Table Rocks have always exuded power and spirituality. The flanks grow a variety of vegetation, from bunch grasses near the valley floor up through chaparral, madrona, and Oregon white oak to ponderosa pine stands. On top, seeps and vernal pools support a profusion of roots, wildflowers, and animal communities, including deer. The eye roams far out in every direction, with tall Mount McLoughlin—at 9,500 feet the highest peak in this part of the Cascade Range—rising forty miles directly to the east. When she

3

Lower Table Rock, shown here in an 1877 engraving of a photograph by Peter Britt. Two Indians are sitting on the south bank of the Rogue River. *Courtesy of Oregon Historical Society, no. bb006740.*

goes there, Agnes Pilgrim can "feel the spirit world, I feel our people, I have tears in my eyes."

Still, for all the surrounding wonder, the air was filled with solemnity, not joy, on this occasion that marked the 150th anniversary of the signing of the Table Rock Treaty on September 10, 1853.

To be sure, the proceedings on that distant day, cloaked in formality and earnestness and witnessed by nearly one thousand people in the old Oregon Territory, carried great significance. This was the first congressionally ratified Indian land treaty in the American West. The United States obtained a great deal of land from the Takelmas, Shastas, and Applegate Athapaskans, signatories to the treaty. In return, the United States guaranteed the tribes a permanent homeland. And the 1853 treaty held out the prospect, fervently

Lower and Upper Table Rocks, with the Cascade Range in the far background. Nearly all of the tops and flanks of these iconic, 800-foot-tall southern Oregon formations are now owned by the Bureau of Land Management or by The Nature Conservancy, which designates its area as a nature preserve with hiking trails. *Courtesy of Oregon Historical Society, no. bb006756.*

desired by both the federal government and the tribe, of stemming the killing and bleeding from one of the most destructive of all Indian wars.

Yet, from the Indian side, the solemn promises made at Table Rocks came to naught. The only lasting words are those extinguishing Takelma, Shasta, and Applegate landownership. Otherwise, the treaty accelerated the decline—fueled by wars and epidemics of European diseases—that the Indians of western Oregon had suffered ever since contact with the whites.

The Siletz Tribe that held the 2003 gathering is a confederation. That is, the United States recognizes the tribe as a single sovereign government even though it is comprised of dozens of separate ethnological tribes and bands. The origins of the Confederated Tribes of Siletz Indians, its formal name, trace to the 1853 treaty, the first federal recognition of tribes in the confederation.

A year later, the three signatory tribes agreed under duress to an open-ended supplementary treaty allowing the United States to add to the confederation (but not to the reservation land area) by moving additional tribes to the Table Rock Reservation with those new tribes to "enjoy equal rights and privileges."

The terms of the Table Rock Treaty of 1853 did not hold. The principal speaker at the commemoration, Robert Kentta, Siletz tribal member and cultural director for the tribe, tall and forceful in a gentle way, put it to his fellow tribespeople in words true to history: Indian people and the treaty itself were assaulted by "white men suffering from gold fever devoid of sense and recognizing no law." And so miners swarmed over the land in spite of the treaty, and hostilities broke out again. The United States terminated the Table Rock Reservation and, as allowed by the 1853 treaty, President Franklin Pierce proclaimed in 1855 an expansive reservation on the Oregon Coast with headquarters at Siletz. Federal officials, with military support, then moved tribes from all over western Oregon to the newly proclaimed Coast Reservation, thereby adding many tribes to the confederated tribe created at Table Rocks. (Contemporaneously, as part of this hasty and often arbitrary series of events, other western Oregon Indians were moved to a temporary encampment at Grand Ronde to the east of Siletz, later to become the reservation of the Confederated Tribes of Grand Ronde.)

The forced removal from homelands and the attendant consolidation of distinct peoples on the Coast Reservation—this massive display of social engineering, the largest confederation of Indian tribes in the country—brought heartbreak, confusion, illness, injury, and death. The transportation of Indians from the south and the north to Siletz was done by terrifying voyages on jam-packed, ocean-going vessels and by laborious, lock-step, overland marches along the rugged Oregon Coast. At the 2003 event at Table Rocks, Professor David Hubin, historian and executive assistant to the president of the University of Oregon, described the removals as "abrupt and cruel. Being forcibly relocated from a land as beautiful and traditional as this is horrendous."

Just as geography made the relocations difficult, so too did it shape the traditional cultures. In aboriginal times, most of the people moved onto the Siletz Reservation lived in villages in the Rogue River watershed and up and down the Oregon Coast. The terrain is mountainous and broken up by many rivers and streams. Separate tribes, with languages and dialects of their own, controlled watersheds and sub-watersheds. Despite the tribal differences—and sometimes rivalries—these societies were thrown together against their will. For the United States, removal and confederation were matters of administrative convenience.

For the tribes, all ability to resist gone, they had no choice, hard though it was, but to accommodate to a new and desperately different reality.

At least they had the land and, however foreign it may have been to many of the tribes, what a land the 1855 Coast Reservation was. Spectacularly endowed with coastal seafood, game, and commercial timber, it was one of the largest and most magnificent of all Indian reservations. The 1853 treaty guaranteed that this reservation would be their "permanent residence."

The Coast Reservation, like Table Rock, could not hold. Settlers and timber companies wanted the land and they got it, save a few thousand acres, by the end of the nineteenth century. Then, in 1954, Congress "terminated" the remnants of the tribe and its land.

It was all gone. The broad beaches and the misty forests. The oyster beds and the fishing rocks for salmon. The sacred sites, Table Rocks, Medicine Rock, Neahkahnie Mountain, Saddle Mountain, all the others. The places for gathering medicines. The dance places. The burial places.

In 2003 the gathering at Table Rocks drew many tears over wrongs to land and culture. How could the land be taken so quickly, so summarily? How could hundreds of generations of possession be erased in just a blink of time?

The wonder of it all is that there ever could have been a commemoration in 2003, and that is the other and better part of the Siletz story. The tribe regrouped in the 1970s and, though poor and small in numbers, persuaded Congress to reverse the termination statute of 1954, restore federal recognition to the Siletz Tribe, and establish a small reservation. Since then, all the trend lines for health, education, and economic well-being have gone steadily up. The tribal government carries out valuable functions. The Siletz have brought back tribal traditions. Among them is a return to Nee Dosh, the traditional feather dance, that appropriately topped off the 2003 Table Rocks commemoration at dusk, as the buck-skinned dancers in their basket caps swung into the old rhythms, with Bud Lane leading the songs sung in Athapaskan, all done to the sweet music of jingling dentalia and abalone shells that adorn the women's regalia.

It is this aggregation of loss and revival, subjugation and self-determination, sadness and joy, that makes up the essence of Siletz history and that infused the remarks of Robert Kentta amid the cross-currents of emotions at Table Rocks. "Our people have many hurts to be healed," he concluded slowly. "Let us remember to be kind to each other and to help each other along the way, toward better days for all our people. We have much to be proud of. Today we celebrate our survival . . . against all odds."

PART ONE

THE LONG ABORIGINAL EXISTENCE

VILLAGE SOCIETIES INLAID IN THE LAND

"Every year we go to the center of our world."

B Y FAR, THE GREATEST PART OF WESTERN OREGON INDIAN HIS-
tory took place over the course of thousands of years before the arrival
of Europeans. The paper record is sparse. These aboriginal societies
left no written accounts. We have some journal entries and letters, dating to
the late 1700s and early 1800s, by European visitors who set forth their observations and recounted conversations with Natives. Anthropologists began to
conduct scholarly interviews with western Oregon Indians much later, beginning around 1900 with a surge in the 1930s. Many of the people interviewed
lived in the 1840s and 1850s. While by then the population had been dramatically reduced by European diseases, they experienced tribal life when it was
still largely intact and they heard stories from many years before that. Further,
and critically, the exacting oral tradition has kept aspects of centuries-old history alive and known by contemporary Siletz tribal people.

One core principle of Oregon aboriginal life stands out, as it does for
Native people everywhere: the land threatens, shapes, and enriches human
life. Just as the Sioux lived in lodges of bison hide and pursued the herds
across broad stretches of the Great Plains for sustenance and the Pueblo people lived in homes of adobe and farmed with the Southwest's bright sunlight,
so too were the cultures of western Oregon embedded in that dramatic landscape—at once harsh and giving—of gusty shores, strong rivers, thick forests,
open meadows and valleys, and lofty peaks.

The nature of aboriginal life is directly relevant to an understanding of
modern Siletz society. The old ways, under assault by 125 years of assimilation-

ist pressures, went dormant but never died out. Over the past two generations, in a profound and moving saga, the Siletz people have engaged in a cultural revitalization. While they live in American society and embrace it in many ways, tribal members made up their minds to do the painstaking work, step by step, of bringing back old traditions. The creation story is told again, the baskets are woven, the dentalium shells strung, the language taught. Acorns, eels, camas, and other traditional foods grace family and potluck tables. Nee Dosh, also called feather dance or the ten-day dance, carried out in the cedar dance house, is again a grand occasion. Love of the land, respect for elders, and nurturing the young are values seriously discussed and practiced.

It cannot again be the way it was. Cultures evolve and being part of American society brings many benefits—and life before the white people, while good, had its challenges. Still, the traditional ways have inspired Siletz people, despite all the forces of eradication, to make their ancient history a living part of today's world as well.

In their own stories, Native people have lived in the landscape of western Oregon as long as there has been time. For their part, modern archaeologists have determined through excavations of Paisley Cave and Fort Rock Cave that people first reached the south-central portion of Oregon at least 14,300 years ago and lived in the Willamette Valley between 8,000 and 9,000 years ago. Pinpointing the arrival of the first inhabitants to the Oregon Coast has been more difficult. The ocean submerged many ancient village sites over the millennia, as rising sea levels and sinking coastlines left what scholars call a "dearth of early [known] sites." Nonetheless, authenticated archaeological sites along and near the Oregon Coast indicate the presence of people between 6,000 and 10,000 years ago. Permanent settlements, with societies fully ensconced in the land-river-ocean environment, date back at least 4,000 to 5,000 years. Field research steadily pushes these dates farther back in time.

An estimated 50,000 people lived on the Coast, along the lower Columbia River, and in the Willamette and other inland valleys. Cultures were dynamic over the millennia before contact with non-Indians, evolving as political institutions matured; commercial relationships expanded over larger areas; hunting, fishing, and gathering techniques grew more sophisticated; and religions became more elaborate.

The village was the center of social, political, and economic life. Steep-sided mountains and hills hugged much of the Oregon Coast, but a dozen or so large rivers and many smaller ones broke through with their canyons and ravines, making a chopped-up, rugged landscape. Each of these watersheds was home to villages, ranging from a few families to several hundred people, at the river mouth and upriver on the main stem and major tributaries.

North-south travel on foot was often arduous and the most extensive intervillage relationships tended to follow river systems. Villages within each watershed traded with one another, used the same trails and sometimes the same sacred sites, held social events and athletic competitions, and made accommodations in those years when the precious salmon runs were down. Land-based peoples, they inevitably felt a strong connection with others who pulled salmon from the same runs, hunted the same deer herds, worshipped from the same mountain tops, spoke the same language, and lived with the same tides and rains and stars.

In spite of the difficulties of travel, villages carried on relationships beyond their watersheds. Groups traveled on an extensive trail system—along which most modern highways and roads have been constructed—for the same kinds of reasons as they did within watersheds, and runners used the trails to spread news. Large, sturdy ocean canoes allowed for trade south to today's California and north to Puget Sound and Vancouver Island. Every village's social and economic contacts radiated out in all directions.

In describing the original societies, the newcomers often departed from this village system. Anthropologists, political scientists, and American treaty negotiators grouped villages, based on their perceptions of language groups and geographical proximity, into what they called tribes, such as Tututni, Chetco, Takelma, and Tillamook. Those classifications are mostly arbitrary constructs of outsiders. In other words, a person designated by the anthro-pologists or treaty negotiators as "Tututni" would be surprised to be identified by that name unless he or she came from the village of Tututin—the name that non-Indians applied to the entire language group. Still, these definitions of tribes can be useful today in understanding Native societies because they refer to groups of villages that had social and economic ties and affinities of language and geography. Also, the term "tribe" has been used for so long and so often in scholarship, laws, and public discourse (including by Indian people themselves) that it would be artificial to try to deny its validity for some pur-poses, especially in modern times.

Despite the commonality among villages, each individual village—not an artificial notion of a "tribe"—had political authority and was autonomous.

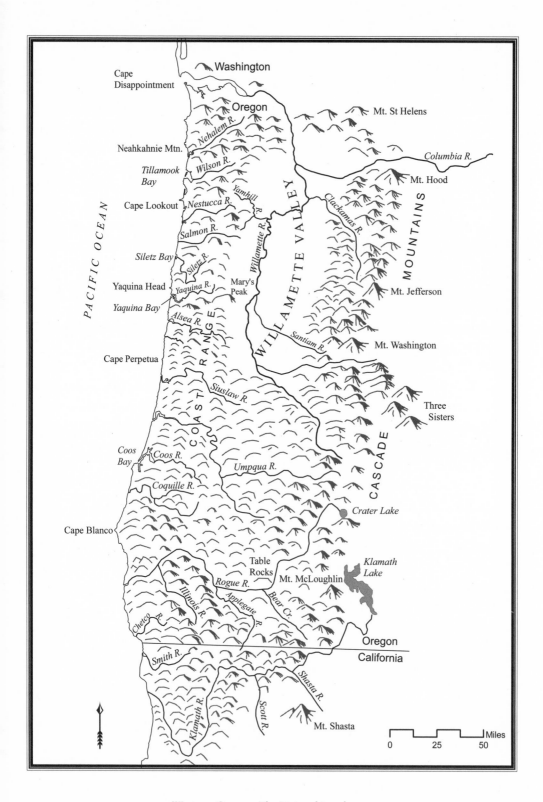

Western Oregon: The Natural Landscape

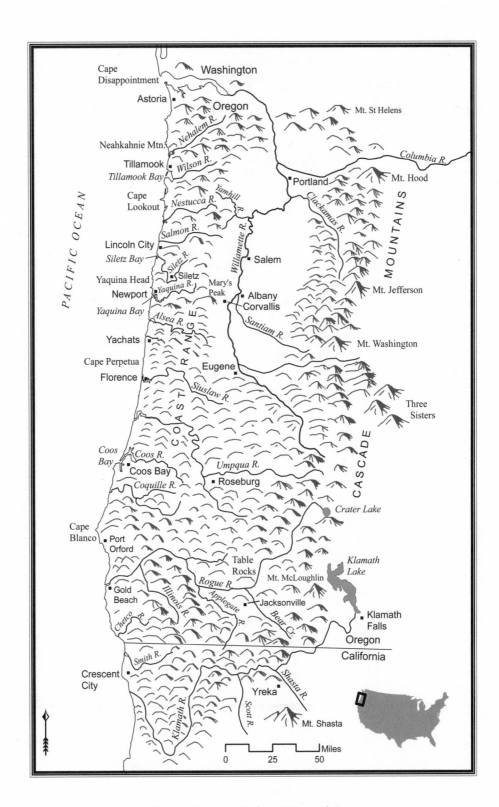

Western Oregon: Modern Cities and Towns

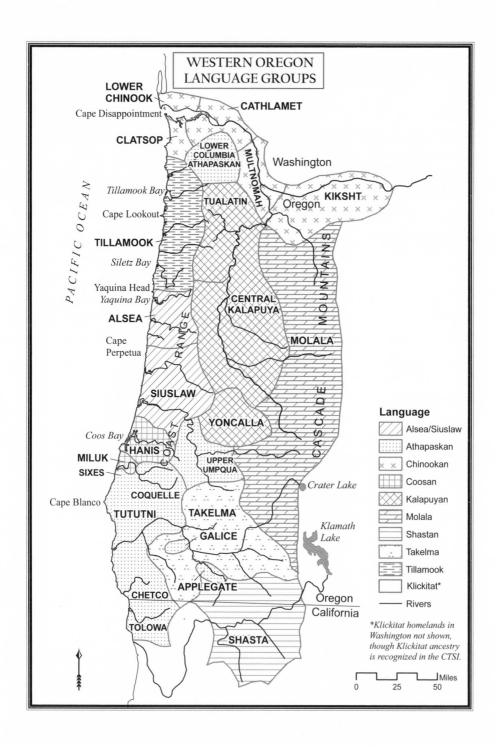

WESTERN OREGON
LANGUAGE GROUPS

Language

- ⬈ Alsea/Siuslaw
- ⋮ Athapaskan
- ✕ Chinookan
- ▦ Coosan
- ▨ Kalapuyan
- ☐ Molala
- ☐ Shastan
- · Takelma
- ▦ Tillamook
- ☐ Klickitat*
- — Rivers

*Klickitat homelands in
Washington not shown,
though Klickitat ancestry
is recognized in the CTSI.*

Miles
0   25   50

Each village exercised its sovereignty, its governmental authority, through an elaborate system of laws and enforcement mechanisms that determined both internal matters and relationships with other villages. In the common marriage laws that bound the villages together, these societies were exogamous—the men always took their brides from other villages and the women became citizens of their new places.

The village as a place carries powerful emotional content. The multidimensional Athapaskan word *duh-neh* means "the people of the place" and also encompasses "the blood line." It is "the place where your family has always been buried." There is no comparable concept in the English language, and I have seen Siletz people strain to articulate the intensity and specificity of the term. The village is at once concrete and dynamic. While it is a fixed place on the land and the people are tied to it, the population changes because of births, deaths, and the law of intermarriage, causing some people (women) to move from one village to another. Yet, for both men and women the tie to the village is immutable. *Duh-neh*: This is the one place where a person is from, where all the people all the way back are from, where the ancestors are buried. This is the only place, the heart place. There can be no other place.

One of the most populated places in aboriginal western Oregon was along the southern Coast where the Rogue River reaches the Pacific, at a level, spread-out stretch of sand beaches. This is the aboriginal territory of what Europeans called the Tututni Tribe, encompassing Athapaskan villages that account for a significant part of the membership of the modern Siletz Tribe. Tututni country reached north to the Sixes River, upriver on the Rogue fifteen miles or so, and south to the Pistol River. The Tututni villages populated nearly every river and stream flowing into the ocean and many of their tributaries.

The largest village, named Tututin and meaning "People of the Water Place," was located inland on the Rogue River. Life in that village reflects society in the other Tututni villages and, as well, the Athapaskan villages to the south, including the Chetco and the Tolowa tribes of the Smith River watershed in northern California. Even more broadly, all the tribes of western Oregon and their villages had a great deal in common with the Tututni and its major village. While every tribe had its cultural variations and some tribes to the north developed entirely different practices (for example, the forehead flattening of the Alsea, Tillamook, Clatsop, Chinook, and Kalapuya), the way

SOUTHWEST OREGON ATHAPASKAN
LANGUAGE GROUPS

of life at Tututin generally represents the worldviews and the social, political, and economic organization of the aboriginal peoples of western Oregon.

The people established Tututin close to the full-bodied Rogue River about six to seven miles inland. The village, oriented to the southeast to capture light and the warmth of sunny days, sat on a low bluff in an open meadow that paralleled the river for nearly a mile. Behind the settlement, the dense, nearly impenetrable, cedar-spruce-hemlock forest rose up sharply to a ridge high above the river. The town, one of the largest Athapaskan settlements, surely held a population of several hundred residents in aboriginal times. In all, Athapaskans on the south Coast totaled 4,500 before the lethal epidemics hit.

Tututin was an active place, a center for trade, dances, games, and socializing. Visitors regularly came in by canoe and trail, sometimes from distant villages, more often from smaller, neighboring settlements, some of which can fairly be called suburbs. Wolverton Orton said that "Tutuden was a big town and [the people] used to be out lots nights." It was, he laughed, like "a modern big town of the whites."

The village was made up of three distinct areas. For habitation, the Tututni had "living houses" and sweathouses. The living houses, of which there were dozens, were large, made possible by the gift of western redcedar, the durable softwood that the men split with wedges to make planks. The houses at Tututin ranged from 10 feet square to 20 by 30 feet, the largest an abode of the tyee, or headman. They were partly subterranean, dug down 3 or 4 feet. The men set the planks vertically to form the house sides and then laid longer planks for the roof, leaving a smoke hole above the cooking hearth. The sweathouses, similar in construction but fewer and smaller, were in continual use. Men and boys slept in groups in the sweathouses, although the men would visit their wives in the living houses during the evenings. Fathers instructed their sons and prepared for hunts there. Coquelle Thompson, who grew up in an Athapaskan village, recalled that "the teller of these stories was always seated in the middle of the sweathouse and told long stories in the dark." Those stories and the times with the men instilled in Thompson "the values and worldview that he carried with him through his long life. It was in the sweathouse that he, and the generations of men before him, learned who they were."

The living houses were the women's place for grinding acorns, cooking, and making baskets and clothing. In more densely populated villages such as Tututin, a separate work space was located away from the living area, where villagers butchered fish and game; shelled oysters and clams; chipped flint; constructed canoes; and worked bones, antlers, and shells for tools and regalia. This labor of daily life produced a refuse pile of leftover materials. In the larger villages, the cemetery would be separated from the living areas to assure peace for the ancestors. In smaller villages, however, refuse piles would be closer to the houses and, in some cases, provided a location for burial. Later, the refuse piles—called middens—would be important resources for archaeologists, since they provided valuable information about diet, work, and other aspects of day-to-day life.

All of Tututin—the young people, the adults, even the ancestors in the cemetery—found deep personal meaning and identity in the mighty Rogue River, which ran in their bloodstreams. The sounds of its current filled the air, murmuring in the strong but smooth eighty-yard-wide stretch opposite the village, roaring loud in the rapids just downstream. It had always been this way, always would be.

Clockwise from top: Wolverton Orton, Tututni (village of Tututin), with Kate Orton and Lucy (Smith) Dann. Courtesy of Curry County Historical Society; Lucy Metcalf, Tututni (village of Tututin). Siletz Tribal Collection; William Smith, Alsea, and Louisa Smith, Siuslaw. Siletz Tribal Collection; Lucy Smith, Tututni (village of Yah-shu-eh). Siletz Tribal Collection.

A large and valuable body of Siletz history was reported by Indian consultants to anthropologists. For generations, relatively few scholars came to the remote Siletz Reservation, with Leo Frachtenberg doing the most extensive work during his many visits in the early twentieth century. By the 1930s, however, Siletz became a hot spot for academic research because so many diverse languages were represented. Among other anthropologists, Melville Jacobs, Elizabeth Jacobs, John Harrington, Cora Du Bois, and Philip Drucker

The Rogue. Shallow near the shores, a clear dark blue out in the center. The chinook and the coho, huge, magical runs, runs without end. A "free highway," the Tututnis called it, to ride the cedar canoes to visit relatives in other villages and to take food from the ocean. The river marked the beginning of each day for the men, who sweated in their steamy lodges and then dove into the bracing water before heading to the living houses for their morning meals. For the people of Tututin, this was *duh-neh*, their place, the only place.

The river and the weather combined to create the rhythms of life for the people of Tututin. A key shift took place in early spring, when the winter clouds and bitter winds began to break and harbingered more than crisp, bright days and warmer nights. Months of hard, coordinated work lay ahead for the village. A lot was at stake. Provisions had to be laid in, for the storms and chill rains would come around again.

Food gathering moved into high gear in late March or early April, as the spring freshets, snowmelt from the watershed's high country, were about to raise the level of the Rogue and make river travel possible for returning salmon. This was the pivotal time, for it signified the spring run of the chinook, bound for their home spawning beds to lay and fertilize their eggs. The Rogue also entertained runs of coho salmon, steelhead, and eels (also called lampreys), as well as resident rainbow trout, but the chinook were the biggest prize, with their ruby red, nutritious meat and enormous size—up to a hundred pounds. All food, including the salmon, was common property, available to everyone in the village.

When the timing was right, Tututnis paddled downriver to the beaches where the Rogue enters the Pacific. There they met families from Yah-shu-eh (sometimes called "Joshua") and other Athapaskan villages and reunited in the annual sacred task of assuring that the salmon would once more return.

To guide and welcome the runs of chinook making their way back from the far reaches of the Gulf of Alaska, the people built a driftwood bonfire of gigantic proportions and torched the brushy hillsides. The light and smoke were visible up and down the Coast and far out to sea. Late into the night, the men danced with fervor and urgency near the pulsing heat of the fire and

---

conducted fieldwork during the 1930s and 1940s. They were able to interview elders in their late seventies and older who lived in traditional fashion in their ancestral villages before being uprooted and moved to the reservation. With the exception of Wolverton Orton, who was born in 1874, the consultants shown here lived in their villages before removal.

The Lower Rogue River. *Photograph courtesy of Lee O. Webb.*

sang out the proper songs to bring the chinook back. The dancing and singing and spectacular displays of flames and sparks and smoke carried on for many nights. When the chinook finally arrived, the families cheered and celebrated the success, once again, of this joined enterprise. Then it was time to return to their villages for another annual ritual manifesting their ties to the natural world.

Before the active harvesting began, the Tututnis, like all northwestern tribes, conducted the first salmon ceremony. At the beginning of the initial run, the people of the village assembled and the first salmon was cooked over an alder fire. A religious leader offered thanks to the fish for returning once again, and before the eating (everyone got a piece of the first salmon, even if only a sliver), the villagers sent out their private thoughts of gratitude. This giving of respect to the salmon—and in other settings to deer and elk, roots and berries, and other gifts from the land and waters—was not some romantic construct. The Tututnis saw themselves as part of the natural world, as citizens along with the plants and animals, and it was proper to show apprecia-

PART ONE. THE LONG ABORIGINAL EXISTENCE

tion. There was a practical aspect as well: they feared that the great fish might not come back if proper respect were not shown.

Salmon harvesting required reliable equipment, strength, and hard work. The fishers constructed fixed weirs—shaped like a V, with the open end facing downstream—with alder frames and a net of hazel or spruce roots or the branches of the sinewy streamside willow bushes. Dipnets and spears were widely used. The large, rounded rocks in front of Tututin made excellent platforms for netting and spearing, with the farthest-out rock the best spot of all. Once the fishers wrestled the struggling salmon out of the water and up onto the bank, the women took over. They butchered the fish and slow-smoked them on alder racks over low fires in smokehouses, which were open sheds.

Late in the spring and summer, the women gathered roots, bulbs, and berries in the woods and clearings. Tututnis ate the salmonberries fresh and stored most of the wild strawberries, black caps (wild raspberries), huckleberries, and carrots. The lily camas, with its blue-violet flowers and dug from moist meadows, was a favorite. Tututnis roasted these sweet onion-like roots in pits and ate them warm or stored them.

The harvesting of vegetation had another objective: to gather material for the baskets so central to the Native cultures of western Oregon. Spring offered a window of just a few weeks to gather hazel sticks and maple bark. Willow and fir tip-sticks were harvested in the summer. Spruce stands placed no seasonal limits on gathering: year-round, the Athapaskans could wade into the deep forest's damp, resistant underbrush of ferns and vine maple to dig into the rich loam and obtain the long, slender, pliant spruce roots. Using these materials, weavers made large numbers of baskets for transport and storage and the distinctive caps worn in day-to-day life and in ceremonies. Just as the Tututnis were Salmon People, so too were they Basket People.

Acorns, harvested in the late summer and fall, were second only to the salmon as a favorite food. The Natives dried and shelled the rich, nutritious acorns of the California black oak and Oregon white oak trees, then stored them in baskets. When ready for use, women shelled them, ground them with a mortar and pestle, and leached the tannic acid out before boiling the fine meal. This *san-chun-tuu-l'*, or "juice of the acorn" (sometimes called mush), would be used in most meals, much like today's oatmeal, mashed potatoes, and bread. Sam Van Pelt, a Siletz ancestor from the Chetco Tribe, explained that in Athapaskan society this mush "was the staff of life, made from the nut of the acorn."

In the fall, Tututnis moved to the mountains, living in temporary brush houses during the deer and elk hunts. The hunters stalked the animals with bows and arrows, sometimes using deer heads as cover, and drove the prey through the forests into traps or hand-dug pits or trenches. Much energy went into the fall chinook and coho runs, and the men caught eels, steelhead, and trout from the Rogue. Cedar canoes carried families downriver from Tututin to the Coast to harvest smelt, mussels, and other seafood.

During the winter, the people continued to hunt deer and engage in other subsistence activities, but on a much smaller scale. The bounty from the more temperate months was stored in large baskets, up to four feet tall and three feet wide, that sat on the plank floors surrounding the lower, earthen cooking areas in the largest living houses. Pounding rains and roiling winds made winter an indoor time of preparing food, making clothing, mending fishing nets, and weaving baskets.

The shorter days, longer nights, and slower pace set the stage for the story-telling that bound together past, present, and future generations. Practiced narrators passed along age-old lessons to young people, who in years hence could present the same stories to their own grandchildren. Male elders instructed the boys in the sweathouses, and women in the living houses passed on knowledge to the girls, as they patiently wove baskets or ground acorns amid the smells of the cedar fire and the cooking. Somewhat more formally, a storyteller gathered young boys and girls in a large, warm plank house for a colorful, dramatic presentation. Later, these stories would be related again verbatim to lodge them in the children's minds.

An elaborate creation story explained the beginnings of the land, the animals, and the people and laid down the obligations of the people. Western Oregon tribes had highly individualized creation stories. Charles Depoe, an Athapaskan who lived in the village of Yah-shu-eh at the mouth of the Rogue River in the early 1850s, recounted the Tututni creation story over and over again to keep it alive after the people were removed to Siletz.

In the beginning, Depoe told the people, all was dark. There was water but not land. "A sweathouse stood on the water, and in it lived two men—Xōwalä´cī [pronounced 'Haa-waa-la'-chee'] and his companion. Xōwalä´cī's companion had tobacco. He usually stayed outside watching, while Xōwalä´cī remained in the sweathouse." One day, they saw a piece of land, which was white, with two trees, a redwood and an alder. Excited, Xōwalä´cī ran experiments to understand this phenomenon:

Then Xōwalä´cī made five cakes of mud. Of the first cake he made a stone and dropped it into the water, telling it to make a noise and to expand as soon as it struck the bottom. After a long while he heard a faint noise, and knew then that the water was very deep. He waited some time before dropping the second cake. This time he heard the noise sooner, and knew that the land was coming nearer to the surface. After he had dropped the third cake, the land reached almost to the surface of the water. So he went into the sweathouse and opened a new sack of tobacco. Soon his companion shouted from the outside, "It looks as if breakers were coming!" Xōwalä´cī was glad, because he knew now that the land was coming up from the bottom of the ocean. After the sixth wave the water receded, and Xōwa lä´cī scattered tobacco all over. Sand appeared. More breakers came in, receding farther and farther westward. Thus the land and the world were created.

Then Xōwalä´cī and the companion took action. They made some mistakes. An attempt to make salmon resulted in a fish without skin. In trying to make humans, Xōwalä´cī instead created dogs and hissing snakes. In time, a beautiful woman appeared, and Xōwalä´cī told his companion to take her as his wife, which he did. "One day Xōwalä´cī told the man [his companion] that all the world had been made for him. Then he instructed him how to act at all times and under all conditions." The man and woman had many children, and they all lived in the Rogue River country. Xōwalä´cī finished his work by giving instructions on how to care for the natural world and create the many tribes:

> Then he [Xōwalä´cī] straightened out the world, made it flat, and placed the waters. He also created all sorts of animals, and cautioned the man not to cut down more trees or kill more animals than he needed. And after all this had been done, he bade him farewell and went up to the sky, saying, "You and your wife and your children shall speak different languages. You shall be the progenitors of all the different tribes."

Countless other stories cascaded down on young people during the winter nights of western Oregon. They heard about Transformer, Star, Salmon, Bluejay, Crow, One-Horn, Big Snake, and many others. The versatile Coyote variously—and often profanely—played the wise man or the fool, the trickster or the trickee. Invariably humorous, the stories usually carried a serious lesson. Coyote might be clowning around in a burial area only to be scared out of his wits, a warning to children not to play in those places. Another story had Coyote, through his hubris, being tricked into believing that summer had come, so he told his wife to throw away all of his old smoked meat. But when Coyote went to the river, he found it barren of eels and realized he had been fooled. It was still winter and, since eels run only in the summer, he would have none of their tasty meat. The moral for young people: conserve your food during the dark months.

Winter was also the best time for gambling, which the Tututni loved. Stick games, played in the sweathouses or living houses, involved teams which had many sticks, including specially marked ones (often by a black, rather than white, band) that became the focal point of the enterprise. Players made dizzying, lightning-fast feints, taking sticks behind their backs to disguise the location of the marked sticks. Many dentalium shells, the prevailing currency, were at stake, and much money changed hands through side-bets by spectators.

Bad weather or no, the Tututni played their favorite sport of *tsa-xwi* or *koho* (also called shinny) in the winter months. Village teams competed against each other, and the large, level meadow at Tututin must have made a pre-eminent playing field. Similar to field hockey, koho was played with a wooden ball the size of a baseball and long sticks, with one end steamed and bent for hitting the ball. The size of each team ranged from just a few to twenty. The objective in this fast-moving, physical game was to drive the ball through goalposts at each end of the field. Koho brought out everyone in the villages. Pride was at stake and so were many strings of dentalia, as spectators placed wagers on the action. Women played a modified version of *koho*, using two small pieces of wood tied together with buckskin in place of the wooden ball.

The Tututni held dances to celebrate specific events or talents, such as first menstruation, a successful battle, doctoring ability, or a hunting expedition, but the major ceremony at Tututin was Nee Dosh.

At Nee Dosh, a dance still held today, the prayers are chanted, one by one, explaining how the world was put together and thanking the Creator for making the land, the people, and the animals and for giving them *duh-neh*, their place. A world renewal ceremony intended to "fix the world," the prayers remind the people of the blessings of the Creator and their responsibility to keep the world right. Held every winter in a dance house or the tyee's living house, with a blazing fire in the hearth, in some years the dance went on for five days rather than ten, but the intensity of these dusk-to-dawn gatherings always ran high. A man from Tolowa, where the dance was the same as at Tututin, remembered this: "Every year we go to the center of our world. In our religion, this is where life began for our people and we dance there for ten nights. We start at about 10 o'clock in the night and then we dance all night;

take breaks but we dance until the sun comes up over the hill."

Both women and men, young and old, attired in their best dentalia and buckskin finery, performed Nee Dosh. Often the people at Tututin invited another village to participate. The dancers formed a semi-circle, with a dance leader setting the rhythm, perhaps by tapping a staff against the floor planks (but not using a drum), while the dancers joined in the leader's songs. Individual dancers broke out of the line, with the women dancing lightly and the men moving more flamboyantly, as if stalking a deer. Spectators shouted out, wishing the dancers good fortune—many strings of dentalia, a fine dress, a high bride price, a good hunt. An early-morning feast followed, and the dancers rested until the evening dance, when they returned to the center of their world.

Historically, settlers and other non-Indians who had contact with American Indian tribes often described them as "uncivilized," "barbaric," and "savage." They could see in tribal life no semblance of governmental organization or legal systems. Some early judges and anthropologists made similar judgments with respect to tribes generally and western Oregon tribes in particular.

A deeper understanding of aboriginal political justice systems has since taken hold. The classic work is E. Adamson Hoebel's *The Law of Primitive Man*. Hoebel, an eminent anthropologist, looked to a formulation by Professor (and later Supreme Court Justice) Benjamin Cardozo that defined "law," which is the essential attribute of a sovereign government, as "a principle or rule of conduct so established as to justify a prediction with reasonable certainty that it will be enforced by the courts if its authority is challenged."

In exploring the role of law in aboriginal societies, Hoebel explained that some tribal justice systems look like "courts" to the Anglo eye; other tribal systems do not, but still fulfill the function of courts in Cardozo's sense. As an example of the second kind of system, Hoebel cited the Yurok Tribe of northern California, a tribe having much in common with the Oregon coastal tribes. He emphasized the success of the Yurok dispute resolution system, which relied on mediators similar to the Tututnis' *gwee-shut-naga*, a "person who walks between."

The practices of the Tututni demonstrate all of the elements of the Cardozo and Hoebel definition of law: rules, regularity, courts, and enforcement. "The society operated on a rather complex set of rules," anthropologist

Philip Drucker reported, the *gwee-shut-naga* was an intermediary, and there were prescribed fines for several offenses. As an overarching matter, Drucker underscored the informal but very real societal pressures that ensured enforcement: "This desire, or even need, to save one's face, regulated the legal system." Anthropologist Cora Du Bois concluded that "the rich man [tyee] functioned as a state surrogate" and that "this system of referred responsibility functioned precisely and directly to produce social alignment."

The legal and political system of the Tututnis and other western Oregon tribes, then, differed from American and European conceptions in many respects. Authority was completely decentralized, with all responsibilities carried out by the villages. But these villages were sovereigns, living governmental institutions that had matured over the millennia. They were "organizationally complex," as anthropologist Rebecca Dobkins describes them, and they worked smoothly for those societies. The fact of their sovereignty is why, for example, the United States used the treaty device—the mechanism with which sovereigns made agreements with each other—and negotiated with the tyees as the acknowledged leaders of the major villages.

The tyee, a principal institution of the Tututni and all other tribes in western Oregon, came from the richest, or one of the richest, families, and the title was passed down patrilineally, subject to consensus within the village. When a headman made a decision, his political and legal authority was buttressed by his other services to the community as facilitator, mediator, planner, and support-giver. He planned village events and organized work parties. When necessary, he ordered reductions or shut-downs of salmon harvesting to keep peace with upriver villages or to sustain the runs. The tyee provided food to the old, the infirm, and the poor and sometimes paid fines on behalf of villagers who had few resources.

The tyee had much to do with administering the village justice system, which was based on payment of monetary fines and an elaborate set of rules. Family fishing sites and sometimes gathering and hunting areas were protected as property rights. Marriage, accomplished by payment to a wife's family, required refund upon divorce. Mourners' rights protected a widow for a period after the death of her husband.

Crimes carried sanctions, to be paid in fines. Sanctions applied to such things as personal injury, theft, swearing, insults, and even refusing food, which violated the principle of showing respect for others. Names were property, and it was taboo to speak the name of a deceased person until a child received that name. When a crime or tort (a civil wrong, such as an accident

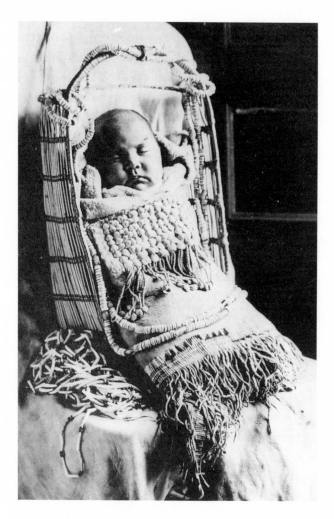

A Siletz baby in the early 1900s, with clamshell money draped around the basket and abundant dentalia and other shells and decorations as regalia. *Siletz Tribal Collection.*

caused by negligence) took place, families might well agree on a fine between themselves, for villagers knew the range for a particular offense. If families did not agree, they might line up against each other and hurl insults in mock warfare, or retaliate with physical force, which would itself call for a fine.

The impulse, however, was to keep peace in the village, so most unresolved disputes went to a *gwee-shut-naga*. This neutral and respected person could be the tyee, but others sometimes assumed the responsibility. Importantly, this system applied to disputes with other villages, as when a hunter took an elk in another village's drainage or when one village raided another in a feud. The tyee of the offending village negotiated the fine and made the payment if his guilty villager was poor.

The principal medium of exchange—within villages, between neighboring tribes, and in the trade network that reached up and down the Northwest Coast and into the Columbia River watershed—was the dentalium shell. These small, slender seashells were found mainly off the western shores of Vancouver Island, far to the north in modern-day Canada. Tapered at one end, the prized shells could easily be strung on a thin thread. In terms of value as currency, after dentalia came shell disk money (clamshells ground to about the size of a nickel with a hole drilled for the thread), followed by pendants and beads made from abalone shells.

The practice of explicitly basing a criminal justice system on the payment of monetary fines might seem discordant, but the Tututni and other Oregon tribes had their reasons for it. The overriding concerns were making the victim and injured family whole and maintaining village stability and harmony. Sanctions such as imprisonment or capital punishment did not address the needs of the wronged family, since the injured or deceased person likely had made needed contributions to the family. Fair payment, rather than imprisonment, created less resentment among the guilty party's family members and, since these village populations were relatively small, allowed him to be a productive member of the community. Restoring order and promoting peace and harmony in the village were also furthered by the rule that once a fine was decided upon and paid, it was final—even bringing it up later could generate a fine. Murder was an exception: in addition to receiving the heaviest fine, a murderer "was considered to be stained by blood for life . . . and could not be active in certain ceremonies after causing wrongful death." While some tribes used banishment from the community as a punishment, it seems not to have been used by the Athapaskans.

The idea of restorative justice, practiced by western Oregon tribes, is holistic in that it aims at repairing the harms of crime by focusing criminal law on compensating the victim and the affected family and on promoting overall community well being. It was employed by other tribes, and those systems have been praised for their effectiveness and civility. Today, restorative justice is used in many countries, including New Zealand, Germany, and Canada. The opposite approach is retributive justice, which emphasizes punishing the offender. In America, criminal law has traditionally been premised mainly on retributive justice, but in recent times elements of restorative justice have been incorporated into American state and federal criminal systems.

Societies craft their justice systems based on their own values and circumstances, and the question is whether their chosen systems are fair, smoothly running, and civil. In the case of the Tututni and other western Oregon tribes, the expectations of the citizens of the relatively small villages were universally understood. Material wealth was important, and the requirement of payment for breaches of those expectations satisfied the aggrieved parties, served as a significant deterrent to unacceptable conduct, and promoted order and individual responsibility.

Individual wealth—which included canoes, fishing spots, dance regalia, and number of wives, as well as currency—played a larger role in the cultures of Pacific Northwest tribes than it did nationally. Wealth came into play in a number of ways. It determined who was eligible to assume leadership as tyee. It gave prestige to individuals. When trouble came, it could be relinquished in settlement of disputes and crimes.

Wealth had another, perhaps more significant, function: it carried with it a high responsibility to the village and encompassed a philanthropic mission. In addition to providing food to the needy and sometimes paying fines on behalf of the poor, responsibilities included sharing canoes, fishing sites, and off-shore rocks valuable for collecting seagull eggs or harvesting sea lions. Wealthy families sponsored dances and supplied the dancers with regalia, skillfully woven basket caps, and buckskin attire adorned with glistening, red woodpecker scalps, abalone shells, and feathers. They provided many strings of dentalia as well. As Bud Lane explained, "When you bring your wealth to a ceremony and the dance people put them on, you are helping the dancers, helping the community, keeping the world right."

In the case of marriage, the groom's family made payment—sometimes called bride purchase—to the bride's family, and the amount of the payment was much noticed in both villages. The term "bride purchase" can be misleading. Since the bride would join the husband's village, her family would be losing a significant worker; logically, the family should be compensated for that loss. As Cora Du Bois observed, "a premium was placed on a woman's capacity for work." Usually the parents made financial arrangements after two young people had fallen in love and decided to marry. "Marriage," Robert Kentta explained, "was not a dry, unfeeling exercise. Romance was important to us. Many of our songs are love songs. There were some arranged marriages, but courtships were much more common."

Slavery existed at Tututin and among the southern Oregon tribes, but only marginally. The rich families, particularly the tyees, had some indentured servants, usually a poor or infirm relative or a villager with no wealth whose fine the tyee had paid. These debtors left the tyee's house when the obligation was fulfilled. As Philip Drucker put it, slaveholding was "scarcely an institution" and might be better understood as "a sort of adoption."

In any event, despite the emphasis on wealth, Tututnis had an egalitarian, not a rigidly stratified, society. Their notion of wealth differed from American capitalism in two important ways. There was no interest imposed on debts, and it was a community responsibility to provide for the downtrodden. "There is no hint," Cora Du Bois wrote, "that money was ever very important in determining whether a man were well or poorly fed and housed." Instead, these communities were imbued with what Du Bois called a "democracy of manners." As one Tolowa villager put it, "If a boy is brought up by his grandma and believes everything she says, he gets to have good sense; he knows everything, he talks the same way to all kinds of people no matter what kind of clothes they wear."

If a single theme runs through life in Tututin and other western Oregon villages, it is the distinctive and demanding set of moral obligations to the vanguards of their existence: the Creator, fellow villagers, other villages, the animals, and the land and waters. They sometimes came up short of their ideals when individuals strayed or raiding parties attacked other villages. Nonetheless, the cluster of ideas that made up the core of their philosophy—the complex entwining of reverence, respect, and duty—ran so deep that they set aside ten days, dusk until dawn, to go the center of their world and reaffirm their beliefs.

PART ONE. THE LONG ABORIGINAL EXISTENCE

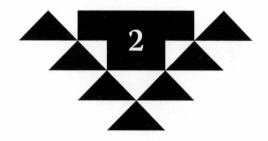

LANDSCAPES THAT FED THEIR PEOPLE

"Nothing is too good for salmon."

L IFE IN TUTUTIN IS A BENCHMARK FOR THE CULTURAL CHARAC-
teristics of the aboriginal people of western Oregon because the many
tribes and bands had much in common. They held similar worldviews
and developed similar institutions of society and governance. But a person
traveling south or north along the Coast would notice increasing variations
in the life patterns of those villages. Visits to the tribes of the interior valleys
of the Upper Rogue, Umpqua, and Willamette rivers would unveil still other
ways of living in the region. The landscape was varied and the peoples who
lived within it reflected that diversity.

Differences were evident even among the Athapaskan villages of southwestern Oregon. The people of Tututin, for example, made social visits to
the Coast in their canoes and might bring back shellfish, but the six-mile
upriver haul made it difficult to transport heavy loads back home. The coastal
Athapaskan villages had much closer ties to the ocean. Each village had rights
to the whales that drifted ashore on the adjacent beach, and within villages,
families had property rights to specific sections of the whale. The sea lion
hunt was the province of the bayside and seaside villages. When one of the big
animals slumbered on the rocks, hunters might make a kill with clubs. Out in
the open water, they pursued sea lions in canoes, using harpoons with detach-
able points attached to a cord. They wrestled the smaller sea lions into a canoe
and towed the larger ones to shore. As with deer and elk hunts, the hunters
sang songs, went through ritual purification, followed other protocols before
a hunt, and offered thanks and respect to the sea lion after a kill.

"ROCK OYSTER QUEEN NEWPORT, OREGON"

Chetco Anna with basket. Harvesting rock oysters (actually rock-boring clams) is hard work, requiring a hand sledge to break them out of the sandstone. These bivalves are considered a delicacy. *Siletz Tribal Collection.*

Storms and swells required that the ocean canoes be larger and sturdier, which made them less nimble, than the river canoes used at upriver villages. Ocean canoes took the better part of a year to craft, from selecting and cutting downed redcedar trees through the process of drying, hollowing, and fixing seats to the shell. These vessels—which went undecorated, unlike those farther to the north—ran as large as forty feet long, with twelve pullers and a captain. They could travel great distances, probably as far north as British Columbia, and could haul tons of cargo.

Down the Coast from the Rogue River lived the two southernmost Athapaskan tribes, the Chetco and the Tolowa of California's Smith River country. The Lower Rogue villages, Chetco and Tolowa, had extensive relations and much in common. The largest Chetco villages were established at the mouths of the Winchuck and Chetco rivers. Chit K'wut (pronounced Chetco by settlers) is the name of the large village on the Chetco's south bank.

The Chetcoes had productive beds of oysters and mussels that women harvested and stored in large baskets worn like backpacks. In addition to salmon, the tribe depended heavily on game and found excellent deer and elk hunting in the high country of the Chetco watershed, now a part of the Kalmiopsis Wilderness Area. As Sam Van Pelt, a Chetco, reported, "The only thing that was cultivated was tobacco, and that was sown in the shade of the myrtle bottoms along the rivers. The reason for planting in the shade was so it would be mild and pleasant to inhale."

The Chetcoes and other coastal tribes have stories of a great flood—such as the tsunami that overwhelmed the Oregon Coast in 1700—that destroyed many villages and took numerous lives. Billy Metcalf told the Chetco version, which, through the travails of a youth, gives stern warning of the consequences of a lack of readiness:

> There was once a time when a youth continually went around in the night. Then at that time everything appeared to be different. So then when that occurred he began to run toward the mountain. He kept running. Now then he thought to himself, "I used to be a good runner." So then he kept running toward the mountain. Now then while he was running like that then the ground was becoming soft. That is why he ran to the top. He ran among all kinds of animals there, all of them were growling as he ran among them. Now then he pushed their faces aside there to make space for himself. Now he stayed with them. Now then the (flood) water stopped coming toward there (because) it did not flow over the top. That is why only those who were on the mountain were safe (on the earth now), because the ocean did not rise to the top. That is why they were all safe. Now then he stayed there only two days. Then it became dry. The water was not flowing there (anymore). Then he heard people crying. Gradually all the voices died down. Then all the voices he had heard died down. Now then he no longer grieved. He just thought, "There is nothing to be done. My people are all dead."

Typical of those stories, which so often taught conflicting lessons, both sour and sweet, Billy Metcalf's tsunami account holds a ray of light. It turned out that not all of the people were lost. A young woman had climbed a little hill and it "floated up with her" and kept her safe. She met up with the youth and "presently they took each other in marriage [and] they lived together very well." To this day, Mount Emily, which rises above the Lower Chetco River and is the locale of the story, remains a sacred site.

Southwestern Oregon and northern California, described as "one of the most complex linguistic regions of North America," are apt places to mark down the array of languages that hampered tribal relations during aboriginal times and stifled community-building when the tribes were thrown together on the Siletz Reservation in the mid-1850s. The people of western Oregon developed strategies to ameliorate the difficulties. Many became bilingual and trilingual. The Athapaskan language is sometimes described as a "chain of dialects," but people from different villages usually communicated well with each other; rather than the dialects being mutually unintelligible, conversations would be much like exchanges between English speakers with British and American accents. The Chinook Jargon, drawn in part from the language of the Chinook Tribe at the mouth of the Columbia River, evolved to ease intertribal communications in the Pacific Northwest. The Jargon—a language of just 250–500 words designed mainly to facilitate trade, flexible and easy to learn—was a significant cultural innovation.

The Upper Rogue country also presented formidable linguistic problems. The region had three wholly different language families—Takelman, Athapaskan, and Shastan—and the Galice and Applegate Athapaskan-speaking tribes were cultural islands within the Takelma territory of the Upper Rogue. Linguist and anthropologist Edward Sapir, who interviewed Takelma people in the early twentieth century, wrote that the characteristics of the Takelman language "are such as to mark it off most decidedly from those of the neighboring stocks."

The Takelma Tribe, which played such a central role in the cataclysmic mid-nineteenth-century events of resistance, treaties, war, and removal, lived aboriginally in different geographic circumstances than most tribes of the Siletz Reservation. Takelma country lay in the Upper Rogue River terrain, about fifty miles from the Coast in a drier, warmer, sunnier clime. In contrast to the Lower Rogue and the Coast, the upper valley, while forested in the higher elevations, had a floor of level terrain and rolling hills carpeted with stretched-out expanses of grasslands. Nonetheless, daily life in both landscapes bore many similarities.

The structures in Takelma villages were like those at Tututin, save for walls made of sugar pine planks rather than cedar. Similar, too, were the governmental systems of tyees, mediators, and fine-based justice. Most of the social customs tracked each other. At puberty, the Takelma women, like the

Athapaskans, received distinctive tattoos with three parallel stripes, beginning just below the lower lip and running down over the chin.

Because of the distance from the ocean, there was no fresh seafood in the Takelma villages. The river was faster and rockier than down below, and while canoes (and rafts made of logs tied together by pliable hazel switches) were used, mostly for portage, transportation by river was much less frequent than among the people who lived on the lower river. The salmon runs were somewhat smaller in Takelma country because returning fish veered off into the Illinois and Applegate rivers and other tributaries. Also, the fish were less desirable, having lost some weight and food value by burning off fat during their upriver journey. The Takelma relied more heavily on game and acorns from the California black oaks.

Still, the salmon was important to them. The fishing was robust near Table Rocks, and just downriver, near the present town of Gold Hill, the village of Dilomi had more than a hundred residents. We can be sure of the reason for Dilomi's location. A nearby waterfall created a prime dipnet site. Molly Orton, a Takelma woman who lived there before the treaty, described one of the best

Frances (Harney) Johnson, from the Takelma village at Jumpoff Joe Creek, participated in the Rogue River War of 1855–1856 as a teenager and lived until 1941. She was the principal Takelma language and ethnographic consultant to Edward Sapir (1906) and John Harrington (1930s). She is shown here with her niece, Eveline (Harney) Baker, in the 1930s. *Siletz Tribal Collection.*

fishing spots near the waterfall, a rock called the "Story Chair." The name reportedly came about because an elder would net the first salmon of the year, conduct the first salmon ceremony, and tell the story of that place: "The first owner of the place (Evening Star) challenged all who came there to a wrestling match, and killed them. He allowed no one to fish. At last someone (Swallow) managed to vanquish him, 'and gave the salmon to be free to all the people.'"

In the middle 1800s, Takelmas gained the reputation among Americans of an aggressive, combative society. The tribe launched a ferocious defense of its homeland when steadily increasing numbers of Americans came through their territory on the California-Oregon Trail and when lawless miners openly called for "extermination" of the Upper Rogue River Indians. The Takelmas' conduct was definitely warlike, but many view it as valiant—and largely, if not entirely, justifiable. In any event, those wars tell us little about the tribe's pro-clivities before white settlers arrived. Edward Sapir tentatively advanced the proposition that "on the whole the Takelmas seem to have been a rather war-like tribe," but we have scant data about how bellicose they and other western Oregon tribes actually were. We know only that villages sometimes mounted raids on villages of other tribes, and sometimes people were killed. So we should be cautious, as Sapir was, in drawing conclusions about how violent these tribes were in aboriginal times.

Shastan speakers, the third distinct language family in southern Oregon, like Takelmas, lived in the drier, inland climate. Also as with the Takelma lands, Shasta lands were coveted by settlers and miners during the incendiary years of the mid-nineteenth century. In addition to living in the Klamath, Scott, and Shasta valleys of northern California, the Shastas made villages in southern Oregon in open valleys and rugged mountain-forests in the upper parts of the Applegate River and Bear Creek valleys in the Rogue River watershed. Before whites came to the region, the total Shasta population was approximately 3,000 strong.

Even though the Rogue River Athapaskans were their long-time enemies, the Shastas shared many of the same traits as their Takelma and Athapaskan neighbors to the north. They highly valued dentalium shells, their men slept in sweathouses, they used baskets to store and transport goods, and they preferred acorns from the black oaks over all other native acorn species. The Shastas also gambled, including playing the stick game. As on the Coast, girls at the age of ten, eleven, or twelve received the "111" chin tattoo, along with the promise that whatever dreams they had during the night after the tattooing would come true.

While Shasta hunters brought in large amounts of elk and deer meat, salmon was a principal food source. Every year, an individual was sent out to watch for the first salmon traveling upriver. The first fish was allowed to pass, because the people believed that all the other salmon followed the earliest fish. The salmon could then be caught, but none could be consumed until the first catch was dried and eaten by the fishing party. According to Sargeant Sambo, the son of an Oregon Shastan tyee, at mealtime the children all sat quietly on one side; they were told to eat slowly or "people will say you don't know much, you don't have any feeling for yourself."

Over on the middle Coast north of the Rogue, the Coos (Hanis and Miluk), Siuslaw, Lower Umpqua, and Alsea tribes totaled about 7,600 people before contact. Although the overall pattern of culture and government was consistent with the tribes to the south, these four tribes formed a transition area where the beliefs and practices of the Lower Columbia River tribes were also in evidence.

The mouth of the Coos River formed Coos Bay, one of the few harbors along the Oregon Coast. (The Rogue River, for example, while it is the largest river between the Klamath and the Columbia, had no harbor.) The Natives lived in about seventy villages, mostly around the bay's twenty-some miles of usable shoreline, and thrived on the ocean and river resources. The living houses were about 20 by 50 feet, smaller than those of the Columbia River tribes, but larger than houses on the south Coast. While their river canoes resembled those of the Athapaskans, the Coos relied on ocean canoes, sometimes with carved and painted birds and animals on the prow. The Siuslaw established approximately thirty villages in the broad, protected river areas a few miles from the mouth of the Siuslaw River. In the summer, they moved to camps at prime hunting grounds and salmon and eel harvesting spots. They, too, used colorful ocean canoes.

MIDDLE OREGON COAST LANGUAGE GROUPS

In spite of language differences, geography bound the Coos, Siuslaws, and Lower Umpquas together. South of Coos Bay, the mountains, blanketed with Sitka spruce, come right down to the sea, leaving steeply angled cliffs and drop-offs. Far to the north, just above the mouth of Siuslaw River, where Siuslaws located most of their villages, the imposing promontory of Heceta Head

This sketch accompanied William Wells's report on Indian fishing by torchlight on Coos Bay in an 1856 issue of *Harper's New Monthly Magazine*: "The operation seemed simple enough. . . . The light of the fire seemed to possess some attraction for the finny denizens of the bay; for as the light passed along the surface of the water, they would dart upward toward it and become the sure prey of the spearsman. . . . At my request the [Indian woman] paddled me alongside a canoe, the proprietor of which handed me a spear; but though he pointed out dozens of salmon, some of them glorious fellows three feet long, my unpracticed hand met with no success. In an hour the novelty of the thing had passed and I gave the signal to return. There were about five hundred fish taken in that time."

announces a return to the mountains-and-cliffs terrain that makes travel so laborious north of there. In between lies a striking natural feature—a fifty-mile stretch of flat, broad beach and dunes directly north of Coos Bay (now protected as the Oregon Dunes National Recreation Area). Especially at low tide, when the sand was wet and firm, Indian people made good time on foot. As Annie Miner Peterson explained, for thousands of years, with north-south travel by land along most of the Coast so brutal, this was the "highway" of the Coos, Siuslaws, and Lower Umpquas.

Peterson also talked about the Indian doctors who, with variations, existed in all the western Oregon tribes. The Coos had two kinds of people, men

Annie Miner Peterson, subject of Lionel Youst's biography *She's Tricky Like Coyote*, was a principal consultant to linguists on both Hanis and Miluk Coos dialects. She is photographed here in about 1910, in a shredded cedar or maple bark dress and other regalia. *Photograph courtesy of Earl Edmonds, great-grandson of Annie Miner Peterson.*

or women, who possessed supernatural powers. The *ilaxquain* was a doctor, while the *mitadin* sometimes did healing but was known more for "poison power" and could bring sickness to people. Peterson believed that the "good" doctors, at Siuslaw and Lower Umpqua as well as Coos, were every bit as effective as western-trained physicians. Indian doctoring, however, was a perilous profession. At Coos and elsewhere, the relatives sometimes killed the doctor if the patient died.

As for the *mitadin*, Annie feared them, but she had a mind of her own. When she was a young woman, a *mitadin* named Old Lyman asked her to marry him but she considered him "pretty horrible." Knowing he might use his medicine to kill her if she turned him down, she nonetheless took the "chance of her life" and refused him.

Farther north, a majority of the Alsea tribal villages clustered around Yaquina Bay, just south of the imposing edifice of Yaquina Head, the ocean

The Alsea, Siuslaw, Lower Umpqua, Coos, and Lower Coquille people consider "Big Stump," remnant of a redwood tree and located just south of Waldport, to be the center of the world. *Siletz Tribal Collection.*

point jutting out just north of today's Newport. The Alseas adopted even more cultural practices from the tribes of the Columbia River and the Coast north of there. They engaged in head flattening of babies and buried their dead in canoes or small houses. Their use of slaves was more extensive than in the south, and the women did not use the "three-stripe" chin tattoos favored there. Still, they had many similarities with south coastal tribes, including the roles of Indian doctors and the structure of extended families. Symbolizing their midway position, Alseas had extensive and peaceful relations with both Tillamooks to the north and especially Siuslaws and Lower Umpquas to the south, whom they considered to be their close relatives.

The geography of Alsea country proved to be a blessing in aboriginal times but a vulnerability after contact. The excellent harbor of Yaquina, with timbered hills and solid, level ground down by the water, was perfect for locating villages and launching ocean canoes to pursue sea lions and seals. The

Emma John, who was born before removal in the Takelma village of Sumolk near the mouth of the Applegate, wore this pack basket at the turn of the twentieth century. The tump line, or burden strap, was usually worn across the forehead or shoulders, but this thinner version of the strap was situated lower. *Photograph provided by the Lincoln County Historical Society.*

bay also held outstanding oyster beds. But after Oregon statehood, developers and commercial fishers learned of the deep water port and the oysters, which spurred them in 1865 to obtain the first of several major reductions of the Siletz Reservation.

The Tillamook, Chinook, and Clatsop are the three northernmost coastal tribes in the Siletz confederation. The Salishan-speaking Tillamook, with an estimated 4,000 members, lived on an eighty-mile stretch of Coast that was five or so degrees chillier than the Rogue country in the winter but not much different in the summer. Tillamook country encompassed Siletz, Netarts, Tillamook, and Nehalem bays and bold coastal formations, such as Cape Lookout, Cape Falcon, and Tillamook Head. The territory included sacred Neahkahnie Mountain, rising up 1,600 feet from the rocky beach just north of Nehalem Bay, its vertical stone front facing straight into the west winds and rains. The Tillamook homeland reached inland to Saddle Mountain, at 3,200 feet one of the tallest spots in the Coast Range and blessed with 360-degree views of the Pacific Ocean, the Columbia River, and the Cascades.

The Chinook and the Clatsop were closely tied. With about 2,000 members between them, they spoke the same language, called Chinook, and inhabited

Neahkahnie Mountain, the most dramatic edifice on Oregon's north Coast, is the home of the Tillamooks' God. *Ekahnie* is the Tillamook word for the Creator and *ne* means "place of." *Photograph © Larry N. Olson.*

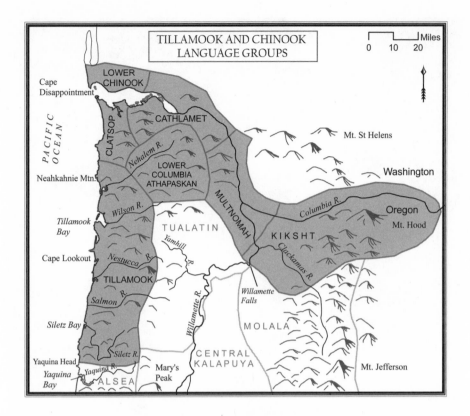

the dramatic mouth of the Columbia River, four miles across at present-day Astoria—Chinooks to the north, Clatsops to the south. That strategic spot led to extensive trade with tribes up and down the Coast and into the Columbia interior. The magnet that was the Columbia also drew in early European and American ships and the killing germs that their seamen sometimes carried.

Recent field research has suggested that the coastal villages may have been more resilient than previously assumed by archaeologists, who believed that people abandoned their villages after the cataclysmic earthquake and tsunami of January 1700. Robert Losey studied Tillamook sites at Nehalem and Netarts bays showing that villagers hung on after the events, with the Nehalem villages managing to continue their reliance on salmon and the Netarts changing their diets to rely more heavily on small fish, mussels, and land mammals.

The Tillamook, Chinook, and Clatsop had many customs in common with coastal tribes in present-day Washington. Their houses were bigger, averaging 20-100 feet in length and holding several families; in the case of the Chinook and Clatsop, houses could be over 300 feet long. Their canoes were ornate, and they flattened the foreheads of their children. At the same time, their societies operated in much the same way as the villages down the Coast. While

Medicine Rock, an exposed stone formation along a stretch of the lower Siletz River where the riverside is mostly forested or grassy, is a sacred site for tribal members. It is a place of healing and respite, and it is said that a person who leaves an offering there will receive safe passage and good luck. *Siletz Tribal Collection.*

the details of the first salmon ceremony varied among the tribes, the spirit of that yearly event prevailed everywhere. Clara Pearson, Tillamook, born in the 1860s or 1870s, spoke reverently about the ceremony: "Real old-timers used flint to cut the first salmon with. They had to do that because a salmon is an awfully particular fish. Not one drop of blood should be allowed to drop on the ground in cleaning the first salmon." The fish were cleaned on decorative rush mats. As Pearson explained, "Nothing is too good for salmon."

The Clatsop and Chinook villages were located on the Columbia River, one of the world's greatest salmon producers, and Tillamooks sometimes traveled north to fish there. Working durable, well-designed nets, weirs, and spears, they knew the best fishing sites and the times of year when the salmon were running. The tribes took prodigious amounts of salmon. Historically, the

Columbia River tribes (those tribes throughout the full reach of the river), consumed an estimated 42 million pounds annually. For Oregon coastal rivers other than the Columbia, the estimated aboriginal take was about 10 million pounds (roughly 2-5 million fish) per year. By comparison, with all the habitat degradation from dams and other development, the annual commercial salmon harvest in Oregon and Washington between 2000 and 2008 averaged 2 million pounds.

With these immense harvests, why did the runs on the Columbia and the coastal rivers not crash? Why, by every account, were the runs strong when the settlers arrived? The best answers lie in a future-looking pragmatism. Overfishing would mean reduced runs and hard winters in years to come, and it would also antagonize other villages on the river. Accordingly, tyees or other leaders would call for a closure if further fishing would exceed physical sustainability or violate duties to neighbors. "The fact remains," historian Robert Bunting writes, "that indigenous peoples apparently possessed the population and skill to have decimated the region's salmon, yet they looked for security and safety in extensive relationships with the land and other peoples. Fishing beyond a certain limit was simply irrational."

For the Tillamook, Clatsop, and Chinook, as was the case up and down the Coast, wealth largely determined individual prestige. Unlike the tribes to the south, however, the Clatsop and Chinook held potlatches (giveaways). These were not nearly as bounteous as the ceremonies at Puget Sound and beyond, but they manifested a value found in the tribes to the north and on the southern Oregon Coast as well—that the wealthy had a responsibility to share with the larger community.

The Chinook and Clatsop, and to a lesser extent the Tillamook, built slavery into their societies to a much greater degree than the other Oregon coastal tribes did. They held many more slaves, left their heads rounded, and allowed almost no social mobility. Viewed as property, slaves were thrown into makeshift graves or into the water when they died, and western observers reported that some were left to starve when their owners died so they could "serve their masters in the other world."

Slavery hardly set these Columbia River tribes apart from other societies. We know that "slavery has been one of the most ubiquitous of all human institutions, existing in many times and most places and persisting in some variants even at the start of the twenty-first century." England did not abolish slavery until 1833. When the Chinook, Clatsop, and other Oregon tribes negotiated treaties with the United States in the 1850s, slavery prevailed in .

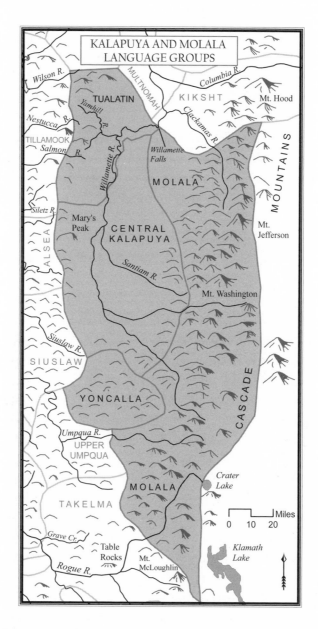

nearly half of the states in the nation and was sanctioned by the United States Constitution.

The Siletz confederation of tribes includes members from the Kalapuya, Molala, and Klickitat tribes, who lived in the Willamette and other inland valleys. During the helter-skelter years of the 1850s and 1860s, when federal troops marched

Indian people from their homelands to the new reservations, arbitrariness often trumped order. Just as some individuals from tribes designated for the Siletz Reservation (that is, people from the Coast and Rogue River regions) ended up on the Grand Ronde Reservation, which was intended mostly for inland tribes, so too were some people sent to Siletz while the main bodies of their tribes went to the Grande Ronde Reservation. Thus majorities of the Kalapuya and Molala tribes went to Grand Ronde and most Klickitats were taken to the Yakama Reservation in Washington, while some individuals came to Siletz.

The Northern Molala lived partly on the eastern side of the Willamette Valley and the flanks of the Cascade Range, while the Southern Molala, a smaller group, resided in the Upper Umpqua and Rogue watersheds. Both had close relationships with the Klamath Tribe, but the Molala language bore no similarity to any other in the region. Molalas favored mud and bark-covered winter homes, not plank houses. Large game, mainly deer and elk, was an essential source of food and clothing for these people who migrated between lowland winter settlements and summer harvest locations in the high mountains.

Members of the Klickitat Tribe, from today's western Washington, came south of the Columbia River after European epidemics in the 1820s and 1830s had devastated Willamette Valley populations, forcing the remaining Kalapuyas to reach an agreement allowing the Klickitats to stay. Their men were excellent hunters on horseback with bows and arrows, and Klickitat women were known for their sturdy baskets. Highly mobile, Klickitats moved as far north as Puget Sound and south to the interior Rogue River watershed, where they were active in trading arms to the Upper Rogue River tribes. Some Klickitat people from the southerly group were eventually enrolled at Siletz.

The Kalapuya, a large tribe (estimates range from 4,700 to 15,000 members) with some thirteen bands, occupied much of the oak-savannah floor of the Willamette Valley and its western foothills. While the Kalapuyas took salmon and eels from the Willamette River and its tributaries, they lacked access to the prime fishing grounds at Willamette Falls. Several tribes fished there, but the Chinooks who controlled the Falls excluded the Kalapuyas. As a result, the meat of deer, elk, and bear superseded fish and eels in importance. Kalapuyas had large homes and some slavery, although not to the extent of the Chinooks and Clatsops, and some of the bands flattened their children's foreheads. The Kalapuyan language was mutually unintelligible with all the surrounding languages, although accommodations were made through learning other languages and through the creation of the Chinook Jargon.

Fire management played an important role in the lives of the Kalapuya

The legendary fishing grounds at Willamette Falls were used by many tribes and are still visited today, as in this photograph, by Siletz tribal members harvesting eels. *Courtesy of Siletz Tribe Natural Resources Department.*

and other western Oregon tribes. For generations, American scholars viewed Indians through a romantic stereotype—the "pristine myth," as it has been called—that Native Americans lived in an untamed, virgin landscape. That notion has now been roundly debunked, and there is a broad understanding that aboriginal societies worked the land and sometimes altered it. In western Oregon, just as Indians harvested monumental amounts of salmon, they also made extensive use of fire. Perhaps because of the preeminent agricultural values of the Willamette Valley, the various fire management practices of the Kalapuya are especially well documented.

While some Kalapuya deer and elk hunting was done with snares and by single bow-and-arrow hunters wearing deer hides, fire played a major role in wildlife harvesting. Large community hunts used fire to surround a large territory and drive the game to the center. A Santiam Kalapuya, Joseph Hudson, gave this account to an *Oregonian* reporter in about 1880:

> This annual hunt was conducted under the orders of the most famous war chief, and all others had to receive instructions and live up to them. There

was considerable skill required to do this correctly and effectively. . . . Possibilities were carefully calculated in advance and pains taken to plan operations early in the fall of the year, when storms were not frequent and the game easily controlled. . . . At a given signal, made by a fire kindled at some point as agreed, they commenced burning off the whole face of the country and driving wild game to a common center. . . . If badly managed, the game could break through and escape to the mountains. . . . When the circle of fire became small enough to hunt to advantage, the best hunters went inside and shot the game.

Manipulating the habitat with fire also produced verdant plant growth that promoted deer and elk habitat. Robert Bunting describes it this way: "Late-summer and early-fall burns fertilized the ground with ash and fostered a luxurious growth of grasses following the first rain. Without those annual burns, grassland areas would have been circumscribed, as well as the large deer and elk populations that depended on the grass for winter feed." Kalapuya game hunters also benefited from burning the undergrowth, which increased their range of vision.

Northwest Native peoples were agriculturists as well as "hunter-gatherers," which is the traditional description of them. Before Indian contact with whites, the fertile Willamette Valley soil, assisted by annual burnings, grew a cornucopia of camas, wapato, onions, carrots, berries, and hazelnuts. The fires also improved the harvesting of two other staples of the Kalapuyan diet. The oak trees did not burn, but acorns dropped to the ground and this, along with the increased visibility caused by torching the underbrush, facilitated acorn harvesting. The handling of tarweed—used for meal and cooking oil—was made much easier by burning off the plant's sticky resin.

The Kalapuyas' fire management, which went on for thousands of years, changed the environment of the Willamette Valley. Through their fires, the Natives preserved the valley as an oak savannah, but the savannah is a seral stage, meaning that under natural conditions it will give way to another stage—a Douglas-fir and bigleaf-maple forest, in the case of the Willamette Valley. The Douglas fir and bigleaf maple did begin to encroach on the savannah after the 1840s, when serial malaria epidemics killed so many Natives and when white settlers—wrongly believing that fire injured the savannah they wanted to farm—forced the remaining tribal members to stop burning. One of the many ironies of the collision between the two societies was that Kalapuya fire practices created an open, fertile Eden for the new arrivals, who failed to appreciate the contributions of the peoples they considered primitives.

Siletz people, today and yesterday, will sometimes wax nostalgic about life before the Europeans. Late in her long life, Annie Miner Peterson testified in a 1931 court case about the Coos Tribe's loss of land. At the end of her testimony, she was asked if she had anything she wished to add. She replied: "Long years ago my parents were living happy in their own homes. They have abundance of food of all kinds such as fish and game from the forest of the Coos Bay country. Immediately after the whites came to our country we then right away experience hardships and we have no way of remedying conditions that we once enjoyed. That is all." Sam Van Pelt, Chetco, said: "There was a strip of territory about a mile wide by ten miles long skirting the ocean, where all kinds of game could be seen all day long. We had the grey wolf, panther, bear, and wildcat by untold numbers. Elk and deer were the principal meats used. . . . Then they would kill and butcher what they would have and this was all divided with old first, then the rest would take their share. . . . The hunters then would turn to the ocean for the various kinds of fish and seal. . . . There was plenty of time for pleasure—dancing and all kind of games."

Life has its challenges and sorrows, and the Coos, Chetcoes, and the others had their share, but look at the facts underlying the descriptions of Annie Miner Peterson and Sam Van Pelt. Their traditional homeland was literally the most productive, in terms of mammals, fish, and other seafood, of anywhere in western North America; western Oregon Indians understandably revered these "landscapes that fed their people." Their environment was so mild in climate—often rain- and windswept to be sure, but ultimately so easy on a person. The land was physically magnificent, with its green ridges and mists and changing coastlines and endless sea. Everyone was buried there, from way back, and all the stories were told there. This was where it began. The reverence for their homeland, for *duh-neh*, their place, is so complete, so profound, that their religion has no heaven separate from earth. When people pass on, they simply remain here, in their paradise.

And they had their sovereignty, their right to follow their own star, the self-determination for which indigenous and ethnic cultures the world over yearn. All of this stood in the starkest contrast to what was to come.

PART TWO

WAR AND REMOVAL

INTRUDERS ON THE LAND

"The sickness came from the south—it just came by itself."

THE FIRST BLOW HIT INDIAN PEOPLE BEFORE THEY EVEN SAW the faces of the intruders. The killing germs may have invaded Oregon as early as the 1520s. The spark, set off by an arriving Spanish seaman infected with smallpox, ignited in what is now the Dominican Republic. The disease spread like wildfire, to the mainland, then up the East Coast, into the Midwest, out to the Great Plains. All of that is documented. What is not finally known is whether the smallpox moved beyond the Rocky Mountains. Some researchers believe that it did, while others consider the evidence incomplete.

But there is no question that European diseases ravaged Oregon by the 1770s. Smallpox epidemics came first, but the helpless people of the Siletz tribes who lacked immunity to the foreign germs also were infected by measles, malaria, gonorrhea, typhoid, tuberculosis, and other diseases. The attacks were relentless, hitting Oregon tribes at least every decade from the 1770s through the 1850s and beyond.

The effect was grotesque beyond any understanding. In his major contribution to the history of the Pacific Northwest, *The Coming of the Spirit of Pestilence*, historian Robert Boyd documented the epidemics, estimated the aboriginal populations of Pacific Northwest tribes, and compared them to the post-epidemic population numbers. For the tribes in the Siletz confederation, the estimated population declined from approximately 52,000 to 4,200. In less than a century, they lost roughly 92 percent of their people.

Where did the affliction come from? When did it start? The most likely culprit is a crew member infected with smallpox on the 1775 voyage of two

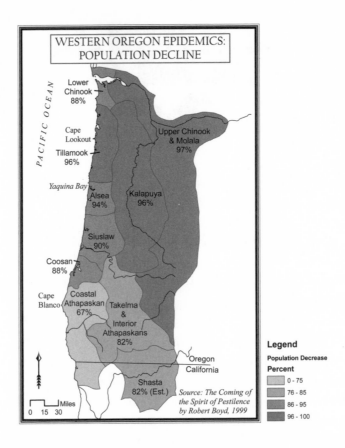

WESTERN OREGON EPIDEMICS:
POPULATION DECLINE

PACIFIC OCEAN

Lower
Chinook
88%

Cape
Lookout

Tillamook
96%

Yaquina Bay

Alsea
94%

Siuslaw
90%

Coosan
88%

Cape
Blanco

Coastal
Athapaskan
67%

Takelma
&
Interior
Athapaskans
82%

Upper Chinook
& Molala
97%

Kalapuya
96%

Oregon
California

Shasta
82% (Est.)

Source: The Coming of
the Spirit of Pestilence
by Robert Boyd, 1999

Miles
0   15   30

Legend

Population Decrease
Percent

	0 - 75
	76 - 85
	86 - 95
	96 - 100

Spanish ships, the *Santiago* and the *Sonora*, captained by Bruno Hezeta and Juan Francisco de la Bodega. The explorers met with Indians at the mouth of the Trinidad River, 225 miles to the south of Yaquina Bay, and at the Quinault River, nearly that far to the north. The Trinidad encounter is especially suspect because a large Tolowa village—with close social relations to the Tututni and other Athapaskan tribes of southern Oregon—was depopulated at about this time, probably from a smallpox attack. The disease easily could have moved north from there. But wherever the source of this first reported incident—and some scholars have speculated about even more distant origins—smallpox is a speedy, long-distance traveler that comes invisibly, in the dark of night, and then it is too late to react.

At first, Indian people were mystified by the invader. Amelia Brown, a Tolowa, recounted: "Old timers said that the sickness came from the south—it just came by itself." In time they pieced the puzzle together. The link to white people was confirmed by a particular kind of event, replicated elsewhere and the subject of many tribal stories, that took place at Fort Astoria, the fur-trading post near the mouth of the Columbia River. In August 1811,

PART TWO. WAR AND REMOVAL

Duncan McDougall, the head man, angered by the massacre of the crew of the ship *Tonquin* at Nootka Bay on Vancouver Island and wrongly believing that Columbia River tribes were implicated, decided to strike fear into the Clatsops and Chinooks:

> He assembled several of the chieftains who[m] he believed to be in the conspiracy. When they were all seated around, he informed them that he had heard of the treachery of some of their northern brethren towards the Tonquin, and was determined on vengeance. "The white men among you," said he, "are few in number, it is true, but they are mighty in medicine. See here," continued he, drawing forth a small bottle and holding it before their eyes, "in this bottle I hold the small-pox, safely corked up; I have but to draw the cork, and let loose the pestilence, to sweep man, woman, and child from the face of the earth."

The "smallpox in a bottle" display terrified the Chinook and Clatsop leaders, whose people had been ravaged by the disease. One can be sure, with the ease of canoe travel and the elaborate trail system linking the tribes, that the word spread everywhere. The white man's cannons and rifles seemed to be weapons enough. Now this, which was far worse.

Suffering swept over the tribes. Coquelle Thompson of the Coquille solemnly explained the dread. "They were afraid to call it by name. They spoke of 'That kind of sickness.' One little spot and a person would die. It was just like cutting brush. . . . Men, women, children—all go. . . . No one could cure for that kind of sickness. They were afraid, you know. Terribly." Daloose Jackson (Coos) thought he heard cries from the old people buried in the graveyard. He knew the cries were a warning: "Oh, the smallpox is going to go through again." A federal agent taking a census on the southern Oregon Coast found that the death toll of smallpox and measles epidemics in the Chetco and Rogue watersheds was so great that "many of their once populous villages are now left without a representative." Of the Clatsop and Chinook tribes at the mouth of the Columbia, Meriwether Lewis wrote in his journal on February 6, 1806, that

> the smallpox has distroyed a great number of the natives in this quarter. It prevailed about 4 years since among the Clatsops and destroy[ed] several hundred of them, four of their chiefs fell victyms to it's ravages. . . . I think the late ravages of the small pox may well account for the number of remains of villages which we find deserted on the river and Sea coast in this quarter.

Deeply ingrained tribal customs aggravated the effects of the unfamiliar diseases. When a person took ill, it was a tradition for medicine men, family, and others to gather around and give support. This hastened the spread of the viruses. The sweathouses, places of healing in precontact times, also contributed. The heat of the sweat, and especially the subsequent plunge into a river or the ocean, could seal the fate of the victim.

Terrible though the smallpox epidemics of the late 1700s and early 1800s were, the "fever and ague" crisis of the 1830s may have been worse. Robert Boyd calls this outbreak of malaria "the single most important epidemiological event in the recorded history of what would eventually become the state of Oregon." The devastation started at Fort Vancouver and spread to the mouth of the Columbia, moved upriver a hundred miles, and raged through the Willamette and Upper Rogue valleys and into northern California. Chinooks and Clatsops were among the first to suffer:

> During its worst years, the few surviving natives of the lower river could no longer bury their numerous dead in their usual manner. Corpses, denied canoe interment, piled up along the shores to fatten carrion eaters, and famished dogs wailed pitifully for their dead masters. Surviving natives dared not remove or care for the bodies as they normally so meticulously did. Nor dared they molest markers in the river in fear of more fever. Natives burned their villages attempting to destroy the contamination. For years skeletons of victims would bleach on gaunt and dreary shorelines like so many pieces of driftwood.

While Indians made up most of the dead, whites also were infected. Ezra Hamilton, an early settler who survived, left this account of the epidemic's torment:

> [Of] the fever and ague, intermitent feavor and other malarial diseases, the fever and ague was the worst and acted peculiar. I was struck with it seven Sundays in succession. Would not have it durig the week. The act at work kep it of[f]. I have had shakes that lasted 2 ours, fevor two ours. It was no chill, but a geneuine shake. Seamed I would freeze. All the covers you might put on would not keep you warm. I used to rape [wrap] the covers around my feet and take the corners in my mouth. When got through shakig I found I had chewed the corners of the blankets. The fever and ague was about 4 feet deep all over that country!

The "fever and ague" cut deeply into Willamette Valley tribes, the once-populous Kalapuya and Molala tribes, until they were all but extinguished, fragments of their former selves. Farther south, the Takelma and Shasta lost many people. All tribes endured serial attacks, as numerous other epidemics of smallpox and other diseases were close behind.

With most of their people gone—nearly every tribe lost more than 80 percent, with the more remote south coast Athapaskans losing about two-thirds—one wonders how the survivors could cope. Who among us today can fully comprehend losing nearly the whole population of our own town or city? Most of our family and friends? And, at the same time, amid the loss, confusion, and fear engendered by the epidemics, other pressures were bearing down on the Indian villages.

The Spanish, British, Russian, and American sailing ships that worked the Northwest Coast during the late eighteenth century found one great economic treasure: sea otters. These animals grew to five feet in length—their skins could be stretched even further—and their soft fur made exquisite garments, with China and Russia the major markets. By the 1790s, Americans had captured the trade because of strict British regulations that effectively barred British merchants from sea-otter commerce with China. This system was a new kind of institution. Before outsiders were involved, intertribal commerce was extensive but the tribes, who did harvest large amounts of animals, took only what they needed and left what sustained the resources. The Americans exploited the resources and, within a few generations, drove down and jeopardized the populations of salmon, sea otters, and beavers. Further, commerce with Indians often had an ugly cast as the relationship quickly moved from trade to control. Historian Frederic Howay captured an all-too-common dynamic between American traders and the coastal Indian villages:

> Haswell [on Robert Gray's ship, *Columbia*] records in his first log the
> method adopted (as he says) by Meares to obtain sea-otter skins from the
> Indians through force and fear. Many similar cases are to be found in the
> journals. The traders had no hesitation in acknowledging that they them-
> selves had resorted to such practices, though, of course, they always had

some plausible excuse. In such high handed acts lay the root of so-called unprovoked attacks by the natives upon the trading vessels. Force breeds force. . . . The wrong had been done by one vessel, and the Indians, believers in vicarious responsibility, took revenge on the next ship that happened to visit them—if the opportunity offered. If it did not, they waited patiently for a ship less carefully guarded.

After the Lewis and Clark transcontinental expedition, the Northwest fur trade received increased interest. John Jacob Astor, an American millionaire, established his post on the Columbia River in 1811, but the enterprise, which never made money, was short lived. Two years later, he sold out to the North West Company, which in 1821 merged with the Hudson's Bay Company. In 1825, Fort Vancouver opened for business on the north shore of the Columbia River near present-day Portland. This trading post, operated by the powerful HBC, would be a main force in Oregon for a generation.

The HBC directed its efforts toward beavers, whose hair made a superior felt for hats that were much sought after in London, Paris, and other European cities. Some of the inland Native villages had already encountered a few Astorians trapping beaver in the Willamette Valley and a small party led by Alexander Ross of the Northwest Company party in the Umpqua Valley. Now much longer HBC forays led by Peter Skene Ogden, Alexander McLeod, and others worked the interior rivers. Some American trappers made their way into the Northwest from the south, and HBC and American expeditions trapped on their own and traded for pelts with the tribes.

The barriers created by language, culture, and radically disparate priorities and worldviews proved formidable for all concerned—tribespeople and immigrants, and political leaders on both sides. There were glimmers of hope, of reaching "middle ground" in which both sides would establish informal and formal relations, make accommodations, and coexist. Sadly, to the ruin of the Siletz, obstacles prevented the sides from achieving common cause. For most western Oregon Indians up through the 1820s, the fur traders were the first whites they saw, and those dealings displayed the kinds of differences, misunderstandings, and stresses that would make a middle ground unreachable for generations to come.

The fur traders had business to do and they saw Oregon as free and open country, available for their enterprises. To their eyes, Indian people were uncivilized, in need of Christianity and western education, clothing, and housing. They were "lazy" because they relied on salmon rather than farming.

Such words as "savage" and "barbaric" punctuated common discourse, and the use of the term "Great Father" stood as a fit metaphor for the newcomers' paternalistic view of Indian people.

John McLoughlin, head of HBC operations at Fort Vancouver, strived for the most part to stay on good terms with the Indians for business reasons. At the same time, the HBC believed in exacting quick and brutal vengeance when they thought it necessary. George Simpson of the HBC described the company's policy as an "invariable rule of avenging the murder by Indians of any [HBC] servants, blood for blood, without trial of any kind," an approach that could cause great injustice.

A notable example—of both the HBC policy and the misunderstandings—took place in 1832. Alseas killed two HBC hunters because they had run a long trapline and taken many animals in Alsea territory without getting permission from the tribe. Coquelle Thompson, an Athapaskan who learned of the incident many years later from Yaquina John, a survivor of the subsequent HBC attack, told anthropologist John Harrington that the hunters "came trapping to that lake inland of where Seal Rock is, and the party stayed there all winter, getting beaver skins, sea-otter skins, muskrat skins just piled up. [The Alsea and Yaquina people] did not know [how many] beaver hides they got, maybe 200 lbs, and fisher skins like sea-otter."

McLoughlin ordered a take-no-prisoners raid on a nearby Yaquina village, which had no connection with the original incident, killing many tribal members. He subsequently thanked Michel Laframboise, the HBC interpreter responsible for carrying out his command:

> I think it but right that you send word to these sauvages—that what we have done is merely to let them see what we can do, and that as we do not wish to hurt the innocent we expect that themselves will Kill the remainder of the Murderers of our people.—if they do not we will return and will not spare one of the tribe—

Despite the fact and threat of violence, the Natives saw some benefits from the fur trade. They had not developed iron and they found the new material most useful, whether for rifles, axes, knives, traps, or hooks. They also liked to trade for beads and baubles that could be used on ceremonial garments. But Indians smarted at the many slights and strong-arm tactics in the trade. They bitterly resented the epidemics that had taken so many of their people. While there are no known examples of the intentional introduction of infectious diseases in the Pacific Northwest, the "smallpox in a bottle" episodes (which traders other than Duncan McDougall exploited) scared Indian people and gave them cause to believe that the epidemics were deliberate.

The most fundamental grievance of the Siletz was the repeated failure of the traders to respect the tribes' powerful sense of territoriality. Tribal boundaries were well known—the Tututin, Coos, and Siuslaw, for example, were clear on where their lands ended and another tribe's began, and village sovereignty extended to outlying areas used for hunting, fishing, and gathering. As anthropologist Dennis Gray put it, in making a detailed assessment of Takelma, Applegate Athapaskan, and Galice Creek territoriality, "it is self-evident that the Native Americans knew precisely where they lived." Villages often allowed other tribes to come on to their lands to hunt or fish, but permission had to be granted and some form of compensation was usually expected.

Both American and British law recognized Indian land rights. In America, in one of Chief Justice John Marshall's leading opinions, the Supreme Court ruled as early as 1823 that Indian tribes "were admitted to be the rightful occupants of the soil, with a legal as well as just claim to retain possession of it, and to use it according to their own discretion." This right of occupancy, then and now a fundamental part of American real property law, was a shared right with the United States. The Supreme Court has ruled that the United States, as the militarily superior party, can extinguish Indian title. Nonetheless, the Indian rights continued in force until tribal land titles were extinguished by treaty. Before then, any entry onto aboriginal Indian land was a trespass under settled American law.

The Siletz tribes, then, held their land by law and long possession. Their land helped define them, and their connection and commitment to their homelands were passionate and profound. And, like the HBC, the tyees believed in avenging bad conduct.

Tensions were on the rise in the 1820s as HBC trappers steadily pushed into new territory and the tribes grew ever more threatened. Then the 1828 expedition of Jedediah Strong Smith—an American in the pantheon of storied fur traders and explorers, along with Jim Bridger and Kit Carson—laid bare the sensitivity of the situation and foreshadowed the bloody wars that lay ahead.

Smith was obsessed with pushing the boundaries of the American fur trade ever farther west. He set out from St. Louis in 1821 with the famed Ashley-

Henry expedition and trapped the Upper Missouri River country in what is now Montana and Wyoming. After forming a fur trapping and trading firm, Smith, Jackson & Sublette, he and his party traveled all the way from Bear Lake, Utah, to California in 1826 by way of a southern route. For the return to Bear Lake, Smith chose a more northerly course, crossing the Sierra Nevada, the first white man to do so.

The next year, in a fateful journey, he led his men to southern California and, in the spring of 1828, up through the Sacramento Valley. Fur trading was a substantial business and Smith led a substantial entourage. His expedition, which must have been intimidating to Natives, included Smith and his 17 men, 47 traps, more than 300 horses and mules, and an unknown number of rifles. Smith had his own rules, not much different from the HBC's: "A Christian and a soldier, the Bible and the rifle were his inseparable companions, and the mild teachings of the one never diminished in any way the vigor with which he used the other."

Near today's town of Red Bluff, Smith and his party turned northwest toward the coastal mountains. Indians harassed the trappers, shooting arrows into some of their horses, and the Americans tried to chase them off, but to no avail. On April 16, Smith took matters into his own hands. "In order to intimidate them," as he wrote in his diary, he shot two of them. The next day he shot two more.

The expedition then proceeded laboriously through the rough mountain country before reaching the Klamath River country and the Coast. They

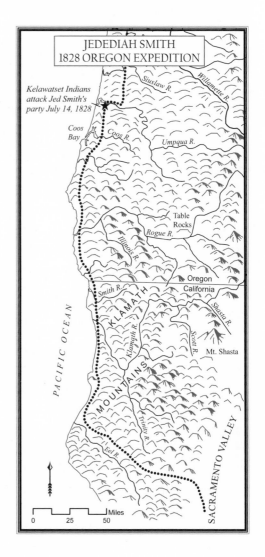

JEDEDIAH SMITH
1828 OREGON EXPEDITION

Kelawatset Indians attack Jed Smith's party July 14, 1828

Siuslaw R.

Willamette R.

Coos Bay

Coos R.

Umpqua R.

Table Rocks

Rogue R.

Illinois R.

Oregon
California

Smith R.

KLAMATH

Shasta R.

Klamath R.

Scott R.

Mt. Shasta

PACIFIC OCEAN

MOUNTAINS

Trinity R.

Eel R.

SACRAMENTO VALLEY

Miles
0   25   50

crossed the Smith River and on June 23, 1828, entered Oregon—at least by the white peoples' maps—by passing from Mexico into lands claimed by Great Britain. The next day, Smith found a deserted Chetco village. It is probable that Smith's killings in northern California explain why the village emptied out and why trouble lay ahead. "Word traveled from village to village ahead of the expedition," one of the expedition chroniclers reported, "that a company of hostile white men was passing through the country." At the mouth of the Rogue River, Tututnis, edgy in the face of this imposing force entering their land, shot arrows into several of the expedition's horses. Smith moved on up the Coast, and his horses received still more arrows, now from Coquilles and Coos. On July 11, the group reached the Umpqua River.

Harrison Rogers, Smith's clerk, recorded in his diary that the first Umpqua village had seventy or eighty residents. They "appear friendly," he wrote, and the Smith party traded for fish and berries. The next day, about three miles above the mouth of the Umpqua River, Rogers described an ill-boding incident: "one of the Ind. stole an ax and we were obliged to seize him for the purpose of tying him before we could scare him to make him give it up. Capt. Smith and one of them caught him and put a cord round his neck, and the rest of us stood with our guns ready in case they made any resistance, there was about 50 Inds. present but did not pretend to resist tying the other."

The Kelawatsets, a band of Lower Umpquas, may not have seemed offended to Rogers's eye, but the humiliation of their fellow tribesman deeply angered them. One chief wanted to attack, while another thought they should hold back. Later, George Simpson of the HBC, who understood Indians as well as any of the whites in the Northwest, made it clear that the ax incident had been mishandled. He rebuked Smith for the "harsh treatment on the part of your people towards the Indians who visited your Camp some of whom you had beaten, and one of them bound hand and feet for some slight offence."

On the Umpqua River, Jedediah Smith sensed trouble. Before leaving to scout a route for the upcoming travel on the morning of July 14, he instructed Rogers not to let any of the Umpquas into camp. Regardless, when about one hundred Indians appeared, for some reason Rogers allowed them in. The Umpquas certainly had not forgotten the ax incident, and, worse, that morning Rogers apparently forced himself on one of the Indian women sexually. As a general matter, the sheer size and might of Smith's party may well have amounted to an invasion in the minds of the Indians. Beverly Ward, who interviewed many tribal elders, reported all of these factors and several other slights. Whatever their motives, the Indians charged, and with axes, knives, and rifles they killed fourteen of Smith's men. Only Smith, who was scouting upriver, and three others survived.

Smith fled to Fort Vancouver to request help from the HBC to retrieve his beaver skins, traps, and horses. The HBC did manage to recover much of the lost property, but decided not to retaliate against the Umpquas. Alexander McLeod had met with the Umpqua chiefs, and his findings were included in George Simpson's long report to the HBC in London. This remarkable document shows as well as anything how the simmering mix of ambitious white exploration, determined tribal nationalism and territoriality, and varying degrees of misconduct (minor theft by an Indian and sexual assault by a white in this instance) held sway in western Oregon from the 1820s through the 1850s. Simpson wrote:

> On arrival there Mr McLeod Summoned the principal Chief and his followers to the Camp, which they obeyed, and in answer to the queries put to them as to the cause of the Massacre, they said, that previous to Smith's arrival they had notice of the approach of his party, from some of the Tribes he had passed, with intimation that they were Enemies destroying all the Natives that came within their reach. That this information was in some degree confirmed by their severely beating and binding the hands and feet of one of their own Tribe who had pilfered an axe (a very slight offence in their estimation). That they declared themselves to be people of a different Nation from us, and our Enemies, and therefore intended to drive us from the Columbia where we were intruders on their Territory. —
>
> These circumstances, they said, induced them to look on the party with suspicion, but they had not formed any plan of destruction, until one of them "Rogers" a Clerk, in Smith's absence, attempted to force a Woman into his Tent, whose Brother was knocked down by Rogers while endeavouring to protect her; upon which, seeing the opportunity favorable, as some of the people were asleep, others Eating and none on their guard, they rose in a body and dispatched the whole party except the man who fled.
>
> Some parts of this Statement, Smith denies; but the whole story is well told, and carries the probability of truth along with it. —

The Oregon fur trade fell into decline in the 1830s. Beaver populations dropped as HBC trappers, increasingly familiar with the terrain, grew more efficient. Then the company, fearing United States influence in the Northwest, intentionally created fur deserts, hunting areas completely out of beavers to discourage American trappers. The death knell for the once-flourishing trade came in the mid-1830s, when new silk hats became all the rage and demand for high-topped beaver hats plummeted. From that point on, British influence in the Northwest waned and American fortunes surged.

The early arrivals from the United States included notables other than homesteaders. Jason and Daniel Lee came to the Willamette Valley in 1834 and established a Methodist mission for the purpose of educating Indians. "Christianizing" Native Americans had been the goal of federal policy since the late 1700s, and in 1819, Congress took the step—extraordinary by modern lights—of subsidizing Christian missionaries to set up churches and schools in Indian country. The Lees' mission, the first in Oregon, initiated the Christian proselytizing that would play such an insistent role in Natives' lives.

In the years after Lewis and Clark's expedition to the Pacific, the Willamette Valley gradually gained the status of legend in American eyes. In that heyday of the Jeffersonian Ideal, the valley's extraordinary agricultural potential stood out. Ample salmon runs coursed in the full-bodied flows of the Willamette River and its many tributaries. Promoter Hall Jackson Kelley read the Lewis and Clark journals and in the 1830s fueled "Oregon fever" and promoted the valley as a "New Eden." By 1834, a trickle of pioneers opened the Oregon Trail, which came down the Snake River and the main stem of the Columbia.

Traffic also began moving north from California, bringing trouble along with it. In 1834, the mountain man Ewing Young, with fifteen men, drove more than 150 horses on the California-Oregon Trail north to the Willamette Valley. Young's colleagues, who had no regard for Indian lives, shot eight Natives while in California. When they reached the Rogue River, two Takelmas came to their camp. Because some of Young's men had contracted "fever and ague," the Americans feared that the Indians would report the sickness back to the tribe and put the expedition in danger. To prevent that, they shot both Takelmas. Three years later, Young led another California-to-Oregon expedition, this time driving some 600 cattle north to establish Oregon herds. They shot a Takelma man and boy and an unknown number of other Indians. In 1840, a large HBC party rounded up 4,000 sheep and 2,000 cattle in California and drove the gargantuan herd north to the Willamette Valley, tramping through the meadows and forests of Takelma and Shasta territory.

The Upper Rogue would remain the flashpoint for Indian-white tensions for a generation. The Willamette Valley was the new arrivals' destination, but conflicts with the tribes of the Willamette were unlikely since nearly all had been killed off by the epidemics. The Coast Range separated the coastal tribes from the Willamette and the interior Rogue Valley. The lands of the Takelmas, Shastas, and Applegate Athapaskans lay on the main route.

The Willamette Valley had a white population of just 137 in 1840, but by 1850 the American citizenry in Oregon, most of it in the valley, swelled to over 12,000. Most of the newcomers came from the north on the Oregon Trail, which roughly followed the path of modern-day Interstate 84. In 1846, Jesse Applegate and others opened a more direct route—the Applegate Trail, also called the Southern Route—that took off to the south from Fort Hall and then met up with the California-Oregon Trail to go through the Upper Rogue River Valley. Now the Takelma and other tribes had settlers from the east, as well as from California, moving across their territory.

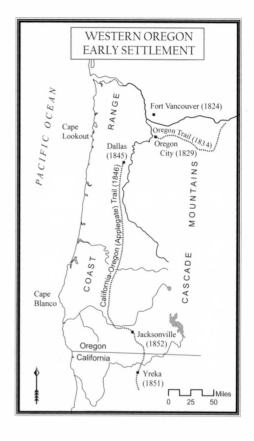

The United States had its ambitions fixed on controlling the continent, from the Atlantic to the Pacific, and Oregon was a big part of the mega-politics. The cry was "Manifest Destiny," and in 1844 the voters chose James Knox Polk as the president to accomplish it. Polk put forth three main planks in his platform: bring the Republic of Texas into the nation; take the Southwest from Mexico; and eliminate Great Britain's claim to the Pacific Northwest. He achieved all three goals and, Jefferson's Louisiana Purchase notwithstanding, brought more land under American control than any other president. The Oregon Compromise, memorialized in a treaty with Great Britain, was completed in 1846, bringing Oregon—and Washington, Idaho, and parts of Wyoming and Montana as well—under U.S. jurisdiction and ownership.

The next step for the new Oregonians, even though the population was not yet large enough to qualify for statehood, was to obtain territorial status so that they could have a delegate to Congress and gain an interim, but still official, legislature and courts. Congress acted and the Oregon Territory came into existence in 1849; almost all of its citizens lived south of the Columbia River, but the sprawling territory encompassed present-day Washington and Idaho and reached to western Montana. The territorial statute provided that Indian land rights would remain in place until extinguished by treaty.

Statehood would not come for another decade, in 1859, but now the immigrants had momentum on their side. The settlers wanted sovereignty, but they also wanted land. Even before the 1846 treaty with Great Britain was signed, bills were introduced in Congress to lay the foundation for land grants to American homesteaders in the Oregon country. Once the treaty became law, pressure for land rights intensified. Then, with territorial status, Oregon had a representative in Washington, D.C., who, while nonvoting, could advance the cause for land in Congress. The first territorial delegate, Samuel Thurston, more than filled the bill: "He was an indefatigable promoter of a Donation Land Act for his Oregon constituents. In the East he interviewed editors, Congressmen, and executive officers, always urging a land grant."

The breakthrough came in 1850, when Congress adopted the Donation Land Act in order to promote settlement in Oregon. Resident white males were entitled to grants of 320 acres and resident married couples could receive 640 acres (a full square mile). For those arriving during the next three years, a single person could claim 160 acres, a married couple 320 acres. The grants were free upon showing settlement on the land and cultivation of crops for four years.

The generosity of the Donation Land Act fueled even more excitement for Oregon land, and the inrush of settlers mushroomed. This early Oregon settlement law, which served as a model for the Homestead Act of 1862, has been roundly praised by American politicians and scholars. It inspired one observer to exult that it "came very near to meeting the classic homestead ideal—award of the best farmland to the actual settlers."

But "the best farmland" was Indian land, and "the actual settlers" did not include Indians. Congress knew there was a problem, namely, that the United States held shared land title with Indian tribes and could not grant the land without first resolving Indian title. To address this, Congress adopted a parallel and complementary policy that put western Oregon Indians and their homelands squarely in the sights of federal power: The Oregon Indian Treaty

PART TWO. WAR AND REMOVAL

Act directed the negotiation of treaties for "the extinguishment of their claims to lands lying west of the Cascade Mountains" and, if practical, "for their removal east of said mountains."

The national legislature could hardly have been more blunt: Indians may have land rights but we will adjust them through treaties dictated on our terms. Western Oregon is for white settlers, not Indians.

In the villages, Indians in 1850 could see that changes were coming. The steadily increasing march of white people into Oregon left no doubt about that. Diseases had taken most of the people, and the epidemics continued to do their horrible work as smallpox swept the south Coast in 1836–1837; measles hit the Lower Columbia, the Willamette Valley, and the Umpqua Valley in 1847–1848; and a smallpox epidemic ravaged the Lower Columbia River and northern Oregon Coast in 1853. Only thousands remained where once there had been tens of thousands.

Still, in many respects the old ways held. People still lived in their villages, speaking their languages, governing themselves, telling the old stories, and dancing the old dances. Salmon still filled the rivers and the coastal reach remained a cornucopia. They even tried to adapt to the new circumstances. As Robert Kentta explained, "The relationships between our tribal people and the settlers changed slightly or radically depending on the rate of population influx and the main activity of the new population, as the focus switched in different areas from fur trade to permanent settlement activities. It doesn't appear that our ancestors resisted settlement to the point that they thought *all foreigners* needed to be kept out, but instead tried to accommodate settlers who were respectful."

Respect. There had been some of that before 1850. Fur traders adopted some Indian ways. Some farmers acted as neighbors. Some took Indians as spouses. Looking to the future, during the Indian treaty era that Congress set in motion in the 1850s, some federal officials honestly kept the best interests of the tribes in mind along with their federal duties. Yet that respect for Indian rights, shaky but still holding promise, never took hold. New personalities, hard-edged and mean-spirited far beyond the trappers or the farmers, threw the lives of the Siletz people into a chaos of insensitivity and virulent racism from which it seemed they could never emerge.

GOLD FEVER

"Extermination!"

THE DISCOVERY OF GOLD IN CALIFORNIA IGNITED EXPLOSIVE changes that soon reached Oregon's Indians and non-Indians alike. Communications and transportation being what they were, word of James Marshall's historic strike on the American River near Sutter's Mill on January 24, 1848, did not make it back to the East Coast and to other nations in time for goldseekers to travel to the Sierra Nevada foothills that year. Instead, the skyrocket that was the California Gold Rush blasted off with the Forty Niners, and "Gold Fever" generated one of the greatest migrations in human history. In 1848, an estimated 14,000 non-Indians lived in California. By 1852, the population had shot to 223,000.

The California Gold Rush made the expansionists' dream of "Manifest Destiny" a reality by installing an economic powerhouse in the Far West. In short order, the mines were producing nearly half of the world's gold. Mining brought waves of economic benefits in addition to the value of the precious metal itself. Supply towns—Sacramento, San Francisco, and many others—expanded and prospered. All manner of manufacturers and shippers, many far beyond the Golden State, profited from this burgeoning new source of business. The output of the gold fields also cemented the international standing of the young nation. Writing in the *Oxford History of the American West*, Keith Bryant Jr. concluded: "The gold production alone transformed the role of the United States in world trade and led to rising foreign investments in the West. . . . The trade surplus generated by western mining encouraged the expansion of credit and brought the United States into the mainstream of the world economy."

Events raced ahead. Traditionally, aspiring states had to bide their time by first being recognized by the United States as territories. Alone among western states, California—although it lay off by itself, a thousand miles west of the nearest state—vaulted over territorial status and went straight to statehood in 1850. America's political leaders and its citizenry smiled on the miners and the many benefits they produced.

For all the wealth and perceived good that the Gold Rush brought, the actual conduct of miners on the ground wreaked havoc on Indian tribes. The mining camps were rough-hewn, chaotic tent cities. The miners, more than 90 percent male, were mostly hard-working, hard-drinking, rootless men who had no stabilizing family lives. Avid to locate and hold new claims, they spread out over the landscape and took charge, oblivious to impacts on people or the land. They "were not settlers or pioneers in the tradition of America's westward migration," J. S. Holliday wrote. "These people came as exploiters, transients, ready to take, not to build." When the goldseekers encountered Indians—which was common, since California was nearly all Indian land in the early Gold Rush days—many miners, regarding Indians as little more than wildlife, chased them off their ancestral land or shot and otherwise abused them.

Needless to say, a movement as frenzied as the Gold Rush would not be constrained by political boundaries. In the highly regarded "Shirley Letters," Dame Shirley (the pen name of Louise Amelia Knapp Smith, wife of a miner at Rich Bar and one of the few women in the camps) observed that "our countrymen are the most discontented of mortals. They are always longing for 'big strikes.' If a 'claim' is paying them a steady income, by which, if they pleased, they could lay up more in a month, than they could accumulate in a year at home, still, they are dissatisfied, and, in most cases, will wander off in search of better 'diggings.'" Mark Twain, who toured the gold country, reported that "every few days news would come of the discovery of a brand-new mining region; immediately the papers would teem with accounts of its richness, and away the surplus population would scamper to take possession." A Sacramento paper described the waves of miners as "a sea whose tide knows no law—a rumor or a reality will fill a canon with thousands of human beings."

And so, by 1850, miners swarmed into northern California and the southernmost river valley in Oregon—the Rogue.

The Takelma, Athapaskan, and Shasta tribes had endured more than two decades of steadily increasing traffic through the Upper Rogue River country, where the broad, level terrain offered generally good passage for wagons and herds traveling between California and the Willamette Valley. They were on guard. In their eyes, every entry onto their territory was a provocative act. The incoming whites were jittery, too. For them, every arrow was provocation. Yet it is hard to deny that, more than Jedediah Smith and the other fur traders, more than the farmers, the "wild, reckless" character of the miners lay at the center of the violence that raked the Rogue River country from 1850 through 1856. As Oregon historian Albert Walling put it,

> Good men were there and bad. The same vicious qualities which charac-
> terized the ruffian in more settled communities marked his career in this,
> except that circumstances may have given him a better chance here to
> display himself. . . . A portion were ready to do the Indian harm, and cir-
> cumstances never could have been more favorable to their malice. Law and
> justice were not; and whenever and wherever a white man's lust or love of
> violence led him then and there an outrage was perpetrated.

In the spring of 1850, Takelmas and incoming miners clashed at Rock Point, in a steep canyon downriver from Table Rocks. During the skirmish, the Indians made off with the pack horses, loaded with pouches of gold. Furious, the miners continued on to the Willamette Valley and enlisted the help of Joseph Lane, the territorial governor, who promptly rode by horseback to the Upper Rogue country. It is here that we first see the confluence of two of the four political leaders—Lane and Apserkahar, the Takelma tyee—who would be so prominent during the 1850s. Joel Palmer and Tyee John would come to the fore later.

A general in the army and a war hero during the Mexican conflict, Joseph Lane necessarily focused his energies as territorial governor on relations with the tribes, one of the major public issues in Oregon during the 1840s and 1850s. Handsome and outgoing, Lane had a way of engendering affection and trust, an attribute that would serve him well during his rise in state and national politics. While he was paternalistic and hardly sympathized with the tribes' objectives—especially their desire to retain large amounts of land—he was patient and willing to listen. Lane was ever firm in his representation of the United States' interests—and later would turn on the Indians by, among other things, opposing any reservations west of the Cascades—but in these early dealings Indian leaders liked and respected him.

In his journey to the Upper Rogue River Valley, Lane took with him fifteen whites and fifteen members of the Klickitat Tribe, who were hostile to the Takelma. Upon his arrival, he sent out word that he wanted to meet with the Takelma chiefs in two days to discuss a treaty of peace and friendship.

Tyee Apserkahar (Horse Rider) and some seventy-five men, all unarmed, crossed the Rogue River in canoes and arrived at the appointed time and place, near Table Rocks. Apserkahar and Tyee Sam were tyees of a large village nearby. Tall and slim, just past middle age, Apserkahar, known as a man of peace among both Indians and whites, was especially influential with other Takelma villages and with the Shasta and Applegate Athapaskan tribes as well.

The talks had barely begun before another group of about seventy-five Takelmas rode in, armed with bows and arrows. They agreed to put their weapons aside, but the mood had grown tense—Lane exchanged "significant glances" with Quatley, chief of the Klickitats and Lane's main protector, before continuing with his presentation. He explained that the United States insisted on peace and the ability of its citizens to pass through Takelma territory in safety. When Lane finished, Apserkahar began translating the speech but his tribesmen rose in anger, shouting war cries. Quatley leapt into action, grabbing Apserkahar and putting a knife to his throat. Lane pulled his loaded revolver. When the dust settled, the Indians agreed to return in two days—but Apserkahar would remain a prisoner.

During the captivity, Apserkahar and Lane became friends, so much so that Apserkahar asked Lane if he would give him his name. From that time on, Apserkahar was known as Tyee Joe. When the negotiations resumed, Lane obtained his treaty along with Tyee Joe's personal promise to help in keeping the peace.

The 1850 peace lasted, with intermittent breaches, for a year. But too many miners were working the creeks and too many homesteaders were establishing Donation Land Act claims. In the end, despite their good intentions, neither Tyee Joe nor Lane could control their people.

The spring of 1851 saw many and grievous hostilities. On the Coast, Captain William Tichenor with his crew of nine brought a steamship, the *Sea Gull*, into the harbor at Port Orford, with the intent of establishing a settlement there. The location, Tichenor reasoned, would make a good spot for a supply town to serve

Battle Rock, where Captain Tichenor's men positioned themselves. Local Indians approached from the bluff located to the right of the photograph on June 18, 1851, before being fired upon. *Siletz Tribal Collection.*

the inland miners. Leaving his crew behind to establish a townsite and scout out the area, he embarked in the small steamer for Portland to obtain supplies.

The remaining Americans, seeing a small group of Indians on the cliffs, grew concerned about their safety. They decided to camp on the flat, timbered ground atop the massive formation attached to the shore at all but high tide, that now carries the name Battle Rock. There they set up a cannon. Word of the ship's arrival spread among the Tututnis, and the next morning a large group of Indians assembled on the cliffs. They approached Battle Rock, not knowing of the loaded cannon.

J. M. Kirkpatrick ignited the cannon at close range with an ear-shattering explosion. The ammunition—"bar lead cut up in pieces of from one to two inches in length"—tore into the Indians, killing as many as thirty and wounding many more. In the aftermath, the Indians carried away their dead and the ship's crew of nine, abandoned by Captain Tichenor and the *Sea Gull*, fled to the north on foot.

PART TWO. WAR AND REMOVAL

History cannot finally tell us who the aggressor was at Battle Rock—the first Indian-white clash on the southern Oregon Coast since Jedediah Smith had entered Umpqua territory thirty-four years earlier. Kirkpatrick, who fired the cannon, laid the blame on Tututnis, claiming that a leader "with at least one hundred of his braves, started for us with a rush." Anson Dart, the newly appointed superintendent of Indian Affairs who arrived at Port Orford about two weeks after the cannon blast, concluded that "instead of an Indian massacre of a white settlement, it was an atrocious massacre of peaceable and friendly Indians."

More misunderstanding and violence soon erupted on the Coast. Port Orford business people, eager to hook up with inland commercial traffic, decided to explore a connecting route up the Rogue River to the California-Oregon Trail. In August 1851, William T'Vault agreed to head up the expedition, which soon turned into a boondoggle. They made only halting progress in the steep, rugged country. When they finally reached the Big Bend of the Rogue River, exhausted and nearly out of food, half of the party turned back. T'Vault and nine others struck out to the north, bushwhacking out of the Rogue watershed and into the Coquille. There, Indians befriended the bedraggled Americans and offered to take them downriver to the Coast.

At the mouth of the Coquille, everything turned sour—"the most awful state of confusion . . . it appeared to be the screams of thousands, the sound of blows, the groans and shrieks of the dying," as T'Vault described it. For reasons that remain unclear—one historian wrote that "T'Vault and Williams [another survivor] seem to have left out some element necessary to make sense . . . of the story"—T'Vault's men and Indians from a large Coquille village were suddenly locked in mortal combat. Five Americans were killed.

T'Vault made it back to Port Orford and spread his story of the massacre. To avenge the deaths, Colonel Silas Casey took sixty soldiers back up the Coast to the Coquille and for four days rowed up the river. All the villages were empty. On November 21, they finally came upon Indians, never mind whether they had any connection to the earlier combat. Casey's charge to his men was "Boys, take good sight, throw no shots away, give them hell!" Two American privates and fifteen Indians lost their lives to punctuate the sorry, confused episode.

Major combat also broke out inland. May and early June of 1851 brought several skirmishes on the Upper Rogue and the adjoining Klamath rivers. Indian attacks on incoming miners and settlers, along with raids by volunteer armies of miners, took dozens of white and Indian lives. Whites in the Upper Rogue Valley sent a petition to Territorial Governor John Gaines, urging him to raise a volunteer company to fight the Indians. Gaines, wanting to see the situation himself before bringing in citizen soldiers, headed down to the Rogue country. But events overtook him. Before he arrived, Major Philip Kearney and his troops moved into action.

Major Kearney, who was in the Umpqua Valley scouting a route for a military road, learned of the conflicts in the Upper Rogue Valley and set out with his twenty-eight soldiers for the Table Rocks area. Learning that a large number of Indians had camped in a wooded area about ten miles upriver of Table Rocks, he proceeded up the Rogue. On June 17, the military charged the Indian impoundment. They lost one man, Captain James Stuart, but otherwise the major's surprise attack was a one-sided bloodbath. As Jesse Applegate, Kearney's guide, wrote:

> It was a most admirably chosen battle field [from the Indian standpoint], and could the Indian runner have succeeded in giving his friends notice only of a few minutes, the daring charge of the Major into this stronghold might have resulted in a terrible tragedy and defeat. But the highest ground in the peninsula being along the bank of the river, it seems the whole body of Indians had rushed there to ascertain what was going on up the river; the charging cavalry had cut them off from the lagoon almost as soon as they were seen; they were not prepared to fight a whirlwind or thunderbolt, and seemed only intent on escape, and by the river was their only chance. But the troubles of the savages were not ended. As the sabers of Capt. Stuart's Company were strapped to their saddles in such a way that they could not get at them, they used their firearms only, but the flying Indians had barely reached the opposite bank of the river, when Capt. Walker was upon them, his troops sword in hand. Here many were slaughtered; the writer of this saw Capt. Walker cut down two of these helpless wretches with his own hand.

Kearney returned five days later, his ranks fortified by a hundred volunteers. They engaged in another successful battle, tracked down some Indian warriors, and "scoured the country from the ferry to Table Rocks, returning in the evening to Camp Stuart, when the campaign was considered as closed." The U.S. Army had killed fifty Indians, wounded many more, and taken thirty women and children as prisoners in preparation for the treaty negotiations they expected to take place between the tribes and Governor Gaines. The

Indians, mostly Takelmas, were despondent. Joseph Lane, who had come on the scene, said the Indians complained to him "that white men had come on horses in great numbers, invading every portion of their country. They were afraid, they said, to lie down to sleep lest the strangers should be upon them. They wearied of war and wanted peace."

To consummate the peace, Governor John Gaines met with a group of Takelmas and other Upper Rogue River Indian leaders, and the two sides signed a treaty on July 14, 1851. It was a brief "peace and friendship" treaty, meaning that it did not involve a land transfer: in the less-than-comprehensive treaty, the parties mutually promised "a lasting peace" and agreed to return all prisoners. The agreement of a year before, negotiated between Joseph Lane and Tyee Joe, was not a true treaty since Lane had resigned as territorial governor shortly before the negotiations and could not speak for the United States. The Gaines document of 1851, however, was intended to become a formal treaty but never went into effect because the United States Senate failed to ratify it.

Unratified treaties played a major role in federal Indian policy in Oregon in the 1850s. In the case of the Gaines treaty, the tribes lost nothing tangible due to the lack of ratification since no land was involved and no binding promises were made. Different were the more expansive land treaties, where western Oregon tribes were promised permanent reservations in exchange for ceding most of their aboriginal lands. In 1851, between them, Governor Gaines and Superintendent of Indian Affairs Anson Dart negotiated no fewer than nineteen land treaties—none ratified—with western Oregon tribes: four with Kalapuya bands, two with Molala bands, and one with the Clackamas Tribe in the Willamette Valley; six with Chinook bands and one with the Clatsop on the Columbia; three with Tillamook bands on the northern Coast; and two with Tututni and Coquille bands on the southern Coast. Congress scuttled them all because some settlers claimed land within proposed treaty reservations and because Joseph Lane, by 1851 Oregon's territorial delegate to Congress, objected to any Indian reservations in the Willamette Valley.

As a matter of law, the lack of ratification should have worked in favor of the tribes: absent Congress's approval of the treaty, their cession of land to the United States did not go into effect; as a result, they continued to hold title to their vast aboriginal homelands. It failed to work that way in practice. Administrators acted as though the lands had been ceded legally and allowed

Donation Land Act claims and mining claims to move ahead. Native people, poor in terms of the new currency and unsophisticated in the white man's laws, had no access to attorneys to protect their land rights. Pushed off their aboriginal lands by settlers but lacking any reservations, they were saddled with all of the negatives and benefited from none of the positives of the 1851 treaties that they solemnly signed but Congress failed to ratify. The resulting anger and distrust made the brewing unrest stronger yet.

The southern Oregon tribes—the Coos, Umpqua, Chetco, and Tututni on the Coast and the upriver Takelma, Shasta, and Athapaskans—had all encountered the invading miners during the early spillover from California in 1850 and 1851. The violence in those two years was all linked in some way to mining through the actions of aggressive individual miners or the ambitious entrepreneurs looking to supply the Oregon mining boom they hoped would come. Rough and trigger-happy, the miners were plainly dangerous—but they were not numerous, probably totaling no more than a few hundred in southern Oregon. Further, because none of them made big strikes and were always on the move, always in a rush, the peripatetic newcomers made no permanent settlements.

Then came Jacksonville. In January 1852, James Cluggage took his bowie knife, scraped around in the creek-side gravel of a canyon (soon to be called Rich Gulch) on Jackson Creek, and uncovered an abundance of bright, chunky nuggets. Ebullient, Cluggage knew there would be much more, that this was the real thing. He and his partner, J. R. Pool, tried to keep their find a secret, but word of such a bonanza could not be contained. Within a month, the rush was on and the gold was there for the taking. As with the early days and years of the California Gold Rush, miners worked placer deposits—loose nuggets and flakes in gravel and soil. Placer mining did not require the elaborate tunnels and shafts and backbreaking pick-axe labor required to extract lode deposits, where the precious metal is embedded in rock. In the early years, most of this Oregon gold, which had washed down the mountainsides over the eons, was found in highly accessible placer deposits, mixed in with the sand and gravel of the banks and beds of streams at the bottom of canyons.

The new town of Jacksonville—the first in southern Oregon—boomed to a population of 1,000 by summer. Miners, nearly all male, continued to flood in.

Jacksonville in the mid-1850s—a town where none existed just a few years earlier. The artist of the somewhat romanticized painting is Peter Britt, who came to Rich Gulch penniless, made a strike, and began a successful career as a photographer and painter. Tyee Jim, a signer of the 1853 treaty, was shot and killed from one of these houses as he walked down the street in 1854. *Courtesy of Southern Oregon Historical Society, no. B330.*

Tents were followed by cedar cabins and clapboard buildings for residences, bars, and gambling establishments. With Jackson Creek mostly taken up by claims, newly arriving miners moved on to other profitable sites at Gold Hill, Sterling, and the Applegate River. Riding on the population surge from the rich mineral deposits, rowdy Jackson County quickly outstripped the agricultural communities and became the largest county in Oregon. The miners may also have made Jacksonville the largest town. Oregon City had just 933 people and Portland had only 805 in the 1850 census.

These were not homesteading families, intent on farming and building communities. Men came to Jacksonville for one reason, to strike it rich—and whether they made it big or not, to move on to another prospective gold field or return home. Although Jacksonville was lawful when it came to the business of mining (claim-jumping, for example, was rare and quickly punished when it occurred), as a society it was otherwise lawless and violent. In particular, while some individuals were moderate and sensible, the dominant mindset labeled Indians as dangerous nuisances. There were no compunctions about killing them on the spot.

The first major hostilities broke out in the summer of 1852, soon after Jacksonville's founding. Alarm spread among Upper Rogue River Indians when they learned that the killing of a miner in the Siskiyou Mountains of northern California had been blamed on them. The rumors spread to Jacksonville, where citizens organized a vigilante force of some seventy-five men. Vigilantes also came up from California, bringing with them Indian hostages for protection. With danger in the air, Judge A. A. Skinner stepped in to help. Skinner, recently appointed federal Indian agent and committed to justice for the tribes, arranged a peace talk with the Takelmas at Big Bar, near Table Rocks. Tyee Joe and Tyee Sam brought their men to the north bank but, seeing the imposing assemblage on the other side, grew reluctant to cross the river. Skinner, thinking it was safe, coaxed them, and eventually the two leaders and some of their tribesmen came across the Rogue.

Almost immediately, one of the Californians overreacted. Thinking that a hostage was attempting to escape, he shot him dead at close range. Fighting erupted, but the Takelmas were overmatched. Thirteen Indian men were shot and killed, many of them as they attempted to swim the Rogue.

The vigilantes spent the next few days marauding, tracking down and killing still more Indians, including several women. Finally Tyee Sam, his band surrounded, agreed to peace negotiations moderated by Agent Skinner. The miners, wanting more blood, argued for continuing the battle but the settlers urged a moderate course and finally prevailed. The Takelmas promised peace and also received it, but on stern conditions: if the Indians committed any crimes, the whites could "do with [Tyee Sam] as they think proper, even to the taking off of his head." As another sign that both language and action had taken an ominous turn, the newcomers of Jacksonville and the Upper Rogue River Valley had adopted a commonly used term to describe the future of the local Indians: *extermination.*

By the pivotal year of 1853, Indians and whites in southern Oregon, and especially in the Upper Rogue Valley, stood on the brink of all-out war. Both sides had their strengths but the scales had tipped in favor of the newcomers. True settlers—farmers and townspeople who intended to stay—had steadily grown in numbers. Donation Land Act claims in Jackson County went from 8 in 1851 to 53 in 1852, and then to 129 in 1853. The settlers' population about equaled the Indians'. But the dramatic influx of miners made all the difference and put Natives in the minority for the first time in history.

The outlook turned increasingly grim. In that frontier society, the miners, sometimes supported by the settlers, took the law into their own hands. They organized as "volunteers," a term usually applied to citizens who step forward to serve on a short-term basis when United States military forces run short of regulars. In southern Oregon, however, many of these groups acted independently of official military leadership and paid no heed to the promises of "peace and friendship" in the treaty that Governor Gaines had negotiated two years earlier. These vigilantes, who would make life miserable for the tribes and interfere with federal officials for the next three years, committed many slaughters and atrocities, including lynchings.

For their part, the tribes also had people who carried out raids, thefts, and killings. Some villagers believed they were not governed by the treaties; the Gaines treaty, for example, was signed by only eleven tyees, who could not speak for all of the dozens of independent villages. Others, members of villages represented in the treaty, operated outside their people's laws by ignoring the spirit of the peace treaties.

It is a mistake, however, to think of this and later stages of the Rogue River War in terms of equivalency, as a conflict where blame should be equally allocated between the two sides. By 1850, the tribes had reached an accommodation with the settlers; the implicit live-and-let-live understanding was an uneasy, delicate one to be sure, but it had promise. The Gold Rush changed everything, as the miners and their vigilante groups threw southwestern Oregon into turmoil. Joel Palmer, superintendent of Indian Affairs for the Oregon Territory from 1853 to 1857 and the senior federal Indian official in the region, wrote these sentiments in 1856. It was a view shared by other leading Americans, including Judge Matthew Deady, General John Wool, and John Beeson:

> The cause of the present difficulty in southern Oregon is wholly to be attributed to the acts of our own people. . . . The Indians in that district have been driven to desperation by acts of cruelty . . . that would disgrace the most barbarous nations of the earth. . . .

The region now had a great deal of firepower. The miners had come to the gold fields armed, and Native peoples had always been expert with bows and arrows. In particular, Takelmas carved sharp and deadly arrowheads and could deliver them accurately at distances of 100 yards or more. But now the Indians also had stocked themselves with rifles through trade with the whites, and later with the Klickitats. By 1853, they likely had more firearms than the settlers and miners combined. Though outnumbered in terms of fighting men, the tribes were formidable adversaries, courageous and committed.

Indians were ever more determined to hold their land as the impacts of white invasions became evident. Placer mining, which flushed large amounts of water through sluices to separate the gold from the surrounding material, wreaked havoc on the salmon runs by sending tons of soil, gravel, and debris into the rivers, clouding the water and destroying spawning grounds. Domestic hogs on the loose dug up roots and ate acorns. Packers for the miners grazed large numbers of mules on luxuriant prairies, especially in the Upper Rogue country; these and other domestic animals ate or trampled camas and other native foods and medicines. Fenced and plowed farms put traditional gathering and hunting areas off limits entirely.

Events beyond the Rogue River country also contributed to the incendiary environment. Killings of miners in the Umpqua River watershed to the north and the Klamath River to the south were often blamed on Rogue River Indians, and accused Indians from the north and south escaped to the Rogue, usually with vengeful posses in pursuit. The widely publicized Whitman massacre of 1847 near present-day Walla Walla, Washington, instilled continuing alarm and fear throughout the Oregon Territory. Kamiakin, a Yakama chief, raised the hackles of federal officials by traveling to other Northwest tribes and urging them to unite in resistance to the whites.

Tyees Joe and Sam continued on, determined to keep the peace. Historian Albert Walling wrote that

> the Indians began, in the spring of 1853, to court the friendship of the whites. . . . Several highly respected pioneer inhabitants of Jacksonville, including two or more ladies, have now . . . given testimony concerning the unvarying courtesy and gentleness of the principal chiefs of the tribe, when met in times of peace. Sam and Joe, they say, were favored guests in private homes; and by their dignified and manly ways, won the approbation of all who could appreciate their simple yet honorable character.

Tyee Joe's daughter, Mary, also was a "familiar figure" in Jacksonville and acted as a peacemaker on other occasions. Yet their efforts, and those of many whites as well, went for naught. During the violence that erupted in 1853, 100 to 120 people died in combat from June through August. At least ten Indians were hanged. Two events stand out among the many battles, raids, and skirmishes of 1853.

On August 6, Daniel Giles, a seventeen-year-old clerk in an Applegate Valley store, rode his mule over to Jacksonville. On the way, he was confronted by a group of Indians. He might have lost his life had he not previously befriended the son and daughter of Tyee John, the respected Shasta leader. The son, Charley, was in the group and persuaded his colleagues to hold off. When Daniel reached Jacksonville, he realized how raw the emotions were. Miners were forming vigilante groups and killing Indians based on dubious evidence, or none at all. He saw the bodies of several Indians hanging from oak trees in Jacksonville. Another man witnessed ten or twelve Indians dead by the side of the road outside of town.

Combat broke out shortly after Daniel Giles returned to the Applegate Valley. About twenty volunteers, led by Lieutenant Burrell Griffin, rode from Jacksonville to the Applegate and destroyed an Indian village. Then they met with resistance. This was the first engagement between whites and the Applegate leader, Tyee John, who would play such a major role in southern Oregon over the next three years. John and his men retreated up a side canyon and took cover. The Shastas surprised the pursuing federal troops and overpowered the Americans, driving them off, killing one and wounding Griffin, their leader:

> The engagement, which lasted three-quarters of an hour, was closely contested, and bravely and skillfully fought. The Indians, better sheltered than the whites, met with a heavier loss, as they acknowledged five killed and wounded. The soldiers were compelled to retreat finally, leaving the battlefield to the Indians. The savages probably outnumbered the whites by at least two to one, and had the additional advantage of being at home. But more than anything else that contributed to this success was the fact that Old John, their redoubtable war chief, led them, and by his strategy and foresight secured a victory. If their chief was so warlike the individual warriors of his band were hardly less so. Of one of them, "Bill," who was wounded at the fight on Williams' creek, General Lane once said that he never met a braver man in peace or war.

The final battle of 1853 took place in the mountains northwest of Table Rocks. Joseph Lane, at his home in the Umpqua Valley, heard of the warfare

"Princess" Mary, daughter of Shasta war leader Tyee John, in 1896. *Courtesy of Oregon Historical Society, no. bb006082.*

Indian Mary, daughter of Tyee Joe from the village of Grave Creek, in the early 1900s. *Courtesy of Oregon Historical Society, no. bb006084.*

on the Upper Rogue and hastened to the scene, arriving on August 21. Because of his military fame and relationships with the Native people, especially Tyee Joe (formerly Apserkahar), he assumed overall command of the federal troops and volunteers. The crucial battle took place three days later under the most difficult conditions for both sides, who endured intense summer heat, smoke from forest fires, and brushy, rocky terrain.

Tribal warriors, led by Tyee Joe, had retreated and camped at a rugged, secluded site on Upper Evans Creek, close to the 4,000-foot peak that would soon be named Battle Mountain. They assumed that they had eluded their pursuers. But the whites had stayed on the Indians' trail, even though the brush grew too thick for horses, and their charge on foot caught the Natives off guard. The fighting was furious. Lane took a shot in his right arm just below the shoulder. Three of his soldiers were killed and three wounded. The tribes had the worst of it, with eight dead and twenty wounded.

Within an hour, the Indians called out for a truce. They wanted to speak with Lane, who had been taken to the rear of the company. The general

PART TWO. WAR AND REMOVAL

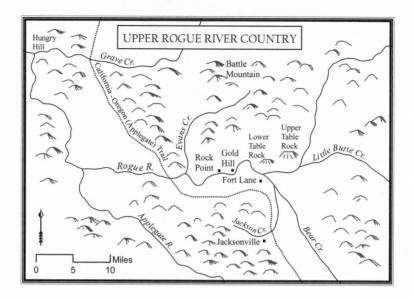

returned to the front wearing a bulky coat to conceal his heavily wrapped arm and shoulder. "On going into their camp, Lane found many wounded; and they were burning their dead, as if fearful they would fall into the hands of the enemy. He was met by chief Jo, his namesake, and his brothers Sam and Jim, who told him their hearts were sick of war." Lane wrote, "I told them who I was and why I come. That I was tired of fighting and come to talk with them, to eat, sleep and smoke with them."

The tyees and Lane talked at length and laid plans for peace talks and a formal treaty at Table Rock. Then, in a gesture of humanity and hope for a brighter future, Indian soldiers served as bearers of the stretchers that carried the wounded Americans some fifteen miles back to their camp. Of this, historian Hubert Howe Bancroft observed wryly that "I find no mention made of any such humane or christian conduct on the part of the superior race."

5

TABLE ROCKS, 1853

"The white man is as plenty away over

the mountains as the trees in the woods."

TYEE JOE AND GENERAL JOSEPH LANE AGREED, AT THE END OF the battle of August 24, to meet seven days later at Table Rocks. The tyees needed several days to assemble Indians hiding out in the hills so that all could hear the momentous discussions that would, they hoped, finally bring peace. A feeling of harmony settled in during the next few days, as tempers cooled and both sides grazed their horses together on the open meadows near the massive rock formations. Still, when the appointed date came, the tribes were not ready to talk. Tyees Joe and Sam knew Lane well and trusted him. Tyee John (Tecumtum, "Elk Killer"), the Shasta warrior who had defeated the Americans in his home Applegate Valley, however, was much less familiar with Lane. As Joel Palmer wrote in his diary, the other tribal members must have been even more apprehensive, for when he and Lane went out to meet with the Indians "but a few could be found. They affeared treachery on our part and are very shy. It is with the utmost difficulty that they can be approached."

Nevertheless, Palmer and Lane pushed forward, toward a treaty. Lane held a council on September 4 with several Takelma tyees: Joe, Sam, Jim, George, and Lympy. The talks led to a preliminary treaty on September 8. This peace and friendship treaty, which laid the groundwork for the formal and comprehensive negotiations two days later, described the territorial limits of the Upper Rogue River tribes, declared peace, and, while it did not identify a particular locale, promised a permanent home for the tribes. The document did not refer to the most sensitive issue of all, the sale of tribal land. On September 9, Palmer held another council with tribal members and, in an emotional presentation, urged the tribes to cede most of their aboriginal lands to the United States because of the force and inevitability of the flood of settlers: "The white man has come and they will continue to come for they are as plenty away over the mountains as the trees in the woods."

By this time, the Table Rocks area had become the site of a major assemblage. Hundreds of Indian people rode in. Several companies of troops arrived in order to beef up the American military presence. And many leaders, Indian and white, were in attendance. As one historian accurately put it, "The occasion was a remarkable one; and brought together many remarkable individuals." The principal Takelma, Athapaskan, and Shasta tyees were there. On the American side, save for the territorial governor, the leading dignitaries in the state came to Table Rocks to resolve the bitter conflict that was of such moment in the Oregon Territory and California.

To the Americans, the occasion carried significance far beyond the Rogue River country. The agreement signed on September 10, 1853, signaled the implementation of a newly formed federal policy calling for permanent tribal reservations, where Indian people could learn the art of agriculture and become "civilized." The Table Rock document broke new ground in another respect: it was the first ratified land treaty with Indian tribes in the American West.

Lane, fresh from reelection as Oregon's territorial delegate to Congress, and Joel Palmer, just installed as superintendent of Indian Affairs in May, acted as lead representatives for the United States. Palmer, who had farmed in Indiana and served in the state legislature, came west by wagon with his family in 1845 and quickly joined the inner circle of Oregon politics. By 1847, he held three posts at once in the short-lived provisional government—superintendent of Indian Affairs, commissary general for the Cayuse War, and peace commissioner. An adventurer and outdoorsman, he took a pack train down to the California gold fields in 1850 before returning to Dayton in the Willamette Valley to farm and engage in various business enterprises.

Palmer—who would be the dominant figure in Indian Affairs during the critical years of 1853–1856, when Indian land title was extinguished in most of Oregon and the western Oregon tribes were removed en masse—came to the Indian superintendency with respect across the board. His political connections and tenure as commissary general (he was sometimes referred to as "General") sat well with the whites. Of Quaker upbringing, he had a deep-

Joe Lane, left, and Joel Palmer represented the United States during the early and mid-1850s, when the tribes of the Upper Rogue River Valley were so prominent because of their numbers, strategic land holdings, and imposing military strength. The work of the two men led to the creation of the Siletz Reservation. Lane, a former general and governor of the fledgling Oregon Territory beginning in 1850, gained the trust of tribal leaders, although he later opposed the interests of western Oregon Indians when he was a United States senator. Palmer, superintendent of Indian Affairs for the territory from 1853 to 1856, was accorded broad discretionary powers not usually vested in superintendents in order that Oregon Indian policy would be conducted with humanity and in accordance with treaties. In the early 1870s, Palmer served as Indian agent for the Siletz Reservation. *Courtesy of Oregon Historical Society, nos. bb003659 (Lane) and bb006242 (Palmer).*

dyed sympathy for the tribes and wanted to do well by them consistent with the political realities of the era. Palmer "seems to have had an unusual amount of compassion and understanding of our people's situation—at least for a man of his time," wrote Siletz tribal historian Robert Kentta. "He would soon be known and respected among our people by a name that translates as 'knows in his head.'"

In addition to the influential James Nesmith, a future superintendent of Indian Affairs and United States senator, and LaFayette Grover, a future congressman, senator, and governor, another Oregon luminary, Judge Matthew Deady, attended the treaty council. A lawyer who joined the bar in Ohio, Deady crossed the country to Oregon in 1849. He gained election to the territorial assembly the next year and then secured appointment to the Territorial Supreme Court. At statehood in 1859, he became Oregon's first United States district judge, holding that position until his death in 1893. He is regarded as one of Oregon's greatest judges.

While Deady stood up for African Americans and Chinese immigrants as his tenure on the bench went on, he did not generally champion the concerns of minority groups in his early professional years. He supported slavery in the 1850s and had no particular sympathy for the travails of Chinese laborers in the mining camps or on the railroad crews. Like Palmer, however, Deady's experience with Oregon's Indian-white conflicts led him to conclude that the whites were usually the aggressors. In 1876, Deady, known for his careful writing style, wrote that "it ought never to be forgotten, that in all disputes and controversies between the whites and Indians upon this Coast concerning the occupation of the soil (or almost anything else for that matter) it may be safely assumed that the latter are not in the wrong."

One of the judge's earliest exposures to such wrongs came on September 3, 1853, when he rode on horseback to hold court in Jacksonville and then to participate in the Table Rock Treaty convocation. He stopped over at the Bates House, in the territory of the Grave Creek Athapaskans, and was confronted by the barbarism in southern Oregon that did such violence to the most basic principles of American law:

> There I found Captain J. K. Lamerick, in command of a company of volunteers. It seems he had been sent there by General Lane after the fight at Battle Creek, on account of the murder of some Indians there, of which he and others gave me the following account:
>
> Bates and some others had induced a small party of peaceable Indians, who belonged in that vicinity, to enter into an engagement to remain at peace with the whites during the war which was going on at some distance from them, and by way of ratification of this treaty, invited them to partake of a feast in an unoccupied log house just across the road from the "Bates House," and while they were partaking, unarmed, of this proffered hospitality, the door was suddenly fastened upon them, and they were deliberately shot down through the cracks between the logs by their treacherous hosts.

Near by, and probably a quarter of a mile this side of the creek, I was shown a large round hole into which the bodies of these murdered Indians had been unceremoniously tumbled. I did not see them, for they were covered with fresh earth.

🦅 ⚙ 🦅

The massacre at Grave Creek underscored how agonizing a path the peacemakers had to walk. Local miners and settlers wanted extermination, not accommodation. In early September, a letter to the *Oregonian*, referring to Palmer and Lane, warned that "the whites of Rogue River valley will pay but little attention to any treaty stipulations entered into by those in authority with the Indians," and the *Oregon Spectator* observed that "extinction of the entire race in that region is the almost unanimous sentiment." Tribal and federal leaders, however, all of whom felt the many wounds and losses of the collision of the two races, pressed ahead with determination if not certitude.

In terms of substantive issues, the Indians wanted an end to the botched and unwise federal policies, actions, and inactions of the past several years. They were being overwhelmed by people who had no respect for Indian land rights or lives. Leaving aside the Americans' inability to control their own people, two practices especially rankled: the unratified treaties and the efforts to remove the Indians of western Oregon to lands on the eastern side of the Cascade Range.

From the beginning of American settlement in Oregon, state and federal officials were well aware of Indian land title and the need to obtain tribal land before homesteading could legally begin. Lane, as the first territorial governor, made the necessity of extinguishing Indian title the first topic in his initial speech to the territorial legislature. The subject was directly raised in Congress. Despite the continuing conflicts between settlers and Indians, Congress passed the Donation Land Act in 1850 without dealing with Indian title one way or the other. This shortsighted action immediately led to increasingly heated disputes over landownership between settlers and Indians, especially in the Willamette and Rogue River valleys.

In the same year, Congress adopted the Oregon Indian Treaty Act, which authorized commissioners (in practice, the U.S. superintendent of Indian Affairs for Oregon) to negotiate land treaties with tribes. Reflecting the view of Lane and Samuel Thurston, the territorial delegate, the statute directed that the negotiations with western Oregon tribes include cessions of their ancestral lands and "if found expedient and practicable, for their removal east of [the Cascade] mountains."

The threat of moving tribes across the Cascades fouled up the treaty negotiations. None of the tribes wanted to go. The salmon were fewer and the vegetation was different. There were no treasured acorns from the black oak trees. It was colder and arid across the mountains. The tribes there would object to having foreign tribes brought in. Most of all, for the western tribes it meant leaving their homelands. All the ancestors, all the memories were there.

When Superintendent Dart and Territorial Governor Gaines went out to negotiate in 1851, the "east of the Cascades" policy put them in a bind. The tribes—whether from the Willamette Valley, the Columbia Valley, or the Coast—held their ground and insisted on reservations within their ancestral territories. Then, when Dart and Gaines sent their nineteen treaties to Congress, Joseph Lane, the new territorial delegate, blocked ratification—in significant part because the proposed reservations lay west of the Cascades. In turn, the tribes, in addition to despising the "east of the Cascades" policy, were frustrated and angry with the Americans' on again–off again practice of negotiating treaties but failing to ratify them.

By 1853, a revised national Indian policy had crystallized and Table Rock was a proving ground. For its first half-century, the United States took the easy course (for the Americans if not the tribes) of designating areas to the west of settlement as "Indian country" or the "Indian territory." The assumption was that this land could safely be set aside for tribes because it was unlikely to be needed for settlement, at least not in the foreseeable future. The first such line was drawn in 1796 and ran through Cleveland, then southwest through Ohio and Indiana, then southeast through Kentucky, Tennessee, the Carolinas, and Georgia. American citizens would settle east of the line. To the west would be Indian country.

As the East began to fill up, Congress moved the line farther west. By the 1840s, the Indian country consisted of the land west of the Louisiana, Arkansas, Missouri, Iowa, and Wisconsin borders. The most notable series of events involved the "Trail of Tears," the heartrending removals in the 1830s of the so-called Five Civilized Tribes—the Cherokee, Chickasaw, Choctaw, Creek, and Seminole—from their homes in the southeast to the "Unorganized Indian Territory" (later, the state of Oklahoma). The southeastern states simply refused to tolerate the existence of the tribes within state boundaries. Their success, greatly aided by President Andrew Jackson, in enlisting federal troops to remove Native people to the Indian country both brought unmitigated tragedy to the Five Civilized Tribes and epitomized how the pressure for land was trampling American ideals of respecting minority rights: at the same time that Chief Justice John Marshall was handing down one of his most luminous opinions, acknowledging the right of tribes to be free of state laws, Congress at the behest of the states was granting the president unfettered power to abrogate treaties and remove the southeastern tribes from their homelands.

The notion of a separate Indian territory west of American settlement finally blew apart during the James Polk presidency of 1845–1849, with the nation's greatest spate of expansion through the annexation of Texas and treaties with Mexico and England. The United States held, as against all European nations, all land between the Rocky Mountains and the Pacific. Indian title remained in place. Now it was clear that Americans wanted to settle all of it.

The transfer of Indian responsibilities from the War Department to the new Department of the Interior in 1849 provided the opportunity to reformulate Indian policy and institute the reservation system. When Luke Lea took office in 1850 as commissioner of Indian Affairs, he was handed the task of developing an Indian policy to replace the "Unorganized Indian Territory" approach. Lea, a Mississippi lawyer who took for granted the inferiority of Indians, believed that, although it would take time and effort, Indians could be assimilated into the general society. Until then, the tribes must be kept separate: "Civilization and barbarism . . . cannot coexist together." This would be accomplished by permanently setting aside separate, isolated tracts of land for tribes. Lea formally announced the new policy of creating a reservation system in his 1850 annual report to the Congress:

> There should be assigned to each tribe, for a permanent home, a country
> adapted to agriculture, of limited extent and well-defined boundaries, within
> which all, with occasional exceptions, should be compelled constantly to
> remain until such time as their general improvement and good conduct may
> supersede the necessity of such restrictions. In the mean time the govern-
> ment should cause them to be supplied with stock, agricultural implements,
> and useful materials for clothing; encourage and assist them in the erection
> of comfortable dwellings, and secure to them the means and facilities of
> education, intellectual, moral, and religious.

This major shift in policy had its inconsistencies. How could Indians be assimilated while kept separate? How could lands be permanently set aside if the ultimate goal was assimilation? But the charge—the creation of "permanent homes"—was clear, and federal officials set out to implement it.

Joel Palmer, convinced that white settlement could proceed in a way humane to the tribes, found the new policy entirely consistent with his own views. His compassion and idealism came out in his June 1853 report to George Manypenny, now commissioner of Indian Affairs:

> It is too clear to admit of argument—vice and disease, the baleful gifts of civilization are hurrying them away, and ere long the bones of the last of many a band may whiten on the graves of his ancestors. If the benevolent designs of the Government to preserve and elevate these remnants of the Aborigines are to be carried forward to a successful issue, there appears to be but one path open, —a home, remote from the settlements must be selected for them, then they must be guarded from the pestiferous influence of degraded whitemen . . . let comfortable houses be erected for them, seeds and proper implements furnished and instruction and encouragement given them in the cultivation of the soil; let school houses be erected and teachers employed to instruct their children, and let the missionaries of the gospel of peace be encouraged to dwell among them. Let completeness of plan, energy, patience and perseverance characterize the effort, and if still it fail, the Government will have at least the satisfaction of knowing that an honest and determined endeavour was made to save and elevate a fallen race.

As superintendent of Indian Affairs for the Oregon Territory, Palmer turned his attention to finding the best location for "a home, remote from the settlements" for the tribes of western Oregon.

In Palmer's mind, the Oregon Coast presented by far the preferred option. The Willamette Valley would be a breeding ground for conflict: it already had many settlers and more were on the way. The "east of the mountains" policy was unworkable: the tribes would not agree to move there. But the Coast, though Palmer had not yet visited it, was so rugged that it would never have large numbers of whites. It did, he was told, have small valleys for the farming way of life that Palmer and the policymakers in Washington envisaged for Native peoples.

In the beginning, even though the poisonous atmosphere in southern Oregon presented his greatest challenge, the superintendent apparently assumed that a large Coast Reservation would serve the tribes of the Willamette Valley and the Lower Columbia River. However, while a temporary site would initially be designated in the Table Rocks area, the impossibility of peaceful Indian-white relations in southern Oregon would soon cause federal officials to look elsewhere for a permanent home for the Upper Rogue River tribes. The early focus on the Coast, put forth by the chief federal Indian policymaker in the region, played a defining role in the climactic decisions of the mid-1850s regarding land and treaties.

During the summer of 1853 Palmer enlisted federal employees and several Indian tyees and planned an expedition to the Coast to evaluate the area's suitability for a reservation. The idea was to assess the area between Coos Bay and the Tillamook River, about 125 miles of terrain. In late August, the party was ready to embark. But events to the south intervened. The battle on Evans Creek had just concluded and Palmer received a missive from Joseph Lane that Palmer's attendance was "imperatively required." And so Palmer packed up and rode down to Table Rocks for the peace talks.

The atmosphere, the tone, of United States–Indian treaty negotiations varied from one tribe to another. All were solemn—the federal representatives had important business to do and tribal leaders knew that the proceedings were momentous in their peoples' histories. Still, some of the gatherings lacked a sense of loftiness. Several of the 1851 Anson Dart treaties with Willamette Valley and Columbia River tribes, for example, involved once-populous tribes that had been reduced by European diseases to just a few families. Other treaty convocations were large, formal gatherings filled with high ceremony. Two years after the Table Rock Treaty of 1853, Joel Palmer and the other Americans at the Walla Walla negotiations were awestruck as the Nez Perce rode in, "a thousand warriors mounted on fine horses and riding at a gallup, two abreast, naked to the breech-clout, their faces covered with white, red, and yellow paint in fanciful designs, and decked with plumes and feathers and trinkets fluttering in the sunshine."

The scene was also dramatic when Joseph Lane, Joel Palmer, Matthew Deady, and James Nesmith headed out on the morning of September 10 by horseback on the two-mile ride from Lane's camp on the meadow to the upthrusting edifice of Lower Table Rock. Against Nesmith's advice, the

PART TWO. WAR AND REMOVAL

American military force, numbering in the hundreds, remained on the valley floor. Nesmith warned Lane of the hundreds of Indians who had gathered at Table Rocks—danger lay ahead and the men should be accompanied by soldiers—but Lane, having promised Tyee Joe that he would come only with unarmed men, insisted on keeping his word.

Lane and two other men rode part of the way up the eastern flank until the thick chaparral of buckbrush and manzanita made further travel on horseback impossible. Nesmith described the scene:

> We dismounted and hitched our horses and scrambled up for half a mile over huge rocks and through brush, and then found ourselves in the Indian stronghold, just under the perpendicular cliff of Table Rock, and surrounded by seven hundred fierce and well armed hostile savages, in all their gorgeous war paint and feathers. Captain Smith had drawn out his company of dragoons, and left them in line on the plain below. It was a bright, beautiful morning, and the Rogue River Valley lay like a panorama at our feet; the exact line of dragoons, sitting statue like upon their horses, with their white belts and burnished scabbards and carbines, looked like they were engraven upon a picture, while a few paces in our rear the huge perpendicular wall of the Table Rock towered, frowningly, many hundred feet above us.

Judge Matthew Deady also recalled the moment:

> The scene of the famous "peace talk" between Joseph Lane and Indian Joseph—two men who had so lately met in mortal combat—was worthy of the pen of Sir Walter Scott and the pencil of Salvator Ross.
>
> It was on a narrow bench of a long, gently sloping hill, lying over against the noted bluff called Table Rock. The ground was thinly covered with majestic old pines and rugged oaks, with here and there a clump of green oak bushes. About a half mile above the bright mountain stream that threaded the narrow valley below sat the two chiefs in council. Lane was in fatigue dress, the arm which was wounded at Buena Vista in a sling from a fresh bullet wound received at Battle Creek. Indian Joseph, tall, grave and self-possessed, wore a long black robe over his ordinary dress. By his side sat Mary, his favorite child and faithful companion, then a comparatively handsome young woman, unstained with the vices of civilization. Around these, sat on the grass Captain A. J. Smith—now General Smith of St. Louis—who had just arrived from Port Orford with his company of the First Dragoons;

Captain Alvord, then engaged in the construction of a military road through the Umpqua Canyon, and since Paymaster General of the U. S. A.; Colonel Bill Martin of Umpqua, Colonel John E. Ross of Jacksonville, Captain, now Gen. John F. Miller, and a few others. A short distance above us on the hillside were some hundreds of dusky warriors in fighting gear, reclining quietly on the ground.

The day was beautiful. To the east of us rose abruptly Table Rock, and at its base stood Smith's dragoons, waiting anxiously with hand on horse the issue of this attempt to make peace without their aid.

The talks did not begin immediately. The Takelma, Athapaskan, and Shasta representatives wanted Tyee Jim, an accomplished negotiator and leader who had married Tyee Joe's daughter, Mary, to participate in the talks. Lane had agreed. Jim had not arrived, and the tribal and American leaders took the opportunity to share a peace pipe. When Jim did make his appearance, he began the talks with a formal statement. According to LaFayette Grover, "I recollect he stood up there like a native orator, and began to talk. He spoke at least half an hour in the Indian dialect. There was no [Chinook] jargon about it. You never heard the most polished orator use more perfect intonations and gestures—and the effect [of it] was the effect of true oratory." Then Tyee Joe spoke. The only known version of his remarks is by Grover:

He made his speech in his own tongue. He made his speech for us, and it was interpreted to us. He said: "We have sent for you to come here to make a treaty of peace. We inten[d] what we say. A few days ago some white men sent for the Indians to come in to Applegate creek to have a talk and to make peace. They went and while they were eating their feast the white men came in and killed them all. Now here you are, five of you. We sent for you to come here, and to leave the soldiers behind, six miles off. We told you to come without arms, that we wanted to make peace. We intended what we said. The white men killed the Indians when they said that to them. You are 5 & we are 200 all armed. We could kill you all now." But the Indian Chief meant what he said:

"The Indian is nobler than the white man." He spread himself up there and looked really a nobleman.

It confounds the mind that such a stately ceremony, with hundreds of Indians in attendance, took place at all. The germs had taken more than 80 percent of the population of these Upper Rogue River tribes, and hundreds had been lost to war and other killings. Yet the Indians knew how much was at stake, how the future of their nations hung in the balance. Further, they had some leverage. While the tribes currently held an advantage in rifles and other weaponry, the United States population and industrial capability assured that it would prevail in protracted conflict. But the Native fighting men had proven themselves magnificent warriors, and further combat would be costly to the Americans. The tribes found the resilience to rise up to their full height. The Americans had sent their top leaders and many battalions to bring an end to the major Indian conflict in the West, to obtain title to Indian land, and to implement the nation's new Indian policy. The talks were ready to begin.

The formality of the occasion sharpened the gulf between the two cultures. During the days leading up to this final council, leaders from both sides had gone over the issues and doubtless reported back to their people. Nonetheless, the language differences made for slow-moving, laborious negotiations. If, as Nesmith reported, Tyee Joe made a speech to Lane, it would have been translated from Takelman, then into the Chinook Jargon, then into English—and Lane's reply would have gone from English into the Chinook Jargon as translated by Nesmith and then into Takelman:

> Long speeches were made by General Lane and Superintendent Palmer; they had to be translated twice. When an Indian spoke in the Rogue River tongue, it was translated by an Indian interpreter into Chinook or jargon to me, when I translated it into English; when Lane or Palmer spoke, the process was reversed, I giving the speech to the Indian interpreter in Chinook, and he translating it to the Indians in their own tongue. This double translation of long speeches made the labor tedious, and it was not until late in the afternoon that the treaty was completed and signed.

Federal-tribal treatymaking has always been plagued by the problem of language. With such large and often technical matters at issue, the question has often arisen as to whether the Indian and American negotiators fully understood each other. When the agreement was put in writing, it was always done in English—in words the Americans wrote and the Natives could not read.

In the Pacific Northwest, the common language was the Chinook Jargon. The Jargon, an amalgam of phrases from different tribes (principally the

Chinook), came into use before non-Indians arrived as a basis for discourse in the far-flung trade network among tribes with a large number of distinct languages. When foreign traders came, they learned the Jargon and contributed some words of their own. By the time of the Table Rock negotiations, the language had an estimated 250–500 words. Scholars of the Chinook Jargon emphasize the importance of the quality of the translations. "To a great extent, effective communication through the Jargon depends on the ingenuity and imagination of the speaker." Thus, "the way a word is spoken has a tremendous influence on meaning." In addition to the subtlety that is required to speak and understand the Jargon properly, discourse cannot be a wooden linguistic exercise and must take account of Native culture:

> The most important knowledge to possess . . . is a thorough understanding
> of the Indian point of view; that is to say, how the Indian thinks, the mental
> process by which he arrives at an idea and, in addition to this, a knowledge
> of his method of expressing this idea. Without this knowledge you can never
> speak Chinook [Jargon], or any Indian language, fluently.

We do not know how accomplished James Nesmith and Robert Metcalfe, listed as interpreter on the treaty, were as translators in and out of the Jargon.

The Chinook Jargon was poorly suited to serve as the medium of discourse over grand abstract notions such as sovereignty, landownership, and the future relationship between the tribes and the United States. As explained by Judge George Boldt, who conducted the most far-ranging judicial examination of Pacific Northwest treaties and whose conclusions were affirmed by the United States Supreme Court in 1979: "The Jargon was capable of conveying only rudimentary concepts, but not the sophisticated or implied meaning of treaty provisions about which highly learned jurists and scholars differ." The courts have developed common-sense rules for construing Indian treaties, requiring that all doubts be resolved in favor of the tribes—just as judges interpret residential leases and bank loans in favor of the tenant or the borrower and doubts are resolved against the landlord and the bank, the more powerful party and the one who drafted the document. The rules are even stronger for Indian treaties, where the United States is a trustee and is considered to be acting in the best interests of the beneficiaries, the tribes. Judge Boldt ruled, in a principle universally accepted in Indian treaty law, that "the treaty must therefore be construed, not according to the technical meaning of its words to learned lawyers, but in the sense in which they would naturally be understood by the Indians. . . . How the words of the treaty were understood by this unlettered people, rather than their critical meaning, should form the rule of the construction."

Any doubts, ambiguities, or uncertainty, then, in the words written down and agreed to under the cliff at Lower Table Rock, and approved by the United States Senate, should be resolved in favor of the Indians and in a manner consistent with their understanding.

The negotiations, although burdened by the re-translations of all the speeches, were orderly save for one exception. In the afternoon, a young Indian runner, sweating heavily and exhausted by his race from the Applegate Valley, broke into the proceedings, shouted out a brief speech, and collapsed. The congregated Natives were furious—the runner had reported that whites in Captain Owens's volunteer company had tied an Indian named Taylor to a tree and shot him. Nesmith recalled: "I saw some Indians gathering up their lass-ropes, while others drew the skin covers from their guns, and the wiping sticks from their muzzle."

Lane, always resourceful, always keeping his eye on the objective, prevented an outbreak. He told the assemblage that Owens was "a bad man," that he would be punished, and that the Americans would give compensation for Taylor's death. The danger passed and the discourse returned to the treaty.

The fundamental principles of the Table Rock Treaty of September 10, 1853, were applied in the many treaties between the United States and Indian tribes that resolved land title to most of the Oregon and Washington territories. (The Washington Territory was carved out of the Oregon Territory in 1853.) The first to put into action the new national federal policy announced by Luke Lea, the treaty rejected extinction as an option, promised a permanent tribal homeland, and provided aid to the tribes in making the transition to an agricultural lifestyle. Isaac Stevens, governor and superintendent of Indian Affairs for the Washington Territory who negotiated Indian treaties from Puget Sound to western Montana, later expressed his gratitude to Joseph Lane for his example and tutelage in dealing with the tribes.

The Table Rock Treaty dealt with a number of relatively minor matters. The government agreed to provide farming equipment and clothing to Indians and to build houses for the three principal tyees, Joe, Sam, and John. The tribes guaranteed safe passage for whites traveling through their reservation. Crimes committed by Indians against whites would be tried in federal courts. The United States promised to indemnify the tribes for horses or other property stolen by whites.

Land was the overriding issue. In article 1, Takelmas, Shastas, and Applegate Athapaskans ceded to the United States most of their aboriginal land in Oregon. The transfer encompassed the Upper Rogue River Valley, including the Applegate Valley, all the way to the crests of the Cascade and the Siskiyou mountains. This magnificent landscape of about 2,400 square miles held extraordinarily valuable resources, including the mineral deposits in the Jacksonville area and other goldbearing regions, old-growth forests, and broad valley floors for farming. As payment for the land, the United States promised to pay the tribes $60,000, of which $15,000 would be retained by the federal government to pay for "property of the whites destroyed by [the Indians] during the late war."

The tribes did not want to sell their land, and it was a delicate subject during the several days building up to the main treaty. The peace and friendship treaty signed on September 8, 1853, made no explicit mention of a cession of land although it did describe the aboriginal domain and promised that the tribes "shall hereafter reside in the place to be set apart for them." When Palmer met with tribal members on September 9, he was disappointed by the small turnout. "I fear your people are not all here. Why should they be afraid to come and see us and hear us talk?" Knowing the widespread apprehension about the treaty in general and land in particular, Palmer made a long and impassioned plea for a land sale. He said this in the most detailed account that we have of the words spoken at Table Rock:

> Our great chief, your father, who lives a long way over the mountains has
> sent us to see you and to talk with you—our chief has a good hart, he wishes
> all his read children to live in peace and be happy, he dose not want them to
> go to war with the whites or with one an other.—He has a great many red
> children. A long way to the east they are a happy people, they live in homes,
> have cattle, sheep, hogs, they raise wheat, corn, potatoes. . . .
>
> We do not want to deceive you, but like our chief our harts are good and
> we give you good talk. . . .
>
> The chief sent here to advice, protect and assist you, cannot see you all—
> but he will do all he can to prevent our people from doing you harm. If you
> are good and do not injure our people and their property. We think it is good
> that you should sell our great chief your land and then you can be supplied

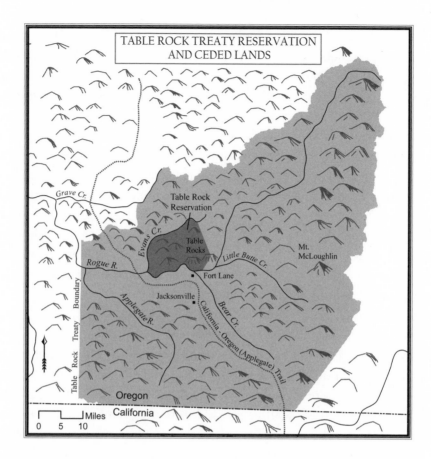

TABLE ROCK TREATY RESERVATION
AND CEDED LANDS

with blankets, clothing & food—and have houses, cattle, & horses—and be taught how to grow wheate and other food and your children how to read and write so that when they are grown to be men and women they can understand good from bad, and now a greate deal like the good whites, and have good medicine when they are sick—and be warm in winter and [live] happy.

And now, I will make you a proposition, If you will sell our great chief your country as bounded & described in the Treaty of peace made and concluded yesterday between Genl. Jo Lane, and the chiefs of the Rogue River bands of Indians we will agree for our great chief on the part of the United States to give you [fifty five] sixty thousand dollars. Fifteen thousand . . . or so much of that sum as may be necessary to pay the amount of damages done to the property of the whites in the Rogue River Country.

Toward the end of his oration, Palmer drove his main point home: "The white man has come and they will continue to come. . . . We cannot stop them. It is no use to make war upon them for if one be kiled ten will come in his place."

The provisions for tribal land evidenced the superior position of the United States. Article 2 of the treaty called for a reservation of just one hundred square miles, about 4 percent of the tribes' aboriginal domain. Though minuscule in comparison with the ceded land, the reservation preserved important tribal values and, at an average of eight miles north to south and thirteen miles east to west, had some size to it. It included all of Lower Table Rock, with its great cultural and spiritual meaning, and part of Upper Table Rock. Tyee Sam's valley and other flatlands held traditional roots and tarweed seed-gathering grounds and were suitable for farming. The northern reaches, up to Evans Creek, offered forested lands and good hunting. Since the reservation bordered the Rogue River from above Upper Table Rock down to the mouth of Evans Creek, tribal members had excellent salmon fishing on a stretch of about fifteen river miles on the Rogue and on the east bank of Evans Creek as well. Painfully small, but good land, heartland.

The Table Rock Treaty came with a proviso that was rare among Indian treaties nationally but not in Oregon, where it was of great moment in the years to come. Palmer and Lane both feared that the local hatred might never relent and that continuing violent acts would make it necessary to remove the tribes to another location, far from populated areas. The treaty, therefore, provided that the tribes "shall be allowed to occupy temporarily" the Table Rock Reservation. The temporary reservation would remain fully in effect, as tribal land under federal protection, until replaced by a permanent home: Table Rock *"shall be deemed and considered an Indian reserve, until a suitable selection shall be made by the direction of the President of the United States for their permanent residence and buildings erected thereon, and provisions made for their removal."*

The Table Rock Treaty was signed by Tyees Joe, Sam, Jim, John, and Lympy, on behalf of their peoples. Joel Palmer signed for the United States. The Senate ratified it seven months later.

The 1853 treaty guaranteed the tribes a permanent reservation. The initial reservation at Table Rock was "temporary," but the treaty required that it would remain in place indefinitely until a president declared a "permanent" reservation. The treaty allowed only those two outcomes: a temporary but ongoing reservation at Table Rock or a permanent one elsewhere.

The question soon became whether the Table Rock Treaty, and the six other western Oregon treaties that followed its template, could hold. The law, even the supreme law of the land, can be overwhelmed when citizens take the law into their own hands and nowhere in American history has that been more prevalent than when an angry, determined, and violent majority sets its sights on the rights of a small minority.

THE ROGUE RIVER WAR

"Now the earth went bad."

THE ROGUE RIVER WAR LASTED FROM THE SPRING OF 1851, WHEN the cannon blast from Captain Tichenor's crew at Battle Rock killed some thirty Indians, through July of 1856, when Tyee John finally surrendered after the furious battle in the wild country of Big Bend on the middle Rogue River. This five-year struggle was episodic. There were gaps, occasioned by treaties, between most of the major battles, which numbered about two dozen. Yet the citizenries, Indian and non-Indian alike, could never find respite from disagreements, raids, shootings, and lynchings.

Taking into account all of the major Indian wars fought by the United States—about forty in total not including numerous battles, skirmishes, and other armed conflicts—the Rogue River War ranks as one of the most violent and destructive. The death toll in southern Oregon reached 600 or more: the tribes had an estimated 418 to 446 killed, while the whites lost 182. The deadliest United States–Indian wars were the conflict of 1790–1795 with the Miamis, Shawnee, Wyandot, and other midwestern tribes; the Creek War of 1813–1814; the Sioux wars of 1862–1877; and the Apache War of 1861–1886. In each of those wars, the total casualties approached or exceeded 2,500. The Seminole Wars of 1817–1818 and 1835–1842 exacted approximately 1,000 lives. Otherwise, the death tolls in the other major Indian conflicts were lower than the Rogue River War. The conflict in southern Oregon was the largest in the Pacific Northwest and, save for the Sioux and Apache wars, the most costly in the western half of the country. The human losses exceeded those in such well-known conflicts as those between the United States and the Navajos, Nez Perces, Comanches, and Cheyennes.

The number of fatalities in the Rogue River War is not high by today's lights but the impact on those societies was grievous. The American population in southern Oregon amounted to only 2,000 or so, and the loss of 182 people, with many more suffering serious wounds, was immediate and personal. Fear and uncertainty gripped a citizenry that felt fragile, unsure of its safety and stability on that far frontier.

Indian people also saw their hold on the land, the very existence of their societies, as hanging in the balance. They had lost most of their population to diseases. Now, with a populace of not much more than 2,000 between the coastal and upper valley tribes, they lost more than 400 men, women, and children to the battles. Every family, especially in a culture of extended families, must have been directly affected, probably multiple times. Late in his life, John Adams (Applegate Athapaskan and Shasta) recounted the horror that the war brought to his childhood years—and to three generations of his family:

> Pretty rough times! Awful hard time when I'm baby. Rogue River Injun War that time. Well, soldier come, everybody scatter, run for hills. One family this way, one family other way. Some fighting. My father killed, my mother killed. Well, my uncle he come, my grandmother. Old woman, face like white woman, so old. "Well my poor mother, you old, not run. Soldiers coming close, we have to run fast. I not help it. I sorry. Must leave you here. Maybe soldiers not find you, we come back. Now this little baby, this my brother's baby. Two children I got myself. I sorry, I not help it. We leave this poor baby, too." That's what my uncle say.
>
> Course, I small, maybe two years, maybe nearly three years. I not know what he say. Somebody tell me afterwards. Well, old grandmother cry, say: "I old, I not afraid die. Go ahead, get away from soldiers."
>
> Well, just like dream, I 'member old grandmother pack me round in basket on her back. All time she cry and holler. I say, "Grandmother, what you do?"
>
> "I crying, my child."
>
> "What is it, crying, grandmother?"
>
> "I sorry for you, my child. Why I cry. I not sorry myself, I old. You young, maybe somebody find you all right, you live."
>
>   * * *
>
> [The two survived winter together and then his uncle returned and stayed with them.]

Pretty soon soldiers come again. That's the time they leave my old grandmother cause she can't walk. Maybe she die right there, maybe soldiers kill
her. She cry plenty when my uncle take me away. Well, all time going round
in the woods. After while my uncle get killed. Then I'm 'lone. Klamath Injun
find me, bring me to new reservation.

Venomous though the miners were in the early 1850s, public opinion
among white Oregonians grew ever more hostile as the war moved toward
its climax. The cry of "extermination," rather than a slogan among a few hot-
blooded miners, became the editorial policy of the local *Table Rock Sentinel*,
the *Oregon Statesman* in Salem, and the *Oregonian* in Portland. Those public officials planning to remain in office supported a hard line against the
tribes. Politics allowed Territorial Governor John Gaines to negotiate a peace
and friendship treaty in 1851, but George Curry, who served during the last
three years of the war, was left with little leeway other than to approve local
requests to call up volunteer groups to fight the tribes. On at least one occasion, the request to Curry was unvarnished: "The people there [in southern
Oregon] now demand extermination of the hostile Indians, and are resolved
not to stop short of it." Joseph Lane, who knew better but had his eye on
still higher office, assured his colleagues in the House of Representatives that
Oregon Indians were "treacherous and ungrateful" and had "commenced all
the wars which have taken place between them and the white settlers."

A few moderate voices were heard. Joel Palmer, who as superintendent
of Indian Affairs probably had more information at hand due to the amount
of time he spent with the people involved, Indian and non-Indian, displayed
extraordinary patience and courage in his efforts to stave off violence and the
extermination that he knew to be possible. Palmer believed to his depths—
and, at the risk of his job, expressed such sentiments publicly—that "the present difficulty in southern Oregon is wholly to be attributed to the acts of our
own people. . . . The future will prove that this war has been forced upon these
Indians against their will." Another leading Oregonian taking the Indian side
was Judge Matthew Deady, who knew how determined Tyee Joe, Tyee John,
and other Indian leaders were to preserve the peace promised in the Table
Rock Treaty.

The regular military, bound by the rules of war, carried out its duties with
considerable distinction. This was especially true of General John E. Wool. A
veteran of the Indian wars in the south and commander of all United States
forces in the Pacific Department, Wool described the local volunteers as "sig-

PART TWO. WAR AND REMOVAL

nally barbarous and savage" and regularly refused to cooperate with them. In 1856, he relayed a report from Oregon that "many citizens, with a due proportion of volunteers, and two newspapers advocated the extermination of the Indians. This principle has been acted on in several instances, without discriminating between enemies and friends, which has been the cause in southern Oregon of sacrificing many innocent and worthy citizens." Wool realized, contrary to conventional military thinking of the time, that a primary obligation of the military, particularly after the treaties, should be to protect Indian people from local hostility. He has been called the first of the "humanitarian generals" in the West.

One of the most compelling figures during the height of the war was John Beeson, a settler in the Rogue River Valley who dared to take up the Indians' cause. Beeson came west with his family from Illinois, where he was well known for his fervid commitment to abolition and temperance. In 1853 they homesteaded in the Upper Rogue River Valley near present-day Talent and farmed. Never before concerned with Indian matters, he and his son Wellborn found Indian campsites on the property they farmed. Although Beeson knew that the Natives had ceded most of their traditional territory lands to the United States and had been moved to the Table Rock reserve, his occupation of Indian land sat on his conscience. Ever the reformer, John Beeson had found a new cause.

Beeson was captivated by the beauty of the landscape but found most local people to be lawless and ignorant of the nation's traditions, "for they denied to the poor Indian the common prerogative, peaceful enjoyment of 'life, liberty, and the pursuit of happiness.'" Conversations with neighbors and exhortations at public meetings made it clear to him that community leaders had nothing but contempt for their country's promise of peace in the Table Rock Treaty. People told him that "they should not be satisfied until every Indian was destroyed from the Coast to the Rocky Mountains." He knew settlers who disagreed, but none dared come forth.

Moralistic and driven, Beeson could not keep his views to himself. He spoke out in community gatherings and wrote letters to Oregon newspapers—and, when they refused to print them, sent them to out-of-state papers. He ran unsuccessfully for the territorial legislature as a defender of Indian rights. In 1855, as vigilantes were about to launch the murderous raid at Little Butte Creek, he urged moderation but, even in the Methodist Church, no one was willing to support him publicly. In January 1856, he rented a meeting hall in Jacksonville and sent out flyers with the hope of convening a civil discussion on the Indian issue. Nothing of the sort happened, as exterminationists took over the meeting. Other Indian sympathizers had promised to come but did not. Beeson finally gave a long explanation of his views, broken by repeated interruptions, all to no avail: "the meeting broke up, with but one voice raised in behalf of peace."

The Rogue River Valley became too dangerous for Beeson. One of his articles in the *New York Tribune* made the rounds in Jacksonville, as did one addressed to the *San Francisco Herald* that was intercepted at the local post office. An angry group called a meeting to denounce him, but he was not allowed to present his side to the raucous gathering. "The following evening, a friend sent me word that the excitement was getting fearfully high. Several companies of Volunteers were discharged. They encamped near my house; and, as I was informed, some of the most reckless among them, were deter-mined on vengeance." Beeson's wife and son, who worried that some would as soon "kill him as an Indian just because he has spoken the truth out bold," agreed there was only one course. Beeson left home in the dark of night and made it to Fort Lane, where he received a military escort north to safety in the Willamette Valley. Other than a visit, probably in 1868, he did not return to Talent until the early 1880s. He died there in 1889.

John Beeson's midnight escape hardly ended his career as a defender of American Indians. Lecturing widely in the East and publishing many articles and pamphlets, he gained some national prominence. Were it not for Oregon senators Harding and Nesmith, who blocked his nomination, he might have become the commissioner of Indian Affairs.

But John Beeson's greatest legacy was his thin volume, *A Plea for the Indians*, where he set out in full his views on the Rogue River War in particular and Indian Affairs in general. Anchored in his own day-to-day experiences and personal con-tacts in the crucible of the most violent years of the war, the book carried authen-ticity. While he documented violence by the whites, he did so as a pious man who came forth out of duty: "If at every point of this melancholy story, I awake unfavorable reflections on the conduct of our fellow-countrymen, it is not because I either will or wish it. Would to God I had sufficient authority to do otherwise. But feeling as I do, that the Indian, though of a different Race, is a brother of the same great family, I should not be true to our common nature were I to withhold a faithful statement of the wrongs I have witnessed."

For Beeson, Americans failed to receive the truth because of the way that the zeal and influence of the local exterminationists controlled the debate. If the public had received the truth, "surely this state of things could not long exist.

John Beeson, outspoken champion of Indian rights, was forced to flee western Oregon in 1856 because of his views. Much later, he felt it safe to return and is shown here in the late 1880s as the graduation speaker at the Wagner Creek School, near his home in Talent. *Photograph from Beeson's* A Plea for the Indians *(a reprint of Beeson's 1857 book) by Bert Webber, Webb Research Group, www.pnwbooks.com.*

The impulsive humanity of the Nation would rise against it. And, doubtless, the reason why there is so little done, is, for the want of data, as to facts." Instead, public impression was driven by "the varied statements, almost all of them over-charged with a cruel and bitter prejudice against the Indians, who cannot write, or proclaim their own grievances by any competent mode of speech."

A Plea for the Indians attempted to set the record straight. Beeson disputed the accuracy of some alleged Indian attacks on whites, but more fundamentally he put the Indian-white conflict in a broader context. Repeatedly, he showed, the tribes were not the aggressors: their attacks were made in "self-protection." "The main body of Indians," Beeson wrote, "evidently acted with the greatest discretion, keeping entirely on the defensive." Even given their superiority in terms of rifle power and knowledge of the land, the tribes wanted peace:

Had the Indians been disposed to destroy and slaughter all they could, there would have been hardly a house left in the Valley; and it was often a subject of remark, that they did so little damage. And so far as Volunteers and Forts were concerned, many thought that fifty determined Indians, bent on their object, could have overthrown and burned the whole in a week.

To illustrate the motives of the tribes and his central belief in the humanity of Indian people, Beeson used as example Tyee John, the great Shasta war leader during the war years of 1855 and 1856. Beeson described John as "a very sagacious and energetic man. He was greatly esteemed by his people, and under ordinary circumstances would have commanded respect in any community." John, who appreciated the importance of diplomacy and signed the Table Rock Treaty, "was faithful in the observance of the treaty, and often lamented the necessity his people were under [in] retaliating upon the Whites."

Tyee John, while an exceptional warrior—Binger Hermann wrote that "of all the Pacific Coast Indians Chief John ranks as the ablest, most heroic and most tactical of chieftains"—was committed to the rules of war and knew that the regular officers in the army acted accordingly. His trust was not always rewarded. Beeson recounted an incident where miners in California accused John's son and a fellow tribesman of murder. John knew them to be innocent. So did Captain Andrew Smith, but duty required him to have the case tried in a United States court in Yreka, California. John reluctantly agreed. The grand jury refused to issue an indictment against the two Indian men but on the way back to Oregon, with a military escort and through no fault of Smith's or the other officers, the miners caught the guards by surprise and brutally murdered the two men. John Beeson eloquently put forth the confusion and deeply held sense of injustice that Tyee John and other Native people endured in this terrible clash of cultures:

When the aged Chief became acquainted with the fate of his son and his companion, he was astonished and outraged, beyond the power of language to describe; for he had had full confidence in the sincerity and power of the Military to secure their present protection and ultimate justice. He had been impressed with the idea that our Great Father, the President, and all his men, the Soldiers, were the Red Man's friends; but, in the bitterness of grief, he saw that they were either unable or unwilling to save them from their enemies. He had long foreseen the gradual but certain destruction of his people;

but he now saw that the great train of extermination was in rapid progress. Another conviction was also forced upon him. He saw that the "bad Bostons" were no more under the control of the Great Father, than bad Indians were under his own. And, doubtless, the many cases of insult and wrong which he had borne and witnessed, and from a repetition of which he had no guaranty, crowded on his memory, inciting him to vengeance, and strengthening his resolution to be his own defender. Will any one who believes that man has a right to defend himself, say that the Chief had not the strongest and truest reason for war? Compared with his wrongs, the petty infringements of which our Fathers complained sink into insignificance and become trivial.

A Plea for the Indians, while it went into three printings, never received the attention it deserved. It was published in 1857, while the Indian wars still raged or, in the case of the Rogue River War, had freshly ended. The two books similar to Beeson's work in scope and tone, Helen Hunt Jackson's *A Century of Dishonor* (1881) and *Ramona* (1884), were in a much better position to capture a favorable public reaction. By then, nearly all the wars had been fought and the nation, however limited its responses may have been, was more sympathetic to the Indians' plight.

The final years of the Rogue River War, after a long, inspiring, and often successful tribal resistance, ended in a costly but nearly complete victory for the whites. The exterminationists did not achieve their literal objective, but they killed many Native people and, upon Tyee John's final, sorrowful surrender, drove the rest of them out. The mobs also drove John Beeson out, and by 1857 both Joel Palmer and General John Wool, scalded by public derision (Joseph Lane called Wool a "military fogie"), had left their positions. And so we are reminded that heroes, however much they may give guidance and inspiration to future generations, often fail in their own times.

The Table Rock Treaty of 1853 provided only a brief interlude before violence broke out. Another gold rush was shaping up, this time on the Coast. In 1851, miners had discovered beach gold in the sands at the mouth of the Klamath River in California. The word spread, but the fabulous finds in Jacksonville drew most of the prospectors there. By 1853, however, production from the mines in the Upper Rogue country began to level off—and the gulches were crowded.

The high bluffs along the southern Oregon Coast offered much the same conditions for beach gold as did northern California. Storm waves ate away at those bluffs, tearing out soil and the gold placers buried in some of them. Then the undertow pulled out the lighter soil, leaving the heavier black sand—and some gold flakes—on the beaches. By the summer of 1853, miners from Jacksonville and elsewhere were pulling out gold in paying quantities from the black sand beaches near the mouths of the Coquille, Rogue, and Chetco rivers and other spots along the Coast.

The miners in these wood-shanty mining camps harbored the same dark mindsets about Indians as those in the Sierra Nevada and Jacksonville. Trouble broke out at the mouth of the Coquille. Annoyed by minor insults—thefts of paddles, "insolent" and threatening conduct, and asserted firing of a gun near the whites (the tyee said he was hunting ducks)—the miners swung into action. They called one meeting, then another, in early 1854. In the second meeting, they solemnly adopted a resolution requesting federal assistance and sent it to Agent F. M. Smith.

Before daybreak the next morning—obviously, Smith had had no opportunity to respond—a mob calling themselves volunteers set upon a sleeping Coquille village, slaughtering fifteen men and one woman and torching the buildings. When Agent Smith finally did arrive, he found the raid wholly unjustified. "Thus was committed," he concluded, "a massacre too inhuman to be readily believed."

Miners then took up arms against the Chetco. To serve the new mining camps, A. F. Miller started up a townsite that overlapped a Chetco village. Miller also attempted to take over the vessels of an Indian ferry, now profitable due to the mining, but the Chetco ferry operators refused. The next morning, Miller led eight others on a raid of the Indian village on the north bank of the Chetco, shooting twelve men and ordering two Chetco women, friendly to Miller, to burn down lodges, killing three more. Having received "random fire" from the village on the south bank during that operation, the raiders attacked the second village the next day. Both villages were then burned to the ground. In all, twenty-three Indian men and several women were killed. The military arrested Miller and saw that he was brought to court, but the local justice of the peace dismissed the charges for want of sufficient evidence: all the witnesses were Indians, and territorial law prohibited Indians from testifying against whites.

Violence also struck the Tolowa of Smith River in California, the Athapaskan tribe closely related to the Chetco and Tututni. In 1853, whites burned a

PART TWO. WAR AND REMOVAL

large village, killing seventy. A year later, when three miners drowned crossing the river, locals assumed that Tolowas were responsible. They set fire to Indian lodges and, while the death toll is not known, Edward Curtis reported that "many of them" were killed.

Word of the killings on the Coast undoubtedly spread throughout the Indian villages in southern Oregon. In the Upper Rogue River country, the tribes faced a steady drumbeat of killings, rapes, and burnings. The promises of peace in the Table Rock Treaty seemed to make little difference. If anything, the treaty stirred up many of the non-Indians because, to them, it set aside too much land that should be available for mining and homesteading. Indian people lived in terror. Historian A. G. Walling wrote that

> it is a fact that after the Lane treaty was signed, its provisions were repeatedly broken by whites, who deliberately murdered unsuspecting and helpless Indians. . . . [T]he class of exterminators alluded to keep up their efforts to kill off as many Indians as they could, regardless of any moral restriction, whatsoever. Revenge was the motto, and these men lived up to it. Not half of the outrages which were perpetrated on Indians were ever heard of through newspapers.

The whites lived in terror too. Indians made sporadic raids, burning homes and barns and murdering some miners and settlers. Tipsu Tyee was especially flamboyant and notorious. A Shasta, he refused to recognize the Table Rock Treaty or submit to moving his band to the reservation. Tall and handsome, with a goatee, the charismatic Tipsu Tyee "effectually terrorized a tract of country reaching from Ashland to beyond the Klamath, and during many months made unexpected descents upon white settlements, or robbed towns, with almost entire impunity." Federal troops could never catch up with Tipsu Tyee, but in May 1854, a fellow Shasta, Tyee Bill, killed him because Tipsu's actions were causing retribution against the Shasta people.

In the absence of any local voice for Indian people other than the maligned and isolated John Beeson, public sentiment in the Upper Rogue River Valley grew ever more toxic. The exterminationists wanted war to finish off the tribes, their reservation, and the treaty; the army, however, under General Wool's command, and the Indian Office, under Joel Palmer, would have none

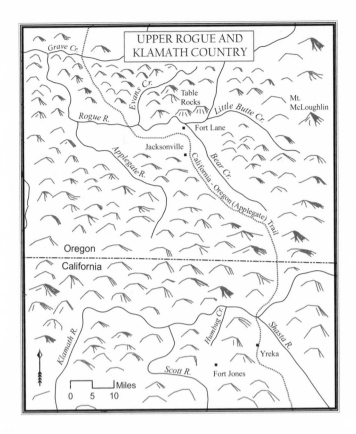

of it. To the consternation and bitter resentment of most southern Oregon whites, Wool and Palmer judged non-Indians as the instigators in most cases and saw their jobs, as federal officials, to safeguard the Indians rather than wage war against them.

By the summer of 1855, the locals were ready to take matters into their own hands. Any pretense would do. All sense of restraint was thrown off in the horrible massacre at Little Butte Creek, which blew the lid off the cauldron of emotions in the Upper Rogue River country.

Two events, mostly taking place in the Klamath River watershed in California, set the stage for Little Butte Creek. The first, on Humbug Creek near Yreka in July, exemplified the confusion and misunderstandings that characterized these times. Miners and Indians died in a drunken brawl of pistol and rifle shots; accounts differ as to who fired first. The next day, an Indian raid took up to a dozen miners' lives. The miners then killed some twenty-five Indians. Each side had indiscriminately lashed out against the other, with most of the dead having nothing to do with the sorry encounter that incited

PART TWO. WAR AND REMOVAL

Klamath Charley, a Shasta, witnessed the incident at Humbug Creek and accompanied Tyee John to Yreka when John reluctantly turned his son and a fellow tribal member over to federal authorities for trial. The two men were acquitted and then murdered by locals. Later in life, living on the Siletz Reservation in the early 1900s, Klamath Charley served as a consultant to Roland B. Dixon in his anthropological research on the Shastas. *Photograph by R. B. Dixon; courtesy of American Museum of Natural History Library, no. 12532.*

the mayhem. The Humbug incident caused temperatures to rise in the Rogue River Valley, both because of the proximity and because five or six Indians from the Table Rock Reservation were in the Humbug area and—though the historical record does not prove it either way—the miners in Yreka believed that Indians on the Oregon side were involved. For Hoxie Simmons, Galice Creek Athapaskan, this was when the die was cast: "Now the earth went bad."

The second round of incendiary incidents involved surviving members of Tipsu Tyee's band. In August, they began a series of raids mostly resulting in property damage—thefts, burnings, and shootings of livestock, predominantly on the California side. In late September they attacked a wagon train ascending the Siskiyous on this California-Oregon Trail from the south, killing and mutilating two male settlers. No doubt the event aroused even greater anger due to memories of the depredations of the hated Tipsu Tyee.

The first week in October was "court week," and Judge Matthew Deady traveled to Jacksonville for hearings, which drew people to town. Extermination talk filled the air. The regular army gave no support to the crowd—General Wool's disdain for the volunteers was well known. At Fort Lane, Captain Andrew Smith knew how much generalized anger was directed toward the Indians, most of whom wanted peace. He saw his primary duty as protecting the Natives on the reservation. This left the field to Major James Lupton. Like many "majors," "lieutenants," and "colonels" in the volunteer armies, he had no formal military title—the locals had bestowed "major" on him. This was one of the many cases in which "volunteers" was a euphemism: Lupton's recruits were vigilantes, a mob, thugs.

Their target was a band of Table Rock Indians living in brush huts at their traditional summer camping site near the mouth of Little Butte Creek. They were off the reservation, which was for the Indian Office and the army to enforce, but otherwise they had done nothing wrong. Lupton called two meetings in Jacksonville to propose his attack. John Beeson rode up from Talent for the meetings and at the second implored the group not to go ahead. No one backed him up.

> I arose, and spoke with all the feeling, and all the power I had, in the behalf of the poor Indians. . . . I begged them, by every principle of humanity and justice, to inflict no wrong upon the helpless. . . . I strongly urged them, as citizens and Christians, to raise a voice of remonstrance, or to call on the Authorities for the administration of justice, and thus avert the impending calamity.

The summer village site at Little Butte Creek was close to the reservation, within sight of Upper Table Rock. Small grassy openings, where the Natives constructed their lodges, were hemmed in by thick vegetation—an underbrush of vine maple and a tall canopy of oaks and willows reaching up a hundred feet or more. But if it was well protected, it was hard to see out: Little Butte Creek enters the Rogue out in the flats of the main valley so that the creek and its banks made only a shallow indentation in the landscape. There was no nearby high ground for a lookout.

As they had vowed to do at the second meeting in Jacksonville, the exterminators raided the Indians on Little Butte Creek on October 8, 1855. Some forty vigilantes crept to the perimeter of the village during the dark and made their charge before the sun rose. Although Lupton took a fatal arrow to the chest and another raider died, all the other dead were Indians. "Lupton and his party fired a volley into the crowded encampment, following up the sudden and totally unexpected attack by a close encounter with knives, revolvers,

PART TWO. WAR AND REMOVAL

and whatever weapon they were possessed of. . . . These facts are matters of evidence, as are the killing of several squaws, one or more old decrepit men, and a number, probably small, of children."

There is no precise count of the carnage. Beeson reported "twenty-eight bodies, fourteen being those of women and children. But as many dead were undoubtedly left in the thickets, and no account was taken of the wounded, many of whom would die, or of the bodies that were afterward seen floating in the river, the above must be far short of the number actually killed." One newspaper account reported forty Indian casualties. Captain Smith estimated eighty. Joel Palmer received a report that one hundred and six Indian people had been killed.

News of this horror swept across the reservation and out to those villages where people still lived in spite of orders to settle on the reservation. Tyee Joe, who might well have argued for restraint, had passed away the year before. Tyee Sam, determined to hold the peace, decided against a reprisal. But for the others, this outrage, coupled with all the others, was too much. The deaths had to be avenged. People rallied around Tyee John, who came to the fore as the dominant force among the Rogue River tribes as the region plunged into all-out war.

The tribal warriors gathered at Table Rocks on the morning of October 9 and immediately launched a ferocious campaign of revenge. The first act was both inflammatory and symbolic. Tyee John himself, who had stayed with his band on the Upper Applegate rather than move to the reservation, killed a young man named William Guin, whom the Indian Office had hired to build a house for John at the Table Rock reserve, one of the houses named in the treaty. In his rage over the slaughter at Little Butte Creek and all the other killings and indignities, Tyee John shouted: "I want no house! I am going to fight until I die!"

John and his men then headed down the Rogue, toward the deep wild country and support from lower river tribes, raiding and burning and killing as they went. Soon joined by the bands of Tyee George and Tyee Lympy, downriver Takelmas who had stayed off the reservation, they lashed out against women, and sometimes children, as well as men. On October 9, they killed between fifteen and twenty-seven whites. The whites, miners and farmers alike, whatever contempt they might express toward the Indians, knew that they were fierce and able warriors—well armed and determined. "It would be difficult," Walling wrote, "to picture the state of alarm which prevailed when the full details of the massacre were made known.

Self-preservation, the first law of nature, was exemplified in the actions of all. The people of the Rogue river valley, probably without exception, withdrew from their ordinary occupations and 'forted up' or retired to the larger settlements." As for the tribes, women, children, and elderly men needed protection at least as much: they could not possibly remain in the villages at the mercy of the miners. Some received military protection at Fort Lane or the Table Rock reserve, while many others went down into the canyons with the warriors.

It is unnerving the extent to which the majority society, even with the perspective of time, conceived of Indians as completely apart from the Oregon populace—apart, it seems, even from the human race. Walling wrote in 1884 that "the ninth of October, 1855, has justly been called the most eventful day in the history of Southern Oregon." Even Frances Fuller Victor, one of the finest nineteenth-century western historians, writing in 1894, called October 9 "altogether the bloodiest day the valley had ever seen." Yet, catastrophic and brutal though that day was, even more blood had been spilled the previous day on Little Butte Creek.

The whites furiously put together an imposing military force. Even Joel Palmer, with his sympathies for the Indians, knew that the time had come. On October 13, he wrote George Ambrose, the agent at Table Rock: "Great wrongs have undoubtedly been done the Indians, but when war comes between the races who can hesitate to act!" A month later, he underscored the seriousness of the crisis in a letter to Commissioner Manypenny: "War is upon us, and whatever its origin, when defenseless women and children are murdered and the property of our citizens destroyed by the ruthless savage, no one can hesitate as to the course to be pursued towards those in the attitude of enemies." Governor Curry issued emergency calls for volunteers, and within a fortnight some 500 men had enlisted under the command of John Ross. By November 1, the volunteer force reached an estimated 750 recruits. The regular army also jumped in: Captain Smith had 105 soldiers at Fort Lane. They and still others would be needed, for the tribes, in passionately defending their homeland, presented singular challenges to this foreign army. There were an estimated 400 warriors and, according to Victor, "four times that number of white men would be required to subdue them on account of their better knowledge of the country, their ability to appear simultaneously at several points, and of disap-

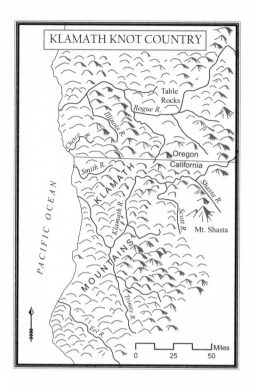

KLAMATH KNOT COUNTRY

pearing rapidly in the approach of troops, wearing out the horses and men engaged in pursuit."

By mid-October, American military leaders knew only that tribal fighting men from the valley to the Coast had gathered in the canyons and meadows below Grave Creek. They did not know how many warriors there were or where they had set up camp. And they did not know the country: John had led his people deep into the northern reaches of what geologists call the Klamath Knot— the 150-mile mass of mountains, gorges, ravines, and gashes stretching from the Trinity River to the Klamath and the Rogue, one of the three or four most remote and inaccessible regions in the continental United States. Even today, the majestic but unforgiving terrain of the Rogue River watershed below Grave Creek is lightly settled; Congress has established two large wilderness areas and declared this stretch of the Rogue as a Wild and Scenic River. The landscape had become as central to the Rogue River War as the two opposing military forces.

The tribes battered the Americans in three early encounters. Captain William Lewis had set up headquarters at Galice Creek for his volunteer forces. On October 17, tribal warriors attacked the facility. Lives were lost on both sides, but the assault forced Lewis's company to retreat from the area. A week later, by complete accident a group of ten regular army soldiers, led by Lieutenant A. V. Kautz, were scouting for a suitable wagon road route when they stumbled upon the main body of tribal warriors in the steep forest land above Lower Grave Creek. Indian soldiers charged Kautz's group, killing two and capturing several pack animals, but the Americans managed to escape to Fort Lane.

Despite its misfortune, Lieutenant Kautz's expedition provided key information to the Americans. Now they knew where Tyee John's men were encamped. Captain Smith promptly set out for Grave Creek with a force

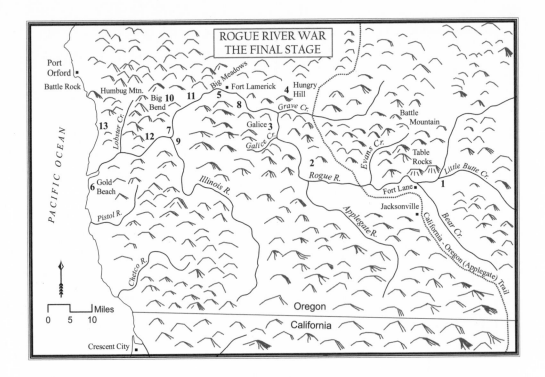

Major Events
1) *Little Butte Creek Massacre (Oct. 8, 1855)*
2) *Indians attack settlements (Oct. 9, 1855)*
3) *Battle of Galice Creek (Oct. 17, 1855)*
4) *Battle of Hungry Hill (Oct. 31-Nov.1, 1855)*
5) *Battle of the Meadows (Nov. 26, 1855)*
6) *Indians burn Gold Beach (Feb. 22, 1856)*
7) *Troops burn main Mackanutuni village (March, 1856)*
8) *Troops attack Indians at Battle Bar (April 27, 1856)*
9) *Oak Flat council (May 20, 1856)*
10) *Battle of Big Bend (May 27-28, 1856)*
11) *Indians Come in to Big Bend for removal north (May 30 -June 15, 1856)*
12) *Troops attack Shasta Costa and Painted Rock Village (June 5-6, 1856)*
13) *Tyee John surrenders (July 2, 1856)*

of about 100 regulars. Colonel Ross brought 250 or more volunteers. While enthusiastic, these armies had a rag-tag, makeshift quality to them. Walling described the volunteers as "ill-organized, unpaid, ill-fed, ill-clothed and insubordinate." They also were ill-armed, carrying "sabers, pistols, squirrel guns, and almost anything they could call a weapon." The regulars had military training and were better paid and clothed, but they, too, suffered from a lack of quality arms: two-thirds of them had only musketoons, short-barreled, inaccurate rifles with limited range.

PART TWO. WAR AND REMOVAL

The combined American forces marched to the vicinity of the tribal encampment at Hungry Hill on the evening of October 30. Estimates vary, but probably about 200 Indians were positioned there. The next morning, the day of the intended assault, Captain Smith's men made a crucial error, building campfires to cook breakfast and capture some warmth in the chilly autumn morning. In addition, two companies of volunteers, seeking to stake a position opposite from the regulars and create a surround, climbed a ridge and inadvertently came into full view of the Indians. Seeing the smoke and the soldiers, the Indian fighting men made ready.

The Battle of Hungry Hill lasted two days. The Indians, fighting from the concealment of pine trees and thick underbrush, repeatedly repulsed charges from the Americans. The volunteers' attempt to trap the tribal warriors from the rear failed because of the exposure they faced coming down the bare ridgeside. Heavy fire raged for most of the day. On the second day, the Indians surrounded their opponents but were beaten back. By the afternoon, the Americans had had enough. Eleven regular and volunteer soldiers had died, and twenty-seven were wounded. Exhausted and short of water, the regulars and volunteers made their way back to Fort Lane and other parts of the Upper Rogue River Valley.

The tribes lost the most men, twenty, but all acknowledged that they were the victors in this pitched battle: they had defended their homeland and forced the retreat of the largest American fighting force ever assembled in Oregon. No doubt could remain about their staying power and military capability. A letter to the editor in the *Oregon Statesman* lamented: "God only knows when or where this war may end. . . . These mountains are worse than the swamps of Florida." Lieutenant George Crook, who met the returning American soldiers at Fort Lane, called the Indians the "monarchs of the woods."

The Battle of Hungry Hill gave a bracing dose of confidence to southern Oregon tribes. As a teenage girl, Frances Johnson, a Takelma and niece of Tyee George, participated in the battle, as did a few other females. Frances remembered the excitement. "Boy, those bullets sounded funny when they fly by your head! Hwhoooo . . . Hwhoooo . . . Hwhoooo. . . ." She also took lifelong pride in the way her people had risen up and beaten back the Americans. "You bet your life," she would say firmly in her later years. "That night I danced with white man's scalp on a stick."

This photograph is believed to be of Tyee John. If it is in fact an image of the tyee, it was presumably taken late in John's life, which ended in 1862. The historian Hubert Howe Bancroft, looking at another photograph (location unknown) of John with his son, described him as having "an intelligent face" and "the look of an earnest, determined enthusiast." Bancroft added that his features were "marked with that expression of grief which is often seen on the countenances of savage men in the latter part of their lives." B. F. Dowell, an Oregon attorney who knew Tyee John, "always thought his features, height, and shape resembled General Andrew Jackson." *Courtesy of Oregon Historical Society, no. ba018607.*

Tyee John moved his people, women and children as well as warriors, still farther downstream to Little Meadow, part of the "Meadows" area, thickly forested but interspersed with occasional grasslands for grazing the horses. Slashed with ravines and the woods full of downed timber and chaparral, the Meadows presented even more difficulties for the American troops. On November 26, some 400 soldiers began an assault on the tribes' stronghold on the north side of the Rogue. But the Indians learned they were coming and, as American soldiers began to ford the Rogue, tribal riflemen rained bullets down on them from the ridges above. The Americans withdrew later that day. Tyee John's forces had again prevailed. Then, for months the cold and rain of a severe winter kept the Americans from making large movements of troops.

Along the Coast, as in the valley, daily life in late 1855 was punctuated by regular incidents instigated by Indians and non-Indians alike. Call them skirmishes or scrapes, but it was rattling and tragic whenever a person was shot, hanged, or scalped or when a farm house or cedar plank lodge went up

PART TWO. WAR AND REMOVAL

in flames. The relentless displays of violence soured everyone's daily lives.

Tututnis, while not directly subjected to extermination threats, knew of the violence in the upper valley and the beach goldminers' unprovoked attacks to the north and the south. Now a vigilante group calling itself the Gold Beach Guard set up shop at the mouth of the Rogue. Fearing the worst, the tribes took preemptive action.

On February 22, 1856, Tututnis and some Chetcoes and Mackanutinis conducted an all-out, early morning raid on Gold Beach. Of the twenty-three murdered, one of the first was Ben Wright, an Indian agent who for months had been meeting with both sides, trying to keep the lid on. The Indians then proceeded to burn the town of Gold Beach to the ground. The following days brought more killings and burnings. The coastal tribes were squarely in the Rogue River War.

General Wool ordered troops from forts in Vancouver and California and from Fort Lane to the east, to converge on southern Oregon and launch a spring offensive "for terminating the Rogue river war by United States troops." The string of Indian victories was about to come to an end, for Joel Palmer spoke the truth at the Table Rock negotiations when he told the assembled Takelma, Athapaskan, and Shasta people: "I have said the white man have come and more are coming. . . . It is no use to make war upon them for if one be kiled ten will come in his place."

Wool appointed Colonel Robert Buchanan to head up field operations. After arriving in late March, the colonel sent nearly 200 regulars to attack and burn Indian villages, including the main Mackanutini village, on the Lower Rogue up to the Illinois River. Troops from California fought Chetco and Pistol River bands on their way north, and volunteer groups from Gold Beach, Port Orford, and Coquille raided Tututni villages. Indians were killed and taken prisoner—and they scattered under the pressure, further diminishing the tribal military capability.

Buchanan knew that Tyee John's forces were holed up in the Meadows area but decided not to mount his offensive on them during the heavy spring rains. By early April, several volunteer groups were moving down the Rogue toward the Meadows. The weather was miserable, with heavy snows. Nonetheless, within weeks General John Lamerick of Jacksonville had 535 volunteer troops at the Meadows under his command, and they were in no mood to wait for Buchanan. They found that Tyee John had abandoned the encampment at Little Meadows and moved most of the Indians downstream yet again. Scouting the area further, the Americans soon discovered a large camp on the south

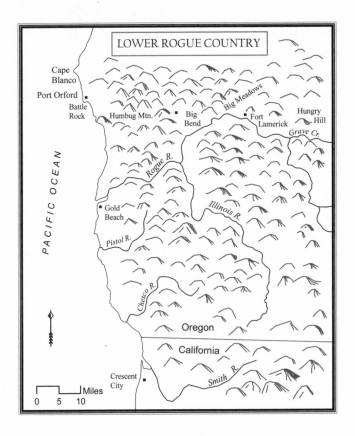

bank of the Rogue, now called Battle Bar, occupied by Tyee Lympy's band.

In the early morning light of April 27, Colonel John Kelsay, with 100 men, charged the camp. It was a rout:

> Many Indians had not yet got out of their huts. The soldiers poured a heavy fire on them. Men, squaws and children were all together in great confusion—nothing saved them but the river. The enemy took positions behind rocks and trees (and fired). The squaws and children disappeared in a dense growth of fir. The enemy lined themselves behind trees above their camp and while they were watching our movements, the detachment (150 men) under Major Bruce came down in great haste without being discovered. Capt. Abel George poured in the whole fire of his company. A fire was kept up during the day. There were 20 or 30 of the enemy killed.

Intermittent firing continued for two more days—the volunteers lost but one man—after which the surviving Indians were forced to escape downriver toward Big Bend. The volunteers then made a significant strategic move: they constructed Fort Lamerick on Big Meadows on the north side of the river and staffed the stockade with 200 soldiers.

The Indian fighting force had been weakened and Tyee John's men were caught in the pincers created by the upriver volunteers at Fort Lamerick and the army soldiers on the Coast. And, given months of experience, the Americans had gained a much better sense of the lay of the land. They knew the hiding places, ambush sites, and escape routes.

In early May, Colonel Buchanan marched his 200 regulars up the Rogue and sent word to Tyee John and the bands aligned with him that he would like to hold council at Oak Flat, near the mouth of the Illinois River, to talk peace. A large delegation, including the tyees, came down from Big Bend for the meeting, set for May 20. By then, Joel Palmer, although he could not make it from Portland in time for the Oak Flat gathering, had solidified plans to remove all southern Oregon Indians north to the new reservation at Siletz. At the grassy bench above the surging Illinois, Buchanan urged the leaders to surrender and agree to move north. At first, the Indians refused to go to the reservation, but then Tyee George and Tyee Lympy agreed, recognizing the overwhelming number of American troops. They would bring all their people to Big Bend in one week to surrender formally and be escorted to the Coast for the transit north.

But Tyee John would not relent. The chief, probably now in his fifties, still believed that he and his warriors could prevail in battle. He addressed Colonel Buchanan and made his stand with some of the most memorable words in Oregon history:

> You are a great chief. So am I. This is my country; I was in it when those trees were very small, not higher than my head. My heart is sick with fighting, but I want to live in my country. If the white people are willing, I will go back to the Deer creek and live among them as I used to do. They can visit my camp, and I will visit theirs; but I will not lay down my arms and go with you on the reserve. I will fight. Good-by."

Buchanan stayed at Oak Flat. When the time came to meet at the broad meadow on the north side of the Rogue at Big Bend, he sent Captain Smith and his 200 men of Company C from Fort Lane to receive the surrender. Tyee John and his comrades met them, not with a white flag but with an extraordinary, last-ditch campaign to preserve their freedom and their homeland.

The Indians failed to show at the Big Bend meadow on the appointed day, May 26. Sensing trouble, and warned by Indian boys, Smith moved his men out of the open, flat meadow to high ground in order to establish a more secure site. After dark, they ascended a narrow, north-south ridge above and to the west of Big Bend. The slope at the south end of the ridge gave the Americans a defensible position and there they located their howitzer, dug trenches, and established breastworks. The trenches, eroded away, remain visible today. It was a good defensive posture from the American point of view: the Indians could never attack from the west, which was a virtual cliff, and the terrain dropped off sharply in the other directions as well. This battlefield was compact. The ridge was only 200 yards long—with most of the action taking place at the south end—and the ridge's crown spread just 12 to 30 feet across. In the Battle of Big Bend, the opposing forces would be right up against each other.Early on May 27, John's warriors began arriving at the meadow below. Although some of the Indians had intended to surrender, Captain Smith and his men knew that Tyee John—historian Frances Fuller Victor termed him "the iron chief"—would renew his colleagues' resolve. As many as 300 or 400 Indian fighters moved up the hillsides toward the ridge and took their positions. At about 11:00 in the morning, with John barking orders, they opened fire. The fighting went on all day and, for the second night in a row, the army soldiers went with little sleep, food, or water. In spite of the steep terrain and Company C's strategic location, the Indians had the Americans nearly surrounded.

On the next day, both sides, but especially the exhausted Americans, continued to take heavy losses: seven Americans were killed and twenty injured and the tribal losses were severe, although there is no known count. Tyee John took to taunting Captain Smith. At the Oak Flat council, Smith had made the mistake of telling John "we will catch and hang you, sir; but if you go on the reservation, you can live in peace." John resented the threat, and he knew that, despite Smith's assurances and given the broken promises under the Table Rock Treaty, there would be no "good life" at the new reservation. Perhaps Captain Smith himself would like to live there? John made his points and inspired his warriors by getting within hearing distance of Smith and waving a rope that the Shasta general soon intended to place around the captain's neck:

Hello, Captain Smith! You go on the reservation? You go on the reservation? Hiyu chick chick (many wagons travelling); Hiyu ikta (a great many good things); hiyu muckamuck (much food); Hiyu clothes; wake klatawa reservation (not go to the reservation); take rope Capt Smith; do you see this rope Captain Smith?

By mid-afternoon, Tyee John's forces had the clear edge and seemed poised to claim yet another victory. Military historian Jeffery Applen, who conducted on extensive site survey, reports this:

> After 30 hours of fighting the soldiers were in extreme peril. The battle situation was simple and uncomplicated; the soldiers were surrounded by Indian warriors and had suffered so many casualties that their fighting efficiency and capabilities had been degraded by at least 28% based on casualty figures alone. For the soldiers, after the first few hours of combat, their tactical options became limited, a breakout maneuver was not possible without abandoning their dead and wounded. Consequently, they were limited to fighting the battle to its conclusion where they stood. For the Indians, because their initial assaults failed to overpower the soldiers of Company "C", their options too became limited. Without overwhelming strength in manpower to defeat the soldiers outright, the Indians were limited to containing the soldiers within their defensive position, and reducing their strength by fire. Given time, this course of action would ultimately lead to the erosion of the soldier's capability to resist until, by weight of numbers, the Indians could carry their position.

But the Indians were not given time. Late in the afternoon, the balance tipped the other way. As a precaution before moving out of the meadow, Captain Smith had sent a rider to Colonel Buchanan at Oak Flat to get reinforcements. Captain Auger finally arrived with seventy-five dragoons. Although two of those men were killed and three injured, the Americans now had the advantage and the ferocious Battle of Big Bend was effectively over. The Indian warriors fled the battlefield, leaving behind a pile of ropes that Tyee John had expected to use to hang Captain Smith and the army soldiers.

Joel Palmer, who had arrived with Captain Smith, engaged the tyees in their scattered camps, urging them to assemble at Big Bend for surrender, a march to Port Orford, and transport north by ship to the reservation. Hundreds of people straggled in over the next two weeks. Others went voluntarily to Port Orford or were rounded up and brought in by regulars and volunteers. Even though the tribes were resigned to the move north and, combat over, Governor Curry ordered the volunteers to disband on May 31, some of the volunteers wanted more Indian blood. On June 5 they burned a Shasta Costa village and shot four Indian men while they were fishing. The next day they attacked a village of men, women, and children on Painted Rock Creek, killing at least twenty.

Tyee John's people, 35 men and 180 women and children, were the last to come in. The agreed-upon place was Reinhart Creek, north of Gold Beach. Trying, perhaps, to revive the never-say-die heroism they had displayed for the past many years, John and his soldiers shouldered their rifles and fired, but their shots were off mark and landed harmlessly. The soldiers returned fire and John's men retreated to the woods. John insisted that he and his men be allowed to keep their arms, but Captain Smith refused. Then, during the afternoon and evening, John's people gradually filed in and turned over their weapons.

Finally, Tyee John himself walked into the circle of American soldiers and ceremoniously laid his rifle against a rock. Even then, he rebelled against the surrender. Probably as much from instinct as design, the tyee suddenly grabbed his rifle. The fifty soldiers were quicker and leveled their weapons at him. And so Tyee John—Tyee John of the iron will; Tyee John of the blood commitment to his people and his land; Tyee John, one of the great Northwest war chiefs along with Leschi, Kamiakin, and Joseph—handed over his weapon.

At that moment, on July 2, 1856, the Rogue River War came to an end.

THE COAST RESERVATION

"A suitable selection shall be made by the President

for their permanent residence."

T HE CHURNING VIOLENCE, AND THEN ALL-OUT WAR, THAT FOL-
lowed the Table Rock Treaty of September 1853 did not constitute all
the Indian history made in southern Oregon during 1854 and 1855.
Indeed, the turmoil made policy decisions and diplomatic initiatives, embodied in treaties, all the more imperative. If it is true that whites were most often
the aggressors, that fact took a back seat to Commissioner George Manypenny's policy that, whoever might be at fault, Indians must be removed to permanent homes in remote areas to separate them from American settlement.
To this formulation the commissioner added a new element. With so many
tribes and bands, creating separate reservations for each would be inefficient.
Instead, Indian peoples in western Oregon would be moved and confederated
on just one reservation. In 1855, the Coast (or Siletz) Reservation was established. Two years later, a separate and smaller reservation, the Grand Ronde,
was created on the eastern border of the Coast Reservation.

Joel Palmer drove the events from the federal side. In the early 1850s, he
had played second fiddle to Joseph Lane, but the conflict at Battle Mountain in
1853 was Lane's last military excursion, and the ensuing treaty at Table Rock
marked his final face-to-face negotiations with tribal leaders. Lane continued
to work on some Indian issues; as territorial delegate he pressed hard to move
western Oregon tribes east of the Cascades and he supported reimbursement to
Oregon citizens who suffered damage from conflicts with Indians. He directed

his efforts in Congress, however, primarily toward achieving statehood for Oregon, addressing the slavery question, and, not inconsequently, furthering his own political ambitions that would give him a place on the Democratic ticket in the presidential election of 1860. Commissioner Manypenny took a keen interest in western Oregon—after all, this was the proving ground for his new policy—but he was in distant Washington, D.C. Joel Palmer worked in Oregon and, for the most part, his decisions were the decisions of the United States of America.

Right or wrong, like him or not, the tall, strapping, and gregarious Palmer was as active and committed a public official as one will find. He was the principal person charged with carrying out Manypenny's policy—but it was Palmer's policy, too. It is hard to exaggerate his fixation on finding a "permanent home" for the tribes, separate from the whites. To him, only separation and stable land tenure could stem the violence and give tribes a chance to survive. He genuinely cared both for the dreams of the burgeoning numbers of American settlers and for the humanity of Indian people. He wanted Indians to have land and peace, and he unflaggingly rode rough wagon roads and trails across nearly all of western Oregon and to the Upper Klamath country beyond the Cascades in his quest to find the best place.

Still, many American citizens in Oregon comfortably incorporated the word "extermination" into their daily discourse. With that approach foreign to Palmer's thinking, the prevailing public opinion about him ranged from distrust to disdain and led to his downfall in 1856. Against this backdrop of conflict that made bilateral federal-tribal policy so essential, Joel Palmer was the architect of the system that removed Indians from the daily lives of western Oregon settlers, inflicted enormous pain and upheaval on the tribes, and held out the promise—if the promise could be kept—of a better future for Native people.

Palmer moved at a fast pace in his crusade to locate western Oregon Indians on separate reservations, away from the ever-increasing settlers. The Table Rock Treaty of 1853, signed in September, was followed several days later by the ratified treaty with the Cow Creek Band of Umpquas, which also provided for a temporary reservation, to be followed, if necessary, by a permanent home. In March 1854, Palmer signed a treaty with the Tualatin Band of Kalapuyas, promising them farm implements, clothing, other assorted goods, and $300 in cash. In exchange for its lands in the northern end of the Willamette Valley, near Portland, the tribe received no specific reservation, only the assurance of one in the future. As with so many of the Willamette Valley treaties, Congress never ratified it.

With the Oregon Coast and the Klamath country east of the Cascades much on his mind as the best locales for permanent reservations, Palmer set out with pack trains on exploratory visits to both. In April 1854, he reported on the profusion of coastal shellfish, crabs, and berries and noted that "Salmon and other fish in perpetual Succession visit the streams." But he conceived of Indians as Jeffersonian farmers, not as the gatherers they had been for millennia. Accordingly he emphasized, because of the "dense forest" and narrow valleys, that only the more level uplands would "admit of cultivation and [have] a fertile soil." Now, in his first visit to the area, he was "less favorably impressed" than he had expected to be with a 100-mile stretch of the north-central Coast as the permanent Indian homeland:

> Between the Si us Slaw and Neachasna [the Salmon] a country enough to Settle all the Indians in the Willamette and Umpqua Valleys and on the Coast, but they would be required to live in Small communities, in Scarcely accessible valleys; and a great number of farmers, mechanics, teachers, and Agents would be required for their proper instructions and control.

In August, to examine the alternative site, Palmer ventured across the Cascades to the Upper Klamath River watershed, home of the Klamath Tribe. This could be the place to move some western Oregon tribes, who would presumably be interested in grazing and farming: "An abundance of nutricious grasses borders these lakes and Streams. . . . The Soil is rich and appears suited to the growth of cereals, and the usual production of the garden." Klamath country, it followed, was "suited to the colonization of the Indians of the Willamette and Umpqua Valleys," and, while those tribes had "expressed a decided opposition to removing east . . . their consent can now be easily obtained." This was a curious statement because the valley tribes had been steadfast against the "east of the mountains" proposals from the beginning. The optimistic superintendent may have been caught up in his enthusiasm over the Klamaths' agricultural potential. A year later, Palmer dispensed with the idea altogether.

Upon returning from Klamath country, Palmer received a noteworthy letter from Commissioner Manypenny. The United States now added a critical element to the new Indian policy. The circumstances in Oregon, Manypenny ordered, required that large groups of tribes be confederated and coexist together: "It is of great importance . . . that . . . the numerous small bands of fragments of Tribes be united into tribes, and concentrated upon reservations as limited in number as possible."

It is true that a kind of confederation had already been accomplished in the Table Rock Treaty, where three tribes were involved. That grouping in 1853, however, resulted from an ethnological confusion in which whites routinely referred to the linguistically distinct Takelma, Shasta, and Athapaskan tribes as "the Rogue River tribe" and so the treaty described them all as being a single tribe. Now, a year later, the United States made confederation into official policy, especially in the Pacific Northwest.

None of the tribes and bands wanted to confederate. They had built societies and governance around their own village systems and were separate peoples who often spoke different languages. Sometimes age-old grievances scarred relationships between tribes. None of this mattered to the United States. For the government, confederation was more efficient and less expensive and it became the predominant organizational device in Oregon, Washington, and other states as well.

With the policy of confederation now fully in force, Palmer went into a new round of treatymaking. He traveled to southern Oregon to negotiate a supplemental treaty with the three tribes on the Table Rock Reservation. The occasion lacked the high theatre of the year previous. Palmer came with a small company, and the tribal leaders, determined to hold the fragile peace, never threatened military action. But Tyees Joe, Sam, and John balked when Palmer proposed moving additional tribes and bands onto the Table Rock reserve. Divisiveness among the three tribes already on the reservation, they argued, "would be increased by the residence of strange Indians." The Indian agent pressed on, reminding the tyees that the 1853 treaty made no allowance for schools, blacksmith shops, or a hospital; those and other benefits, including oxen, wagons, and clothing, would be provided if the additional Indians could be moved onto the reservation. In the end, Palmer prevailed. The new treaty, signed on November 15, 1854, gave unfettered federal authority to add tribes to the reservation—the ability, really, to redefine the basic natures of these societies by deciding with whom they would live.

Palmer's next order of business, which he accomplished three days later, was to bring new groups onto the Table Rock reserve and obtain land cessions from them. This treaty was negotiated downriver, at the mouth of the Applegate River, with tyees from the Shasta bands from Deer Creek on the Upper Applegate; the Scotons, a Takelma village just below Galice Creek; and the Grave Creek Band of Takelmas. These groups strenuously objected to being amalgamated with the foreign tribes on the reserve, but to no avail. Palmer obtained signatures that both acceded to confederation and relinquished Native ancestral lands.

Palmer continued on, seeking to clear Indian title in western Oregon and consolidate tribes on temporary reservations, knowing that removal to still other lands would likely follow. He brought together Umpqua and Kalapuya bands of the middle Umpqua Valley and obtained a treaty that located them on a temporary reservation. This agreement of November 29, 1854, gave the United States sweeping authority to add still more bands to the confederation created by the treaty and to move all of them to a permanent reservation.

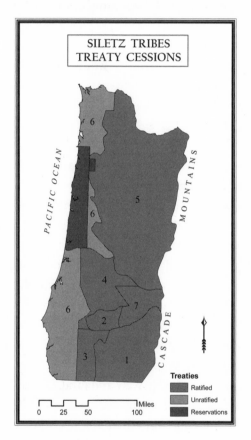

Then Palmer made a major move, bringing together nearly all of the Willamette Valley tribes and bands in January 1855. Following his pattern, he obtained the cession of Kalapuyan, Chinookan, and Molala aboriginal land and required the tribes to confederate. As with all the tribes, Palmer acknowledged that his "most difficult task [was] to obtain their consent to leave their old homes." But he had the force of empire on his side and persuaded

Number	Treaty	Date
1	Table Rock Treaty	Sept. 10, 1853
2	Cow Creek Treaty	Sept. 19, 1853
3	Chasta, Scoton, and Grave Creek Treaty	Nov. 18, 1854
4	Umpqua and Calapooia Treaty	Nov. 29, 1854
5	Kalapuya Treaty	Jan. 22, 1855
6	Unratified Coast Treaty	Aug. 11 - Sept. 8, 1855
7	Molala Treaty	Dec. 21, 1855

them to move to a temporary reservation with the promise that a permanent reserve would follow. This treaty, the largest single land acquisition from the tribes of western Oregon, secured for the United States 7.5 million acres (about 12 percent of Oregon), the entire Willamette Valley to the middle of the Columbia River. Settlement on those prized agricultural lands was now fully legal under American law. The tribes received about 3 cents per acre as compensation.

With this burst of treatymaking, save for the lands of the coastal tribes and a small southern band of Molalas, Joel Palmer had obtained Indian title to all of western Oregon. All of the reservations were temporary. These agreements, which were ratified by the Senate, were just the beginning of a removal to new lands and the confederation of diverse peoples. Still ahead lay the largest removal of all, probably to the Coast. Once treaties with the coastal tribes were signed, the final piece of the elaborate federal strategy would be put in place.

As Indian superintendent for the entire Oregon Territory, Joel Palmer had obligations elsewhere and, as of the early spring of 1855, could not immediately pursue his grand plan of treating with the coastal tribes and then locating all western tribes on one large reservation. Instead, working closely with the aggressive Isaac Stevens, both governor and superintendent of Indian Affairs for Washington Territory, Palmer traveled to the middle Columbia River on important business. American settlement along the Columbia did not come close to the relative boom in the Willamette Valley, but the region had excellent potential for farming. Also, there was some tension with the tribes, especially with Yakama Chief Kamiakin. It was time to negotiate treaties with the inland Columbia River tribes.

Stevens and Palmer negotiated four major treaties in May and June, obtaining tens of millions of acres from tribes and bands of the region and establishing the modern-day Warm Springs, Yakama, Umatilla, and Nez Perce reservations. Except for the Nez Perce, the mid-Columbia treaties all followed the prevailing policy of creating reservations of several confederated tribes and bands.

Upon his return in July, Palmer turned his full attention to the western Oregon tribes. He was gratified on one score. Before leaving for the mid-Columbia, he had resolved the central question plaguing him since taking office: where should the western tribes be permanently located? He had become satisfied that they simply would not agree to go east of the mountains. The solution was the Coast Reservation he had imagined two years before, even before the Table Rock Treaty had been signed.

Palmer had taken decisive action. On April 17, 1855, he filed formal papers designating an Indian reservation of stupendous scope—from the divide between the Siuslaw and Umpqua rivers in the south to Cape Lookout in the north, a distance of 105 miles, reaching 23 miles inland in the south and 12 miles in the north. The reservation would be made permanent through treaties with the coastal tribes. The same day, Palmer wrote to Oregon newspapers and candidly explained his reasons for the proclamation, which closed the entire area to settlement by whites:

> I would be pleased to have you call the attention of settlers particularly to this subject as it is one of great importance to the well being of these waning tribes, no less than to the maintenance of good order and morals in our community.
>
> There may be found persons seriously objecting to the selection of a reservation in the district indicated. But the habits of the Coast Indians, their mode of subsistence and the absence of any natural, facilities for sustaining life east of the mountains, argue strongly against their removal to the interior. . . . [N]o part of our line of Coast affords equal facilities for the Indians Reservation with so few attractions, for white settlements as this one selected.
>
> In order to avoid any conflict of claims growing out of occupancy by settlers, I have deemed it best to give timely notice so that persons may not select claims within the tract described.

Three months later, Palmer could rightly conclude that setting aside the coastal lands had caused little stir. This is not to say he lacked detractors. The apparently unfounded allegation that he was sympathetic to the nativist, anti-immigrant Know Nothing movement hurt him with his own Democratic Party and caused him to think he might be removed from office. No one, however, doubted his ability, commitment, or energy.

And plenty of energy would be needed to persuade the Coast tribes to relinquish most of their land, confederate, and move to the new reservation. Since they were located along the whole Coast from the Columbia River to the California line, the negotiations would have to be done in stages and would require elaborate advance planning. Goods—agricultural equipment, tools, kettles, clothing, blankets, beef, flour, and presents such as calicoes, beads, knives, hatchets, and tobacco—would have to be provided at five separate council sites. To do this, Palmer issued orders to accommodate deliveries to strategic coastal points: a shipment by steamer from the Willamette Valley to the mouth of the Columbia; the construction of a new trail for a pack train over the Coast Range to Tillamook Bay; a delivery by pack train to the mouth of the Umpqua; and shipment of goods, including two tons of flour, by steamer to Port Orford. As for his own travel, even though rivers and creeks would be running low in the summer, the rugged terrain would make his journey arduous. Still, we can doubt that Palmer much minded all this. He was a prodigious traveler and loved getting out of town on horseback to Oregon's backcountry. This would be especially true for the treaty tour, which he hoped would make his vision for western Oregon a reality.

Both sides of Joel Palmer's Indian policy showed through on this long-distance expedition. Fearful that Indian people might be annihilated altogether, he desperately wanted to give them a chance to survive and prosper. But, as an officer of the United States, he was bound to serve the American population and would be resolute in fulfilling that duty. He would establish by treaty the large reservation he declared on April 17 as a permanent Indian reserve, which he viewed as a fair and generous homeland. The tribes would cede to the United States of America all other land "from the middle of the channel of the Columbia River" to "the southern boundary of the Oregon Territory," and west of the summit of the Coast Range.

Knowing he would be holding five separate councils of tribes and bands that would be confederated by the treaty, Palmer took the unusual step of drafting in advance just one treaty that would be signed successively by tyees at each council site. No changes would be made. There would be talks, translated in the Chinook Jargon by John Flett, a Canadian Native employed by the United States as interpreter, who had participated in most of the western Oregon treaty convocations. Doubtless, Palmer and the handful of other federal officials would listen politely and give explanations. But Palmer would stand firm on the treaty he had composed. These councils would be signings, not negotiations.

Palmer's cavalcade of three pack trains set out on its lengthy journey down the Coast in early August. The formal treaty proceedings commenced on August 11 with a council of northern tribes at Yaquina Bay. Forty-one tyees from four bands of Tillamook, Alsea, and Yaquina put their "X's" on the document. Just six days later, Palmer and his men held council farther down the Coast at Coos Bay with leaders from the Coos, Siuslaw, and Lower Umpqua tribes. While there are no formal minutes from, and few reports on, these councils, we can be sure that the reaction of the Indian people on that day at Coos Bay reflected the sense of loss held by all the coastal tribes as, with no real choice, they submitted to land cession, confederation, and removal to new lands:

> Some old Indians said after the treaty was signed, the Indians gathered on Tar Heel point and held a special ceremony. Old chiefs who had ruled their people with a firm but gracious hand said a few words. Then they bowed their heads and a medicine man called on the Great Spirit. The Indians buried a stone hatchet in the ground, and the waves beat a mournful dirge along the shore.

At the meeting with Coquille tyees on August 23, Palmer pressed a theme that he doubtless urged at all of the councils. The tribes would benefit by moving to the new reservation and being separated from the whites:

> If we have a bad man who shoots an Indian, and Indian goes & sees the agent before he gets there the bad man has gone and we cannot get him. . . . They sometimes give them disease and it is spread among other of their people, it is bad—we know these things are so, we want to prevent this—we want to do them good & make them a people, it is for these reasons that our chief thinks it best to have a country of their own, where no whites will be allowed to live among them.

Palmer's party then held council with the Tututnis and Chetcoes. "The council ground," wrote Rodney Glisan, an army doctor, "was located in a beautiful myrtle grove on the south bank of the Rogue river, three miles from its mouth." The Indians knew that the treaty convocations were monumental, historic events for their people, and the councils with coastal tribes were all well attended. On the Rogue River, for example, Dr. Glisan reported that 1,220 Indians gathered in the myrtle grove, where fifty-five Tututni and Chetco representatives affixed their marks.

The last of the councils for the 1855 treaty took place with bands of Upper Coquilles on September 8. Coquelle Thompson was a boy then and his father was one of the signatories. His account of the session includes this questioning of Joel Palmer:

"You say you take us Willamette. What kind of place?" "Well," Julian Palmer say, "just like here, only more open place. The Willamette is a big river." Question again from chief, "I want to know, any deer in there?" "Deer? Of course there's deer in there. Lots of deer in there!" "Any fish in there?" "Oh yes! Lots of spring fish. All kinds of fish, just like you got here." "Any eels?" "Oh yes! Lots of eels, Oregon City. Big falls there! Lots of eels, hang that way!"

. . . Oh everybody glad now. Indians ready to give up now, ready to go. "Any elk there?" "Oh yes, elk there! Everything you see here, everything there! Bear!" "Any berries there?" "Oh yes, everything you have here: strawberries, blackberries, salmonberries, everything you got here, just same there." That's all they want to know, you see. All leaders stand up before treaty people. They say, "We'll go now, we give up now." Oh Jerry Palmer clap his hands.

The exchange demonstrates the difficulties of language, the inadequacy of the Chinook Jargon as a vehicle for treaty negotiations, and the power differential between the federal and Indian sides. It is unclear why Palmer would have referred to the Willamette Valley, since the treaty calls for removal to the Coast Reservation. Perhaps he was misleading the questioner, or perhaps he was thinking of the additional area at Grand Ronde, adjacent to the Coast Reservation but in the valley, a plan that he would formally propose a few months later. Even then, though, tribal members would have no right to fish in the Willamette River or at Willamette Falls since those places were a good distance beyond the borders of the Grand Ronde site Palmer may have had in mind. And Coquelle Thompson was just six in 1855. Perhaps his memory, or his recollection of the account his father related to him, was faulty. Perhaps the Coquilles heard one conversation and Palmer another.

What we can be sure of is that any good faith and honorable intentions were choked off by the atmosphere for Indian-white relations in Oregon of the 1850s, which was afflicted by misunderstandings, distrust, a wide and deep cultural and language gap, and threats and fears of violence. Nonetheless, from one perspective the Coast Treaty of 1855, with all its imperfections, offered some hope. With the signing of the treaty by Palmer and tribal representatives and the presumed approval by the Senate, the tribes seemed to be assured of a large, magnificent, and permanently secured homeland. But the saga of Indian land rights on the Coast had only begun to be written.

Despite all the effort by Palmer and Indian leaders—and despite the congressional and administrative determination not to repeat the destabilizing mistakes of the past in failing to ratify Oregon treaties—Congress never ratified the 1855 Coast Treaty. This was not due to objections to Palmer's plan for locating the coastal tribes on a permanent reservation or even to concerns about the size of the reservation. Instead, confusion wrought by rudimentary long-distance communications, the outbreak of the Rogue River War, and legal uncertainties over presidential power led, not to a ratified treaty, but to an executive order by President Franklin Pierce establishing a reservation nearly identical to the original April 17 reserve Palmer had proposed. When the Interior department received the Coast Treaty just a few days after the president signed the executive order, the Senate was in recess. Soon thereafter, the department submitted several treaties when Congress resumed business, but the Coast Treaty sat in the Interior department for fifteen months before it was sent to the Senate. Commissioner Manypenny reported that the treaty had been "overlooked." The muddled process left in its wake a tangle of problems that would plague western Oregon Indians for generations.

Returning to his office in the Willamette Valley town of Dayton after negotiating the Coast Treaty, Joel Palmer, who had no way of knowing that time would be of the essence, waited nearly a month before sending the treaty and his report back to Washington on October 3, 1855. The treaty package literally went by slow boat, first by steamship to San Francisco and then by a three-to-four-week ocean journey from San Francisco to New York via the Panama railroad route, which had opened in 1855. Presuming that the trip from New York to the nation's capital was accomplished in just a few days, mail from or to Oregon took between five weeks and three months.

Earlier in the year, in reporting on his declaration of the Coast Reservation on April 17, Palmer had asked for ratification of this set-aside land; he had been given basic instructions and accorded broad authority, but he had acted unilaterally and understandably wanted confirmation of this sweeping administrative action. In addition to the slow pace of the mail, two additional

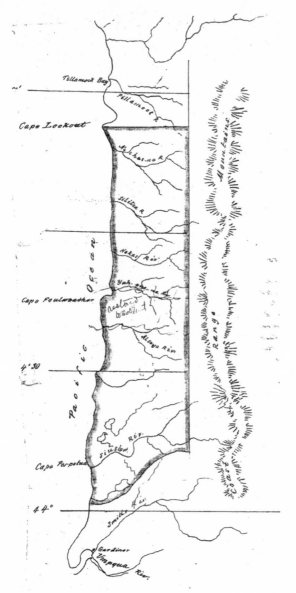

Joel Palmer's original map of the Coast Reservation, developed in April 1855 in connection with his closing the area to homesteading by non-Indians and taking the initial step toward establishing it as a reservation for the exclusive use of the Coast, Willamette, Umpqua, and other tribes. President Pierce's executive order of November 9, 1855, establishing the Coast Reservation, was based on Palmer's request, which included this map.

months had been taken up by a malfunction: Palmer's letters had arrived, but he had sent the map in a "tin case," which had been delayed in transit. In the meantime, the Interior department advised Palmer to notify land officers to assume that the designation of Indian land was valid and that no settlements by whites should be authorized.

By September, the map of Palmer's April set-aside had arrived and the commissioner of the General Land Office recommended to the secretary of the Interior the creation of "a large reservation of land, for the Coast, Umpqua, and Willamette Tribes." The GLO commissioner, who had no way of knowing that out in Oregon Palmer had just obtained the last signatures on the Coast Treaty, further recommended that a presidential order be obtained.

Secretary McClelland then requested a full report from Commissioner Manypenny, who responded at some length on October 29. He reviewed

Oregon Indian policy and Palmer's request that his August 17 set-aside "be made a permanent Indian reserve." Manypenny then advised that "this course does not conflict with the uniform policy of the Government, and is in keeping with that pursued in the case of the treaties in Oregon already ratified." The commissioner emphasized that action on Palmer's request could not have been taken earlier "in the absence of the map." With the map now in Washington, however, and because "very great embarrassment must result to the service because this subject has not been determined," Manypenny agreed that the permanent reservation recommended by Palmer should be established, subject to later adjustments by treaty or legislation:

> As therefore, the policy of concentrating the Indians upon one or more reservations, is that already adopted in the State of California, by Act of Congress, and I know no reason why the recommendation made by the Supt. is not the best in view of all the surrounding circumstances that can be devised, I respectfully recommend that the tract of land designated on the accompanying map from the General Land Office as that "proposed for Coast & Umpqua & Willamette Indians," be reserved from sale or settlement, and set aside for Indian purposes—subject however to such curtailment in dimensions as treaties here after to be made and ratified and a better knowledge of the requirements of the Indians may admit under the direction of Congress. It is only by some such action that the salutary provisions for treating with the Indians of Oregon for a cession of their lands to the United States, and their consequent concentration at any point can be carried into effect, without the delay of further legislation, if not war and bloodshed.

Having received Commissioner Manypenny's report, Secretary McClelland made his recommendation to the president on November 8:

> Before submitting the matter to you I desired to have a more full report of the subject from the Indian Office, and the letter of the head of that Bureau, of the 29th ultimo . . . having been received and considered, I see no objection to the conditional reservation asked for, "subject to future curtailment, if found proper," or entire release thereof, should Congress not sanction the object rendering this withdrawal of the land from white settlement at this time advisable.
>   A plat marked A, and indicating the boundaries of the reservation,

accompanies the papers, and has prepared thereon the necessary order for
your signature, should you think fit to sanction the recommendation.

The matter went to President Pierce's desk the following day. Because of the
slow course of the mail, the officials in Washington still did not know that
two months before, Joel Palmer and tribal leaders had executed the Coast
Treaty, which called for a reservation very similar to the one referenced in
the executive order. The treaty would arrive in Washington just five days after
the secretary presented the executive order to the president, but by then the
president had already signed the executive order:

> November 9, 1855
>
> The reservation of the land within denoted by blue-shaded lines is hereby
> made for the purposes indicated in letter of the Commissioner of the Gen-
> eral Land Office of the 10th September last and letter of the Secretary of the
> Interior of the 8th November, 1855.
>
> Frank'n Pierce

The executive order can be viewed in three different ways. First, and most
likely, it can be understood as fulfilling the president's duties in the Oregon
Indian treaties to provide "permanent" reservations if tribes are moved from
their temporary reserves. Second, President Pierce's order could be viewed
as a separate, stand-alone action, providing the kind of rights that attach to
those executive orders not related to treaties. Third, the order might be read
as creating a lesser kind of executive order reservation—one that is "conditional."

These distinctions have considerable legal consequences. Treaty land is
fully owned by the tribe. It is not subject to unilateral action by a president;
only Congress can remove land from the reservation. If treaty land is taken
(Congress does have the power to abrogate Indian treaties), the tribe is entitled to full compensation under the Fifth Amendment to the Constitution.

Stand-alone executive orders, unrelated to treaties, are different. While
Congress in the twentieth century granted important protections to executive order reservations, the courts had long upheld presidential rights to adjust
reservation boundaries. As late as 1942, the U.S. Supreme Court ruled that
executive order tribal land is "subject to termination at the will of either the
executive or Congress." Unlike treaty land, if Congress does take executive
order land, then it is not subject to compensation under the Fifth Amend-

ment. Finally, if the Coast Reservation were "conditional"—that is, temporary—then any tribal rights would be minimal, especially in the days before Congress took steps to give additional protections to executive order reservations.

The difference between reservations being altered by Congress or by a president acting alone would prove to be of great moment at Siletz. A decade after President Pierce created the Coast Reservation, President Andrew Johnson unilaterally—and probably illegally—signed an executive order divesting the tribe of 200,000 acres, about one-fifth of the reservation.

President Pierce based his order in part on Secretary McClelland's brief and seriously flawed one-paragraph letter, which purported to accept Commissioner Manypenny's recommendation for a "conditional" reservation. The commissioner, however, never used the term "conditional" and did not intend such a result. In addition, McClelland misquoted Manypenny's letter, which nowhere described the proposed reservation as being "subject to curtailment, if found proper." While Manypenny employed the term "proper" three times, he always tied it to whether the reservation should be established in the first place. McClelland's combining of the two passages can be read as applying "if proper" in a different sense, to the curtailing—that is, termination—of the reservation. And, although he never made the claim, perhaps McClelland's letter suggests that it is the president, not Congress, who decides when it is "proper" to remove land from the Coast Reservation.

Secretary McClelland's letter to President Pierce was terse in the extreme and may have been written hastily. He almost certainly failed to think through the effect of the Oregon treaties, which did not allow the president the option of creating a "conditional" reservation. To some extent, that was understandable. The use of presidential executive orders to create Indian reservations was brand new at the time, having been used only three times, all earlier in 1855, to establish reservations in Michigan and Minnesota. None of them involved prior, ratified treaties.

But, whatever one may make of McClelland's communication, there is no reason to believe that President Pierce was attempting to infringe on Congress's authority over Indian treaties. The executive order never used the term "conditional" or asserted a presidential prerogative to abridge this reservation, which traces to promises in the Oregon treaties. Even treaty reservations can be altered or terminated, although it must be done by Congress, not by the president. That is why, in recommending a permanent reservation, Commissioner Manypenny was careful to qualify it in order to acknowledge congressional authority under existing law: "subject, however, to such curtailment in dimensions as in treaties hereafter to be made and ratified . . . *under the direction of Congress.*"

In fact, while presidents had broad power to create executive order reservations, the special nature of the western Oregon treaties significantly narrowed that authority. The Table Rock Treaty of 1853 first implemented the policy of establishing a temporary reserve that the president could curtail if, and only if, "a suitable selection shall be made by the direction of the President of the United States for their permanent residence." The Cow Creek Band of Umpqua Treaty included the same language, and the other five ratified treaties all promised those tribes that the president could move them from their temporary reservations only to permanent reservations.

Once the president was involved, then, the overriding law came from the ratified Oregon treaties. The high stakes, complexity, lack of direct Indian involvement, and the Interior department's trust relationship to the tribes all make this a classic situation for applying the basic Indian law principle that ambiguities and uncertainties in treaties, statutes, and executive orders are interpreted in favor of the tribes. President Pierce's executive order is properly understood as establishing a permanent treaty reservation, especially considering the controlling nature of the treaties and the text of the executive order itself, which never referred to any conditional or temporary status.

Within just three months after the executive order was signed, federal officials began conducting mass removals to the Coast Reservation. The original idea behind the reservation was that the Coast, Willamette Valley, and Umpqua Indians would be moved there, and many were. Then an exigency of the highest order arose. Although no one in Washington knew it, the Rogue River War had broken out with the massacre at Little Butte Creek a month before President Pierce signed the executive order. With the Takelma, Athapaskan, and Shasta people at the Table Rock Reservation in terrible jeopardy, Joel Palmer wrote Commissioner Manypenny that he was "satisfied of the futility of attempting a permanent Indian Settlement on the Table Rock Reserve and that its abandonment at once is the wiser course." He proposed that the Table Rock tribes be removed to the Coast Reservation and that the initial plans to place the Willamette Valley tribes be changed. For them, he proposed a new land base, initially a temporary encampment and later, he hoped, a second and separate reservation—the Grand Ronde. Palmer then immediately carried out the removal of the people of the Table Rock tribes who remained peaceful under the protection of Fort Lane. After their march north, they stayed at the Grand Ronde encampment until facilities were made available on the Coast, when most of them were moved to the Siletz River Valley within the Coast Reservation. At the close of the Rogue River War, they were joined by their fellow tribespeople from the upper- and mid-valley Rogue River country.

The establishment of the Grand Ronde Reservation in 1857 sheds light on the status of the Coast Reservation. Smaller at 69,000 acres and located at the headwaters of the Yamhill River on the west edge of the Willamette Valley, Grand Ronde was hand-in-glove with the neighboring Coast Reservation as a matter of policy. Grand Ronde was often called an "extension" of the Coast Reservation, and Palmer described it as "the key to the entrance of the Coast Reservation." Grand Ronde was proposed mainly for Willamette Valley tribes, although this massive social reordering was anything but tidy: some individual Indians from the valley went to Siletz and some from the Coast and southern Oregon went to Grand Ronde.

By 1857, the Buchanan administration had come in with a new Indian commissioner and Interior secretary. Commissioner James Denver, a lawyer, had a long and diverse career in which, in addition to two separate stints as Indian commissioner and many years in law practice, he served as state senator and secretary of state of California, congressman, governor of Kansas (which then included Colorado, where the capital city was named after him), and brigadier general in the Union Army. In a detailed report, the commissioner recommended to Secretary Jacob Thompson the confirmation of the encampment at Grand Ronde as a permanent reservation. Denver reasoned that members of several tribes with ratified treaties already resided there and that "the treaty provisions with the Willamette tribes, as well as with the others above named, are such as clothe the President with the amplest power respecting the location of a reserve for their permanent home."

The secretary approved the recommendation and forwarded it to President James Buchanan, with the provision that it be established "particularly for the Willamette tribes, party to the treaty of January, 1855." The president proclaimed the Grand Ronde Reservation on June 30, 1857.

This treaty-based analysis invoked by President Buchanan was also the law when President Pierce created the Coast Reservation. That reservation was established for the Coast tribes, who did not have a ratified treaty, but also for the Willamette Valley and Umpqua tribes, who had four ratified treaties among them. The Molala signed a treaty for a permanent reservation in December 1855, and the Rogue River tribes, with their treaty promise of a permanent homeland, if removed from Table Rock, were sent to the Coast Reservation.

Knowledgeable figures of the day treated the Coast Reservation as permanent. Commissioner Denver, in his report to the secretary of the Interior about the Grand Ronde executive order, set out the law and policy framework with sophistication. James Nesmith, who attended the Table Rock negotiations and was named superintendent of Indian Affairs for Oregon, wrote in 1858 that Palmer's initiatives for the Coast and Grand Ronde had together created "a permanent home for the Indians of the Willamette, Umpqua, and Rogue River valleys." The main architect of the Table Rock Treaty, Joseph Lane, who was by 1860 a U.S. senator, addressed the issue of white settlement on the Table Rock reserve. His bill, S.142, designed to clarify that homesteaders' rights to settle on the former Table Rock reserve should be confirmed, passed the Senate and was sent to the House, though it never went to a vote there. The text of Lane's bill explained with precision this important episode in Oregon history: how the Rogue River tribes were removed from Table Rock and now resided at Grand Ronde and Siletz, with rights to permanent residence there by virtue of treaty. Lane's bill stated that "the Indians inhabiting said tract temporarily set apart for their use were removed to the Grand Ronde and Siletz reserves, which had been selected for their permanent residence."

Ever since the arrival of white people in the Pacific Northwest and for many generations beyond, the legal rights of western Oregon Indians were no more substantial than a summer mist along the Oregon Coast. A leading instance is the failure of federal officials to acknowledge the truth that the Siletz Reservation was a permanent treaty reservation that could be altered only by the unequivocal direction of Congress. In a right world, that truth would have prevailed, not only because it was American law but also because it was born of the grit of Siletz ancestors, who, even as their leverage was slipping away, had the wisdom and determination to insist that their treaties include the right to a permanent reservation. But the world was not right, and in the wake of the treaties came the agonies of the ancestors' removal from their cherished homelands and, not long thereafter, the breakup of the magnificent reservation that had been promised to Siletz people forever.

TRAILS OF TEARS

"Walk on, and don't look back."

THERE ARE TWO NARRATIVES ABOUT THE UPROOTING OF SOME 4,000 western Oregon Indians in 1856. With few exceptions, federal officials and other non-Indians wrote clinical and matter-of-fact, even cold, accounts of severe weather, starvation, illness, and death. The Indian narrative is very different, a white-hot description of ordeals, including beatings, rapes, and killings, that were inhumane in the extreme. That narrative is alive today. In virtually every family, twenty-first-century Siletz people tell stories handed down by ancestors of the brutal removals.

The physical ordeals were coupled with the sadness of being forced out of their ancestral homelands. Shortly after removal, J. Ross Browne visited the Siletz Reservation and reported to the secretary of the Interior. He included verbatim accounts of talks with several tribal leaders. "For my own part my heart is sick," said Tyee John. "Here the mountains are covered with great forests. It is hard to get through them. We have no game; we are sick at heart. . . . I will consent to live here one year more; after that I must go home. . . . I am unable to go to war, but I want to go home to my country." Takelma Tyee George asked why "we should be removed so far from our native country. . . . to us it is a great evil. If we could even be on the borders of our native land, where we could sometimes see it, we would be satisfied. . . . My heart is not bad; it is sick. . . . We are sad now; we pine for our native county. Let us go back to our homes, and our hearts will be bright again like the sun." The Tututni tyee, Jim, agreed. "I think we have been here long enough. We came from the mouth of the Rogue river. There we had plenty of fish. It is a good country. We want to go back to our old fishing and hunting grounds. What George said is our heart."

More than a century later, the wound was still open. In emotional testimony, Pauline Bell Ricks told Congress in 1976 of her grandmother, Ki-Ya-Na-Ha, "who lived in the beautiful Rogue River Valley. . . . She was happy there, the soil was rich, she had a home, canoe, and food in abundance, she remembered a lot of happy times there." But then came removal:

When they [got] to Siletz, she told of how hungry, how tired and weary, and yes how heart sick, for here they were on the most rugged part of the coast. Lands were not clear, the climate was different, it was like going to a foreign country. She remembered a lot of people dying from many different kinds of diseases unknown to her. Probably chicken pox, tuberculosis, she didn't know. For she always believed most of them died of depression, heartbreak, and mis-treatment.

The displacement of the twenty western Oregon tribes took several shapes. More than 1,400 people endured harrowing shipments by sea. Some groups had to march fifty miles by land. Two agonizing overland marches encompassed more than 250 miles. All of the removals inflicted incalculable physical and psychological injuries on the people. One distinguishing aspect of the Oregon experience was the lay of the land: the steep, tangled terrain and strong rivers made the marches especially wearing and treacherous.

The first removals to the Siletz Reservation took place in the winter of 1856: Kalapuyas and Molalas from their villages in the Willamette Valley; Umpquas from their temporary reservation in the Umpqua Valley; and Takelmas, Athapaskans, and Shastas in a cavalcade from the Table Rock reserve on the Upper Rogue River. Two journeys, mostly by sea, followed in June and July, from Port Orford to Grand Ronde. Later in July was the overland trek from Port Orford to the Siletz Reservation. These removals from Port Orford were preceded, for most of the Indians, by round-ups at Big Bend or other points on the Rogue and marches to Port Orford. There was also a "voluntary" removal, when members of tribes to the north—the Tillamooks, Clatsops, and Chinooks—were eligible for residence and enrollment at Siletz, but were not forced to go. And finally, there was a removal that stretched out twenty years or more. Some families and individuals initially eluded the government and remained in their aboriginal territories. Others escaped from the reservation. Over the years, federal agents and contractors tracked down, and some-

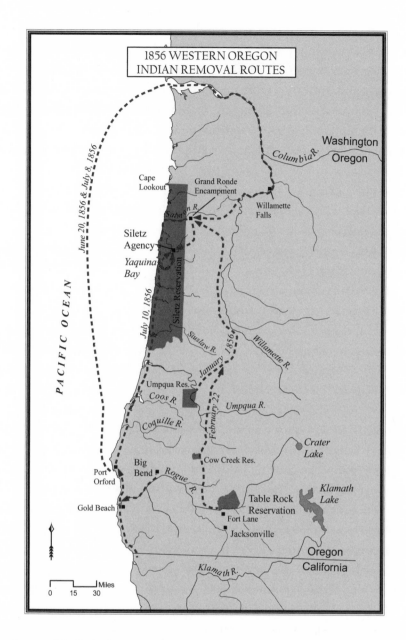

1856 WESTERN OREGON
INDIAN REMOVAL ROUTES

Washington
Oregon

Columbia R.

June 20, 1856 & July 8, 1856

Cape
Lookout

Grand Ronde
Encampment

Salm. R.

Willamette
Falls

Siletz
Agency

Yaquina
Bay

PACIFIC OCEAN

July 10, 1856

Siletz Reservation

Siuslaw R.

Willamette R.

January 1856

Umpqua Res.

Coos R.

Umpqua R.

Coquille R.

February 22

Crater
Lake

Cow Creek Res.

Port
Orford

Big
Bend

Rogue R.

Klamath
Lake

Gold Beach

Table Rock
Reservation

Fort Lane

Jacksonville

Oregon
California

Klamath R.

Miles
0   15   30

times shot and killed, these resisters, whose only crime was love of homeland.

Joel Palmer, driven by treaties that provided for temporary reservations and then moves to permanent ones and by the policy of confederating many tribes together, began planning for the removal of western Oregon tribes as soon as he became Oregon Indian commissioner in 1853. Then, the massacre at

Little Butte Creek in October 1855 and the tribes' campaign of revenge triggered emergency action. The Indians on the Table Rock reserve faced daily peril unless and until they were transported out of southern Oregon. Palmer notified Commissioner Manypenny of his plans and requested a military escort. Although he had no doubt that a rapid exodus had to be carried out, he lamented that the basest attitudes of the white citizenry made it necessary:

> The future will prove that this war has been forced upon these Indians
> against their will; and that too, by a set of lawless vagabonds for pecuniary
> and political objects and sanctioned by a numerous population [volunteers
> seeking pay for their service] who regard the treasury of the United States a
> legitimate subject of plunder.
>
> The Indians in that district have been driven to desperation by acts of
> cruelty against their people. Treaties have been violated and acts of barbarity committed by those claiming to be citizens that would disgrace the most
> barbarous nations of the earth, and if none but those who perpetrated such
> acts were to be affected by this war, we might look upon it with indifference.
> But unhappily this is not the case.

The Siletz Reservation was not yet ready to receive the arrivals. Homes and agency buildings promised in the treaties had not yet been constructed. In addition, while the Indians would be marched north from Table Rock on the California-Oregon Trail to the Willamette Valley, no road had yet been built to connect the valley with Siletz. Palmer decided to have the government purchase several homesteads from settlers on the South Fork of the Yamhill, a tributary of the Willamette River, to serve as an encampment, or staging area, until the tribes from Table Rock could be moved to Siletz. Palmer also envisioned making the encampment a permanent extension of the Siletz Reservation, where the Willamette Valley tribes could settle. In 1857, by presidential executive order, it became a separate reservation, the Grand Ronde.

War or no war, George Ambrose, the agent at Table Rock, was not enthusiastic about Palmer's proposal for immediate removal of the Rogue River Indians. Taken aback by the hurry-up attitude, Ambrose's reply in December laid bare some of the realities of removal in the dead of winter:

> Winter with all its severity has fully set in, snow is several inches deep on
> the ground at the time of my writing and falling fastly yet. From all appearances it may be very deep before night. I regard it as almost impossible to

PART TWO. WAR AND REMOVAL

remove the Indians at this time for several reasons. First the unusual severity of the winter at this early season. Secondly, they are destitute of winter clothing not having received their annuities but very few of them have either shoes or stockings, many of them are sick. . . .

. . . I do assure you a trip to the Willamette at this inclement season of the year could not be accomplished without a vast deal of suffering among them. Again it will be impossible to move them without an escort which cannot be obtained for two or three weeks to come.

Capt. Smith of Fort Lane with all of his disposable force is now engaged with those hostile bands of Indians near sixty miles distant from here from which he will not be disengaged for several weeks. Mr. Metcalfe who has just travelled over the road, also entertains the opinion that it would be worse than folly to endeavor to remove them without an escort.

Hence we will not be able to start so early as you expect; necessity compels that humanity would require a delay at least until comfortable preparation can be made for their accommodation.

Two months later, on February 22, 1856, close to 400 Indians set out on their daunting removal journey, led by Ambrose and troop escort. The procession moved along the California-Oregon (or Applegate) Trail, the wagon road that roughly followed today's Interstate 5, from the soon-to-be-abandoned Table Rock Reservation to the Willamette Valley. The frigid weather had relented somewhat since Ambrose's plea to Palmer; the cold nights left frost in the morning but no snow. The wagon road, however, which wound through steep, up-and-down terrain, was rough to begin with and received plenty of rain. Ambrose kept the assemblage moving—an average of eight miles a day— but the going was slow, sloggy, and fatiguing.

While Ambrose finally secured shoes and blankets for the marchers, the conditions remained deplorable. "Our teams now numbered eight which I feel will not be sufficient. Thirty four Indians are disabled from traveling by reason of sickness aside from the aged & infirm, who will as a matter of course have to be hauled." The great majority, healthy or not, were forced to walk. As the trip dragged on, the number of sick people increased.

The Indians, and Ambrose as well, were "in constant alarm" that the Jacksonville crowd would raid the entourage. Timcolean Love from Jacksonville dogged the group during the early days as the march moved down the narrow canyons through present-day Grants Pass toward Wolf Creek. On the fifth day, near Jumpoff-Joe Creek, Love rode up and shot and killed an Indian man, sending shock waves through the group. Ambrose sent a message to Captain Smith at Fort Lane for help; Smith ordered Love arrested and turned over to civil authorities for prosecution.

After three weeks, they reached the level, open space of the Willamette Valley. The weather lifted and although the wagon road was muddy, travel on the flatland was much easier. As had been the case throughout the journey, ferries on the relatively well-traveled California-Oregon Trail took them across the rivers and streams. Still, while the dangers of Jacksonville lay behind them, their fears of mayhem could not have been much allayed. War tensions were at their height and the "extermination" sentiment had spread throughout western Oregon. Finally, after thirty-three days and a forced march of 263 miles, the Takelma, Athapaskan, and Shasta people reached the temporary encampment at Grand Ronde. The journey had taken the lives of eight Indians.

The Rogue River people joined 500 Umpqua, Molala, and Kalapuya tribal members at the Grand Ronde encampment in Polk County. Even before the removal began, Ambrose had heard from a resident of the county: "I will not be surprised if every Indian brought in . . . is immediately killed. . . . The people of Polk have be come so excited about it they held a meeting at our Court house to day & passed resolutions disapprobating like course, and the people of the country are determined the Rogue River Indians shall not settle in our midst or on our boundary."

The Kalapuyas at the encampment had lived on the floor of the Willamette Valley and the Molalas in the Cascade foothills on the eastern side of the valley. Their journeys were shorter than the Rogue Rivers' and on a more level landscape. The Umpquas, facing difficult terrain and bad weather, vehemently objected to any removal from their reservation in the Umpqua Valley. Joel Palmer, concerned for their safety if they remained, spent three days urging them to leave, without success, but John Flett, the Canadian Native who had served as interpreter at the Umpqua treaty negotiations, finally gained their consent after all-night meetings with the principal tyees.

The Umpquas were force-marched in January away from their homelands of millennia, in what Hubert Howe Bancroft called a "heavy storm of rain and snow." Their ordeal lasted nearly a month, and they lost four people to sickness and one to murder. Once at the encampment, their misery continued. Joseph Jeffers, Joel Palmer's hired hand, wrote that many contracted the flu "to the extent that it makes humanity shudder . . . and those that are sick suffer with the cold at night a nuff to kill them . . . the suffering of these people haunts me day and night."

PART TWO. WAR AND REMOVAL

The largest removals to the Siletz Reservation came from the southern Oregon Coast. Port Orford was often described as the launching point, and it is true that ocean steamers did depart from that port and overland marches were organized there. But for most Indians, their long journeys began earlier—and still farther away from Siletz—when they were rounded up from battlegrounds and homes after the Rogue River War. A main departure point was Big Bend.

By trail, the Big Bend of the Rogue River lay about fifty miles from the river's mouth. This is the wild, gashed country where the last battle of the war was fought. Travel on the sheer canyon sides and across the many gorges and tributary streams was slow and arduous "owing to the nature of the Country," as Joel Palmer put it. It took soldiers five difficult days to march groups of Indians from Big Bend to the mouth of the Rogue.

In late May 1856, on the final day of the Battle of Big Bend, Captain Auger and his troops had decisively turned the tide in the Americans' favor, sending the Indian warriors into retreat to the surrounding forests. Palmer and others promptly sent out word to the Indian camps that they should come in to Big Bend peaceably and surrender. Then they would be marched to the mouth of the Rogue and north to Port Orford and the Coast Reservation far beyond.

For the tribes, the long, last stage of the war became a community affair. They had no choice. The extermination-minded miners would have had a field day with their rifles and nooses if Indian families had stayed behind in their villages near the Upper Rogue River when the warriors established their tactical positions in the remote country downriver. So the women and children moved down the wild Rogue with Tyees John, George, and Lympy and other tyees and their soldiers.

Captain E. O. C. Ord, one of the officers assigned to oversee the encampment at Big Bend and transport Indians to the Coast, wrote empathetic diary entries of western Oregon removal. He recounted how Indians, hundreds in all, gradually straggled into the camp day after day. By June 7, many of the Indian men, probably feeling release from war, played games and sang and danced. The Indian women, though, continued to unleash their despair at the loss of lives and homeland: "A few yards off from under the crowd of brush huts and low blanket tents issues the never-ending melancholy wail of the squaws in mourning." On June 8, Captain Ord wrote:

4 men 9 squaws and some children came limping and crying (these squaws) into camp . . . poor devils—the decrepid and half-blind old women are a melancholy sight to see—to think of collecting such people for a long journey through an unknown land—no wonder the men fight so desparately to remain—after they have driven all the white settlers too out of it—it almost makes me shed tears to listen to them wailing as they totter along—one old woman bringing up the rear, her nakedness barely covered with a few tatters—and barely able to walk—they had been a long time getting here and many of them have lost all they had by the capsizing of the canoe. Some others were near drowning—the girl was on the back of a man who was swimming ashore with her—he had a boy, too—the girl was washed off—canoe smashed as it went over the rapids.

Captain Ord led 100 Indians down the river from Big Bend. It was a hard, tedious hike, tough on the elderly and, the captain acknowledged, tiring for him as well. One child died and another was born. At Oak Flat at the mouth of the Illinois River, the procession met with some 600 Indians in a temporary camp overseen by Captain Auger.

Continuing on, Ord found an encampment of about 165 Indians on the ocean shore at Gold Beach. This was a layover point for the three-day, thirty-mile leg up the Coast to Port Orford. Indians were steadily coming in—some by canoe, some by mule, most on foot—from the Chetco and Pistol rivers to the south as well as the Rogue. By mid-June, the rush was on to get the Indians to Port Orford to meet an ocean steamer for transport north. Captain Ord described how the steamer schedule and the need to get Indians away from the local volunteers—"vols"—created pressure to keep weary people moving:

Indn women packing the mules—thick set sturdy packers—they are—land party stopd—said twas too rough & the packing women were tired & the old were sick & one old man was dead & they would go on to Mollout but I sent Drysdale and Foster over to em, to say the vols were coming & they must push on—which they did suddenly—but it was a sorry sight to see—fat & lean staggering along—the old too tottering under heavy burdens.

With Indians and soldiers filing in, for a period of six weeks or so Port Orford became one of the busiest places on the West Coast. By June 11, some 1,100 Indians had been marched in, while several hundred troops kept watch. The number grew, for about 1,700 Natives would be moved north over the course of the next month. Tensions ran high among both Indians and the local citizenry. Many white Oregonians were out for blood, and by June of 1856 the tribes, who had relinquished their weapons, were defenseless.

The federal representatives, whether soldiers or Indian Affairs officials, made no mention of the troops killing any Indians to keep order, but the accounts handed down by Indians being removed tell a different story. The removal was not optional and the military meant to enforce it. After reaching Siletz, no Indians would be allowed to leave the reservation without written permission from the agent. Violators would be shot by the military or civilian contractors. Coquelle Thompson recalled that "when some [Indians] refused to go [to the new locations,] the soldiers were summoned and they were forced and in many instances killed in front of their loved ones to show that the government meant business. What was the poor Indian to do but go?" Ki-Ya-Na-Ha, grandmother of Pauline Bell Ricks, "began to cry for she saw her people gathered up like herds of sheep. Some families were even broken up, maybe a mother in one bunch and her children in another bunch. Many fled to the mountains, for they did not want to leave their home. But they were hunted down by the white soldiers and shot. They learned very quickly that if they wanted to live they dared not protest."

The steamship *Columbia* arrived at Port Orford about two in the morning of June 20 and anchored a few hundred yards offshore. The goliath was 200 feet long and sported bright lights and a tall smokestack. Few of the Indian people had ever seen, much less ridden on, such a vessel.

If the *Columbia* were not intimidating enough, the Indians were terrified of the troops, with whom they had clashed in pitched battle just a few weeks before. Rumors spread that the army planned to throw them overboard once the steamship got out to sea. The undertaking had the feel of finality: the Indians had been ordered to leave their belongings behind and bring only what they could carry; for many, that meant whatever they could stuff into a medium-sized traditional basket. Some, but surely not all, were assuaged by the assurances of a safe voyage by Palmer, whom they trusted in an arm's-length way. He promised to accompany them on the trip, and he did.

Getting more than 700 Indians out to the *Columbia* was no easy matter. Port Orford was a port but not a harbor; the headlands to the north gave some protection from the winds and heavy seas, but there was no enclosed harbor and, with no docks, the *Columbia* had anchored in open water. The Indians' cedar canoes took some people to the schooner, but most waded out through the cold, low waves. The boarding was rushed and chaotic. Lillie Butler's

The steamship *Columbia* in 1856 transported southwest Oregon Indians, in two desperately overcrowded trips of 700 people each, to the Willamette Valley and the new reservation. In 1858, the *Columbia* carried Tyee John and his son, Adam, from Vancouver on the Columbia River to military prison in California. *Courtesy of Oregon Historical Society, no. bc001739.*

grandparents (Tututni and Chetco) "took only as much as they could carry and kept leaving behind stuff as they were marched to Port Orford. When they waded out to the boat they lost all their belongings." Coquelle Thompson sorrowfully described this sharp dividing line between the long-held ways and an unknown future: "We left behind many fine canoes, homes, tanned hides, and other belongings found in an Indian colony at that time. We were all heart sick."

Belching black smoke, the *Columbia* rumbled away from Port Orford on June 20 with its load of 710 Indian people and their military overseers. As Coquelle Thompson explained, dread and seasickness plagued the people: "It was our first night at sea, many of the Indians got seasick—some tried to jump overboard and swim back. It was an awful night; many were sick and could not eat." With the vessel severely overcrowded—the *Columbia*'s average passenger load was 100—most people had to stay on deck in the turbulent weather. Historian Terence O'Donnell painted the scene:

It turned out to be a terrible voyage. The seas were rough, and the . . . Indians, accustomed to the calm of estuary waters, were terrified by the giant, break-

PART TWO. WAR AND REMOVAL

ing swells. And more than terrified, for all succumbed to seasickness, made worse by their being crowded into the limited quarters of the little ship. Also, blankets and apparel were in short supply, and so, exposed on the decks, they suffered the assaults of wind and spray and the driving rains. [The passengers were] jostling one another for space on the crowded decks, flung this way and that by the heavy seas, cowering in the cold and in terror of the tempest, and finally their retching sickness soiling everything—it must have seemed to them the coming of a foul death. Such were the conditions in which "the monarchs of the woods" departed their land.

This was a far quicker journey, though, than the marches that preceded it and the exhausting overland trip that other Indians would take the next month. The steamer, making good time despite the turbulent sea, reached the mouth of the Columbia River the second day. Now, on the calm river waters, the passengers felt some relief. Not only were the rough seas gone, but the Natives could see that they really were going to the Willamette country, as

Coquelle Thompson Sr. was the son of Coast Treaty signer Washington Tom. A principal Athapaskan language consultant for many linguists and a Siletz tribal leader in many capacities over his long life, he is the subject of *Coquelle Thompson, Athabascan Witness* by Lionel Youst and William R. Seaburg. He is pictured here in Siletz in about 1940. *Courtesy of The Oregonian.*

Palmer had told them. As Coquelle Thompson recalled, "Now everybody is glad. They had been scared they take somewhere else."

After reaching Portland on June 23, the troops transferred the Indians to a smaller river ship for passage up the Columbia River to Willamette Falls. From there they used even smaller craft to reach Dayton and a camp where Palmer's farm was located. Now the idea was to march the Indians to the layover camp at Grand Ronde and, with the wagon road now mostly constructed, on to the Coast Reservation, a total of about fifty miles. Palmer hired Courtney Walker, a former fur trader and missionary, to lead the procession and ordered teams of oxen for the aged and the infirm. The others hiked. The group, with a troop escort, headed out from Dayton on July 14.

It was quite a scene when the entourage reached Grand Ronde, where there were already some 1,500 Willamette Valley, Umpqua, and Upper Rogue River Indians. With the arrival of the south Coast group, the total swelled to well over 2,000, making it the largest population center in Oregon (Portland, Salem, and Jacksonville all had populations under 1,500 at the time). During this stopover, Coquelle Thompson witnessed an event, as reported to George Maxwell of the Oregon *Journal*, that impressed on him ever more how this new life would be different:

> While detained at Fort Yamhill [located within the Grand Ronde encampment] this Indian boy received his first lesson in the white man's humanity when he witnessed the hanging of a Rogue River Indian who had endeavored to incite an insurrection among his tribesmen. Troops summoned all Indians to the scene of the grewsome affair and now, after 80 years, Coquille Thompson has vivid remembrance of the garroted Rogue swinging from the gibbet days after the execution. The affair was staged to impress and discourage other Indians inclined toward rebellion.

There was no fully common experience, no single story, for the thousands of removed western Oregon Indians. The faces at the Grand Ronde gathering surely reflected that. Many endured serious physical injuries and disease, for the European germs continued to exact their tolls. Others—including women and children who had witnessed the brutal battles on the Rogue—suffered from what we now know as post-traumatic stress disorder. Sadness must have shown everywhere.

There were other emotions as well. The Upper Rogue River tribes had been split: many people had gone down the Rogue in combat and then come north by steamer; others had remained at Table Rock and marched the California-Oregon Trail with George Ambrose. They must have been energized by this reuniting at the western edge of the Willamette Valley, bringing each other up to date on family deaths and births, reminiscing about former times. Some looked forward to fitting in with the Americans and gaining benefits from the newcomers' society. Others—Ki-Ya-Na-Ha and Coquelle Thompson seem to have been of this mind—felt resignation and, as well, a determination to make their new lives fruitful, and were optimistic about it. And with so many tribes coming together for the first time, new friendships and rivalries may have sprung up with young men—as was the case on the meadow at Big Bend a few days after the defeat in the war's last battle—breaking into games, probably *koho*. Elders would have looked on, smiling through the heartbreak.

The entourage that came north on the steamship and their military escort then proceeded west to the mouth of the Salmon River and, on July 23, 1856, became the first arrivals to the Coast Reservation. They were joined a few days later by most of the 729 Indians on the second *Columbia* voyage, which departed Port Orford on July 8 and followed the same Portland–Dayton–Grand Ronde route. This camp on the ample south bank of the Salmon, with proud Cascade Head rising across the river, certainly presented a welcome interlude for the weary travelers. It was not home, but it was the same Oregon Coast, wind-swept, magnificent, and giving. Coquelle Thompson, even as a young boy, rejoiced in the mussels, juicy and creamy, just like he knew them farther south.

Although some would stay in this area at the north end of the reservation, there were no homes or other structures at Salmon River and it would be temporary for most of the uprooted Indians. Removal was playing out fast, and the army and Indian office couldn't keep up with it. Even as the second group of *Columbia* relocates was arriving, Joel Palmer was further south on the Coast finalizing his decision on the best location for the government's operations. Finding many prairies and good timber along a stretch of the middle Siletz River and especially impressed by a 1,500-acre prairie—perfect, he thought, for agency facilities, a fort, and homes—near but safely above the north bank of the river, Palmer decided on what is now the town of Siletz as the site of the new reservation's headquarters. For people at the Salmon River, yet another locale lay two tough days away.

The mouth of the Salmon River, where the first group of Indians from southern Oregon arrived on the reservation in July 1856. Cascade Head lies to the north. *Photograph courtesy of Duncan Berry.*

The next removal, the grinding overland march north from Port Orford to Siletz, holds a central place in Siletz history. Perhaps more than any single event, it symbolizes the Siletz tribal experience. Sometimes called the "Death March," it encapsulates all the horrors over all the years since white people came. It also stands as a monument to the valor of the ancestors and their will to survive. "Batter us as you will," they announced through their intrepid actions, "we shall endure." The image perseveres today through public display as well as in the minds of the people: on a prominent wall of the first floor of the tribal office building in Siletz, a painting depicts the long line of ancestors trudging in pain and defiance up a demanding slope on a narrow trail rising above the beach and rock below, leaving behind beloved old places and heading toward uncertain new ones.

When Tyee John ended the war by surrendering at Rinehart Creek on July 2, troops took him and his 225 followers north to Port Orford. John reached that harbor before the second *Columbia* voyage, but Palmer and the military

PART TWO. WAR AND REMOVAL

Peggy O'Neal's rendering, *Ahnkuttie Tillicums (Ancestors)*, of Tyee John's band being marched north into Port Orford under military escort, after his surrender on Reinhart Creek. The acrylic is a tribute to *Ahnkuttie Tillicums*—"The ancestors of the People." © *Peggy O'Neal 1996. No portion of this image may be reproduced without the written consent of the artist.*

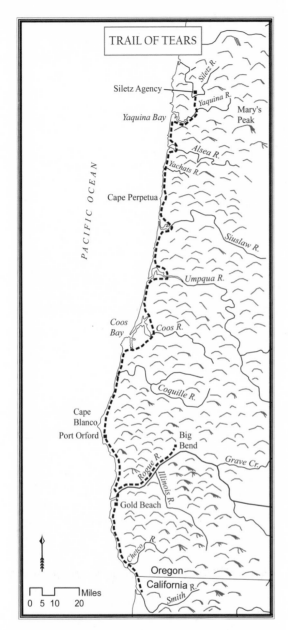

decided that he and most of his people would go to the reservation on foot. It was a form of punishment. Tyee John—"the famous Old John and his band, the terror of Southern Oregon"—had been all the talk in the journals and correspondence before and after the surrender. While Captain Smith had agreed that John and his men would not be prosecuted for their wartime actions and, while everyone had a healthy respect for his abilities, the military—and Palmer as well—resented the costs of the conflict and the leader of the opposition. As a result, even though the steamship had been used precisely because it was much cheaper and quicker than the grueling, one-month onshore trek, the Americans were determined to send John by land. They did allow some women, children, and elders in John's band to go by sea and the sick and wounded remained in Port Orford. Several resisters from the Chetco and Pistol rivers also were consigned to march. Coquelle Thompson's father, an Upper Coquille tyee, marched and perhaps tyees from other tribes did as well.

This throng set out from Port Orford on July 10, 1856. In addition to infants, 125 Indian men, women, and children were accompanied by no fewer than 90 troops under the command of Major John Reynolds to keep order and prevent escapes. With the terrain far too rough for wagons, they brought 200 mules,

160 to be used as pack animals. Although game and seafood (especially mussels) were readily available, the primary fare was cows: Coquelle Thompson related that "people who came overland had to drive cattle. Every time they camp they kill one beef. That made enough so each person get one piece."

The distance from Port Orford to Siletz by today's road system is 161 miles but in the mid-1850s it was likely 200 miles or more. There were neither bridges nor road-cuts back then and the route confronted five substantial bays at the mouths of the Coos, Umpqua, Siuslaw, Alsea, and Yaquina. Crossing the large rivers and the dozens of good-sized streams brought fatigue, delay, and danger. Palmer acknowledged this in his early planning for removal: "The number of Indians . . . the numerous streams to cross on the route and the difficulty in transporting the requisite supplies most necessarily, cause great delay." At numerous spots, the old Indian trails (which is what the caravan was following) left low ground to twist up and around coastal mountains, ridges, and drop-offs. Even on flat land, the rains created bogs, marshes, and small lakes. The areas of open beach, including the fifty-mile stretch of dunes north of Coos Bay, allowed mostly unimpeded passage but hiking on sand is physically draining. Even with the troops pushing hard, the group could make only six or seven miles a day, making the trip an ordeal of about a month.

There are no known journals or field reports written by soldiers on this march, but Siletz people handed down numerous accounts. Terry Russell is one of many tribal members who grew up hearing stories about the rivers: "The people had to swim the rivers on the march north. People died along the way and the survivors couldn't stop and bury them. Instead, they were forced to keep walking. Women had to swim the rivers and had their babies swept from their arms." Pauline Bell Ricks related the experience of her grandmother:

> Our trail of tears began. Ki-Ya-Na-Ha was not one of the ones that rode on the ship or a wagon, for she remembers walking most of the way. She told of women being abused, misused, and even kicked around by the white soldiers, especially if a mother tried to protect her young daughters. If men came to the rescue of their families, they were badly beaten and in some cases shot, and left, for they were not allowed to stop and bury any one that died along the way. She also remembered little children being kicked around if they fell too far behind.

Agnes Pilgrim, Takelma, received accounts of the removal from three different relatives who made the overland journey to Siletz: "The terrain was

Lucy Dick, pictured here in her beloved Chetco homeland, ca. 1939. *Photograph courtesy of Jeanette Giddings, great-granddaughter of Lucy Dick.*

harsh and our young were trained to watch out for the elders. When the elders stopped or fell, the kids went back, but the guards beat them."

Lucy Dick was a full-blooded Chetco, born in the early 1840s in a large village at the mouth of the Chetco River, who made the long walk to Siletz. Years later, she and her husband, Chetco Dick, received permission from the agent and returned to her former home. Living to nearly 100 years, she became a respected citizen of the town of Harbor, assisting in the births of numerous children. Lucy never forgot the march north, for she heard the gunshot that killed her father. When she began to turn around, her mother told her: "No. Walk on, and don't look back."

The Siletz ancestors reached Yaquina Bay in late July. From there, it took three more days to hike inland through the forest and over the low divide between the Yaquina and Siletz watersheds to reach the 1,500-acre prairie above the Siletz River. With well over a thousand people coming down from the Salmon River and across from Grand Ronde, the removal was nearing

PART TWO. WAR AND REMOVAL

completion. The unsettling fact that the Coast Reservation was not remotely ready to receive such a large, exhausted, and often sick or injured population is a matter to which we will return.

The fourth category of removal involves the fewest number of Indian people and varied fundamentally in that it was voluntary. In Joel Palmer's crusade for a Coast treaty in the summer of 1855, Yaquina Bay was the site of the first of five councils. The assembled tribal leaders from the north Coast signed away their ancestral lands, from the Salmon River to the Columbia. As with the southern Oregon tribes, the original idea was to relocate the northern coastal tribes on the new reservation. But there were no forced marches for the Clatsop, Chinook, and Tillamook tribes.

It was a matter of politics. On the south Coast, in the mining camps of southern Oregon, and in the Willamette Valley, the American population was adamant: they had warred with the tribes, wanted no more of it, and insisted on removal. In the far northwest part of the state, the settlers viewed the Indians as good workers, willing to labor at rail splitting and farming—at, not incidentally, low wages. There had been scattered conflicts but no wars, and the whites did not expect any in the future.

Part of the calmer relations with the northern tribes traces to measles, smallpox, and other diseases. With the whites coming to the Lower Columbia so early and often, the epidemics hit those tribes especially hard, killing so many people that the combined population of Chinooks, Clatsops, and Tillamooks plummeted from an estimated 6,300 before contact with Europeans to just 431. When Palmer met with them in council in 1855, only 41 representatives came.

Spared compulsory dislocation, these families made their individual decisions. Some went down to the Siletz Reservation, where they were entitled to be enrolled. Other Chinook and Clatsop families became members on the Grand Ronde Reservation or the Quinault, Shoalwater Bay, and Chehalis reservations in Washington. Still others simply stayed in their homes on the Lower Columbia and northern Oregon Coast.

The final form of removal involved a problem that, as the federal government came to learn, was inevitable as the United States carried out removals in other parts of the country, including the Southeast, where the Cherokee, Choctaw, Creek, Chickasaw, and Seminole Indians were moved to Oklahoma in the Trail of Tears, a term often applied to the Siletz. In its various removal programs—the Seminoles from the nearly impenetrable Florida swamps to the Navajos from their redrock canyon hideouts to western Oregon Indians from their deep forests—the United States came up against Indian people who hid out and refused to go or who escaped and returned to their homelands. In Oregon, as elsewhere, federal agents sternly insisted that everyone relocate and that no one leave the reservation. To the United States, the rounding up of the resisters amounted to a mop-up operation; to the resisters, it meant a profound violation of personal freedom. Federal policy acquired an even sharper edge with the removal of Joel Palmer from office on August 15, 1856, just as relocatees were streaming into the reservation. Commissioner Manypenny, facing ever-increasing political pressure from Oregon, had no choice but to dismiss the superintendent: Palmer's policies had offended just about every American in Oregon as being too pro-Indian and, to boot, he had failed to be a sufficiently loyal Democrat, committing the sin of making his hires based on merit rather than party. Rounding up recalcitrant Indians would have to proceed without Palmer's moderating influence.

Soon after the initial waves of removals, reports came in that numbers of Indians still had not moved and (subject to the usual questions as to who started what) that some of them were committing raids and killings. Absalom Hedges, the superintendent for Oregon, retained William Tichenor of Port Orford as a special agent, or "bounty hunter," to track down south Coast Indians. No friend of the Natives, Tichenor had captained the *Sea Gull*, which had moored in the Port Orford harbor in 1851 and whose crew had discharged the cannon that killed and wounded dozens of Indians at Battle Rock. In his most controversial incident involving removals, in May 1858 Tichenor ordered nineteen Chetco and Pistol rivers Indians shot and killed when they attempted to escape during their march to the reservation. He claimed that they had committed crimes and "were the most desperate and murderous of all the Indians on the coast." In examining the incident, James Nesmith, by then superintendent of Indian Affairs for Oregon, carefully avoided the question of whether "shoot to kill" was official policy for those who tried to escape removal. He delicately concluded that "in relation to the conduct of special Agent Tichenor while in charge of those Indians, various reports have reached this office. If his own representations, and that of certain others are to be relied upon as correct the Indians were killed in attempting to escape from his custody which I consider as sufficient justification for his firing upon them."

Tichenor and his men apparently brought in several hundred Indians. He sent eighty-five north from Port Orford on the *Columbia* in November 1856 for the third and last removal voyage on that vessel. The exact numbers are unknown, but other special agents and soldiers were also active in rounding up resisters.

With the place-based peoples of Siletz enduring such a violent rupture of their connection with place, people longed to return home and the early decades were rife with attempted escapes. Given the heavy Indian Affairs and military presence—Indian agents, bounty hunters, and the forts at Siletz, Fort Hoskins to the east, and Fort Umpqua to the south—any such thoughts were fraught with danger. In April of 1857, Lieutenant Philip Sheridan learned that several tyees at Siletz were planning an escape. "I . . . told them the consequences of such a step," he wrote, "and that they would have to regard the Seletz as their future home, and that they must not only abandon all intention of leaving but would have to stop talking about it." The fear that gripped them, and the risks of returning home, are reflected in Ki-Ya-Na-Ha's story of her sister's experience:

> She made up her mind that she would go back to the Rogue River and live out her days there. She was very unhappy in Siletz so she left and went back to the Rogue River to die. This is exactly what happened, she made it there, but her sister's happiness was short lived, for the story goes she was shot one day for crossing the river in a canoe. But in later years, Ki-Ya-Na-Ha was told her sister was attacked by three white soldiers, and again the same old story. But by then she knew the words, raped and murdered and thrown into the river. Ki-Ya-Na-Ha never really knew the truth of her sister's fate, for her body was never found.

Some did make it back. One woman was protected by a sympathetic white family who, when the soldiers came by, hid her in their flour barrel. Another, Lucy Smith, recalled eluding the military as a little girl:

> The last time they came after Inds. to Chetco it was I who ran away. I was 3 years old. The officers already had me + my mother, and we were being led away when she suddenly said: I have forgotten my sewing materials. As

she said this I dove into the brush + my mother after me. They never got us. We remained at Gold Beach. And that was the last time that officials ever attempted to carry back Inds. to Siletz—they never came again.

Many ancestors remembered swimming the rivers, both on the way north and sometimes going back home. Amelia Van Pelt, a Chetco who married Tom Van Pelt, a non-Indian, had such an experience. Although Indian women married to white men were allowed to remain, Amelia was taken to Siletz while Tom was in the army and away from home. Siletz tribal member Sally Engstrom records that, upon return from duty, Tom went straight to the reservation to recover Amelia and their child, Charles. He "walked all the way to Siletz and all the way back—had to swim the rivers in between, holding the baby above the water, as they swam."

For everyone, the removal era shattered their experience of living Native cultural lives, of being tribal Indians. The people in the north escaped a forced removal, but the germs had taken nearly their whole tribes. The women who avoided removal through marriage to non-Indians could try to raise children with a sense of Indian values, but those families were mostly isolated from fellow tribal members. Somehow, in a few pockets in the remote Cow Creek watershed and in the wild Rogue and Chetco country, Indians hid out from their pursuers, but they were forced to live as fugitives. Some Coos and coastal Umpquas stalled removal to Siletz by living at the temporary encampment near Fort Umpqua; later, many of them would find ways to live in towns in their aboriginal territory rather than be forced to move to Siletz. But they had no land. As for Siletz, spectacular though the reservation was as a physical place, living conditions were severe at best and the federal enforcers had a mission to deny them their culture. Their hearts were sick for their ancestral homes.

Removal was yet another assault, stifling what western Oregon Indians had lived for and believed in. The Native seeds of culture and sovereignty were there, but they lay deep underground, buried and choked by layers of actions by the new people. And many more layers were still to come.

PART TWO. WAR AND REMOVAL

PART THREE

THE RESERVATION YEARS

SURVIVAL IN A NEW LAND

"It is your peace that is killing us."

ONCE AGAIN, INDIAN PEOPLE AND THE AMERICANS HAD DIFferent perceptions and expectations, this time about the nature of governance and society on the Coast Reservation. The tribes, knowing they had retained land in the treaties, believed that the reservation would be a true homeland governed under their own self-determination. The United States saw it differently and now held all the power: Indian people found themselves squarely under the authoritarian rule of the military and the Bureau of Indian Affairs.

The guiding dogma was assimilation, but "assimilation" had a fundamentally different meaning than its use in immigration policy, where foreign nationals come to America, become citizens, and begin a new life. Immigrants face many obstacles and sometimes keep aspects of their native cultures, but their process of assimilating into American society has an underlying measure of voluntariness.

Not so with the federal policy of Indian assimilation, also called civilization, Christianizing, and Americanizing. Native American assimilation involved official suppression, control, and force, sometimes physical. Indian people were confronted—in their homelands—by American bureaucrats and their surrogates, educators and men of the cloth, all bent on stripping them of what the Americans believed to be primitive, pagan ways. To one Siletz man, assimilation meant "to tame, to put in a corral, like you do with a new horse."

The central premise of assimilation policy—that being Indian was bad, that being white was good, and that the federal government should remake these fishing, hunting, and gathering peoples with their own religions into agricultural, Christian Americans—was in place long before the removals to Siletz. By the 1850s, however, with most Indians concentrated on reservations and stripped of military power, assimilation became easier to enforce—and with an iron hand if need be.

Assimilation kept its grip on the Siletz for more than a century. Over that time, it took gradually shifting forms. At the outset, the Bureau of Indian Affairs launched a high-pressure program to denigrate traditional ways, champion farming and Christianity, and promote American and Christian values in heavily disciplined BIA and church schools. The government then turned it up a notch by removing children from their homes and placing them in BIA boarding schools. By the end of the nineteenth century, based on the justification that communal tribal landownership was "unproductive," most of the land was gone. In the 1920s, with Siletz people now living in close contact with whites and (to the eyes of federal officials, at least) mostly assimilated, the BIA shut down its reservation office and pulled out most of its services. Finally, in 1954, Congress imposed on the Siletz the most extreme form of assimilation: outright termination. This eliminated federal recognition of tribalism and Indian identity. It is rare for public policy to remain largely unquestioned for a full century and a half, yet that held true for assimilation, which was not dislodged until the self-determination era that began in the 1970s.

Like Indian policy in all eras, assimilation was the product of many motives. The dominant programs and events at Siletz during the second half of the nineteenth century—assimilation and the taking of land—are stained by racism, greed, and insensitivity. Nonetheless, a good many policymakers and Americans sincerely believed that Indians would gain by receiving the benefits of the majority society. In 1868, Commissioner of Indian Affairs Nathaniel Taylor, while romanticizing the changes and understating the ability of the Five Civilized Tribes of Oklahoma to retain aspects of their cultures, displayed the idealism—genuine in some cases, strategic in others—that accompanied the assimilation effort: "How can our Indian tribes be civilized? It so happens that . . . certain tribes of our Indians have already emerged from a state of pagan barbarism, and are to-day clothed in the garments of civilization, and sitting under the vine and fig tree of an intelligent scriptural Christianity."

Indian people knew that some measure of adaptation was necessary. There was no denying that they had been overwhelmed and would need to adjust. The problem was that most Indians wanted to keep many of the ways of their

Although the Siletz River Tillamooks were said to have been
completely extinguished by
disease, Doctor Johnson, shown
here about 1910, was one who
managed to survive. A Tillamook and an Alsea speaker,
his right hand was mauled by
a bear. Doctor Johnson never
wore shoes. *Siletz Tribal Collection.*

own world and resented the change that was forced on them so harshly and in such absolutist terms.

A centerpiece of the civilization movement—the federal boarding school system—demonstrates what a sledgehammer assimilation was. The BIA, with enthusiastic support from Congress, opened the Carlisle Indian Industrial School in 1879, the first of many boarding schools where Indian children were sent to be Americanized. (The second boarding school, Chemawa in Salem, Oregon, where many Siletz young people were educated, became one of the two "crown jewels" in the system: Pennsylvania's Carlisle in the East and Chemawa in the West.) A military man, Captain Richard Henry Pratt, one of the principal boarding school proponents and the founder of Carlisle, believed that through education, Indians could be moved away from what he believed was their primitive state: "There is no resistless clog placed upon us by birth. We are not born with language, nor are we born with ideas of either civilization or savagery. Language, savagery, and civilization are forced upon us entirely by our environment after birth." Pratt left no doubt about which direction boarding school education should take: "All the Indian there is in the race should be dead. Kill the Indian, and save the man."

It leaves a lasting sadness that Siletz people had to endure so many generations of being branded "lazy," "incompetent," "savage," and worse. Less obvious, though the hurt and disorientation must have run at least as deep, was mainstream America's failure to honor cultural values that, to the Siletz, had such worth and beauty. How could the white people have failed to appreciate the intense labor of making salmon nets, spears, and cedar canoes and then harvesting the catch, often in driving Oregon rains? The weeks of preparation, the precision, and the spirituality that bathes the traditional Nee Dosh dances in the dance houses constructed of cedar planks? The grace of a fine basket crafted of spruce roots and hazel sticks with intricate design and the long labor it took to gather and twine the materials?

These would be hard times. The BIA was a suffocating presence and the Siletz people had little understanding of how to engage that large, powerful, and foreign government. Having arrived at the reservation with only what they could carry, the more than 2,700 souls who made up the early population of the Siletz Reservation had nothing but their individual resourcefulness, the strength of their families and cultures, and the land.

Although the reservation was not familiar or fully appreciated at first by those who were required to call it home, it was breathtaking in its size and value, whether value be measured tangibly by economics or intangibly by beauty. Running 105 miles from Cape Lookout in the north to the town of Dunes City in the south, the reservation encompassed 1.1 million acres, about one-third of the Oregon Coast. It reached twenty-three miles inland in the south and twelve in the north: by today's roads, the eastern boundary lay about five miles west of Globe on Route 126 from Eugene to the Coast at Florence; just east of Eddyville on Route 20 from Corvallis to Newport; and six miles west of Grand Ronde on Route 18 from Salem to the Coast. The Siletz Reservation included dramatic shoreline rock formations, sheer cliffs rising from the ocean rocks and foam, and long beaches. The ocean presented a bounty of sea life, diverse and abundant.

The spruce, fir, and cedar forests of the Coast Range were among the most commercially valuable in the world. The Siuslaw, Yachats, Alsea, Yaquina, Salmon, Siletz, and Nestucca rivers were all major producers of Pacific salmon, with coho (also called silvers) and chinook the mainstays; the small streams and creeks also had robust runs. Most of the Coast Range afforded good, if not excellent, habitat for deer, Roosevelt elk, bear, and small game. Despite the existence of healthy ancient forests, in the decade before creation of the reservation, large fires, including the Yaquina Burn, killed or scorched hundreds of thousands of acres of old-growth timber; thick brush took over the landscape, making hunting and traveling difficult on most of the burned terrain within the reservation. Fallen dead timber was the bane of both game and its pursuers in the mountains, but the bottomlands, most

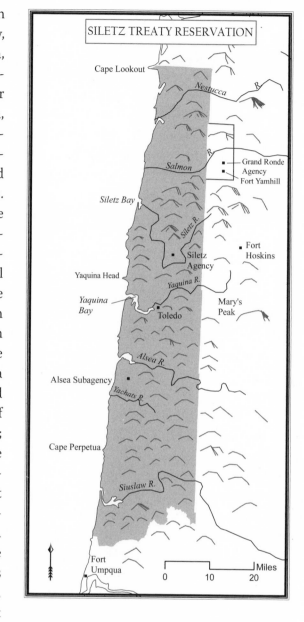

of them maintained as open grasslands by regular traditional burning for centuries if not millennia, continued to be excellent habitat for large elk herds.

The heavily forested land, poor soils, chill summer evenings, and overcast and rainy skies discouraged farming, however, and agriculture could not thrive on most parts of the reservation. There was also no major port. Yaquina Bay did provide a workable harbor on the reservation coastline, but it could not receive larger vessels. Still, the Coast Reservation—perceived in the mid-

1850s as too remote for profitable commerce and likely to remain so—would soon begin to show its many strengths. As a homeland, both for living and doing business, the Siletz had reserved a wondrous landscape.

The Indians who straggled into the Siletz Reservation in August and September 1856, exhausted, hungry, destitute of belongings, and mourning their dead, would need time to appreciate their surroundings. They found no improvements on the broad meadow, the planned site of the BIA agency and tribal housing, that spread across a bluff above the Siletz River. There were no buildings, not even tents. Food was limited. Heavy rains poured down. Panic-stricken, Absalom Hedges, the new Indian superintendent for Oregon, pleaded with Washington for help: "No means have been provided for their sustenance or shelter during the winter which is before us nor are there any funds. . . . They have left their homes and come to a strange land reposing their faith in the word of the agent of their Great Father."

That first winter, the stormiest in years, wrought great suffering. A schooner bearing lumber and flour made it to the Yaquina harbor in October, but with supplies already running low, the December shipment met with disaster. The schooner, captained by the omnipresent William Tichenor, met an extreme wave event and wrecked at the mouth of the Siletz River, losing a load of potatoes and thirty tons of flour. By April, according to J. Ross Browne, a journalist who conducted investigations for the Interior department, "the Indians were in a state of starvation. In a few days more, they would have been driven by the laws of self-preservation to abandon the reservation and seek relief by attacking the settlements." With appropriations chronically late, the government had bad credit and the local agent, Robert Metcalfe, had no choice but to contract for inferior flour, much of it "sweeps"—leftovers swept off the floor, "only fit for cattle." The housing in that unusually wet, blustery winter was no better: the agency was able to put up only twenty-seven houses for Indians. The early chaos may have been too much for Hedges, who resigned as superintendent and was replaced by James Nesmith in the spring of 1857.

The move to Siletz had been jolting for everyone, but most of all for the Upper Rogue River tribes. While the more northern geography was different for the coastal tribes, the contrast was greater for Takelma, Shasta, and Athapaskan bands who were used to a drier, sunnier climate. The California black oaks, with their nutritious and tasty acorns, a staple food for the Upper Rogues, did not grow as far north as the Siletz Reservation. The consequences of disease and change of climate were horrendous. By 1858, Metcalfe reported that 205 of 590 Upper Rogue River Indians had died: "Almost daily we hear of the death of some of those people. . . . A few more years will put an end to the most fierce and warlike race of people west of the Rocky Mountains." Some Upper Rogue River people had remained at Grand Ronde, and the loss of life was at least as great there. Like many Siletz people, Agent Metcalfe believed that depression was part of it: "Many of the more sensitive have died from a depression of spirits, having failed in the last desperate struggle to regain their country, where they once roamed free as air, unmolested by the white man, and knew no bounds to their liberties and savage ambition." The Shastas, Takelmas, and Applegate Athapaskans were losing more people than they had in the war. Superintendent Nesmith wrote that they took to telling him, "It is your peace that is killing us."

The reservation was an unstable, often violent place in the early days. Fighting among the many different tribal groups was commonplace. Diseases also continued to threaten, and traditional cures offered only limited success against the European illnesses, now compounded by near starvation and depression. Indian doctors were caught in a bind. When a family member died, the survivors sometimes killed the doctors, who were believed to possess great healing powers and who had a responsibility to cure their patients. To the Americans, it seemed logical that the seemingly immense reservation would be open to all, share and share alike, but it was more complicated than that. In the first year, for example, a major confrontation broke out on the "D" River, at the north end of the reservation. A group of Rogue River people began fishing that small but productive stream, but the "D" had long been a traditional fishery of a band of Tillamooks. A battle ensued and many people died.

The desire to return home continued to burn bright. When J. Ross Browne met with the tyees in 1857, the leaders expressed how "heart sick" they were and asserted that Joel Palmer had promised them they could in time go back. Takelma Tyee Sam said: "Captain Smith, U.S.A., Palmer, Metcalf, and others, promised us that as soon as the war was over we would be permitted to return to our country. Now the war is over. Why are we kept here still? This is a bad country. . . . My people are all dying. There will soon be none left. The graves of my people cover the valleys. We are told that if we go back we will be killed. Let us go, then, for we might as well be killed as die here." Tyee John remembered the same promise: "A long time ago we made a treaty with Palmer. There was a piece of land at Table Rock that was ours. He said it should remain ours, but that for the sake of peace, as the white settlers were bad, we should leave it for a while. When we signed the paper that was our understanding; we now want to go back to that country."

Nothing in the written record mentions such assurances, and it is not clear why this subject would have come up at the 1853 Table Rock negotiations as Tyee John seemed to suggest. On the other hand, it does appear that prior to the massacre at Little Butte Creek, there were plans to make the Table Rock reserve permanent. Then, with talk of extermination much in the air in 1856, it could well be that vacating the reserve on a short-term basis was discussed; perhaps assurances were never written down or the two sides misunderstood each other due to the limitations of the Chinook Jargon. Joel Palmer's removal from office in 1856 undoubtedly muddled things, since he would have been the person to make verbal promises. In any case, the government was not about to change course. The Indians would remain at Siletz unless given permission to leave temporarily.

The area gradually became more settled. Palmer had selected Siletz for the agency because it was less affected by ocean weather and the level meadows lent themselves to the buildings, homes, and farms that the BIA hoped to establish. The government put its offices, residences, and farms at Agency Farm. The blockhouse there would remain in military use for a decade. Using Indian labor, the military grew grain for its own use and staged drills on Agency Farm. Trails and wagon roads fanned out to places important to tribal members and federal officials. About seven miles from the Coast as the eagle flies, the agency was farther than that by trail. The mouth of the Siletz River was twenty-five miles to the north and west. The Yaquina harbor lay thirteen miles to the southwest, although Depot Slough, where shipments could be unloaded and transported by wagon road, was six miles upriver at today's town of Toledo and about seven miles from the agency.

The area in and around the agency headquarters, soon to be the town of Siletz, was the heart of the reservation and where most of the Indians made their homes. Four large prairies, about 5,000 acres in all, became the main areas for houses and farms. In much the same spirit as immigrant ethnic groups who settled into separate neighborhoods in American cities, allied tribes and bands at Siletz set up residence together. Upper Rogue River tribes—the Shasta, Takelma, and the Applegate and Shasta Costa Athapaskans, as well as Cow Creek Umpqua—settled in Upper Farm, six miles above the agency. On nearby Rock Creek, Galice Creek Athapaskans established a colony. Shasta Farm lay just downriver from Upper Farm. The Chetco, Tututni, Joshua, Euchre, Sixes, and many other Athapaskan bands located

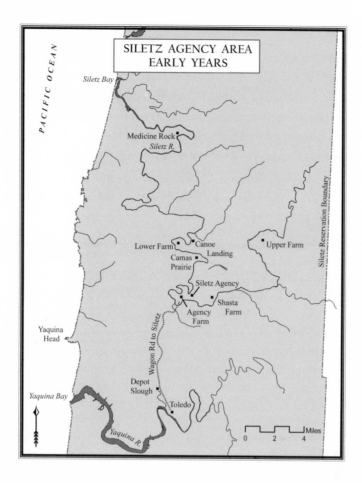

**SILETZ AGENCY AREA
EARLY YEARS**

PACIFIC OCEAN

Siletz Bay

Medicine Rock
Siletz R.

Siletz Reservation Boundary

Lower Farm • •Canoe
Landing
Camas •
Prairie

Upper Farm

Siletz Agency

Shasta
Agency Farm
Farm

Yaquina
Head

Wagon Rd to Siletz

Yaquina Bay

Depot
Slough

Toledo

Yaquina R.

Miles
0   2   4

their homes near Agency Farm. South Coast Indians, some Tututni bands, and the Coquille occupied Lower Farm, downriver from the agency. The BIA operated the Alsea sub-agency on the Coast at Yachats, where the Alsea, Coos, and some Lower Umpqua Indians were located. While a number of Indians lived in the area, the BIA's Salmon River Station to the north lacked a usable harbor and was discontinued early on.

One piece of unadulterated good news came in during the difficult early times. In the first few years at Siletz, the salmon runs were weak, and widespread frustration set in among Siletz people. Then it became apparent that the Siletz River was a very good salmon stream after all. To be sure, for chinook the Siletz could not match the Rogue, which was by far the best of all coastal Oregon chinook rivers, with fish up to one hundred pounds and more. But for coho, which averaged six to twelve pounds and could go up to thirty, the Siletz was superior. The Siletz also carried good runs of succulent eels. Dipnets, weirs, and spears became a valued and necessary part of the reservation scene. When Hoxie Simmons was a boy and the runs came in, he fished, and so later did his son. They ate most of their catches and sold the surplus to homesteaders: "[We would] net, and at certain times spear them on the riffle. Where we live, there was a rapid. When the freshet come, salmon generally stop there, not moving. My oldest son is fifty-five now. When he was boy, he run down there before breakfast. He catch hundreds and catch hundreds— that is fifty before breakfast—and sell them to white people."

THE TRIBES OF THE SILETZ CONFEDERATION
(as posted on the tribal Web site)

Compiling a list of tribal groups that became incorporated into the Confederated Tribes of Siletz Indians as a tribe, or who had individual members who became incorporated into the Confederated Tribes is in itself a daunting task. The easiest way to accomplish it is to mention only the more general term for the language group or larger tribal affiliation, rather than getting down into the specifics of village based identity. However most of the old-time people and many tribal members even today prefer to identify their tribal ancestry with as much detail as possible. Some examples of more general terms would be "Tillamook Tribe" rather than "Salmon River, Siletz, Nestucca or Nehalem Band of the Tillamook Tribe" or "Kalapuya Tribe" rather than the "Yamhill, Yoncalla or Luckimute Band of the Kalapuya Tribe."

Going by the preferred method stated above, the following is what [the tribal Cultural Department] generally considers to be an inclusive list of "our tribes": Clatsop, Chinook, Klickitat, Molala, Kalapuya, Tillamook, Alsea, Siuslaw/Lower Umpqua, Coos, Coquelle, Upper Umpqua, Tututni (including all the Lower Rogue River Bands and those extending up the Coast to Floras Creek and down to Whales Head), Chetco (including all of the villages from Whales Head to the Winchuck River), Tolowa, Takelma (including the Illinois Valley/mid-Rogue River and Cow Creek peoples), Galice/Applegate, and Shasta. Each of these tribes has a unique individual history, culture, and legal relationship with the federal government, all of which was brought into the Confederated Tribes of Siletz Indians.

At Siletz as elsewhere, the BIA agents were overseers, strict taskmasters. Their marching orders required it, for they were directed to erase Indian religions, cultures, languages, diets, ways of holding land, clothing—all that made up their worldview. Agents attempted much of this through persuasion, relentless and growing ever more stern for backsliders, and by withholding benefits. Depending on the agent's nature, whippings, beatings, or imprisonment might be meted out for fighting and other violent conduct, leaving the reservation without a pass, and disobeying other BIA rules. Ben Simpson, agent from 1863 through 1871, easily the longest tenure of any nineteenth-century Siletz agent, was the most domineering. Quick to inflict punishments, he personified the malevolent side of the Great Father. Simpson employed whipping and the buck-and-gag, where the offending Indian would have his hands and feet bound, a stick placed in his mouth sideways and secured by a tightly bound cord, and then left to endure the pain for hours at a time, often in public. Alexander Chase, an anthropologist who met the agent during a visit in the late 1860s, described Simpson's "indomitable energy and will, and the complete control that he exercises over the Indians. . . . You notice that he has deep-set eyes, with over-hanging brows, broad forehead, wrinkled with lines indicative of power . . . and begin to realize that his is one of the few faces met with that have 'power of command' stamped plainly." As Siletz people quickly found out, for Indians the BIA truly was, as one study put it, "our brother's keeper."

Yet the Siletz agents were a varied lot that included the compassionate Joel Palmer and on many occasions displayed empathy and a sense of obligation toward the Siletz people. They mostly took seriously their duty to protect the Siletz from violent settlers; even Ben Simpson, for example, insisted on bringing to justice a non-Indian who murdered an Indian. For decades, agents pressed their superiors to urge ratification of treaties in order to quell concerns of tyees, understandably uneasy about the prospect of another move being forced upon them. With closure of the Alsea sub-agency looming, agent William Bagley flatly stated that it was wrong to move the Alsea Indians to Siletz and was particularly concerned that closing the school was "ruinous to this branch of the service (the attendance yesterday, being larger than ever before) and is much regretted." Letters from agents are rife with concerns about funding to address the Indians' basic needs: essential purchases such as flour and beef, the lack of physicians and blacksmiths, and the inability to pay those employees they did have. Despite budgetary constraints, sometimes the agents extended personal kindnesses that went far beyond the call of duty,

Lower Farm on the Siletz Reservation, ca. 1939, where a number of coastal tribes set up their villages and worked the fields under the direction of a "Boss Farmer." Because the Coast Treaty of 1855 was never ratified and treaty appropriations were unavailable, Siletz agents funded the farming operations with a minimal budget. Euchre Mountain, elevation 2,446 feet, named after one of the coastal tribes placed on Lower Farm (and the southwestern Oregon creek on which they once lived), rises in the background to the north. *Siletz Tribal Collection.*

as James Condon learned upon reporting to the Siletz Agency in 1861: "I am informed that a short time before he left the Agency, my predecessor John F. Miller, Esq. had two small houses removed from the vicinity of the Agency buildings, and given to Indians either of which would have made a very good office for the Agent or Physician."

The mandated change from hunting, fishing, and gathering to farming lay at the heart of the policy to "civilize" Indians, but the approach did not fit circumstances of Siletz. Unlike the Willamette Valley, flat with rich soils and sunny summers and a superb locale for agriculture, the coastal region was ill suited for farming. The terrain was heavily forested with many steep slopes and shallow soils. The weather brought too much rain, too many cold evenings, and not enough sun. Farming takes place in coastal Oregon on pockets

The fields of Upper Farm, about 1905. A good portion of the 1853 and 1854 Rogue River Treaty funds was dedicated to making farmers out of the hunting, fishing, and gathering Siletz people. Just this side of the right end of the bridge is where Frances Johnson sat in an orchard in 1906 with Edward Sapir, recording her Takelma language onto wax cylinders. *Siletz Tribal Collection.*

of open meadows, such as those at Siletz, but farmers must be content with marginal operations at best. Other than some riverside bottomlands with rich alluvial soils, the area within the Coast Reservation is classified by the U.S. Soil Conservation Service as Class VI—"generally unsuited to cultivation." Without the help of modern soil science, Joel Palmer early on recognized the challenge of farming on the Siletz Reservation: "Our [horse] teams should be engaged in plowing under our foul ground to another crop; for we have tested the advantages of fall plowing, and twice plowing in the spring before sowing. In this way alone can we hope to subdue the dense and rapid growth of sorrel, lupin, and other weeds peculiar to this soil and climate."

At least as prominent as the physical barriers was the premise of making Indians into farmers. It would seem natural for any human to look askance upon effectively being instructed "thou shalt become a farmer" and this was notably true of Indians at Siletz, most of whom were unenthusiastic about the prospect. They loved wild plants, especially the acorns, camas, tarweed, and berries, but they had no history of farming. The only crop they actually cultivated was tobacco.

Nevertheless, the agents earnestly pressed ahead. In his first report to Nesmith, Metcalfe was optimistic about the Indians' willingness and ability. While some tribal members took to farming and managed to work the land in spite of the many challenges, the difficulties soon rose up. The wheat crops were disappointing. Some garden vegetables grew well, but corn and beans failed due to the cold nights. Sorrel, bracken fern, and other weeds invaded farmland. Tribal members regularly quit the farm fields—even though every able-bodied person who refused to farm would be punished—and got food for their families, and some income, from the forests and rivers.

Federal institutional problems made matters worse. Low funding levels and delays in sending the money west, problems that afflicted all aspects of the agency's work, forced Siletz farmers to work with inadequate plows, wagons, and other equipment. The BIA made bad management decisions: the first grist mill was constructed across the Siletz River on a hard-to-access site and, according to Corporal Royal Bensell, "never grained 100 bushels." The white employees hired to manage the farms—"Boss Farmers" to the Indians—sometimes worked out, more often not. Many were political appointees, inexperienced in agriculture, and turnover rates were high. Especially troubling was their tendency to treat the Indians as day laborers. The physician at Siletz reported critically in 1863 on a chronic problem: "The hard labor which the women are obliged to perform, consisting principally of carrying heavy weights on their backs, sometimes for long distances, is the cause of much sickness."

Home gardens became a satisfying part of life for many families and put some vegetables and grains on the table. A few took to ranching and later raised horses and competed in rodeos. The assimilationists' aim of creating agrarian societies where farming brought in significant income, however, never came close to fruition on most reservations. Certainly at Siletz it was the wrong idea and the wrong place, and the people had other inclinations. Production, never high, tailed off in the 1890s and continued to decline as farmland passed out of Indian ownership.

Education received much less attention than farming in the early years of the reservation. A schoolhouse built in 1857 was promptly abandoned. Education at the agency resumed but proceeded sporadically, with the school, which had no stove or fireplace, operating in some years and not in others. The teachers—hard to hire, harder yet to retain—complained that the parents, mostly traditional people with no formal education, served as bad examples. They recommended a boarding school in Siletz to keep the children "entirely separated from the noxious influences of savage life" found in Indian homes. The complaint of Margaret Gaines, who taught for a year in the early 1860s, captured the common sentiments:

> The parents are more interested in supplying the present demands of the body than in the intellectual training of their children. . . . Some of the larger [children], who have visited our cities and towns, have returned, feeling quite ambitious to become Bostons, as they term the white people, but, finding this cannot be accomplished in a day or two, they are content to remain Indians.

A major boost for assimilation, and education in particular, came in the early 1870s when President Ulysses S. Grant pronounced his Peace Policy. With the army being withdrawn from many reservations and the BIA coming under mounting criticism, a promising new approach to "Americanizing" Indians came to the fore: give churches primary administrative authority on the reservations. The BIA would continue to administer the reservations, but the churches would have far-ranging powers. The Peace Policy was designed to bring radical change and the president put forth the central idea in his 1870 Message to Congress:

> I determined to give all the [Indian] agencies to such religious denominations as had heretofore established missionaries among the Indians, and perhaps to some other denominations who would undertake the work on the same terms—*i.e.*, as a missionary work. The societies selected are allowed to name their own agents, subject to the approval of the Executive, and are expected to watch over them and aid them as missionaries, to Christianize and civilize the Indian, and to train him in the arts of peace.

Commissioner of Indian Affairs Ely Parker expounded further on the ideals that drove the policy:

Not, therefore, as a dernier resort to save a dying race, but from the highest moral conviction of Christian humanity, the President wisely determined to invoke the cooperation of the entire religious element of the country, to help, by their labors and counsels, to bring about and produce the greatest amount of good from the expenditure of the munificent annual appropriation of money by Congress, for the civilization and Christianization of the Indian race.

The Peace Policy made its mark through increased funding and, even more importantly, missionary zeal. Each reservation was assigned to a denomination, which then could name the agent. Employees came from that denomination. The church had carte blanche to proselytize and the BIA employees pressured the Indians to attend church and otherwise become good Christians. The plan put a premium on education.

The policy remained in place for about a decade but then fell into disfavor. "The romantic ideal of depoliticizing the Indian office and the administration of the agencies by the appointment of high-minded, religiously motivated individuals," historian Francis Paul Prucha wrote, "ran up against the hard rock of practical operations within an old political system." The Peace Policy, however, gave the churches an even greater presence in Indian country and it did not begin to diminish until generations later.

Siletz was assigned to the Methodists, who moved quickly to establish a congregation of a hundred or more (the reservation also had a smaller Catholic congregation). The first agent under the Peace Policy regime was none other than Joel Palmer, who conveniently converted from the Society of Friends to Methodism in 1870 and thus could be appointed as Siletz agent in 1871. A breath of fresh air to the Indians, he soon came under fire from the church and the BIA for being insufficiently zealous; the Methodists were unmoved by his view that "it is useless to preach Christian conversion to a starving man—first feed him." Because of the attitudes of his higher-ups, the inadequate budget, and the enormity of the poverty and other social problems, the assignment turned out to be a disappointment to Palmer and he resigned in frustration after just a year and a half.

The Methodists revived the school at Siletz and added a new one. The children attended Sabbath School and the agents, believing that "Christianity is the best civilizer," often held religious services on weekdays as well. With the Methodist control of agency administration waning but the Chris-

Students line up for morning class at the BIA boarding school at the turn of the century. A few local non-Indian children attended the school. They and the Indian students studied in the same rooms, but the two groups were strictly segregated at recess. *Siletz Tribal Collection.*

tian influence at least as strong, schooling at Siletz gradually expanded and evolved. By the 1890s, the agency was operating a reservation boarding school with an enrollment between sixty and ninety, most of the school-age children on the reservation. About ten students per year went to Chemawa, the off-reservation school in Salem. A few went away to Carlisle in Pennsylvania and Haskell Indian School in Kansas. On the reservation, assimilation was making inroads: most people, children and adults, were wearing American clothes. But the changes went much deeper than that. As the superintendent of the boarding school at Siletz reported in 1895:

> The children, one and all, use the English language: in fact, there are a great many who can not speak a word of their mother tongue. I did not at any time hear a word of Indian language spoken during the school year, and it is a fact to be commended that not once was there an occasion to use or to hear that old-time and oft repeated command, "Stop talking Indian," that is so often used in so many Indian schools by the employees.

Daughter of the Molala chief Yelkus, Molala Kate grew up in a village near Willamette Falls. Strongly traditional, she lived to approximately one hundred years of age and passed away in the 1940s. *Siletz Tribal Collection.*

Siletz basketmaker Minnie Lane is shown here in the early twentieth century. The examples of her work are, from the left, a large hazel hamper with a lid, two double-handled baskets, an openwork flat carrying purse, and a large hamper with a spruce root over hazel warp. *Courtesy of Oregon Historical Society, no. bb006163.*

The early reservation years were an unsettling, confusing time for Siletz people. Facilities were primitive, poverty and sickness were everywhere, and federal and church employees were punitive at worst and ineffective at best. The pressure to become white was pervasive, but that world seemed foreign. While some tribes with ratified treaties received annuities, the Coast Treaty still had not been ratified. It caused hard feelings: why should those tribes be treated differently? The memories of the old days were powerful but the chances of recovering them grew fainter with each passing year. Would it be possible to be like the Americans? Would it be worth it? Should a man be a farmer or a fisherman, or both? Should a woman keep weaving the baskets? Should a person fight the Bureau or go along? Should a person leave the reservation and go out into the outside society?

The tribes had lost so much power. They had laid down their arms and now were beset by an occupying force. There was something else. They did not understand the ways of this foreign government, how to influence it, how to move it. Still, they were resourceful people. They developed survival strategies, ways for a person to remain traditional, become modern, or invent something new, something in between.

Part of it was cataloguing the problems, making a record. Compelling stories, when told, sometimes take hold in America, though it may take years or generations. In 1862, a group of tyees met with William Rector, Oregon superintendent of Indian Affairs. The Chetco tyee, William, related this:

> We are Slaves. Nine of our people have died last Winter from hunger and cold. I do not like the Agent to abuse my people. We are willing to stay here, and believe we can make our own living if we are furnished with things to work with. We should have one wagon, and two yoke of cattle for each tribe. Our women are packed like Mules. They have all the potatoes and pack all the wood. They packed most of the things the ship brought, from the Depot to the Agency (a distance of Six Miles) and got one cup of flour for a days work.
>
> We do not want to be Slaves. We want to work for ourselves.
> This is my mind.

Es-chus-sa, a Sixes tyee, spoke to a problem that would soon be alleviated:

> I want a gun. If I had a gun I could Kill some Elk. I want my people to be permitted to go outside to work for clothes. I want Something done with the Mills. I have never received any good from them. My people want Camp Kettles, and other things to cook in. We want to live like white people. And we look to you for help. I hope that you will let me have a gun.

Another Sixes tyee, George, used humor to address issues of diet, hunting, assimilation, and treaties:

I think our people have improved some, and would become like white people if they had any help. Palmer told me that I would be a white man in two years. I have been here five years and am not a white man yet. I don't know but I will soon be a horse, as I am eating oats. Do you know of any Country where white people eat oats like horses?

Our people have had to eat frozen potatoes, that are rotten, and the carcasses of dead horses. They are dying very fast, and my heart is sick. I think rotten potatoes are not good for any people. I can Eat Oats but don't like them.

My people complain of hunger and want to go back to the Sixes River again. I would rather have our Treaty ratified, and have the things we bargained for and Stay on the reservation. Do you think you are paying us for our country by giving us one blanket to every four or five Indians, and giving us such things as oats and rotten potatoes to eat? If I was allowed a gun I could Kill some elk.

Tyee John, so fiercely independent during wartime, remained utterly unreconstructed. The respect, and consequent close surveillance, that government officials had given him since his surrender in July 1856 continued on the reservation. James Nesmith sized John up accurately: "He is a daring, restless man, possessed of great sagacity and courage, and likely at any moment to head a war party."

In October of 1857, one of John's sons, Cultus Jim, attacked an Indian doctor, accusing him of witchcraft. According to Agent Metcalfe, when he and two army officers attempted to arrest Cultus Jim, he resisted, pulled out a gun, and fired at the two men. Metcalfe and the officers then shot and killed Cultus Jim. Coquelle Thompson heard a different version from his elders—Cultus Jim was drunk and the Americans shot him while he was unarmed because they feared what he might do. For months, Tyee John and another son, Adam, threatened Metcalfe, who finally had them arrested in April of 1858.

The two Shasta men were sent to Fort Vancouver and then on to San Francisco Bay on the steamer *Columbia* for imprisonment at the Presidio. On the second day at sea, Tyee John and Adam tried to take over the steamer. John attacked his guard and, to the terror of the other passengers, let loose an "ear-piercing" scream. The two men were eventually subdued.

Tyee John and Adam spent nearly four years in prison. We can be sure John hated those years. On the way down to San Francisco, he was briefly held in custody at Fort Vancouver awaiting the steamer. When LaFayette Grover visited him, John, who was in chains, said, "A few days ago I was a great Chief, now I am a dog." In 1862, Superintendent Rector visited John's family, who lived at Grand Ronde, and "his daughters made a very strong appeal for their release and return to their families." Three years earlier, Superintendent Geary had considered releasing John, but decided against it: "I would not at present hazard the return of old John as I fear his indomitable spirit might impel him to some deed of violence or to spread discontent among the Indians at the Siletz." Rector, however, was now persuaded by the family's pleas and the positive impact his return might have: "His tribe are now nearly all dead And I am of the opinion that it would not be detrimental to the public good, to return him to his family, while perhaps [with] the knowledge he has obtained during his exile . . . he may turn to good account by imparting it to his brethren." The military acceded, and John, who moved back and forth between Siletz and Grand Ronde, returned to Grand Ronde that year.

Back on the reservation, Tyee John's spirit burned as hot as ever. Apparently bristling over being required to obtain a pass to leave the reservation and convinced that the tribes, not the military, should be setting the rules on their homeland, Tyee John turned the tables. He took to demanding that all soldiers must possess a pass before entering the reservation, proclaiming that he would "souse every Soldier in the River who would not show a pass."

Shortly thereafter, Royal Bensell, a corporal in the army stationed at Fort Yamhill near Grand Ronde, entered two poignant entries in his journal. On May 13, 1862, he wrote: "Cloudy and Misty, a cold Sea Breeze blows off the Coast. 'Ty John' and 16 other Rogue Rivers passed here en-route for their old hunting grounds." Ten days later he reported: "Nothing of interest to-day except 'Tyee John,' the famous warring chief of the Rogue Rivers has returned." That hunting trip must have filled up the old man's heart and soul. "This is my country; I was in it when those large trees were very small, not higher than my head," he pronounced at Oak Flat in his defiant refusal to surrender. "My heart is sick with fighting, but I want to live in my country." Living there was no longer possible, but at least he had this chance to walk the old trails and stalk the plentiful deer in the forests of his youth.

Tyee John, a man of iron who never lost his spirit or love of homeland, passed away on June 6, 1864, at Fort Yamhill.

Perhaps it was in response to Tyee John, or to the Sixes tyees who pleaded to have their rifles back and to hunt in their southern forests, or to the wide dissatisfaction among all the tribes, but in 1862 Agent Biddle and Superintendent Rector relented and agreed to issue passes for individuals to leave the reservation to hunt on ancestral lands. Just a single piece of freedom, but a bright and welcome one.

The ability to leave the reservation, whether with a written pass or a wink and a nod, whether temporarily or for good, became a necessary part of the survival strategy. Early on, it became clear that farming at Siletz provided only limited opportunities. Gardens could help feed individual families but commercial sales were minimal. The land could not produce sufficient quantities of vegetables and, even if it could, transportation from out-of-the-way Siletz to the markets was unrealistic. The real agricultural production came from the Willamette Valley. Working on farms or in other businesses in the valley, on the other hand, could bring decent wages.

The liberal policies of Agent Biddle in granting passes came to an abrupt halt under the harsh regime of Ben Simpson, when he was named agent at Siletz in 1863 and stayed on for eight years. Simpson enforced the pass requirement religiously. People who left without permission would receive forty lashes and those who overstayed the length of their passes were locked up. The agent believed in equal treatment for women. Lucy Smith remembered the punishment her mother received after she was apprehended and brought back to the reservation: "After being publicly whipped, her hair was cropped and tar and feathers were applied to her scalp." Simpson's real interest lay, not in encouraging productive outside opportunities for Indians but in hunting down tribal members who were off the reservation. In 1864, for example, he conducted a grand sweep of southern Oregon and brought back one hundred Indians, mostly from the Rogue and Chetco country. He was gone for seven weeks and logged 1,200 miles.

Beginning in the late 1870s, more paying work became available. Increasingly, jobs at the agency, although mostly menial, were being done by Indians. The tight agency budget allowed for some part-time work, such as cleaning the boarding school, harvesting timber, making and repairing roads, and hauling goods, especially arriving shipments of flour. Seamstresses, blacksmiths, and cooks also found some work. In 1899, Robert DePoe, who had attended Carlisle, taught at the agency school.

After Simpson moved on, the number of people leaving the reservation with temporary or long-term passes increased. Picking hops in the fields of the Willamette Valley paid good wages. Tribal members, generally viewed as good laborers, also did other farm and ranch jobs in the valley. Siletz people

L a n d.
18758--1891.

Department of the Interior,

OFFICE OF INDIAN AFFAIRS,

WASHINGTON. May 28, 1891.

T. Jay Buford, Esq.,
    United States Indian Agent,
        Siletz Agency,
            Toledo, Oregon.

Sir:

I am in receipt of a letter dated May 15, 1891, from Judge
Depoe, one of the Judges of the Court of Indian Offences for the
Siletz Agency, complaining that you persistently revise sentences
imposed by him upon persons convicted of Indian offences; that
frequently when he sentences a party to twenty days confinement
you make it thirty days, and that when he makes the sentence ten
days, if the party is your friend, you make it five, etc; that sometimes you come and tell him a certain party is pretty good, that
he is your friend, and not to sentence him; that "somebody is in
jail all the time,—sometimes two or three;"that his people are
kept a good deal of the time holding court or in jail; that it makes
him and his people feel bad, so he writes to this Office all about
it to resign and say he does not wish to be Judge any more; that
he told you on the 14th of May that he would be Judge no longer;
that you put an Indian in jail without a trial, for six months, and
that when he asked you why the Indian did not have a trial, you replied that you sentenced him at your own will, that you are the
Agent and that you can do as you please; that you put this Indian
man when a prisoner to work to tear down a shed, and while at such
work the shed fell on him and he is now disabled by his injuries.

He further says that school Superintendent, Mr. Walker, beats
the school boys and uses them very badly; that on the 12th of May
1891, he knocked a boy down, knelt upon him, and choked him until he
was nearly suffocated; and that there are many other acts of injustice and tyranny which can be proved, if an investigation is
ordered.

The regulations prescribed to govern the Court of Indian Offence
give you the power to revise to a certain extent, the judgments of
that Court, and you should advise the Indian Judges when they complain of such revision, of this power of discretion placed in your
hands by said regulations. But there is nothing in the regulations of the Indian Department or in instructions to Indian Agents,
known to this Office, that gives you power to imprison an Indian
for an Indian offence without a trial, and instead of *stretching* the
power placed in your hands, you should, as far as possible, throw all
cases into the Court of Indian Offences so that punishment may be
imposed in the regular and lawful manner.

As to the charge of cruelty practiced by the school Superintendent, Mr. Walker, upon the children under his charge, I desire that
you investigate the matter and report all the facts in the case to
this Office at an early date.

Very respectfully,

(Signed) R. V. Belt-

Acting Commissioner.

(Murchison)
    W.

This letter from Acting Commissioner of Indian Affairs R. V. Belt is a reply to an 1891 handwritten letter to the Secretary of the Interior, signed "Judge Depoe (Indian)," detailing objections to interference by the BIA agent in Siletz tribal court matters and stating that "my heart is sick, the way I see things being done at this Reservation." Judge Depoe's criticisms reflected the grievances of Siletz people at the time. The force of Belt's response is surprising; the BIA in this era was not known for giving credence to Indian complaints, however well presented. *Siletz Archival Collection.*

Depoe Charlie, in addition to being recognized as a headman and serving as a tribal judge, was a colorful and respected figure in both Indian and non-Indian communities. Born in the Yah-shu-eh village at the mouth of the Rogue River, he worked various jobs after removal and took his name from driving government teams between Siletz and the agency depot near what became the town of Toledo. After he and other family members received allotments on a small bay north of Newport, the area became known as Depoe Bay after this well-known tribal leader. In the 1870s, he was a dedicated practitioner and leader of the Warm House Dance, a traditional revival movement. *Siletz Tribal Collection.*

PART THREE. THE RESERVATION YEARS

Rogue River Jenny, Takelma, was one of the few Indians allowed to remain in her homeland. *Courtesy of Oregon Historical Society, no. bb006423.*

Tribal members sometimes set up basket camps to sell their wares. This one, in the brush above Newport Bay, was photographed in 1905. On the right are Bradford Charlie and his wife, Mary. She is wearing a basket cap, and her chin tattoo shows up more prominently than in most photographs of that period. Jane Simpson, on the far left, and Mary Hill are also pictured. *Courtesy of University of Washington Libraries, Special Collections, no.NA1510c.*

also capitalized on their knowledge of chittum, a bark that has medicinal properties, by gathering and preparing the herb to sell in local towns. Another pursuit drew on one of the most prized of all traditions and was profitable as well. Modern canning technology allowed for salmon to be preserved and sent to distant markets, and Indian fishermen had new customers for their catches when local canneries started up in the 1880s. Salmon proceeds, sales of chittum, and hop-picking wages regularly exceeded sales of reservation-grown hay, grain, and stock.

Although the numbers were not large in the nineteenth century, some people moved permanently to Portland, Salem, and smaller valley towns to find work. Coos and other tribal members left the reservation and located in the Coos Bay area. Many were accepted into those communities but complaints, based on the usual combination of cultural misunderstandings and bigotry, did arise. A banker from Albany complained that the Indians "steal more or less, will get whiskey, and have fights, and [committed] one murder. . . ." He added that "their dances and pow wows at night are disturbances and in behalf of all our best citizens we ask, as a favor, and a right, that you demand of your agents to keep their Indians on their reservations."

The strategy for moving into a new world had to include anchors in the old. Dancing had always been a way for the Siletz tribes to express their culture and their blessings, obligations, and aspirations. In the 1870s and 1880s, in a major episode in Siletz history, dancing became the medium for a cultural revival. In addition to its own importance, the rise of the Warm House Dance stands as part of the long continuum that includes Nee Dosh (Feather Dance) that preceded contact with whites, the Indian Shaker Church of the twentieth century, and the Nee Dosh revival of the twenty-first century.

In 1873, a Shasta from California named Bogus Tom brought a variation of the Ghost Dance to Siletz and Grand Ronde. Ghost Dance promised the return of ancestors who had passed on "before their time" from the white man's disease and violence and also the return of tribal autonomy. This was the vision of Wodziwob, a Paiute from Nevada, who first conceived it in 1869. In 1889, Wovoka, also a Nevada Paiute, had a similar vision. Ghost Dance spread quickly across Indian country and led to the tragedy at Wounded Knee in 1890, when the Sioux believed that their Ghost Dance shirts would protect them from the army's bullets.

Word of the Ghost Dance spread to the Northwest in the early 1870s. Coquelle Thompson and others heard that Bogus Tom was holding his version of the Ghost Dance, what he called a Warm House Dance, in the Willamette Valley. "I saw the first dance at Corvallis," Thompson remembers. "They put up a round canvas fence, about 20 feet in diameter. You paid about one dollar to get in. . . . There were Indians from Siletz there who were out on passes from the agent to work on the harvests for one or two months." Bogus Tom came over to Siletz and held a Warm House Dance at Upper Farm. As Thompson explained, "He said we were Indians and should not believe the white ways. 'They put things down in books, anything they want. We Indians see what is right. We have to give these dances. They are right for us.'"

The Siletz built six Warm House Dance houses. The first was at Shasta Farm, built by Klamath Jack. Tyee Galice Creek Jim constructed the next and the largest, about 20 feet square, at Upper Farm. A year later Depoe Charlie, a Ya-shu-eh, put in a third at Lower Farm. Others were constructed at Rock Creek, Klamath Grade, and Siletz. The dance houses were subterranean, dug down five to six feet, and, except for the carefully smoothed and polished center pole, were generally similar to the dance houses long used. Hoxie Simmons described the scene: "When you went in, you had to turn around once in place at the entrance before taking your seat, just the way the Shakers turn around in front of the altar now [in the 1930s]. There were no real seats, just blankets spread on the floor. They kept the floor packed solid and swept clean. . . . From one hundred to one hundred and fifty people could get in them. There was no fighting allowed in the Warm House. They were fined if they tried."

While the interior of the dance houses created a familiar setting, the dances themselves had new elements. The songs were delivered in the Shasta language, which only members of that tribe could comprehend. The dancers wore headbands made of the quill feathers of the yellow-shafted flicker (often called the yellowhammer). The music, driven by split elderberry limbs slapped on the hands rather than drums, was very fast. As in the old dances, women were active participants. And, as Coquelle Thompson spelled out, the dances were major community events: "When the dance house was finished at Upper Farm, everyone was notified to come and dance. [Tyee Galice Creek] Jim ordered lots of food, potatoes, meat, coffee, sugar, and flour. They had tents outside to cook in. It began Monday morning and lasted all week. They danced all night and slept during the day. After a night's dancing, they feasted in the morning. Everybody had a good time. The old people danced hard, but the young ones didn't join in much because they didn't believe."

The Warm House Dances lasted throughout most of the 1870s. In 1877, Coquelle Thompson took a long trip that brought the Warm House Dance to several towns on the Oregon Coast; admission fees were charged and curious non-Indians sometimes attended. But soon the BIA had had enough. As Frank Simmons explained, "The soldiers didn't want the Indians to have that dance, that culture," and government employees burned all six dance houses to the ground in the late 1870s.

Then interest waned. One reason, in addition to the BIA coercion, was that many Indian people were disappointed when, despite all the energy put into the dances, the ancestors never did come back. Hoxie Simmons related the experience of a relative, Baptiste, "who went crazy over the Warm House Dance." One morning, after coming out of the dance house, he saw his daughter, who had passed away years before: "He thought the dead had started to come back and he was happy. He planned what he would say to her when he went [back to the family home] and saw her sitting there. He went in and looked all around and couldn't find her. That shook his faith and he gave up the dance."

There are indications that Warm House Dances continued to be conducted for decades afterward and that some tribal members held their beliefs at least into the 1930s. With assimilationist pressures swirling all around, the Warm House Dance afforded a much-needed link to the great dancing traditions of the western Oregon tribes. With all of its limitations, the Warm House Dance helped keep old embers burning.

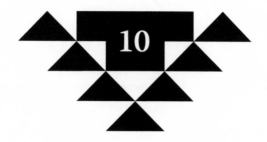

LOSING THE LAND

"We want to hold this land. . . . I will not leave."

I N THE EARLY YEARS OF THE RESERVATION, SILETZ PEOPLE STRUG-
gled to adapt to a new land, the aggreressive federal overseer, forced
farming, the government school, church proselytizing, and tenancy in
common with other tribes. Concurrently, they had to contend with familiar
outside forces—the ones that the remoteness of the reservation was supposed
to protect against. On the one hand, the westward movement had its high
ideals. Americans now had an unparalleled opportunity as the government
adopted homesteading policies that guaranteed free land across the American
West. But westward expansion had its ugly side, and it was not just the miners at Jacksonville and the other camps. There were many other people and
reasons to settle the Pacific Coast, Indian reservation or no.

Yaquina Bay began attracting the attention of shipping and Willamette
Valley agricultural and recreational interests in the early 1860s. After the
shipwreck at the shallow mouth of the Siletz in 1856, the BIA brought shipments into Yaquina harbor and then six miles upriver, to Depot Slough, which
served as the unloading site for the reservation. Word of the Yaquina spread.
It had a tricky, shifting channel, but was the only usable harbor on the central Oregon Coast. Enthusiasm spiked in 1863 with the Americans' realization
of what the Alsea Tribe had always known: Yaquina Bay held excellent beds
of oysters—small, but "thickly clustered" and "finely flavored." Then an alert
went out that the Yaquina sands held paying quantities of beach gold.

Illegal encroachment on Indian reservations plagued Indian tribes
throughout the nineteenth century. At Siletz, where trespassers began to

move in soon after the reservation was proclaimed, the government took some steps in the early 1860s to discourage settlers and seekers of timber, gold, salmon, and oysters. Soldiers directed gold miners to leave the reservation, and Oregon Indian superintendent J. W. Petit Huntington notified the public that the reservation was closed to homesteading. Agent Ben Simpson, in an effort to cut down the oyster traffic, gave an exclusive harvesting permit to Winant & Company out of San Francisco. The $1,000 fee was dedicated to agency programs.

The encroachments continued. In 1864, a group of valley men working some seventy-five mule teams opened up a passable wagon road from Corvallis to Yaquina Bay, and for the first time the central Coast became accessible to citizens of the Willamette Valley. By the summer of 1864, tourists from the valley were traveling to the Coast to enjoy the sights and sounds of crashing waves and the wealth of birds and other wildlife. Two mining outfits worked the sands, although the area was never as rich as advertised. Oceangoing vessels dropped off goods for transport to the valley by wagon, Winant & Company opened a general store to supplement its oyster business, and other buildings went up.

With unauthorized entries reaching alarming levels, the government took action to block outside access to the reservation. Richard Hillyer had brought his ship up from San Francisco and began harvesting oysters. When warned that Winant & Company had the exclusive oystering rights, Hillyer thumbed his nose and refused to stop. Ben Simpson called in Lieutenant Herzer from Fort Hoskins, who arrested Hillyer. Hillyer, however, had connections and telegraphed the commanding general in San Francisco, who overruled the lieutenant. When the general learned the facts, he withdrew his order but by then it was too late. Hillyer had loaded his vessel with oysters and headed back to San Francisco.

When Hillyer sued Agent Simpson in Oregon circuit court in Corvallis, the government moved to dismiss the case. Hillyer argued that the bay was "outside" the reservation, but from the government's side the oysterman had attacked the very existence of the reservation. As Superintendent Huntington warned, "The reservation might as well be abandoned at once," because allowing settlers "to locate upon the numerous bays and inlets of the Coast . . . will be practically the same as if the whole district were opened to settlement." While the case was pending, the defiant Hillyer responded by returning in September for a quick oyster harvest protected by fifteen "roughs." In November 1864, Judge Riley E. Stratton rejected Hillyer's claim, finding that the government had the right to remove trespassers on the reservation. Huntington acted quickly, directing Simpson to "without delay cause the immediate ejection of all such persons, whether they are engaged in cutting timber, taking oysters, or cultivating the soil."

Even as the government fought and won Hillyer's suit, the ground was shifting dramatically under the Siletz Tribe. The new wagon road had opened the eyes of the non-Indians to the Yaquina Bay area and its ocean resources, sand beaches, prime forests, and potential as a port. Pressure quickly built to establish a townsite for settlers and businesses. This would give farmers in the central Willamette Valley—who currently took their produce to Portland and then had it shipped out the Columbia and down the Coast—a forty-five-mile direct route to the ocean at Yaquina harbor, saving four to six days. Oyster and salmon fishers would also benefit from the services afforded by a town.

The matter of opening Yaquina Bay to non-Indians for settlement came to the desk of Commissioner of Indian Affairs William Dole in the late summer of 1864. Dole advised the secretary of the Interior that such a proposal "should not be entertained except for the most urgent considerations." But Dole wanted to hear more and requested the secretary to order a full report from Oregon superintendent Huntington, which the secretary did.

Huntington's reply in December 1864 was a blockbuster. His reasoning closely tracked the arguments being made by A. D. Barnard, a Corvallis farmer who urged that a townsite be established at Yaquina Bay. But he went much further. Barnard argued that the meadows in and near Siletz gave ample land for farming, and the Siletz watershed offered good fishing and hunting. The tribes should be removed away from the settlers and the whites should have Yaquina Bay—and the entire watershed. Huntington emphasized the benefits to "the counties of Linn, Lane, and Benton, and part of Polk (the best agricultural district of the Pacific coast)" and enthused that "the thrifty town which must grow up at the head of navigation will be no mean source of wealth to the nation as well as to the State."

Superintendent Huntington agreed but did not stop there. The southern boundary of the reservation should be moved more than fifty miles north, "somewhere between the Yaquina and Siletz." The Oregon superintendent, supposedly the trustee for the Siletz Tribe and its members, had recommended to the Interior secretary—just ten years after the creation of the reservation and in the name of supporting shipping facilities at one medium-sized harbor—that two-thirds of the reservation be eliminated!

By this time, James Nesmith had won election as United States senator and chaired the Indian Affairs Committee. As a participant at the Table Rock Treaty negotiations in 1853 and superintendent of Indian Affairs for Oregon from 1857 through 1859, he knew the Siletz situation well. A veteran of the Rogue River, Cayuse, and Yakama wars, Nesmith never had much sympathy for Indians and was quick to respond to the desires of his non-Indian constituents. He cooperated closely with the Interior department in drafting papers to support a presidential executive order to open up the Siletz Reservation. In addition to recommending that the Yaquina watershed parcel be removed from the reservation, he wrote that "I also set forth in the memorial that there were no Indians on the strip proposed to be vacated." This was untrue and, in light of his service as superintendent, it is hard to imagine that he believed it.

Secretary of the Interior James Harlan, assuring the president that Yaquina Bay was "a small and rugged portion of the reservation . . . not occupied or desired by the Indians," recommended an executive order to President Andrew Johnson on December 20, 1865. The area to be removed ran from a point two miles south of the Siletz agency south to the Alsea River and then east to the reservation boundary near the crest of the Coast Range: twenty miles of the Coast and fifteen miles east to west. This was less than half the size recommended by Huntington, but it amounted to a full 200,000 acres, more than 300 square miles. On December 21, President Johnson signed the executive order:

> The recommendation of the Secretary of the Interior is approved, and the tract of land within described [in the secretary's recommendation] will be released from reservation and thrown open to occupancy and used by the citizens as other public land.

While the Siletz lacked the means to challenge the executive order in court, the president's action was illegal and would probably have been struck down if the case had been properly litigated at that time.

The courts have been precise about mapping out the separation of powers between the Congress and the executive branch when it comes to Indian affairs in general and Indian treaties in particular. The Constitution lodges authority over Indian affairs in the Congress: under the Commerce Clause, Congress has power "to regulate Commerce with foreign Nations, and among the several States, and with the Indian Tribes." The Supreme Court has described that authority as "plenary and exclusive." Thus, if treaty rights are to be abridged, it must be done by Congress, not the president.

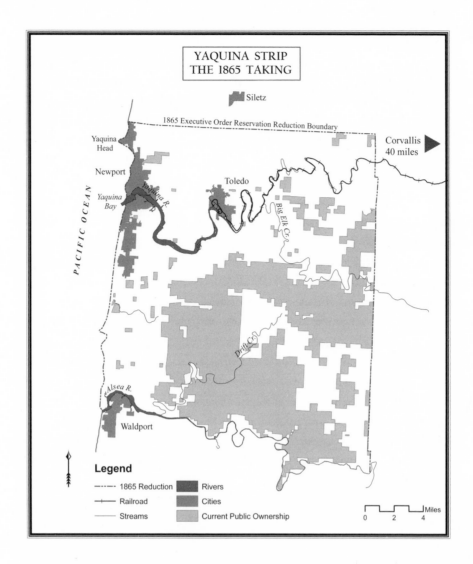

YAQUINA STRIP
THE 1865 TAKING

Siletz

1865 Executive Order Reservation Reduction Boundary

Yaquina
Head

Corvallis
40 miles

Newport

Toledo

PACIFIC OCEAN

Yaquina
Bay

Yaquina R.

Big Elk Cr.

Drift Cr.

Alsea R.

Waldport

Legend

------- 1865 Reduction   Rivers

—+—+— Railroad   Cities

———— Streams   Current Public Ownership

Miles
0   2   4

From the earliest days of the Republic, Supreme Court opinions and statutes have required that tribal lands can be sold or taken only with the approval of Congress. Early twentieth-century cases invalidated executive actions by the Interior department that allowed homesteading by non-Indians of reservation lands. In a major 1999 Supreme Court opinion, *Minnesota v. Mille Lacs Band of Chippewa Indians*, the Court struck down an 1850 executive order abrogating treaty hunting and fishing rights. Calling it "black letter law," the Supreme Court began its analysis by quoting with approval a statement by the lower court: "The President's power, if any, to issue the order must stem either from an act of Congress or from the Constitution itself."

Looking back on it, we can understand with some clarity what happened in 1865. Both in Washington, D.C., and in Oregon, most federal officials had lost track of the direct connection between the ratified treaties at Table Rock and elsewhere and President Pierce's 1855 executive order creating the Siletz Reservation. It wasn't that the government was cavalier about Indian treaties. To the contrary, all three branches—while they knew Congress could break treaties—accepted the clear structure for altering treaties, which required going through Congress.

The practice of creating reservations by presidential executive orders, brand new in 1855, threw a monkey wrench into the recognition of Siletz rights. Federal officials correctly realized that stand-alone executive orders were different from treaties, which Congress—with express constitutional authority—had approved. People focused on the Siletz Reservation as tracing to an executive order and missed the central constitutional fact: *by treaty*, the western Oregon tribes could be moved off their temporary reservations only to a reservation "made by the direction of the President of the United States for their permanent residence." Once President Pierce established the Siletz Reservation, Congress could change that treaty promise of a lasting homeland but a president could not.

Yet once again, as in the 1850s, hunger for land overrode all else. President Johnson's executive order, void in law but not on the Oregon Coast, triggered a land rush at Yaquina Bay. Especially troubling were Senator Nesmith's statement that "no Indians" lived at Yaquina Bay and Secretary Harlan's assur-

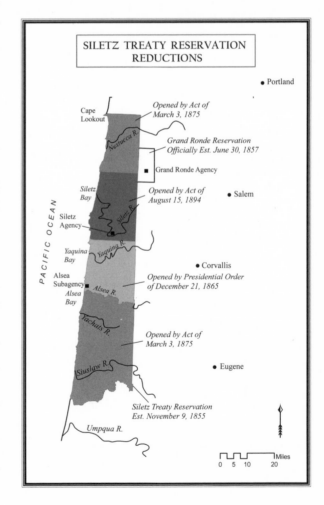

SILETZ TREATY RESERVATION REDUCTIONS

Portland

Cape Lookout

Opened by Act of March 3, 1875

Grand Ronde Reservation Officially Est. June 30, 1857

Grand Ronde Agency

Siletz Bay

Opened by Act of August 15, 1894

Salem

PACIFIC OCEAN

Siletz Agency

Yaquina Bay

Corvallis

Alsea Subagency

Alsea R.

Alsea Bay

Opened by Presidential Order of December 21, 1865

Yachats R.

Opened by Act of March 3, 1875

Siuslaw R.

Eugene

Siletz Treaty Reservation Est. November 9, 1855

Umpqua R.

Miles
0   5   10   20

With the area removed from reservation status in 1865, Nye Beach in Newport quickly became a favorite for tourists. *Courtesy of Oregon Historical Society, no. bb006164.*

ance to the president of the United States that Yaquina Bay was "not occupied or desired by the Indians." To the contrary, "a large population lived full time at Yaquina Bay, gathering crab, oysters, clams, mussels, spearing flounder, and [harvesting] other native foods from the estuary. There were also 2 trails from the Siletz community for the people to come and gather foods." Nonetheless, there was no attempt to gain tribal consent and perhaps find some acceptable middle ground, as Superintendent Huntington had recommended. Even Huntington, who had so strongly urged the opening of this part of the reservation, was outraged by the treatment of Indian people. As he wrote in 1867:

> Upon this tract were located some Indians who had been encouraged to open farms, erect buildings, and establish themselves permanently. The effect upon them and upon the other Indians was most disastrous. They had all been promised protection in the possession of their lands, and that pro-

tection had hitherto been afforded them; but now the agent was powerless, and whites occupied the lands as they pleased. . . .

After the promulgation of the order by which the tract was thrown open to settlement, (which I may remark was very sudden, and gave no time for preparation on the part of the government or the Indians,) the whites rushed in upon the tract, seized upon the Indian farms, occupied their houses . . . by force, and immediately commenced the settlement of the country. The effect was deplorable. The Indians were dispossessed of their homes and property. . . . They were discouraged because they could not feel any assurance that they would be protected in any other settlement they might make. They had no incentive to labor. A part were induced by Agent Simpson to remove above (north of) the vacated tract, and are now opening farms near the Siletz agency, but they are doing so timidly and haltingly, and during a late visit to them I constantly met with the inquiry "when the whites were coming there to settle." It is idle to expect any improvement in a people so harassed and discouraged. . . .

The whole treatment of the government towards these Indians has been full of bad faith.

Although their homes and canoes were either taken over by whites or destroyed, and other personal belongings similarly lost to them, the Indian people at Yaquina Bay never received any compensation.

The settlers moving to the Coast and their inland sympathizers allowed no respite for the Siletz people. In the spring of 1870, a petition circulated to throw open the entire reservation. Whites told tribal members that "it was useless for them to plant their crops, as they would be removed before they could harvest them." The Indians, remembering how quickly the Yaquina land had been taken, were angry and scared. Some fled the reservation, and a cloud of gloom settled over those who remained.

Within months, the Oregon Legislative Assembly adopted a memorial to Congress calling for termination of the reservation. Citing the need for land for "agricultural and other purposes," the legislature resolved that "it would be beneficial to both Indians and whites if both the [Siletz] reservation and [Alsea] sub-agency . . . could be vacated and the Indians removed to other reservations not immediately surrounded by American settlers, and all the

Indians in Oregon concentrated upon Klamath reservation, thereby saving a large amount to the Treasury of the United States." Congress took no immediate action, but the ferment in Oregon continued.

In 1873, white settlers to the north circulated a petition calling for opening to settlement all reservation land north of the Salmon River, mostly in Tillamook country. To the south, similar efforts called for elimination of the lower one-fourth of the reservation, the Alsea sub-agency, which had been separated from the rest of the reservation by the 1865 executive order. Oregon Superintendent T. B. Odeneal gave his support to the proposal, throwing his weight behind the elimination of more than two-thirds of the already-reduced Siletz Reservation. Although Odeneal believed that removing the Indians to Siletz would "better the[ir] condition," he did recommend that "their consent to the changes should of course be obtained."

To look into the matter, Commissioner of Indian Affairs E. P. Smith directed a study and report by Inspector Edward Kemble of the Washington, D.C., office. The inspector, who had been tasked to assess Indian and non-Indian attitudes, went out to Siletz and convened a council, which 135 tribal members attended on a blustery December day. George Harney, chief of the Siletz confederated tribes and the nephew of Takelma tyees Lympy and George, spoke first:

> A long time ago the whites defeated the Indians in battle and brought them here. They are still troubling us. They have taken a part of our reservation, and now want the rest. A year ago last fourth of July they killed one of our chiefs, and now want to drive us from our homes. The President believes in God; so do you, and so do I, and I would like the President to help Indians, and we want you to help us. . . .
>
> I want the whites to stop troubling us about our land and about removing us. What have we done? We believe in God. We are trying to do good. Why should they want to drive us away? All that is sorry in my heart I tell you. I want you to tell President that the Indians desire to remain here. We do not want to be driven away. We were driven here, and now this is our home, and we want to stay.

Depoe Charlie, Joshua Band of Tututni, said this:

> You told us not to speak about anything except great things. I am sorry for one thing; I am sorry to have you leave to day in this storm; I would like you to stay here to-day; will tell you one thing, and I want you to put it in your

heart. I don't want them to take this land from us; want you to keep this in your heart. You have a good heart; so have I. I think now we are beginning to do better. Church-members have come here and taught us, and now we are all trying to be good. Do you think it would be well for these bad white men to come and drive off good men both white and Indian?

William Strong, Tututni, spoke forcefully:

I am proud and glad to see you. . . . Have been waiting for you. Our agent told us you were coming. Am sorry you have to go away. It is a bad, stormy day. Was glad to hear you speak yesterday at church. Am glad you want to help the Indians. . . . Our present agent and employees are good people. There are bad people at Yaquina. . . . Now I want to be good. We want to hold this land. We all want it. After my chief was killed we did not try to get revenge. Now we don't want to leave. They may send soldiers, but I will not go. If they want to hang me they can do so, but I will not leave.

Kemble found "these Indians desirous, to a man, to retain their reservation."

He also went into Newport, the largest non-Indian town in the area, and was surprised by what he found. "The call for the removal of the Siletz," Kemble wrote, "was started by a handful of speculators two years ago as part of a scheme to invite settlement and capital into this part of Benton County. . . . There is now no agitation of the subject. The sensible portion of the little white community on the Yaquina, abating from the enthusiasm of last year, are disposed to regard the reservation rather as a help than as a hindrance." The inspector was reporting what farmers had already learned—that the Siletz made good workers at a low cost. On the Coast, where the heavy forests and steep terrain threw up so many obstacles to transportation, the Siletz "had put one thousand days' work on the roads in the vicinity of their reservation."

In his report, Kemble came down firmly against any reduction of the reservation. "Under all the circumstances, I can but advise the dismissal of the complaints against these Indians, and"—referring now to ratification of the 1855 Coast Treaty—"express the hope that the present Congress will not adjourn without confirming their right to the lands they now occupy."

Such was not the political mood in Oregon. Indian Affairs had fundamentally

PART THREE. THE RESERVATION YEARS

changed since the Table Rock Treaty of 1853. Back then, the tribes actually outnumbered the Americans. Indian issues, along with achieving statehood and promoting settlement, were at the top of the political agenda. The delegation at Table Rock included two future U.S. senators, one who almost achieved that status, and the territory's leading jurist. The office of Indian superintendent was a political plum, as was the position of agent at Siletz. By the middle 1870s, Indian Affairs had gone from the main current in Oregon public policy to a side eddy. Over the course of a generation, the white population had increased several times over and Indian numbers had steadily declined, due partly to war, mostly to disease. The tribes lost their military capability and, their own economies smashed, lived in abject poverty with inadequate housing, insufficient food, and debilitating health problems. Non-citizens, they lacked the vote.

The center was gone. There were no moderating influences left. As a matter of social justice as well as strategy, Joe Lane and Joel Palmer had tried to find solutions that reflected the legitimate interests of the tribes as well as the Americans. Now the stage was left to men like John Hipple Mitchell and Ben Simpson.

The imposing and courtly Mitchell, who was first elected U.S. senator in 1872 and served four terms until his death in 1905, came to Oregon from California in 1860. A powerful attorney for railroad companies, including the Northern Pacific, he rose above allegations of bigamy to become a major figure in Oregon politics. "The one constancy of Mitchell's public and private career," historian William Robbins wrote, "was his unstinting belief that the interests of business and government were one." Late in his career Mitchell was indicted in the Oregon timber and land frauds—his supporters vigorously argued that the charges were politically motivated—and died in office while his conviction for bribery was on appeal.

After his eight years as Siletz agent, where he was known for handing out brutal punishments, Ben Simpson pursued his lofty political ambitions. He held the position of surveyor general of Oregon from 1872 through 1876 and eventually served six terms in the Oregon legislature. As agent, he opposed a break-up of the reservation in the 1860s, perhaps because it would cost him a job, but as surveyor general he was more than happy to assist Senator Mitchell in eviscerating the Siletz Reservation.

Simpson had business entanglements with developers eyeing the central Coast, as did two Oregon Indian superintendents, Alfred B. Meacham (1869–1872) and T. B. Odeneal (1872–1873). Their dream was to put through a Wil-

Ben Simpson, left, and Senator John Mitchell. After the 1865 Siletz Reservation reduction, Simpson, as surveyor general of Oregon, and Senator Mitchell teamed up and were relentless in pursuit of opening still more reservation land for settlement. They achieved their goal in 1875, when their efforts led to the removal of 700,000 acres from the reservation. *Courtesy of Oregon Historical Society, nos. bb006241 (Simpson) and ba019648 (Mitchell).*

lamette Valley–Yaquina Bay railroad to complement the wagon road and to obtain the lucrative federal land grants that accompanied rail lines. Successive articles of incorporation were filed, with Odeneal a signer in 1867, Simpson and Meacham in 1871, and Simpson in 1872. With the sorry 1865 reduction offering precedent for still more takings of land and with petitions circulating to that end, federal and state officials in the late 1860s and 1870s should have avoided the specter of serious conflicts of interest and taken a hands-off stand toward railroad development, which plainly would spur pressure to open still more reservation land to settlement.

Learning of Inspector Kemble's strong recommendation against a breakup of the reservation, Senator Mitchell moved quickly. In January 1874, he came out in favor of the large-scale reduction of the reservation, as urged by the Tillamook County petition and approved by Superintendent Odeneal. Simpson advised Mitchell on the issue the senator likely cared about most,

PART THREE. THE RESERVATION YEARS

confirming that opening the big-tree forests "will greatly accommodate the whites as they can use the timber which the Indians have no use for." John Fairchild, the agent at Siletz, had initially opposed the idea. He well knew of the tribal opposition, having been told by various chiefs "that all of them desired to remain" and that "they desired above all things to be let alone and allowed to die in the country the Government has given them." Yet, he wrote Commissioner Smith that "there would be no difficulty in overcoming their objections."

Mitchell brought his proposal, which would reduce the reservation by two-thirds, to the floor of the Senate in early 1875 as an amendment to an appropriations bill. It was a classic example of the disputes between western and eastern senators during the halcyon years of the westward expansion— Vernon Parrington called it "the great Barbeque"—with the western senators on the move and the easterners urging restraint. Senator William Boyd Allison of Iowa believed that the Indians in the north and south parts of the Siletz Reservation should not be removed "without their consent being first obtained." John Sherman, senator from Ohio and a leading congressional figure on monetary policy and later secretary of the treasury, dug even deeper and saw the problem for what it was:

> It is manifestly the purpose to disturb this Indian reservation in order to extend the white settlements over a portion of this reservation, a part of it having already been taken, and this mandatory provision requiring the removal of these two or three hundred Indians is to be carried out by money paid out of an appropriation made nominally for some other purpose, perhaps made for the education and support of these very Indians, which will be used in removing them forcibly against their will to some other portion of this same reservation. That is the way it appears to me.

Mitchell argued that his proposal would provide budget savings due to the closure of the Alsea sub-agency. As for Sherman's concerns, he responded disingenuously or worse. His reference on the floor of the Senate to two inspections glossed over Kemble's comprehensive report, which strongly recommended against reducing the reservation, and the fact that the second report mentioned the issue inconclusively and in passing:

> I desire to say in answer to the honorable Senator from Ohio that he assumes that this whole proceeding, this recommendation of the Commis-

sioner of Indian Affairs and of the Secretary of the Interior has been without any investigation of the matter on the ground, without any reference to
whether or not the consent of the Indians has been obtained. I will state for
the benefit of the Senate that this matter has been investigated not only by
the agents of the two reservations but by two Indian inspectors, and their
reports are on file in the Indian Department, and upon them the Secretary
of the Interior and the Commissioner based their recommendation.

Mitchell's proposal did pass, although Senator Allison's consent requirement
was added to it: "Provided, that these Indians shall not be removed from their
present reservation without their consent previously had."

The way in which "consent" was obtained is a textbook example of how
western senators usually prevailed—one way or the other—in confrontations
with their eastern colleagues over western lands. In notifying Siletz Agent
John Fairchild of the amendment and charging him with obtaining the needed
consent, Commissioner Smith made clear that the consent of the Indians was
required, but he authorized Fairchild to use "such other inducements as will
seem proper and reasonable."

Fairchild, however, hit brick walls in both the north and the south. At
Tillamook, he called a council on the first of June. Joseph Duncan, one of the
tyees, told him that "we all want to stay in our country and take up land like
the whites. Our people all think alike on this subject." Fairchild poured on
the pressure, warning that if they stayed "bad white men will debauch your
women, and bring in bad diseases among you, and in many other ways work
evil to you" and that "the orders of the Great chief in Washington cannot
be disobeyed with impunity." The tyee of the Nestuccas, a band of Tillamook,
refused to attend the meeting, but he knew of the consent provision and reportedly declared that "he would die before he would leave his country."

In the council at Alsea on June 17, the sentiment was the same. Fairchild
explained to the tyees that he had been sent by Congress "to talk strait and
true" in obtaining their consent, but warned that "all Indians must obey the
laws of Congress." The tyees unanimously refused to give up their land. Their
objections were forceful.

Tyee John, Siuslaw:

As long as I live on my land I am not sorry if I have nothing. My people have
all the same mind as I have on this point. . . . I understand the Washington

Chief wants to send us money What for? I know the mind of my people They do not want money It is long since we had money and we no longer care for it I have only a little place and no money. Yet my heart is not sick. . . . At first, the whites promised many things The people will never do again as they once did sell their land If I was to talk many days I should say the same thing. . . . Gen Palmer gave us this country and I will never give it up That is all.

Tyee Joe Scott, Umpqua:

I have long had a sick heart on account of Mr Fairchild coming today. . . . Today I am in good heart because I see my words written down I don't want to do as Mr Fairchild advised Perhaps the Great Chief will make us poor but we don't want to do this thing We don't want it even talked about This was not always my Country

I am a driven man I will not give up my land on that account This is my Country now and no one has any right here

Tyee Jeff, Coos:

Yes it is like the whites had made us poor by driving us from our old country I have a heavy heart on account of the treaty we made with Gen Palmer (unratified) We came a long distance from that Country It was not a small Country we give the whites It was a large Country You see me Mr Fairchild today You do not see me have much property When we sold our land we never received any pay You do not see me with team or wagon I do not owe anybody anything but the Great Chief owes me a great deal for the Country we sold We have left two countries now [the Coos Bay and Fort Umpqua reserves] I think on that account the Great Chief will not insist on our leaving this Country.

In his report to Commissioner Smith, Fairchild concluded: "From their entire unanimity of sentiment and strong feeling on the subject, I doubt the possibility of their peaceful removal."

Then—one can surmise, through the intervention of Senator Mitchell— Ben Simpson got involved. Commissioner Smith made him a special agent to obtain the consent that Fairchild could not. In his instructions, Smith twisted the consent requirement in the statute, writing to Simpson that while the Indians "should not be coerced in their preference," the special agent was to assure that they "understand that they are expected to comply."

Simpson convened a second council at Alsea on August 24 and 25. He came on strong, telling the tyees of "the great importance of obeying the wishes of the Department" and "the necessity of complying." When the tyees from Coos and Umpqua refused to consent, Simpson handed out beef and tobacco and adjourned the council for the day. The next day, as Simpson reported, the tyees continued to hold their ground, "though in a milder form than before." Contrary to the June council and the normal formality for such gatherings, there was no transcript or detailed notes, and the summary report by Fairchild's clerk, M. N. Chafeman, is the only other first-hand account of the tyees' consent (or lack of it) at the August council: "Quite a number of the Indians spoke, all mildly declining to make the proposed change and stating that they preferred to stay where they were, some remarking that their fathers had lived upon salmon and grown old and died and that they were content to do likewise. Altogether, considering their circumstances and surroundings their contentment was remarkable."

Agent Fairchild did not attend the council, deputizing Chafeman to act on his behalf. In his report to Commissioner Smith, Fairchild never reported the tyees' statements, as related to Fairchild by his clerk, that the Alseas had "mildly declin[ed]" to move. Instead, he relied on information purportedly given by George Harney, Depoe Charlie, and William Strong, who attended the August council at the request of Simpson and Fairchild, to "notify" the Alseas and to "prepare their minds for the coming council." Fairchild wrote to Commissioner Smith that southern tyees had told the three Siletz chiefs that "they expected to move to Siletz, but only wanted time to prepare themselves for the change." This statement should be given great weight, Fairchild advised, because "being of the same race, and speaking the same language, [the Siletz chiefs'] opportunities for forming correct conclusions, are far greater than any white man could possibly have." Based on those statements, Fairchild, as Simpson also urged, recommended that the government begin removing public property from Alsea and preparing Siletz for the arrival of the Alseas.

None of the three reports—from Simpson, Chafeman, or Fairchild—claimed that the Alseas had consented to move. The first two stated that their objections were "in a milder form than before" and that the Alseas all "mildly declin[ed]" to move from their lands, and Fairchild referred only to the views—never mentioned by Simpson or Chafeman—of the three Siletz chiefs. Correspondence other than the formal reports give a fuller picture. Simpson and Fairchild were furious with Litchfield, the Alsea agent, who refused to apply the pressure that Simpson and Fairchild wanted. Simpson, frustrated with the Alseas' refusal to comply, wrote Senator Mitchell that "it was a terrible mistake making him one of the commissioners, as he is opposed to the removal of the Indians. He said he could not say to the Indians that it was best for them to go, when he did not believe it."

The resolution at Tillamook was at least as unsatisfactory. In mid-September Simpson went to Tillamook country to hold another council. Again, there was no transcript or detailed account. He described the outcome of three days of negotiations in a letter to Commissioner Smith:

> On the third day however, after repeated meetings, they consented to abandon their country at once, and locate on Siletz reservation as defined by Law at the mouth of the Salmon River. To accomplish this result they were promised assistance from the Government. . . . That each head of a family of two would be allotted forty acres of Land . . . they would be furnished with lumber and nails for the erection of suitable houses and also the aid of one white man to assist in the construction of the same. It was further promised that they should be provided with plows and teams to break and cultivate their land and that they should have seed potatoes for the first years planting.

These promises, which finally induced the Tillamook to agree to move, turned out to be empty. The funds to provide assistance to the Tillamook were supposed to come from the Alsea agency, but George Litchfield, the agent at Alsea who had stalwartly represented the interests of Alseas in their unwillingness to move, refused to turn over the money. So the Tillamooks waited by the mouth of the Salmon River throughout the dead of winter, freezing and starving, their homeland already snatched up by eager white settlers.

Apparently Ben Simpson filed no official final report on his efforts with the two groups of tribes. We know only that Kappler's *Indian Affairs*, a congressional publication, has a cryptic footnote to the official text of the statute requiring consent: "Consent reported by Special Agent Simpson, October 28, 1875."

And so the 1875 statute went into effect, tearing away a full 700,000 acres from the Siletz Reservation. Unlike the 1865 executive order, there is no question that Congress had the power to act, but a serious question arises as to whether the administration complied with Congress's precondition to the break-up that tribal consent be obtained. In a similar situation in the twentieth century, the California termination statutes had a precondition—that the BIA put in water facilities for the terminated rancherias. When, after many years, the agency failed to construct the facilities, the courts held that the termination statute had never gone into effect and was void. Under that reasoning, the failure to obtain meaningful consent might well have been a basis for overturning the 1875 statute. But this was a century earlier, and it was John Mitchell and Ben Simpson, not the Siletz people, who knew how to pull the levers of government.

The 1.1 million-acre reservation had been reduced to 225,000 acres. Some Coos, Lower Umpquas, and Siuslaws went to Siletz, but more remained in southern Oregon and, a century later, achieved separate federal recognition as a tribe. As for the Tillamooks, many members of the Nestucca Band, just north of the Salmon River, moved a short distance south to live within the remaining Siletz Reservation among their southern relatives. Farther north, some Tillamooks went to nearby Grand Ronde or Siletz, while others stayed in their aboriginal area but without any rights to land.

Toward the end of the nineteenth century, as the national campaign for assimilation picked up ever more speed, the federal government moved on the most central issue of all: land. The churches and schools were making inroads on traditional lifeways, but ties to the land permeated the Indian worldview, the assertedly primitive mindset that the radical reformers meant to erase. So long as American Indians remained land-based peoples, so long as they had their hunting and fishing grounds, so long as they worshipped at their traditional sacred sites, true assimilation would remain incomplete. With the passage of the landmark General Allotment Act in 1887, the Siletz found themselves caught in yet another raid on their reservation, this one even harder for them to judge than the others, laced as it was with apparent benefits, economic and legal traps, unintended consequences, and well-disguised greed.

The idea of providing Indians with allotments—80- or 160-acre parcels of land owned by individual Indians—had been put to work in a number of treaties but never on a comprehensive basis. Support grew among lawmakers for announcing allotment as a top-priority policy to cement assimilation in place. Congress could delegate authority to the Interior department, which could then establish allotments for reservations, tribe by tribe. Henry Dawes, a well-regarded congressman who, like most Americans, believed that Indians would gain by abandoning their traditional cultures, took the lead. The General Allotment Act that resulted, and that was applied to many but not all tribes, is often called "the Dawes Act."

Part of the context for the allotment statute was the surging interest in bringing scientific knowledge to the making of public policy. An influential group of social scientists, notably anthropologist Lewis H. Morgan, a proponent of "social Darwinism," believed that human advancement took place in evolutionary stages of savagery, barbarism, and civilization. In their eyes— and in those days who would much disagree?—Indians were primitives who needed to move toward a civilized state. A stronger federal assimilationist policy was needed and special attention should be given to land: holding land in communal ownership was a hallmark of primitive societies, while more advanced, civilized societies prospered through basing their economies on private ownership of property.

Of the few members of Congress who followed Indian issues, almost all believed in allotment in some form. The major exception was Senator Henry Teller of Colorado, who stood stoutly against it:

> If I stand alone in the Senate, I want to put upon the record my prophecy in this matter, that when thirty or forty years shall have passed and these Indians shall have parted with their title, they will curse the hand that was raised professedly in their defense to secure this kind of legislation, and if the people who are clamoring for it understood Indian character, and Indian laws, and Indian morals, and Indian religion, they would not be here clamoring for this at all.

Although he failed to come forward when the Interior department was imposing allotment plans on the Siletz and other Oregon tribes, Oregon Senator Joseph Dolph was convinced that Indians would sell or be tricked out of their allotments as soon as they received full land titles and that "we shall have a quarter of a million paupers, or more, on the hands of the Government."

While most decision-makers in Washington, D.C., in the 1880s could not foresee the costs of allotment, one person saw what was coming with complete clarity. John Wesley Powell knew more about Indian people than any non-Indian in the country. The storied geologist-ethnologist had gained prominence by exploring the remote canyons and spending time with Indian societies of the American Southwest in the 1860s and 1870s; later he served at the same time as director of both the U.S. Geological Survey and the Bureau of Ethnology. In the darkest episode of his career, Powell wholeheartedly supported and pushed allotment precisely because he understood the depth of Indians' relationship with the land. He knew that only by forcing Indians off the land could the radical reformers achieve the wholesale assimilation of Indians. In February 1888, Powell wrote this cynical, treacherous letter to Senator Henry Teller:

> The Indian religion is localized. Every spring, creek and river, every valley, hill and mountain as well as the trees that grow upon the soil are made sacred by the inherited traditions of their religion. These are all homes of their gods. When an Indian clan or tribe gives up its land it not only surrenders its home as understood by civilized people but its gods are abandoned and all its religion connected therewith, and connected with the worship of ancestors buried in the soil; that is, everything most sacred to Indian society is yielded up.

He concluded by underscoring the ultimate consequence of allotment, that it would wrench away all that was sacred to Indian people: "Such a removal of the Indians [from their land] is the first step to be taken in their civilization."

Needless to say, with Manifest Destiny the political battle cry in the West, opening up the reservations resonated with the public. Many Indian reservations contained good farm land and held valuable mineral deposits or, like the Siletz, timber stands and fisheries. The lands and resources were not being made "productive" under the tribes, but they could be made so by the Americans.

Tribes nationally were no better equipped to influence Congress than the Siletz. The self-styled, East Coast–based Friends of the Indian directed the brunt of their criticism at BIA mismanagement, incompetence, and corruption rather than at the policy of assimilation and allotment. Many of these people, who saw themselves as representing Indians although most of them had no contact with tribes, concluded that the best approach was total assimilation, including breaking up the reservations and sacking the BIA. With virtually no other voices purporting to speak for the Indians' best interests, the allotment program never received the scrutiny it badly needed. With the warnings of Senators Teller and Dolph failing to gain traction, the bill went through Congress with little serious opposition.

The idea behind the General Allotment Act of 1887 was deceptively simple and seemingly innocuous: to make Indians into farmers by carving lands out of tribal reservations and providing every tribal member with an individual allotment—a plot of land, usually eighty acres. No new land would be brought into Indian ownership, since allotments were taken from tribal lands.

Tribal land is held in trust by the United States through the Interior department, meaning that it cannot be sold or taxed. Individual allotments were held in trust but, unlike tribal land, not indefinitely. Trust allotments remained in trust for twenty-five years—a period that the BIA had the power to shorten or lengthen—at which time the tribal member received a patent (the same as a deed). At that point, the tribal member held title in fee simple absolute (complete ownership) and the fee-patented land could be sold and taxed. This was a potential danger point. Most Indian people were unfamiliar with the world of land sales, property taxes, and liens, and Indians across the country lost millions of acres through fraudulent transactions and tax sales after their allotments passed out of trust. The warnings of Senators Teller and Dolph had all too much merit.

The tragedy played out at Siletz. The father of Gladys Bolton had an allotment east of Kernville on the Lower Siletz River. "It was beautiful land," she recalled, but he was forced to sell it in order to afford heart medicine for his father. Eddie Collins grew up on his grandfather's allotment land. When he returned from the army after World War II, "the allotment was no longer there"—his grandfather had lost it at a tax sale. "I would have liked to have kept the land myself, but I was overseas," he said. Frank Simmons relates that his grandfather, Hoxie Simmons, had an allotment on scenic Rock Creek, a prime fishing spot for salmon and eels. Hoxie Simmons, a young man at the time, lost the land at a tax sale. In 2007, looking back, Frank Simmons explained that "many Siletz people lost their allotments as a result of failure to pay taxes. Siletz people were asked if they would pay property taxes and they would say yes, but they didn't understand what they were getting themselves into."

Frank Simmons's point is understandable. Few people, inside or outside Washington, on or off the reservations, comprehended how the now-discredited allotment program would play out. For their part, Siletz people had been asking for allotments, for the land to be "divided" among the membership, at least since the early 1870s. For years, BIA and church people had harped on the virtues of private ownership. The Indians, knowing they would need to take on some white ways in order to function in society, could see some

A main Tututni headman by the late 1870s, William Strong stood firm against pressures to break up the reservation. He had a broad following among the Siletz, but the forces behind allotment would not relent: "It looks as though this will happen regardless of what the Indians say." *Siletz Tribal Collection.*

advantages in having their own parcels. It seemed safe and secure and a move away from their tormenter, the BIA. When Inspector Kemble came to Siletz on that stormy December day in 1873 to assess the Indians' view on opening the reservation, William Strong made his powerful stand: "We want to hold this land. . . . I will not leave." But he then added: "I want the land divided. . . . I want the land divided . . . so that we can do something." Several other speakers that day spoke of wanting the land "divided," and that sentiment continued into the 1890s, when the reservation was allotted.

In American language, policy, and law, "divided" meant "allotment," a term that carried much additional baggage. Did William Strong and his tribespeople really mean to have the family home available for sale? For it to be subject to property taxes? Did they really mean to pay cash for tax bills when their economy still relied so heavily on subsistence and barter? If some of them did understand and accept those ramifications of the word "divided," how many other Siletz people did?

PART THREE. THE RESERVATION YEARS

And, for those who did accept sales and property taxes, how many thought of "divided" as including "surplus lands"?

The surplus lands provision was the most toxic of all the poison pills in the General Allotment Act. Like "divided," in this setting "surplus" is an ultimate euphemism: since allotment meant that Indians would abandon their traditional ways and become farmers rather than hunters and gatherers, it followed logically that tribal hunting lands, fishing rivers, and sacred sites—most of them on reservation lands—would no longer be used. Those lands, therefore, would be "surplus to their needs" and would be eliminated from reservations at the time the allotments were made.

"Divided" and "surplus" were indeed large words. Allotment remade Indian country once again. When Congress enacted the statute in 1887, Indian land-holdings nationally totaled about 140 million acres. By 1934, when Congress abandoned the discredited policy, tribal land holdings had plummeted to about 52 million acres, a loss of nearly 90 million acres, an area almost the size of Oregon and Washington combined. President Theodore Roosevelt called the Byzantine workings of allotment "a mighty pulverizing machine, to break up the tribal mass."

By 1892, the Interior department had authority to issue trust allotments, but designating surplus lands and throwing them open for settlement by non-Indians required an agreement with the tribes and congressional approval. It was time to close the deal at Siletz. Three federally appointed commissioners came to the reservation on October 17, 1892, to reach a surplus lands agreement. Like Joel Palmer, when he negotiated with the Coast tribes in the summer of 1855, they came to dictate, not negotiate. Unlike Palmer, they did not include a shred of generosity or fairness in the terms they planned to impose.

The commissioners, former justice of the Oregon Supreme Court Judge Reuben Boise, William Odell, and H. H. Harding, met with tribal members in two well-attended councils on October 17 and 29, 1892. Detailed transcripts were prepared for both. A seven-member committee of tribal members then met privately with the commissioners on October 31; that meeting involved "long explanation and discussion," but no transcript was taken. The tribal committee reached agreement with the commissioners, and 118 male tribal members signed the agreement (the tribal membership, including minors, was about 550). Although the commissioners and federal officials rationalized the tribal members' ability to understand complicated business dealings by emphasizing their high degree of assimilation, half of

In his brief tenure as Siletz agent in the early 1870s, Joel Palmer urged the tribe to organize a government. George Harney, a Takelma and brother of Frances Johnson, became the first elected chief of the Siletz confederation. This photograph, with his first wife, Klamath Maggie, was taken in 1874, when a delegation of tribal leaders met with federal officials in Washington, D.C. *Siletz Tribal Collection.*

the signatories to the agreement gave their approval with "X" marks. Despite the importance and complexity of the land transaction, the tribe had no lawyer.

The seven-member tribal committee was a matter of some controversy. The transcript of the October 29 meeting states that the tribal members in attendance elected the committee. Hoxie Simmons, in his twenties at the time, later testified in a tribal claims case that the committee was appointed by the agent, T. Jay Buford. "Our agent instructed them," Simmons said. "They do whatever he say." He also said that two members of the Indian committee, George Harney and John Adams, did not want to sell the land: "They wanted to keep for the next generation, the last allotment, made for even little baby not born." As for the rest of the membership, Simmons said that "some" wanted to sell but "not the people. They holler in the Indian language, 'Keep the land, don't sell it.' "

The commissioners knew what they wanted and did not intend to budge.

PART THREE. THE RESERVATION YEARS

They reiterated that they were being "fair" and acting in "good faith." They also talked tough. When Judge Boise said that the forest lands had "very little value," George Harney disagreed, saying, "I think there is a good many timber on that land, and a good many timber is money." Harding called Harney's statements "rash" and threatened to "terminate this negotiation at once." It was an effective threat. These were destitute people, and while many were reluctant to sell, they obviously wanted to receive a fair price. They knew, too, that the government had already taken most of the reservation without any payment at all and feared that terminating the meeting could lead to another uncompensated taking.

The three representatives of the United States repeatedly made statements they knew to be false. The commissioners refused to say how much surplus land they had in mind, probably because the large amount of land affected would alarm the Indians. When U. S. Grant, a tribal member, asked "We want to know how much land is left outside of the land that is allotted?" Odell responded, "We cannot tell because it is not all surveyed. We can only guess at it." The commissioners never gave even an estimate. Yet, when they submitted their report to the secretary of the Interior a few weeks later, the number came easily: "The amount of land ceded is over 175,000 acres." Later, the number was found to be about 179,000 acres—80 percent of the entire reservation.

At the councils, the commissioners hammered away at the supposedly low value of the land. "The Government does not think that these lands are of much value to you." "The government does not buy these lands because they want them, or need them. They are buying to give away to the settlers, the same as their other public lands. . . . the Government will get nothing for them." "They are of so little value that the Government has not even employed a surveyor to survey them, knowing that they could not sell them if they did."

The official reports to the secretary and the Congress painted a very different, and much more accurate, picture. The commissioners wrote that the surplus lands were "densely timbered with good fir and cedar trees, and well watered with rapid running streams, which will furnish a good means of getting the timber and lumber out." In his assessment, Commissioner of the General Land Office W. M. Stone advised the Interior secretary that, with "said lands . . . being generally valuable for the timber growing thereon," the surplus lands should be sold to the public at "not less than $2.50 per acre." The agreement provided for a total payment to the tribe of $142,000, or 80 cents per acre. George Harney, speaking for the tribal members, requested $1.25 per acre but the three commissioners held firm.

The enormous value of timber on the former Siletz Reservation soon became clear. Fraud on the western federal lands had been rampant throughout the nineteenth century, but it rose to its zenith in the rich timber forests of the Pacific Northwest in the 1890s and early 1900s. The usual ruse centered on "dummy homesteaders," who claimed to be agricultural settlers. Hired by speculators, they had no intention of homesteading—especially in dense forests where farming was impossible—but they nevertheless (under penalty of perjury) filled out the necessary paperwork with the General Land Office. As soon as these bogus homesteaders received their patents, they turned them over to their corrupt sponsors.

The former Siletz tribal forest lands became a prime target for these racketeers precisely because they had such high value. Apparently, none of Senator John Mitchell's ill-begotten transactions involved these lands—he preferred forests in the Cascades—but others of his ilk were hard at work on the Coast. The exposé on Oregon land fraud, *Looters of the Public Domain* by Steven A. Puter, dedicated a full chapter to the rampant fraud at Siletz. Several prosecutions ensued, although many of the patents were never revoked. Tens of thousands of acres of spruce-fir and cedar forests eventually passed into the hands of, and brought much profit to, timber companies.

The three commissioners, then, obtained exactly the surplus lands agreement they had aimed for from the beginning. In round numbers, the 225,300-acre reservation was carved up as follows:

1. 179,000 acres for surplus lands, to be thrown open for acquisition by non-Indians.
2. 43,000 acres for 551 individual allotments for tribal members living on the reservation. Later, in a separate development under section 4 of the General Allotment Act, 387 western Oregon Indians living off the reservation received allotments, not from the reservation but from federal public domain lands.
3. Five sections, or 3,200 acres, for a timber reserve for the tribe.
4. 700 acres for agency-related purposes—farmland, saw mill, and BIA and church buildings.
5. The total payment to the tribe amounted to $142,000. Of this amount, $100,000 would be deposited with annual interest at 5 percent, with the proceeds to be paid to members of the tribe in March of each year (with

slightly over 500 tribal members at the time, this annual payment would amount to approximately $10 for each member). The remaining $42,000 would also be deposited at 5 percent and $75 would be paid out to adults annually until the fund was exhausted, which would occur in just a few years.

Congress approved the agreement in 1894.

At least the allotments remained. These parcels, located where Siletz families lived at allotment time, had become homes during the half century since the removals. Most of Upper Farm, Shasta Farm, and Lower Farm, for example, went into allotments. The story differed for each family as the twentieth century wore on. Some land was lost early, some remained family land for generations and a very small amount still is. Even when the allotments were lost, people often stayed in the area. This landscape, with all of the treachery wrought there, still had its rivers and creeks rich with salmon and eels; forests that held deer and roots, barks, and grasses for basketmaking; and the rugged, giving coastal shoreline with its mussels, oysters, smelt, crabs, and magnificence. The Siletz no longer owned it, but it had become their second homeland.

The year 1900 marked the all-time low point for the American Indian population. The accepted estimate of aboriginal populations before Europeans came is in the range of 5 to 7 million people. In 1900, after the diseases, wars, and removals, it had dropped to just 250,000, a loss of 95 percent or more. When Siletz tribal members had arrived after the removals, the 1857 reservation population was an estimated 2,700. By 1900, the population stood at about 500 people.

In spite of such depressing numbers, it may be that the turn of the century marked the point at which Siletz people began to rebound. At long last, although tuberculosis would be a problem into the 1940s, there was relative freedom from the European epidemics. The removals lay behind them. The salmon ran strong and game was plentiful. The clean, fresh coastal mist smelled and felt like home. Even with the many separate tribal histories, there was now a shared sense of culture, of being Siletz. Economic opportunities lay ahead: in particular, although one can doubt the rightness of their ownership of the forests, the timber companies would generate a decades-long

Son of Rogue River Johnny and his Coquelle wife, Sissy George, Archie Johnson was
orphaned early. He was sent to Chemawa, where he helped clear the grounds for the new
campus at Salem, and then to Carlisle Indian School in Pennsylvania, before returning to
Siletz. He trained for spiritual power along the Upper Klamath River, under the teaching of
his mother-in-law, Bessie Snelling. One of the last great Siletz canoe makers, he is pictured
here in the mid-1960s at the approximate age of ninety, standing on the last canoe he ever
constructed. *Siletz Tribal Collection.*

boom—and Siletz men made damn fine loggers. It was not enough, not nearly their due, and many wrongs would still be inflicted upon them, but at least, after the long run of endings, Oregon Coast Indians could now claim some beginnings.

CHANGE AND PERSEVERANCE

"I didn't know why they were strapping me."

T HE FIRST HALF OF THE TWENTIETH CENTURY MARKED THE time when national and local pressures for assimilation, at work for generations, finally took hold. The great majority of Siletz tribal members were born into a society shaped as much by their federal overseers as their parents. They had never lived in the ancestral homelands. With the reservation shattered, non-Indian homesteaders moved in among them. As a result, in contrast to tribes with large, remote reservations, such as those in the Southwest and Upper Great Plains, tribal culture at Siletz necessarily coexisted with the larger society.

Until the Termination Act in 1954, the 1900s saw no single event that even came close to the several dramatic crises of the 1800s. Nonetheless, this was a time of great change. Tribal members experienced continuing land loss, discrimination, poverty, and health problems. Pressures in the schools, towns, and workplaces pushed them to adopt America's values and economy wholesale. There was another aspect, a positive one. The mainstream world had its attractions—friendships, automobiles, radio, paying jobs, hospitals, and universities. The only counterforce to final immersion, frail though it may have been, was a conviction in the hearts and minds of Siletz people that the traditional culture, with its ceremonies and fellowship and its love of the extended family and the land, gave comfort and fulfillment in ways that the white world could never match. The context was different but the central question remained the same as it had been in the 1800s: could the Indian way persevere in western Oregon?

At the turn of the twentieth century the tribe continued to hold the five sections of timber land under the terms of the 1894 Siletz allotment statute. Almost all of the 551 eighty-acre individual allotments remained in trust. The original idea under the General Allotment Act was that allotments would stay in Indian hands—safe from taxes, creditors' claims, and sale—until 1919, when the twenty-five-year trust period expired. By then, the reasoning went, allottees would be acclimated to the American system of landownership and could manage their affairs. There was a kicker, though: Congress created ways to shorten the trust period and make the allotments taxable and available for sale. Indian agents, attentive to whites with their eyes fixed on Siletz farm and timber land, were all too happy to facilitate the sales of property. As the map on page 232 shows, settlers and developers had much to gain. Siletz allotments lay on nearly every stretch of river and major tributary and, as well, on most of the twenty-five mile coastline.

The Bureau of Indian Affairs was so eager to free up Siletz lands for non-Indian settlement that it devised entirely new and devious strategies to wrench allotments out of trust status. In 1901, the Interior department persuaded Congress to pass the Siletz Inherited Lands Act, which forced any Siletz Indian who inherited an allotment—and thereby held more than one eighty-acre allotment—to sell it. That accomplished, later in the same year the BIA went after all Siletz inheritances, whether or not heirs already held land. The agency recommended legislation that allowed heirs to sell deceased tribal members' allotments, arguing to Congress that "there is too much idle land" at Siletz and that the example of good white farmers would encourage other allottees to farm: "Many of these people would be benefited by the sale of these lands and the mixing in of respectable, thrifty, white farmers." Congress, instead of limiting the policy to Siletz, went further and applied the proposal nation-wide in the so-called "Dead Indian Act" of 1902.

Between them, the two statutes mandated that all allotments of deceased Siletz tribal members either automatically be put up for sale or made eligible for sale with the consent of the heirs—and the BIA could be counted on to pressure heirs to sell. Thus started the drain of allotment land. Not surprisingly, despite the BIA's assurances to Congress, there is no reason to believe that the presence of "respectable, thrifty, white farmers" ever inspired Indians to farm since Siletz tribal agricultural production steadily declined.

Congress then carved out an even larger loophole. In response to demands

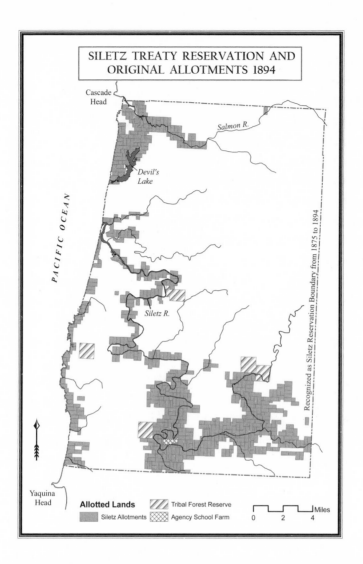

SILETZ TREATY RESERVATION AND
ORIGINAL ALLOTMENTS 1894

for Indian land, the Burke Act of 1906 permitted the issuance of fee title to those allottees whom the government declared "competent," defined only as a person that the secretary of the Interior "in his discretion" found to be "competent and capable of managing his or her own affairs." Following Interior department policy during the first two decades of the twentieth century, BIA officials aggressively moved land out of trust status. Indian Commissioner Cato Sells, for example, argued in 1917 that eliminating trusteeship over allotments would be "the beginning of the end of the Indian problem." Traveling "competency commissions" were established to determine competency, as determined by factors including an individual Indian's industriousness, education, degree of assimilation, and blood quantum, and led to the transfer of large numbers of allotments out of trust. Many of the allotment sales at Siletz were the notorious "forced-fee" patents, which BIA agents across the country imposed on Indian people by declaring them "competent" under the Burke Act and then pressuring them into disposing of their land or watching it be sold at a tax sale.

These policies, a major part of the legacy of the allotment regime, brought ruin to Indian country. Nationally, in addition to the 60 million acres taken as "surplus" lands and opened for settlement under the homesteading laws, 27 million acres of allotments—two-thirds of all land allotted and nearly half the size of Oregon—passed out of Indian hands.

At Siletz, where the rate of allotment land loss was higher than at most other reservations, people found themselves caught on the horns of a dilemma. Virtually everyone was destitute—unemployment was not officially calculated, but it surely reached 50 percent or higher—and yet they had to meet the demands of the cash economy. Few, if any, wanted to sell. After all, one of the few positive aspects of allotment was that Siletz allottees had their choice of parcels before the remaining lands were declared "surplus," and they had selected the best locations. But they needed cash to live. The allotments were their only assets and, with the trust lifted and the land sold, they could spend the proceeds for day-to-day needs. Of course, if an allotment were taken out of trust and failed to sell, money had to be found to pay the taxes—and if that proved impossible, then the land would go up for a tax sale. "Once this machine is put into place," Bob Tom lamented, "we won't know where [the allotments] went. We'll just know they're gone."

The land loss was steady and substantial. By 1905, nearly half of the allottees had passed away and the Siletz Inherited Lands Act allowed heirs, usually encouraged by agents who fast-tracked the process, to sell those allotments. The agent reported that "this land is in demand and brings good prices." While these allotments may have been selling at market value and recognizing that it is difficult to make accurate judgments with the hindsight of a century, one can doubt whether Siletz allottees received a fair return: in 1907, for example, the BIA annual report disclosed that forty allotments (a total of 2,671 acres) of deceased tribal members were sold at an average of just $7.12 per acre—about $180 in current dollars.

When the Burke Act took effect in 1906, any tribal members declared by the Interior department to be "competent" became eligible to divest themselves of their land. (Siletz people were "competent" to do many things, but managing a block payment of cash was seldom one of them.) Historian D. S.

PART THREE. THE RESERVATION YEARS

Otis, writing from the perspective of 1934, when Congress finally put a hold on transferring allotment land out of trust, identified the allotment program's basic dynamic in his comprehensive report to Congress: "For if white land seekers and business promoters did not create the allotment system, they at least turned it to their own good use. Where the land was valuable white interests formed a ring about the Indian reservation; a ring which exerted a relentless pressure in all directions, until the force was felt in Washington itself."

With reservation farming in steep decline and almost no commercial sales of agricultural products, the main function of the Siletz agency was to serve as a real estate office. By 1920, 60 percent of all allotments had gone out of trust and into the hands of non-Indians. The second largest source of annual reservation income—though it would usually be quickly spent—came from allotment sales. When the Siletz agency was closed in 1925, Agent Edwin Chalcraft, a fervent assimilationist, urged in his final report to the commissioner of Indian Affairs that the work of taking allotments out of trust should continue apace because "competent" Indians "should be required to assume their responsibilities" of paying property taxes. In 1931, however, a Lincoln County agricultural agent testified in Congress and told how the unfamiliar but inexorable requirement of paying taxes burdened the Siletz people and separated them from their land:

> Many of the best farms on the Siletz were held by the Indians. . . . Gradually, from year to year, when the patents were obtained—and in my own mind I

Opposite: Allotment affected Siletz land, resources, and people in many ways, not all of them obvious. Before allotment, when nearly the entire Siletz River watershed still remained tribal land, Siletz agents made requests for a tribal commercial salmon canning operation. Each was denied. Then the reservation lands ceded under the 1892 allotment agreement (ratified in 1894) were opened to homesteading in 1895. In 1896, construction began on the Kern Brothers cannery (shown in the upper photograph in the early 1900s) on the Lower Siletz River on former Indian land. The cannery owners operated a large and efficient fish wheel nearby, scooping fish out of the river—salmon that otherwise would have gone upriver to spawn or be caught by tribal families. The new system was unsustainable: overfishing, logging operations upstream, and other factors led to sharply diminished runs. The lower photograph of the interior of the cannery shows the size of the "June Hogs" (the spring chinook salmon run) that were common in the Siletz River in the early 1900s. *Both photographs courtesy of North Lincoln County Historical Museum.*

wondered at that time a great many times as to how they had issued them and why, because of a knowledge or thought in my mind a great many of the Indians were not ready to handle their own personal business. I believe there are some of the Indians here to-day that will tell you that their patents were more or less forced on them. . . . As soon as these patents were given to the Indians they either failed to pay their taxes or through the opportunity to borrow on the land when they owned it themselves, . . . a great deal of the land was mortgaged and the mortgage sold, either foreclosed or directly sold. So that from that time to the present time the better lands on Siletz have passed out of the hands of the Indians.

Two other decisions led to land loss. Driven by the same day-to-day financial demands that drove tribal members to sell their allotted lands, support grew for a transfer of the five sections of timbered lands that the tribe had reserved in the 1892 allotment agreement. In 1907, seventy-seven Siletz men petitioned President Theodore Roosevelt for sale of the five sections, saying that "the money derived from the sale of this Reservation would be of vast help to us." The request fit nicely with the Interior department's agenda of breaking up reservation landholdings. The departmental memorandum to the House Indian Affairs Committee on the transfer proposal made clear that "the policy of this department has been to withdraw its control and guardianship over individual Indians and Indian tribes as soon as it becomes apparent that they are possessed of the means and ability to care for themselves." In an ominous foreshadowing of termination, the memorandum added: "I am convinced that it is only a matter of a very short time before patents in fee can be granted these Indians and all governmental supervision withdrawn." Congress passed a bill authorizing the sale of these lands in 1910, although just one of the sections was sold.

Another land provision was included in the 1910 legislation. When the government shut down the boarding school on Government Hill in the town of Siletz in 1908 and switched it to a day school, the official explanation was that "the land allotted to the Siletz Indians is quite productive, and it is essential that the older children receive thorough training [in agriculture]. . . . There are, however, much better facilities at the Chemawa school . . . than there were at the Siletz boarding school . . . ; this will be for the best interest of these Indians as well as a saving to the Government." This was just a euphemism. While true that the allotments were "quite productive," by 1908 it was clear that most of them would be sold, not farmed by Siletz people. To the government, it was long past time to get serious about cutting Indian expenditures, and shutting down the boarding school would save money.

So, what should be done with the Siletz boarding school land—some 200 acres of level, productive ground that had been set aside for Indian purposes? Apparently no thought was given to transferring it to the tribe. Instead, the 1910 legislation declared that the land would be "sold for town lots, or for such other purposes that [the BIA] may deem advisable." In particular, the forty acres known as Government Farm "shall be laid out as a town site and sub-divided into town lots" and put up for sale to non-Indians. The town of Siletz then rose up on that land. After all, the future belonged to the settlers, not the Natives.

By the early 1950s, the job of moving Siletz allotments out of trust was more than 85 percent completed. Only 76 of the original 551 allotments—5,390 acres out of 44,470—remained in trust. The tribe also owned four of the five timber sections from the Allotment Act. Then, with the Termination Act in 1954, Congress broke off the trust relationship altogether: the four tribal sections were sold off and the remaining land in allotment status was transferred to Siletz people by the issuance of fee patents.

Siletz children attended Chemawa boarding school in Salem in the 1800s, but Chemawa began playing a larger role in tribal life with the conversion of the Siletz boarding school to a day school in 1908 and with the closing of the BIA day school in 1918. Most students went to the local public schools, but Chemawa appealed to many parents because of its discipline and its status as one of the two flagship boarding schools in the country. For students, the boarding school offered the chance to be around Indians from other tribes. After the BIA office at Siletz shut down in 1925, Chemawa, which then housed the Siletz BIA office and health clinic, was perhaps the most significant federal presence for the tribe.

Chemawa was strict. With administrators and teachers pushing Americanization in every aspect of school life, students wore uniforms and the "cardinal rule" was "No Indian Talk." Although national BIA policy prohibited corporal punishment in 1904, whippings and other forms of severe punishment continued to be administered. The school aimed to send students to non-Indian communities, not the reservations. When graduates did return to their own reservations, Chemawa's reaction was disappointment: they "have

Drawn by a Chemawa student, this 1908 cartoon extols the benefits of the school. The smaller figure is Army Lieutenant Melville Wilkinson, the school's founder. *National Archives and Records Administration–Pacific Alaska Region.*

been fitted for better things; we cannot do less than fit them for things far above the old reservation surroundings." During the height of the effort to turn fee patents over to "competent" allottees in the 1910s, the express objective was to designate graduating students as "competent" (and open up the possibility of land loss); "every such capable young man and woman should be given a certificate of competency or a patent in fee."

Like other boarding schools, Chemawa has been controversial among Indian people. In part, it depends on the era. During the early years, from the 1800s through the early 1900s, schooling at Chemawa was a blunt instrument, racist and sometimes brutal. Many Siletz people, including Aurilla Tom, who went to Chemawa in the early 1900s, hated the punishment: "They beat us if anyone was caught talking Indian." In the twentieth century, the physical punishment diminished and the quality of education improved, although the schooling continued to be dominated by hard-edged assimilation ideology and a lack of respect for tribal cultures. By the 1980s, with the modern Indian revival, Chemawa evolved into a far more progressive school. Today, it offers several courses in Indian history and arts and emphasizes that education is carried out "in keeping with the tribes' cultural traditions."

One thing was for sure until the past generation or so: the experience was a jolting challenge and the young people who endured it, and often made it through to graduation, showed a resolve and strength of character that is much to be admired. Researcher Sonciray Bonnell, who conducted numerous interviews with Chemawa alumni, found that regardless of how much people disliked the experience while actually in school and despite the many criticisms that can be made, many Chemawa graduates offer "positive appraisals" and hold the school in "high regard."

The experiences of Siletz students at Chemawa were varied and reflected the blizzard of bruises, confusion, successes, anger, and satisfaction that all Indian people encountered during the first half of the twentieth century, as they haltingly encountered still-foreign and often insensitive Anglo communities. Kay Steele recalls that her father, Daniel Orton, learned the trade of tailoring at Chemawa; through his handiwork, the men in his family were known for being well dressed. When June Austin moved to Chemawa, she appreciated the indoor showers and toilets—and the luxury of sleeping in her own bed—and discovered "a whole new world with stores." A Siletz girl at Chemawa from 1927 through 1933 remembered a kind BIA employee who bought clothes for her and other girls: "We got the dresses and we got shoes that fit our feet, we got to have something to have beside black stockings. Oh, we were white girls then. Really, we were like the kids [in] Salem. . . . He just took us out of the dark ages and put us in the new ages." In 1934, with talk of closing Chemawa in the air, Wilbur Martin of Siletz argued that "we should not give up Chemawa. Chemawa belongs to our Indian people. It is one of the greatest government institutions. I think our children should go to public schools and when they are fit to go to Chemawa they should go there."

Although Native traditions were denigrated at the boarding school, much more often than not Chemawa students kept their minds open to the songs and stories of their ancestors. Something visceral told them that they could gain a white education and still remain Indian. Later in life, after graduation, most consciously honored their Indianness even if they were living in a city. One tribal member, for example, was raised by his grandmother in the traditional fashion because his father was being treated for tuberculosis in a hospital. Then in 1934, at the age of five, he was taken away to Chemawa and his world was turned upside down. He was so young that "I didn't know why they were strapping me for using the language I had been raised with," he remembered. Yet he rose above all that, served in the Marines for twelve years, and in time became a respected elder at Siletz.

At Chemawa, students felt the undercurrent of faithfulness to Indian culture that ran strong beneath the Americanization. Students gave the name "Pigsville" to the enclave where the hogs were kept, a place where they could claim some privacy. One time, when Gilbert Towner was six or seven, he and

The Wanamaker Expedition, funded by Rodman Wanamaker, heir to the Wanamaker department-store fortune, visited many Indian reservations and came through Siletz in 1913. The expedition, led by Joseph K. Dixon, professional photographer, lecturer, and former Baptist minister, was designed to instill patriotism in members of the "vanishing race." In this photograph, taken by Dixon, tribal members are folding a large flag presented to the tribe by the expedition. *Siletz Tribal Collection.*

some of his friends staged an impromptu pow-wow in Pigsville, tying tin-can bells around their ankles, shaping feathers out of cardboard, and using a washtub for the drum. School officials heard the rhythms and, "to put disgrace on us," called everyone to the gymnasium, where they forced the boys to perform their pow-wow in front of the whole school. But the punishment backfired. "One by one, everyone came out dancing," even the instructors. Towner beamed when he told that story, including its aftermath: "We still got strapped."

From the time when western Oregon Indians were located on the reservation in 1856, they continually faced a poverty considerably deeper than the nation experienced during the depths of the Great Depression. The federal support trumpeted during treaty negotiations never amounted to much and it dissi-

Visits by anthropologists often had a celebratory quality to them. Leo Frachtenberg, who visited Siletz several times between 1909 and 1916, is seated at the lower left in this photograph taken at a picnic with the families of Agent Knott Egbert; Arthur Bensell Sr., Macka-nutini; and Robert Depoe, Ya-shu-eh. *Siletz Tribal Collection.*

pated over time. After the BIA closed the Siletz agency in 1925, the only federal employee with responsibilities for Siletz, and Grand Ronde as well, was a clerk located at Chemawa. The BIA no longer provided regular health care, much less general welfare support, and even discontinued rations. Lincoln County made some welfare payments, but they were small. The frame houses on the reservation were forty to fifty years old and not in good condition. Tuberculosis and other diseases continued at high levels, with most people unable to obtain proper medical help. Hoxie Simmons testified to federal officials: "You turn an old horse loose in a poor pasture to die. That is the condition of the old Indians to-day."

The land offered some seasonal jobs. Men worked on company road crews and at low-paying but welcome New Deal jobs—usually outdoors on road, trail, and small-building projects—with the Civilian Conservation Corps and Works Progress Administration. Picking was more widespread. Oregon was the nation's second-largest producer of hops, used to flavor beer, and most of

The BIA agency was an active place in the early 1900s. This photograph shows the buildings on Government Hill and the farmland in what is now the town of Siletz. *Siletz Tribal Collection.*

Siletz boys learning how to brand cattle. *Siletz Tribal Collection.*

Hoxie Simmons in 1945, with a load of ferns to be sold to the florist trade, once a common way for Siletz families to earn money. *Courtesy of* The Oregonian.

Abe Logan Sr., Tututni, on the left, and Arthur Bensell Sr. harvesting oats in the 1930s. *Siletz Tribal Collection.*

CHANGE AND PERSEVERANCE

the state's harvest came from the Willamette Valley. Siletz also labored in the strawberry, prune, and bean fields. Pickers in the 1930s earned about $1.25 to $1.50 per hundred pounds, allowing skilled workers to earn $3 or $4 a day.

The early fall expeditions to the fields were big events, with most Siletz families heading over to the valley in horse-drawn wagons and, later, flatbed trucks. The children had the luxury and excitement of riding on top of the bundles of clothes and hop sacks as the vehicles bounced along on the roads. Many other Oregon tribes worked the harvest: in the 1934 season, for example, an estimated 3,000 Indians picked hops in the Willamette Valley.

The journeys had a cultural grounding. As Lionel Youst explained in his biography of Coquelle Thompson, "The hop harvest fit perfectly with the Indian tradition of seasonal migrations for harvests of various kinds. After eels in the late spring, 'Oat harvest next, then hops, then salmon.'" On the Coast, the lush forests provided another venue for commercial gathering. Florists coveted the ferns, salal, moss, huckleberry branches, and foxglove leaves, all used by Indian people traditionally.

The forests of the former reservation brought even higher-paying jobs in another way—the harvesting of the spruce, cedar, and Douglas fir stands. The era of intensive logging, beginning in the 1920s, provided the largest stream of income yet seen and amounted to one of the most significant events in the history of the Siletz Tribe.

Commercial logging on the Oregon Coast started up in the mid-1800s with horse teams, later to be replaced by "steam donkeys," engines that powered winches equipped with ropes and steel cables for hauling and yarding the big logs. Then, in the early twentieth century, using the "surplus" lands that were taken from tribal ownership by the 1894 agreement, the government put most of the Siletz watershed up for homesteading in 160-acre parcels. It made for a booming real estate market and rampant fraudulent claims, usually in the form of "homesteaders" obtaining patents to heavily forested land without ever erecting the residences and cultivated crops that the law required. A. W. "Jack" Morgan, who bought and sold timber claims in Lincoln County during the first half of the twentieth century, had a twinkle in his eye as he tiptoed through the fraud issue in his engaging memoir, *50 Years in Siletz Timber*:

I sometimes feel thankful that they did not get us homesteaders indicted for

A stand of the giant Sitka spruce trees that once stood in the lower Siletz watershed. With nearly all of the spruce logged off, basket weavers no longer have access to roots from these prized trees. *Courtesy of University of Washington Libraries, Special Collections, no. UW120*

fraud or something of the kind, as people were apparently stampeded for awhile. There was some skullduggery going on in the way of someone who had money and wanted to get timber cheap, would have a locater pick up idle men around towns and get them to file timber claims on vacant land, and furnish them money to pay the $2.50 per acre, which was the price then, and give them a few hundred dollars to deed the land to them. . . . There was so much agitation about timber frauds at that time that I think some people thought it was a crime to get any timber from the Government whether it was legal or not. I heard a number of people say the Siletz should never have been open for homesteads, but I think this was mostly from those who were sore because they did not get in on it. In other places, where it was open for timber claims and script, it was soon gobbled up and sold to big corporations, usually for a small price. My observation was that the homesteaders here were mostly good, honest people who took care of their money when they sold their claims and as a rule used it wisely.

CHANGE AND PERSEVERANCE

World War I transformed the timber industry in the Pacific Northwest. Several mills in Lincoln County were already cutting dimension lumber, but the combat in Europe sparked a tremendous demand for the strong, light Sitka spruce that was ideal for construction of aircraft. Sitka spruce thrived in the "fog zone," reaching no more than fifteen miles inland along the central Oregon Coast, and the lush forests of the Lower Siletz watershed offered prime habitat. These were virgin old-growth stands in an area that had never undergone a major burn.

The U.S. Army created the Spruce Production Corporation, an enterprise that erected a "war mill," one of the largest wood-processing facilities in the world, at Toledo, nine miles south of Siletz. The operation was not fully completed by the end of World War I, but the corporation was up and running, harvesting and milling nearly 54 million board feet annually of former Siletz Reservation timber at the height of the war, with workers housed in a giant tent city.

When the war ended, with final construction of the mill almost completed, the government decided to divest itself of its Toledo operations. A consortium headed by C. D. Johnson jumped at the opportunity, making the purchase on what historian William Robbins characterized as "generous terms." The private company, the Pacific Spruce Corporation (soon to be the C. D. Johnson Company and acquired by Georgia-Pacific in 1952), with its Toledo mill, quickly became a major Lincoln County institution, the leading employer for most of the twentieth and early twenty-first centuries. It acquired vast amounts of timber land, especially in the Siletz watershed. By 1924, it owned 14,600 acres on the Lower Siletz, holding an estimated 835 million board feet. The Blodgett Tract south of Newport was similarly valuable. Many other purchases were still to come during the historic logging boom, as Oregon became the top timber-producing state in the Union.

The many timber operations on the central Coast (at the high point, sixty-eight mills operated in the Toledo area alone), but especially the Johnson company, employed hundreds of Siletz men over the years. In order to get Siletz timber to the mill, Pacific Spruce Corporation punched a railroad line from Toledo north to serve "Camp 12," a log-collecting center built on the hill just south of the town of Siletz. "Camp 11" was located at the lower end of the watershed and "Camp Gorge" was later built upriver from the town. The Siletz men worked mostly in the mills or out in the woods, felling, bucking, and yarding the towering trees. To this day, tribal members believe that

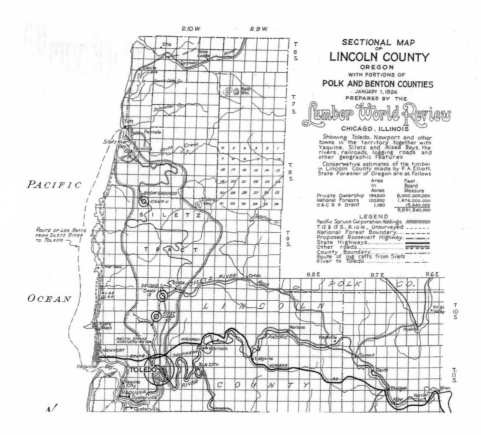

The C. D. Johnson Company logging road map for Lincoln County as of 1924. High-volume extraction was already in full swing by this time but the road system would expand greatly over the next two generations.

discriminatory practices kept them from higher-paying jobs operating heavy equipment. And logging was dangerous—at least four Siletz men lost their lives and many were injured, for even the felling of limbs from those goliaths could cause havoc.

Nonetheless, for generations logging produced good-paying jobs. In the 1940s, tribal members made $225 to $250 a month, and by the late 1980s an experienced logger could make up to $17 per hour. Other Siletz men ran their own logging operations. The industriousness of the men and their skills in the woods were a matter of great pride. They took satisfaction in having, as their workplace, the deep forests where Indian people had always hunted and gathered. Although later in life Eleanor Logan said she would raise her children to get college educations, her approach was different during her child-raising years in the mid-1900s: "My boys will be loggers. My girls will marry loggers." From the 1920s through World War II and beyond, that formula defined the workaday world for a great many Siletz families.

⚼⚜⚼

While few people realized commercial returns, hunting and fishing continued to be of importance for subsistence and barter. As was common with the Salmon People of the Pacific Northwest, when Gladys Bolton grew up in Siletz in the 1920s and 1930s, "there were always eels and salmon hanging in the family smokehouse." Clayburn Arden was one of many who made good use of the river and ocean resources that were so plentiful through the years after World War II. He netted salmon and took eels on the Siletz River, storing them in cans for the winter. He also took oysters and clams, as well as seaweed that he washed on boards and dried on the roof on screens until it was baked crisp. Arden hunted deer and elk as well.

At one point, conflict developed with Oregon wildlife officials over whether, with the reservation mostly broken up, tribal members could fish and hunt under tribal rather than state regulations. The matter was resolved by 1938, when the Oregon attorney general issued an opinion recognizing that the state had no right to control fishing and hunting on trust land, that is, on allotments (a number of which had river frontage) and the four remaining tribal timber sections. The BIA issued tags to tribal fishermen to certify the primacy of tribal and federal law on those lands. More broadly, tribal members carried the belief that they could rightfully hunt, fish, and gather throughout the former reservation. For hunting and fishing outside of trust land, the state—in a time when competition for fish and game was still relatively low and habitat degradation had yet to take its toll—enforced its license requirements, seasons, and bag limits sporadically, if at all. As Reggie Butler put it, "I didn't grow up thinking hunting was against state law. No one did."

Siletz people had a special affection for eels, especially into the 1950s when the runs were still strong. (Scientists classify these lampreys, with their toothy, suction-cup mouths, as fish but Siletz people, like many others, refer to them as "eels.") They were plentiful in the Siletz River and its tributaries and, on the other side of the Coast Range, at Willamette Falls. Eeling was primarily a nighttime activity with fishermen—to the light of lanterns or large bonfires—using gaff hooks fixed on long poles. The eels attached themselves to rocks with their mouths. Fishermen, working from ledges or rocks or boats in open water, dragged their hooks along the rocks and then threw the eels on the banks for the women and children to stuff in gunny sacks. They gutted the eels, cut off the heads, and took out the backbones, the translucent cartilage the Siletz called the "gristle."

The cleaned eels were then hung by their tails on strings in the smokehouses to dry. Usually they would be "smoked and baked"—smoked for two or three days and then put in the oven briefly to finish the cooking. The eels made a real delicacy: oily but subtle in taste, not "fishy."

All the fishing, eeling, hunting, and gathering made for a community of sharing and bartering. People came together to help neighbors build a house or dig a well. "If a woman didn't have a man, they'd stock her woodpile." Most people had home gardens and nearby patches of Oregon blackberries—the tangly, snarly gifts that kept on giving. Trading and exchanging cans and jars of preserved seafood and fruit were commonplace.

Then, in the 1930s, the BIA built an elaborate cannery, including two large ceramic tubs for fruit, on Government Hill. It never worked as originally intended, as an economic development project, but the Siletz women made it a fine nonprofit community facility. Families, including the children, pitched in to do the canning. "If we wanted to eat," LaVera Simmons laughed, "we'd have to help." With the elaborate, commercial-type machinery, her family would end the season with 600 to 700 jars packed with salmon, eels, fruit, berries, and vegetables. Although Siletz people as a whole were well below the poverty line, even with the income from logging, the ever-giving land and community support etched a different picture. June Austin spoke for most Siletz families when she said, "We didn't know we were poor."

Gradually, Siletz people began going to college. The first, James Collins, graduated from Oregon State College (now University) in 1888. Coquelle Thompson Jr. followed in 1927 and graduated while starring on the football team as a fullback. Art Bensell studied at Heidelberg College in Ohio, graduating in 1932 as a small-college, All-American football player. Reuben Saunders, a graduate of Willamette University in Salem, Oregon, was an all-around athlete; like Bensell, he was inducted into the American Indian Athletic Hall of Fame, as a member of the inaugural class of 1972, along with Jim Thorpe. In the 1930s, Bensell's sister, Mary Alice Bensell Munsee, graduated from the Oregon Normal School in Philomath and in the 1950s earned a degree from the University of Oregon. Elwood A. Towner obtained a law degree from Willamette University in the 1920s. In 1947, Ken Hatch became one of the first American Indians to graduate from West Point.

The Siletz Nee Dosh, or Feather Dance, was an attraction up and down the Coast. This gathering took place in the late 1800s on a wooden plank street, common in that era, in Newport's bay front. Note the man on the far left in a feather shirt and the man second from the right in a headdress of flicker tail-feathers. *Siletz Tribal Collection.*

Living as Siletz people did, intermixed with whites, their society was not as separate as those tribes whose reservations remained intact. Many Siletz people had good social relationships with non-Indians from workplaces, schools, churches, and neighborhoods. Nonetheless, racial discrimination, while it did not raise its head everywhere, remained an unpleasant fact of life for the Siletz. Oregon law had a miscegenation statute—not repealed until 1951—that outlawed marriages between Indians and whites, causing numerous couples to take their vows across the Washington line. Federal law prohibited liquor sales to Indians in Indian country, and many tavern owners refused to sell to Siletz people even when their taverns were no longer covered by the law after termination in the 1950s. Some restaurants displayed "No Indians Allowed" signs and many a fight broke out in those bars and taverns that did serve Indians. Too often, children faced discrimination in the schools. In the white-dominated Bureau of Indian Affairs, some employees refused to work for Art

　　　　　　　PART THREE. THE RESERVATION YEARS

Five generations of a Siletz family in 1909: the baby, Stanley Strong (a future tribal leader), is pictured with, from the left, Jane Yanna (great-great-grandmother), Molly Carmichael (great-grandmother), Mamie Strong (mother), and Mary Catfish (grandmother). *Siletz Tribal Collection.*

Bensell, a college graduate who held a supervisory position. Even today, when discrimination is greatly reduced, the emotion over such past treatment is palpable among older Siletz people.

Chemawa boxing team in the 1920s, coached by Reuben Saunders (*upper left*), Siletz star athlete.

Hoxie Simmons and Tom Jackson in the 1920s. Jackson (*right*) served as a tribal policeman and became one of the first Indian photographers. Princeton University acquired a collection of his work. *Siletz Tribal Collection.*

Just as the Warm House Dance resonated with many Siletz people in the 1870s and 1880s, so did the Indian Shaker Church call out to Siletz spirituality in the first half of the twentieth century. The origins of the church go back to 1885 and John Slocum of the Squaxin Island Tribe at the southern end of Puget Sound. In 1881, Slocum had been taken for dead but miraculously sprang back to life and, in his mind and in some others', the experience was evidence that he had supernatural powers. A year later, when Slocum again took seriously ill, his wife Mary prayed over her husband and fell into uncontrollable sobbing and trembling—a "shaking." When Slocum recovered, Mary's actions were interpreted as medicine from God and he came to be viewed as a prophet. Word spread from Slocum's church at Mud Bay, near Squaxin Island, to Puget Sound tribes and Yakama east of the Cascades, then to Warm Springs and Umatilla in Oregon. By the time Slocum passed away in 1897, the Shaker Church had gained many adherents despite attempts by missionaries and Indian agents to suppress it.

A syncretic religion with both Native and Christian elements, the church resonated with Indian people forced toward assimilation but tugged by their traditional values. Shakers believed they could heal sick people through the shake, resulting from the intensity of prayer, dance, and doctoring while in a trance. Adherents give many accounts of such healings, including one of a Tillamook woman who had severe depression that was cured after a man encouraged her to attend a service: "Whoever believes this thing can learn for himself and after a while they'll shake. You will shake yourself; you can't help it. Any evil people who do not believe cannot learn this. They cannot shake."

Siletz people heard of the religion as early as the 1890s, but a local congregation was not established until the early 1920s. Leone Letson Kasner, who knew many Siletz tribal members, wrote that

> The [Shaker] approach to worship was spontaneous and individualistic which recognized the Indian attitude toward the Spirit world. . . . On the [Siletz] reservation where many Athabascans . . . had already joined Christian missions the missionaries saw, by 1928, that white orthodox churches were losing ground to faiths more comfortable to the demonstrative Indians. White religious standards were too severe. Indian Shaker beliefs were intuitive, emotional—comparable to aboriginal myths and legends."

Anthropologist Lee Sackett found that

the equalitarian nature of the Shaker church was . . . a strong attraction. In the Shaker church there was no white leader telling the Indian congregation how to behave. And members could wear any type of clothing without feeling that they were being talked about. In sum, they were all brothers and sisters in the eyes of the Lord, and in their own eyes also."

Eleanor Logan, a Yurok whose Siletz husband, John, led the Siletz congregation for many years, said simply, "God gave Indian people something to meet the Indians' needs, the Shaker Church."

The first Siletz Shaker services were held in homes at the north end of Lincoln City on the site now occupied by the tribal casino. In 1926, with so many church members in Siletz having to make the twenty-mile journey on horseback or by horse and buggy to attend the services, the Shakers bought land on East Swan Avenue in Siletz. Jakie Johnson, leader of the congregation, and John Albert soon purchased lumber and put up a church building.

A year later, Jimmy Jack Hoppell, a Yurok Shaker from California married to a Siletz woman, was having little luck recruiting adherents, and he asked the Siletz for help. Given the historic ties to northern California, the Siletz were quick to respond. Thirty followers, joined by a group from Klamath, traveled to the mouth of the Klamath River. By the end of three weeks, they had recruited thirty new members and witnessed the formation of the Weitchpec–Old Mill Indian Shaker Church. On their way home, the group stayed with friends and relatives of the Tututnis' sister tribe, the Tolowa of Smith River. The trip sparked congregations there and at Hoopa. The California expedition marked the southernmost reach of the Shaker religion, and the church at Smith River is still active today.

Not long after returning home from California, the Siletz Shakers built a larger church behind the existing structure on East Swan, using wood salvaged when the government boarding school was torn down. The older building then served as a kitchen and community dining hall.

The late 1920s and early 1930s marked the highwater point for the Shakers at Siletz. A majority of Indians in the Siletz area were members and about seventy attended regularly. Even among non-followers, the church was held in near-universal high regard. As the Siletz sub-agency superintendent, James McGregor, perceptively wrote at the time, "the Indian Shaker Church ritual allows dancing as a means of expression, which to the Indian is more definite than mere gestures and words."

In a church distinguished by the bright, clear sound of bells, the large bell on the top of the building on East Swan rang three times on Friday nights: the first bell at about six o'clock to invite people to the evening meal, the second to announce the beginning of testimony, the third to signal that "church is starting." Entering the neat, one-room building, Shakers—all dressed in white—faced the altar against the far wall and saw a large stove directly left of the entrance. A twelve-piece chandelier hung from the ceiling. Benches lined the side walls up to the altar; a few rows were placed as common church pews are, with an aisle down the center and space left open in front of the altar. After songs, true to the religion's emphasis on equality, the leader would say to the gathering, "I am going to have this person do the service this night," and then indicate the person who would give the sermon.

After the sermon and testimonies, the ceremony began. The preacher called for anyone who needed healing and that person would come to the middle of the open floor and stand. Men who wanted to participate picked up bells from the altar while women took candles, and they stood beside the altar in two lines. With a word, the healing began, and the men and women fell into a circle around the sick person. The preacher alternated between praying and singing Shaker songs, which carry a traditional Indian rhythm and feel, and the circle joined in. Everyone danced in a procession, moving around the room counterclockwise three times, feet softly but purposefully tapping to the driving, jingling rhythm of the bells and songs. Reflecting the Shaker commitment to sobriety, Archie Johnson told stories of the church's early days when visitors would attend the church, standing along the sides and back. The Shakers would dance up to them, eyes closed, and reach into their pockets and take out cigarettes, or whatever else they weren't supposed to be carrying, and dispose of them.

During a healing, which often took two or three hours, women danced out of line and, using the candles, pulled the sickness off a person and burned it. Men healed by shaking their bells in front of the sick person. The church filled with prayer, song, and ringing bells, a rich and full layer over the focused and methodical rhythm of the healers' thoughts as they danced with closed eyes, allowing the spirit to move them. The services continued deep into the night, and sometimes worshippers walked from the church in the early light of day.

The Shaker Church at Siletz started to lose momentum in the late 1930s. Even though membership declined, services continued in the traditional fashion under the leadership of Ethel Gardipee and, later, John Logan. Some tribal members, although not Shakers, came to dinners at the church. Then the cookhouse suffered severe wind damage in 1964 and was rendered unusable. When John Logan, aging and ill, moved to California, the Siletz knew the end of the church was near. In 1969, services ceased and the bells rang for the last time.

Though its membership today is small, the Shaker Church holds a place of respect among Indians in the Northwest. The members are earnest, church doctrine has authentic Native roots, and the services are moving. At Siletz, there have been no services since the 1960s, but some tribal members travel to Shaker services in Mud Bay, Smith River, and other places.

The legacy of the Siletz Shaker Church is manifested in the values and actions of the people it influenced. As a young woman, Gladys Muschamp's problems with alcohol affected her exceptional basket-making talents. She joined the Shaker Church in its early days at Siletz, became a loyal adherent, and made many pilgrimages to Mud Bay and Smith River to attend Shaker gatherings. The experience changed her life. She never took another drink and, in time, became the greatest of all Siletz basket makers. Generous with her time, she passed on her artistry to young people who in turn have taught others. Through spirituality, dance, and basketry, Gladys Muschamp became one of the many Siletz people who maintained the culture through challenging times.

STRUGGLES TO MAKE
THE WHITE MAN'S LAWS FIT

"My Father spent much of his life working on the claims.
The payments were a slap in the face."

EVER SINCE THE REMOVALS OF 1856, SILETZ PEOPLE CALLED FOR just reckonings of their land rights. For decades, they urged the ratification of the 1855 treaty. In time, the truth sank in: the treaty would go unratified. Then the reservation was torn apart in 1865, 1875, and 1894. That bitter truth sank in, too: the land was gone. The sense of wrong, however, never died and was manifested in court cases to recover compensation for the value of the land taken from them. Poverty-stricken western Oregon Indians needed that money, but from their standpoint the long campaign to prosecute the claims cases also was suffused with the morality of achieving some measure of justice.

George Bundy Wasson Sr., of Coos and Coquille blood, initiated the first claims case and dedicated his adult life to the effort. The flame was lit early by his spirited grandmother, Gishgiu, who had avoided removal north to Siletz by hiding from the soldiers, first in a hollow log and then in a tiny storage space under a living-room staircase. When Wasson was a little boy in the 1880s, Gishgiu took him to a bluff overlooking Coos Bay and put out words that would stay with him always: "All this land belongs to your *hiyas papas* (grandfathers). Someday, Chawtch (George), you get it back." Even at a young age, George knew that he was the one. "I was the fourth son and according to the legends of the Coos Indians, I was the member of the family supposed to have the best qualifications for the work she wanted me to do."

Wasson grew up in the Indian society around Coos Bay, went off to Chemawa and Carlisle Indian Industrial schools, and then returned to southern Oregon to learn the craft of timber cruising—surveying forest land, identifying species, and estimating potential harvest volume. In 1916, he went to a meeting of Coos, Lower Umpqua, and Siuslaw Indians, whose aim was to recover the value of their lost land. The group agreed that Wasson, with his college education and reputation as an expert timber cruiser, should take the lead. Hearing his grandmother's words, he pronounced himself "raring to go."

Prosecuting tribal land claims at that time forced Indians to fight their way through one of the gnarliest thickets in all of the law. A chief tormentor of the Siletz and other tribes was the doctrine of sovereign immunity, which has its origins in the Common Law of Olde England. This followed from the maxim that "the King [or Queen] can do no wrong," a principle justified by the notion that the sovereign's authority—originating as it did in the will of God—was absolute and higher than any person on earth. "The law," an early English legal scholar asserted, "supposes it impossible that the King himself can act unlawfully or improperly." Citizens, in other words, can't sue their own governments.

From the earliest days, American courts adopted the Common Law doctrine of sovereign immunity. Incorporating English legal principles usually worked well, but not when it came to the antiquated, rigid idea that "the king can do no wrong." Because sovereign immunity caused so many injustices, Congress established the Court of Claims in 1855, waiving sovereign immunity and allowing lawsuits to be brought against the United States for many types of claims involving illegal federal actions. Eight years later, however, Congress backtracked and denied this simple matter of fairness to tribes: no matter how serious the grievance, tribal suits against the federal government for treaty violations were not permissible. For tribes, federal sovereign immunity remained in place.

This meant that the Coos, Siuslaw, and Lower Umpqua tribes could not file suit directly against the United States for the taking of their land. Instead, the only avenue was to persuade Congress to enact a "special jurisdictional act" that would waive sovereign immunity and give the Court of Claims authority to hear the tribes' case. Congress sometimes did respond to tribes in this fashion, but the legislators wanted to see plenty of documentary evidence and this process would take time—thirteen years in the case of Wasson and the three tribes. And even if the tribes proved that their land was wrongly taken,

George Bundy Wasson Sr., of Coquille/ Coos ancestry, spearheaded claims cases for coastal tribes. The results fell short of Wasson's and the tribes' objectives, but his use of litigation, in an era when few tribes were seeking relief in court, was a bold and creative stand for tribal rights. *Courtesy of the Wasson family.*

the Court of Claims could award only money damages. Congress had a firm policy against returning tribal lands.

The Coos, Siuslaw, and Lower Umpqua plea was straightforward and, if Congress gave the Court of Claims authority to hear it, seemed likely to be successful. The three tribes occupied portions of the Oregon Coast long before white people came. Under settled American law, as announced by Chief Justice John Marshall, the tribes owned those aboriginal lands. In the Coast Treaty of 1855, the tribes agreed to cede most of their lands to the United States and to move north to the Coast Reservation. Because the treaty went unratified, the tribes' land cession never went into effect and, legally, the tribes continued to own their aboriginal lands. The United States, however, ignored the tribal rights and opened the land for settlement and transfer to settlers. Therefore, the tribes' argument went, they should be entitled to monetary compensation for the loss. (Half a century later, some tribes, mostly in the East, successfully brought suits under similar circumstances to recover the land rather than monetary compensation. In Wasson's day, due to the legal community's lack of familiarity with Indian law, tribes were not advised of the possibility of getting back land.)

Wasson gave it everything he had. It was one thing to know—as all the Indians did—of the long-time tribal possession of the Oregon Coast and another to prove it to skeptical, uninterested federal officials 3,000 miles away. He went door-to-door, meeting with families, locating historical letters, photos, and papers, and writing down personal reminiscences. Although each leg took several days by rail, he made many trips to Washington, D.C., to present the facts to BIA officials, congressional staff, and legislators.

The Interior department actively fought the tribes' efforts. During the 1920s, assimilationist policies raged, with BIA Commissioner Charles Burke and consecutive secretaries Albert Fall and Hubert Work ordering the suppression of dances, healing ceremonies, giveaways, and other traditional customs. Work personally wrote to Congress and opposed bills that would grant the Coos, Siuslaw, and Lower Umpqua the right to be heard in court.

Finally, in 1929, Congress overrode Interior's opposition and agreed to allow the Court of Claims to hear the case, styled as *Coos Bay, Lower Umpqua, and Siuslaw Indians v. United States*. Now expenses would be higher since the tribes would be going to court; those families that could afford it pitched in five dollars a month.

The claims cases brought by western Oregon tribes would produce a number of judicial low points, and this first case was one of them. When the Claims Court decided the *Coos* case in 1938, the key evidence was court-administered testimony on aboriginal possession of land given by seventeen Coos, Siuslaw, and Lower Umpqua tribal elders in North Bend, Oregon, in 1931. With the long passage of time, most of them did not have personal memories of their homeland as it existed before 1855, but they all had learned from their elders and had themselves lived all or most of their lives on the south Coast in Indian societies. The witnesses offered detailed knowledge of hunting and fishing techniques, basket making, village locations and names, trade with other tribes, and other aspects of traditional life. They were clear on the specific areas each of the three tribes occupied. For example, several witnesses focused on the north boundary of the Coos, and southern reach of the Lower Umpqua, as Skayedgemitch or Ten Mile Lake. As James Buchanan, eighty-five years old and a member of the Coos Tribe, explained, "The biggest half of the lake is owned by the Coos Bay Indians. . . . The Lower Umpqua tribes own the other half of the *Skayedge* lake."

The oral testimony given by the elders was consistent with all existing knowledge and seemed to resolve the main issue in the case, whether the tribes occupied the land *before* contact with the whites. The court was sidetracked, however, and wrote mostly about events *after* aboriginal times: the unratified treaty of 1855, the removal north, the 1892 allotment agreement

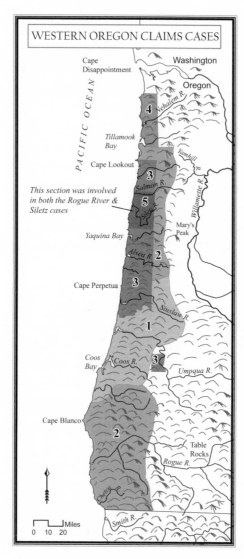

WESTERN OREGON CLAIMS CASES

Cape Disappointment

Washington

Oregon

PACIFIC OCEAN

Nehalem R.

4

Tillamook Bay

Cape Lookout

3

Salmon R.

Yamhill R.

This section was involved in both the Rogue River & Siletz cases

5

Siletz R.

Willamette R.

Mary's Peak

Yaquina Bay

Alsea R.

2

Cape Perpetua

3

Siuslaw R.

1

Coos Bay

Coos R.

3

Umpqua R.

Cape Blanco

2

Table Rocks

Rogue R.

Chetco R.

Miles
0 10 20

Smith R.

1. Coos, Lower Umpqua, and Siuslaw Indians v. United States
Tribes: Coos, Lower Umpqua, and Siuslaw
Year: 1938
Claim: Taking of aboriginal title
Award: None

2. Alcea Band of Tillamooks v. United States
Tribes: Chetco, Tututni, Coquille, Tillamooks
Year: 1950
Claim: Taking of aboriginal title
Award: $3.3 million ($520-3,200 per member)

3. Rogue River Tribe of Indians v. United States
Tribes: 27 western Oregon tribes and bands
Year: 1946 and 1950
Claim: Taking of Siletz (Coast) Reservation and Upper Umpqua-Kalapuya Reservation
Award: Rogue River and other tribes and bands for taking of Siletz (Coast) Reservation: $0
       Upper Umpqua, Kalapuya, and Molala Tribes: $342,450.

4. Tillamook Band of Tillamooks v. United States
Tribes: Tillamook and Nehalem Bands of Tillamooks
Year: 1955
Claim: Inadequate payment for taking of aboriginal lands
Award: Nehalem Band: $72,000; Tillamook Band: $97,000

5. Siletz Tribe of Indians v. United States
Tribes: Confederated Tribes of Siletz Indians
Year: 1959
Claim: Inadequate payment for "surplus lands" in allotment agreement
Award: $368,000 ($400 per member)

and statute in which the Siletz tribes ceded away most of the reservation, and recent intermarriage with other tribes. When the court opinion did turn to the crux of the *Coos* case—aboriginal possession—it described tribal possession in terms easily sufficient to support the tribes' case but then swept away the court's own conclusion with a single unsupported sentence:

> There is no doubt but that the plaintiff Indians established their villages along the coast, and subsisted primarily upon sea food, making infrequent excursions inland to procure berries and other products of the soil. They were decidedly peaceable and friendly Indians. Their bands were small in

number, never hostile nor practicing the savage customs of other tribes. *It is impossible to establish with any degree of certainty the location of these tribes prior to 1855.* (Emphasis added.)

Establishing the exact areas of aboriginal habitation should not have been a sticking point. Courts in Indian claims cases, often faced with difficulties in knowing precise tribal territories, have regularly set approximate boundaries. There seem to have been two core problems in the *Coos* case. First, the tribes produced no expert testimony by academics, which is normally required to prove ancient events, although the court could easily have made an exception since the United States had no basis for contesting the tribal occupation. Second was the court's ethnocentrism, unintended though it may have been. The opinion shows distrust of the tribal witnesses, and the several references to irrelevant post-1855 events suggest that the court may have believed that assimilation was taking its toll. This was the era of viewing the Indian as the "vanishing race," when tribes were supposedly disappearing, and the judges may have doubted the continuing existence of modern tribes.

In 1938, then, twenty-two years after George Wasson began his campaign, the Court of Claims rejected the elders' uncontradicted testimony, ruled that the Coos, Siuslaw, and Lower Umpqua tribes had failed to prove aboriginal title, and dismissed the case outright. The U.S. Supreme Court declined to review the decision, making it final.

Other western Oregon tribes were moved by Wasson's vision and work, especially after Congress passed the 1929 special jurisdictional act. The Tillamook, Coquille, Tututni, and Chetco, all signatories to the unratified 1855 treaty, were the next to pursue their own claims cases. They, too, were bucked by the administration in their effort to obtain a special jurisdictional act from Congress, even though the climate in Washington had changed for the better. President Herbert Hoover—influenced by the Meriam Commission Report of 1928, which recommended broad-based reforms of Indian policy—promised a new direction for Indian Affairs and appointed Charles Rhoads, a respected Philadelphia banker and Quaker, as commissioner of the BIA. Rhoads did bring some fresh air to the agency but it was of no use to the Oregon tribes. He fought the Tillamook, Coquille, Tututni, and Chetco claims with the same vehemence that his predecessors had opposed those of the Coos, Siuslaw, and Lower Umpqua.

The tribes hit a roadblock in 1931 when Congress failed to override Interior's opposition. A year later, Congress did pass the bill in spite of the department's position, but Wasson and the tribes came up short at the White House. Professing that "I want full justice for our Indian wards," President Hoover nonetheless levied a veto, citing technical grounds. Very likely the real reason for trumping justice for Indians lay in the last sentence of Hoover's veto statement on April 25, 1932: "I am further constrained to this action at a time when the Government cannot assume additional and unknown burdens of expenditure." As it turned out, that specter of large money payments, all from the public fisc, later played on the minds of judges as well.

When Franklin Roosevelt took office in 1933, the BIA under John Collier—a staunch advocate for tribal sovereignty and culture—moved far beyond the modest advances of the Hoover years. Now equity for the tribes might have a chance of rising above fiscal concerns. With Interior department and presidential support for the claim, Wasson succeeded in obtaining a special jurisdictional act from Congress, signed by the president, in 1935.

The Tillamooks, Coquilles, Tututnis, and Chetcoes promptly filed suit in the Court of Claims. The case was titled *Alcea Band of Tillamooks v. United States*, even though there is no Alcea Band of Tillamooks (the Alseas are a separate tribe). The *Alcea* case, while it suffered one setback of gigantic proportions, would nevertheless be the most successful of all the western Oregon land claim cases.

As a starting point, there was every reason to believe that the *Alcea* case would suffer the same fate as the *Coos* case. These tribes had the same theory—that aboriginal lands ceded and opened for settlement should be compensated—and the aboriginal territories of the several tribes in the two cases lay next to each other along the Coast. In addition, all were parties to the unratified 1855 Coast Treaty. If the proof of aboriginal title in the first case was insufficient, then how could the result be any different in the second?

The 1945 Court of Claims opinion by Judge Littleton, who had supported the dismissal of the *Coos* case, found that the attorneys for the tribes in the *Alcea* case had submitted "a great deal more and much stronger evidence." The decisive information was the testimony of Dr. John P. Harrington, a respected ethnologist in the Bureau of American Ethnology. Harrington had no doubt about the tribes' aboriginal possession and testified that "beyond any shadow of a doubt . . . these tribes and bands of Indians which fringed the Coast were the ancient and original inhabitants, and . . . have been to all intents and purposes where they were at the dawn of history." The Supreme Court affirmed the Court of Claims decision.

Harrington's words served the tribes in the *Alcea* case well but delivered a galling message to the tribes in the *Coos* case: however accurate oral tradition may be, courts were (and to a lesser extent still are) moved, not by the knowledge of tribal elders but by the opinions of experts as defined by the larger society. The realization that, not for the first time, the two sources of information stood in full agreement on the aboriginal history of the Oregon Coast came too late for the Coos, Umpqua, and Siuslaw.

"INDIANS WIN LAND CLAIM OF $16,515,604" screamed the *Oregonian* headline on January 4, 1950. The Court of Claims, having decided the foundational question of whether the Alcea tribes had land title, took evidence on the value of the 2,773,000 acres owned by these four tribes and taken by the United States. The total land value as of 1855, when the taking occurred, was about $3.3 million. The far greater amount of the award accrued from interest, at the rate of 5 percent from 1855 to 1934 and 4 percent from 1934 to 1950.

Attacking the interest award of $13.2 million, the government took the case to the Supreme Court on an issue that had never been decided. Courts had always held that for government takings of "recognized" Indian title—land guaranteed by a statute or ratified treaty—tribes were entitled to interest. But the claim in *Alcea* was for the loss of the tribes' "right of occupancy," which had existed since time immemorial but had never been recognized by a ratified treaty. As explained in Chief Justice John Marshall's opinions, that long possession had always been considered in federal law as a kind of land title.

The government argued that the right of occupancy is not as high a property interest as "recognized" title. In a tactic that has been criticized as overly zealous but that may well have swayed the court, the attorney general—representing the tribes' trustee, the United States—made this incendiary assertion without any support: "It is hardly likely that Congress would deliberately provide, in this and related Indian legislation, for interest payments to Indians which are likely to exceed the sums proposed by the President, in his recent budget message, for foreign military and economic assistance."

"INDIANS TO LOSE INTEREST ON CLAIMS DATING TO 1855," the *Oregonian* announced on April 10, 1951, after the Supreme Court denied interest—and reduced the total award from $16.5 million to $3.3 million— in a superficial, three-paragraph opinion. The tribes were awarded (after attorneys fees and various off-sets) $960,000 (Tillamook and Alsea), $625,000 (Coquille), $321,000 (Tututni), and $353,000 (Chetco), with

'Now Can I Go to Harvard?'

The optimism in this 1946 cartoon would be dashed five years later. *Courtesy of* The Oregonian.

individual tribal members to receive $3,200 (Tillamook), $2,100 (Coquille), $425 (Tututni), and $520 (Chetco).

The *Oregonian* called the payments a "windfall" and undoubtedly many of the newspaper's readers saw it that way. For the tribes, wounded by the reduction of the award, it was partial justice only but, after many sterile decades, at least some justice. At Siletz, members held celebratory salmon bakes with dancing and partying. For nearly everyone, the payments salved the poverty, although the money did not last long. George Bundy Wasson, who passed on in 1947, lived to read the first *Alcea* decision upholding the aboriginal land title, but not the 1951 decision striking down most of the award.

Numerous land claims cases were inevitable given the many separate ethnological tribes, treaties, and takings of land. A third major case, *Rogue River Tribe of Indians v. United States*, also went to the Court of Claims on a special jurisdictional act of 1935 (yet more work of George Bundy Wasson). This comprehensive litigation, with twenty-seven tribes and bands as plaintiffs, was an effort to recover fair compensation for many violations of the seven ratified treaties signed between 1853 and 1855. Most important, the tribes sought compensation for the land grabs that took more than three-quarters of the Coast Reservation in 1865 and 1875.

In 1946 and 1950, the Court of Claims handed down opinions, both authored by Judge Marvin Jones, in the *Rogue River* case. The court addressed rights under the Treaty of November 29, 1854, which set aside 67,820 acres "as a reservation" for bands of Umpquas and Kalapuyas in the Upper Umpqua River watershed not far from the California-Oregon Trail. The treaty did not describe the reservation as "permanent" but the court treated it as such, following the rule that tribes receive the benefit of the doubt in construing Indian treaties. The tribes had been removed from the reservation in December 1855, and the claim was brought to recover compensation for the taking of the land. In determining the value of the reservation, the court found that "in 1855 this reservation was located in an area where settlements on its edges were thriving and increasing in population. There was a demand for the agricultural products and the timber of this area." Tribal witnesses set the 1855 value at $4.00–$5.00 per acre, while government appraisals estimated the value at less than 10 cents per acre. The Court of Claims ruled that the land was worth one dollar per acre, a total of $67,820. With interest at 5 percent from December 1855, the award was $342,450, so that Upper Umpqua and Kalapuya tribal members received several hundred dollars apiece.

The Molala Tribe, another party in the *Rogue River Tribe* case, agreed in its treaty of December 21, 1855, to confederate with the tribes of the Umpqua and Kalapuya and to settle on that reservation. The Molala award, which was based on a proportionate share of the Umpqua and Kalapuya award, came to $34,996.

Whether the Umpqua, Kalapuya, and Molala received a fair return for the loss of their reservation is difficult to ascertain from our vantage point a century and a half later. The value of one dollar per acre for western Oregon timberland, even as of 1855, seems suspiciously low, but the opinion did present what appeared to be a thorough discussion of timber, farm, and range values at that time. The remainder of the case, dealing with most of the tribes in the *Rogue River* litigation, is much harder to swallow and stands with the *Coos* case as an archetype for the legalisms and inequities that all too often afflicted Indian claims litigation.

No award at all was made to the "Rogue River Tribe" of the Table Rock Treaty of 1853; the Cow Creek Band of Umpquas under its 1853 treaty; the

Shastas, Scotons, and Grave Creek Band of Umpquas of the 1854 treaty; and the several tribes and bands in the Confederated Bands of the Willamette Valley Treaty of 1855. Under the Table Rock Treaty, and the others as well, tribes held "temporary" reservations until they were removed to "permanent residences." The language means that the temporary reservations remained in full force until the president declared a permanent reservation. The court should have acknowledged, as a result of the treaties and executive orders by Presidents Pierce and Buchanan, that the Siletz and Grand Ronde reservations were permanent and awarded to the tribes the value of any land taken, plus interest. Instead, with no analysis, Judge Jones wrote that recognizing the tribes' vested rights in the land would amount to this:

> The Coast or Siletz Reservation contained 2,000 square miles of territory. To sustain the contention that simply because tribes comprising a few hundred Indians were permitted to occupy this reservation under an Executive order they acquired a full title to this immense tract of land would be an extreme interpretation of the obligations of the United States Government toward the Indian. It would be as if the owner of a large ranch should tell one of his employees he was ultimately going to provide a home for him and that in the meantime he could reside at the ranch headquarters. Surely no one would contend that the employee acquired a vested interest in the entire ranch.

There is no mooring for this radical "ranch hand" proposition. The courts have always recognized tribal ownership of treaty lands, which the Coast and Grand Ronde reservation lands were, and acknowledged that tribes are entitled to be compensated under the Fifth Amendment when treaty lands are taken. Even aboriginal lands, which have fewer legal protections in American law, were owned by the tribes, who were not remotely akin to "employees of a large ranch." As Chief Justice Marshall ruled, the tribes "were admitted to be the rightful occupants of the soil, with a legal as well as just claim to retain possession of it, and to use it according to their own discretion."

Judge Jones's characterization may have stemmed from ignorance or venality, or his argument that the tribes had no ownership interest in the Coast Reservation may have reflected the Court of Claims' resolve to protect the federal budget. If the court acknowledged the treaty status of the Coast Reservation, the tribes would be entitled to extremely high damages—plus interest—for the breakup of the 1.1-million-acre reservation.

Whatever the reason, Judge Jones demeaned the tribal plaintiffs and their legal rights with his wholly unsupported characterization of Indian people as ephemeral ranch hands on their ancestral homelands. By labeling them as supplicants before the court, his words poisoned this and other proceedings by denigrating the solemnity and legitimacy of the proceedings at Table Rock in 1853 and other treaty sites. As a result, the summary elimination of the temporary reservations in the 1850s, the strong-arm marches to new lands, and the rakings of the Coast Reservation in 1865 and 1875 were never vindicated, not by an acre, not by a penny.

The court did find that the Rogue River Tribe and the others were entitled to recover several thousand dollars in damages for payments and services provided for in the treaties but never made. Even those crumbs were denied by virtue of the "gratuitous offsets" doctrine, creating deductions against the tribal award, a legal rule that was much discredited and later abandoned. But the order of the day was to calculate the government's services to the tribes, with the Court of Claims then subtracting from the tribal awards the value of health and education services, administrative expenses, clothing, tools, farm implements, housing, and the like that the government had provided to tribal members over the years.

The gratuitous offsets doctrine diminished most of the Oregon claims awards. These "gratuitous" services for western Oregon Indians in fact had been carried out in accordance with the government's trust duties that flowed from the treaties, a necessary part of the "Great Father's" promises to help Indian people make the difficult transition to a new way of life. Overall, to give a sense of the magnitude of these offsets, during the years that the western Oregon tribes had cases before the Court of Claims, total awards nationally were approximately $49 million; gratuitous offsets amounted to $29 million, reducing recoveries by nearly 60 percent. So the tribes in the *Rogue River Tribe* case were told that the gratuities "equal" their awards and "there is no balance due them for which judgment can be awarded and as to them the petition is dismissed." The Supreme Court denied review. There were no salmon bakes on the Oregon Coast.

In 1946, in an effort to improve the unwieldy process of special jurisdiction acts, Congress passed the Indian Claims Commission Act. Rather than seeking congressional approval, tribes now had five years to file suits for money damages directly with the newly created Indian Claims Commission for any land disputes that had not been taken to the Court of Claims. Gratuitous off-sets were sharply curtailed, and other progressive provisions were included, such as the broad invitation to file "claims based upon fair and honorable dealings that are not recognized by any existing rule of law or equity."

The Indian claims legislation was heralded by President Harry S Truman as a gracious measure that would mark the dawn of "a new era for our Indian citizens." It would resolve, he predicted, all the age-old grievances and put the tribes on a level playing field "without special handicaps or special advantages." The improved system did bring financial benefits to some tribes but it did not do away with the essential problems as perceived by the tribes. Return of land, their real objective, remained off the table. The clunky, legalistic machinery slowly ground along, often for decades. Further, the 1946 claims legislation had a dark underside: by settling accounts with the Indians, the thinking went, the nation had laid the moral foundation for termination, for finally resolving the "Indian problem." For Siletz and other Indian people, this "new era" with no "special advantages" would mean a program for selling off the reservations.

By the time the act went into effect, most western Oregon Indian claims had already been filed with the Court of Claims, but two remaining cases went to the Indian Claims Commission. The Tillamook and Nehalem bands of Tillamooks had been parties to an 1851 treaty with the United States, negotiated by Anson Dart. The treaty was never ratified but the Tillamooks moved off the land, about 224,000 acres, which was then opened for homesteading. The treaty called for payments to the bands, and the United States made those payments, but they were less than the value of the land. The ICC awarded $72,000 to the Nehalem Band and $97,000 to the Tillamook Band.

Since any recourse for the 1865 and 1875 reservation takings had been scuttled by the *Rogue River* case, the Confederated Tribes of Siletz Indians brought a claim based on the 1894 Allotment Act, which had opened most of the remaining reservation lands—more than 170,000 acres—to settlement as surplus lands. At the time, the tribe was paid $142,600, but the ICC found that amount "unconscionable." Although the 1894 act was passed before timber prices soared in the early twentieth century, the Siletz forest still had commercial potential—just as tribal leaders had argued to the commissioners at the ill-fated council meetings in 1892. The ICC valued the land at $3.00 per acre, a total of $575,400. Less the $142,600 already paid, the award came to $432,800. It was later reduced by attorneys' and witness' fees to $368,000. Tribal members received checks for $400.

The long, drawn-out claims struggle left Siletz tribal members with a bitter brew of confusion, resentment, and dashed hopes. Indian people initially saw the claims process as a noble crusade for redemption—and, in many minds, impossible though it was, for a return of land. Government administrators, legislators, judges, and lawyers treated the claims as a fiscal accounting chore, and a minor, tedious one at that, with the objective being to hammer and peck away at the tribes' requests so as to keep the commitment of federal dollars to a rock-bottom minimum. Archie Ben was one of many tribal leaders who did what he could to rectify the "unconscionable" payment made for gutting the Siletz Reservation in 1894. His son, Ed, described his father's view, which represented the general sentiment at Siletz:

> My father spent much of his life working on the claims decisions. Finally, when the money was handed out the Indians only ended up with about $400 a person. The lawyers took their cut, the government took their cut, and the Indians ended up with nothing. This was really a slap in the face for my father.

Over roughly the same time span, another branch of federal policy drew tribes into debates and decisions over tribalism and land. The Indian Reorganization Act, like the claims cases, would be marked by complexity and misunderstanding and it, too, would leave little other than a bitter brew.

After generations of hard-line assimilationist policies aimed at ending the so-called Indian problem by eliminating tribal cultures, a shift began to take place in the late 1920s. The blue-ribbon Meriam Commission, sponsored by the Institute for Governmental Research (known as the Brookings Institution), blasted allotment, detailed how it had decimated the tribal land base, and urged that the policy be abandoned. The commission also recommended reforms in education, health, and economic policy, proposing, for example, that schools show "more understanding of and sympathy for the Indian point of view." The Hoover Administration responded by taking limited measures, but with the election of Franklin Roosevelt in 1932 came the appointment of BIA Commissioner John Collier, a social worker and outspoken defender of the rights of the Pueblo Indians of the Southwest. Collier was the first true Indian advocate to hold the office of commissioner.

The driven, idealistic Collier, who sometimes got out in front of both congressional and tribal opinion, promptly put together a comprehensive reform package, his proposed Indian Reorganization Act. With support from the president and Secretary Harold Ickes, the bill was put before the Congress and also became known as the Wheeler-Howard Act after its primary congressional sponsors, Senator Burton K. Wheeler of Montana and Representative Edgar Howard of Nebraska. A major purpose of the IRA bill was to encourage tribes to exercise greater self-governance by adopting constitutions and corporate charters. Collier also proposed to bring allotment to an end but coupled it with two especially controversial provisions aimed at tribalizing existing allotments: the Interior secretary would be allowed to transfer Indian allotments to the tribes to help consolidate tribal land bases; further, when allottees died, their allotments would pass to the tribes. The forty-eight-page IRA bill met with congressional objections—especially, even though he was a sponsor, from Senator Wheeler, chair of the Senate Indian Affairs Committee—and drew concern from some tribal leaders as well. Legislators and Indians alike worried over the sweeping nature of the measure and looked askance at the procedures for tribalizing individual allotments."

Convinced that the tribes would support the bill, Collier took an unprecedented step. He scheduled ten regional meetings—"congresses," he called them—so that Indians across the country could comment. The United States government had never before shown such solicitude for tribal opinion. His decision to include tribes in the legislative process was, as Vine Deloria Jr. and Clifford Lytle termed it, "a radical step" and it made a difference, for amendments to the IRA draft bill traced in part to the Indian voices expressed at the congresses.

The congress for the Northwest tribes was held at Chemawa Indian School on March 8 and 9, 1934, and attended by some five hundred Indians, split about equally between those in favor and those against the bill. Respect for Collier was accompanied by distrust of the government and confusion over the provisions of the bill. Several Siletz tribal members participated. Abe Logan—speaking through a translator, as did many of the participants—was positive: "What I have heard from you gentlemen seems to please me. I am going home now to my mother who is over 90 years old and the younger people and tell them all that you have said." Both Coquelle ("Tom") Thompson Jr. (son of Coquelle Thompson) and Elwood Towner, the Siletz tribal member and lawyer, also supported the proposal. George Wasson, who had already endured nearly two frustrating decades on the *Coos* claims, was skeptical. Pointing out that the government's much-heralded General Allotment Act had wrought so much suffering, Wasson asked what his children and grandchildren could expect in the future: "Will another commissioner come out from the seat of government and tell them this community system is a failure [?]"

After the congresses, the IRA bill went back to Capitol Hill for reworking. The amendments included deleting the provisions for transferring allotments from individual owners back to the tribes. When the bill passed later in 1934, the heart of the Indian Reorganization Act remained the same: allotment was brought to an end and tribes could elect whether to organize under the IRA by adopting federally approved constitutions and business charters.

The Siletz took up the question of whether to adopt an IRA constitution in an atmosphere of apprehension, distrust, and a sense of powerlessness. At one meeting, "Tom" Thompson acknowledged the doubts among his people. "I've noticed in these meetings, we find people who jump up and say: 'We can't do that.' But have you really tried? Be frank with yourself. Have you? In your own home where your minor governing problems come up, have you ever tried?" He also raised the specter of federal withdrawal and argued that exercising IRA self-determination would ease the transition that loomed: "In time, when we are ready to be turned loose to walk for ourselves and speak for ourselves, we will be familiar with the laws on the outside and we can carry on. I know you are asking: 'Will there be any such day when we will be turned loose?' We do not know but suppose there is, will we be capable of taking care of ourselves?"

The IRA question coincided with the gestation of several claims cases. The two were not related—organizing under the IRA would not affect the claims—but the conjunction of the two muddied the waters. Bensell Orton was one of many who showed concern: "Uncle Sam has to fulfill his promise and settle up with this treaty business. . . . I think we should put this [IRA constitution] off for a while and let them tend to this treaty business first." Another confounding matter was the bill's original language—later stricken—calling for the transfer of some allotments to the tribe. As with allottees from other tribes, Siletz allotment holders opposed those provisions, and that controversial proposal, even though not included on the IRA as passed, clouded the later vote on organizing under the IRA.

Support for the IRA never came together at Siletz. Attorney Elwood Towner, for example, vacillated on the issue. He spoke for it at the Chemawa congress and after a visit from John Collier, but on election day, according to sub-agency Superintendent Ryan, he "talked against the Bill, and it is believed that his arguments swayed a large number of votes against the bill." In a larger

Coquelle ("Tom") Thompson, pictured here on the left in 1951, was a tribal leader from the 1930s through the 1950s. *Courtesy of Reggie Butler.*

sense, as Robert Kentta explained in *The First Oregonians*, "the Siletz people were afraid" of the IRA because of the original allotment provisions and because "it was difficult to trust the legislation's positive intentions after so many devastating laws had been passed against tribal people."

On April 6, 1935, Siletz tribal members voted against organizing under the IRA by a vote of 123 to 109. That count exaggerated the actual pro-IRA sentiment: 55 eligible voters did not vote but, under BIA rules, non-voters were counted as votes in favor.

In retrospect, while the episode gives insights into tribal attitudes in the 1930s, the Siletz vote on whether or not to adopt an IRA constitution was of little consequence to tribal affairs. True, tribal members vigorously debated it and, along with other tribes, treated it as a major issue. How could it be otherwise? The BIA trumpeted the importance of IRA constitutions, and Indian people knew from long and unhappy experience that policies from distant Washington could reap large consequences for Indian land, governance, and day-to-day life. Nevertheless, for the Siletz, the matter of adopting an IRA constitution paled in comparison with the IRA's historic rejection of allotment and the prosecution of the claims cases. Tribes possessed their own sovereignty with or without an IRA constitution. The IRA and Secretary Collier encouraged tribes to spread their wings, but IRA constitutions created no new tribal powers. The real question was how active a tribe would be, under the IRA or otherwise, in exercising its inherent right of self-determination.

While there was no magic to an IRA constitution, the tribe did suffer some disadvantages from the lack of a written governing document. In 1940, BIA officials held a lengthy open meeting with an estimated 175 tribal members to discuss problems with federally funded programs. In particular, the Civilian Conservation Corps had funded useful community projects and provided badly needed jobs in the thick of the Depression. The BIA discontinued funding to Siletz for the CCC and other projects because different groups at Siletz expressed conflicting preferences. As Superintendent Earl Woodridge told the group, "We have been continually faced with unreasonable demands from individual Indians and from the Business Committee. . . . My own thought . . . is that the Siletz people are not properly organized to present their views."

Tribal members, however, had organized, although not in the form the BIA wanted. They held community meetings and, following the traditional residential pattern, selected seven representatives—four from the town of Siletz, and one each from Upper Farm, Lower Farm, and Salmon River. Tom Thompson emphasized to Collier that "you may be assured that the Indians of Siletz will be represented from among their own numbers and by people of their own choosing."

Federal officials would not accept that. The whole tribe—including members in the Willamette Valley and beyond—needed to vote. Further, it was essential that the tribe be "organized," that is, that it have "an approved [by the BIA] constitution and by-laws." The constitution, the officials emphasized, did not have to be an IRA constitution, but there had to be a constitution—some organization acceptable to the BIA—if the funding were to be resumed.

Tribal people, who had governed themselves for millennia without written documents, had questions that went to both definitional details and philosophical precepts. Fay Fitzpatrick asked, "What do you mean when you say that you want them to organize? The Indians here as a tribe are all together." After further discussion, Elmer Logan returned to the premise. "I don't think that mine or Mrs. Fitzpatrick's question was answered fully. Explain what you mean by properly organizing. I don't think that you should come out here and say that we are not properly organized. We have our own committee that was elected by us. Please explain this—just what do you mean by properly organized [?]"

The government men could see that they and the Indians were at loggerheads. Realizing that a written constitution was not in the cards and coping the best they could within their institutional constraints, they presented to the group resolutions approving the work programs so that, failing the desired "organization," at least the pressing issue of jobs could be addressed. "How many

Tribal member and attorney Elwood Towner, on the left, was influential during the claims process, Indian Reorganization debate, and termination deliberations. As for termination, he seemed supportive of the idea at first but later changed his opinion. *Courtesy of Oregon Historical Society, no. bb006225.*

Elmer Logan served on the Siletz Tribal Council during the late 1940s and early 1950s, when pressure for termination grew ever more intense. *Siletz Tribal Collection.*

of you would like to express your opinion today on these things? All those who want to vote, or express themselves, today please raise your right hand."

But the weight of history was too great. The tribe had already organized in its own way. The Siletz were suspicious for good reason and had been for generations. Neither their regard for John Collier nor the balm of jobs could erase that. The majority refused to raise their right hands, knowing that the proposal would go down and the programs would likely go unfunded.

As it turned out, their intransigence did not cost the Siletz in the way that the BIA threatened. Probably due to a reluctance to deny good programs to people who so badly needed them, federal officials apparently restored the funding in question and kept levels fairly constant. From the Indian side, the reluctance continued. Several years later, in 1949, the tribe voted down another proposed tribal constitution.

The votes on proposed constitutions exemplified how far sovereignty in western Oregon had sunk since aboriginal times, when villages governed themselves according to established norms and customs. By the middle of the twentieth century, the Siletz were left with the least of governmental powers—the right to say no to documents that amounted to little more than paperwork. BIA suppression had gone on so long and was so embedded in the agency's culture that sovereignty—and its synonyms of self-governance and self-determination—lay nearly inert. The BIA ran the reservations and the IRA, with all its good intentions, did little to change that. At Siletz and else-where, the movement to regain sovereignty would not begin to gain traction until the 1970s.

The bright promise of the John Collier years quickly dimmed. In 1939, the Senate Committee on Indian Affairs sharply criticized Collier's emphasis on tribalism and reiterated complaints that his approach amounted to communism. In 1943, a subcommittee advocated the end of the reservation system and an outright withdrawal of federal support to Indians. A year later, the Portland area office of the BIA issued a ten-year plan for the Siletz Reservation that called for "decreasing Government assistance during the next ten years" and—invoking the term that would become official federal policy a decade later—"final termination of such help at the end of that time." Cut off in every direction, Collier resigned in 1945.

World War II brought increased, although short-term, economic benefits to Siletz. Lincoln County timber production jumped in support of the war effort. Local shipyards, including the Siletz Boat Works in Kernville, went into operation and some Siletz men and women found employment in the mammoth shipyards in Portland and Vancouver, Washington. A few tribal members staffed a lookout tower in Siletz and scouted the horizon for Japanese air attacks. The income for these war years was the highest ever for tribal members.

Much has been written about the extraordinary wartime response of American Indians, who in the twentieth century served in the military at a rate three times higher than the general population. They also served with distinction. General Douglas MacArthur observed that "as a warrior the Indian's fame is world wide," and another general stated that the Native American was "the best damn soldier in the Army" due in part to his "imperturbability." In Indian country, the high rates of enlistment and quality of service are a source of enormous pride.

All of this was true at Siletz. In World War I, seventeen Siletz men enlisted. In World War II, forty-eight served, probably more than one-third of the adult males. Among tribal members, military service in wartime may well be the highest honor of all.

Upon returning home from the war, the veterans, and their fellow tribespeople as well, faced difficult circumstances. The claims cases were grinding toward mostly dismal endings. Nearly all of the land was gone, and, save for the timber industry, jobs were scarce. Houses were dilapidated and eighty families were homeless. Discrimination stifled individual progress.

None of that gave pause to the advocates of termination. It would be simple. The Congress would pronounce the Siletz and other tribes in similarly dire circumstances self-sufficient—fully ready to be cut off from all federal recognition and support—and then terminate them by statutes that would sell the reservation land and eradicate the treaties once and for all. It would, they intoned, be fair. With exquisite cynicism, the architect of termination, Senator Arthur V. Watkins from Utah, wrote that the woefully inadequate claims process, which had so little to do with morality, would be used as a moral validation for the false freedom of a new policy: "a basic purpose of Congress in setting up the Indian Claims Commission was to clear the way toward complete freedom of the Indians by assuring a final settlement of all obligations—real or purported—of the federal government to the Indian tribes."

THE SILETZ VETERANS OF WORLD WAR I

U.S. Army: Edward Charley • Leonard Evans • James Logan • Tony Reed • Darvin Watts • Paul Washington • Edward Felix (1st & 2nd) • Lee Evans • Abeson Logan • Elmer Reed • Fredrick Simmons • Louis Towner • Andrew (Gippy) Washington

U.S. Navy: Archie Lane • Marvin Downey • Alfred Lane

U.S. Marine Corp.: Gilbert L. (Buster) Towner

THE SILETZ VETERANS OF WORLD WAR II

U.S. Army: Calvin Bell • Everett (Gabby) Butler Sr. • Ernest (Fatty) Chapman • Edward (Booty) Charley Jr. • Griffin John • William Lane • Sidney Lawson • David (Sam) Martin • Lawrence Orton • Clayton Pond • Randolph Strong • Edgar Williams • Willie Williams • Chester Butler • Eddie Collins • Maxwell Collins • Everett (Buck) Downey • Louis (Dinky) Klamath • Joe Lane Sr., • Manuel Lawson • Alfred Pond • Manuel Rilatos • Harding Simmons • Albert (Tootsel) Reed • Byron Strong • Stanley Strong (and Navy)

U.S. Navy: Edmond Ben • James (Phumps) Blacketer • Bennie Brown Sr. • Alfred Lane Jr. • Edward (Ochie) Rilatos • Phillip Rilatos • Alfred Kekua • Herman Bell (and Coast Guard) • Eddie Bensell • Fritz Chapman • Lindsey John • Joseph (Sharp) Williams • Joseph (Dugan) McCoy

U.S. Air Force: William (Bill Buck) Batise • William Towner

U.S. Marine Corp.: Floyd Day • Kenneth Blacketer • Leonard Logan • Donald Bellinger • Larkie Logan Sr. • Elwood Towner

---

TERMINATION

"Historic Indian policy has been swept away.
Assimilation must be the goal."

FEDERAL INDIAN POLICY ALWAYS HAS BEEN CHARACTERIZED BY the tension between two broad and opposing ideas—separatism and assimilation. Initially, separatism dominated. Witness the original "Indian Country" beyond the Appalachians with the line steadily moved west and, later, the Coast Reservation, both assumed to be for Indians only, beyond the needs of the settlers. After the Civil War, the government moved to assimilation, epitomized by "No Indian Talk" boarding schools and allotment, which opened many reservations for settlement by non-Indians. Beginning in the 1970s, Congress adopted the self-determination policy, based on a measured separatism in which tribes are the principal, although not exclusive, governments on the reservations. In between the boarding school–allotment version of assimilation and modern self-determination—roughly from the mid-1940s through the 1960s—lay the most extreme form of assimilationist policy: termination. Congress would not just encourage assimilation but force it by eliminating the reservations and breaking up tribal communities.

Termination can be defined simply—an end of all reservations, federal obligations, and tribal sovereign rights, including those promised by treaties. Termination's specific provisions and impacts—and the ethos—cannot be explained so easily. In fact, perhaps the single most distinguishing feature of termination is that when Congress began passing termination acts in 1954—the Siletz statute was in the first wave—the new policy was a generality, not much more than a slogan. Indian people had no realization of what it meant. The same was true for most, perhaps all, of the federal leaders and employees who worked on termination—members of Congress and Interior department officials in the Washington, D.C., and regional officers who failed to do any serious examination of history, culture, or economics. For all concerned, it was an experiment dreamed up in the dark.

Understanding of the real meaning of termination set in as the fourteen termination laws—covering 109 tribes and bands, 11,466 individuals (about 3 percent of all Indians), and 1,362,000 acres (3.2 percent of Indian land)—went into effect and took hold. Tribal land was sold off, and individual allotments, released by termination from the Indian Reorganization Act's ban against allotment transfers, once again went on the market and passed from Indian hands. Communities broke up and dispersed. Economic and social conditions worsened. In the 1960s, as the tribes that escaped termination began asserting their sovereignty and hunting, fishing and water rights, terminated tribes were left on the sidelines. And, immeasurable but all too real, members of terminated tribes felt a profound pain as termination ruptured tribal ties and slashed their very sense of personal identity. As one terminated Oregon Indian agonized, "I mean, even the [other] tribes looked at us as, 'You're not Indian any more.' And that's basically what the Termination Act said, 'They will no longer be Indians.' How do you deal with that?"

E. Morgan Pryse arrived in Portland in 1946 as the new BIA district director for Oregon, Washington, and Idaho. A veteran BIA employee, he started his career at the Klamath Reservation in 1920 and made several stops before being promoted to district director. From the beginning Pryse was enthusiastic about cutting off federal responsibilities to the Siletz. Severing relations with tribes was emerging as the basic departmental policy; the idea made sense to Pryse as a general matter and the Siletz, as an essentially landless tribe, was a logical candidate. While the tribe's termination may have been inevitable, Pryse was the one who made the case.

He had a good foundation to build on. Commissioner John Collier's promotion of tribalism and federal trust duties had made him few friends on Capitol Hill. Beginning in the early 1940s, various committees and individual members of Congress proposed shutting down Indian health and education programs, removing Indian lands from trust status, and virtually eliminating the BIA—termination in everything but name—and called for the "emancipation" of Indians from BIA control and the removal of Indian land from trust. With pressure building, one of the clearest examples of the shift in federal policy was the testimony of acting BIA Commissioner William Zimmerman before a Senate committee in 1947. Zimmerman, a Collier loyalist required by duty to respond to the committee's directive, identified tribes for which BIA services could be eliminated. He also specified four criteria that Congress might use in identifying tribes for termination: (1) degree of acculturation; (2) economic resources and condition of the tribe; (3) willingness of the tribe to be relieved of federal control; and (4) willingness of the state to assume jurisdiction. While Zimmerman did not intend it as such, termination advocates proceeded to use his "plan" as a blueprint.

In addition to the mood in Washington, Morgan Pryse also enjoyed favorable conditions in Oregon. Two years before being named district director, his predecessor had prepared a detailed ten-year program for the Siletz that served as a useful precedent. The 1944 document set an ultimate goal: "Decreasing government assistance during the next ten years and final termination of such help at the end of that time." It appears that this was the first time that the word "termination" was used, at Siletz or elsewhere, to describe federal Indian policy. U.S. Senator Guy Cordon of Oregon offered assistance on withdrawal of federal services at Siletz as early as 1947 and Governor Douglas McKay, who took office in 1948, supported termination.

With gusto, Pryse set about the job of laying the foundation for Siletz termination legislation. Within a few months after arriving in Oregon, he took up the matter of closing the short-staffed Grand Ronde–Siletz agency administered out of an office at Chemawa Indian School and then shut it down in 1947, shifting the work to the Portland office. In 1948, Pryse announced a major initiative, giving notice of meetings with committees of every tribe in the district "to determine when the federal government may withdraw its supervision and turn over Indian property, etc. to the tribes." He would later tell Congress that he "spent much of his own time on Saturdays and Sundays from 1948 to the present [1953] in meeting with various Indian groups, county and State officials in proposing withdrawal of the Indian Service over affairs of the western Oregon Indians." Tribal consent was considered important, though not essential, to termination and the Siletz Tribal Council minutes show that he did often attend the meetings. He may, though, have spent little time in one-on-one or small group meetings. Tribal council member Dan Orton complained to Senator Cordon of "Morgan Pryse who has never been in our Indian homes at Siletz."

There are no known photographs of E. Morgan Pryse at Siletz. Here, he is shown making an argument for termination at the Lummi Reservation in Washington, where termination legislation was never introduced. The stilted, uncomfortable atmosphere prevailed at Siletz also. *National Archives and Records Administration, Pacific Alaska Region (Seattle), RG 75 BIA, Portland Area Office, Tribal Operations Branch, General Subject Files, ca. 1934–1951 (George P. LaVatta) Box 1511.*

The decisive year was 1950, which saw an alignment of interests in Washington, Portland, and Siletz. Policy hardened, and termination was just a matter of time.

In the years leading up to 1950, federal policy was a blend of John Collier's commitment to tribalism and some form of reasonably rapid assimilation. In addition to the calls issuing from members of Congress for federal withdrawal, the 1948 report of the influential Hoover Commission, chaired by the former president and charged with examining governmental efficiency in light of post-war needs, addressed Indian policy and found that "the basis for historic Indian culture has been swept away. . . . Assimilation must be the dominant goal of public policy." Yet no Indian reform legislation was introduced, much less passed.

The Interior department was of two minds. William Brophy, appointed commissioner in 1945, sympathized with Collier's views but, to appease the changing sentiments in Congress, acknowledged withdrawal as a long-term goal. He took ill early in his term, assigned many duties to Zimmerman, his top assistant, and left office in June 1947. Zimmerman—like Brophy, caught in the middle—continued as acting commissioner until the appointment in March 1949 of John Nichols, who held the post for less than a year and made no mark. The Bureau of Indian Affairs had been rudderless for half a decade.

That changed abruptly on May 5, 1950, when Dillon S. Myer, a Truman appointee, took over as commissioner. Lacking any background in Indian matters, his calling card was his service as director of the War Relocation Authority, the detention camp system for Japanese Americans during World War II. Myer was honest and known for his diligence and efficiency: he knew how to set a mission, hire the right people, and push resolutely to achieve his goals. Always the hard charger, the new commissioner had received sharp criticism on civil liberties grounds during his WRA years for his treatment of Japanese Americans—who were United States citizens. He had exacted harsh sanctions, including isolation, on perceived "troublemakers"; required loyalty oaths of all detainees; and consigned those who refused the oaths to especially overcrowded and undesirable concentration camps. Myer's work at the WRA included an analogue to termination, the step-by-step dismantling of the system after the war's end. Within months after taking office at the BIA, he announced his objective: terminate tribes "as fast as possible."

Myer cleaned house in the BIA. Holding little regard for Collier or his ideas, he forced out Zimmerman and other holdovers and replaced them with his own people, many from the WRA. Early on, he made deep changes to facilitate termination by asserting his approval power over attorney contracts to eliminate assertive tribal lawyers, adopting a "relocation" program to encourage reservation Indians to move to the cities, and placing boarding school students in non-Indian, Christian families. Myer made the most of BIA reorganization efforts in 1947 and 1949, which consolidated widely scattered offices into eleven areas, one of which was located in Portland under Pryse. With his own people in the key Washington, D.C., and area offices, the commissioner established a smooth-working engine to do his bidding. As historian Francis Paul Prucha explained:

> By effectively reducing the division directors in Washington to staff officers, [Myer] concentrated administrative decision in his own hands, and by giv-

Senator Arthur V. Watkins of Utah (*left*) and Dillon S. Myer, BIA commissioner (1950–1953), were the principal leaders of the termination policy. Watkins: *used by permission, all rights reserved, Utah State Historical Society.* Meyer: *courtesy of the Bancroft Library, University of California, Berkeley.*

ing substantial authority to the area directors, who would play a key role in termination activities, he strengthened the move toward withdrawal. Officials below the area level lost many of their responsebilities. The changes not only tightened the machinery of the bureau, with centralized power in the hands of the commissioner, but they eliminated to a large extent residual Collier influence among the division heads and among the field superintendents.

Myer knew how to present his ideas to the public and, like other terminationists, used a language that resonated. He rejected the reservation system, which he called a "glass case policy" that treated Indians like "museum specimens," and favored bringing Indian people into "the sunlight of independence." They should not be "wards" of the BIA. Rather, they should have "freedom." This language reached its high-water mark with Senator Arthur V. Watkins, the terminationist from Utah, who, flirting with a comparison of himself to Abraham Lincoln, proclaimed of his termination bills that "following in the footsteps of the Emancipation Proclamation of ninety-four years ago, I see the following words emblazoned in letters of fire above the heads of the Indians—*THESE PEOPLE SHALL BE FREE!*"

Myer and the others had a point. Anyone who visited an Indian reservation—Siletz, Navajo, Crow, or any other—could see the problem with their own eyes, and those who didn't go to Indian country saw it through news reports and popular literature: The poverty was unspeakable, the worst of any place in the country, and alcoholism and malnutrition were rampant. With the Bureau of Indian Affairs keeping the clamps on, individual initiative had no chance. All of this in America, which after the long war was surging, giving life to individual initiative to a degree never seen before. "Freedom." That rang true.

So there was a clear problem. Everybody knew it, the general public and Indian people at Siletz and everywhere else. Termination was the only solution on the table, and its proponents had little opposition. Indian country was too poor, too disorganized, too scared to offer an alternative. A few contrary voices sounded. John Collier came forward and called termination "social genocide," and Harold Ickes, the longest-serving Interior secretary in history, who oversaw the Indian Reorganization era, charged Myer with being "Hitler and Mussolini rolled into one." But they were old news in a new America and their entreaties were dismissed as sour grapes.

As a result, questions were never asked, at least in the beginning, and the Siletz were very much part of the beginning. There is a serious breakdown here, but is termination the right answer? Do the last remnants of Indian land have to be taken away to make Indians full citizens? Is it right to break all the treaties? If the BIA is denying Indians freedom, shouldn't the BIA be changed? Could the tribes govern themselves on the reservations and find freedom that way? In all likelihood, such questions would have been brushed aside even if asked. The time was wrong, and all the momentum was with Myer and the others. Termination was the only game in town and it moved ahead with a vengeance.

In 1950, out in Oregon, Morgan Pryse was getting down to business. The area director welcomed a directive from Myer that "makes mandatory our close attention to the possibilities of this advanced thinking for Northwest Indians," referring to plans to discontinue federal supervision over tribes. In response, Pryse drafted a report entitled "Program for the Early Termination of Selected Activities and Withdrawing Federal Supervision over the Indians at Grand Ronde–Siletz and Southwestern Oregon," which was completed in

December 1950. Fitting as it did with Myer's agenda, the document put Siletz termination on the front burner.

The 1950 Program was brief—just nineteen pages of text covering three tribal groups—superficial, and wholly out of character for the seriousness of the matter. The first two elements for termination under the 1947 Zimmerman analysis were "degree of acculturation" and "economic resources and condition of the tribe," but Pryse's program was devoid of data or discussion of those factors. By any standard, analysis of these issues was critical. If they were not met, how could a tribe be ready for termination? Detailed socioeconomic information had traditionally been part of BIA reporting, all the way back to the annual reports in the early days of the reservation. The "Ten-Year Program, 1946–1955," prepared in 1944 by Pryse's immediate predecessor, for example, had examined the tribes' economic and social situation in considerable detail and sounded a warning that cried out for discussion in Pryse's report. After detailing the high number of Siletz jobs in defense-related industries during wartime, the Ten-Year Program was pessimistic about the future: "This picture, however, will change materially after the war and it is feared unemployment conditions, similar to those experienced during the CCC program, will return."

Why the 1950 Program departed from the practice of thorough reporting is unknown. Pryse was a good bureaucrat, and his annual reports to Washington, D.C., show an attention to detail. He may have felt that he had to act quickly here, due to real or perceived pressure from the commissioner's office. By then it was clear that Siletz would be one of the first tribes that the BIA would put forth to Congress under the new program. Myer wanted action.

Or perhaps the facts were inconvenient. Just a few months before, Pryse had reported to the commissioner that "there appears to be quite a number of indigent Indians of the [Grand Ronde–Siletz] district who demand assistance" in meeting their health needs. A year earlier, referring to the sharp downturn in the local timber industry, Pryse commented that "due to the gradual closing down of the mills and logging camps within the vicinity of Siletz, Oregon, some Indians were feeling the difficult times for lack of employment." The district office gave a grave assessment of Siletz housing in the "Ten-Year Program, 1946–1955." The homes, many dating back to early reservation days, "are old and weather-beaten, needing considerable repair or replacing." The Ten-Year Program further reported that the situation had not changed since a 1938 study, which found that there were "more than 80 families without houses." The report continued: "There is only one resident family engaged in private business."

Inadequate though it was, the 1950 Program had one great strength from the government's point of view. The last two pages contained a November 12, 1950, resolution by the Siletz tribe approving termination. This seemed to fulfill the third Zimmerman criterion, the standard that most fully represents the government's trust relationship to the tribe: the "willingness of the tribe to be relieved of federal control." Or did it?

The question of tribal consent was a contentious and difficult issue for every terminated tribe. Termination advocates used approval by tribes to justify termination, to show that it was both right and fair, yet every tribal consent contained powerful elements of coercion and inevitability. It was also the case that federal officials and Indian people had different perceptions of the meaning of termination. The terminationists had a crisp, clear understanding. Termination closed down an outmoded set of federal financial, social, and legal obligations and moved the country one step closer to being "One America." The tribal understanding was much more vague. The vast majority of Indian people, tribal leaders included, had no experience with major federal policy initiatives. To a person, they did know that the BIA regime had a deadening effect that diminished and demeaned them. Being "free" of that sounded good, but beyond that point the conceptions in Indian country did not equate with the words that made their way into the statute books and the realities that followed. It was not clear to them that this freedom was linked to the loss of land, treaty rights, federal services, community, and individual identity.

Each terminated tribe had its own individualized experience. In regard to consent at Siletz, Morgan Pryse was not far from the mark when he wrote in the 1950 Program that "many Siletz people have long expressed a desire to free themselves of all further supervision or (what they term) interference by the government." Pryse's parenthetical comment, however, acknowledges that the government had one objective and the tribe another, more limited one. What Siletz tribal members wanted—to be "free of interference" by the BIA— is illustrated by an incident recounted by Lionel Youst and William Seaburg in their biography *Coquelle Thompson, Athabascan Witness.*

In 1937, Coquelle Thompson, then in his nineties and blind, and his wife, Agnes, lost nearly everything when their house burned to the ground. They moved into one of the cottages on Government Hill, built the previous summer for "aged and indigent" Indians. Because of the tragedy, the agent sent Coquelle $25 from his Individual Indian Money account (IIMs are government accounts that hold moneys received by tribal members from such things as an Indian's lease of his or her allotment). In addition, the agent gave the couple a purchase order for beds and bedding.

Unfortunately, the purchase order was of no use to them because, as Agnes wrote to the agent, "the Red Cross has been very effective in helping us" by providing a bed and ample bedding. Instead, she asked the agent to send her $150 from her IIM, which had a balance of $174.69, so they could buy what they actually needed, furniture and two stoves. The agent responded with a check for $50. He had found, "after carefully studying your request," that national BIA regulations placed a cap of $50 per month on withdrawals from IIMs.

Further entreaties to a new agent came out no better. The hurt and frustration is evident in this plea from Agnes, a nurse, who wrote on behalf of her husband, a person of great stature in the tribe:

> Dear Sir: Please send me the amount of money that I asked for $150. I am surprised that I am not in trust of my own money after all these years. . . . Do you know how I am living? I suppose you think I squander it away, well you may at any time investigate my record and see my character status. I am in need of this money so please send it at once.
>
> Truly yours,
Coquelle Thompson, Sr.
by Mrs. A. Thompson (wife)

Frustration with BIA oversight and the humiliation of having to beg for assistance was widespread. This was coupled with a steady decline in federal services beginning in the late 1930s. By the 1950s, the Portland area office allowed only the most minimal health care for Siletz, and children could go to Chemawa and perhaps qualify for a bare-bones BIA college scholarship. Otherwise, there was little left to the federal relationship save the degrading and arbitrary control over land and individual money accounts.

Siletz tribal members had other perceptions of termination. With the high poverty rate, people wanted access to the scant resources in BIA hands. As Joe Lane, tribal chair in the 1970s, explained, among the Siletz "the word 'termination' was not used. That was a new word in our vocabulary. The term which was used was 'liquidation.' And the Indians at that time felt liquidation meant they would probably be compensated for some of the timber that had been taken and some of the land." In this view, the four remaining tribal timber sections—containing 2,600 acres, scattered and not much used by tribal members—could be liquidated, with the sale proceeds distributed among tribal members.

Lane's explanation is consistent with years of requests from tribal leaders. In 1947, Hoxie Simmons asked the Interior secretary for assistance in obtaining "permission for the tribe to manage its own . . . affairs." Tribal chairman Elmer Logan, writing on behalf of the tribe, wrote Commissioner Myer that "our tribes want immediate liquidation." In 1951 the tribe requested that the four timber sections be sold. Just as Coquelle Thompson had to plead for the release of funds from his IIM account, so too did the tribal council in 1949 and 1950 implore the BIA to distribute $150 per capita payments to tribal members from the tribe's trust account, which had been accumulating funds from timber sales on tribal land. The tribe's anger toward the BIA during the years leading up to the vote on whether to consent to termination was expressed in Vice Chairman Daniel Orton's 1949 letter to Senator Cordon:

> You will recall that over a year ago our people sent a petition to you and others there in Washington asking that our timber sales money be paid out to us. You have our correspondence relative to the same. This however Senator Cordon is a dire emergency and something must be done and soon.
>
> I think that you know that the Indian Bureau there in Washington has consistently opposed any payments of our timber money on the Siletz Reservation to our people in per capita payments and they persist in controlling our funds. Our boys fought and died in two wars or more against this sort of Indian Bureau dictatorship and paternalism and we are tired of it and we are capable of managing our own property and financial affairs and we feel that the Indian Bureau with its misfits and parasites should be liquidated and the sooner the better for all concerned.

There were other misunderstandings. Siletz people hoped that termination could bring down the curtain on their perceived second-class citizen status. They resented the federal laws that prevented them from purchasing alcohol at restaurants, bars, and package stores. They chafed at Oregon's law prohibiting interracial marriages and believed that termination would cure that. Maybe, as the BIA assured them, termination would bring a new era that would end racial discrimination. Wilfred Wasson, chairman of the Coquille Tribal Council, spoke to that notion:

> The Bureau of Indian Affairs officials had told us they were going to remove all the special liabilities and limitations of being Indian and thereafter we would be just like white people. This, of course, did not happen. Employers, teachers and government officials still treated us like Indians. We still felt like and thought of ourselves as Indians. The only difference was that we no longer had health services, we no longer had education benefits and we could now pay property taxes just like non-Indians.

In understanding the Siletz state of mind about termination, there is also the matter of possible BIA coercion. We know that Senator Watkins withheld claims payments for the Menominee and Klamath tribes until they agreed to termination. These payments came from court cases the tribes had won, but actual disbursement of funds depended on congressional action through the appropriations process, which normally was routinely done. In 1950 the claims were all the talk at Siletz: four separate cases involving nearly all the tribes in the confederation were in the Court of Claims or Indian Claims Commission; in the largest one, the *Alcea* case, the Court of Claims had just ruled for the Tututni, Chetco, Coquille, and Tillamook tribes in the amount of $16 million (this is the award that the Supreme Court reduced to $3.3 million a year later).

There is no conclusive evidence that Pryse, Myer, Watkins, or others made threats to the Siletz about withholding claims funds. Tribal members, though, were jumpy about these cases, all trudging toward completion after their long journeys through the courts. At Siletz and other reservations, there was a widespread belief that, at the very least, the BIA implicitly coerced the tribes by delaying claims awards. Much later, during the Siletz restoration effort in 1976, BIA Commissioner Morris Thompson ordered a thorough review of the coercion issue in response to a request from the Senate Indian Affairs subcommittee. He found no evidence in the agency files and noted that Pryse had unequivocally testified to Congress that there was no such pressure. Although it is probable that coercion will never be finally proven, Commissioner Thompson pointedly noted one tantalizing piece of circumstantial evidence. As the Siletz termination bill went through Congress, the appropriation bill for the *Alcea* judgment followed right behind it in both the Senate and the House. The appropriations measure became final just seventeen days after the termination statute was signed into law.

Archie Ben was a central Siletz figure for decades. He served regularly on the Siletz Tribal Council and was stalwart in preserving tribal traditions. Admired for his commitment to the old ways, he instructed young people in Nee Dosh, arranged for public dances in area locales, and helped put on dances in peoples' homes. *Courtesy of Ed Ben.*

Whether or not the BIA used claims payments as a prod or a club, Morgan Pryse was unrelenting. As of early 1950, his case for Siletz termination lacked a proper constitution and governing body; there was no acceptable legal structure or voice to provide the tribal consent that Pryse wanted. In 1935, the BIA had pushed for an IRA constitution to activate Collier's idealistic vision and the tribe voted it down. In 1940, the agency urged a constitution and governing body to regularize administration of the Civilian Conservation Corps and other federal grant programs for Siletz, and the tribe balked. In 1949, the BIA—now under Pryse—came back again with a different motive, to pave the way for termination, and once again the Siletz had rejected the proposal.

Pryse would not give in. In September 1950, with his urgency now joined by Dillon Myer's, he came back to the tribe once more. This time the constitution and by-laws were adopted at an open tribal meeting. Although the BIA made much of tribal involvement, claiming that members of the tribal business committee "were especially busy in drafting the constitution and assisting all along the line," this was a government-issue constitution: Ever

The buildup to termination was a stressful time at Siletz, but people still found time for celebrations. Here, in 1948, tribal members do a "good time" dance—an informal, social version of Nee Dosh—to welcome back Arthur Bensell Jr. and his wife, Margaret, who were returning to the reservation to operate the general store in Siletz. Archie Ben is singing and drumming on the far right, joined (*from right*) by Griffin John, Mary Washington, Aggie Williams, and Helen "Nellie" Orton. *Siletz Tribal Collection.*

since the IRA, tribal constitutions were mostly boilerplate charters drafted by the BIA with few differences from tribe to tribe. No matter. Now, with this constitution, there was a seemingly respectable legal framework for obtaining agreement to termination.

Pryse came back for the tribal consent just two months later. It was a confusing time for tribal members. So much was swirling around Siletz in 1950—so many highfalutin' words, so many misconceptions, so little common understanding between the tribe and the federal officials, so much pressure. Dr. Hiroto Zakoji, the long-time BIA anthropologist in the Portland area office in the 1950s, who witnessed termination first-hand, was satisfied that there was "very little understanding of what termination was all about" at Siletz. "I don't think there was more than a handful of people who knew what

Termination was," recalled Hardy Simmons, who came back home after serving in World War II. "Most people only knew about Termination through rumors. . . . The big words the BIA used to talk about termination made it hard for people to understand, especially the older people." Archie Ben, a tribal council member since the 1930s, was of the same mind. "The vote came very quickly and I do not think that the members of the Council really understood all of the things that Termination stood for."

A sense of inevitability dulled the Siletz response to the program that Pryse brought to them. The congressionally established American Indian Policy Review Commission, which held hearings and conducted interviews at Siletz and Grand Ronde in the 1970s, found that there was "an attitude held by many tribal members that termination was inevitable and would happen no matter what the Indians decided." The new generation of Siletz tribal leaders saw the final action as preordained. As Joe Lane said, "We had people in the amounts of 25 or 30 or less than that attending meetings of the tribes. They thought, 'Well, we are going to be terminated anyway.'" To Dolly Fisher, "the Bureau pushed hard. It had to happen." As a young woman, Jo Anne Miller attended many of the termination meetings. "I just figured it was going to happen and that was it."

Pryse sought formal tribal consent at a general council meeting on November 12, 1950. There is no record of how many of the 786 tribal members attended the meeting, but few tribal meetings in those days exceeded 40 members. It is a byword in Indian culture that people who are against a proposal will stay home or attend a meeting and refuse to vote. The resolution in support of the principle of withdrawal (the word "termination" was not used), doubtless drafted by Pryse's office, stated—without indicating the numbers of votes for or against—that "we have advanced in education, customs, and knowledge . . . [and] we feel that we are able, willing, and should assume the duties and responsibilities of full American citizenship." The voters resolved "that the Federal Government withdraw all restrictions and services now existing . . . at the earliest practicable moment." Pryse reported to Commissioner Myer that it had been "an enthusiastic meeting" although he did not mention the size of the vote.

One further procedural matter lay ahead. The tribe had approved withdrawal in principle but also needed to sign off on the actual bill itself. Interior department attorneys in Washington drew up the language and on August 10, 1951, the commissioner's office telegraphed the text of the bill out to Oregon for approval by the Siletz and Grand Ronde tribes. Now the bill referred to "termination" rather than "withdrawal," although the substance was the same—the final and complete separation that the federal officials had been espousing all along. But the gap between the conceptions held by Interior officials and the Siletz leaders, much less the general membership, had not been closed. When Pryse wrote Myer on September 11 there seemed to be a considerable rush, which led to an unseemly recommendation: "I believe the Commissioner would be justified in starting immediate action on this proposed legislative bill without awaiting formal resolutions from the Indians, since it has been discussed with many of them and not a single member has objections." When these discussions took place is not clear. Pryse made one visit to the Coast in August, but it "coincid[ed] with the day of per capita payments, a funeral," and jobs in the hop fields and the woods. As a result, although "copies of the bill have been distributed among tribal members," Pryse found that "it was not possible to get affirmative action" on the proposal. The next tribal meeting at Siletz was on September 30, but Pryse could not attend. Action was tabled for a week by a vote of 23 to 0.

Approval of the draft bill came before a special general council meeting on Sunday, October 7. Just thirty-four tribal members attended. Pryse, who read a letter from Commissioner Myer, led the discussion. This time there was a vote count. When the matter came up, thirteen approved and no opposition was reported. Less than 3 percent of the adult population of the Siletz tribe had approved the termination bill.

A month later, at the regularly scheduled tribal meeting for November, tribal members brought forth an important matter. Some fifty-seven acres of land, small in size but heartland, were in federal ownership. By resolution, the tribe requested that the agency area, the day school, the cemetery, the canal, and the mill sites—Government Hill and places where people had held meetings, enjoyed social events, run a cannery, attended school, worked, danced Nee Dosh, and been buried—be transferred to a tribal corporation to be established under state law. This was the only change to the legislation that the tribe requested, but it was not added to the bill.

Grand Ronde–Siletz termination bills—among the first to be brought forward for any tribe and actually out in front of Congress's announcement of the termination policy a year later—were introduced in April 1952 and went quickly to subcommittee hearings in both Houses on May 21, 1952. Associate Commissioner Rex Lee presented testimony for the administration before the Senate subcommittee, and Commissioner Myer spoke on the House side at the perfunctory proceedings. No Siletz people attended. The bills stalled and never got out of committee, perhaps because relatively few congressional working days remained in that presidential-election year. Besides, while the Interior department strongly endorsed the bills, there was no committed base of support in Congress for immediate action, especially in the Democratic Party, which controlled both Houses.

Indian policy changed dramatically after the election of 1952, with the rapid-fire adoption and implementation of termination. It was not due to the new president. Truman, a Democrat, had appointed the termination-minded Myer, and the Republican Eisenhower decided not to keep him on because he had become a lightning rod for criticism. In all, however, administration policy remained the same. Former Oregon Governor Douglas McKay, who favored termination, moved to the capital as secretary of the Interior and, along with Commissioner Glenn Emmons, continued the policies and personnel in place under Myer. There is no sign that McKay gave any particular attention to terminating the western Oregon tribes.

The difference came in Congress, where Republicans took over both chambers. Even so, it was not exactly a matter of party. For years, the small group of legislators, mostly westerners, who paid attention to Indian affairs had agreed in principle that something big needed to be done. Termination, the only proposal put forward, had no congressional detractors but few people in Congress had strong feelings about this new strategy. What broke through the legislative passivity was the rise of the incoming chairman of the Senate Indian Affairs Committee, a veteran lawmaker who fervently believed in termination and knew how to pull the right levers of Congress so that a handful of true believers could control the legislative process.

Arthur V. Watkins, a self-made man who grew up in rural Utah and became a farmer and lawyer, earned election to the Senate in 1946 on a clean-government platform. He gained stature for his stands on principles; in the mid-1950s, for example, he was the first Republican to condemn the excesses of Wisconsin senator Joseph McCarthy for his Red-baiting crusade. A crusader himself, the white-maned Watkins—who came to Indian Affairs with little or no contact with Natives—believed that if he could pull himself up by his bootstraps, so could Indians. The senator, a tough, aggressive chairman who politely led favorable witnesses in the desired direction and often badgered and insulted dissenting witnesses, made that point many times over. To Governor Maytubby of the Chickasaw Nation, he asked, "Why can [Indians] not do the same as the white man does. . . ? I wanted to be a lawyer. The Government did not come around and offer to pay my tuition and pay my board. . . . I had to get out and work long, hard hours for it." To Gordon Keshena of the Menominee Tribe, who doubted the readiness of many of his tribespeople for termination, Watkins asserted: "All you have to do is to agree now to grow up—that you are no longer children." On another occasion, he charged that Indians "want all the benefits of the things we have, highways, schools, hospitals, everything that civilization furnishes, but they don't want to help pay their share of it."

For Watkins, the only solution was termination—and soon. While one can doubt his tactics and his wisdom, he seemed convinced of the rectitude of termination. In all probability the Siletz bill would have passed soon anyway, but the determination and leadership of Watkins and a few others made it a certainty.

As a cornerstone, the terminationists wanted a strong, clear statement of policy so that bills terminating individual tribes would be identified as carrying out the will of Congress. Congressman E. Y. Berry, a business-oriented Republican from South Dakota, introduced House Concurrent Resolution 108 to declare termination as official congressional policy. Henry Jackson, a Democrat from Washington who had favored termination-style proposals in the House before his 1952 election to the Senate, carried the resolution in the Senate. With Berry and Watkins chairing the two Indian Affairs subcommittees, HCR 108 passed both Houses smoothly and went into effect on August 1, 1953. Now the United States Congress had announced its future course of action with respect to Indian tribes, people, and land:

> Whereas it is the policy of Congress, as rapidly as possible, to make the Indians within the territorial limits of the United States subject to the same laws and entitled to the same privileges and responsibilities as are applicable to other citizens of the United States, to end their status as wards of the United States, and to grant them all of the rights and prerogatives pertaining to American citizenship; and
>
> Whereas the Indians within the territorial limits of the United States should assume their full responsibilities as American citizens: Now, therefore, be it

Resolved by the House of Representatives (the Senate concurring), That it
is declared to be the sense of Congress that, at the earliest possible time, all
of the Indian tribes and the individual members thereof [in certain tribes]
. . . should be freed from Federal supervision and control and from all dis-
abilities and limitations specially applicable to Indians.

The resolution listed several tribes, including the Klamath, although for reasons unknown it did not refer to the western Oregon tribes, who were in fact
at the head of the list. HCR 108 directed the BIA to prepare, by the end of the
year, recommendations to terminate other tribes. To avoid alarming congressional colleagues, the resolution never spelled out the real effects of the new
policy: treaty abrogation, sell-off of Indian lands, and the end of federal programs for impoverished Indian people.

With the overarching policy announced, Congress could now begin the
business of terminating tribes, one by one. For expediency, the hard-driving
Watkins chose to move individual termination bills through Congress by
means of joint Senate-House hearings; one hearing would thus suffice for both
Houses. The Senator also sought to push through a large number of termination bills, and 1954 became one of the most active years in the long history
of Indian lawmaking. To begin the parade of joint hearings, he selected three
groups: the Southern Paiute Tribe of Utah, the Alabama-Coushatta Tribe of
Texas, and the western Oregon tribes. The hearings would be held on three
consecutive days beginning on February 15, 1954.

The subcommittee hearings for the Utah and Texas tribes make depressing reading. In both cases, tribal members were dirt poor and had little formal
education. No tribal members testified. Non-Indians, however, had plans to
exploit the tribes' land. The Southern Paiutes had received an inquiry from a
mining company that wanted to lease tribal land "without going through the
usual procedure." The Alabama-Coushatta had 4,000 acres of "good forest
land." In time, both termination bills passed. These tribes obviously needed
help, but was termination the right approach?

Next up was the bill for the Siletz, Grand Ronde, and, to be certain that
no western Oregon Indians were overlooked, a long list of small tribes and
bands in southwestern Oregon (mostly families formerly associated with the
Siletz Reservation.) The joint Senate-House subcommittee took up the bill
at a hearing on February 17. Morgan Pryse had done some rewriting of his
1950 Program, but his presentation—the principal supporting document for
termination—remained woefully weak. As in 1950, the agency produced no

data whatsoever on the central issue of economic readiness for termination. Instead, his assessment, which portrayed Siletz people as prosperous and indistinguishable from the white population, was subjective, glib, and wildly overstated. Pryse's report on the subject of "social and economic progress" amounted to this:

> Almost every employable male person of Indian blood is gainfully employed. Some are in business for themselves, in logging, fishing, and other pursuits. Others are employed in the lumber mills and logging camps, and some are employed in offices and banks. More women of Indian blood are accepting employment of all types. There are a number, both men and women, who teach in the public schools. Practically all of these Indians have been integrated into the social structures of their respective communities.

Under the section on "Justification for Federal Withdrawal," Pryse offered this assessment:

> *1. Ability to handle own affairs*
> The younger generations are mixed bloods and in most cases have the appearance of white people; they are literate, have practically all of the mannerisms of the average white person, are practically all gainfully employed either in their own businesses or by others, and are capable of attending to their own affairs to the same extent as other citizens.

The director went even further in his responses to Senator Watkins's leading questions:

> SENATOR WATKINS. Based on what I have heard here today, it appears that these Indians have made great progress.
> MR. PRYSE. They have, indeed.
> SENATOR WATKINS. They have made progress in being able to take care of themselves. Do you have any theory, or any observations to make, as to why they seem to be out in front?
> MR. PRYSE. Well, sir, I would say because they have been so well integrated among the non-Indians or the whites down there, that they generally have attended public schools and attended the same churches, lodges, and have had to get out and make a living for themselves all up and down

the coast among the white communities, and the Indians have more or less become a part of the community in which they live.

SENATOR WATKINS. For the most part they are able to take care of themselves, and they provide for their own welfare, and they are not on State or county welfare rolls?

MR. PRYSE. To no greater degree than their white neighbors; about the same number as their neighbors. They are well integrated.

SENATOR WATKINS. They have not had any great amount of property given to them?

MR. PRYSE. No.

SENATOR WATKINS. That is, not through the Federal Government?

MR. PRYSE. They have had to take care of themselves, and you will find many of them range from fifth-grade education clear on up through college graduates. They are very fine, and many are well-educated people, and many have responsible positions.

SENATOR WATKINS. I wonder if there were any special reasons there why these Indian groups are so far out in advance of many other Indian tribes in the United States.

MR. PRYSE. I think it is because they have lived in these scattered communities all up and down the coast among the non-Indians, and they worked with them and for them; and they have gone to the same schools, churches, social events, and so forth; and they have more or less become citizens of the community.

SENATOR WATKINS. They have the same type of homes, I suppose?

MR. PRYSE. Yes; you often cannot tell an Indian home from another. They drive nice cars and dress nicely, and you often cannot distinguish them from non-Indians.

The report also was notable for a significant omission on the issue of tribal consent to termination. The document includes the November 12, 1950, resolution in which the tribe approved withdrawal in principle, but the resolution of a year later, on October 7, 1951, was more relevant: rather than addressing the concept of withdrawal, it approved specific language in a draft bill. Unlike the 1950 resolution, which did not include the vote count, the 1951 tribal resolution included the vote of 13 to 0. Could the later resolution have been left out of the report to Congress because, by documenting the excruciatingly low Siletz participation, it would have sent up a red flag that something was terribly wrong with the consent process?

To their credit, both Pryse and Rex Lee raised the issue, not included in the bill before the subcommittee, of transferring the fifty-seven acres of federal lands on Government Hill and elsewhere in Siletz to a tribal corporation after termination. This was the amendment—the only one—that the tribe requested at the tribal council meeting on the draft bill in October 1951. The government men raised the tribal concerns perfectly, saying that "we think it would be less disrupting . . . to give this [land] to the community," for it "is being used 100 percent by the tribe [as opposed to the government] now as a community center, and the building there and the cemetery and there are about 10 cottages . . . which are occupied by old Indians that would have no other place to go." Neither Senator Watkins nor Representative Berry showed any support for the idea. Instead, after termination became final the Interior department conveyed these lands, which held so much meaning for Siletz people, to the City of Siletz.

No tribal people testified at the hearing.

The Siletz tribe stood in a position different from most of the other terminated tribes and it came from the legacy of the nineteenth century. Notably, the Siletz did not lose a magnificent reservation in the way that tribes such as the Klamath and Menominee did; those were landed tribes and the impact of a potential breakup of their reservations was obvious to anyone. The Siletz was once a landed tribe and suffered a similar loss, but not at termination. In that sense, they were not as badly affected as many of the other terminated tribes.

It also may be true that the Siletz were somewhat more assimilated then most reservation Indians in that they had more day-to-day contact with non-Indians. That, too, came as a result of the break-up of the reservation as white people moved in and made their homes on the compelling Oregon Coast. But the Siletz were not fully assimilated, not nearly as assimilated as Morgan Pryse claimed them to be. This was a time when many Indian people kept their identity under wraps. Jim Metcalf, a former Coquille tribal chairman, explained that "a lot of Indians didn't want to admit they were Indians. It was a lot easier to get a job if you weren't. Indians were the last hired and first fired." But the Siletz were still Indians, people who heard and respected the old calls.

Economic life was nothing like the picture painted by supporters of termination. It was not true, as Pryse reported to the Congress, that "almost every employable [Siletz male] is gainfully employed." The Siletz people were poor, high in unemployment, and low in formal education. We know that Indian unemployment nationally in the 1950s was about ten times higher than the rate in the country at large and that precious few Native people had gone to college. Things were somewhat better for the Siletz because of the logging jobs, but not by much. In the mid-1970s, when reliable statistics were finally available, Siletz unemployment was estimated at 44 percent and average income was one-half, or less, than that of the general population in Lincoln County. Nearly half of Siletz young people did not finish high school. True, termination made things worse, but circumstances were dire in the early 1950s and the Bureau of Indian Affairs was wrong to paper that over in its presentations to Congress.

Although there was probably more understanding in the BIA than anywhere else of the wreckage that termination would bring, virtually no one in the Bureau stood up against termination at Siletz or elsewhere. Dissent was not brooked in the agency. The sense of momentum was overwhelming from the day Dillon Myer entered office, and lockstep was expected and enforced. Nevertheless, one person did stand up. That was E. Morgan Pryse, who had the courage to tell Senator Watkins and Congressman Berry at a joint Senate-House subcommittee hearing of how termination would inevitably cause the Klamath to lose their land.

One might wonder why Pryse was so brave at the Klamath hearings and so lacking in bravery at Siletz. The reasons may trace to his personal background at Klamath, the losses of the nineteenth century at Siletz, and the complexity of a radical policy that no one fully comprehended. Pryse had begun his career at Klamath and likely was moved by the prospect of the Klamath losing their grand expanse of ponderosa pine and river country in central Oregon, fully sixty miles north to south, twenty miles east to west. He could see what a wonderland the Klamath had to lose. The Siletz, who once had a comparable reservation, had nothing like that in the 1950s. The best use of the remaining tribal timber lands was to liquidate those isolated parcels, as tribal leaders had urged.

As for what the Siletz actually had to lose, it turns out that all manner of losses were discussed barely or not at all during the termination process. Giving Pryse the benefit of the doubt, perhaps he did not see them or he badly underestimated them. After termination, when the state cracked down on tribal hunting and fishing, the reduction in subsistence use affected the diets and health of most Siletz families. The elimination of education benefits, which included partial college scholarships, and limited health benefits, minimal though they were, mattered to the many people below the poverty line. While the tribe held only the timber sections, there were seventy-six family allotments totaling 5,390 acres. That is a lot of Indian land, and most of the allotments were prime parcels, on the rivers or the Coast. After termination most of that land was lost in distress, sold for badly needed cash or auctioned off in tax sales. With those home places mostly gone, people moved out—a diaspora—and the sense of community crumbled. Perhaps Pryse did not foresee all of that. Virtually nobody did.

Such can be the case when the nation's legislature imposes an untried idea with too much force, in too much of a rush, and with too little thought.

On August 13, 1954, President Eisenhower signed the Siletz Termination Act into law. Two years later, Secretary of the Interior Fred Seaton approved the final tribal roll so that $792.50 could be paid to each tribal member from the sale of the tribal timber lands. The United States had terminated its special relationship with the Siletz Tribe—ridding itself of all the treaties, all the promises, all the obligations—once and for all.

PART FOUR

THE MODERN ERA

RESTORATION

"We want to be restored."

THE EFFECTS OF TERMINATION SET IN BY ACCRETION, NOT DELuge. One by one, Siletz people lost their allotments through failure to pay taxes and, with no other way to come up with basic living expenses, by selling their homes and land. Tribal members with cancer scares or strokes, conditions still covered by the Indian Health Service in the early 1950s, could not afford medical help. Traditional fishermen, who once had BIA tags allowing them to gillnet on their allotments, now faced arrest by the state. Deer hunters, who hunted free before termination and whose families depended on the venison they carried home, learned they had to pay the state license fee and could take just one buck per year. There were no jobs at the BIA, which gave a hiring preference to Indians but not members of terminated tribes; one woman lost her teaching job at Haskell Indian School in Kansas because she was no longer a member of a "recognized" tribe. The employers who had refused to hire Indians before termination still refused. The City of Siletz evicted the eleven elders living on Government Hill—maybe the city owned that land now, tribal members asked, but how could the city do that? Family after family, confronted with the loss and disruption, moved out to Salem, Portland, and points beyond.

The socioeconomic statistics were dismal. Tribal members endured skyhigh unemployment, over 40 percent, and basement-level income, half that of the general population. Most adults between seventeen and twenty-five never finished high school. Alcoholism afflicted almost every family.

There is an open question as to how much of this traces to termination.

Certainly not all of it. Despite the rosy descriptions of Siletz life by BIA officials during the rush to termination, the tribe faced widespread poverty before Congress withdrew its support. And larger economic forces were at work. The Lincoln County timber harvest dropped from an annual average of more than 400 million board feet to less than 300 million, with much of the decline occurring from 1968 through 1970. This cost tribal members good jobs and forced some to relocate. If, as Indian people believe, Indian employees were the first to be let go when labor reductions were made, then the cuts disproportionately affected the Siletz. But whatever the specific contributions of termination, by the mid-1970s the Siletz people faced dire economic and social circumstances.

Intangibles were just as important. The spirited sense of community, created and preserved by countless generations of ancestors, lost vitality. With the departure of two-thirds of the Siletz people living in Lincoln County, there were still some traditional dances and an occasional pow-wow, but not nearly as many. With no tribal business to conduct, tribal meetings lapsed and gatherings were now held by families rather than the larger tribal community. There was a lingering sadness, broken hearts, at a life with few dances, songs, and stories—and no land.

The perception—the charge—of "not being an Indian anymore" especially hurt. Ed Ben remembered, in anger and frustration, that "after termination we would go to pow-wows and recognized Indians would talk down to us. When we told them we were Siletz, they would say, 'oh yeah, you're those terminated Indians.'" "It made me feel vulnerable, deficient, ready to fight anyone who said we weren't Indian people," Agnes Pilgrim said. "I hated that word 'termination.' It was like 'extermination.' I felt like I lost my identity."

The gravity of termination sharpened during the 1960s as new advantages to federal recognition emerged. Government programs for Indians improved and recognized tribes began to make tribal sovereignty mean more than just John Marshall's words on a page. One termination-era policy—the transfer of the Indian Health Service from the BIA to the Department of Health, Education, and Welfare—proved to be a boon to Indians. Relieved of the dead-end image of the BIA, the IHS became more professional, congressional funding increased, and health care for Native people improved. Congress initiated new Indian education programs and stepped up funding for BIA schools, special programs for Indian children in state elementary and secondary schools, and college scholarships. The War on Poverty, initiated in 1964, gave a shot in the arm to tribal governments by funding community action projects designed and administered by the tribes themselves. All of these programs benefited only recognized tribes.

With the advent of "Red Pride" in the late 1960s, American Indians began thinking differently about their Indianness—and so did the American public. A number of events put exclamation points after both the grievances of Native Americans and their burgeoning sense of worth. The nation gave its sympathy and support to the Indians who occupied Alcatraz Island in San Francisco Bay. Vine Deloria's *Custer Died for Your Sins: An Indian Manifesto* hit the best-seller lists and raised spirits across Indian country. The American Indian Movement may have gone too far in its takeover and trashing of BIA headquarters in Washington, D.C., and the paramilitary standoff with federal forces at Wounded Knee in South Dakota, but particularly in its early days, AIM's proud, charismatic leaders trumpeted the values of Indian spirituality and inspired young Indian people.

For the first time in generations, tribes took bold actions to assert their sovereignty and treaty rights. Tribes in Maine sued to recover ancestral land. South Dakota tribes succeeded in passing a statewide initiative protecting their sovereign jurisdiction so that lawsuits would go to tribal, not state, courts. In the Pacific Northwest, Oregon and Washington tribes, fed up with decades of arrests and jail time, filed suits to enforce their treaty rights to take salmon at their traditional off-reservation fishing sites. In historic rulings, federal judge Robert Belloni upheld robust treaty rights for the Columbia River tribes in 1968 and Judge George Boldt followed suit for the Puget Sound tribes in 1974.

Trailblazing activity took place in Washington, D.C. The BIA began to loosen its grip on the reservations, spurred in part by the appointment of Robert Bennett, an Oneida Indian from Wisconsin who in 1966 became the first Native American BIA commissioner in nearly a century. After a half-century struggle, in 1970 the Taos Pueblo of New Mexico persuaded Congress to return to the pueblo its sacred Blue Lake and surrounding lands. In the same year, President Richard Nixon delivered his influential message to Congress proposing his policy of "Self-determination." That formulation, which called for recognition and support of the sovereign authority of tribes—not the BIA—on the reservations, became the keystone of federal Indian policy and remained so into the twenty-first century. And in April 1972, the Wisconsin congressional delegation introduced the Menominee Restoration Act, designed to repeal the Menominee Termination Act, an event duly noted by Joe Lane, soon to become the first tribal chairman in modern Siletz history.

In the early 1970s, Siletz tribal members, feeling the material and spiritual needs of their people, began the process of putting the tribe back together. Many ancestors lay in the Paul Washington Cemetery on Government Hill, named in honor of the grandson of Shasta Tyee Push Wash, who died on the battlefields of Europe, the first Siletz Indian to give his life in World War I. Blackberry patches marched on the cemetery, and so many people had moved away that maintenance was difficult. Local people—the Ben, Brown, Bensell, Simmons, and Strong families among them—formed work crews and established the Paul Washington Cemetery Association. Within a few years that memorial area once again became a place of grass rather than brambles. Tribal members also took on the pressing and tangled matter of alcoholism. With a small grant from the state, they established and staffed the Siletz Alcohol and Drug Program. Many Siletz people had moved to Portland, where the Indian community was becoming active. Siletz tribal members Joe Lane, Francella Griggs, and Adolph Tronson Jr. formed the Portland Urban Indian Center to provide a community gathering place in the city.

Then, based on meetings at the Portland Urban Indian Center and the realization that Congress could terminate the federal relationship with the Siletz tribe but could not terminate the tribe itself, tribal members decided to revive their government. The first meeting, held on September 30, 1973, at the VFW Hall in Siletz, was widely advertised and drew a crowd of fifty-four tribal members. After a discussion, the group unanimously voted to reorganize and form a government. The tribal council elected that day consisted of Joe Lane, chair; Robert Rilatos, vice chair; Rowenda Strong, secretary; Dolly Fisher, treasurer; and members Stanley Strong, Ed Sondenaa, Ed Ben, Pauline Bell Ricks, and Lindsey John. The idea took off. During those formative years, the monthly meetings—usually held in the one-room, cinderblock Siletz Grange Hall—drew two hundred or more tribal members and the discussions were lively. They adopted a constitution and by-laws and obtained a charter as a nonprofit under Oregon law.

It was a frenetic time. Lane, in his fifties and trim, somehow at once both low-key and a dynamo, seemed to be everywhere, traveling in an old Winnebago motor home on his many trips from Portland to Siletz. To get around the tribe's terminated status, the Siletz contracted with the Warm Springs Tribe—which as a recognized tribe was eligible for grants under the Comprehensive Employment and Training Act—to set up a local CETA-Manpower

Senator Mark Hatfield (*far left*), soon to become the congressional champion for Siletz restoration, attended the tribal council meeting in June 1974 and presented the tribe with an American flag. Tribal Chairman Joe Lane is third from the left. Others, from the left, are Art Bensell, then mayor of Siletz, and tribal council members Ed Sondenaa and Robert Rilatos. *Used with permission from the* Newport News Times/Lincoln County Leader.

program under the aegis of Warm Springs. With the alcohol and drug program and CETA-Manpower program both in place and with the tribal council needing space for administration and meetings with members, the tribal council rented a modest building known as the "A-Frame" and set up a drop-in center convenient for members.

The tribe also took steps in the political arena. To raise public consciousness, the council issued a proclamation, which it submitted to Governor Tom McCall, complaining of a one-sided highway historical marker about an 1850s battle and pointing out that "those signs are wooden books which many people read." On one occasion, Senator Mark Hatfield—soon to become a major figure in Siletz history—spoke at a monthly tribal meeting.

Then Joe Lane, having learned of passage of the Menominee Restoration Act in December 1973, called his sister Gladys Bolton. "Sis, what do you think of being an Indian again?" Shortly after that, John Volkman, a legal aid lawyer in Portland, looked up from his desk to find Joe Lane standing in the doorway. Lane got straight to the point. "We want to be restored."

❦ ⚘ ❦

Volkman warned that it would not be easy. As a starting point, the Menominee were a special case. Unlike the Siletz, they still had their large and splendid reservation—250,000 acres of deep forests, full rivers, and plentiful wildlife, including major deer and bear populations—and it was at immediate risk. The land, no longer held by the United States in trust, was taxable and the terminationists' overblown descriptions of Menominee economic health did not prove out. The tribal corporation could not meet the tax bills and the corporate officers sold off thousands of acres of pristine forest land to non-Indians for second homes. With more sales in the offing, tribal members rose up and received statewide sympathy. The Menominee also made an overwhelming showing of economic, health, and educational needs.

As the Menominee bill went through Congress, many legislators worried that other terminated tribes might use it as precedent for their own restoration. Reversing termination had federal budget ramifications, raised questions of state taxation and regulation, and brought forth hot-button issues of fishing, hunting, water rights, and land return. The widely held view on Capitol Hill was that Menominee was a one-of-a-kind relief measure.

Worse yet, Lane had come to Volkman's office just after the Boldt Decision was handed down, decreeing that northwest Washington tribes had the right to take 50 percent of the salmon harvest. Non-Indian fishermen were picketing Judge Boldt's federal courthouse, hanging him in effigy and loudly proclaiming their refusal to abide by his ruling. It looked like his reasoning would be applied to the Columbia (as it soon would be), so that Oregon was directly implicated. Volkman knew—and it was no surprise to Lane—that powerful commercial and sport fishing organizations in Oregon would spare nothing to prevent "restored" Indians from getting legislation through Congress, reviving expansive fishing rights, and stretching their gillnets across the Siletz and other coastal rivers. It would not matter that the Siletz had no intention of using restoration as a vehicle for gaining fishing rights. The fishermen felt cornered and they would fight.

Still, the new tribal council wanted to push ahead. Volkman drafted a restoration bill and Wendell Wyatt, congressman for the central Coast, agreed to introduce it in June 1974. Wyatt, who was about to retire, did not push the measure and it failed to receive a hearing.

This was no setback. Bills that go nowhere can be revived in a new congress. In this case, the Siletz had yet to build the apparatus needed to propel major and controversial legislation through Congress. But they were making a good start. Were they ever.

The tribe, knowing it had an uphill road to travel, plunged into the task of making a persuasive presentation to the public. Proving the many current difficulties it faced was critical, but there was almost no documentation of the tribe's plight. Members began by meeting with the schools to obtain data on Siletz students. The volunteer information-gathering gradually merged into the Statistical Profile of tribal members, completed in December 1976, with the assistance of Volkman and Jonathan Sayers, holder of a master's degree in social work. The findings, comprehensive and accurate, showed much the same societal breakdown as the Menominees had suffered.

Through small grants, the tribe also commissioned a short film by filmmaker Harry Dawson, entitled "The People Are Dancing Again." Featuring Gladys Muschamp gathering basket-making materials and then weaving them, the film was honored by the Northwest Film Festival in Portland and was shown on television through the Public Broadcasting Service. The 26-minute video made for a fine presentation at public gatherings and fundraising meetings.

The tribe had something else on its side: the support of Senator Hatfield. Governor from 1959 through 1967 and elected to the first of his five U.S. Senate terms in 1966, the dashing Hatfield had earned deep and broad public support for his courageous and independent stands, including opposition to the Vietnam War. The senator would not be cowed by opposition to restoration if he believed the objections were wrong-headed.

This was when I first became involved with the Siletz Tribe. In the winter of 1974, Joe Lane called John Echohawk, executive director of the Native American Rights Fund, a nonprofit law firm located in Boulder, Colorado, and requested assistance from NARF. I had worked on Menominee restoration, and Echohawk talked to me about whether NARF should take on Siletz restoration. In his view, the Menominee had broken new ground but the Siletz— the only terminated tribe actively pursuing restoration at the time—now had special importance: passage of a Siletz bill, significant in its own right, would also establish Menominee as precedent and open the door for all the terminated tribes. From the look in my eye, John could see what my decision was, and we both laughed.

Robert Rilatos, passionate vice chairman of the tribal council during the restoration years and an influential council member and tribal leader thereafter, emphasized the creation of traditional dancing, basketry, and language classes. *Siletz Tribal Collection.*

Joe Lane and Vice Chairman Robert Rilatos flew out to Boulder—probably on their own hooks, I realized later—to meet with a group of staff lawyers. I was reminded how tenacious Indian people are: unratified treaties, broken ratified treaties, war, removal, break-up of a great reservation, allotment, termination, yet refusing to give in. John Volkman's name came up at the meeting and I later gave him a call. John, who chooses his words carefully, said the Siletz were definitely the real thing. NARF took the case. Don Miller in NARF's Washington office, and later Sharon Gordon, a Eugene attorney, would work on it with me.

My first meeting with the Siletz Tribal Council was on April 5, 1975. As I flew out to the Portland airport and then drove over the Coast Range, representing Siletz had taken on additional, unexpected meaning for me. A few months after the Boulder meeting, I had taken a position on the law faculty at the University of Oregon in Eugene, just a two-hour drive from Siletz, and NARF asked me to continue with Siletz restoration on a contract basis when I started teaching in the fall. I didn't know exactly what the proximity of Siletz and Eugene meant, except that it would probably lead to a deeper involvement and a greater time commitment. What would these people and this place be like?

The meeting at the Grange Hall in Siletz took me aback. If anything, Joe Lane, Robert Rilatos, and John Volkman had understated the level of enthusiasm and commitment at Siletz. The place was packed, with people standing in the back and on the sides. Everyone could feel it. It was one of those moments that sometimes come to pass in the histories of dispossessed peoples when the air seems to take on a different physical character, charged with the heat of injustice suffered and simmering for generations and, as well, fired by a belief that this might be the time when justice would answer the call.

Several tribal council members made reports. The treasurer passed around a coffee can for contributions (the take was about seventy dollars). We had done some redrafting of the bill, and I explained those changes. I gave my assessment, which was that the tribe had a tough road ahead but—particularly given what I'd seen and felt that day—had a realistic chance if they could complete their efforts-in-progress of documenting their difficult circumstances and building a broad base of support, especially in Oregon. They would need to respond effectively to the attacks from fishermen, which were sure to come.

It was a long discussion. They knew well the importance of the words in the draft bill and people needed to hash and rehash them. Nearly all the comments and questions were on point, and those that weren't had the virtue of being colorful and loud. A potluck featuring venison and salmon followed, and I had the chance to visit with people. Driving back to the airport, I knew this would become a big part of my life.

The rest of 1975 brought far more work than anyone imagined. Siletz people looking back on those days roll their eyes at the sheer number of meetings and how hard it was on their families. There were two saving graces. Citizens across Oregon and beyond responded well to the Siletz experience, both the history and the current dilemma. Also, this was not an effort in which a small number of people did all the work. While tribal council members properly carried heavy loads, scores of other people, both Siletz and those from outside the tribe, volunteered in countless ways, from making presentations to preparing food at potlucks to licking stamps.

There were so many venues. Staffers for the Oregon congressional delega-

---

SILETZ TRIBAL COUNCIL

The following people served on the Siletz Tribal Council during the restoration years from 1973 through 1980: Joe Lane, Robert Rilatos, Rowenda Strong, Dolly Fisher, Stanley Strong, Ed Sondenaa, Ed Ben, Pauline Bell Ricks, Lindsey John, Jim Cook, Kay Steele, Arthur Bensell, Delores Pigsley, Kathryn Harrison, Robert Tom, Sister Francella Griggs, Alta Courville, Mae Bostwick, and Linda Merrill.

---

tion, the interior committees in the Senate and House, and the governor's office had to be regularly briefed. Relationships needed to be established and maintained with reporters and editors for the two Portland newspapers and the papers in Salem, Corvallis, Eugene, and the coastal towns. The effort never raised large amounts of funding, but several thousands of dollars came from the United Churches of Oregon; individual churches, especially the Lutheran and Presbyterian; the American Friends Service Committee; the League of Women Voters; the Daughters of the American Revolution; and others. The tribe broadly solicited letters and resolutions of support, which often required meetings as well as mailings and phone calls. In Oregon, endorsements from the coastal towns were important, as were those from church and civic organizations. No Indian bill can pass without support from the Indian community and endorsements had to be obtained from the Northwest tribes, including the Warm Springs and Yakama; the regional intertribal organizations, including Affiliated Tribes of Northwest Indians and Small Tribes of Western Washington; the National Congress of American Indians, the largest national Indian organization; and other Indian groups, such as the Survival of American Indians Association. Relationships with state and federal agencies, notably the Bureau of Indian Affairs and the Oregon Department of Fish and Wildlife, also needed to be maintained. Lawyers could help with some of this, but most of these people wanted to see tribal leaders and members, not attorneys.

There were other duties. Tribal members wrote papers on history and culture for briefing purposes. They participated broadly in "The People Are Dancing Again" film, providing information during script development, appearing on camera, and then reviewing rough takes for accuracy. Restoration could not proceed without the Statistical Profile of tribal members, which provided socioeconomic data that underscored the tribe's urgent current needs. Siletz volunteers did much of the legwork, which required extensive interviewing since so little data were in existence.

That fall, activity stepped up a notch for the best of reasons. Senator Hatfield not only was eager to introduce the bill. Beyond that, he wanted to hold early committee hearings, assuming that the tribe felt ready.

Autumn also brought storm clouds. The tribe, in gathering support, had contacted many people about the bill that would soon be introduced. There was little resistance to addressing the tribe's economic, social, and cultural issues, but the fishing rights issue was explosive. Salmon and steelhead fishing was sacred for hundreds of thousands of Oregonians. John McKean, director

Pauline Bell Ricks, a leader in the restoration movement and respected tribal member for several terms, has been honored by the naming of the Pauline Ricks Memorial Pow-Wow Grounds on Government Hill. *Photograph by Ron Appelbaum.*

of the Oregon Department of Fish and Wildlife and the most powerful voice in state government on salmon issues, had been set back on his heels by court cases ruling in favor of fishing rights for the Klamath and Columbia River tribes. In November, the influential Fish and Wildlife Commission, the governing board for the department, came out in opposition to Siletz restoration. A big, strong-willed man, McKean sent out flares to his constituency, sports and commercial fishing advocacy groups, and to the press.

The issue was joined before the bill had even been introduced. The *Sunday Oregonian*, with by far the largest circulation in the state, editorialized against the tribe. Pete Cornacchia, outdoors writer for the Eugene *Register-Guard*, set the tone that would characterize the debate from the fishing and hunting side. "Nets in the Alsea all fall and winter, from the first of the silvers to the last of the steelhead? Deer and elk in the coast range under fire all year, day and night, even more so than now? It could happen." He warned, "Circle the wagons, boys, here they come again."

The conflict would plague Siletz restoration all the way through Congress. With several cases upholding tribal treaty rights, Oregonians were attuned to the issue of fishing rights, often front-page and top-of-the-broadcast news. Most of the public did not understand all the ins and outs of the complicated issue, but a large segment thought of it as an "us against them" matter caused by antiquated, technical federal laws.

Tribal fishing and hunting rights mean that the tribes, rather than the states, regulate their own members by setting bag limits, seasons, and licensing requirements and then policing tribal fishers. The rights, especially in the Northwest, may apply at traditional off-reservation sites as well as on the reservations. In addition, tribes in the Northwest are entitled to a "fair share," usually 50 percent, of the resource. The reasoning, a fair reading of history, is that tribal treaty negotiators, as salmon people, insisted on protecting their basic means of subsistence when they agreed to surrender most of their lands and be placed on smaller reservations.

The issue in modern times can be characterized as a turf battle, with the state commission fighting to protect its regulatory jurisdiction and its non-Indian constituents. While this is true, it was not that simple, certainly not that simple politically. A great many people and communities depended on commercial fishing in the 1970s—more than today—and, however fair it might be to the tribes to enforce these rights, the economic and human hardships for non-Indians can be considerable.

The Siletz understood the sensitivity and included a provision that the bill would be neutral on the treaty issue: restoration would not grant or restore any new hunting or fishing rights. At the same time, it was possible that the tribe still possessed some rights that preexisted and survived termination, although it was uncertain how extensive they might be. John McKean, his commission, and the fishermen's organizations wanted language extinguishing all existing Siletz fishing and hunting rights. The tribe saw this as a hold-up and did not want to agree to such confiscation. But, reasonable or not, arguments by the commission and its allies vividly portraying effects on hardworking fishermen, their families, and their communities carried great weight. The Siletz restoration effort had been pushed perilously close to the third rail of Northwest politics.

Senator Hatfield expected strong opposition and would not be thrown off track. He unequivocally favored Siletz restoration and assigned Tom Imeson, one of his top aides, to work on the bill. On the fishing issue, Hatfield agreed with the tribe's approach: the bill should not create any new rights but it would be wrong to extinguish any rights the tribe might now have. Comfortable with his grasp on the issues, he was unimpressed by parades of horribles and confident that he would not be blindsided by some unexamined point of law. Politically, he was safe.

It was harder for Les AuCoin, a Democrat who succeeded to Wendell Wyatt's seat for the district that included the central Coast. AuCoin sincerely backed Siletz restoration, at least so far as health and education matters were concerned, and agreed to introduce the bill in the House. The fishing issue troubled him though, and Indian legislation was new territory for him. A newcomer to Congress, he lacked Hatfield's bulletproof security in office. The House bill would move more slowly than its counterpart in the Senate.

The Siletz Restoration Act was introduced in both Houses of Congress on December 17, 1975. The bills had influential co-sponsors from Oregon, and on the Senate side, Senator Hatfield also lined up members of the interior committee, where the bill would go. Best of all, Senator Hatfield promptly set the Senate subcommittee hearings for March 30 and 31. It deserves mention that it is rare in the extreme for a small minority group to organize, build support, and bring their concerns to congressional hearings within the span of just two and a half years.

The Siletz made two trips to Washington, D.C., in early 1976. On the first, a few council members briefed legislators, staff, and agency officials. By then, Art Bensell, mayor of the City of Siletz and proprietor of the Siletz general store, was tribal chairman. He had not been active in the restoration effort at first, but by mid-1975 he was firmly committed. Soft-spoken and grandfatherly, Bensell was knowledgeable, articulate, and fair. People took to him immediately and trusted him. The same can be said of the tribal council as a whole. Passionately committed to their cause, they nonetheless avoided overstatements and inaccuracies. Their effectiveness was a main reason why—even given the explosive nature of the fishing issue—the reporting in the press was mostly positive, public officials responded well, and personal confrontations were few and far between. On their first trip back east, the council members won many supporters.

The entire council went back to the Capitol for the March hearings. Because of the full-court press applied by John McKean, the Fish and Wildlife Commission, and fishing interests, the bill had received broad attention in the press and at public forums. Siletz representatives had met with several commission members and with Beverly Hall, the lawyer in the state attorney general's office who was assigned to the commission. Sessions with commercial and sports interests, which often disagreed with each other but cooperated on Indian fishing issues, were intense but respectful. They had one-on-one meetings with Governor Robert Straub, who supported the bill; Attorney General Lee Johnson, who supported Siletz restoration generally but took a hard line on the fishing issue; representatives of local municipalities (Lincoln City gave support); and other public officials.

A multifaceted public attitude had settled in and would remain in place throughout the five-year legislative process. The Siletz had been badly treated historically and faced serious current problems. The tribe deserved to be recognized once again, and its members should receive health, education, and other federal services. The tribe had good leadership, people who could be trusted. As for the fishing issue, public opinion was all over the map.

For the council members, the trip was daunting, but spirits were high. None had ever testified before Congress and most had never been to Washington, D.C. As Kathryn Harrison, who had been on an airplane just once, put it, "We were like kids. [It was] just a thrill to be there." She fondly remembered the support of Senator Hatfield, Tom Imeson, and other staff members. "We could feel that warmth on the plane—that they were waiting for us." Just before take-off from Portland, they received surprising but welcome news that their hard work was paying off. One of the leading fishing organizations, the All Coast Fishermen's Marketing Association, had come out in favor of the bill.

The council members and Joe Lane—no longer chairman but still active in the restoration effort—divided up the topics and prepared written testimony in advance. To put them more at ease, Tom Imeson had arranged to keep the Senate hearing room open beyond normal closing hours for a "dress rehearsal" the night before the hearing. After dinner, the council members gave their testimony in the chambers. The lawyers and Senate staff members acted as senators, firing the kind of questions they might receive over the next two days, and the council members responded.

The next morning, the testimony of council members was informative, well-delivered, genuine, and moving. Observers were spellbound as Pauline Bell Ricks presented nineteenth-century history through the eyes of her grandmother, Ki-Ya-Na-Ha, who had been brutally taken from her homeland on the Trail of Tears to Siletz. Joe Lane recounted the tribe's reorganization in the early 1970s and documented how the tribe's "consent" to termination was not freely and knowingly given. Others addressed health, alcoholism, education, economic conditions, current tribal membership, and tribal administration. Art Bensell gave an overarching account of the importance of restoration and touched on the bill's provision that neither granted nor extinguished any fishing or hunting rights. Capitol Hill veterans in the audience later agreed that this was how such a hearing should be done.

Siletz representatives testify in Washington, D.C., in front of the Senate Indian Affairs Committee on March 30, 1976. From the left are Delores Pigsley, Joe Lane, Robert Rilatos, Art Bensell, Katherine Harrison, Robert Tom, Pauline Ricks, Alta Courville, and Sister Francella Griggs. *Siletz Tribal Collection.*

The second day of hearings opened with rousing testimony from Senator Ted Kennedy, who made a surprise appearance:

> Mr. Chairman, as indicated in testimony taken yesterday, the Federal agencies charged with delivering programs to federally recognized tribes stand ready to begin work with an already elected council. This council has shown its initiative, its leadership ability, and its commitment by presenting to the Senate a clear and compelling case for restoration. I associate myself with their presentation and fully support enactment of S.2801. It would be especially fitting for Congress to enact this bill in our bicentennial year, so that we might show by deeds as well as words that we are a nation of honor, that we can admit our mistakes of the past, and that we are prepared to act fairly and justly towards Indian tribes in the future.

The mood shifted dramatically when Beverly Hall seated herself at the witness table. While opposition to the bill came from several quarters, this assistant in the state attorney general's office was the main spear-thrower, a role she assumed with relish. Articulate and smart, but combative and unyielding in her zeal to extinguish Siletz fishing and hunting rights, Hall wielded great power. Charged with giving the Fish and Wildlife Commission advice on the red-flag matter of Indian treaty rights, she could—and did—use scare tactics to alarm state officials and the public. To some extent, Hall was a creature of her times: assertive sovereign tribal governments were new on the scene and attorney general offices in all the western states were stoutly defending the sovereignty of their states. But Hall crossed the line by never relenting, by insisting on abrogating Siletz treaty rights, and, failing that, by spuriously arguing that broadly supported neutral language on treaty rights was not neutral and was affirmatively dangerous.

Congress had three options with regard to Siletz fishing and hunting rights. First, the legislation could grant such rights to the tribe, a course the Siletz decided not to pursue. Second, the bill could extinguish any rights that might exist. This was the so-called McKean Amendment, supported by the commission and Hall. Third, the bill could be neutral—that is, maintain the status quo by neither granting new rights nor extinguishing existing ones. This was Senator Hatfield's position. Section 3(c) of the bill, drafted to be direct and easily understandable, read: "This Act shall not grant or restore any hunting, fishing, or trapping rights of any nature to the tribe or its members." On the first day of the hearing, Reid Chambers, the top Indian law expert in the Interior department and an eminent attorney, had testified that section 3(c) was neutral and did not create any hunting or fishing rights.

SENATOR HATFIELD . . .

Now, Mr. Chambers, if the Siletz fishing and hunting rights did not survive the termination act, is it possible this provision in some manner could confer special hunting and fishing rights upon the tribe?

MR. CHAMBERS. No. That is impossible, Senator. The plain language of the section says it shall not confer any such rights and if there was any conceivable doubt about that in deciding that kind of question, courts would refer to this kind of legislative history by the sponsor of the bill in committee hearings and would conclude—it means clearly a court would conclude that this act does not confer any special hunting or fishing rights.

In Hall's tense, ninety-minute testimony, she evaded and bickered with Hatfield's questions, raising fears that the bill was not neutral but unwilling to submit corrective language. When she advocated for the McKean Amendment, the extinguishment option, Hatfield replied that "we might as well kiss the bill goodbye today if we are going to follow that procedure." He knew that tribes nationally would actively oppose the bill with that amendment because it would set a precedent for abrogating treaty rights. Also, the Office of Management and Budget would shoot it down on budgetary grounds, since the tribe would have to be compensated in an unknown amount for any treaty rights that might exist. But for Hall, displaying a lack of respect for Hatfield that the senator chose to ignore, it was extinguishment or nothing, plain and simple:

> It is unconscionable for the Congress to attempt to assuage the Nation's guilt complex for its past mistreatment of Indian citizens by simply ignoring, because of political convenience, the issues this proposed legislation raises concerning the protection of fish and wildlife.

Siletz restoration, out of nowhere a major public issue in Oregon, saw no formal congressional activity for more than a year following the March 1976 Senate hearing. Hall's arguments generated numerous exchanges of memos on legal points and historical developments. John McKean proposed alternative legislation, the "Siletz Health and Welfare Act," which would make tribal members eligible for federal benefits. The draft bill, rejected outright by the tribe, did not provide for recognition or creation of a reservation. It never gained traction.

In the summer of 1977, with the identical restoration bills moving toward committee action in both Houses, the issue reignited in the press. After the Senate committee voted the bill out favorably, the measure was scheduled for House committee action on September 23. Then, six weeks before the hearing, the new attorney general for Oregon, James Redden, circulated a memorandum written by Beverly Hall. She argued that the passage of the bill would automatically restore tribal jurisdiction over all land and persons, Indian and non-Indian, within the boundaries of the pre-termination reservation. Redden's cover letter reflected his doubts, calling the opinion a "rough draft" and emphasizing that it "does not constitute a formal or informal opinion of this office." He apologized that the memorandum had already been leaked to the press. Hall's incendiary document was a scare tactic and was quickly exposed as such. Congressman AuCoin referred the matter to the Library of Congress for an opinion, and the Library had no trouble in concluding, within just a week, that the bill "would not have the territorial ramifications" claimed in the memorandum.

With one exception, the bill received only technical amendments during its journey through Congress. The original bill called for the BIA to develop a reservation plan in negotiations with the tribe and to submit the plan to Congress for approval within six months. The implicit assumption was that the forty acres on Government Hill would be the reservation. The statute, as passed, called for a more elaborate study to be conducted over a period of two years. Some of the other provisions placed limits on the tribe—for example, all reservation land must be in Lincoln County, and Public Law 280, which applied in Oregon except for the Warm Springs Reservation, would be in force for Siletz and would give the state broader jurisdiction than on non-Public Law 280 reservations. More importantly, the revised reservation-plan provisions (including the two-year time period) were much more broad-gauged than conceived in the original bill and laid the foundation for a larger reservation. The bill went through both Houses easily, and President Carter signed the Siletz Restoration Act into law on November 18, 1977. The celebrating took place some 3,000 miles away.

Once the bill passed both Houses, the tribe had less than two weeks to arrange an all-out, three-day celebration to commemorate the historic occasion. Tribal staff coordinated with the White House so that President Carter would sign the Siletz Restoration Act into law—and repeal the termination act—on Friday, November 18, 1977. That night, people directly involved in restoration would have a potluck at the Grange Hall, followed by speeches and reminiscences in the Siletz high school gym. Saturday would be the big public evening, a potluck and a major pow-wow, "the social event of the year in Lincoln County," as one local newspaper described it, and one of Oregon's biggest Indian gatherings. Sunday would be low-key, with a service and time for people to talk, reflect, and let it all sink in. The word went out by newspaper, radio, and the moccasin grapevine.

Siletz people from the Willamette Valley, the greater Northwest, and beyond, forced away by termination, came back in numbers to celebrate the new beginning. The dancers, drummers, and spectators included Indians from tribes in western Oregon, across the Cascades, and in Washington and California. Among the dignitaries were Victor Atiyeh, state senator and soon to be governor of Oregon, and many officeholders from the Coast who had stuck with the Siletz in spite of the opposition. Many locals, knowing that something good was up, came by. Siletz women, headed up by Pauline Bell Ricks, chairperson for the celebration, cooked food for hundreds of people. High school and junior high boys and girls, organized by teacher Tom Ball, a Klamath tribal member, set up tables and chairs and cleaned up.

No facility in Siletz was large enough, so the Saturday pow-wow was held at the Lincoln County Fairgrounds in Newport. It exceeded all expectations. That was certainly true of the weather, which produced the kind of late autumn Oregon chill that seeps into every bone and organ. Preparations had been made to hold the pow-wow indoors, except that the fire marshal, seeing the overflow crowd, ordered that all the doors remain wide open. When the tribe brought in propane heaters, the marshal considered them too dangerous and ordered them shut down. Condensation formed on the ceiling and dripped down, making the chill sink in even deeper. More than thirty years later, people still rhapsodize about that magical evening, but invariably they begin with the weather. "It was *soooo cold.*"

The pow-wow was an explosion of color and sound and emotion, with the drummers pounding out the old rhythms and the singers reaching, their neck muscles tight and their veins bulging, for the piercing high notes. The grand entry was stunning, as the Indian people came in, bedecked in their best regalia, the basket hats, dentalia and other sea shells, buckskin, beads, shawls with swaying fringes, and headdresses with eagle feathers, some adorned with the bright red of pileated woodpecker scalps. The grand entry went on for well over an hour. Drum groups from Umatilla, Warm Springs, Yakama, and intertribal groups, most with eight drummers seated around the large central drums, performed their songs when called by Bob Tom, the master of ceremonies. When you are within the driving rhythms of Indian drums and songs, enveloped by them, they are captivating, utterly mesmerizing, and that was especially so, on the Oregon Coast that night, when we were enveloped as well by full-blown justice and the knowledge that our nation's system, with all its flaws, can sometimes respond to dispossessed peoples, can simply do what is right.

After the grand entry, the tribe held an elaborate giveaway to express appreciation to the many people who had supported their cause. The gift-giving was a fit reminder of the generosity and civility that so distinguished the conduct of tribal people during their four-year journey from reorganization to restoration. The pow-wow then moved into specialty dances—war dances, social dances, hunting dances, a gourd dance by Native American Church dancers—with a drum taking each dance. The first dance was for the veterans, the second for the elders. Well past midnight, the drummers performed the last song and people were sent on their way by a prayer on this night when termination died off, tribalism was restored, and the oldest music of the Coast, the ancestors' melodies, rang out once again with their full beauty and vigor and hopefulness.

"I thought the first restoration bill was hard," reflected Delores Pigsley, then tribal secretary and treasurer, "until it got even more difficult when we had to build a government and obtain a reservation." The tribe had committed to a number of tasks, including writing a new constitution, setting up the capability to administer federal and foundation grants, constructing a tribal center, and obtaining lands for a reservation. As for the reservation, under the 1977 restoration statute, the BIA had two years to negotiate with the tribe and submit a plan to Congress, which would decide whether to pass a second Siletz statute creating a reservation.

The restoration act gave few specifics about the reservation plan. How much land should be in the reservation? Where would it be located? What should be the reservation's purpose? The only assumption was that Government Hill would go into trust—if the City of Siletz agreed to transfer it back to the tribe—and be a part of a new reservation, or perhaps all of it.

Early in the work of setting up a tribal structure, it became apparent that federal recognition would be a big help. The health and education programs addressed critical needs and the tribe received significant direct funding for administration and construction. Still, federal programs standing alone could not assure a secure financial future. At the early strategy sessions, the tribal council concluded that the reservation should have two main objectives: To provide cultural and recreational opportunities for tribal members and to produce a steady flow of income for tribal governance, economic development, and job creation. The council knew that this meant a reasonably large land base, something that had not been much discussed. It also would require a comprehensive planning effort—more than the council had anticipated. Using BIA funding, the tribe retained CH2M Hill, the internationally known engineering and planning firm that had its international headquarters in Corvallis (the home office has since been moved to the Denver area). Marcy Schwartz and

William Blosser were the point people at the firm for the Siletz contract.

As CH2M Hill's economic analysis came in, it became clear that the logical source for income was timber, the traditional economic engine in Lincoln County. Recreation—a resort, a rustic inn, and campground—were also considered, but the thinking was that the way to pursue those projects would be through investing timber revenues. How much forest land would be needed? Studies showed that the tribe would require about $600,000 annually to support the comprehensive program it envisioned. The idea, then, would be to seek a transfer of land that would provide that level of income. It was a long shot but the only way to reach the tribe's goal.

The planners developed maps showing all land ownerships in Lincoln County. The Siuslaw National Forest was located in the northern and southern parts of the county, far from Siletz, and it was likely that the Forest Service and environmentalists would strongly oppose taking land out of a national forest. A meeting with R. E. Worthington, regional forester, confirmed that national forest lands would not be available. There was one sizeable block of private lands near Siletz: the old C. D. Johnson holdings, now owned by Georgia-Pacific. The tribe made a formal proposal to the company and asked for a meeting with Robert Floweree, president and CEO. In a meeting in Floweree's Portland office, he told the tribal delegation that no, the company was not willing to transfer any land to the Siletz. He also said that Georgia-Pacific would be perfectly happy to have the tribe as a neighbor, if it obtained federal land near the company's operations. The company would in no way oppose a reservation for the Siletz.

That left the Bureau of Land Management. Most of the BLM's holdings in the country were marginal grazing lands in the arid West. The exception was in western Oregon, where the BLM held valuable old-growth Douglas fir stands, prime lands for timber harvesting. Unlike the Forest Service, the BLM's mission and traditions included transferring land out of federal ownership when appropriate. The agency might be willing to relinquish some land to the tribe.

CH2M Hill located 3,630 acres of BLM land in the Upper Siletz River watershed with high timber potential. The land was not contiguous—there were thirty-seven separate parcels—and some of it was steep and difficult to log. It was rough and remote enough that it would not offer much recreation use. The stands contained few old-growth trees—most of them were 90 to 120 years old, having grown back from the 1849 fire—but it was mature, marketable timber. These parcels could be expected to produce the target amount of

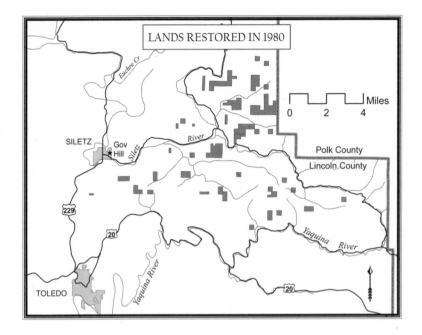

LANDS RESTORED IN 1980

SILETZ · Gov Hill · River · Polk County · Lincoln County · Yaquina River · TOLEDO · Yaquina River · Euchre Cr · Siletz · 229 · 20 · 20 · Miles 0 2 4

$600,000 per year. The total value of the land was estimated at $26 million or more.

What would the BLM say? The proposal to the agency was lengthy, detailing the tribe's history of land loss, its current needs, the planning process under the restoration statute, and the BLM lands the tribe had identified. The decision point came at a Portland meeting with Murl Storms, state director of the BLM, a crusty, no-nonsense veteran of public lands controversies who had grown up in ranch country. Storms, in effect, would make the final decision. BLM officials in Washington, D.C., favored the tribe's plan, but they would almost certainly defer to the staff in the field, namely Storms. We had no idea what he would do.

At the BLM's Portland office, Art Bensell laid out the tribe's position. Storms, seated at the other end of the long conference table, said nothing during Bensell's lengthy presentation and asked no questions afterward. When Bensell finished, Storms remained silent and stared down at his folded hands. Then he looked up and announced his decision. "OK. I'll keep my pistol under the table if you will." We all laughed. There was still a long way to go but this was a monumental accomplishment for the tribe. The BLM Washington office soon endorsed the arrangement.

Government Hill, the other parcel in the reservation plan proposed by the Siletz, was just forty acres, but it held great meaning. Graced with mature Douglas fir and Sitka spruce trees and level on top, the low but scenic hill rises a hundred feet or so above the east side of town. A center for tribal existence since the earliest days of the reservation, Government Hill was the locale for the BIA buildings that housed the Siletz agency back to the 1800s. Most of those structures—the agency headquarters, the hospital and meeting hall, the tribal cannery, and tribal cottages—had collapsed or been torn down, since the city had made no use of the area other than building a water storage tank and treatment facility. Only the Paul Washington Cemetery had been maintained, owing to the labor of Siletz people. Looking to the future, the tribe planned to construct its main tribal buildings on the hill, including offices, a clinic, a community hall with a large meeting room and kitchen facilities, and a gymnasium. There would be a pow-wow ground and children's play area. Now the question was whether the City of Siletz would return to the tribe the land that it obtained at termination.

The city began its decision-making process in the fall of 1979. The Planning Commission voted unanimously to transfer the land to the tribe, but the city council, which had authority to make the transfer, was divided and decided to put the matter to an advisory election on November 1. The two-year period for

Art Bensell, tribal chairman during the passage of the 1977 restoration statute and the 1980 reservation statute, is shown here in the early 1970s, viewing some of the wreckage of termination—the BIA health clinic abandoned two decades earlier. *Siletz Tribal Collection.*

Government Hill Advisory Ballot

One of the friendlier cartoon depictions of Siletz Indians in the 1970s, this one from 1979 portrayed well the tribe's dreams for Government Hill—but the attire was hardly the chosen style at Siletz. *Used with permission from the* Newport News Times/Lincoln County Leader.

the Interior department to submit the bill to Congress expired just seventeen days later.

The tribe believed their request was fair: the tribe's past and future uses were well documented and, besides, the city had received the land for free. Some citizens, though, wondered about a legitimate issue. The hill, overgrown though it was by blackberries, could be cleared and used as a city park amid the tall trees. Should the city be giving away municipal land that it might develop for public purposes in the future? Further, a small number of non-Indians stirred the pot with racist remarks. One of Leonard Whitlow's more moderate statements was that "we're not going to give those people city land so they can build their White House up on the hill and play . . . Indian all day long." The group launched unfounded charges, such as assailing the tribe for intending to use the area for a house of prostitution.

City officials believed that the turnout was the largest for any Siletz election ever held. Tribal members were a large part of the voting population although not a majority because many lived near Siletz but outside the city limits. A sizeable number of non-Indian residents supported the tribe. They and dozens of tribal members spent election day in a get-out-the-vote campaign, and drove people to the voting booths.

I remember that evening so vividly. A group of us waited anxiously for the results over at the BIA offices. Art Bensell, the former mayor, served as an election official and ran over from the A-Frame several times to give us tallies. "We're behind by five." "Now we're ahead by seven." Then finally, Art burst

The Siletz City Council, lower left, deliberates the return of Government Hill to the Siletz Tribe in a tense room packed with citizens and newspaper, radio, and television reporters. *Used with permission from the* Newport News Times/Lincoln County Leader.

through the door, shaking and flushed in a way I'd never seen him. "We WON!!"

The vote was 148 to 134. It was close enough that the opponents pressured the City Council, reminding them that it was only a straw vote. But on November 13, the Council voted 3 to 1 to transfer the land back to the tribe.

The City Council vote came just in time to meet the November 18 deadline for submitting the reservation plan to Congress. The plan received broad local and state-wide support, with the *Oregonian* editorializing that "the Siletz Indian Tribe must have a reservation on the central Oregon Coast. A tribe without land is like a native bird shorn of its nesting area." Oregon Attorney General James Redden, who had chaired a committee of representatives of state agencies that monitored the development of the plan, reported to Governor Atiyeh, who himself supported the plan, that "I think it is fair to state that the members of your committee . . . approve the Reservation Plan." Senator Hatfield promptly introduced a bill to approve the plan. Then came a surprise: Les AuCoin refused to follow suit in the House.

AuCoin never had been entirely comfortable with Siletz restoration and now his doubts came out in a scattershot of concerns about the proposed reservation. He worried about economic feasibility: "What will be the impact of this bill on land use in the area? Is the plan economically workable? Are the timber projections realistic? What is the taxpayers' liability if it proves to be uneconomical?" Although federal and state officials had regularly been briefed as the plan progressed and the BIA Portland area office, with Doyce "Spec" Waldrip taking the lead, had been constantly involved, AuCoin criticized the role of CH2M Hill and the tribe in developing the plan: "Thus far it is not evident that the [Interior] department has been anything other than a forwarding agency for the tribe."

But it was the fishing issue that was front and center in AuCoin's mind. Although the neutral language in the 1977 act was repeated in the Hatfield bill approving the reservation plan, AuCoin asked, "Will it or will it not enhance prospects for superior hunting and fishing rights? The answer is far from clear." He also asserted, although there is no indication of this in the public record, that "the Siletz tribe have known for two years" that a final settlement of the rights issue was "fundamental" to his support.

The tribal council was left with a dilemma. There was by then a broad understanding, including by Attorney General Redden, that the neutrality language did assure that no new rights would be created. But some of the sports groups still insisted on eliminating whatever rights the tribe might already possess—and Les AuCoin was carrying their water. He would block the reservation bill until Siletz fishing and hunting rights were abrogated or otherwise settled.

The tribal council and attorneys went into negotiations that took nearly six months. The Northwest Steelheaders, the largest and most vocal group opposed to the bill, took the lead for the fishing interests and dropped their insistence on extinguishment of rights in favor of a limited tribal fishery. The state was taking a more moderate position this time around. Jack Donaldson had replaced John McKean as director of the Fish and Wildlife Department, and Attorney General Redden kept Beverly Hall under wraps. As Herb Lundy, chair of the Fish and Wildlife Commission candidly put it, the "commission has been adamant on this matter, but that position is not tenable any more."

In time, a compromise emerged and an agreement was signed by tribal, state, and federal officials on April 22, 1980. The tribe would have a cultural—not a commercial—fishery and tribal members would be allowed to take up to 200 salmon at sites on Euchre Creek, Dewey Creek, and Rock Creek. Tribal fishers would not be required to obtain state licenses; a sixty-day season would be set by the State Department in consultation with the tribes; and—contrary to state law—tribal fishers could use dip nets, spears, and gaff hooks. The state would be required to provide the tribe with 4,000 pounds of edible salmon carcasses for tribal ceremonial and subsistence purposes. Tribal members could also obtain sport and commercial licenses under general state laws.

The agreement further provided that tribal members could take a total of 375 deer and 25 elk each year from the Stott Mountain and Alsea Management units. State licenses would not be required, but tribal hunting would be during regular state seasons. As for gathering, the tribal members would have a broad right to take eels, seaweed, and freshwater mussels for non-commercial purposes. The state also agreed to provide special permits that the tribe would issue to tribal members to gather sea anemones, rock oysters, and saltwater mussels for ceremonial and subsistence purposes.

The negotiations included special provisions for approval. A federal court judge would be asked to issue a consent decree approving the agreement and making it into a federal court injunction. This would be a "friendly lawsuit" with the tribe, the state, and the Interior and Justice departments all seeking court approval. Congress would then approve the agreement as part of the reservation legislation.

The consent decree went before U.S. District Judge James Burns, who held an expedited hearing on May 2, 1980. Federal, state, and tribal attorneys explained the background and the agreement. Burns knew of the long-running public issue and was pleased to see that it had been resolved short of lengthy litigation. Three Siletz tribal members filed a statement of objection, supported by fifty tribal members, arguing that the tribal council lacked authority to sign the agreement and that the matter should go before the full general council. Judge Burns was satisfied that the tribal council had authority to adopt the agreement, however, and signed the consent decree, making the agreement controlling law. AuCoin, who had followed the negotiations closely and approved of the consent decree, attended the court hearing and promptly introduced a bill endorsing the reservation plan.

The tribal council's decision to enter into the consent decree was controversial within the tribe then and remains so today. It could hardly be otherwise. Fishing, hunting, and gathering rights are sacred to Indian tribes, and the idea of compromising them is repugnant. Tribal members can fairly ask whether the decision was right. Why so few fish? Why so much state involvement? Why the rush? Why not just stand on our rights and stay firm until AuCoin saw the light or left office?

To a person, tribal council members themselves held these concerns. The decision was reached only after long and intense meetings. They knew AuCoin was not bluffing: there would be no reservation on his watch unless there was a settlement of the fishing issue. At stake was 3,630 acres of valuable timberland that could provide needed revenues for critical tribal functions and jobs. Obtaining the transfer of these BLM lands was a great achievement—beyond anyone's expectations when the planning process began—and the offer of those lands was fragile and could be repudiated by a future administration or Congress. As for going to court, the fishing and hunting rights of the tribe had never been formally adjudicated or otherwise defined, leaving the tribe with extensive and uncertain litigation over the effect of allotment and termination on tribal rights.

Few governing bodies face decisions as wrenchingly complex and emotional as do American Indian tribal councils. The decision to support the consent decree was laden with the weight of history, legal technicalities, great economic value, the impossibility of knowing the predilections of future judges and members of Congress, and the social, economic, and cultural needs of a land-based people. And it may be that the council in 1980 received imperfect advice from their lawyers, of which I was one. One thing is for sure: Siletz Tribal Council members gave it their all, committing every necessary hour, asking every question, reading every memo, hearing out every tribal member, and heeding every last call to conscience.

After the consent decree, the reservation bill sailed through Congress and received President Carter's signature on September 3, 1980. It was finally time to return to the tribe a small but significant part of the ancestral lands. The formal land transfer was set for the morning of September 20, to be followed by an afternoon parade down the streets of Siletz and an evening pow-wow. More than a thousand celebrants flowed into Siletz all day long from all over Oregon and the Northwest, their numbers larger even than the celebration three years earlier.

The transfer ceremony was held on Government Hill at the old picnic site adjacent to the Paul Washington Cemetery. Once there had been a log and shake structure, an open-sided lodge for shelter, and a large stone fireplace constructed by Siletz workers under the auspices of the Civilian Conservation Corps. Now only the fireplace stood, but it remained a favorite tribal place, set

Tribal council member Stanley Strong delivers a ringing message at the ceremony on Government Hill celebrating the creation of the reservation in 1980. *Siletz Tribal Collection.*

among giant spruce and fir. The weather that morning was moderate, and the forest and some 250 people were graced by a thick coastal mist that softened the ceremony and bound us together.

There were a few speeches from tribal and federal officials and a chance for other Siletz people to comment and reflect on the occasion. The feelings deepened as the moment for the return of land grew close.

The crowd went silent. Paul Vettrick of the BLM formally handed the federal patent for 3,630 acres to Art Bensell. Mayor Roy Weaver of the City of Siletz gave him the deed to Government Hill. Bensell then gave the documents to Bernard Topash, BIA superintendent for Siletz, who presented Bensell with trust certificates for the land. The men shook hands. Then the tribal chairman held the documents aloft and cried out with an emotion-packed voice: "I proclaim this your reservation forever! Let the celebration begin!" And the war-whoops and applause and shouts sounded out and mixed with the mist, for at last a clear marker had been laid down forever. The Siletz Tribe was back, truly and finally back.

REBUILDING SOVEREIGNTY

"We will *survive."*

R ATHER THAN BEING AN END IN ITSELF, RESTORATION PROVED to be only a beginning. The tribe—its members scattered, most of its land taken, and its governing authority dormant for a quarter of a century—had to establish its identity and create a governing structure in a new time. Looking back, the tsunami that was termination left much wreckage for the Siletz Tribe of the 1980s, but the upheaval held out one great benefit: free of accumulated baggage and blessed with flexibility, the tribe could step back, assess the possibilities in the midst of the most progressive era for Indians in history, and craft institutions and priorities designed to fulfill the best dreams of its people.

Over time, an approach emerged. The highest calling of the Siletz Tribe is to preserve and restore the culture. The second is to rebuild and maintain a strong and compassionate sovereignty. The third, with the first two as the foundation, is to provide for the health, education, and financial well-being of the 4,500 tribal members. While inevitably there are many shortcomings and numerous advances still to be made, the Siletz Tribe has made progress beyond anyone's imagination on the day in 1980 when Siletz people and their friends celebrated the land return.

Nationally, modern Indian tribes are undergoing cultural revivals, socioeconomic conditions on reservations are improving, and tribal governments have become members of the community of governments in contemporary America. At the same time, the general populace has a limited understanding of modern Indian tribes. They ask how tribes can be sovereign governments.

Isn't that the role of the federal and state governments? Are there really very many Indians who still follow the traditional cultures? Why are tribes allowed to operate casinos? And where does the money go?

The evolution of the modern Siletz Tribe is a fascinating story of how a dispossessed people has, through its own resilience and creativity, wrought a reconstruction uniquely fitted to its own historical and contemporary circumstances. This has been done through a combination—at first blush, an unlikely one—of governmental excellence, traditional values, and wise entrepreneurship. No tribe, including the Siletz, has found all the answers, but by the early twenty-first century, it is fair to conclude that the Siletz and many other tribes may have put in place fundamental attitudes and institutions that will lead to the fulfillment of their ambitious goals.

Siletz people are clear that their tribe has little ownership of land under American law, that most of the aboriginal landscape and the treaty reservation have been wrested from tribal hands. Those realities are different from morality, though, and tribal members hold firm to a moral claim to the land their ancestors walked. Certainly there is an overwhelming sense of belonging. This is their place.

Most people go to Siletz country by car from the Portland area. You drive south on I-5 through the welcoming Willamette Valley, where Kalapuyas fired the grasses to encourage them to grow and where Siletz tribal families later picked hops after driving over the bumpy road from the reservation. At Salem you turn west on Route 22. Now in the foothills of the Coast Range, you take Route 18, the Salmon River Highway. This was the route taken by Coquelle Thompson Sr. and the other south Coast Indians in 1856 under the watchful eye of their military escort, after their confounding steamship voyage. Thompson's people found some respite when they reached the sea smells and the mouth of the Salmon River, so promising in scrumptious mussels and returning coho.

Route 18 goes past Spirit Mountain, the Grand Ronde Tribe's casino. The Lincoln County line lies about five miles farther on. About fourteen miles from the Coast at this point, this is the eastern border of the 1855 treaty reservation.

So far, the drive across the Coast Range has mostly been through private land, which has been heavily logged over, leaving patches of ground in different stages—middle-aged trees 100 feet or taller, smaller growth, and stripped-bare hillsides. The trip down the west side of the range takes you through the Van Duzer Scenic Corridor, with its old-growth Douglas fir stands of the sort that blanketed the area for thousands of years.

Near the Coast, the modern highway bends south, away from the old route to the mouth of the Salmon. You find yourself on the outskirts of Lincoln City, every inch of which was once allotted land held by Siletz tribal members. When you enter the north end of town, the first thing you come to, on the beach side of the road, is the Siletz Tribe's Chinook Winds Casino Resort. It is Lincoln City's largest landmark and largest business as well.

Chinook Winds operates at something of a competitive disadvantage, since potential customers from the Portland area reach the Grand Ronde casino first and may eschew the additional thirty-minute drive to the Coast. The Siletz, however, seem to have struck a chord with billboards proclaiming "It's Better at the Beach." Also, it may have helped that *Native American Casino Magazine*—for reasons that remain unclear—named Chinook Winds the "Sexiest Casino in the Country." Chinook Winds is a force.

Since time immemorial, western Oregon tribes have played elaborate stick games and engaged in other forms of gambling, but Chinook Winds' direct origins are more recent, tracing to the 1970s when Indian tribes first asserted their right to engage in high-stakes gambling operations. The states immediately pounced, challenging tribal bingo halls and poker rooms on the grounds that they violated state laws and county ordinances (the states did in fact allow poker rooms and gaming operations run by churches and fraternal organizations, but the tribal laws allowed higher stakes and longer hours than their state counterparts). The tribes relied on the most basic proposition of federal Indian law: that, for most purposes, state laws do not reach onto Indian lands, where sovereign tribal laws govern.

The states, characterizing their attack on Indian gaming as a moral crusade, raided Indian bingo halls and shut them down. The Seminole Nation of Florida and the Morongo Tribe and Cabazon Band of Mission Indians of California prevailed in lower court rulings, which upheld tribal sovereignty. The much-watched cases from California went to the United States Supreme Court, which ruled for the tribes in a 1987 opinion. "Tribal sovereignty," the Court held, "is dependent on and subordinate to, only the federal government, not the states." The opinion squarely addressed the importance of successful commercial ventures, such as gaming, to poverty-stricken tribes: "Self-determination and economic development are not within reach if Tribes cannot raise revenues and provide employment for their members."

States and non-Indian gaming interests, knowing that Congress could outlaw tribal gaming even if the states could not, proposed a ban on Indian gaming. In the end the national legislature, with Senators Daniel Inouye and John McCain and Congressman Morris Udall taking the lead, decided in the Indian Gaming Regulatory Act of 1988 to regulate tribal gaming but not prohibit it. IGRA provides that in most instances tribes have the "exclusive right" to regulate gaming on land under tribal jurisdiction, subject to federal oversight by the National Indian Gaming Regulatory Commission. In a provision that would later work to the Siletz Tribe's disadvantage, "Class III" operations—that is, casinos and other high-stakes ventures—are subject to tribal-state compacts, which IGRA required the states to negotiate in "good faith." The federal oversight in IGRA is rigorous but has preserved for tribes the opportunity to produce substantial revenues.

By 2008, annual gross revenues from tribal gaming nationally had soared to about $27 billion annually, a whopping figure, but still less than 30 percent of the national yield from gaming. Now almost a quarter of the states, many of which protested loudly and sanctimoniously against Indian gaming, allow casino gambling, and most states run their own large-scale lotteries to generate budget funds. Although the exact figure is not known, net revenues for all gaming tribes combined in 2007 were probably about one-third of the gross, or $8 billion for the year.

The 225 tribes that allow gaming fall into three groups. About 20 tribes raise roughly 40 percent of all Indian gaming revenues. Several—mostly near large metropolitan areas in New England, the Great Lakes area, and California—have small memberships, and per capita distributions to tribal members, which are subject to income taxation, reach six and even seven figures annually. Another group of a few dozen tribes in remote areas struggle to make any positive return at all, and some of them may eventually fail. (For those tribes, even though the bottom line may be flat or worse, the casinos are useful. With unemployment high, casino jobs are prized.)

The third group, by far the largest, is composed of tribes with casinos that show a net annual return of roughly $10-$25 million a year. This revenue stream is critical to those tribes, but not because of the modest per capita payments, which will not make any tribal members rich. Rather, the gaming proceeds go to governmental operations so that tribes can have a chance to reach their highest ideal—making their reservation true homelands. Casinos provide funding for health, education, housing, law and order, natural resource management, and the many other programs that make modern Indian tribes full-service governments. The Siletz Tribe is in this group.

By the late 1980s, the Siletz tribe was reeling financially. The tribal timberlands obtained through restoration were caught up in the forces crippling timber production all across Oregon: the weak economy drove demand down and concern for endangered species restricted harvesting of mature stands. BIA funding declined. Tribal Chairman Delores Pigsley put it starkly: "I was afraid the tribe would go bankrupt. I really was."

In 1991, with revenues weakening and facing budget deficits in some years, the tribal council began to examine gaming in light of the promising returns that some tribes were seeing. Council member Jessie Davis, the tribe's first chair of gaming, visited the Oneida casino in upstate New York, the Sycuan casino in San Diego, and the Shakopee Mdewakanton Sioux casinos in Minneapolis-St. Paul, where she witnessed tribes transforming "a few trailer houses" into "mega casinos."

The first Siletz effort was full of promise. The tribe purchased a sixteen-acre farm in Salem near the heavily traveled I-5 freeway through the Willamette Valley. Under IGRA, however, the tribe had to accomplish two things: the secretary of the Interior needed to take the land into trust and the Oregon governor, Barbara Roberts, had to approve the transfer into trust. The casino had support from Salem business interests but drew stiff opposition

Longtime tribal council member Jessie Davis played a leadership role in the establishment of Chinook Winds Casino. *Siletz Tribal Collection.*

from, as a federal study described it, "fear of competition" by operators of low-stakes bingo halls and poker rooms and "anti-Indian sentiment and moral resistance to any form of gaming." When the Salem City Council, which had initially supported the project, voted 5 to 4 against the casino, Governor Roberts announced her opposition and later refused to approve the land-into-trust transfer. In her view, the tribe should not operate a casino on acquired land beyond its reservation in the Siletz area. The Interior department, which favored the casino as a matter of policy, had no choice but to decline to take the land into trust. The tribe sued in federal court, to no avail.

The Siletz tribe turned to land in Lincoln City. While Governor Roberts was more favorably disposed toward the Coast proposal than the one on I-5 because it would be within the original Coast Reservation boundaries, the tribal council decided not to risk another defeat through the administrative channels. Instead, the tribe went directly to Congress to have the land taken into trust.

Bill Richardson, a congressman from New Mexico and supporter of tribal initiatives, sponsored the measure. Introduced in June 1994 and joined with several other Indian projects, the bill quickly passed the House. Senator Inouye carried the proposal in the Senate. Like many, Senator Hatfield opposed casino gambling as a general matter but recognized that Indian gaming involved special circumstances; he declined to co-sponsor the bill but supported it when it came to the floor. The legislation was signed into law on November 2, 1994. The tribe then completed negotiations on a compact with the state, signed by Governor Roberts, and the BIA took the land into trust.

Although the die was already cast, some local citizens and city officials objected to the new enterprise. Lincoln City, a long, thin town that hugs the coastline, had aspirations to expand its tourist potential and the casino raised worries that it would compete with tourism and further ensnarl the already congested stretch of the Oregon Coast Highway. Acknowledging that Chinook Winds might boost the economy, local bookstore owner Robert Portwood argued that "money isn't everything. This town has changed from being a small city to being a Newburg or McMinnville, a strip-city of fast-food outlets and malls. . . . I'd rather make less money and have a quieter town." For months, "No Casino" signs sprouted outside city council meetings and informational sessions about the casino.

In the years since the casino opened—a temporary facility began operation in May 1995, with the permanent casino starting up in June 1996—relations between the tribe and the town have markedly improved. Some of this is due

Chinook Winds Casino. *Siletz Tribal Collection.*

to Chinook Winds itself. While indisputably a gambling house, with a glittery, jingling ambiance, the casino welcomes visitors into an open atrium with plants and a 19-foot waterfall. Indian art and Siletz historic photographs are abundant, and the facility includes a 35,000-square-foot convention center with conference rooms named after tribes in the Siletz confederation. Since the casino's opening, the tribe has purchased and remodeled an adjacent ocean-front resort hotel and added an 18-hole golf course on the inland side of the highway.

In 2006, the *Newport News-Times* published a six-part, ten-year retrospective on Lincoln City's experience with Chinook Winds. The study concluded that, contrary to fears in the 1990s, the casino did not cause an increase in the crime rate, force restaurants out of business, drive up the price of property, or cause Lincoln City to be known as a "Casino Town." It was impossible to know whether traffic congestion had increased, the study reported, but the tribe had contributed $262,000 for planning designed to help alleviate the problems caused by the increased number of visitors. Since 1995, the tribe has paid Lincoln City $170,000 each year to compensate for municipal services related to the casino.

There can be no disputing the economic boon to the city. The *News-Times* article found that despite some continuing criticism to the contrary, "Clearly, people who come to the casino, whether as a primary stop or secondary one, spend their time and dollars elsewhere in Lincoln City. . . . It is impossible to say where or how much, but to say it isn't happening at all is not so much wrong as it is illogical." Local residents also benefit directly. Chinook Winds—the largest employer in Lincoln County along with the Georgia-Pacific timber mill in Toledo—has a workforce of more than 800 and generates an estimated 720 jobs indirectly, all at a time when the Coast's natural resource employment, especially in logging, has been steadily declining. The casino donates 5 percent of revenues, nearly $1 million a year, to charity. The Lincoln City Chamber of Commerce has twice honored Chinook Winds as "the Large Business of the Year."

The greatest contribution of Indian gaming to the Siletz has been what Jessie Davis and her fellow tribal members dreamed of from the beginning. Creating the casino, coupled with other management decisions, has brought financial stability to the tribe, helped fund a full-service government, and supported strong cultural and natural resources programs.

The allocation of net gaming revenues demonstrates the future-looking way that the tribe views gaming. Acknowledging that casino glitz is "untraditional," Chairman Pigsley emphasizes that it was "the only way we can get to where we want to go." She sees the casino as "a stepping stone, not an end in itself," and Siletz tribal members comment that they work on the assumption that gaming may not always be the resource it is now. As a result, by tribal ordinance, about one-third of net revenues go to investments and economic development in other ventures. Five percent is used for charitable contributions. The remainder goes to tribal government for programs, general assistance (welfare), and taxable per capita payments of about $1,000 a year for every tribal member (with elders receiving additional amounts). Casino funds, which make up more than one-third of the tribal budget, help support, among other things, full scholarships for all full-time students beyond high school; desktop computers for every tribal family and laptops for students; a cultural resources program that includes a repository for cultural artifacts, historic photographs, and documents; a fitness center and gym; special programs for elders; and a K-12 charter school that places a heavy emphasis on tribal culture and offers early college credits.

The journey from the business arm of the tribe to the seat of Siletz government takes you south through Lincoln City. You soon come to Siletz Bay, a wide, marshy estuary, open and tranquil with its light green reeds and salt marshes. It was here, on the seaward side of the bay, during the first—and dismal—winter of 1856 that the newly arrived and nearly starved Indians received yet another setback when a schooner bearing potatoes and flour bound for the reservation crashed at the entrance to the bay and lost its cargo.

Continuing south, after passing in and out of thick dark forests, you reach Yaquina Head, one of the largest juts into the Pacific of any landform on the Coast. Native people thrived at this site, full of power, the incessant waves pounding at the rocks. The shellfish, birds, seals, and sea lions—and their people's tenure there—must have seemed without end.

Newport and Yaquina Bay lie just a few miles beyond. The town's Nye Beach has been a prime tourist destination since this part of the reservation was broken off in 1865, and the ocean-going fishing fleet perseveres at the harbor docks. Heading east from town on Highway 20 and then taking a left onto Highway 229, the drive to Siletz takes about twenty-five minutes, up and down through forested terrain.

You'll know you're in Siletz when you cross the bridge over the Siletz River. Off to the right sits the most prominent building in town, the tribal administrative center. A sturdy two-story log affair with a bright green roof, it fits the landscape. As you walk into the sunny entryway adorned with traditional tribal artifacts and history, the receptionist will direct you to the department you're looking for—natural resources across the hall, child and family services to the left, tribal court upstairs, and so forth.

This is a busy place, housing as it does many of the tribe's employees. It is hard to imagine that thirty years ago there was naught but a double-wide with four people working for a government possessed of not much more than the hope and excitement bred by restoration. Now the tribal government's workforce of about 300—this does not include Chinook Winds and other enterprises—is larger than Lincoln County's. The government's size has created a need for land in town beyond the Government Hill area obtained at restoration. Although the tribe's active land reacquisition program has led to the purchase of thousands of acres of rural forest land, the tribe also has acquired significant acreage in and near the town of Siletz for tribal housing, health and recreation facilities, buildings for administration and programs, and other purposes.

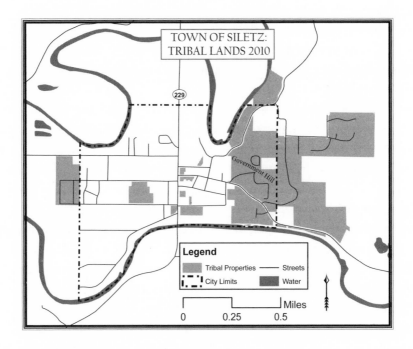

TOWN OF SILETZ:
TRIBAL LANDS 2010

Legend
Tribal Properties —— Streets
City Limits ▮ Water

Miles
0   0.25   0.5

American Indian tribes, assertive and productive once again after a century and a half of forced inaction, are unique and interesting entities: each carries out governmental, landowning, corporate, and community functions. On the government side, tribes are one of three sources of sovereignty in the United States along with the federal government and the states (with cities and counties being creatures of state sovereignty). While tribes are closely tied by history and law to the United States government, they are separate: federal sovereign power derives from the Constitution, while tribal sovereignty has much earlier origins in the practice of self-government by aboriginal societies. Tribes are greatly affected by federal laws and policies—Congress has sweeping authority under the Commerce Clause to "regulate Commerce [which is very broadly defined] with foreign Nations, and among the several states, and with the Indian Tribes"—but tribes are independent governments, not federal instrumentalities.

The separate governmental status of tribes has ramifications that distinguish them from all other American governments. For example, tribal members have a number of prerogatives, including reserved hunting, fishing, and water rights, because of their status as citizens of a sovereign government. The Siletz Tribe can and does have a tribal-member preference for jobs in Chinook

Winds, where tribal members hold 100 jobs including 25 in management, and tribal governmental programs, where more than half of all jobs and nearly all top staff positions are held by Siletz people. This is a matter of citizenship, not racial discrimination.

The status of tribes also involves religion. The First Amendment prohibits Congress from making any "law respecting an establishment of religion." Courts have found that the Fourteenth Amendment imposes this Establishment Clause on the states, but nothing in the Constitution applies the Establishment Clause to Indian tribes. Congress, which has made many Bill of Rights provisions binding on tribes under its general power over Indian affairs, has never imposed religion limitations on tribal governments. As a result, a hallmark of Siletz governance is the way that the tribe meshes into its official actions various religious and spiritual traditions and practices, ranging from prayers at the beginning and end of meetings to supporting the age-old dance, Nee Dosh.

At first glance, it may seem quizzical that tribes would be considered sovereigns. The word, which packs potent emotional content, evokes great authority, indeed absolute power. How can tribes, small in population and reliant in part on the United States for funding and protection, be sovereign?

The term sovereignty traces to sixteenth-century European philosophers

Mary A. "Dolly" Fisher was elected to many terms on the Siletz Tribal Council, including stints as chairman and vice chairman, from restoration days through the early 2000s. She served on numerous tribal committees and as a delegate to the National Congress of American Indians and Affiliated Tribes of Northwest Indians. *Siletz Tribal Collection.*

who, seeking theoretical rationales to justify political stability, described the king as sovereign—holding unlimited, undivided power and answerable only to God. In post-revolution America, with its intricate system of checks and balances, the notion made no sense. This caused Thomas Jefferson to declare that the absolutist formulation of sovereignty was "an idea belonging to the other side of the Atlantic."

The American usage of sovereignty is synonymous with government authority: the power to make laws and enforce them. Sovereign, or governmental, authority can overlap (some crimes can be tried in either federal or tribal court) and one sovereign's authority can override another's. Pointedly, especially in the West, a main limitation on state sovereignty is tribal sovereignty: states have little power on Indian reservations and trust land. So in this country we have many sovereigns with varying degrees of political power, and none omnipotent.

Like all grand ideals, such as freedom and justice, tribal sovereignty operates on different levels. Sovereignty is an elegant, inspiring philosophical concept, the call to true liberty for Native peoples, an emblem and cause worth fighting for. It is also highly specific, a daily reality that springs to life in the actions and activities, large and small, of the political leaders, employees, traditional practitioners, and individual members of Indian tribes. For Siletz tribal leaders, a principal objective of restoration was to reactivate tribal sovereignty.

Today you can see and feel the sovereignty at Siletz, relatively small though the membership and land holdings may be. Government officials, corporate officers, and citizens regularly come to the tribe to make requests, negotiate, provide information, and otherwise conduct business. They take their seats at the table in front of the nine elected council members at their raised semi-circular table in the formal council chambers, make their presentations, and receive questions. The session will be civil, efficient, and leavened with humor, much like a presentation to a state or federal legislative committee. When the outside officials' work is done and they walk down the stairway and depart the administrative building, they will know. Yes, this is a government, a sovereign.

By the 1970s, tribes were focused on reforming the Bureau of Indian Affairs, the bane of Indian country. The BIA presence was an affront, symbolically and practically, to the sovereignty that was guaranteed in the treaties and that the tribes wanted to see take flight. Reform came, but it took time. In 1975, Congress passed the Indian Self-Determination and Education Assistance Act, which made a good start by allowing tribes to contract with the BIA and Indian Health Service to do the work on specific projects. If one of those agencies planned, say, to build a road or health clinic, then the tribe could contract with the agency and do the project itself. A breakthrough to be sure, but the BIA moved slowly and the scope of the act allowed only piece-by-piece transfers of authority to the tribes.

In 1988, the tribes succeeded in convincing Congress to broaden the concept to "self-governance," meaning that tribes could now enter into a "compact"—not a "contract"—a comprehensive agreement authorizing the tribe to take its entire share of the BIA budget and allocate the funds in accordance with tribal priorities (this was extended to the IHS budget in 1991). There were many kinks to be worked out, but a "demonstration project" went ahead with seventeen tribes. In 1992, the demonstration project was expanded to thirty additional tribes; one of them was the Siletz.

The tribe's self-governance compacting in the early 1990s closely tracked the gaming effort. Combined, the two were transformational: they increased both revenues and sovereignty. Today, Chinook Winds provides about 37 percent of the tribal budget, and self-governance funds from the BIA and IHS about 30 percent. "We thought we could make better decisions and we have," reports Brenda Bremner, the tribe's general manager and tribal member. The influence of the BIA has diminished to the point, as Bremner puts it, that the agency has "very little impact on us." "They do have some influence in law but mostly that only slows us down and doesn't stop us. If we request waivers we are able to receive them. Basically, we have a good working relationship with the Bureau."

But now it is a sovereign-to-sovereign, not guardian-to-ward, relationship.

Self-determination, with its heady infusion of independence and pride, has a high value of its own, but carrying it out for the betterment of society is challenging for any government. Indian tribes, the oldest governments in the land but the newest in their modern incarnations, have faced especially daunting circumstances. At Siletz, while the gaps are narrowing, socioeconomic indicators continue to lag behind national averages. History has run roughshod over the Siletz and it will take time to catch up. Now, though, it is on their

Delores Pigsley was a Siletz Tribal Council member during the restoration effort and has led the tribe during most of the modern era. As of 2010, she had served as tribal chairman for a total of twenty-five years. *Siletz Tribal Collection.*

terms and they are crafting the future in their own way.

The Siletz Community Health Clinic is adjacent to the administration building. This single-story facility houses most of the fifty tribal health-care employees. It provides direct medical and dental services and optometric care; operates a diabetes program; houses a pharmacy and laboratory; and runs an alcohol and drug program (the tribe has three area offices in Eugene, Salem, and Portland, and they, too, offer alcohol and drug services but not the other health-care programs). When hospitalization or more specialized treatment is required, the tribe contracts health services with hospitals and physicians in urban areas. Using an innovative approach that provides health care to both Indian and non-Indian residents in the Siletz area, the clinic receives funding from both the state of Oregon and the IHS. The tribe is one of the few providers on the Oregon Coast that accept Medicare and Medicaid patients.

The clinic has become an integral part of the tribal community. Many elders who live elsewhere make the trip to Siletz for clinic visits and checkups; for them, the two- to four-hour drive is well worth the financial savings and the comfort of a community clinic—as well as the chance to visit with friends. The clinic, which receives over 40,000 physical visits per year and thousands of phone-in requests for prescriptions, has outgrown the existing building. In 2009 ground was broken for a new and larger facility on Government Hill. Two other health facilities opened in 2008: a workout facility called the Tillicum Fitness Center and a neighboring gymnasium, both of which are open to non-Indian residents of Siletz.

REBUILDING SOVEREIGNTY

A top tribal priority is to provide housing for the considerable numbers of Siletz people who have wanted to return to the Siletz area since restoration. The Siletz Tribe, with a housing department staff of twenty, administers an array of programs. Eighty-three homes for purchase by tribal members, such as those shown above, are available in the home-buyer program and the inventory of properties is steadily growing. The tribe also leases sixty low-cost rental units. Depending on need, financing is available in both the home-buyer and rental programs. In addition, on non-tribal parcels the tribe offers down-payment assistance, rental assistance, and emergency support for members undergoing eviction from rentals or foreclosure. *Siletz Tribal Collection.*

From the tribal council on down, the government searches for ways to address the causes of diseases and conditions that disproportionately afflict Indian people. This includes diabetes, largely traceable to the change of diet from fishing, hunting, and gathering to fast foods; alcoholism, which is psychologically entwined with the whole saga of colonization; and depression, lack of self-esteem, and debilitating negative attitudes reflecting a sense of displacement and disempowerment.

Siletz health professionals make telling comments about this. George Nagel, a non-Indian who is the tribe's mental health specialist and has worked for Siletz for eighteen years, says that "for pretty much all people I see there is that historical trauma," a variant of post-traumatic stress disorder (PTSD). Janet Wicklund, a non-member who has worked for the tribe for twenty years and is now program director for the alcohol and drug program, elaborates on generational trauma and her belief that Siletz addiction problems are largely

Elected many times to the Siletz Tribal Council, Reggie Butler, shown here with his grandson, Isaac Butler, has specialized in housing issues. *Siletz Tribal Collection.*

the result of scars inflicted on Siletz people dating back to the Rogue River War. "People are experiencing anger as the most comfortable way to deal with difficult feelings of stress and depression," she says. "There was a whole generation taken off to boarding schools. The generation after the boarding schools didn't have parenting models. Relocation and termination were huge things to go through. I feel like there are a lot of specific reasons for generational trauma."

The early research on generational trauma, also called intergenerational trauma and historical trauma, involved descendants of Holocaust victims. Subsequent scholarship found other examples of psychological wounding across generations in sexual abuse victims, war veterans, and other groups, the most notable of which have been indigenous groups—Australian Aborigines, Canadian Natives, and American Indians. Eduardo Duran and Bonnie Duran explain the impact across generations on American Indians:

> The lifeworld as had been known for centuries became threatened, and in most cases that lifeworld was systematically destroyed. . . . The psychological trauma perpetrated by such an intrusion had collective impact at the

beginning of what was to become a process of ongoing loss and separation. This loss and separation was not only from loved ones, but was also a loss of the relationship the people had with their daily world. These losses were not allowed the time for proper bereavement and grief process, thus adding to the wound in the Native American collective psyche.

In comprehending this psychological phenomenon, it is important to mark down why "trauma" is a necessary descriptor. Teresa Evans-Campbell explains: "The events are usually perpetrated by outsiders with purposeful and often destructive intent. This . . . is critical to the definition of historical trauma. Indeed . . . many of these events are not only human initiated and intentional but also fall under the category of genocide . . . making them particularly devastating."

Much of the scholarship is future-looking and emphasizes the importance of family and community ties, and culture and tradition, in the healing process. Health professionals at Siletz agree and incorporate culture into treatment as much as possible; they refer patients to tribal elders and tribal-member counselors and encourage patients to attend cultural events. George Nagel believes that culture "has to be part of treatment. . . . I am non-tribal, but I can direct people to others in the tribe. . . . When I started there wasn't a dance house. When I started there wasn't a culture program." He encourages

The tribe has an active elders program, for those fifty-five and older, that includes nutrition counseling, in-home services, and some financial benefits. The Elders Council holds regular social and business meetings. Transportation is available on the "Elders Bus," shown above; larger busses are used for trips to other reservations, cultural and sports events around the Northwest, and tribal gatherings such as the conclusion of the Run to the Rogue in southern Oregon. *Siletz Tribal Collection.*

PART FOUR. THE MODERN ERA

patients to participate in cultural events, including Run to the Rogue, a three-day relay. The run ends deep in the traditional Rogue River country at Oak Flat, where Tyee John gave his brave and inspirational speech near the end of the Rogue River War in 1856.

In discussing tribal government, Siletz people will often mention that education is the highest priority and the comprehensive educational effort lends support to that view. Head Start programs in Siletz, Salem, Portland, and Lincoln City enroll over 100 children and maintain an attendance rate of 85 percent or higher. Among many other programs for young people, a Tribal Youth Center in Siletz is open for three or four hours after school. Adult education for vocational training and completion of General Education Development degrees are available in Siletz and the three area offices. The tribe funds all members who seek education beyond high school for the cost of tuition and books; additional grants are available, depending on need, for student living expenses. The number of Siletz students in higher education has increased from 35 in 1995 to 129 in 2008.

The tribe has also embarked on an adventuresome initiative in elementary and secondary education. The town of Siletz, like many isolated rural communities, has been plagued by public school closures. In the 1980s, the Lincoln County school board eliminated the high school, reducing the Siletz public school to a K-8. High school students were bussed to Toledo, nine miles away. In 2003, the school district decided to shut down the remaining 170-student school in Siletz altogether. Amid longstanding concern about the high dropout rate for Siletz students in Toledo High, on short notice the tribe took the lead in salvaging the situation by petitioning for a charter school, and the Oregon Department of Education and the school district approved the application. Since then, the curriculum has been enriched by adding more tribal history and culture, including language classes. Student enrollment increased. The Siletz Valley School, the "Warriors," soon had teams in football, basketball, and other sports. During the 2006-7 school year, the high school was transformed into an "early college academy" under a program created and funded by the Bill and Melinda Gates Foundation to reach low-income communities. The early college academy curriculum allows participating students, working through distance learning provided by Oregon State University, to gain up to two years of college credit while earning their high school degree.

Lillie Butler, in the center-front of this photograph taken at the annual Run to the Rogue, was elected to the tribal council for many terms, served as tribal chairman for one year, and focused on education issues. *Siletz Tribal Collection.*

The charter school is an independent entity, a nonprofit organized under state law, but it is effectively a tribal program. The tribal council contributes an average of $250,000 a year, which, according to school director Van Peters, the school "couldn't operate without," and tribal members make major contributions to the curriculum, especially in the teaching of tribal history, culture, and language. In 2007, the town of Siletz celebrated its first high school graduation ceremony in twenty-five years. The valedictorian called the charter school "by far the best—it changed my whole outlook on life." Then, in the traditional Indian way, every graduate was wrapped in a Pendleton blanket, and Reggie and Lee Butler concluded the ceremony with an honor song for the graduates.

While the Siletz Tribe has tripled its landholdings since the 1980 restoration statute and now owns about 9,100 acres, tribal land still makes up a tiny part of the original reservation. In spite of the small ownership, tribal leaders have taken an assertive environmental stance toward management of what they view as their homeland. This is the landscape where Siletz people have fished, gathered, and hunted back through all the generations and the tribe is bent on restoring the health of the land, water, fish, and wildlife. Progress is difficult. Some programs depend on soft money. Even more basically, the tribe has little direct control over most of the development activities that cause degradation and depletion. The tribe's greatest asset is a good track record and respect for its research and policy decisions; that can and has translated into interest from grant makers and a willingness on the part of state and federal agencies with broad regulatory powers to collaborate with the tribe.

In 1999, the southern Oregon Coast was hit with a major oil spill. The 660-foot cargo vessel *New Carissa* wrecked and broke apart near Coos Bay, spilling some 70,000 gallons of tarry fuel into the ocean and onto the shoreline. When the shattered bow section of the *New Carissa* was towed north, it broke loose and caused yet more coastal damage near Waldport. The accident was a disaster for ocean-front landscapes and marine life, including 262 marbled murrelets, a species listed as threatened.

A court-approved settlement followed, with state and federal agencies and the Siletz and the Coos, Siuslaw, and Lower Umpqua tribes designated as restoration trustees. They were charged with finding habitat that, when protected, would mitigate the destruction caused by the spill.

For years the trustees studied what land might be chosen as habitat, how it should be managed, and who should do it. Finally, in 2006, the trustees located parcels owned by two timber companies—the lands were suitable because the murrelets feed mostly in the ocean but nest in coastal forests, miles inland. These were part of the Siletz Treaty reservation, located near Route 229—the Kernville Road, the inland route from Lincoln City to Siletz—not far from tribal headquarters. A Coast Guard fund contributed the purchase price, $15.5 million.

The trustees initially preferred that a non-governmental organization manage the land but they could not settle on one. They turned to the Siletz Tribe, which was delighted at the opportunity to recover prime ancestral land, nearly 3,900 acres. The trustees and the tribe negotiated a unique agreement that transferred the land to the tribe and provided that it be conservatively managed "in perpetuity" as murrelet nesting habitat. The agreement allows a limited tribal commercial timber harvest "consistent with restoration objectives."

The transaction was made possible because the tribe had proven itself with

Frank Simmons, fisheries technician in the Natural Resources Department and Siletz Tribal Council member for several terms, dip-net fishing for salmon at the Euchre Creek site. *Courtesy of Siletz Tribe Natural Resources Department.*

its sustainable management of the timber lands obtained through restoration. The nine-person Siletz forestry staff coordinates with the Cultural and Natural Resources departments to avoid impacts on cultural and environmental resources. The tribal council has long insisted on an environmentally sensitive timber harvesting regime. Jeff Classen of the Oregon Department of Forestry has observed the tribe's environmental practices. "From what . . . I've seen, they do a good job and manage their lands responsibly. They put a lot of time and effort into what they do out there and don't take this stuff lightly." At the signing ceremony in Salem in 2007 for the transfer of the 3,900 acres to the tribe, the trustees cited the tribe's "long history of forest management and community involvement, a multidisciplinary staff, and a demonstrated ability in resource restoration and species conservation." Lincoln County Commissioner Terry Thompson, who had been a main figure in developing the arrangement, called the tribe "a perfect match for this program. The Siletz Tribe has a proven track record for land management of all types of uses for our forest lands."

A tribal employee transplanting native oysters in Yaquina Bay at low tide. *Photograph courtesy of Dave Pitkin and the National Oceanic and Atmospheric Administration.*

The Siletz have taken many other protective actions through its Natural Resources Department. The department now operates Lhuuke Illahee ("Fish Place"), an innovative fish hatchery on Rock Creek, a tributary of the Siletz River above the town of Siletz. Under the 1980 consent decree, the tribe could establish three cultural fishing sites, one of them on Rock Creek. To provide salmon at the tribal site and to put more coho salmon in the river, the state leased a private hatchery on Rock Creek. The outmoded hatchery, dating to the 1930s, never worked well and the state stopped running it in the 1990s. The tribe then purchased the 200-acre property and put in a hatchery that is not a hatchery: Aquatic Programs leader Stan van de Wetering explains that the term "'hatchery' is really a misnomer. It's more of a refuge where fish can rear and grow and reproduce."

Hatcheries have been controversial on Pacific Northwest rivers and the tribe attempts to avoid the errors of the past. Under tribal management, native wild fish are raised instead of using the common old-style practice of bringing in eggs from other watersheds. The fish are fed on naturally produced foods instead of pellets and no straight-walled concrete pens are used. Tribal employees diverted water from the stream to create a pond in a meadow. The young fish are obtained by opening the pipe from Rock Creek, causing some fish to swim into the pond for food. Tribal Natural Resource Department staffers put wood chips and brush in the pond, creating bacteria and algae. The fish then acclimate themselves in the pond before heading downstream on their own schedule.

Salmon restoration is a long-term process, so final returns are not in, and Lhuuke Illahee is a small project, but this refuge seems to be helping. The indications are that it is gradually bringing back more wild fish to Rock Creek for traditional Siletz fishers and sports fishers as well. This project, like most of the tribe's natural resources endeavors, represents the hallmark of the tribe's approach, a willingness to think in the long term, to recognize that restoring land and water health in the tribe's homeland will take decades, and to put in the necessary time and patience to push ahead, piece by piece, year by year.

The Natural Resources Department has also taken on shellfish restoration. In the Siletz mind, Yaquina Bay oysters evoked two images: succulent seafood that was an aboriginal delicacy and the bay that attracted the commercial harvesters—people who led the charge for the 1865 executive order that took 200,000 acres from the reservation. By the early 1900s, because of commercial over-harvesting and water pollution, the once-bountiful Olympic oysters in Yaquina Bay were in serious decline. The bay no longer supports harvestable numbers of oysters.

In addition to restoring bay habitat, the tribe conducted an oyster restoration project funded by the National Oceanic and Atmospheric Administration. Tribal members traveled north to Netarts Bay, near Tillamook, just north of the 1855 reservation boundary, to collect brood stock of native Olympia oysters. Those oysters were taken to a shellfish hatchery to spawn and mature. Siletz employees then transplanted them on state-owned sites on Yaquina Bay. Frank Simmons, former tribal council member and natural resources technician for the tribe, said this about the project: "How do I feel about this first step to put oysters back? It's the beginning of a new life. We want oysters here, not just for Native Americans, but for all."

Lamprey eel recovery is another priority area. In mainstream American society, attitudes toward eels, with their toothy, raspy, suction-cup mouths, ranged from worthless to plug-ugly to vaguely dangerous. In the Pacific Northwest, eels were targeted for eradication as trash fish. To the tribes, the eels were a key part of their diets, a nutritious and delicious food. Starting

Eels, harvested by tribal members at Willamette Falls, hanging to cure in a smokehouse. *Siletz Tribal Collection.*

in the 1990s, Northwest tribes, with the Siletz taking an active role, stood up for the eel, an anadromous species that is born in freshwater, migrates to the ocean, and returns to its native stream as an adult in a life cycle different from, but similar to, salmon. A broader understanding developed among scientists and policymakers that the lamprey is an important part of the food chain during its life cycle, providing food for small fish, salmon, seals, and sea lions. Now a restoration effort, modest but growing, is operating on many of the region's rivers.

Sharing the same rivers as Pacific salmon and having many of the same habitat needs, eels—like the salmon—have sharply declined due to dams, logging, and other development activity. They also suffer from eradication efforts. Siletz people saw a drop-off in the populations after World War II and a near collapse by the 1980s. The tribe formed the Lamprey Eel Decline Project and began to assemble a database with the assistance of students at Oregon State University. Professor Jefferson Gonor, an oceanologist, agreed to serve as a mentor for Tom Downey, a Siletz tribal member who later earned a degree in environmental health and safety.

Downey headed up a project that culminated in the publication in 1996 of *Skwakol: The Decline of the Siletz Lamprey Eel Population during the 20th Century.*[72] The report included traditional scientific and historical information, but its essence is found in nineteen extensive oral histories that document cultural use, decline of the eels, and current conditions in the Siletz River watershed. The observations in that report and later data-gathering made it clear that the primary cause for the drop in eel numbers was high-yield logging that increased the sediment load and degraded the water by harvesting in riparian zones, using bulldozers to clear out fallen trees in streams, and applying herbicides and other chemicals to promote regeneration of trees.

As with all complex river restoration efforts, the tribe's focus is what it has to be—to improve watershed health—and the time period for significant returns is what it has to be—mid-term or long-term. Project areas now include both the Siletz watershed and the Willamette River, where a group of tribal members still catches eels by hand at the traditional site at Willamette Falls. Strategies include taking water samples, assessing eel toxicity levels, and helping to shepherd the cleanup of a superfund site on the lower Willamette. The Siletz also coordinate with federal and state agencies and other tribes to leverage resources and compare strategies. Mike Kennedy, tribal natural resources manager, emphasizes the compelling reasons for bringing back the eels, scorned for so long as a trash fish. "While we are studying the eel because of its importance as a traditional food source, this is not a single-species project. Lamprey eels are connected to an entire system that supports salmon, crawdads, and other organisms. We are using eels as an indicator of watershed health."

The Siletz Tribe has gained a reputation for sound, steady governance. Stanley Speaks gives his assessment from the vantage point of director of the BIA Northwest Regional Office since 1982. "They had strong leadership at restoration. Now, when they bring in new people, they're able and talented. For stability and continuity, Siletz is right up at the top." This stability comes from the council, where many members over the years have served multiple terms, and from veteran senior staff as well. For one tense stretch of time, however, the system of governing deteriorated and tribal operations threatened to grind to a halt. The episode offers a window into some of the main institutions of Siletz sovereignty: the constitution, tribal council, general council, election board, and judiciary.

The Siletz constitution requires that tribal council elections be held annually on the first Saturday in February. Each year, three of the nine council seats are up for election. The new council then elects a tribal chairman and other officers. On February 1, 1997, in the midst of turmoil over economic development, especially management of the casino, three new council mem-

PART FOUR. THE MODERN ERA

bers were elected. In a 5 to 4 vote, the council then installed a new chairman, replacing Delores Pigsley, who had served for thirteen years.

Throughout the spring, tribal operations continued in more or less the same manner as before the election. The administration of Chinook Winds was controversial, but that had been a problem area for two years. Then, in July, the tribal council, by another 5 to 4 vote, terminated the tribal adminis-trator (the position is now designated general manager). The decision, right or wrong, ignited conflict and sparked talk of a recall of the five council mem-bers who had removed the administrator. There had never been a recall under the Siletz constitution, adopted in 1979.

The dispute grew angrier as the council passed over two tribal-member candidates for the tribal administrator opening. In late August, the council filled the position with an Indian from another tribe. Once again, the vote was 5 to 4, with the breakdown being the same as the alignment for the firing in July.

The recall movement gathered steam as the tribal administrator (who lasted only until February, when he was fired for cause) took heavy criticism for his management style and dismissals of several employees, including the assistant administrator. Attendance was higher than usual at tribal council meetings and at the November 1997 general council meeting, where tribal members lodged many objections to the administrator's performance. (The Siletz constitution provides, in addition to the elected tribal council, for a gen-eral council composed of all tribal members eighteen years of age and older. The general council, which meets four times a year, has limited powers but is an important forum for tribal members to speak and question their elected tribal council members.)

In a petition drive, tribal members succeeded in gathering the signatures of one-third of all general council members, the constitutional requirement for a recall election. The election board set the recall vote for March 23, 1998. Only four council members appeared on the ballot; the fifth had not been re-elected in the February 1998 election.

The four council members up for recall, joined by tribal chairman Pat Duncan (elected to the council in February), went to tribal court and sued the Siletz Election Board to block the recall election, alleging that several of the petitions contained errors. Associate Judge Andrew Viles held three hear-ings, the last just four days before the election, and then issued a long opinion early on the day of the election. After detailing technical defects in the recall petitions and signatures, Judge Viles allowed the voting to be completed but ordered the election board to shred the ballots without counting or inspecting them.

The election board immediately appealed to the Appellate Court, which promptly issued an emergency order blocking the destruction of the ballots until the appeals court issued a final decision. (At the time, by Siletz tribal law, appeals from the Siletz Tribal Court went to the Northwest Intertribal Court System, a consortium of tribal courts. The Siletz Tribe now has its own Appellate Court.) For four months, the tribe was on tenterhooks, waiting for a ruling. The four council members targeted by the recall continued in office.

The Appellate Court handed down its ruling in July. While there were a number of minor errors on the petitions, the court found that there still were enough valid signatures to meet the constitutional requirement of one-third of all general council members. The court directed that the ballots be counted. When that was done, the four council members were recalled by margins of 70 percent or more. Now there were only five sitting council members.

Chairman Duncan, having aligned with the four recalled members, now found herself in a minority of one. The constitution, in addition to allowing the council to select the chairman, provides that council vacancies will be filled by the council upon recommendation of the chairman. Believing that the other four members would likely vote to remove her as chairman and appoint new members, she refused to call a tribal council meeting, putting tribal decision making on hold. The tribal council has a steady stream of responsibilities; at this time, for example, time was running out to finalize the $5 million self-governance contract with the Indian Health Service.

When tribal members gathered for the regularly scheduled general council meeting on August 1, tensions came to a head. The chairman, acknowledging that "we are in turmoil," explained her view of the situation—that allowing the other four council members to take charge would lead to "political unrest for many many years to come." Emotions ran high and the minutes record that, just before the lunch break, "comments continued from the attendees and comments cannot be heard because the attendees were shouting and the meeting was out of control."

The meeting continued after the break and at the end of the session, "after carefully weighing all the options," Duncan resigned. Now the council was down to four members. Under the constitution, no tribal council meeting can be held without a five-member quorum. Addressing the general council, Duncan explained that resignation was the right course because the stalemate would "force the Bureau of Indian Affairs to exert their trust responsibility to hold and conduct a Special Election."

The four remaining council members thought differently. Business needed to be conducted and a BIA takeover would be contrary to, and a black mark against, Siletz sovereignty. They went to tribal court the next day, Sunday, and requested that the court acknowledge the crisis and issue an order allowing the four members to hold a special meeting. They wanted the court to allow them to name a fifth council member, the one who received the next highest vote total in the January election. Then the council, now with a five-member quorum, could select a chairman and fill the four remaining seats under the ordinary procedures of the constitution. Only such an approach, they urged, could meet the highest purposes of the constitution, to "continue forever" the Tribe's identity and to "protect our inherent rights as Indians and as a sovereign Indian tribe."

Chief Judge John Roe, recognizing the extraordinary nature of the situation, ruled on Monday that such a course was "fair," "in the best interest of the Confederated Tribes of Siletz Indians," and "will insure that Tribal business continues without further interruptions." The council held a special meeting on Monday evening in an overflowing council chamber and filled the remaining seats. With that accomplished, the council then proceeded to conduct business.

The episode tested the foundations of Siletz sovereignty and stability. Yet, all governments face their crises and how they handle them is often the truest gauge of a government's worth. Here, the Siletz constitution held, along with the checks and balances it puts in place. The citizenry announced its will through the recall provisions and the courts, election board, general council, and tribal council functioned as they should. It took time—the tribe endured a year's disruption—but the government righted itself and got back on track.

A person can fairly ask whether the Siletz Tribe can continue for the foreseeable future. In one sense, we do not have much data to go on. Modern tribal governments, with their brand of self-determination, have existed for only about forty years, the Siletz a decade less than that. The budget is heavily dependent on Chinook Winds and federal funding. What would happen if either or both of those revenue streams dried up? To many Americans, tribes are anomalies—history-based in a nation that prides itself on modernism—and they are small in population. With all the progress, many tribal members remain below the poverty line. Will the Siletz once again face termination or other debilitating congressional policy?

Still and all, the Siletz Tribe has put building blocks in place that suggest permanence. Money is being set aside for investments and diversity of economic development. The tribe has built up contacts, credibility, and respect, thereby weaving itself into the local, state, and national societies. Somehow, despite all the bad years, from the time of the diseases to termination, Siletz people have found a way to nurture and revive the roots of their culture.

Maybe this cannot hold. Maybe Indian tribes, Siletz included, will become anachronisms, and the passage of time and the force of political and economic powers will erase them away. Maybe the construct of the past two generations is too fragile to last. Maybe, though, the Siletz have built an elaborate infrastructure of governing authority, economic security, and culture—a steel frame that will endure. Maybe Tribal Chairman Pigsley has it right when she announces her mind with clarity and force: "We *will* survive."

CULTURAL REVIVAL

"The people are dancing again."

IN MARCH 1996, ROBERT KENTTA AND SELENE RILATOS OF THE
Siletz Cultural Department traveled to the Bronx. They planned to meet
with the curatorial staff of the National Museum of the American Indian,
which had a number of Siletz artifacts in its collection, and they had a photographer in tow to create a formal record of these Siletz cultural objects.
The trip came about because of the upswelling of cultural concerns among
Indians nationally and at Siletz.

In the 1970s, outrage had spread in Indian country over the way archaeologists and museums treated Indian burials. Although state laws had long protected non-Indian graves, excavation of Indian burial sites was common, with
tens of thousands of Native American skeletons stored in museums. In addition to human remains, museums were also well-stocked with Native American sacred and cultural objects, some purchased legally but many illegally
excavated under federal laws.

A coalition of Indian organizations pressed for congressional action. Initially, the archaeology community was indignant, believing that restrictions
on excavation and storage would impede their scientific research, but by the
late 1980s many archaeologists came over to the Indians' side. The National
Museum of the American Indian Act of 1989 created this museum as the
sixteenth museum within the Smithsonian Institution, and its heralded main
facility has since been constructed on the National Mall in Washington, D.C.,
opening in 2004. The NMAI legislation also required the repatriation, when
requested by tribes, of the remains of some 19,000 Native Americans in the

Smithsonian Institution's collection. The law squarely acknowledged the core issues of morality and sovereignty by using the term "repatriation." Repatriation describes the return by one nation to another of human remains, prisoners of war, money, or cultural objects. Until this legislation, the United States had recognized repatriation with foreign nations, but returns to sovereign tribal nations also fit within the meaning of repatriation, and Congress so decided.

A year later, Congress responded to tribal and religious leaders and passed even more sweeping legislation, the landmark Native American Graves Protection and Repatriation Act. NAGPRA—followed by complementary state laws in some forty states—protected Indian graves on federal and tribal land. It also required, upon request of affected tribes, the repatriation of human remains held by all non-federal institutions that received federal funding. The 1990 statute went a step beyond the NMAI legislation—in provisions that gave cause for the Siletz to head back east—by requiring the museums to repatriate sacred objects and, broader still, cultural objects, not related to gravesites, that had been stolen or improperly acquired.

Out in Siletz, tribal members were just completing a project that cried out for access to the historic Siletz dance regalia in storage at the NMAI Bronx facility. Back in the 1870s, in that era when forcefully eradicating Indian culture was firm federal policy, the agent at Siletz ordered that all six of the traditional dance houses be torched. When any talk of building new ones came up, the BIA shut it down. By the time the Siletz group went to the museum in 1996, nearly two years of work had gone into building a new dance house at the east end of town, among tall fir trees along the river. Many volunteers pitched in, for there was a lot of heavy lifting. Three 60-foot fir logs, supported by vertical fir and cedar log uprights, lay horizontally as the main support beams for the roof. The walls of the house, 60 by 40 feet in all, are thick cedar planks.

Despite government suppression, the ancient dance Nee Dosh never died out. Siletz dancers regularly performed it at local social events such as county fairs, clam bakes, the Cherry Festival, and the Redhead Roundup. Nee Dosh also was done much more traditionally, underground, after the BIA crackdown on ceremonial dances. Spiritual dances were held secretly in peoples' homes in the Siletz area, at the risk of arrest by BIA police up until the 1930s, when Commissioner John Collier revoked the ban. Private-home dances continued into the 1980s.

But there had not been a full, formal Nee Dosh in a traditional dance house

Bud Lane, vice chairman of the Siletz Tribal Council and Language and Traditional Arts instructor, departing the dance house, which he helped to construct. *Photograph by Fredrick D. Joe; courtesy of* The Oregonian.

for more than a century. Now, in March of 1996, the new dance house, true to the old details, was almost ready for its first dance, on the Summer Solstice just three months away. Much additional preparation was in the works. In addition to a dance house, Nee Dosh needs singers, male and female dancers, and songs. The dance is also made up of regalia: feathered headdresses, basket caps, and dresses, pants, and shirts, all festooned with feathers, beads, dentalia, and seashells.

Many people had regalia, some of it old, and some new regalia was being made. But there was excitement about using regalia from deep antiquity, and the inventory that the National Museum of the American Indian had supplied in response to the Siletz inquiry showed that the NMAI facility in the Bronx possessed some very promising items. Formal repatriation of regalia would take time to complete—well beyond June—and, besides, the tribe did not have a suitable storage facility (though in time it would build one). Perhaps the museum would agree to a loan.

NMAI had never done a loan of a piece that would be worn in a ceremony

Robert Kentta, Tribal Council member and director of the Cultural Department. He is shown here demonstrating beargrass braiding during a traditional dress-making class. *Siletz Tribal Collection.*

and Kentta and Rilatos expected resistance. To their surprise, the people at NMAI were most forthcoming. "There wasn't really any opposition," Kentta recalled. "The only concern was that [the dance house dedication] was coming up so soon and we'd need to get the objects ready to travel."

But NMAI got into gear. Working with the tribe, curators decided on six Siletz pieces, all ancient and delicate but able to be danced: a pine-nut-bead dress, a flicker-feather headband, a set of feather dance wands (called matish sticks), a woman's hair plume (a cluster of feathers), a mussel-shell necklace/sash, and a collar-shell necklace (a dentalium collar from which hung a netting of crisscrossed glass beads and shells). Each object was wrapped in specially made packaging for transport. Then the museum, at its own expense, tasked a staff member to fly the objects out to Oregon and deliver them to the tribe's doorstep.

Ever since June 1996, Nee Dosh—performed on the Summer and Winter Solstices—has been a major event at Siletz. But that first ceremony—reclaiming, as it did, 120 lost years—was bathed in an excitement, spirituality, and

In the women's dressing room, just before daylight, Arlissa Rhoan (*left*) prepares to dance in the final round of Nee Dosh on June 23, 1996. Her regalia include the pine-nut bead dance dress loaned to the tribe by the National Museum of the American Indian. She and the other dancers wear combinations of old and newer regalia brought by families to the dance and old regalia on loan from the Lincoln County Historical Society, Oregon State University–Horner Collection and the University of Oregon Museum of Natural History. To Arlissa's left are Sonya Moody-Jurado, Angeline Easter, Pria Shoemake, and Sasha Shoemake. *Siletz Tribal Collection.*

redemption like nothing else. The dance house was "jammed-full" and dozens had to stand outside. "It was really exciting," Kentta remembered. "It felt good to dance with those great pieces of regalia that hadn't danced in a long time. So many people came. People who used to dance brought their kids and grand-kids who had never danced before."

The Siletz, as with many other tribes, has two broad categories of dances. Pow-wows, important Native American cultural institutions, are upbeat, colorful social events, conspicuously intertribal and widely attended by the general population. Some are held in urban areas—universities are increasingly common venues—but most pow-wows are hosted by tribes in Indian country,

Pow-wow drum group. Bob Tom, center, wearing a dentalium necklace, was instrumental in creating the administrative structure of the restored tribe. After serving on the Siletz Tribal Council through the passage of the 1977 Restoration Act, in 1978 he became the first general manager of the tribe and helped in establishing the eight-county (later to become eleven-county) service area that reaches tribal members on the Coast and in the Willamette Valley. He subsequently acted as tribal education director for over seventeen years. *Siletz Tribal Collection.*

mostly in the summer. Drums, usually manned by eight or more drummers and singers, come in from other tribes in the region and beyond. Some of the dances are competitive, with monetary prizes for the winners in fancy dance, victory dance, grass dance, and others. The dances are done to the rhythms of the drums and high-pitched, electrifying songs, many of which originated in the Great Plains. These are the unique, haunting sounds most people identify as Indian music.

The largest pow-wows, such as Crow Fair, Oglala Nation Pow Wow and Rodeo, and Navajo Nation Fair, draw 5,000 or more participants and spectators. Siletz has two pow-wows each year, one in the summer at the Pauline Ricks Memorial Pow-Wow Ground on Government Hill, the other now held at Chinook Winds in November to celebrate passage of the restoration act. The Siletz pow-wows draw thousands of attendees.

Veterans leading the Grand Entry at the Nesika Illahee pow-wow at the Pauline Ricks Memorial Pow-Wow Grounds on Government Hill. On the right is Ed Ben, son of Archie Ben, distinguished council member and tribal leader during modern times, and expert drum maker. To the left, in the second row, carrying the eagle staff, is William DePoe. *Siletz Tribal Collection.*

Tribes also have internal dances that are deeply spiritual. These dances are for the tribal community, and most of the spectators and all of the participants come from within the tribe. They dance only their own songs and rhythms. While there may be drumming, they use flutes and other instruments, and usually the drums are not as dominant as at pow-wows. At Siletz, the traditional dance is Nee Dosh, when Siletz people go to "the center of our world."

I went to my first Nee Dosh in 2005. By then, participation had mush-roomed and so many people had learned the dances that it was hard to accommodate everyone. Young people as well as adults were participating: in grade school, even though some boys stuck to pow-wow fancy dancing, Nee Dosh was "cool." At first, as the revival of Nee Dosh grew stronger after restoration, the cultural confusion of assimilationist pressures led some older tribal members to raise cautions, believing that Nee Dosh was anti-Christian. That attitude has dissipated and some of the families with initial concerns now strongly support the dance. Margo Hudson's family experience is not uncommon. She never danced or followed other traditions when growing up because her mother, to protect her from discrimination, forbade it. She moved away during termination but has returned to Siletz. "It's a loss for me, but now it's completely natural for my kids—the dancing, the weaving—so I get that enjoyment from it."

Nee Dosh, lasting for ten nights in the old days, now goes on for three nights, starting on a Thursday. Although some experienced dancers partici-pate, the first and second nights are usually reserved for those who are still getting to know the intricate ceremony. The regalia is relatively simple and the dancers do just one round, fifteen to twenty songs lasting for an hour and a half or so. On Saturday, Nee Dosh runs from dusk until Sunday's dawn and the dancers—now the most experienced ones—do five rounds, with the rega-lia growing more and more elaborate as the rounds go on.

The dance house, just north of the river, has a stolid beauty and craftsman-ship and a rightness with the land. You enter through an oval door in the mid-dle of the south wall. (In the old days, the entry door was a circle and it was smaller, lower, and located at the east side of the south wall. The change was made to make entry more convenient, especially for elders.) I turned around in a circle after entering, having been told of the custom, which demonstrates that people are leaving behind all the cares of daily life and entering the spirit world. The building, dug six feet into the earth, is more commodious than it seems from the outside.

The dancing on the first two nights was more intricate than I had expected. On Thursday, "practice night," the children, teenagers down to three- or four-year-olds, were amazing. There were slip-ups but their skill level was high. On Friday, "prayer night," before dancing started, people offered prayers for individuals, whole families, and the community. These many entreaties were heartfelt, this intimate place bringing out the slow, kind, sincere thoughts of the sort that we too often leave unsaid. The dancing, now with older dancers and few children, was even more expert. Then, on Saturday evening, I, like I imagine all newcomers, was transfixed by the skill, attention to detail, and power of the dancers who had given so much time in preparing so that this ancient ceremony would be pluperfect.

Four levels of wood-plank, bleacher-style seating line the west, south, and east walls of the dance house, accommodating about 200 people, with more able to stand near the entry. The north end is a cedar wall with two dressing rooms beyond it, men on the left, women on the right. The dance floor is constructed of boards, and in the center of the dance area is a circular fire pit, a main element of Nee Dosh. The fire sends out burning cedar's sweet smell, but the house is not smoky: rather than a smoke hole, the roof has overlapping layers, creating openings so the smoke escapes but the rain stays out. The fire roars, letting us see the dancers and their regalia and giving life to the north wall, turning the cedar planks rosy and displaying the shadows of the dancers.

As darkness gathered on that June Saturday evening, the men and boys started to sing in the dressing room, a signal that the first round was about to begin. Then the men entered the main area of the dance house, walking along the west wall and coming into the dance area from the south. They formed a half circle around the fire. A few of the older men, and strongest singers, stood in the back. The lead singer tapped a staff against the floor planks to keep time and establish rhythm for the singers and dancers to follow.

Before the women entered, the men sang a full song. Then the men invited the women in. They came along the east wall and entered the dance area from the south. Thirty to thirty-five in all, the dancers formed a semicircle between the fire and the north wall—men facing the fire, unmarried females facing the man to their right, married women facing the fire. They were so calm, so accomplished, so proud, so beautiful. The women wore buckskin dresses and basket caps and carried matishes, feathered wands. They also wore necklaces made of many seashells, which would soon be music. Each had a cluster of feathers or a single feather centered in the back of her headdress or cap. With charcoal, they had drawn the traditional "one-elevens" (permanent tattoos in historic times) on their chins. The men were bare-chested, wearing buckskin wraps or kilts tied at the waist, two feathers on their headbands, and necklaces; they carried bows and arrows.

The singing began again, and the women swung into action with grace and energy, creating a brilliant music unique to Nee Dosh—"the song of the dress." Each dancer's seashells, hundreds of them on her dress and necklaces, combined to make a single instrument. Sliding their feet back and forth, bouncing and swinging their bodies, the women brought their regalia to life in a wave of melodic jingling. The dancers were all in unison. The individual instruments joined in concert and became a chorus of seashells, one great and joyous wave, rolling on, rolling on, rolling on . . .

The singing grew louder. A young man jumped out from the line toward the fire. Hopping, crouching, he pulled an arrow from his otter-pelt quiver, decorated with abalone. Athletic and nimble, he was hunting, pursuing his prey. His posterior was so close to the planks, and his movements so quick and strong, that every person over forty must have had a sympathetic reaction— I did—"Oh, my thighs, knees, and calves—they are on *fire!*" After dancing back and forth in front of the line at least three times, he settled back into his position in the half circle. The lead singer signaled that the song was coming to an end by hollowing out his voice and letting out the air in his lungs with a quavering sound. The women waved their feather matishes in tight circles. When the lead singer finished, the line went motionless.

Between songs, the lead singer offered a prayer to the Creator in Athapaskan. Nee Dosh is a World Renewal Dance, a ceremony practiced by tribes on the Oregon Coast and northern California. As the night progressed, the cycle of song and prayer continued—some originating deep in antiquity, some in the past few centuries, a few in recent years. Prayers thanked the Creator for all He had provided, asked for the continuation of these good gifts, and reminded the people of how these things had come to be. Embedded in the entreaties was a sense of responsibility that tribal people were reasserting that night: their obligation and determination to fix the world, to renew and repair it and make it as it is supposed to be.

Just as before, the lead singer began a song and the men all sang the first verse. This time, however, a woman glided out in front of the line, perhaps responding to a signal from a woman in the front row near the fire who has responsibility for taking care of the female dancers and calling out dancers to dance in the middle. This is new. Traditionally, women who have had children did not come out in this way but, just as new songs come into use, this expanded role for women has become an accepted part of Nee Dosh. Her dance, though, was very different from that of the young man who preceded her. She glided so smoothly that I found it hard to understand how she did it. Moving back and forth in front of the line and making at least three full passes, she then dropped back to her place. Later on, during other songs, two or even three women or men jumped out and danced at the same time. A man, in a sign of romance, may invite a woman out of the line.

The second round was performed by visiting dancers from the Siletz' sister tribe, the Tolowa from the Smith River Rancheria just below the Oregon line. They come to Nee Dosh at Siletz in some years and Siletz dancers sometimes travel south. The tribes have worked closely on modern cultural issues, exploring the Tolowa and Tututni varieties of the Athapaskan language and comparing notes on Nee Dosh protocols, songs, and regalia. Smith River also built a dance house in the 1990s, using three ridge poles donated by the Siletz. The men's and women's regalia are nearly identical, except that the Smith River women do not carry matish sticks. This tribe, 200 miles from home, had fewer dancers—just eleven—because of the distance, but the round had all the pageantry, precision, and uplift of the first.

After the second round, at about midnight, I went out the oval door into the brisk, misty air. Volunteers gave out coffee from a small stand. I got a cup and stood off by the side, talking with a few friends. A large group of young people chatted and joked, some of them observers, some dancers. Here it is early Sunday morning and they are at Nee Dosh, not off doing the less honorable activities that I might have pursued on a similar night at their age.

Nee Dosh went to a new level in the third round. The regalia of the dancers was much more elaborate. The women wore dresses and necklaces with many more seashells, creating an even louder and more layered symphony. Most of the men had donned headdresses with large bunches of floppy feathers—the second and third feathers below the primary ones usually associated with eagles. These feathers—"it's a Siletz thing," one dancer told me at the break—bounced and created a sea of movement. Also, more of the men were wearing on their headdresses the prized, glistening scalps of the red pileated woodpecker, large birds up to twenty inches from their feet to the tops of their flaming red crests. Compared with the first dance in the dance house in 1996, there is much more regalia available now. Building on the initial loan from NMAI, the tribe had repatriated some items from museums and had others on loan that were danced in the later rounds of the night. People brought family heirlooms out of storage and were making new regalia. New, that is, but old, their creations mostly faithful to the format of ancient designs and materials.

Late in the third round, a woman seated next to me whispered, "See those shadows on the back wall? Those are the ancestors, dancing with the people here tonight."

All evening, people arrived and left. By the third round, no one was standing but the dance house was otherwise full. When the Smith River dancers

Nee Dosh dancers in the dance house at Siletz. *Siletz Tribal Collection.*

did round four, now way past the usual bedtime, the house was half full. Some people dozed on the benches. Attendance dropped off again for the last dance. The dancers, ever professional, brought out even more elaborate regalia for the last round and danced and sang as purposefully, energetically, and precisely as before, exhausted though they must have been. The last dance, performed as the early light nudged through the low fog and into the break between the double roofs, departed completely from the conventions of the long evening. As one, responding to the lead singer's signal, the dancers jumped out of line and danced individually and wildly, letting out yelps, howls, and screeches. Finally, everyone settled back into the line. The lead singer said a final blessing, *Huu-chan xuu naa-xutlh-xat-le*, "As you depart, may the blessings be with you." This Nee Dosh had drawn to a close, different in some ways from the dances of centuries past, yet the same, ever the same.

Reclaiming Native spirituality and traditional ceremonies is one aspect of reinvigorating culture. The term "decolonizing" is sometimes used to describe these efforts by modern tribal people to respond to generations of assimilationist policy. In addition to Nee Dosh, the Siletz have moved on a number of fronts to protect and revive traditions. One of those is language.

Language loss is a global phenomenon. An estimated half of the world's languages have gone extinct, and linguists estimate that half the 7,000 languages still alive today will be lost by the end of the twenty-first century. Indigenous societies are especially at risk: "politically dominant languages and cultures simply overwhelm indigenous local languages and cultures, placing them in a condition which can only be described as embattled." As James Crawford pungently puts it, "Language death does not happen in privileged communities."

Language and culture are tightly bound together. Language is where a society expresses its worldview, values, and distinctiveness. Linguists and anthropologists, drawing an analogy to the loss of biodiversity, commonly make the point that language loss diminishes the world's intellectual and cultural diversity. Indigenous peoples, powerless as their cultures and languages were run over roughshod, have become keenly aware of the ramifications of language loss. "Language is part of us and part of our genetic structure," said Jessie Little Doe Fermino, a Massachusetts Wampanoag engaged in revitalizing her tribe's language. "Not to acknowledge a part of you is breaking a spiritual law. . . . language gives us a basis for why we view the world the way we do." Darrell Kipp of the Blackfeet Tribe of Montana explained why the tribe's ambitious language program enjoys such broad acceptance among the membership: "Same reason you don't burn down your libraries is why we keep our language. Our language is our library. And Blackfeet is totally unlike English, so it gives the child another thinking blueprint. For example, in Blackfeet, there is no gender, so the world can be suddenly seen in a different fashion."

Worldwide, the indigenous language revival movement began in the 1960s with the Maori of New Zealand. The Maori had one large advantage: although the number of speakers was dropping, 70,000 people still used the language. Today the Maori have an elaborate revitalization program helped by substantial government funding. Hawaiian Natives soon developed their own full-bore language restoration effort, and the number of speakers has grown from 1,500 to 6,000-8,000. As in New Zealand, Hawaiians have created immersion schools, where the native language is not just "studied" but is also the medium of instruction; in many cases, the parents participate and the native language is used at home. The state constitution makes Hawaiian one of the two official state languages.

By the 1980s, tribes in the contiguous states and Alaska had organized to combat language loss and succeeded in 1990 in obtaining passage of the Native American Languages Act. There are now hundreds of tribal language programs, many with some federal funding. University interest has increased, with the tribal efforts contributing to and benefiting from the academic research. Many colleges and high schools allow native language courses to count toward requirements for foreign language. The tribal programs, where it counts most, range from immersion programs to language courses with written study materials to informal "meet and repeat" gatherings.

The mainland tribes and Alaska Natives face an uphill battle. Half of their languages have already been lost, and just thirty-six tribes have more than 1,000 speakers (with 150,000, the Navajo Nation easily has the most). A large percentage of the speakers are elderly or middle-aged, and nearly everyone—especially the youth—is bombarded by English and distracted by daily obligations from learning a "new" and difficult language. Documenting a language requires an enormous amount of time and expertise. The language must be heard orally through interviews with traditional speakers and then transferred into a written language that most can agree on, not just as to spelling but also grammar and nuance. At the same time, anyone who delves into the literature on tribal language revitalization or becomes familiar with individual tribal programs is struck by the earnestness and commitment of tribal leaders, language instructors, and tribal members. The future is unclear but Dr. Janine Pease of the Crow Tribe is right in saying that language revival is no passing fancy: "The work is much too difficult to be a fad."

Linguists designate the Pacific Northwest as a "hot spot." Most of the tribes are close to non-Indian populations as a result of opening reservations to settlement during the allotment era. Western Oregon is a particularly hard and sad case: despite the diversity of languages, nearly every one has gone extinct, or nearly so, through the relentless historical factors that gripped Indian communities for so long. The Grand Ronde Tribe has responded with an innovative language program based on the Chinook Jargon—the widely used language spoken historically by Indians and traders on the Northwest Coast—rather than a specific indigenous tribal language. Chinuk WaWa, as it is called, is taught as a course to adults and also learned by youth in an immersion program, the only one in Oregon.

The Coast Athapaskan language survives but barely, with just five to ten conversant speakers. The language is rich with words and phrases that link the Creator, the people, and the land. For example, *nvn-nvst-'an* is the word for "the world." Literally, *nvn-nvst-'an* means "for you it is made," but the evocative word has much context and many layers. "It is made" means that the Creator tailored each place, each village area, to suit the peoples' every need for climate, food, water, materials, medicines, and spiritual inspiration. This is the image, the place, that is so full as to mean "paradise." There is no need for a separate heaven, and people simply remain in that paradise when they pass on. The people are endlessly grateful to the Creator for the privilege of living there. And this paradise is so fine that the people have many obligations to take care of it and fix it when necessary. It is that large bundle of gratitude, duties, wonder, and emotions that cause the people to hold Nee Dosh.

In 2003, the tribal council recruited Bud Lane to work in the Cultural Department and head up a language and traditional arts program. Growing up, Lane's connection to Athapaskan was typical: he had heard older relatives using words and phrases but it was not the language of daily conversation. In the late 1970s, after restoration and with pride in being Indian surging at Siletz and nationally, he made up his mind to learn the language. He turned to an elder, Nellie Orton. Born in 1910, she grew up with the language but, trapped in the era when people concealed their culture, refused to speak it in public. At first, she declined to work with Lane, but in time she turned teacher and threw herself into it, methodically walking Lane through Athapaskan. By the 1990s, with the help of Orton and, after she passed away, other Siletz elders and Tolowa people from Smith River, Lane had become the Siletz tribal member most fluent in Athapascan.

Lane holds classes at the Eugene, Salem, and Portland area tribal offices and teaches at the Siletz Valley Charter School. About twenty students attend class. The body of materials is steadily growing as Lane has recorded many Athapaskan-speaking elders. For an ultimate reference work, he has transliterated an Athapaskan-English dictionary, *Nuu-Wee-Ya'* (*Our Words*), with 12,000 words and phrases. With the dictionary as a base, Lane and a group of students are creating the "Siletz Talking Dictionary," with keyboard-friendly, interactive audio files containing all 12,000 words and phrases that students can access on the tribal Web site and the Living Tongues Web site as well. Overall, he is cautiously optimistic about the survival of Coast Athapaskan:

> Athabaskan is the last indigenous language still in use of the [ten] languages spoken here since our people confederated here in the 1850s. It is precious beyond description. Like most of Siletz culture, our language never completely left us, but has been greatly diminished by many different factors. It took 150 years to reduce the pool of speakers to what it is today. It will take

some time and effort to reverse that, but it is our determination that our language and all of the history, world views and lifeways it contains, not be relegated to the ash heap of history. So our vital work continues.

Saving a language is as monumental a task as one could posit for a small society. To be sure, over the past generation there has been a great deal of work at Siletz and progress of many kinds. The sounds of the ancient language can now be heard from numerous young people and newly involved adults as well. Important documentation, written and oral, has been done. Students are studying native languages in college. Still, the odds are against the Siletz reviving Athapaskan in the sense of reaching a stage where a substantial percentage of tribal members are fluent. Respected scholars are skeptical about small tribes maintaining their languages. Linguist David Crystal warns, for example, that "a language spoken by less than 100 is in a very dangerous situation." Of all the indigenous languages in the United States, only one—Hawaiian—has shown a net gain in recent years in the number of fluent speakers.

Yet fluency is not the only way to measure progress. People can learn Athapaskan songs, prayers, and stories—and their *context*. Those people can participate as speakers and listeners in schools, public meetings, Nee Dosh, and gatherings to commemorate triumphs and pain. During the past generation the use of tribal languages in this sense has markedly increased across Indian country and at Siletz. It is profoundly rewarding. Tribal members feel it and so do we outsiders.

The language is sacred. It is in jeopardy. The Siletz could not let that lie. As a matter of duty, of honor, the old sounds need to be heard in some meaningful fashion. It is part of survival.

Baskets were pervasive in Siletz traditional life. Some were practical, with day-to-day uses, and could be simple and utilitarian or finely twined and decorative: storage containers, eating plates, floor mats, and aprons. Small lidded baskets held personal items such as medicines and jewelry. Other baskets did heavy work as sturdy fish traps and large conical baskets, backpacks that transported heavy loads of deer and elk meat, shellfish, salmon, or eels. The weave could be so tight as to make a water basket. Cooking baskets with an impressively tight weave allowed tribal members to rustle up deer, elk, or seal dinners by putting water in the bottom and adding hot rocks while constantly

Culture Camp, held every summer. Gilbert Towner, dedicated to teaching the Tututni language to young people, is shown here passing on the technique for scraping a hide. *Siletz Tribal Collection.*

stirring so as not to damage the valuable basket.

The most prized of all baskets were the basket caps used by female dancers in Nee Dosh or by women and men on other important occasions. Small and delicate, these highly decorative caps, tightly and finely woven, were created by experienced weavers. Making a high-quality basket cap—a piece that rises to the level of fine art—takes 50 to 100 hours.

Carefully graded hazel sticks—the warp—give shape to the baskets. Spruce roots—the weft—are woven in, normally accompanied by overlay material such as bear grass, maidenhair fern, woodwardia, dyed porcupine quills, and other materials in a carefully developed and carried out plan for that design. A good basket can last for 100 or even 150 years if kept safe from bugs, out of the sun to keep it lithe and supple, and away from dampness to prevent mold.

Keeping up traditions takes time and commitment to the point of dedication, and basketry is no exception. Needless to say, the weaving requires patience, dexterity, and the teaching of an expert. Moreover, many days precede the construction of the basket. The plant material must be gathered and made ready for weaving. You have to know where it is, when to go, and how to gather, process, and store it.

CULTURAL REVIVAL

National forests hold productive gathering grounds, and logging roads provide good access, so Siletz basket makers may journey in the Coast Range to the Siuslaw National Forest, which closely conforms to the boundaries of the 1855 Siletz Reservation; travel farther south to the Rogue River–Siskiyou National Forest; or cross the Willamette Valley to Willamette National Forest lands in the Cascade Range. Hazel sticks need to be picked in the spring, just as the sap has begun to flow, and spruce roots are best dug (this digging is not easy on the fingers or the nails) in the late spring and early summer, when the roots are moist and supple and before the ground gets hard. Properly, bear grass should be picked from the middle of the plant, carefully selecting a few crowns from each clump. Ferns and bear grass must be picked at their zenith a bit later in the year before they become too brittle.

All the materials need preparation, but spruce roots require the most. They are boiled, peeled, and split the same day they are picked. After peeling off the bark, the root is split to create even-sized ribbons about three feet long. The result is strong, sinewy, smooth strips that are light tan with a shiny patina. All the materials must be carefully stored after the initial preparation work is done.

The number of master weavers steadily declined over the years. Although several people were doing some weaving in the years leading up to restoration, only a very few of the really old-time, experienced weavers remained— Ida Bensell, her two daughters Gladys Muschamp and Carrie Streets, Nellie Orton, and Ruth Watts-Umatata among them. With the culture at a precarious stage, all of them taught—or tried to teach—young people, but none came forward to practice the elaborate art. Then, in the 1980s, Gladys Muschamp began working with three young men to pass on the weaving, and it took. By 2010 about twenty tribal members were serious, producing weavers. To Bud Lane, Muschamp "is one of my greatest heroes."

Renowned Siletz basketmaker Gladys (Bensell) Muschamp sits surrounded by some of her then most recent weaving (ca. 1980). She rarely agreed to have her picture taken, especially in such a posed shot, but a tribal member convinced her that the picture should be taken; several tribal members provided baskets that they had acquired from Gladys for the composed collection shown here. The technique regularly used by Muschamp's family and many other Siletz families is half-twist overlay, where split roots are woven over small hazel stick ribs, spiraling out and changing the number of strands for texture and strength at prescribed intervals. The main design element is made by weaving sun-bleached bear grass and split maidenhair fern stems into each stitch in the design area. The design material is generally softer, thinner, and less durable than the foundation of the spruce root, and so it lies over the top of the spruce root base strand. One contemporary weaver explained that "to appreciate fully the many diverse and beautiful techniques employed by the Siletz and their ancestors, you have to see the baskets and hold them, watch them being made, and observe the time, love, and labor that goes into the preparation of the materials and the weaving." Photograph by Terry Russell provided to the tribe by Gladys Muschamp's son, George "Woody" Muschamp Jr. *Siletz Tribal Collection.*

Passing on traditions from one generation to another is a mystical process, part sense of community, part diligence of elders, part open-mindedness of youth. So it is with the spiritual art of weaving in the Pacific Northwest, where at Siletz and elsewhere in Indian country, "the basket is a song." W. Richard West, former director of the National Museum of the Native American, told this story:

> A northern California basket maker named Mrs. Mattz was hired to teach basket making at a local university. After three weeks, her students complained that all they had done was sing songs. When, they asked, were they going to learn to make baskets? Mrs. Mattz, somewhat taken aback, replied that they were learning to make baskets. She explained that the process starts with songs that are sung so as not to insult the plants when the materials for the baskets are picked. So her students learned the songs and went to pick the grasses and plants to make their baskets.
>
> Upon their return to the classroom, however, the students again were dismayed when Mrs. Mattz began to teach them yet more songs. This time she wanted them to learn the songs that must be sung as you soften the materials in your mouth before you start to weave. Exasperated, the students protested having to learn songs instead of learning to make baskets. Mrs. Mattz, perhaps a bit exasperated herself at this point, thereupon patiently explained the obvious to them: "You're missing the point," she said, "a basket is a song made visible."
>
> I do not know whether Mrs. Mattz's students went on to become exemplary basket makers. What I do know is that her wonderfully poetic remark—which suggests the interconnectedness of everything, the symbiosis of who we are and what we do—embodies a whole philosophy of Native life and culture and speaks volumes about the nature of Native objects to Native peoples themselves.

Most of Siletz culture—the basketry, Nee Dosh, the language, hunting, fishing, and gathering, and the family- and village-oriented lifeways—trace back into antiquity. But tribal cultures evolve, and at Siletz one of the most cherished traditions is of recent vintage. Yet it stands for the whole Siletz experience, from the revered old days through the bad years to the modern revival.

Each September, the Run to the Rogue, 263 miles in all, sends runners on a

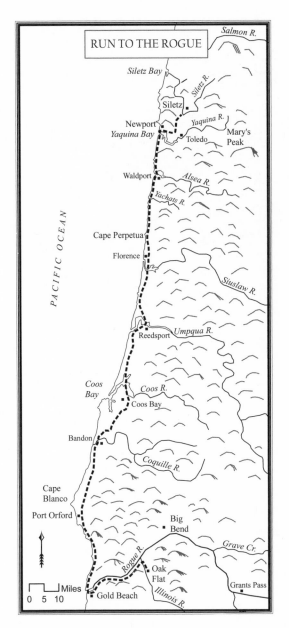

RUN TO THE ROGUE

long-distance relay from the town of Siletz, south down the Coast, and then up the Rogue River to its junction with the Illinois River. Hundreds of people run or walk, help organize, and serve as staff for the three days. Many others gather to watch. On the second night, down south, the people of Port Orford put on a potluck for the Siletz.

In a sense, Run to the Rogue is notable for its ordinariness. Yes, the run has an element of ceremony; it's an event to mark on the calendar and look forward to, but it is unremarkable in its simple logic. The Rogue River country still holds a place in the daily lives of Siletz people. That land and all the stories about it are part of the community. Going to the mouth of the Illinois is as normal and obvious as going across town to visit grandmother.

Still, a solemn mission permeates the run, which is timed to take place on or near September 10, which the tribal council has declared to be Treaty Day, a tribal holiday. Treaty Day is held on the date of the first treaty at Table Rock, but the holiday commemorates all of the treaties, including the unratified Coast Treaty of 1855. The route—trail then, highway now—traces *in reverse* the infamous long march that many of the ancestors made in 1856. Returning by the same route can help salve the memories of the torment of the march and also assure the Coast, the forests, and the rivers that the Siletz have survived and remain loyal to their ancestral place. The destination point is Oak Flat, the meeting ground where

Traditionalist Craig Whitehead, in front, and Frank Petersen were critical organizers and participants in the early years of Run to the Rogue. This photograph depicts the beginning of the run, when many children and some adults gather on Government Hill and walk through town before the staff, carried here by Whitehead (with assistance), is turned over to individual runners and walkers. *Siletz Tribal Collection.*

Tyee John refused Colonel Buchanan's order to surrender and move north and instead chose to fight the final conflict at Big Bend. Downriver is the myrtle grove where the 1855 treaty, never ratified and never honored except by the tribes, was finally signed on September 8. So the Siletz people hold Run to the Rogue each year to remember—and never to forget—the battles, the treaties, the marches, the ancestors, and the land.

The three days of the run, with people making their ways down in various vehicles, including the Elders Bus, are slow-moving and easy, with time for hikes and sidetrips to familiar spots and stories and reminiscing. The ancestors had one or several villages in every valley. Their life was stable and abundant. They had the salmon, eels, shellfish, seals, and sea lions. The thick, green, moist forests gave deer and elk meat, cedar for canoes, and spruce roots for elegant baskets. Picking berries up on the ridge tops, they could survey their vast, generous domain and with a wave of an arm tell their young people *nvn-nvst-'an*, "for you it is made."

Siletz runners on the southern Oregon Coast toward the end of the second day of the Run to the Rogue. *Photograph by Jeff Foster.*

I heard many stories about the landmarks we passed on the times when I took part in the run. Big Stump, the much-weathered redwood stump, right out in the middle of the beach, the center of the world for the Yaquina, Alsea, Yachats, Siuslaw, and Lower Umpqua tribes. The forty-mile-long beach, broad with sand dunes from Heceta Head to Coos Bay and a national recreation area today, that, every bit as much as the big rivers and high cliffs, made the march north so brutal. Cape Perpetua, rising straight up from the waves more than 1,400 feet, where the ancestors built amazing trails into the sheer sides. Battle Rock, near Port Orford, the massive formation where the treacherous seamen fired their killing cannon into a cluster of local Natives in 1851 and where, five years later, Indian people were herded like so many cattle into pens, awaiting the steamers that would take them far north. Humbug Mountain—poorly named, it is no humbug—is another testament to the pain and indignities of the removal; on the coastal side, the goliath is more cliff than slope right down to the waves and so the soldiers marched their captives, most of them barefoot, well to the east across stretches of shale scree to circumnavigate Humbug.

The open, inviting Sixes River Valley. "I never lived in Sixes," one woman told me, "but my people came from there and I've heard so many stories. Whenever I come over that rise, I just feel something in my whole body. It's home to me." At the mouth of the Rogue, Frank Simmons looked back up the river toward his grandfather Hoxie Simmons's home country and reflected on the ultimate meaning of the Run to the Rogue. "We think of our ancestors, of what they went through. Their tracks are still in the sand, their breath still in the air, their hope still in our hearts."

The Illinois River empties into the Rogue about twenty-five miles inland, eight river miles or so below Big Bend, where Tyee John and his people almost won the final battle. On that last leg of the run, steadily uphill, young male and female runners chewed up the early-morning miles, proudly bearing the ceremonial staff—myrtlewood from the Rogue country, embroidered with doe hide and eagle and flicker feathers—as they headed up the Rogue, place of so many good years and then the wars. The canyon tightens. A light rain came in and mist rose up from the river, the white playing off against the bold green that comes down to the banks. Glorious though the landscape is, if you know Siletz history you can't help but feel the presence of the ancestors. The Rogue country is thick with nature, thick with history and humanity.

Two hundred people or so waited at Oak Flat, a level meadow up above the Illinois River. The staff was late by more than two hours but no one seemed impatient. The Run to the Rogue is informal in some ways, ceremonial in others, but it is also a complicated enterprise requiring precision. The organizers have to register sign-ups for 263 one-mile, mostly single, segments and then estimate arrival times and be sure that drop-offs and pick-ups are in order. The people at Oak Flat appreciate that. Another part of it is cultural. No one is in a rush. It's a chance to talk with people and both joke around and feel the larger meaning of the moment.

When the final runner broke into view, he was greeted with smiles and gestures of satisfaction rather than noise. After passing the staff to an elder, he and the other tribespeople walked down a rocky jeep trail, talking quietly, to a wide, rocky beach on the edge of the surging Illinois. A return to a place that once was theirs, a place to stun you with its beauty, a place to break your heart. A commemoration, not a celebration.

The group formed a circle. There was no dancing. A good-time dance would be done later, after the salmon dinner. After a prayer, the tribal chairman welcomed everyone. Some of the elders spoke briefly, honoring the ancestors and talking about how this big-river, big-tree country would always be home. Then the group lapsed into a long silence, awash in thoughts of the ancestors and the land.

The tribal chairman had asked if I would read Tyee John's speech to the gathering. I was glad to do it. When I began this book, I thought I knew the history pretty well. I didn't, and the learning has become a satisfaction of a lifetime. I didn't know of Tyee John when this began. In time he captivated me, partly because of his military skills, more broadly because he was indomitable, because he embodied the staying power of the Siletz. Yes, I was definitely glad to do it.

Now, in the quiet of the group, she said that I would be reading the speech. Choked up, I paused. The people, who felt the same emotions and more, were still. Even the river ceased its rumbling, rushing sounds, the better to hear the words of its old colleague.

> You are a great chief; so am I a great chief; this is my country; I was in it when these trees were very little, not higher than my head. My heart is sick fighting the whites, but I want to live in my country. I will not go out of my country. I will, if the whites are willing, go back to the Deer Creek country and live as I used to do among the whites; they can visit my camp and I will visit theirs; but I will not lay down my arms and go to the reserve. I will fight. Good bye."

The people were still and so was the river. They remained so. Not having planned it, I asked in a low voice whether I should read it again. People nodded in silence, and I did.

NOTES

1 Village Societies Inlaid in the Land

P. 11   *Oral tradition.* In generations past, many anthropologists argued that the only reliable information from Natives about aboriginal life was oral testimony, that is, statements (usually made to anthropologists) by people who actually witnessed events and societal practices. Some anthropologists eschewed the use of oral tradition, accounts of contemporary Indians who received their information from accounts handed down over the generations. The approach to oral tradition has evolved since then. Today, historians and anthropologists critically assess any evidence, including oral tradition, about past events to determine its reliability. As one scholar put it, oral tradition (and, one could add, written primary evidence as well) can be "grotesquely inaccurate" or "extraordinarily accurate." Richard A. Gould, *Archaeology of the Point St. George Site, and Tolowa Prehistory*, p. 5 (Berkeley: University of California Press, 1966) (quoting Roland B. Dixon in disagreeing with Robert Lowie's statement that oral traditions lack historical value).

P. 12   *Native arrival in south-central Oregon and Willamette Valley.* See, e.g., L. S. Cressman, *Prehistory of the Far West: Homes of Vanished Peoples*, p. 73 (Salt Lake City: University of Utah Press, 1977) (on the Cave Rock excavation); also p. 197 (on the Willamette Valley). See also Jo Reese and John L. Fagan, "An Early-Holocene Archaeological Site in Oregon's Willamette Valley," vol. 14 *Current Research in the Pleistocene*, pp. 77–78 (1997).

P. 12   *"dearth of early [known] sites."* Madonna L. Moss and Jon M. Erlandson, "Reflections on North American Pacific Coast Prehistory," vol. 9, no. 1 *Journal of World Prehistory*, p. 14 (1995).

P. 12   *Presence on the Oregon Coast between 6,000 and 10,000 years ago.* The authenticated sites are Tahkenitch Landing, Indian Sands, and Young's River Complex. See ibid., pp. 14–15. See also R. Lee Lyman, *Prehistory of the Oregon Coast*, p. 74 (San Diego, CA: Academic Press, Inc., 1991).

P. 12   *Permanent settlements.* Lyman, *Prehistory*, p. 80.

P. 12   *An estimated 50,000 people.* See Robert Boyd, *The Coming of the Spirit of Pestilence*, pp. 264–65 (Seattle: University of Washington Press, 1999). Boyd has conducted the most comprehensive population and disease analysis. The figure of 50,000 includes his South Coast Epidemic Area (except for the Quinault and Lower Chehalis) and Interior Valleys Epidemic Area (except for the Upper Chehalis and Cowlitz). Boyd did not include one Siletz tribe, the Shasta of northern California and southern Oregon.

P. 17   duh-neh *means "the people of the place."* Bud Lane and Robert Kentta, interview with author, Yaquina Head, Oregon, July 25, 2008.

P. 17   *The largest village named Tututin.* Lane and Kentta, interview, July 25, 2008. See also Loren Bommelyn, *Now You're Speaking—Tolowa*, p. ix (Arcata, CA: Center for Indian Community Development, Humboldt State University, 1995) (this source spells the village name as "Tutuden"); Jay Miller and William R. Seaburg, "Athapaskans of Southwestern Oregon," *in* Wayne Suttles, ed., vol. 7, *Handbook of North American Indians*, p. 586 (Washington, D.C.: Smithsonian Institution, 1990).

P. 17   *Tolowa, Chetco, and Tututni.* Anthropologists regularly comment on the similarities among these tribes. See, e.g., Philip Drucker, "The Tolowa and Their Southwest Oregon Kin," vol. 36, no. 4 *University of California Publications in American Ethnology*, pp. 222, 228 (1937). The scholarly research on the Tolowa is more extensive, probably because of the prominence of Alfred Kroeber of the University of California at Berkeley and the work of his students and colleagues; much of that research is transferable to the Tututni. In modern times, the ties between the Siletz and the Tolowa of Smith River remain strong. In addition to visits back and forth, due to blood relationships and intermarriage, in many years the Siletz host the summer Nee Dosh and the Smith Rivers host the winter Nee Dosh, and dancers from both tribes participate.

P. 18   *Tututin sat on a low bluff.* I have been unable to find anyone, including tribal members, who can identify the exact location of Tututin. The historical accounts differ. Lucy Metcalf estimated Tututin, her home village, at ten miles upriver. Cora Du Bois, "Tututni (Rogue River Athapaskan) Field Notes: Typescript, 1934," 29, *at* University of California, Berkeley, Bancroft Library [hereinafter "Tututni Field Notes"]. The earliest written account is by Paul Schumacher, who visited the site in 1875, and placed the village five miles inland. See Schumacher, "Researches in the Kjökkenmöddings and Graves of a Former Population of the Coast of Oregon," vol. 3, no. 1 *Bulletin of the U.S. Geological and Geographical Survey of the Territories*, pp. 27–29 (January 1877) (locating the village on the north bank, with a map showing it on a bluff). Drucker estimated the location at five to six miles from the river mouth; "The Tolowa," p. 271. It is understandable that people today cannot be specific. After the Tututni were moved north, much of their home area was plowed, as Schumacher noted, and, more recently, this scenic stretch of river holds primary residences, second homes, a luxury resort, a few stores, and a rod-and-gun club. Also, the river is large here and has moved around in flood years, making it hard to correlate today's river with the only known historical map, which is from 1877. Schumacher, "Researches in the Kjökken-möddings," p. 28. After driving and hiking the area, my research assistant, Josh Tenneson, and I did find a low bluff about six to seven miles inland that seemed to us to be the most consistent with historical reports and the villagers' needs: south facing, close to the river but above the floodplain, and endowed with a large, level meadow. In granting me permission to walk the site, the owner asked that I not identify its exact location.

P. 18   *Athapaskan and Tututin population.* Robert Boyd estimates the aboriginal population of the coastal Athapaskans at 4,500. Boyd, *The Coming*, p. 264. The Tututni in the mid-nineteenth century knew that the remnant populations then existing were much smaller than in past generations. Dr. Lorenzo Hubbard's on-the-ground examination in 1856 found their view to be accurate: "According to tradition, many years ago they were far more numerous than at the present time, wars and diseases having in some instances destroyed whole tribes. The marks of old towns and large settlements everywhere found, now entirely deserted, are strong evidence of the truth of their traditions." Reg Pullen, "Overview of the Environment of Native Inhabitants of Southwestern Oregon, Late Prehistoric Era," p. IV-3, report prepared for the USDA Forest Service (Bandon, OR, 1996) (citing Lorenzo Hubbard's *Travels in Southern Oregon*, published in 1856). Cora Du Bois cites one source as setting the Tututin population at 120. Lucy Metcalf recalled fifty-three people in the village, but Du Bois judged that "a most conservative estimate." Du Bois, "Tututni Field Notes," pp. 14, 34. Those estimates came after the epidemics.

P. 18   *Visitors and suburbs.* See, e.g., Drucker, "The Tolowa," p. 244.

P. 18   *"Tutuden was a big town."* See Elaine L. Mills, ed., vol. 1 *The Papers of John Peabody Harrington in the Smithsonian Institution, 1907–1957*, Part 1, Reel 026, Frame 0677 (Millwood, NY: Kraus International Publications, 1981) (containing a microfilm copy of Harrington's handwritten notes detailing an interview with Wolverton Orton).

P. 19   *Tututin "living houses" and other structures.* Tututin has been plowed over and the ground otherwise disturbed so that reconstructing the old settlement pattern is difficult, if not impossible. Paul Schumacher came through early, in 1875, and reported valuable information (see generally Schumacher, "Researches in the Kjökkenmöddings," pp. 29–31). Unfortunately, while he described the existence of many former structures, he offered no estimate of the actual number. A useful reference point, though, is his account of "50 depressions of former houses" at the nearby Tututin village at Pistol River. Ibid., p. 31. Du Bois provides detailed descriptions of the architecture and uses of the structures. See generally Du Bois, "Tututni Field Notes," pp. 36–42. On house sizes, see ibid., p. 38 (dwellings estimated to have been 12 feet square); Miller and Seaburg, "Athapaskans of Southwestern Oregon," pp. 582–83 (largest Tututni houses: 20 x 30 feet; smaller houses: 10 x 15 feet). Accounts of Tolowa villages are also useful. See, e.g., Gould, *Point St. George Site*, pp. 16–27. Gould includes a sketch showing twenty-six living houses (p. 21).

P. 19   *"the teller of these stories."* Lionel Youst and William R. Seaburg, *Coquelle Thompson, Athabascan Witness* (Norman: University of Oklahoma Press, 2002), p. 26 (quoting Coquelle Thompson).

P. 19   *"values and worldview that he carried."* Ibid.

P. 19   *Middens and archaeologists.* On Pacific Northwest middens generally, see Julia K. Stein, ed., *Deciphering a Shell Midden* (San Diego, CA: Academic Press, Inc., 1992), pp. 1–24. Gould describes a separate midden site for a Tolowa village (*Point St. George Site*, p. 43). Robert Kentta and Bud Lane have visited several smaller (one or two living houses) ancestral house pit sites, with middens close to the houses, and told the story of Lucy Metcalf's sister, who passed on at a young age and was buried in front of their house to keep her close to the family (Lane and Kentta, interview, July 25, 2008). To contemporary Indian people, the excavation of middens by scholars and the damaging of them by developers are sensitive matters, especially when burials are involved. Graves may come under protective tribal, federal, and state laws.

P. 21   *Rhythms of life*. Drucker explains the food-gathering cycle well in "The Tolowa," pp. 231–35. See also Miller and Seaburg, "Athapaskans of Southwestern Oregon," pp. 581–82; Lionel Youst, *She's Tricky Like Coyote: Annie Miner Peterson, an Oregon Coast Indian Woman*, pp. 7–8 (Norman: University of Oklahoma Press, 1997).

P. 21   *Food as common property*. See, e.g., Drucker, "The Tolowa," p. 235.

P. 21   *The light and smoke were visible up and down the Coast*. Bud Lane, interview with Josh Tenneson, research assistant, Siletz, Oregon, July 18, 2005. Frank Simmons, interview with author, Lincoln City, Oregon, April 22, 2006.

P. 22   *First salmon ceremony*. Cora Du Bois describes the ceremony in "Tolowa Notes," vol. 34, no. 2 *American Anthropologist*, pp. 258–59 (April–June 1932). See also Philip Drucker, *Indians of the Northwest Coast*, pp. 141–42 (New York: McGraw-Hill Book Co., 1955); Philip Drucker, *Cultures of the North Pacific Coast*, pp. 94–96 (San Francisco: Chandler Publishing Co., 1965).

P. 23   *Respect to the salmon*. Drucker, "The Tolowa," p. 260. For a classic account of the Indian view of unity with the natural world, see Vine Deloria Jr., *God Is Red: A Native View of Religion*, pp. 81–95 (New York: Grosset & Dunlap, 1973).

P. 23   *Large, rounded rocks at Tututin*. See Schumacher, "Researches in the Kjökkenmöddings," p. 30 ("In front of the lower or main settlement are several rocks above water, of which the farthest one out was the principal fishery of the Tu-tu-to-ni . . .").

P. 23   *Gathering basketmaking materials*. Bud Lane, Cheryl Lane, and Robert Kentta described the times and methods of gathering different basketmaking materials in an interview with the author in Siletz, Oregon, May 24, 2005.

P. 23   *Acorns*. California black oak, the most desirable for acorns, has a limited range in Oregon, being found no farther north than Eugene, only west of the Cascades, and in—but never west of—the Coast Range. Acorns from the black oak were a particularly valuable resource for Indians because of their high edible oil content. See Philip M. McDonald, United States Department of Agriculture, "Quercus kelloggii," in vol. 2 *Silvics of North America*, pp. 661, 670 (Washington, D.C.: Government Printing Office, 1990). Tan oak and myrtle acorns also were favored, but were not as geographically widespread in the Lower Rogue River country as the black oak acorns. See Pullen, "Overview of the Environment," pp. IV-10–IV-11. Although the acorns from the Oregon white oak, the most widespread oak in Oregon, were less desirable, meal made from the acorns was still extensively used by Indians for food. Ibid., pp. IV-10 (explaining that these acorns' high tannic acid content makes them difficult to process, and quoting Dixon's description of the resultant "more slimy, glutinous mixture, which was not well liked").

P. 23   *"the staff of life."* Edward G. Olsen, ed., *Then Till Now in Brookings-Harbor*, p. 6 (Brookings, OR: Coastal Printing Co. for the Brookings Rotary Club, 1979) (quoting Sam Van Pelt, "Before the White Man: An Indian's Story," *The Sunday Portland Oregonian*, Sunday Magazine, p. 7 (February 5, 1939), *at* Oregon Historical Society, Portland, Research Library. On mush or juice of the acorn, see Lane and Kentta, interview, July 25, 2008.

P. 23   *Hunting*. Drucker lists a variety of ingenious hunting techniques, summarizing that "before the advent of firearms, the main dependence must have been on traps, though driving with dogs is said to have been common" (Drucker, "The Tolowa," pp. 233–34). See also Olsen, *Then Till Now*, p. 6 (quoting Sam Van Pelt on the use of hand-dug trenches), *at* Oregon Historical Society, Portland Research Library.

P. 24   *Journeys to the Coast.* Lucy Metcalf told Cora Du Bois that in the summer her family "went down to the ocean for about one month during smelt season. Went down for mussels whenever they desired them." Du Bois, "Tututni Field Notes," p. 31.

P. 24   *Storage baskets.* Ibid., p. 38 (Lucy Metcalf's estimation of the size of the storage baskets). For a sketch of the interior of a living house showing storage baskets, see Gould, *Point St. George Site*, p. 23.

P. 24   *Western Oregon creation stories.* Some tribes, like the Tututni, had water-based accounts, while others were land-based. Some treated the Earth as flat. See Katharine Berry Judson, *Myths and Legends of the Pacific Northwest: Especially of Washington and Oregon*, p. 33 (Chicago: A. C. McClurg and Co., 1912) (recounting the Shasta story of Old Man Above stepping down to the "new, flat earth"). Leo Frachtenberg reported a Coos creation story similar to the one summarized in the text here. Livingston Farrand and Leo J. Frachtenberg, "Shasta and Athapascan Myths from Oregon," vol. 28, no. 109 *The Journal of American Folklore*, p. 224n2 (July–September 1915).

P. 24   *Tututni creation story with Xōwa:lä´cī.* On the Charles Depoe rendition, see Farrand and Frachtenberg, "Shasta and Athapascan Myths," pp. 224–28. Robert Kentta also explained the creation story in an interview with the author in Siletz, Oregon, on February 24, 2005. For another version of an Athapaskan creation story, see J. Owen Dorsey, "Indians of Siletz Reservation, Oregon," vol. 2, no. 1 *American Anthropologist*, pp. 58–60 (January 1889).

P. 25   *Western Oregon Native stories.* See generally William R. Seaburg, *Pitch Woman and Other Stories* (Lincoln: University of Nebraska Press, 2007); William R. Seaburg and Pamela T. Amoss, eds., *Badger and Coyote Were Neighbors: Melville Jacobs on Northwest Indian Myths and Tales* (Corvallis: Oregon State University Press, 2000); Melville Jacobs, *Coos Myth Texts* (Seattle: University of Washington, 1940); Livingston Farrand, "Notes on the Alsea Indians of Oregon," vol. 3, no. 2 *American Anthropologist*, pp. 239–47 (April–June 1901); Edward Sapir, "Takelma Texts," vol. 2, no. 1 *Anthropological Publications of the University Museum* (Philadelphia: University of Pennsylvania, 1909); Judson, *Myths and Legends*.

P. 25   *Coyote stories.* Coyote is well represented in all of the sources cited in note 32, above. The winter-summer eel story is from Farrand and Frachtenberg, "Shasta and Athapascan Myths," pp. 228–33.

P. 26   tsa-xwi *or* koho. See, e.g., George W. Riddle, *Early Days in Oregon: A History of the Riddle Valley*, p. 80 (Riddle, OR: Riddle Parent Teachers Association, 1953); see also Edward Sapir, "Notes on the Takelma Indians of Southwestern Oregon," vol. 9, no. 2 *American Anthropologist*, pp. 261–62 (April–June 1907) (describing a "women's substitute for the game of shinny").

P. 26   *Nee Dosh.* See, e.g., Du Bois, "Tolowa Notes," pp. 259–60 (explicitly referring to the five-night dance at Tolowa as "feather dance" and reporting a dance house); Cora Du Bois, "The Wealth Concept as an Integrative Factor in Tolowa-Tututni Culture," in *Essays in Anthropology Presented to A. L. Kroeber*, p. 53 (Berkeley: University of California Press, 1936) (finding the ten-night dance at Tututni "comparable" to Tolowa and Yurok ceremonies); Drucker, "The Tolowa," pp. 264–65, 277; Bud Lane, interview, May 24, 2005; Bud Lane, Cheryl Lane, and Robert Kentta, interview, May 25, 2005. Although Du Bois reported a feather dance at Tolowa in early days, she later questioned whether Feather Dance goes back to precontact times. See Cora Du Bois, "The 1870 Ghost Dance," *Anthropological Records* 3, no. 1 (1939), 34. Robert Kentta believes that Nee Dosh has ancient origins. One reason is that some of the Nee Dosh songs now sung at Siletz contain such "high language," words that are hardly translatable anymore. Robert Kentta, telephone interview with assistant, Cynthia Carter, August 5, 2005. See also the discussion of modern Nee Dosh in the text and accompanying notes of chapter 16, pp. 369–74.

P. 26   *A world renewal ceremony.* A. L. Kroeber and E. W. Gifford, "World Renewal: A Cult System of Native Northwest California," vol. 13, no. 1 *Anthropological Records* (1949), remains the most comprehensive work on the world renewal and new-year ceremonies of the Indians of northern California. Kroeber and Gifford conclude that "the heart of the world renewal religion . . . is antifamine, antidisease, and anticataclysm[;] . . . its purpose is to provide an abundance of food, universal good health, and to renew or repair the earth." Ibid., p. 105. On the philosophical ideas packed into Nee Dosh and other world-renewal ceremonies in northern California and southern Oregon, see also Thomas Buckley, *Standing Ground: Yurok Indian Spirituality, 1850–1990*, pp. 205–44, 261–79 (Berkeley: University of California Press, 2002). Given the many-layered meanings of the Feather Dance, it is hard to understand Drucker's reference to it as "a simple wealth-display dance." Drucker, "The Tolowa," p. 277.

P. 26   *"the center of our world."* Russell Thornton, "Social Organization and the Demographic Survival of the Tolowa," vol. 31, no. 3 *Ethnohistory*, p. 193 (Summer 1984) (quoting a Tolowa's description in 1976 to Charlotte Heth of the ten-night dance).

P. 27   *Early judges and anthropologists made judgments.* For example, Philip Drucker and Cora Du Bois made statements to the effect that the villages had no governmental systems. See, e.g., Drucker, "The Tolowa," pp. 250–51. For derogatory statements by judges, see, e.g., *Cherokee Nation v. Georgia*, 30 U.S. (5 Pet.) 1, 15, 19 (1831) (J. Johnson concurring), and *State v. Towessnute*, 154 P. 805, 807 (Wash. 1916).

P. 27   *"a principle or rule of conduct."* E. Adamson Hoebel, *The Law of Primitive Man: A Study in Comparative Legal Dynamics* (Cambridge, MA: Harvard University Press, 1954), 22.

P. 27   *Yurok and Tututni dispute resolution.* Ibid., pp. 24–25 (Yuroks); the *gwee-shut-naga* of the Tututnis is discussed in the text of this book and accompanying notes.

P. 27   *Drucker's findings.* See, e.g., Drucker, "The Tolowa," pp. 249–51.

P. 28   *Du Bois's findings.* Du Bois, "The Wealth Concept," p. 54.

P. 28   *Villages were "organizationally complex."* Rebecca Dobkins interview with author, Newport, Oregon, July 25, 2008.

P. 28   *The tyee, a principal institution.* See, e.g., Miller and Seaburg, "Athapaskans of Southwestern Oregon," p. 583.

P. 28   *A headman's political and legal authority.* Robert Kentta, "A Piece of Siletz History, Part I," *Siletz News*, p. 27 (November 1999), and at http://www.ctsi.nsn.us/chinook-indian-tribe-siletz-heritage/our-history/part-i (accessed May 12, 2009). This short history, published in installments in the Siletz tribal newsletter and now available on the tribe's Web site, provides a useful overview of tribal history and an informed conceptual structure of these events.

P. 28   *an elaborate set of rules.* Drucker, "The Tolowa," pp. 250, 278.

P. 28   *Names were property.* Robert Kentta, interview with author, Siletz, Oregon, February 25, 2005. See also Drucker, "The Tolowa," 249 (fines imposed for speaking a "dead name").

P. 29   *mock warfare.* Kentta, interview, February 25, 2005.

P. 29   *disputes with other villages.* Ibid. See also Drucker, "The Tolowa," 249 ("All members of group contributed to make up necessary sum, but rich-man had to give larger part.").

P. 30   *Fines as final payment.* Kentta, interview, February 25, 2005.

P. 30   *Murder was an exception.* Bud Lane, interview, May 24, 2005; Kentta, "A Piece of Siletz History, Part I."

P. 30   *Restorative justice in other tribes.* See, e.g., Sidney L. Harring, "Crow Dog's Case [*Ex parte Crow Dog*, 109 U.S. 556 (1883)]: A Chapter in the Legal History of Tribal Sovereignty," vol. 14 *American Indian Law Review*, pp. 236–38 (1989) (describing the Brule Sioux's requirement that a victim of a homicide's family be remunerated with horses, blankets, and other property as achieving the dual goals of "termination of the conflict and the reintegration of all persons involved into the tribal body."). See generally K. N. Llewellyn and E. Adamson Hoebel, *The Cheyenne Way: Conflict and Case Law in Primitive Jurisprudence* (Norman: University of Oklahoma Press, 1941).

P. 30   *Restorative justice in contemporary America and other nations.* Restorative justice is on the ascendancy in the United States. See generally Leena Kurki, "Restorative and Community Justice in the United States," vol. 27 *Crime and Justice*, pp. 235–302 (2000); see also John Braithwaite, "Restorative Justice: Assessing Optimistic and Pessimistic Accounts," vol 25 *Crime and Justice*, pp. 2–3 (1999). Kurki delineates the goals of restorative justice as "restor[ing] the victim and the community, repair[ing] harms, and rebuild[ing] relationships among the victim, the offender, and the community." Kurki, "Restorative and Community Justice," p. 266. Restorative justice has gained widespread recognition and use throughout the world. See ibid., pp. 240, 268–69, 282 (New Zealand, Austria, Germany, and Canada); Braithwaite, "Restorative Justice," p. 4 (New Zealand); Bernd-Dieter Meier, "Alternatives to Imprisonment in the German Criminal Justice System," vol. 16, no. 3 *Federal Sentencing Reporter*, p. 8 (February 2004) ("One of the most important developments during the 1990's [in Germany] has been the legislature's unambiguous support of restorative justice."). Some countries frequently use restorative justice principles for violent crimes. See, e.g., Kurki, "Restorative and Community Justice," p. 269.

P. 31   *Material wealth promoted order.* Cora Du Bois saw this somewhat differently, concluding, "Thus, I feel, that the Tolowa-Tututni wealth attitude was instrumental in creating tensions which easily broke out in acts of violence. That these violences could be deflected by the payment of money atonements does not lessen the underlying conflicts." Du Bois, "The Wealth Concept," p. 65.

P. 31   *"When you bring your wealth."* Bud Lane, interview, May 24, 2005. Cora Du Bois's "The Wealth Concept" is an excellent source on this subject.

P. 31   *"a premium was placed."* Du Bois, "Tolowa Notes," p. 253.

P. 31   *"Marriage was not a dry, unfeeling exercise."* Kentta, interview, February 25, 2005.

P. 32   *Slavery was "a sort of adoption."* Drucker, "The Tolowa," p. 273. See also Du Bois, "The Wealth Concept," p. 55; Kentta, interview, February 25, 2005.

P. 32   *Their notion of wealth.* Du Bois, "The Wealth Concept."

P. 32   *"There is no hint."* Ibid., pp. 51–52.

P. 32   *"democracy of manners."* Du Bois, "Tolowa Notes," p. 251.

P. 32   *"If a boy is brought up by his grandma."* Ibid.

2 Landscapes That Fed Their People

P. 33   *rights to whales.* Philip Drucker, "The Tolowa and Their Southwest Oregon Kin," vol. 36, no. 4 *University of California Publications in American Ethnology*, p. 243 (1937).

P. 33   *Sea lion hunts.* Ibid., p. 234.

P. 33   *Hunters sang songs and went through purification.* Bud Lane and Robert Kentta, interview with author, Yaquina Head, Oregon, July 25, 2008.

P. 34   *Ocean canoes.* See generally David Neel, *The Great Canoes* (Seattle: University of Washington Press, 1995); Stephen Dow Beckham, *The Indians of Western Oregon*, pp. 62–63 (Coos Bay, OR: Arago Books, 1977) (describing and comparing the less ornate southern canoes to the highly decorated ones constructed further to the north).

P. 34   *The Chetco Tribe.* See generally T. T. Waterman, "The Village Sites in Tolowa and Neighboring Areas in Northwestern California," vol. 27, no. 4 *American Anthropologist*, pp. 528–43 (October–December 1925); Drucker, "The Tolowa"; J. Owen Dorsey, "The Gentile System of the Siletz Tribes," vol. 3, no. 10 *Journal of American Folklore*, p. 236 (July–September 1890); Joel V. Berreman, *Chetco Archaeology: A Report on the Lone Ranch Creek Shell Mound on the Coast of Southern Oregon*, pp. 9–10, 33–34 (General Series in Anthropology no. 11) (Menasha, WI: George Banta Publishing Co., 1944); Robert H. Ruby and John A. Brown, *A Guide to the Indian Tribes of the Pacific Northwest*, pp. 19–21 (Norman: University of Oklahoma Press, 1992) (first published 1986); "First Residents Were the Chetco" and "Chetco Life Was Much like Tolowas," *Brookings Curry Coastal Pilot* (February 23, 2001, and March 7, 2001), *at* http://www.currypilot.com/Community/Community/History-of-Brookings (click on the article titles) (accessed May 20, 2009).

P. 35   *"The only thing that was cultivated."* Sam Van Pelt, "Before the White Man: An Indian's Story," *Sunday Oregonian*, Sunday magazine, p. 7 (February 5, 1939).

P. 35   *"There was once a time."* Elizabeth D. Jacobs, "A Chetco Athabaskan Myth Text from Southwest Oregon," vol. 34, no. 3 *International Journal of American Linguistics*, pp. 192–93 (July 1968). Parenthetical material in the quotation is in the original.

P. 35   *"they lived together very well."* Ibid., p. 193.

P. 35   *"one of the most complex linguistic regions."* See, e.g., Jeffrey M. LaLande, "The Indians of Southwestern Oregon: An Ethnohistorical Review," vol. 6 *Anthropology Northwest*, p. 33 (1991).

P. 36   *"chain of dialects."* Jay Miller and William R. Seaburg, "Athapaskans of Southwestern Oregon," in Wayne Suttles, ed., vol. 7, *Handbook of North American Indians*, p. 580 (Washington, D.C.: Smithsonian Institution, 1990).

P. 36   *Chinook Jargon.* Philologists and anthropologists debate whether Chinook Jargon existed prior to European contact. Based upon linguistic, structural, and sociological factors, however, there is ample support for the view that the Jargon existed before contact. See, for example, Barbara P. Harris, "Chinook Jargon: Arguments for a Pre-Contact Origin," vol. 29, no. 1 *Pacific Coast Philology*, pp. 30–32 (September 1994). The extensive trade network and social relations among peoples with different languages would seem to have made a common pidgin language necessary. See discussion and accompanying notes on the Chinook Jargon in chapter 5, pp. 99–101.

P. 36   *formidable linguistic problems.* See, e.g., Joel V. Berreman, "Tribal Distributions in Oregon," no. 47 *Memoirs of the American Anthropological Association*, pp. 28–30 (1937); Lane and Kentta, interview, July 25, 2008.

P. 36   *characteristics "such as to mark it off."* Edward Sapir, "Notes on the Takelma Indians of Southwestern Oregon," vol. 9, no. 2 *American Anthropologist*, p. 257 (April–June 1907).

P. 36   *The Takelma Tribe.* See generally Dennis J. Gray, "The Takelma and Their Athapascan Neighbors: A New Ethnographic Synthesis for the Upper Rogue River Area of South-western Oregon," no. 37 *University of Oregon Anthropological Papers* (1987); Sapir, "Notes on the Takelma."

P. 37   *canoes and rafts used for portage.* Gray, "The Takelma," p. 34.

P. 37   *village of Dilomi.* The British fur trader Peter Skene Ogden visited Dilomi in 1827, well after epidemics had reduced the population, and reported that it contained "six large Houses sufficiently so to contain upwards of 100 Indians." K. G. Davies, ed., *Peter Skene Ogden's Snake Country Journal, 1826–27*, p. 86 (London: The Hudson's Bay Record Society, 1961).

P. 37   *Takelma fishing.* See Gray, "The Takelma," p. 32 (citing John P. Harrington's notes on his 1933 visit with Molly Orton to Ti'lo-mi-kh Falls).

P. 38   *"The first owner of the place."* Drucker, "The Tolowa," p. 296 (transmitting a consul-tant's version of the story). English names in parentheses are in the original.

P. 39   *"a rather warlike tribe."* Sapir, "Notes on the Takelma," p. 272.

P. 39   *Shastas occupied open valleys and rugged mountain-forests.* Roland B. Dixon, "The Shasta," vol. 17, no. 5 *Bulletin of the American Museum of Natural History*, p. 386 (July 1907).

P. 39   *The Shasta population was 3,000 strong.* Shirley Silver, "Shastan Peoples," in Robert F. Heizer, ed., vol. 8, *Handbook of North American Indians*, p. 212 (Washington, D.C.: Smithsonian Institution, 1978).

P. 39   *The Athapaskans were their enemies.* Dixon, "The Shasta," p. 387.

P. 39   *They highly valued dentalium shells.* See A. L. Kroeber, *Handbook of the Indians of California*, pp. 290–93 (Washington, D.C.: Bureau of American Ethnology, 1923).

P. 39   *The Shastas also gambled.* A. L. Kroeber, "Games of the California Indians," vol. 22, no. 3 *American Anthropologist*, p. 275 (July–September 1920).

P. 39   *Girls received the "111" chin tattoo.* Kroeber, *Handbook*, p. 293.

P. 39   *The Shasta first salmon ceremony.* See ibid., 294; Erna Gunther, "An Analysis of the First Salmon Ceremony," vol. 28, no. 4 *American Anthropologist*, p. 611 (October–December 1926).

P. 39   *"people will say."* Catharine Holt, "Shasta Ethnography," vol. 3, no. 4 *University of California Anthropological Records*, p. 339 (1946). Holt's article is based primarily on information she received from Sargeant Sambo, who was the same tyee interviewed by Dixon in 1904, when he was preparing to write "The Shasta."

P. 40   *Tribes of the Middle Coast.* In modern times, the Coos, Siuslaw, and Lower Umpqua have organized as a confederated tribe separate from Siletz. Some people from those ethnological tribes, however, are enrolled at Siletz.

P. 40   *Rogue River largest between the Klamath and the Columbia.* The Klamath and the Rogue are the two largest rivers between the Columbia and the Sacramento. By the time the Rogue River reaches the Pacific Ocean, it runs at an average of 9,000 cubic feet per second (cfs) on an average day during the wet months of December through May, and 2,500 cfs between June and November. U.S. Geological Survey, *Rogue River Near Agness, OR*, National Water Information System, *at* http://www.waterdata.usgs.gov/or/nwis/monthly (Site Name, "Rogue River near Agness, OR," choose Discharge Table of Monthly Mean) (accessed May 20, 2009). The Klamath River runs at an average of 28,500 cfs December through May and 6,700 cfs June through November. U.S. Geological Survey, *Klamath River Near Klamath, CA,* National Water Information System, *at* http://www.waterdata.usgs.gov/or/nwis/monthly (Site Name, "Klamath R NR Klamath CA," choose Discharge Table of Monthly Mean) (accessed May 20, 2009). See generally Arthur C. Benke and Colbert E. Cushing, eds., *Rivers of North America,* pp. 563–73 (Boston: Elsevier Academic Press, 2005).

P. 40   *The Coos and Siuslaw Tribes.* See, e.g., Henry B. Zenk, "Siuslawans and Coosans," in Wayne Suttles, ed., vol. 7, *Handbook of North American Indians,* pp. 573–77.

P. 41   *"Highway" between Coos and Siuslaw villages.* Lionel Youst, *She's Tricky Like Coyote,* pp. 37–38 (Norman: University of Oklahoma Press, 1997).

P. 41   *Annie Miner Peterson.* Youst's *She's Tricky Like Coyote* is a biography of Peterson's long life—she was born in Coos Bay in 1860 and died in 1939—and is especially well conceived and carried out. Similarly excellent is Lionel Youst and William Seaburg, *Coquelle Thompson, Athabaskan Witness* (Norman: University of Oklahoma Press, 2002).

P. 41   *Indian doctors.* See Youst, *She's Tricky Like Coyote,* pp. 55–61. On relatives killing the shaman, see, e.g., ibid., p. 27.

P. 42   *Old Lyman.* Ibid., p. 89.

P. 43   *Head flattening.* The Siuslaw experimented with head flattening quite late, in the mid-nineteenth century, but the tradition never took root as it did at Alsea. See Ruby and Brown, *A Guide to the Indian Tribes of the Pacific Northwest,* p. 206.

P. 43   *The Alseas and north-south influences.* See Livingston Farrand, "Notes on the Alsea Indians of Oregon," vol. 3, no. 2 *American Anthropologist,* p. 239 (April–June 1901); Henry B. Zenk, "Alseans," in Suttles, ed., vol. 7, *Handbook of North American Indians,* p. 568.

P. 44   *Reduction of the Siletz Reservation.* See discussion and accompanying notes in chapter 10, pp. 201–8.

P. 46   *Tillamook, Chinook, and Clatsop Tribes.* See generally Elizabeth D. Jacobs, *The Nehalem Tillamook* (Corvallis: Oregon State University Press, 2003); John Sauter and Bruce Johnson, *Tillamook Indians of the Oregon Coast* (Portland, OR: Binford & Mort, 1974); William R. Seaburg and Jay Miller, "Tillamook," in Suttles, ed., *Handbook of North American Indians,* p. 560; Robert H. Ruby and John A. Brown, *The Chinook Indians* (Norman: Oklahoma University Press, 1976); Michael Silverstein, "Chinookans of the Lower Columbia," in Suttles, ed., vol. 7, *Handbook of North American Indians,* p. 333.

P. 46   *Tillamooks more resilient after 1700 earthquake.* See generally Robert J. Losey, "Native American Vulnerability and Resiliency to Great Cascadia Earthquakes," vol. 108, no. 2 *Oregon Historical Quarterly* (Summer 2007).

P. 46   *houses could be over 300 feet long.* Kenneth M. Ames et al., "Household Archaeology of a Southern Northwest Coast Plank House," vol. 19, no. 3 *Journal of Field Archaeology,* pp. 277–78 (Autumn 1992) (summarizing "considerable variability in plank house size along the lower Columbia," ranging from "extremely large houses" of 60 to 137 meters (196–450 feet) in length to more typical houses that could be anywhere from 6 to 30 meters (20–98 feet) in length).

P. 47   *First salmon ceremony.* Jacobs, *The Nehalem Tillamook,* p. 204.

P. 48   *Columbia River tribes consumed 42 million pounds.* Northwest Power Planning Council, "Compilation of Information on Salmon and Steelhead Losses in the

Columbia River Basin," pp. 66–76 (March 1986). See also Joseph E. Taylor, "Steelhead's Mother Was His Father, Salmon: Development and Declension of Aboriginal Conservation in the Oregon Country Salmon Fishery," M.A. thesis, University of Oregon, 1992, pp. 59–64

P. 48 *Estimated aboriginal take of 10 million pounds.* Chad C. Meengs and Robert T. Lackey, "Estimating the Size of Historical Oregon Salmon Runs," vol. 13, no. 1 *Reviews in Fisheries Science*, pp. 51–66 (2005).

P. 48 *Today the harvest averages 2 million pounds.* Salmon Technical Team, "Review of 2008 Ocean Salmon Fisheries," Pacific Fishery Management Council and National Marine Fisheries Service (February 2009), pp. 300–302, *at* http://www.pcouncil.org/salmon/salsafe08/salsafe08.html (accessed May 20, 2009). In 1986, the Northwest Power Planning Council reported the average annual salmon and steelhead catch to be 5–8 million pounds. See Northwest Power Planning Council, "Compilation," pp. 66–76. The annual commercial salmon harvest has declined significantly since then; the last year that Oregon and Washington's combined salmon harvest exceeded 5 million pounds was 1989. Salmon Technical Team, "Review," pp. 300–302.

P. 48 *Tyees would call for a closure.* See Arthur F. McEvoy, *The Fisherman's Problem: Ecology and Law in the California Fisheries, 1850–1980*, pp. 19–40 (Cambridge, UK: Cambridge University Press, 1986); Deward E. Walker, *Mutual Cross-Utilization of Economic Resources in the Plateau*, pp. 14–15 (Pullman: Washington State University, Laboratory of Anthropology, 1967).

P. 48 *"The fact remains."* Robert Bunting, *The Pacific Raincoast*, p. 12 (Lawrence: University Press of Kansas, 1997).

P. 48 *Potlatches.* See, e.g., Ruby and Brown, *The Chinook Indians*, p. 11; Franz Boas, "The Potlatch," in Tom McFeat, ed., *Indians of the North Pacific Coast*, pp. 72–73 (Seattle: University of Washington Press, 1966).

P. 48 *Chinook and Clatsop slavery.* Ruby and Brown, *The Chinook Indians*, pp. 9–11; Silverstein, "Chinookans of the Lower Columbia," pp. 542–43.

P. 48 *"slavery has been one of the most ubiquitous."* Stanley Engerman, Seymour Drescher, and Robert Paquette, eds., *Slavery*, p. 5 (New York: Oxford University Press, 2001). See also Ehud R. Toledano, *Slavery and Abolition in the Ottoman Middle East*, p. 3 (Seattle: University of Washington Press, 1998).

P. 48 *Abolition of slavery in England.* Paul Finkelman and Joseph C. Miller, *Macmillan Encyclopedia of World Slavery*, p. 7 (New York: Simon & Schuster Macmillan, 1998).

P. 48 *Slavery in United States.* See, e.g., Michael Vorenberg, *Final Freedom: The Civil War, the Abolition of Slavery, and the Thirteenth Amendment* (New York: Cambridge University Press, 2001).

P. 49 *The Molala Tribe.* Ruby and Brown, *A Guide to the Indian Tribes of the Pacific Northwest*, pp. 137–39; Henry B. Zenk and Bruce Rigsby, "Molala," in Walker, ed., vol. 8, *Handbook of North American Indians*, pp. 439–45 (Washington, D.C.: Smithsonian Institution, 1998).

P. 50 *The Klickitat Tribe.* See M. Dale Kinkade et al., "[Plateau] Languages," in Walker, ed., vol. 12, *Handbook of North American Indians*, p. 58; Ruby and Brown, *A Guide to the Indian Tribes of the Pacific Northwest*, pp. 95–97 (explaining that Klickitats strengthened their position in the Willamette Valley after epidemics of the 1820s and 1830s); Thelma Kimmel, "Klickitat," in vol. 2, *Dictionary of Indian Tribes of the Americas* (Newport Beach, CA: American Indian Publishers, Inc., 1980), pp. 374–77. See also

Selma Neils, *The Klickitat Indians* (Portland, OR: Binford & Mort, 1985).

P. 50   *Chinooks excluded Kalapuyas from Willamette Falls.* Melville Jacobs, *Kalapuya Texts: Vol. 11*, University of Washington Publications in Anthropology, p. 188 (Seattle: University of Washington Press, 1945). Peter Kenoyer, a Kalapuyan, reported this of the actions of the Clackamas (Upper Chinooks) against the Tualatins (the northern-most Kalapuyan band): "The Clackamas Indians did not want [the Tualatins] to use seines, to get salmon at Oregon City [Willamette] Falls." Ibid. (quoting Peter Kenoyer, as relayed by his son, Louis Kenoyer).

P. 50   *The Kalapuya language.* Henry B. Zenk, "Kalapuyans," in Suttles, ed., vol. 7, *Handbook of North American Indians*, p. 547; Judy Rycraft Juntunen, May D. Dasch, and Ann Bennett Rogers, *The World of the Kalapuya*, p. 13 (Philomath, OR: Benton County Historical Society and Museum, 2005).

P. 51   *the "pristine myth."* See William M. Denevan, "The Pristine Myth: The Landscape of the Americas in 1492," vol. 82, no. 3 *Annals of the Association of American Geographers*, pp. 369–87 (September 1992).

P. 51   *Aboriginal societies worked the land.* See generally Kenneth M. Ames, "Political and Historical Ecologies," in Thomas Biolsi, ed., *A Companion to the Anthropology of American Indians*, pp. 17–23 (Malden, MA: Blackwell Publishing, 2004); Shepard Krech III, *The Ecological Indian* (New York: W. W. Norton & Co., 1999).

P. 51   *Indians made extensive use of fire.* Robert Boyd, ed., *Indians, Fire, and the Land in the Pacific Northwest* (Corvallis: Oregon State University Press, 1999), provides an excellent examination of this subject. The chapter by Jeff LaLande and Reg Pullen, titled "Burning for a 'Fine and Beautiful Open Country': Native Uses of Fire in Southwestern Oregon," for example, examines inland valley tribes such as the Takelma, Shasta, and Cow Creek Umpqua, as well as those on the Coast. Ibid., pp. 255–76. Nationally, scholars believe that fire was used in some fashion as a land-management tool by nearly all tribes. See ibid., p. 128 (quoting anthropologist Omer Stewart as stating that "nearly every American Indian tribe set fire to the grass and woody vegetation of the area it occupied"); Krech, *The Ecological Indian*, p. 110 (pointing out that while "some have argued that Indian burning was almost universal. . . . practice[s] . . . while widespread, varied from one tribe to another") (internal quotations omitted). See also Bob Zybach, "The Great Fires: Indian Burning and Catastrophic Forest Fire Patterns of the Oregon Coast Range, 1491–1951," Ph.D. diss., Oregon State University, 2003, *at* http://www.nwmapsco.com/ZybachB/DRAFT/PhD_Thesis/index.htm (accessed May 20, 2009).

P. 51   *Hunting with snares.* W. W. Oglesby, "The Calapooyas Indians: A dictation made Aug. 28, 1884," pp. 5–6, *at* Bancroft Library, University of California, Berkeley.

P. 51   *"This annual hunt was conducted."* Boyd, *Indians, Fire, and the Land*, pp. 111–12 (quoting an article written by Samuel Clarke, "The Great Fall Hunt of the Willamette," in *The Oregonian* and drawn from an interview with Hudson estimated by Boyd to have taken place ca. 1880).

P. 52   *fire created a rich grass habitat.* Bunting, *The Pacific Raincoast*, p. 13.

P. 52   *a cornucopia of camas.* See Boyd, *Indians, Fire, and the Land*, pp. 120–22; Thomas J. Connolly, "Anthropological and Archaeological Perspectives on Native Fire Management of the Willamette Valley," pp. 2–3. Paper presented to the American Association for the Advancement of Science, Pacific Division, Fire History in the Pacific Northwest Symposium (June 11–14, 2000), *at* http://www.orww.org/KalapuyaAmin_2006/Program/ConnollyT/Indian_Burning_20000611.pdf (accessed May 20, 2009).

P. 52   *oak trees and acorns.* Bunting, *The Pacific Raincoast*, p. 13; Boyd, *Indians, Fire, and the Land*, pp. 116–17.

P. 52   *tarweed.* See ibid., pp. 113–14.

P. 52   *the savannah is a seral stage.* Ibid., pp. 94–98; Ames, "Political and Historical Ecologies," p. 18.

P. 52   *Farmers stopped tribal members from burning.* Krech, *The Ecological Indian*, p. 117.

P. 52   *Kalapuya fire practices created an . . . Eden.* See Bunting, *The Pacific Raincoast*, p. 15.

P. 53   *"Long years ago my parents."* Youst, *She's Tricky Like Coyote*, p. 171 (quoting Annie Miner Peterson's response to plaintiffs' attorney Daniel Henderson's redirect witness examination).

P. 53   *"There was plenty of time."* Van Pelt, "Before the White Man: An Indian's Story," p. 7.

P. 53   *literally the most productive land.* Donald Callaway, Joel Janetski, and Omer C. Stewart, "Ute," in Warren L. D'Azevedo, ed., vol. 11, *Handbook of North American Indians*, p. 338 (Washington, D.C.: Smithsonian Institution, 1986). See also George Woodcock, *Peoples of the Coast*, p. 13 (Bloomington: Indiana University Press, 1977).

P. 53   *"reverence for their homeland."* Bud Lane, telephone interview with author, Feb. 25, 2009; Bud Lane, interview with author, Lincoln City, Oregon, May 12, 2009. Lane draws his conclusions on a lack of a separate heaven in part from the many prayers and songs offered at Nee Dosh, the tribe's world renewal ceremony. He has never come across any reference to a heaven or other world. The entire focus is on all that the tribal homeland gives to Siletz people. "We take responsibility for caring for everything *here*, we give thanksgiving for what we *have*—not for what we will *get*." Bud Lane, interview with author, Siletz, Oregon, October 24, 2009.

3 Intruders on the Land

P. 57   *The killing germs may have invaded Oregon in the 1520s.* See Russell Thornton, *American Indian Holocaust and Survival*, pp. 62–64 (Norman: University of Oklahoma Press, 1987). Henry F. Dobyns, in *Their Numbers Become Thinned*, pp. 12–16 (Knoxville: University of Tennessee Press, 1983), concludes that this early pandemic did reach the Pacific Northwest. Robert Boyd believes that "the jury is still out." Boyd, *The Coming of the Spirit of Pestilence*, p. 16 (Seattle: University of Washington Press, 1999). Boyd's valuable book, the most comprehensive analysis of infectious diseases among Northwest Coast tribes, examines the region according to tribal groupings.

P. 57   *Total population decline.* See Boyd, *The Coming*, pp. 264–65 (statistical tables showing population loss by regions of the Northwest). The figures in the text were calculated using the data for the Siletz tribes from the south Coast Epidemic Area (excluding the Quinault and Lower Chehalis) and the Interior Valley Epidemic Area (excluding the Upper Chehalis and Cowlitz). For the south Coast, aboriginal population was 18,210 and post-epidemic population 2,523, a loss of 86 percent. For the Interior Valley, population dropped from 33,678 to 1,678, a total of 95 percent. Boyd does not include the Shastas of California and Oregon.

P. 57   *1775 voyage.* See Boyd, *The Coming*, pp. 32–38 (discussing the 1775 voyage and alternative explanations for the outbreaks of the 1770s). The earliest written report of smallpox on the Oregon Coast came in 1788 on a voyage of the fur-trading vessel

Columbia captained by Robert Gray, one of the early "canoes with white wings" that so surprised the Natives. In a landing at Yaquina Bay, Robert Haswell, who kept the log, reported that "two or three of our visitors were much pitted with the small pox." Frederic W. Howay, ed., *Voyages of the "Columbia" to the Northwest Coast*, p. 34 (New York: Da Capo Press, 1969; first published 1941) (entry for August 10, 1788).

P. 58 *Tolowa village smallpox attack.* See Richard A. Gould, *Archaeology of the Point St. George Site, and Tolowa Prehistory*, pp. 96–97 (Berkeley: University of California Press, 1966)

P. 58 *"Old timers said."* Quoted in ibid., p. 96.

P. 59 *"He assembled several of the chieftains."* Washington Irving, *Astoria or Anecdotes of an Enterprise Beyond the Rocky Mountains*, ed. Edgeley W. Todd, p. 117 (Norman: University of Oklahoma Press, 1964). Robert H. Ruby and John A. Brown, in *The Chinook Indians*, pp. 135–36 (Norman: University of Oklahoma Press, 1976), find it highly unlikely that the Clatsops and Chinooks were involved in the massacre of the Tonquin crew. On "smallpox in a bottle" episodes at Astoria and elsewhere, see also Boyd, *The Coming*, pp. 45–46, 112–15.

P. 59 *"They were afraid to call it by name."* Quoted in Lionel Youst and William R. Seaburg, *Coquelle Thompson, Athabascan Witness*, p. 59 (Norman: University of Oklahoma Press, 2002) (quote attributed to anthropologist Elizabeth Jacobs's 1935 interview with Coquelle Thompson).

P. 59 *"Oh, the smallpox."* Quoted in Lionel Youst, *She's Tricky Like Coyote*, p. 129 (Norman: University of Oklahoma Press, 1997).

P. 59 *"many of their once populous villages."* Nathan Douthit, *Uncertain Encounters: Indians and Whites at Peace and War in Southern Oregon*, p. 48 (Corvallis: Oregon State University Press, 2002) (quoting Sub-Indian Agent Josiah L. Parrish in 1854).

P. 59 *"the smallpox has distroyed."* Reuben Gold Thwaites, ed., vol. 4, *Original Journals of the Lewis and Clark Expedition*, p. 50 (New York: Dodd, Mead and Co., 1905) (journal entry of Feb. 7, 1806).

P. 60 *Ingrained tribal customs aggravated the effects.* See, e.g., Elizabeth A. Fenn, *Pox Americana: The Great Smallpox Epidemic of 1775–82*, pp. 24–25 (New York: Hill and Wang, 2001); Boyd, *The Coming*, pp. 18–19.

P. 60 *"single most important epidemiological event."* Boyd, *The Coming*, p. 84.

P. 60 *"During its worst years."* Ruby and Brown, *The Chinook Indians*, pp. 186–87.

P. 60 *"the fever and ague was the worst and acted pecular."* Sheila Whitesitt and Richard E. Moore, eds., *A Memoir of the Indian War*, p. 11 (Ashland, OR: Tree Stump Press, 1987).

P. 61 *Fever and ague among Willamette Valley tribes.* See Boyd, *The Coming*, pp. 84–115, 265.

P. 61 *Early sea otter trade.* See Howay, ed., *Voyages*, p. xxvi; Richard Somerset Mackie, *Trading Beyond the Mountains*, pp. 142–45 (Vancouver: UBC Press, 1997).

P. 61 *"Haswell records in his first log."* Howay, ed., *Voyages*, pp. xxvi–xxvii.

P. 62 *Opening of the Hudson's Bay Company trading post.* See generally Mackie, *Trading Beyond the Mountains*; Robert E. Pinkerton, *Hudson's Bay Company* (New York: Henry Holt and Company, 1931); George Bryce, *The Remarkable History of the Hudson's Bay Company* (London: Sampson Low, Marston and Co., 1910). On John Jacob Astor, see, e.g., Mackie, *Trading Beyond Mountains*, p. 3. On the merger of the North West Company and the Hudson's Bay company, see, e.g., Mackie, *Trading*, pp. 30–31.

On the opening of Fort Vancouver, see, e.g., Mackie, *Trading*, p. 48.

P. 62   *Longer HBC forays and American trappers.* See, e.g., Mackie, *Trading*, pp. 28, 65–66.

P. 62   *reaching "middle ground."* Richard White developed the "middle ground" analysis by moving beyond the one-dimensional stereotype of whites and Indians in continuing conflict and documenting many examples of productive intermingling between the two races in the Great Lakes region. Richard White, *The Middle Ground: Indians, Empires, and Republics in the Great Lakes Region, 1650–1815* (Cambridge, UK: Cambridge University Press, 1991). Nathan Douthit applied the "middle ground" analysis to nineteenth-century western Oregon. See Douthit, *Uncertain Encounters*, pp. 2–4.

P. 62   *The traders deemed them "lazy."* See, e.g., Mackie, *Trading*, p. 81.

P. 63   *use of the term "Great Father."* See, e.g., Michael Paul Rogin, *Fathers and Children: Andrew Jackson and the Subjugation of the American Indian*, pp. 113–25 (New York: Vintage Books, 1975).

P. 63   *Quick and brutal vengeance.* See John Philip Reid, "Principles of Vengeance: Fur Trappers, Indians, and Retaliation for Homicide in the Transboundary North American West," vol. 24, no. 1 *Western Historical Quarterly*, p. 29 (Feb. 1993). This study by Reid, a leading legal historian, is the most thorough examination of the use of vengeance by the HBC and other fur traders.

P. 63   *"blood for blood."* Ibid., p. 42.

P. 63   *HBC hunters, the Alsea, and the Yaquina.* See R. Scott Byram, "Colonial Power and Indigenous Justice: Fur Trade Violence and Its Aftermath in Yaquina Narrative," vol. 109, no. 3 *Oregon Historical Quarterly*, pp. 358–87 (Fall 2008). Coquelle Thompson is quoted at pp. 361–62. Of the four accounts (three from Natives and one from the HBC), Thompson's is by far the most extensive. However, he did not hear Yaquina John's narrative of the 1832 incident until the 1880s and gave his account to John Harrington in the 1940s. The accounts match up in many respects but dramatically conflict with respect to the HBC retaliatory raid: the HBC records state that six Yaquinas were killed while the Indian accounts state variously that the HBC attack killed a whole village, the entire tribe, or 400 Yaquina people. Ibid., p. 376.

P. 63   *"send word to these sauvages."* John McLoughlin, letter to Michel Laframboise (May 9, 1832), *in* Dr. Burt Brown Barker, ed., *Letters of Dr. John McLoughlin*, p. 272 (Portland, OR: Binfords & Mort, 1948). McLoughlin wrote numerous letters relating to the incident. See ibid., pp. 268–73. For other descriptions of the incident, see Stephen Dow Beckham, *The Indians of Western Oregon*, p. 107 (Coos Bay, OR: Arago Books, 1977); Robert Kentta, "A Siletz History, Part III: Fur Trade & Early Exploration," *Siletz News*, p. 27 (Nov. 1999), *at* http://www.ctsi.nsn.us/chinook-indian-tribe-siletz-heritage/our-history/part-iii#content (accessed May 13, 2009).

P. 64   *traders other than Duncan McDougall.* See Boyd, *The Coming*, pp. 45–46, 112–15.

P. 64   *where their lands ended and another tribe's began.* See, e.g., James Arneson, "Property Concepts of 19th Century Oregon Indians," vol. 81 *Oregon Historical Quarterly*, pp. 391, 397–400 (Winter 1980). Although Arneson found that "as the distances from the villages increased the boundaries would begin to fade," it was also evident that "practically all tribes recognized some type of territorial tribal limits." Ibid., pp. 399–400. Additionally, Arneson states that "most tribes claimed a certain territory as their own" and "it would be an unusual tribe which did not claim some territory, as the tribe's survival depended on having a source for the production of food." Ibid., pp. 397–99.

P. 64   *"it is self-evident."* Dennis J. Gray, "The Takelma and Their Athapascan Neighbors: A New Ethnographic Synthesis for the Upper Rogue River Area of Southwestern Oregon," no. 37 *University of Oregon Anthropological Papers*, p. 16 (1987).

P. 64   *permission had to be granted.* See, e.g., Arneson, "Property Concepts," p. 399 (on tribes allowing other tribes onto their land); Douthit, *Uncertain Encounters*, pp. 24–25 (describing payment of tribute).

P. 64   *American and British Law.* On American law recognizing aboriginal land rights, see Felix S. Cohen's Handbook of Federal Indian Law, 2005 ed., §15.04 2) (Newark, NJ: LexisNexis, 2005). For a discussion of the development of the principle in Spain, England, and American colonies, see ibid., §1.02(1).

P. 64   *"admitted to be the rightful occupants of the soil."* See *Johnson v. McIntosh*, 21 U.S. 543, 574 (1823). The rule has consistently been applied by the courts. See, e.g., *County of Oneida v. Oneida Indian Nation*, 470 U.S. 226, 235 (1985) [hereinafter *Oneida II*]. *Johnson v. McIntosh* is often criticized on its additional holding—that the tribes had once held complete land title but that, upon "discovery" of the United States by European nations, complete tribal title was transmuted to a lesser title, shared with the United States, called "Indian title," "aboriginal Indian title," or the "Indian right of occupancy." This "doctrine of discovery" has been described as tracing to racist, centuries-old European attitudes. See, e.g., Robert A. Williams Jr., *The American Indian in Western Legal Thought*, pp. 316–17, 325–26 (New York: Oxford University Press, 1990). On aboriginal title, see also chapter 4, pp. 70, 79 and accompanying notes; chapter 10, pp. 219–21 and accompanying notes.

P. 64   *United States can extinguish Indian title. Lone Wolf v. Hitchcock*, 187 U.S. 553, 566 (1903). In *Tee-Hit-Ton Indians v. United States*, 348 U.S. 272, 279 (1955), the Supreme Court later held that extinguishment of aboriginal title (as opposed to title recognized by treaty) does not require compensation under the Fifth Amendment to the Constitution.

P. 64   *Entry on Indian land as trespass.* See *Oneida II*, 470 U.S. at 235–36. In *City of Sherrill v. Oneida Indian Nation*, 544 U.S. 197, 216–17 (2005), the Supreme Court suggested that trespass claims might be denied by the long passage of time (the tribe had attempted to recover trespass damages tracing to a 1795 treaty), but the case did not disturb the rule prohibiting trespasses on aboriginal Indian land.

P. 64   *Tensions were on the rise in the 1820s.* See Douthit, *Uncertain Encounters*, pp. 19–25.

P. 64   *Smith and the American fur trade.* The standard biography is Dale Morgan, *Jedediah Smith and the Opening of the West* (Lincoln: University of Nebraska Press, 1953). See also Maurice S. Sullivan, *The Travels of Jedediah Smith* (Santa Ana, CA: Fine Arts Press, 1934).

P. 65   *Smith's substantial entourage.* See, e.g., Morgan, *Jedediah Smith*, p. 257.

P. 65   *"A Christian and a soldier."* Hiram Martin Chittenden, vol. 1, *The American Fur Trade of the Far West*, p. 283 (New York: Barnes and Noble, Inc., 1935).

P. 65   *"In order to intimidate them."* Morgan, *Jedediah Smith*, p. 261.

P. 66   *deserted Chetco village.* See Harrison Clifford Dale, ed., *The Explorations of William H. Ashley and Jedediah Smith, 1822–1829*, p. 265 (Lincoln: University of Nebraska Press, 1991) (originally published in 1941); Sullivan, *The Travels*, p. 102.

P. 66   *"Word traveled from village to village."* Sullivan, *The Travels*, p. 107.

P. 66   *the group reached the Umpqua River.* Morgan dedicates a chapter, "The Umpqua Massacre," to this stage of Smith's journey. Morgan, *Jedediah Smith*, pp. 256–79.

P. 66   *"appear friendly."* Ibid., p. 266. Morgan describes Rogers as "educated, intelligent, [and] sharply observing." Ibid., p. 194.

P. 66   *"one of the Ind. stole an ax."* Dale, ed., *The Explorations*, pp. 274–75 (Rogers's journal entry for July 12).

P. 66   *One chief wanted to attack.* See Sullivan, *The Travels*, pp. 123, 125.

P. 66   *George Simpson.* On Simpson's broad knowledge of the Indian trade, see Gordon B. Dodds, *Oregon: A Bicentennial History*, p. 49 (New York: W.W. Norton and Co., 1977).

P. 66   *"harsh treatment on the part of your people."* Quoted in Mackie, *Trading Beyond the Mountains*, p. 65.

P. 66   *Beverly Ward reported all of these factors.* In *White Moccasins*, p. 32 (Myrtle Point, OR: Myrtle Point Printing, 1986), Ward recounts:

> The Umpquas had traded with the Hudson's Bay men, and some had met Douglas on his trip, but Smith's men were different. Most of the men had Indian women that they took along to use as guides, although they were left behind on this long trip. The women-hungry men tried to force their attentions on the Umpqua women when they came to trade. When some of their tools disappeared, they blamed the Indians. They poked fun at the chief when he tried to ride a horse, and one thing led to another. The white men had sealed their fate.
>
> The Indians said some of their children went to the white men's camp, and the white men beat the children and chased them away with clubs. This infuriated the Indians. They attacked the camp, and Smith and three other men were the only ones left to tell the tale.
>
> White men didn't understand the Indians' customs. They thought the Indian women were promiscuous, and could all be had for the taking and this notion still persists today. The Indians had a strange code of ethics. They thought it wasn't any harm to steal, for that proved their cunning, but the Indians kept their word. These were the main contentions between the Indian and the white man.

P. 66   *the Indians charged.* See Morgan, *Jedediah Smith*, pp. 268–69.

P. 67   *"On arrival there Mr McLeod."* Sullivan, *The Travels*, p. 148.

P. 68   *hunting areas completely out.* See, e.g., William G. Robbins, *Oregon: This Storied Land*, p. 32 (Portland: Oregon Historical Society Press, 2005).

P. 68   *Fashion tastes changed.* See LeRoy R. Hafen, ed., vol. 1, *The Mountain Men and the Fur Trade of the Far West*, p. 174 (Glendale, CA: Arthur H. Clark Co., 1965).

P. 68   *established a Methodist mission.* On the Lees and other early Oregon missionaries, see Dodds, *Oregon*, pp. 54–60; Douthit, *Uncertain Encounters*, pp. 42–46. The school later evolved into Willamette University.

P. 68   *"Christianizing" Native Americans.* See, e.g., Francis Paul Prucha, vol. 1, *The Great Father: The United States Government and the American Indians*, pp. 30–33, 145–48 (Lincoln: University of Nebraska Press, 1984).

P. 68   *Congress subsidized Christian missionaries.* Ibid., pp. 151–53. See also Henry Warner Bowden, *American Indians and Christian Missions*, p. 167 (Chicago: University of Chicago Press, 1981).

P. 68   *a "New Eden."* See, e.g., Robbins, *Oregon*, p. 41.

P. 68   *opened the Oregon Trail.* See generally Francis Parkman, *The Oregon Trail* (Garden City, NY: Doubleday, Doran and Co., 1946).

P. 68   *Ewing Young in Oregon.* On Young's expeditions to Oregon, see Kenneth L. Holmes, *Ewing Young: Master Trapper*, pp. 94–136 (Portland, OR: Binford & Mort, 1967). See also Douthit, *Uncertain Encounters*, pp. 38–41; Stephen Dow Beckham, *Requiem for a People: The Rogue Indians and the Frontiersmen*, pp. 32–35 (Norman: University of Oklahoma Press, 1971).

P. 68   *HBC expedition of 1840.* Douthit, *Uncertain Encounters*, p. 41.

P. 69   *white population of just 137 in 1840.* Senate Committee on Interior and Insular Affairs, Jerry A. O'Callaghan, "The Disposition of the Public Domain in Oregon," 86th Congress, 2d Session, p. 4 (Washington, D.C.: Government Printing Office, 1960) [hereinafter The Disposition].

P. 69   *Applegate Trail and American population in Oregon by 1850.* A good article for information on the Applegate Trail is Lindsay Applegate, "Notes and Reminiscences of Laying Out and Establishing the Old Emigrant Road into Southern Oregon in the Year 1846," vol. 22 *Oregon Historical Quarterly*, pp. 12–45 (March–Dec. 1921). On Oregon population and settlement in the 1840s, see also Samuel N. Dicken and Emily F. Dicken, *The Making of Oregon: A Study in Historical Geography*, pp. 64–83 (Portland: Oregon Historical Society, 1979).

P. 69   *"Manifest Destiny."* On the origins and meaning of "Manifest Destiny," see, e.g., Richard White, *"It's Your Misfortune and None of My Own": A New History of the American West*, pp. 73–75 (Norman: University of Oklahoma Press, 1991).

P. 69   *Polk's presidency.* See Charles A. McCoy, *Polk and the Presidency*, pp. 83–112 (Austin: University of Texas Press, 1960). See generally Bernard DeVoto, *The Year of Decision, 1846* (Boston: Little, Brown and Co., 1943).

P. 69   *The Oregon Compromise.* Treaty with Great Britain ("in regard to limits westward of the Rocky Mountains"), June 15, 1846, 8 Stat. 869 (1846).

P. 70   *Indian land rights would remain in place.* Act to Establish the Territorial Government of Oregon, ch. 177, Aug. 14, 1848, 9 Stat. 323 (1848) (not codified).

P. 70   *Land grants to American homesteaders.* The Disposition, p. 31.

P. 70   *"He was an indefatigable promoter."* The Disposition, pp. 31–32.

P. 70   *The Donation Land Act.* For an excellent discussion of the build-up to the Donation Land Act, its passage, and its provisions, see William G. Robbins, "The Indian Question in Western Oregon: The Making of a Colonial People," *in* G. Thomas Edwards and Carlos A. Schwantes, eds., *Experiences in a Promised Land: Essays in Pacific Northwest History*, pp. 53–56 (Seattle: University of Washington Press, 1986). The Act itself is found at ch. 76, Sept. 27, 1850, 9 Stat. 496 (1850) (not codified).

P. 70   *"came very near to meeting the classical homestead ideal."* This was Jerry O'Callaghan's observation in The Disposition, p. 34.

P. 70   *"the actual settlers" did not include Indians.* The Donation Land Act, 9 Stat. at 497, actually did allow grants to "half-breed Indians," but the whole impetus behind the act was to reward white settlers—and, as discussed in the text, to remove Indians east of the Cascades through the treaty process.

P. 70   *Congress knew there was a problem.* See, e.g., Robbins, "The Indian Question," pp. 55–56.

P. 70   *Oregon Indian Treaty Act and "the extinguishment of their claims."* Indian Treaty Act, ch. 16, June 5, 1850, 9 Stat. 437 (1850) (not codified).

P. 71 *The epidemics continued.* See Boyd, *The Coming*, pp. 128–36, 145–70.

P. 71 *"The relationships between our tribal people and the settlers."* Kentta, "A Siletz History, Part III," p. 29 (italics in original).

4 Gold Fever

P. 72 *The discovery of gold in California.* See generally Rodman W. Paul, *California Gold: The Beginning of Mining in the Far West* (Lincoln: University of Nebraska Press, 1947); J. S. Holliday, *The World Rushed In: The California Gold Rush Experience* (New York: Simon and Shuster, 1981); Kevin Starr, *Americans and the California Dream, 1850–1915*, pp. 49–68 (New York: Oxford University Press, 1973).

P. 72 *population in 1852.* Paul, *California Gold*, pp. 24–25.

P. 72 *Manifest Destiny.* On Manifest Destiny as idea and fact, see Richard White, *"It's Your Misfortune and None of My Own": A History of the American West*, pp. 73–75 (Norman: University of Oklahoma Press, 1991).

P. 72 *nearly half of the world's gold.* Paul, *California Gold*, p. 21.

P. 72 *waves of economic benefits.* Keith L. Bryant Jr., "Entering the Global Economy," *in* Clyde A. Milner II, Carol A. O'Connor, and Martha A. Sandweiss, eds., *The Oxford History of the American West*, pp. 195–235 (New York: Oxford University Press, 1994).

P. 72 *"The gold production alone transformed."* Ibid., p. 198.

P. 73 *more than 90 percent male.* Paul, *California Gold*, p. 82.

P. 73 *"These people came as exploiters."* Holliday, *The World Rushed In*, p. 297.

P. 73 *When the goldseekers encountered Indians.* See, e.g., Clyde A. Milner II, "National Initiatives," in Milner, O'Connor, and Sandweiss, eds., *The Oxford History of the American West*, p. 175 ("The impact of the gold rush had destroyed thousands of other Indians. Some California argonauts hunted Indians like wild animals, and all refused to respect Indian land use."); Doyce B. Nunis Jr., ed., *The Golden Frontier: The Recollections of Herman Francis Reinhart, 1851–1869*, pp. 126–27 (Austin: University of Texas Press, 1962) (quoting a contemporary account of a massacre of unarmed Indians as "a brutal affair, but the perpetrators of the outrage thought they were heroes . . . it was like killing chickens or dogs or hogs, and a deed Californians should ever be ashamed of"). The United States negotiated many treaties with California Indians in 1851, but mining interests and California senators blocked congressional ratification. This and other events left California tribes nearly landless. See, e.g., Felix S. Cohen's Handbook of Federal Indian Law, 2005 ed., §1.03(5) (Newark, NJ: LexisNexis, 2005); Chauncey Shafter Goodrich, "The Legal Status of California Indians," vol. 14 *California Law Review*, p. 96 (1925–1926).

P. 73 *"They are always longing for 'big strikes.'"* Carl I. Wheat, ed., *The Shirley Letters from the California Mines, 1851–1852*, p. 131 (New York: Alfred A. Knopf, 1970).

P. 73 *"every few days news would come."* Mark Twain, *Roughing It*, p. 109 (New York: Airmont Publishing Co., 1967).

P. 73 *"a sea whose tide knows no law."* Paul, *California Gold*, p. 85 (quoting the *Sacramento Transcript* of June 28, 1850).

P. 74 *"wild, reckless" character.* Albert G. Walling, *History of Southern Oregon*, p. 192 (Portland, OR: A. G. Walling, Printer, 1884) (quoting J. Ross Browne's description of the mountain men as "a wild, reckless and daring race of men").

P. 74 *"Good men were there and bad."* Ibid.

P. 74 *Takelmas and incoming miners clashed.* The standard source on the Rogue River War is Stephen Dow Beckham, *Requiem for a People: The Rogue Indians and the Frontiersmen* (Norman: University of Oklahoma Press, 1975). This incident is treated at ibid., pp. 43–45. See also Hubert Howe Bancroft, vol. 2, *History of Oregon, 1848–1888*, pp. 219–22 (San Francisco: The History Co., 1888); Nathan Douthit, *Uncertain Encounters: Indians and Whites at Peace and War in Southern Oregon, 1820s to 1860s*, pp. 68–75 (Corvallis: Oregon State University Press, 2002); E. A. Schwartz, *The Rogue River Indian War and Its Aftermath, 1850–1980*, pp. 26–31 (Norman: University of Oklahoma Press, 1997).

P. 74 *Joseph Lane.* For background and useful character sketches of Lane, see James E. Hendrickson, *Joe Lane of Oregon*, pp. 2–3, 14 (New Haven, CT: Yale University Press, 1967); Douthit, *Uncertain Encounters*, pp. 70–71.

P. 75 *Apserkahar.* For information on Tyee Apserkahar (later known as Tyee Joe or Chief Joe), see Walling, *History of Southern Oregon*, pp. 190–91, 202; Douthit, *Uncertain Encounters*, pp. 74–75; Schwartz, *The Rogue River Indian War*, p. 39. The journal of the Cardwell party recounts the efforts of Tyee Joe in protecting the operator of a ferry across the Rogue River against interference from Indians. See Transcript of A. Cardwell, journal from 1850 to 1852, pp. 9–10, *at* University of California, Berkeley, Bancroft Library [hereinafter Cardwell Journal].

P. 75 *"significant glances."* Bancroft, vol. 2, *History of Oregon*, p. 220.

P. 75 *When the dust settled.* The primary account of U.S.–Takelma negotiations was told by Joseph Lane to H. H. Bancroft (and transcribed by "Writer, A.B.") in Portland, Oregon, on June 21, 1878. Joseph Lane autobiography, pp. 90–95, *at* University of California, Berkeley, Bancroft Library. Bancroft accepted Lane's version but later noted that "like many another old soldier Lane loved to boast of his exploits." Bancroft, vol. 2, *History of Oregon*, p. 222n29.

P. 75 *Apserkahar asked Lane for name.* On the tradition of naming Northwest Indians, see Douthit, *Uncertain Encounters*, pp. 71–72. See also Bancroft, vol. 2, *History of Oregon*, p. 222n29 (Joe Lane's version of the naming of Apserkahar Joe).

P. 75 *Lane obtained his treaty.* Although the sources regularly refer to this "treaty," there is no record, either among the ratified or unratified treaties, in Congress of this treaty. See Hendrickson, *Joe Lane of Oregon*, p. 22.

P. 76 *Battle Rock Incident.* See J. M. Kirkpatrick, "The Hero of Battle Rock," *in* Orvil Dodge, ed., *Pioneer History of Coos and Curry Counties, Or.*, pp. 33–50 (Salem, OR: Capital Printing Co., 1898); Beckham, *Requiem*, pp. 53–63; Schwartz, *The Rogue River Indian War*, pp. 33–36.

P. 76 *"bar lead cut up in pieces."* Kirkpatrick, "The Hero of Battle Rock," pp. 35–36.

P. 76 *Indian fatalities.* The estimates vary: Beckham, *Requiem*, p. 51 ("at least seventeen"); Schwartz, *The Rogue River Indian War*, p. 33 ("repulsed about forty Indians, killing half of them"); Robert Kentta, "A Siletz History, Part V: The Early Treaty Making Period of 1851," *Siletz News*, p. 31 (March 2000), *at* http://www.ctsi.nsn.us/chinook-indian-tribe-siletz-heritage/our-history/part-v#content (accessed May 18, 2009) ("about 30 of our people died").

P. 76 *The crew fled to the north.* Schwartz, *The Rogue River Indian War*, p. 34. The nine men, aided by some Indians at Coos Bay, eventually made it to a white settlement at the mouth of the Umpqua River; meanwhile, Tichenor amassed a force of sixty-seven men with whom he returned to Port Orford. Douthit, *Uncertain Encounters*, p. 117.

P. 77   *Kirkpatrick laid the blame.* See Kirkpatrick, "The Hero of Battle Rock," p. 36

P. 77   *"an atrocious massacre of peaceable and friendly Indians."* Schwartz, *The Rogue River Indian War*, p. 34. Schwartz, who seems to accept Dart's basic conclusion, analyzes the competing versions at ibid., pp. 34–36. The useful local history by Beverly Ward, which relies on both Indian and white accounts, notes Kirkpatrick's own account that "the Indians warned them and drew back out of sight so they could leave" before the Indians attacked. Beverly Ward, *White Moccasins*, p. 43 (Myrtle Point, OR: Myrtle Point Printing, 1986).

P. 77   *T'Vault-Coquille encounters.* See Beckham, *Requiem*, pp. 59–63, 65–67; Schwartz, *The Rogue River Indian War*, pp. 40–42; Bancroft, vol. 2, *History of Oregon*, pp. 196–200.

P. 77   *"it appeared to be the screams of thousands."* T'Vault is quoted in Beckham, *Requiem*, p. 62.

P. 77   *"T'Vault and Williams seem to have left out."* Schwartz, *The Rogue River Indian War*, p. 41. The full statement of Schwartz's skepticism reads:

> Neither of the two accounts of this event, one by T'Vault and the other by another survivor, Lorin L. Williams, suggests why the people who found them on the middle fork of the Coquille would have voluntarily taken them perhaps fifty miles downstream before attacking them. Like Lansford Hastings and the men in the McBride party, T'Vault and Williams seem to have left out some element necessary to make sense of the rest of the story. Perhaps T'Vault had compelled the cooperation of the people who took him downstream and the attack was made to free them. Perhaps there was no attack at all but only a misunderstanding in the minds of the fatigued and frightened white men.

P. 77   *"Boys, take good sight."* Quoted in ibid., p. 42; Beckham, *Requiem*, p. 67.

P. 77   *several skirmishes on the Upper Rogue.* See Beckham, *Requiem*, pp. 48–51.

P. 78   *petition to Governor Gaines.* Bancroft, vol. 2, *History of Oregon*, p. 224. Joseph Lane also wrote to Governor Gaines that the Indians would "seriously injure the prospects and interests of the people of this Territory," though he suggested a company of volunteers be raised to make peace. J. Lane letter to J. Gaines, Governor (June 13, 1851), *in* House Doc. No. 2, "Message from the President of the United States to the Two Houses of Congress," 32d Congress, 1st Session, pp. 145–46 (Washington, D.C.: A. Boyd Hamilton, 1851).

P. 78   *"It was a most admirably chosen battle field."* Walling, *History of Southern Oregon*, p. 197 (attachment of Jesse Applegate's version). This is the most complete account of the battle, along with Bancroft, vol. 2, *History of Oregon*, pp. 226–30.

P. 78   *"scoured the country."* Bancroft, vol. 2, *History of Oregon*, p. 229.

P. 79   *"They wearied of war and wanted peace."* Ibid., p. 230.

P. 79   *two sides signed a treaty.* See Treaty with the Rogue River Indians, July 14, 1851 (unratified) *in* Vine Deloria Jr. and Raymond J. DeMallie, eds., vol. 2, *Documents of American Indian Diplomacy*, p. 1287 (Norman: University of Oklahoma Press, 1999).

P. 79   *nineteen unratified land treaties.* For a list of unratified treaties negotiated by Gaines and Dart, see Deloria and DeMallie, vol. 2, *Documents of American Indian Diplomacy*, p. 1238 (listing eleven unratified land treaties negotiated with the following tribes and bands: Santiam band of Kalapuya; Twalaty band of Kalapuya; Luck-a-mi-ute band of Kalapuya; Yamhill band of Kalapuya; Principal band of Molale; Santiam band of Molale; Rogue River Indians; Konnaack band of Chinook; Klatskania band of Chinook; To-to-ton, You-quee-chae, and Qua-ton-wah; Ya-su-chah; Clackamas [The Rogue River Treaty of 1851, discussed in the text, was also listed but is not included here because it did not involve a land cession.]). Subsequently, an additional eight Gaines-Dart unratified treaties were discovered in the obscure Senate Confidential Executive Documents collection. See Charles D. Bernholtz, "The 'Other' Treaties: Comments on Deloria and DeMallie's *Documents of American Indian Diplomacy*," vol. 24 *Legal Reference Services Quarterly*, pp. 107–41 (2005). Those eight 1851 treaties were made with the following tribes: Clatsop; Naalem band of Tillamook; Lower band of Tillamook; Nuc-quee-clah-we-muek; Waukikum band of Chinook; Kathlamet band of Chinook; Wheelappa band of Chinook; and Lower band of Chinook. Bernholtz, "The 'Other' Treaties," p. 122. The Bernholtz paper, which discusses other unratified treaties, explains the Oregon situation at pp. 110, 121–22. The recent "discovery" of these "other" treaties gives additional insight into the confusions, tensions, and insensitivities that plagued Oregon in the 1850s.

P. 79   *Congress scuttled all of the treaties.* On the reasons for lack of ratification of the Gaines-Dart treaties, see Bancroft, vol. 2, *History of Oregon*, pp. 208–18; Terence O'Donnell, *An Arrow in the Earth: General Joel Palmer and the Indians of Oregon*, pp. 137–40 (Portland: Oregon Historical Society, 1991).

P. 80   *Native people had no access to attorneys.* Much later, in the 1960s, tribes, especially in the eastern United States, began to assert their ownership of aboriginal lands that had been the subject of invalid treaties. In response, courts held that the Trade and Intercourse Act, ch. 161, June 30, 1834, 4 Stat. 729 (1834) (codified as amended at 25 U.S.C. §177 [2006]) (replacing the first permanent Trade and Intercourse Act, ch. 13, March 30, 1802, 2 Stat. 139 [1802]), provides that no grant of Indian lands shall be valid unless approved by Congress. Since Congress never ratified the tribal land cessions in the treaties, several tribes—usually in congressional settlements resolving the court cases—regained land and trespass damages. See, e.g., *Joint Tribal Council of the Passamaquoddy Tribe v. Morton*, 528 F.2d 370 (1st Cir. 1975); *County of Oneida v. Oneida Indian Nation*, 470 U.S. 226 (1985). See also Robert N. Clinton and Margaret Tobey Hotopp, "Judicial Enforcement of the Federal Restraints on Alienation of Indian Land: The Origins of the Eastern Land Claims," vol. 31 *Maine Law Review*, pp. 17–90 (1979); Cohen, 2005 Handbook of Federal Indian Law, §15.06. This approach may have been available to tribes in western Oregon in the 1850s if they had had recourse to attorneys. Today, however, many tribes, including those in western Oregon, have received payment for the loss of their aboriginal lands by means of compensation under the Indian Claims Commission Act of 1946 and the courts have ruled that receipt of such compensation extinguishes claims to title of that land. See *United States v. Dann*, 865 F.2d 1528 (9th Cir. 1989). See generally Charles Wilkinson, *Blood Struggle: The Rise of Modern Indian Nations*, pp. 220–31 (New York: W.W. Norton and Co., 2005). See also chapter 12, pp. 268–69 and accompanying notes.

P. 80   *Then came Jacksonville.* See generally Nunis, ed., *The Golden Frontier*, p. 34; Bancroft, vol. 2, *History of Oregon*, p. 186; Muriel Sibell Wolle, *The Bonanza Trail: Ghost Towns and Mining Camps of the West*, pp. 304–6 (Bloomington: Indiana University Press, 1958). On Cluggage's discovery with a bowie knife, see Alice Applegate Sargent, "A Sketch of the Rogue River Valley and Southern Oregon History," vol. 22, no. 1 *Oregon Historical Quarterly*, pp. 3–4 (March 1921). A man named Sykes is credited with making a strike shortly before Cluggage and Pool. See, e.g., Bancroft, vol. 2, *History of Oregon*, p. 186; Nunis, ed., *The Golden Frontier*, p. 34n15.

P. 80   *Gold Rush miners worked placer deposits.* On placer deposits, placer mining, and the extensive use of water in early Jackson County, see Howard C. Brooks and Len Ramp, *Gold and Silver in Oregon*, pp. 32–33, 167–68 (Portland: State of Oregon Department of Geology and Mineral Industries, 1968).

P. 81   *Jacksonville boomed.* See, e.g., Wolle, *The Bonanza Trail*, p. 306 (by the summer of 1852, the population of Jacksonville had reached 1,000); Samuel N. Dicken and Emily F. Dicken, *The Making of Oregon: A Study in Historical Geography*, p. 86 (Portland: Oregon Historical Society, 1979) ("thousands of miners poured into the area" of Jackson County); Nunis, ed., *The Golden Frontier*, pp. 39–41. For general descriptions of Jacksonville, see Thomas Frazar, "Pioneers from New England," vol. 83, no. 1 *Oregon Historical Quarterly*, pp. 37, 40–43 (Spring 1982); David D. Fagan, ed., *History of Benton County, Oregon*, pp. 359–63 (Portland, OR: A. G. Walling Printer, 1885).

P. 81   *Jackson became largest Oregon County.* See Brooks and Ramp, *Gold and Silver in Oregon*, p. 167 ("Word of rich placer deposits spread rapidly and the rush to Jackson County soon made it the most populous county in the state."); Dicken and Dicken, *The Making of Oregon*, p. 86 ("Jackson County may have been the most populous in Oregon."); Sargent, "A Sketch of the Rogue River Valley," p. 5 ("Jackson county in 1855 was the richest and most populous county in Oregon.").

P. 81   *1850 census data.* Dicken and Dicken, *The Making of Oregon*, p. 81.

P. 82   *hostilities broke out in the summer.* For contemporary accounts, see Cardwell Journal, p. 25; A. Skinner, Indian Agent, report to A. Dart, superintendent of Indian Affairs for Oregon (July 26, 1852), *in* House Doc. No. 1, 1852 Commissioner Report, 32d Congress, 2d Session, pp. 455–58. For secondary sources, see Walling, *History of Southern Oregon*, pp. 201–3; Charles H. Carey, *General History of Oregon: Through Early Statehood*, pp. 557–59 (Portland, OR: Binford & Mort, 1971); Schwartz, *The Rogue River Indian War*, pp. 46–49. Walling estimated the Jacksonville vigilante group at 28 or 30, but the figure of 75, or higher, is more commonly accepted. Walling, *History of Southern Oregon*, p. 202; but see, e.g., Carey, *General History of Oregon*, p. 558 ("a company of 75 volunteers"); Schwartz, *The Rogue River Indian War*, p. 48 ("a company of about 80 men"). On the Indian agent, Alanzo A. Skinner, and his protective posture toward Indians, see Douthit, *Uncertain Encounters*, p. 77.

P. 82   *Thirteen Indian men were shot.* Walling, *History of Southern Oregon*, p. 202; Cardwell Journal, p. 25.

P. 82   *vigilantes spent the next few days marauding.* Beckham, *Requiem*, p. 78.

P. 82   *"do with [Tyee Sam] as they think proper."* Carey, *General History of Oregon*, p. 559 (quoting a letter written by soldier J. R. Hardin and published in the Aug. 7, 1852, *Oregon Statesman*, setting out the terms agreed to at the negotiations).

P. 82   *extermination."*See, e.g., Beckham, *Requiem*, p. 78 (quoting Cardwell Journal, p. 26: "The Cry was extermination of all the Indians by the whites . . ."); Beckham, *Requiem*, p. 122 (quoting B. F. Dowell's recollection of a parade through Jacksonville in which the volunteers had carried "a flag on which was inscribed in flaming colors *Extermination*"). See also Schwartz, *The Rogue River Indian War*, p. 49.

P. 82   *Donation Land Act claims.* Douthit, *Uncertain Encounters*, p. 108.

P. 83   *Natives in the minority.* Ibid., p. 109.

P. 83   *Vigilante groups in southern Oregon.* On vigilantism generally, see William Tucker,

Vigilante: The Backlash Against Crime in America, p. 27 (New York: Stein and Day, 1985) ("A vigilante is someone who tries to enforce the law by breaking the law."); Richard Maxwell Brown, *Strain of Violence: Historical Studies of American Violence and Vigilantism*, pp. 95–96 (New York: Oxford University Press, 1975) ("The vigilante tradition, in the classic sense, refers to organized, extralegal movements, the members of which take the law into their own hands."). On groups in southern Oregon organizing as vigilantes, see, e.g., Beckham, *Requiem*, p. 49; Schwartz, *The Rogue River Indian War*, pp. 48–49. On lynchings, see, e.g., Walling, *History of Southern Oregon*, p. 213; Beckham, *Requiem*, pp. 82, 115.

P. 83   *other leading Americans, including Deady, Wool, and Beeson.* See chapter 5, p. 91 (Judge Mathew Deady); chapter 6, pp. 108–9 (General John Wool); chapter 6, pp. 109–13 (John Beeson).

P. 83   *"The cause of the present difficulty."* J. Palmer, superintendent of Indian Affairs for Oregon, letter to J. Wool, major general, U.S. Army (Dec. 1, 1855), in House Doc. No. 93, "Indian Hostilities in Oregon and Washington," 34th Congress, 1st Session, pp. 23–24 (Washington, D.C.: Government Printing Office, 1855).

P. 84   *Indians had stocked themselves with rifles.* Carey, *General History of Oregon*, p. 560; Walling, *History of Southern Oregon*, pp. 210–12.

P. 84   *Placer mining.* The mineral extraction in these early days was all placer mining. Lode deposits—valuable minerals embedded in rocks—were mined later as the more easily mined placer deposits—loose minerals, usually gold, found in soil or sand—played out. Hydraulic mining, involving high-power hoses that blasted away whole hillsides and was even more environmentally destructive, came later. On placer and lode mining, see generally Paul, *California Gold*, pp. 50–66, 150–59; Brooks and Ramp, *Gold and Silver in Oregon*, pp. 32–33.

P. 84   *Hogs ate acorns.* See Douthit, *Uncertain Encounters*, p. 78.

P. 84   *Mules trampled vegetation.* See Stephen Dow Beckham, ed., "Trail of Tears: 1856 Diary of Indian Agent George Ambrose," vol. 10 *Southern Oregon Heritage*, p. 16 (summer 1996); Bancroft, vol. 2, *History of Oregon*, p. 186.

P. 84   *Whitman massacre of 1847.* See, e.g., Douthit, *Uncertain Encounters*, p. 66 ("Although the location of [the killing of Marcus and Narcissa Whitman] was hundreds of miles from the Willamette Valley and southern Oregon, it struck fear into the hearts of white pioneers near and far."); O'Donnell, *An Arrow in the Earth*, p. 182 (by the mid-1850s, the incident still "had not been forgotten").

P. 84   *Kamiakin and uniting of Northwest Indians.* Carey, *General History of Oregon*, p. 560; Angie Debo, *A History of the Indians of the United States*, p. 156 (Norman: University of Oklahoma Press, 1970). On Kamiakin, see generally Richard D. Scheuerman and Michael O. Finley, *Finding Chief Kamiakin: The Life and Legacy of a Northwest Patriot* (Pullman, WA: Washington State University Press, 2008).

P. 84   *"simple yet honorable character."* Walling, *History of Southern Oregon*, pp. 210–11. Walling followed the comments in the text by demonstrating the ethnocentric mindset of the day: "They [Tyees Sam and Joe] were, to be sure, only ignorant and uncultured savages, and perhaps entirely incapable of a high degree of civilization; yet with proper treatment they remained harmless and peaceable individuals, however intractable and fierce a great part of their tribe might have been." Ibid., p. 211.

P. 84   *Tyee Joe's daughter, Mary.* Ibid. See also Joseph Lane, *Autobiography*, pp. 118–22 (Portland, OR, 1878) (recounting a long meeting with Mary on Indian-white relations).

P. 85   *Estimate of 1853 combat deaths and hangings.* For an analysis of the fatalities, see Douthit, *Uncertain Encounters*, pp. 102–3, 200–201.

P. 85   *Daniel Giles and Tyee John's son, Charley.* Beckham, *Requiem*, p. 116.

P. 85   *Ten or twelve Indians dead.* Schwartz, *The Rogue River Indian War*, p. 55.

P. 85   *Applegate Valley combat.* See Walling, *History of Southern Oregon*, pp. 216–17.

P. 85   *"The engagement."* Ibid.

P. 85   *The final battle of 1853.* The fullest account is Walling, *History of Southern Oregon*, p. 218–20. See also Bancroft, vol. 2, *History of Oregon*, pp. 311–17; Beckham, *Requiem*, pp. 119–21.

P. 86   *American and tribal casualties.* Bancroft, vol. 2, *History of Oregon*, p. 317n17 (citing the casualties as reported in the November 15, 1853, *Oregon Statesman*).

P. 87   *The general wearing a bulky coat.* See Walling, *History of Southern Oregon*, p. 219.

P. 87   *"On going into their camp."* See Bancroft, vol. 2, *History of Oregon*, p. 316.

P. 87   *"I told them who I was."* Joseph Lane, *Autobiography*, p. 124.

P. 87   *Indian soldiers served as stretcher bearers.* See Bancroft, vol. 2, *History of Oregon*, p. 317 (citing Joseph Lane, *Autobiography*); Beckham, *Requiem*, p. 121 (quoting a soldier who told the Sept. 6, 1853 *Oregon Statesman* and Sept. 19, 1853 *Alta California* that the litters were carried for "25 miles, through the mountains").

P. 87   *"I find no mention."* Bancroft, vol. 2, *History of Oregon*, p. 317.

5 Table Rocks, 1853

P. 88   *agreed to meet seven days later.* Albert G. Walling, *History of Southern Oregon, comprising Jackson, Josephine, Douglas, Curry and Coos Counties*, p. 220 (Portland, OR: A. G. Walling, 1884).

P. 88   *both sides grazed their horses together.* Ibid.

P. 88   *"They affeared treachery on our part."* Terence O'Donnell, *An Arrow in the Earth: General Joel Palmer and the Indians of Oregon*, p. 152 (Portland: Oregon Historical Society Press, 1991) (quoting Joel Palmer's journal entry for September 7).

P. 88   *council of September 4.* See Frances Fuller Victor, *The Early Indian Wars of Oregon*, pp. 315–16 (Salem, OR: Frank C. Baker, State Printer, 1894). Fuller reports that Lane took several hostages as protection for the talks on September 4 and 8. Ibid. Palmer arrived on September 5 and did not participate in the September 4 council. O'Donnell, *An Arrow in the Earth*, p. 152. Schwartz refers without citation to a September 7 letter from "Timon" to "Bush," stating that preliminary talks were held on September 3. See E. A. Schwartz, *The Rogue River Indian War and Its Aftermath, 1850–1980*, p. 57 (Norman: University of Oklahoma Press, 1997).

P. 88   *preliminary treaty, September 8.* Treaty with the Rogue River Indians, Sept. 8, 1853 (unratified), *in* Vine Deloria Jr. and Raymond J. DeMallie, eds., vol. 2, *Documents of American Indian Diplomacy*, pp. 1300–1301 (Norman: University of Oklahoma Press, 1999). The September 8 treaty was never ratified: while Palmer submitted it to Congress, along with the September 10 treaty, the Senate likely saw no need to ratify it because the only purpose of the September 8 document was to lay the foundation for the full-blown treaty of September 10. On Palmer's submission of the September 10 treaty, see J. Palmer, superintendent of Indian Affairs for Oregon, transcript of letter to G. Manypenny, commissioner of Indian Affairs (Oct. 8, 1853), *at* Archival Collection of the Siletz Tribe Cultural Department [hereinafter Siletz Archival Collection].

P. 89   *"as plenty away over the mountains."* Joel Palmer, "Notes on a Speech Made at Table Rock Treaty Negotiations 1853," Joel Palmer Papers, AX 057, Doc. 33, *at* Special Collections and University Archives, University of Oregon Libraries, Eugene.

P. 89   *"The occasion was a remarkable one."* Walling, *History of Southern Oregon*, p. 222.

P. 89   *policy calling for permanent reservations.* See below, pp. 93–95.

P. 89   *first ratified land treaty.* Earlier treaties in the Southwest and Upper Great Plains had been "peace and friendship" treaties that did not involve land transactions. See, e.g., Treaty with the Apache, July 1, 1852, 10 Stat. 979 (1853); Treaty of Fort Laramie with Sioux and Other Tribes, Sept. 17, 1851, 11 Stat. 749 (1859); Treaty with the Utah, Dec. 30, 1849, 9 Stat. 984 (1850); Treaty with the Navaho, Sept. 9, 1849, 9 Stat. 974 (1850). All of these treaties are reprinted in Charles J. Kappler, ed., vol. 2, *Indian Affairs: Laws and Treaties* (Washington, D.C.: Government Printing Office, 1904). The nineteen treaties negotiated by Governor Gaines and Superintendent Dart in Oregon in 1851 did involve land but Congress failed to ratify them. See chapter 4, pp. 78–80.

P. 89   *Joel Palmer held three posts.* See generally O'Donnell, *An Arrow in the Earth.* See also Stanley S. Spaid, "The Later Life and Activities of General Joel Palmer," vol. 55, no. 4 *Oregon Historical Quarterly*, pp. 311–12 (Dec. 1954); Nathan Douthit, *Uncertain Encounters: Indians and Whites at Peace and War in Southern Oregon, 1820s to 1860s*, pp. 91–92 (Corvallis: Oregon State University Press, 2002); Schwartz, *The Rogue River Indian War*, pp. 49–50.

P. 90   *Palmer "seems to have had an unusual amount of compassion."* Robert Kentta, "A Siletz History, Part VI: The Western Oregon Treaties of 1853–1855," *Siletz News*, p. 2 (April 2000), *at* http://www.ctsi.nsn.us/chinook-indian-tribe-siletz-heritage/our-history/part-vi#content (accessed May 14, 2009).

P. 91   *Judge Matthew Deady.* On Deady's life, see Malcolm Clark Jr., ed., *Pharisee among Philistines: The Diary of Judge Matthew P. Deady, 1871–1892*, pp. xxxi–xxxvii (Portland: Oregon Historical Society, 1975); Malcolm Clark Jr., ed., "My Dear Judge: Excerpts from the Letters of Justice Stephen J. Field to Judge Matthew P. Deady," vol. 1 *Western Legal History*, pp. 79–82 (Winter/Spring 1988). On Deady's stature, see Ralph James Mooney, "Matthew Deady and the Federal Judicial Response to Racism in the Early West," vol. 63 *Oregon Law Review*, p. 629 (1984) (pointing to Deady as Oregon's "most prominent and powerful judicial officer"), and ibid., p. 637 ("for his outspoken defense of embattled Chinese immigrants . . . Clio the muse of history smiles on Matthew Deady"); Charles H. Carey, vol. 2, *A General History of Oregon: Prior to 1861*, p. 495 (Portland, OR: Metropolitan Press, 1936); Robert N. Peters, "The 'First' Oregon Code: Another Look at Deady's Role," vol. 82, no. 4 *Oregon Historical Quarterly*, p. 383 (Winter 1981). For critical views of Deady, see Deborah Niedermeyer, "'The True Interests of a White Population': The Alaska Indian Country Decisions of Judge Matthew P. Deady," vol. 21, no. 1 *New York University Journal of International Law and Politics*, p. 195 (Fall 1988); Peters, "The 'First' Oregon Code," p. 383.

P. 91   *Deady did not generally champion the concerns of minority groups.* See Mooney, "Matthew Deady and the Federal Judicial Response," p, 563.

P. 91   *"it ought never to be forgotten."* Ibid., pp. 580–81n89 (quoting an Oct. 31, 1876, letter from Deady to Major H. Clay Wood).

P. 91   *"There I found Captain J. K. Lamerick."* Matthew P. Deady, "Southern Oregon Names and Events," *in Transactions of the 11th Annual Re-Union of the Oregon Pioneer Asso-*

ciation for 1883, pp. 23–24 (Salem, OR: E. M. Waite, Steam Printer and Bookbinder, 1884) (cited as being reprinted from the *Daily Oregonian* of Dec. 7, 1883).

P. 92 *"the whites of Rogue River valley."* O'Donnell, *An Arrow in the Earth*, p. 151 (the letter was dated Aug. 30, 1853 and published in the Sept. 3, 1853, *Oregonian*).

P. 92 *"extinction of the entire race."* Ibid. (quoting the Sept. 2, 1853, edition of the *Oregon Spectator*).

P. 92 *officials were well aware of Indian land title.* See Senate Committee on Interior and Insular Affairs, Jerry A. O'Callaghan, "The Disposition of the Public Domain in Oregon," 86th Congress, 2nd Session, pp. 21–27 (Washington, D.C.: Government Printing Office, 1960) [hereinafter The Disposition].

P. 92 *Lane's initial speech to the territorial legislature.* See ibid., p. 22.

P. 92 *The subject was directly raised in Congress.* See ibid., p. 33.

P. 92 *Donation Land Act of 1850.* Donation Land Act, ch. 76, Sept. 27, 1850, 9 Stat. 496 (1850) (not codified). See also chapter 3, pp. 70–71 and accompanying notes.

P. 92 *heated disputes over landownership.* See, e.g., O'Donnell, *An Arrow in the Earth*, p. 144 ("daily conflicts erupted between the two groups").

P. 92 *Oregon Indian Treaty Act of 1850.* Oregon Indian Treaty Act, ch. 16, June 5, 1850, 9 Stat. 437 (1850) (not codified).

P. 92 *view of Lane and Samuel Thurston.* See C. F. Coan, "The First Stage of the Federal Indian Policy in the Pacific Northwest, 1849–1852," vol. 22 *Oregon Historical Quarterly*, p. 53 (March 1921) (discussing Lane's view); Hubert Howe Bancroft, vol. 2 *History of Oregon*, pp. 117–18 (San Francisco: The History Co., 1888) (discussing Thurston's view).

P. 93 *"if found expedient and practicable."* Oregon Indian Treaty Act, §1.

P. 93 *None of the tribes wanted to go.* See, e.g., O'Donnell, *An Arrow in the Earth*, p. 138; C. F., "The Adoption of the Reservation Policy in the Pacific Northwest, 1853–1855," vol. 23 *Oregon Historical Quarterly*, p. 7 (March 1922). Coan describes the "east of the mountains" policy as a "compete failure." Coan, "The First Stage," p. 65.

P. 93 *reservations within their ancestral territories.* See, e.g., ibid., p. 56.

P. 93 *Joseph Lane blocked ratification.* See, e.g., ibid.

P. 93 *tribes frustrated and angry at non-ratification of treaties.* See, e.g., Annual Report of Superintendent Joel Palmer, Oct. 8, 1853, *at* Siletz Archival Collection.

P. 93 *"Indian country."* See Francis Paul Prucha, vol. 1, *The Great Father: The United States Government and the American Indians*, pp. 92–93 (Lincoln: University of Nebraska Press, 1984). The description in the text of the first line demarcating Indian country is from *Felix S. Cohen's Handbook of Federal Indian Law*, 1982 ed., pp. 29–30n31 (Charlottesville, VA: Michie Bobbs-Merrill, 1982).

P. 93 *the "Unorganized Indian Territory."* While the Five Civilized Tribes were removed to Oklahoma, as were many other tribes, the territory did extend far to the north, to the Canadian border. For a map, see Richard White, *"It's Your Misfortune and None of My Own": A New History of the American West*, p. 83 (Norman: University of Oklahoma Press, 1991). For a map of other tribes moved to Oklahoma, see ibid., p. 89.

P. 93 *the "Trail of Tears" and the Five Civilized Tribes.* On the Trail of Tears, see, e.g., Angie Debo, *And Still the Waters Run: The Betrayal of the Five Civilized Tribes* (Princeton, NJ: Princeton University Press, 1972); Prucha, vol. 1, *The Great Father*, pp. 271–79; White, *It's Your Misfortune*, pp. 87–89. The opinion by Chief Justice Marshall, referred to in the text, is *Worcester v. Georgia*, 31 U.S. 515 (1832). The statute authorizing removal is the Indian Removal Act of 1830, ch. 148, May 28, 1830, 4 Stat. 411 (1830) (not codified).

P. 94   *The notion of a separate Indian territory blew apart.* See, e.g., White, *It's Your Misfortune*, pp. 89–91.

P. 94   *The reformulation of Indian policy and the reservation system.* On this era, which has been covered extensively, see, e.g., Robert A. Trennert, Jr., *Alternative to Extinction: Federal Indian Policy and the Beginnings of the Reservation System, 1846–51* (Philadelphia: Temple University Press, 1975); Prucha, vol. 1, *The Great Father*, pp. 315–38.

P. 94   *"Civilization and barbarism."* L. Lea, commissioner of Indian Affairs, report to A. Stuart, secretary of the Interior (Nov. 30, 1852), *in* Senate Doc. 1, "Report of the Commissioner of Indian Affairs," 32d Congress, 2d Session, vol. 1, p. 293 (Washington, D.C.: Government Printing Office, 1851).

P. 94   *"There should be assigned to each tribe."* L. Lea, report to A. Stuart (Nov. 27, 1850), *in* Senate Doc. 1, 1850, Commissioner Report, 31st Congress, 2d Session, p. 36.

P. 95   *"It is too clear to admit of argument."* J. Palmer, superintendent of Indian Affairs for Oregon, letter to G. Manypenny, commissioner of Indian Affairs (June 23, 1853), in Senate Doc. 1, 33d Congress, 1st Session, vol. 1, part 1, p. 449 (Washington, D.C.: Robert Armstrong, Printer, 1853).

P. 95   *The Oregon Coast presented the preferred option.* See ibid., pp. 450–51.

P. 95   *The Coast did have small valleys for the farming way of life.* Ibid., p. 450.

P. 96   *Palmer planned an expedition to the Coast.* "Important Explorations," *Oregon Statesman*, p. 2 (Aug. 23, 1853). See also O'Donnell, *An Arrow in the Earth*, p. 148.

P. 96   *"imperatively required."* James E. Hendricksen, *Joe Lane of Oregon: Machine Politics and the Sectional Crisis, 1849–1861*, pp. 76–77 (New Haven, CT: Yale University Press, 1967) (quoting an Aug. 23, 1853, letter from Lane to Palmer, published in the Sept. 6, 1853, *Oregon Statesman*).

P. 96   *"a thousand warriors mounted on fine horses."* Alvin M. Josephy Jr., *The Nez Perce Indians and the Opening of the Northwest*, p. 316 (Boston: Houghton Mifflin Co., 1965).

P. 96   *Against Nesmith's advice.* See James W. Nesmith, "Reminiscences of Table Rock by Senators James W. Nesmith and General Joseph Lane," vol. 7, no. 2 *Oregon Historical Quarterly*, p. 216 (June 1906).

P. 97   *"We dismounted and hitched our horses."* Ibid., p. 217.

P. 97   *"The scene of the famous 'peace talk.'"* Deady, "Southern Oregon Names and Events," p. 25.

P. 98   *He spoke in the Indian dialect.* LaFayette Grover, *Notable Things in a Public Life in Oregon*, p. 35 (San Francisco, 1878), *at* Bancroft Collection, Bancroft Library, University of California, Berkeley. Along with Nesmith's account, Grover's is the most extensive first-hand source on the Table Rock negotiations. Grover later became governor of Oregon.

P. 98   *"He made his speech in his own tongue."* Ibid., pp. 36–37. Although Grover's quotation marks were confusing and most have been omitted, the quotation surely reflects Tyee Joe's intent.

P. 98   *The germs had taken more than 80 percent.* See Robert Boyd, *The Coming of the Spirit of Pestilence*, p. 265 (Seattle: University of Washington Press, 1999). See also chapter 3, pp. 57–61 and accompanying notes.

P. 99   *the tribes' apparent advantage in rifles.* See, e.g., Nesmith, "Reminiscences of Table

Rock," p. 215 ("many of the settlers and miners having traded their arms to the Indians, who were much better equipped for war than their white neighbors"); J. Palmer transcript of letter to G. Manypenny (Oct. 8, 1853), *at* Siletz Archival Collection ("The Rogue River Tribe of Indians are among the most powerful tribes on this coast . . .").

P. 99   *"Long speeches were made."* Nesmith, "Reminiscences of Table Rock," pp. 217–18.

P. 99   *the Chinook Jargon.* The literature on Chinook Jargon is quite extensive. See generally Jim Holton, *Chinook Jargon: The Hidden Language of the Pacific Northwest* (San Leandro, CA: Wawa Press, 2004); Horatio Hale, *An International Idiom: A Manual of the Oregon Trade Language, or "Chinook Jargon"* (London: Whittaker and Co., 1890); George Gibbs, *Dictionary of the Chinook Jargon, or, Trade Language of Oregon* (New York: Cramoisy Press, 1863); George C. Shaw, *The Chinook Jargon and How to Use It* (Seattle: Rainier Printing Co., 1909); Edward Harper Thomas, *Chinook: A History and Dictionary of the Northwest Coast Trade Jargon*, 2d ed. (Portland, OR: Binford & Mort, 1970); George Lang, *Making Wawa: The Genesis of Chinook Jargon* (Vancouver: UBC Press, 2008).

P. 100   *The Chinook Jargon came into use before non-Indians arrived.* The far-flung relationships among aboriginal tribes with distinct languages seem to make the fact of a simple common language a necessity. See, e.g., Thomas, *Chinook*, pp. viii–ix, 10; James G. Swan, *The Northwest Coast or, Three Years' Residence in Washington Territory*, pp. 307, 310 (Seattle: University of Washington Press, 1969) (first published 1857); Barbara P. Harris, "Chinook Jargon: Arguments for a Pre-Contact Origin," vol. 29, no. 1 *Pacific Coast Philology*, p. 28 (Sept. 1994). Others have questioned the precontact origins of the Jargon. See, e.g., Gibbs, *Dictionary of the Chinook Jargon*, p. vi; Horatio Hale, *Ethnography and Philology*, p. 635 (Ridgewood, NJ: Gregg Press, 1968) (first published 1846). See also Lang, *Making Wawa*.

P. 100   *estimated 250–500 words.* By the 1850s, the influential Chinook Jargon compendium by Horatio Hale and described by him as "very nearly complete," listed just 250 words in the Jargon. Hale, *Ethnography and Philology*, p. 636. George Gibbs, writing in 1863, found about 500 words. Gibbs, *Dictionary of the Chinook Jargon*, p. vii.

P. 100   *"effective communication through the Jargon."* Thomas, *Chinook*, p. 53.

P. 100   *"the way a word is spoken."* W. S. Phillips, *The Chinook Book: A Descriptive Analysis of the Chinook Jargon in Plain Words*, p. 6 (Seattle: R. L. Davis Printing Co., 1913).

P. 100   *"The most important knowledge to possess."* Ibid., p. 5.

P. 100   *"The Jargon was capable of conveying only rudimentary concepts." United States v. Washington*, 384 F. Supp. 312, 330 (W.D. Wash. 1974). Judge Boldt's decision was affirmed by the Ninth Circuit Court of Appeals, 520 F.2d 676 (9th Cir. 1975), and the Supreme Court denied certiorari, 423 U.S. 1086 (1976). The Supreme Court ultimately approved the opinion in 1979 in a collateral case. See *Washington v. Washington State Commercial Passenger Fishing Vessel Association*, 443 U.S. 658 (1979).

P. 100   *judges interpret leases and loans.* On these "adhesion contracts," see, e.g., Friedrich Kessler, "Contracts of Adhesion—Some Thoughts about Freedom of Contract," vol. 43 *Columbia Law Review*, p. 633 (1962).

P. 100   *"the treaty must therefore be construed." Washington*, 384 F. Supp. at 331 (quoting *Jones v. Meehan*, 175 U.S. 1, 11–12 [1899]).

P. 101   *"I saw some Indians gathering up their lass-ropes."* Nesmith, "Reminiscences of Table Rock," p. 218.

P. 101 *principles of the Table Rock Treaty.* See, e.g., Alban W. Hoopes, *Indian Affairs and Their Administration*, p. 99 (Philadelphia: University of Pennsylvania Press, 1932) (calling the Table Rock treaty a "prototype").

P. 101 *Isaac Stevens expressed his gratitude to Joseph Lane.* I. Stevens, governor and superintendent of Indian Affairs for Washington, transcript of letter to J. Lane, general (Sept. 19, 1857), *at* Siletz Archival Collection (Joseph Lane Papers available at Lilly Library, Indiana University, Bloomington; also available on microfilm at the University of Oregon, Eugene). On Stevens's life, see Kent D. Richards, *Isaac I. Stevens: Young Man in a Hurry* (Provo, UT: Brigham Young University Press, 1979).

P. 101 *The Table Rock Treaty and minor matters.* See Treaty with the Rogue River, arts. 3–6, Sept. 10, 1853, 10 Stat. 1018 (1854) [hereinafter Table Rock Treaty].

P. 102 *This magnificent landscape.* For a description of the cession, see Table Rock Treaty, art. 1. Palmer estimates the ceded land as 3,500 square miles, see J. Palmer transcript of letter to G. Manypenny (Oct. 8, 1853, *at* Siletz Archival Collection), but that is too high. Review of the topographic maps puts the figure at approximately 2,400 square miles (the ceded area is approximately equal to 2,400 sections; each section equals one square mile).

P. 102 *held extraordinarily valuable resources.* In his transmittal letter forwarding the treaty to Manypenny, Palmer discusses the resources in the ceded area, including "fertile valleys, heavy forests of valuable timber" and lands "rich in gold." Ibid.

P. 102 *payment for the land.* Table Rock Treaty, art. 3.

P. 102 *The peace treaty of September 8.* See above, pp. 88–89 and accompanying notes.

P. 102 *"I fear your people are not all here."* Joel Palmer, "Notes on a Speech Made at Table Rock Treaty Negotiations 1853," Joel Palmer Papers, AX 057, Doc. 33, *at* Special Collections and University Archives, University of Oregon Libraries, Eugene. It is not known exactly how Palmer used these notes—whether he referred to them during his speech or jotted them down afterward as a record of his presentation. The notes are undated but the context makes it clear that he delivered the speech on September 9.

P. 102 *"Our great chief, your father."* Ibid.

P. 103 *"The white man has come."* Ibid.

P. 104 *Article 2 of the treaty called for a reservation.* See Table Rock Treaty, art. 2 (establishing the boundaries of the reservation).

P. 104 *"shall be allowed to occupy temporarily."* Ibid.

P. 104 *The temporary reservation would remain fully in effect.* Ibid.

6 *The Rogue River War*

P. 106 *The death toll.* Nathan Douthit, *Uncertain Encounters: Indians and Whites at Peace and War in Southern Oregon, 1820s to 1860s*, pp. 200–201 (Corvallis: Oregon State University Press, 2002). For the number or whites killed, see also Senate Doc. No. 59, "Communication from C. S. Drew . . . giving an account of the origin and early prosecution of the Indian war in Oregon," 36th Congress, 1st Session, pp. 3–8 (May 9, 1860) (Washington, D.C.: Government Printing Office, 1860). The figures in the text are conservative because they include only southern Oregon and several events took place in California.

P. 106 *United States–Indian wars.* The best source on casualties is Michael Clodfelter, *Warfare and Armed Conflicts*, pp. 203–4, 446–77 (Jefferson, NC: McFarland & Co., 1992).

For Indian Wars generally, see Jerry Keenan, *Encyclopedia of American Indian Wars, 1492–1890* (Santa Barbara, CA: ABC-CLIO, 1997); Gregory Michno, *Encyclopedia of Indian Wars: Western Battles and Skirmishes, 1850–1890* (Missoula, MT: Mountain Press Publishing Co., 2003); William B. Kessel and Robert Wooster, eds., *Encyclopedia of Native American Wars and Warfare* (New York: Facts on File, Book Builders, 2005); and Steve Rajtar, *Indian War Sites: A Guidebook to Battlefields, Monuments, and Memorials* (Jefferson, NC: McFarland & Co., 1999).

P. 107 *"Pretty rough times!"* Quoted in Edward S. Curtis, vol. 13, *The North American Indian*, ed. Frederick Webb Hodge, pp. 94–95 (Norwood, MA: Plimpton Press, 1924).

P. 108 *George Curry.* Curry was acting governor twice, for eight months in 1853 and two months in 1854, before being appointed governor on November 1, 1854. He remained in office until 1859. "Curry, George Law, Gov.," in Howard McKinley Corning, ed., *Dictionary of Oregon History*, 2d ed., p. 68 (Portland, OR: Binford & Mort, 1989).

P. 108 *"demand extermination of the hostile Indians."* Terence O'Donnell, *An Arrow in the Earth: General Joel Palmer and the Indians of Oregon*, p. 148 (Portland: Oregon Historical Society Press, 1991) (quoting a man named Ettinger, who was on a mission to Salem "to inform the government of the state of things in southern Oregon and to get troops"). On such volunteer call-ups, see also Douthit, *Uncertain Encounters*, pp. 141, 143.

P. 108 *"treacherous and ungrateful."* Address by Joseph Lane of March 31, 1856, *Congressional Globe*, 34th Congress, 1st Session, p. 776 (Washington, D.C.: John C. Rives, 1856).

P. 108 *"the present difficulty in southern Oregon."* J. Palmer, superintendent of Indian Affairs for Oregon, transcript of letter to J. Wool, major general of the Pacific Division (Dec. 6, 1855), M2 Roll 5, Doc. 123, *at* Archival Collection of the Siletz Tribe Cultural Department [hereinafter Siletz Archival Collection]. See also Editorial Correspondence of the Tribune, "The Indian War on the Pacific," *Oregon Statesman* (May 27, 1856).

P. 108 *Matthew Deady took the Indian side.* Ralph James Mooney, "Matthew Deady and the Federal Judicial Response to Racism in the Early West," vol. 63, no. 4 *Oregon Law Review*, pp. 580–81n89 (1985) (quoting Deady's Oct. 31, 1876, letter to Major H. C. Wood).

P. 109 *"signally barbarous and savage."* John E. Wool, letter to the editor, "The Indian War in Oregon," *Washington, D.C., Daily National Intelligencer* (May 2, 1856).

P. 109 *"sacrificing many innocent and worthy citizens."* J. Wool letter to I. Stevens, governor of Washington Territory (Feb. 12, 1856), *in* Senate Doc. No. 66, Report of the Secretary of War, 34th Congress, 1st Session, pp. 37–39. For an excellent treatment of General Wool and the military in the context of the Rogue River War, see T. O'Donnell, *An Arrow in the Earth*, pp. 242–44. See also Douthit, *Uncertain Encounters*, p. 142.

P. 109 *first of the "humanitarian generals."* See, e.g., Douthit, *Uncertain Encounters*, p. 142 (referring to Richard N. Ellis, "The Humanitarian Generals," vol. 3, no. 2 *Western Historical Quarterly*, pp. 169–78 [April 1972]). On Wool, see also Robert M. Utley, *The Indian Frontier of the American West, 1846–1890*, pp. 53–55 (Albuquerque: University of New Mexico Press, 1984).

P. 109 *John Beeson.* For a short biography of Beeson, see Bart Webber, "Introduction," *in* John Beeson, *John Beeson's Plea for the Indians: His Lone Cry in the Wilderness for Indian Rights*, pp. 7–29 (Medford, OR: Webb Research Group, 1994). The original edition of Beeson's book, *Plea for the Indians; with Facts and Features of the Late War in*

Oregon, was published in New York in 1857 (stereotyped by Thomas B. Smith; printed by Pudney & Russell). The 1857 edition, which went into three printings, is discussed in *Plea for the Indians*, pp. 26–29. See also Douthit, *Uncertain Encounters*, pp. 107–12, 128–32, 135–36, 144–45 (tracking Beeson's role in Oregon during these years); Stephen Dow Beckham, *Requiem for a People: The Rogue Indians and the Frontiersmen*, p. 152 (Norman: University of Oklahoma Press, 1971).

P. 109 *"they denied to the poor Indian."* Beeson, *Plea for the Indians*, p. 50.

P. 109 *"they should not be satisfied."* Ibid., p. 52.

P. 110 *"the meeting broke up."* Ibid., p. 96.

P. 110 *New York Tribune and San Francisco Herald articles.* Ibid., pp. 106–7.

P. 110 *"the excitement was getting fearfully high."* Ibid., p. 107.

P. 110 *"kill him as an Indian."* Webber, "Introduction," *in* Beeson, *Plea for the Indians*, p. 14 (quoting Welborn Beeson's diary entry of May 22, 1856).

P. 110 *Beeson left home in the dark of night.* Ibid., pp. 14–15; Beeson, *Plea for the Indians*, pp. 107–8.

P. 110 *he did not return to Talent.* Not much of this is known, except that Beeson had made a trip to Oregon and returned to the East by 1868.

P. 110 *might have become the commissioner of Indian Affairs.* "Eastern News," vol. 9, no. 4 *Salem Oregon Argus* (June 8, 1863). On Beeson's career in the East, see Hubert Howe Bancroft, vol. 2, *History of Oregon*, p. 404n17 (San Francisco: The History Co., 1888).

P. 110 *"If at every point of this melancholy story."* Beeson, *Plea for the Indians*, p. 78.

P. 111 *"surely this state of things."* Ibid., p. 79.

P. 111 *"cruel and bitter prejudice."* Ibid.

P. 111 in *"self-protection."* Ibid., p. 68.

P. 111 *"acted with the greatest discretion."* Ibid., p. 83.

P. 112 *"Had the Indians been disposed to destroy."* Ibid.

P. 112 *"a very sagacious and energetic man."* Ibid., p. 86.

P. 112 *"was faithful in the observance of the treaty."* Ibid.

P. 112 *"of all the Pacific Coast Indians."* Binger Hermann, "Early History of Southern Oregon," vol. 19, no. 1 *Oregon Historical Society Quarterly*, p. 67 (March 1918).

P. 112 *"When the aged Chief became acquainted."* Beeson, *Plea for the Indians*, p. 88. On the killing of the two men, see also Albert G. Walling, *History of Southern Oregon*, p. 240 (Portland, OR: A. G. Walling, 1884).

P. 113 a *"military fogie."* Quoted in E. A. Schwartz, *The Rogue River Indian War and Its Aftermath, 1850–1980*, p. 133 (Norman: University of Oklahoma Press, 1997).

P. 113 *beach gold at the mouth of the Klamath River.* See Walter Van Dyke, "Early Days in Klamath," vol. 18, no. 104 *Overland Monthly and Out West Magazine*, p. 175 (Aug. 1891).

P. 114 *Beach mining on the southern Oregon Coast.* See Beckham, *Requiem*, pp. 132–33; Bancroft, vol. 2, *History of Oregon*, pp. 329–30; Van Dyke, "Early Days in Klamath," p. 175.

P. 114 *miners swung into action.* On this incident, see generally Beckham, *Requiem*, pp. 134–35; Schwartz, *The Rogue River Indian War*, pp. 61–62; Douthit, *Uncertain Encounters*, p. 122. While Bancroft asserted that the Coquilles "added to insolence robbery and murder," vol. 2, *History of Oregon*, p. 330, no other account reports any physical attack by the Indians. See also Frances Fuller Victor, *The Early Indian Wars of Oregon*, pp. 323–24 (Salem, OR: Frank C. Baker, State Printer, 1894).

P. 114 *"Thus was committed a massacre."* F. Smith, Indian sub-agent, letter to J. Palmer (Feb.

5, 1854), *in* House Doc. No. 1, 1854 Commissioner Report, 33d Congress, 2d Session, pt. 1, 477.

P. 114 *Miners' raids on Chetco village.* Palmer gave a full description of this incident in his annual report to Commissioner Manypenny. See J. Palmer transcript of report to G. Manypenny, commissioner of Indian Affairs (Sept. 11, 1854), M2 Roll 7, Doc. 9, *at* Siletz Archival Collection. Palmer's report is ambiguous as to the number of Chetcoes killed; I have used the figure of twenty-three in the text, but the actual count may have been thirty-eight. As of 1854, Oregon territorial law barred testimony against a "white person" by "Negroes, mulattoes, and Indians, or persons of one-half Indian blood." See *Statutes of Oregon*, ch. 4, title 1, §6(3) (Oregon: Asahel Bush, Public Printer, 1853) (repealed by 1862).

P. 115 *Violence also struck the Tolowa.* See Curtis, vol. 13, *The North American Indian*, pp. 91–92.

P. 115 *"it is a fact."* Walling, *History of Southern Oregon*, p. 227.

P. 115 *"effectually terrorized a tract of country."* Ibid., p. 233. On Tipsu Tyee, see also Schwartz, *The Rogue River Indian War*, pp. 64–66.

P. 115 *Tipsu Tyee killed.* See T. O'Donnell, *An Arrow in the Earth*, p. 172; Walling, *History of Southern Oregon*, p. 233. For no clear reason miners then brutally killed Bill and two of his men. S. Culver, Indian agent, transcript of letter to J. Palmer (June 1, 1854), M2 Roll 4, Doc. 44, *at* Siletz Archival Collection.

P. 116 *Miners and Indians died in a drunken brawl.* See, e.g., Schwartz, *The Rogue River Indian War*, p. 79 (miner fired first); Walling, *History of Southern Oregon*, p. 238 (Indian fired first).

P. 117 *The Humbug incident.* According to Walling's account of the incident, "Excitement knew no bounds; every man constituted himself an exterminator of Indians, and a great many of that unfortunate race were killed, without the least reference to their possible guilt or innocence." Walling, *History of Southern Oregon*, p. 238. On the role of Rogue River Indians, see ibid., pp. 238–40 (two Indians from the Table Rock Reservation were charged with murder, but the grand jury did not return an indictment; local whites shot both Indians immediately after being released from custody). See also Schwartz, *The Rogue River Indian War*, p. 80; Beckham, *Requiem*, p. 149.

P. 117 *"Now the earth went bad."* Galice Athapaskan text translations from Melville Jacobs's Galice Athapaskan field notebooks, No. 126 (1967), Melville Jacobs Collection Box 104-9, pp. 126–38, *at* Melville Jacobs papers, Special Collections, University of Washington Libraries, Seattle, Washington.

P. 117 *members of Tipsu Tyee's band.* See Beckham, *Requiem*, pp. 150–51.

P. 118 *Captain Andrew Smith.* When volunteers from Yreka came to Fort Lane and demanded that Captain Smith turn over alleged criminals, Smith refused, saying that he would deal only with "properly constituted authorities." See Walling, *History of Southern Oregon*, p. 239. See also Beeson, *Plea for the Indians*, p. 75.

P. 118 *Lupton's recruits were vigilantes.* Walling, *History of Southern Oregon*, p. 243.

P. 118 *The band at Little Butte Creek had done nothing wrong.* Walling, who wrote an extensive account of the raid at Little Butte Creek, asserted that "the reason why the particular band at Butte creek was selected as victims also appears a mystery." Ibid. The only suggestion of any misconduct I have found is Victor's vague comment that "it was suspected that among [the band members] were some who had been annoying the settlers." Victor, *The Early Indian Wars*, p. 343.

P. 118 *"I arose, and spoke."* See Beeson, *Plea for the Indians*, p. 72.

P. 118 *The summer village site at Little Butte Creek.* I hiked this area in August 2006.

P. 119 *"Lupton and his party fired a volley."* Walling, *History of Southern Oregon*, p. 243.

P. 119 *"twenty-eight bodies."* Beeson, *Plea for the Indians*, p. 74.

P. 119 *forty Indian casualties.* See Schwartz, *The Rogue River Indian War*, p. 85 (referring to an article in the *Crescent City* (California) *Herald*.

P. 119 *Captain Smith estimated eighty.* See Walling, *History of Southern Oregon*, p. 243.

P. 119 *one hundred and six Indian people had been killed.* See J. Palmer letter to G. Manypenny (Oct. 19, 1855), *in* House Doc. No. 93, "Indian Hostilities in Oregon and Washington," 34th Congress, 1st Session, p. 75 (Washington, D.C.: Government Printing Office, 1856).

P. 119 *Tyee Sam decided against a reprisal.* See, e.g., Victor, *The Early Indian Wars*, pp. 346–47. Tyee Sam may well have held back because of his longstanding attempt to preserve the peace promised in the treaty. However, Victor suggests that Tyee Sam's motive might have been self-interest: the reservation offers "refuge" from violence by whites and "for while even one chief is friendly the treaty payments go on." Ibid., p. 347.

P. 119 *Tyee John came to the fore.* Suggestions have been made that Tyee John had prepared for war and had his men battle-ready. See, e.g., Schwartz, *The Rogue Indian War*, pp. 86–87; Victor, *The Early Indian Wars*, p. 347. This is probably true. Tyee John signed the Table Rock Treaty but knew the aims of the exterminationists and the recent turmoil in the Rogue River Valley. A determined warrior who believed that the tribes could prevail in battle, it follows that he would be fully prepared for combat. Given that, the massacre at Little Butte Creek would inevitably push him into war. Tyee John is mentioned prominently in many sources about the Rogue River War and the early years on the Siletz Reservation. For a short account, see Sue Waldron, "'I am going to fight until I die': Chief John and the Rogue Indian Wars," vol. 9, no. 5 *Table Rock Sentinel* (Sept./Oct. 1989).

P. 119 *launched a ferocious campaign of revenge.* See, e.g., Walling, *History of Southern Oregon*, pp. 244–45.

P. 119 *"I want no house!"* See G. Ambrose, Indian agent, transcript of letter to J. Palmer (Oct. 20, 1855), M2 Roll 5, Doc. 104, *at* Siletz Archival Collection. See also Frank K. Walsh, Indian Battles along the Rogue River, 1855–56, p. 1 (North Bend, OR: Te-Cum-Tom Publications, 1996); Schwartz, *The Rogue River Indian War*, p. 87.

P. 119 *They killed between 15 and 27 whites.* The estimates of deaths on October 9 vary. See Charles H. Carey, *General History of Oregon: Through Early Statehood*, p. 591 (Portland, OR: Binford & Mort, 1971) (sixteen dead); Walling, *History of Southern Oregon*, pp. 244–47 (approximately sixteen dead, plus three found later); Schwartz, *The Rogue River Indian War*, p. 88 (Dr. A. G. Henry reported fifteen dead); Victor, *The Early Indian Wars*, pp. 344–45 (twenty-seven dead).

P. 120 *"It would be difficult to picture the state of alarm."* Walling, History of Southern Oregon, p. 247.

P. 120 *"the most eventful day."* Ibid., p. 244.

P. 120 *"the bloodiest day the valley had ever seen."* Victor, *The Early Indian Wars*, p. 345.

P. 120 *an imposing military force.* See Walling, *History of Southern Oregon*, pp. 249–50; Beckham, *Requiem*, pp. 154–57; Carey, *General History of Oregon*, pp. 591–92; Schwartz, *The Rogue River Indian War*, pp. 93–96.

P. 120   *"Great wrongs have undoubtedly been done."* J. Palmer letter to G. Ambrose (Oct. 13, 1855) quoted in Stanley Sheldon Spaid, "Joel Palmer and Indian Affairs in Oregon," p. 174 (Ph.D. diss., University of Oregon, 1950). On the same day, Palmer issued a comprehensive order directing that all Willamette Valley Indians party to the Treaty of Jan. 10, 1855 (probably referring to the treaty of January 22, 1855, with the Kalapuya), must be taken to temporary reservations. The order served the dual objectives of protecting the Indians and preventing them from joining up with the warriors. See J. Palmer, transcript of Order (Oct. 13, 1855), M2 Roll 5, Doc. 97, *at* Siletz Archival Collection.

P. 120   *"War is upon us."* See J. Palmer transcript of letter to G. Manypenny (Nov. 12, 1855), M2 Roll 5, Doc. 107, *at* Siletz Archival Collection.

P. 120   *"four times that number of white men."* Victor, *The Early Indian Wars*, p. 347.

P. 121   *The Klamath Knot.* For a fine piece of natural history on the Klamath Knot, see David Rains Wallace, *The Klamath Knot: Explorations of Myth and Evolution* (San Francisco: Sierra Club Books, 1983). See also Rogue River Country–Oregon, Wild and Scenic Rivers, at http://www.roguerivertrips.info/locations/Wild_Scenic_Rivers.asp (accessed May 20, 2009).

P. 121   *Captain William Lewis at Galice Creek.* See, e.g., Walling, *History of Southern Oregon*, p. 251.

P. 121   *Lieutenant A. V. Kautz at Grave Creek.* See, e.g., ibid.; Beckham, *Requiem*, pp. 157–58.

P. 122   *"ill-organized, unpaid, ill-fed."* Walling, *History of Southern Oregon*, p. 248.

P. 122   *"sabers, pistols, squirrel guns."* Beckham, *Requiem*, p. 158.

P. 122   *musketoons.* See Walling, *History of Southern Oregon*, p. 252.

P. 123   *Seeing the smoke and the soldiers.* Ibid., pp. 251–52.

P. 123   *The Battle of Hungry Hill.* Schwartz points out that accounts of this major battle differ in several aspects and does a good job of analyzing inconsistencies. See Schwartz, *The Rogue River Indian War*, pp. 97–100.

P. 123   *Eleven regular and volunteer soldiers had died.* See Beckham, *Requiem*, p. 159. According to Victor, twenty-six volunteers were killed, wounded, or missing. Among the regular troops, three were killed in action, one was killed by accident, and seven were wounded. Victor, *The Early Indian Wars*, pp. 354–55.

P. 123   *"God only knows."* Quoted in Victor, *The Early Indian Wars*, p. 355.

P. 123   *"monarchs of the woods."* Walsh, *Indian Battles*, p. 4.

P. 123   *"Boy, those bullets sounded funny."* Robert Kentta, interview with author, Siletz, Oregon, Feb. 24, 2005. Kentta was told this story by his father, born in 1910. His father knew several people involved in the Rogue River War, including Frances Johnson, who told these words to him. Women generally did not fight as warriors in precontact Oregon, but the grave circumstances of the Rogue River War pushed females into this nontraditional role. As Siletz elder Gilbert Towner explained, "They fought where they needed to and they fought hard. They fought just as well as the men." Gilbert Towner, telephone interview with María Aparicio, research assistant, Oct. 4, 2007.

P. 124   *Tyee John's forces prevailed.* See, e.g., Victor, *The Early Indian Wars*, pp. 362–63; Beckham, *Requiem*, pp. 160–62.

P. 125   *relentless displays of violence.* See, e.g., Beckham, *Requiem*, pp. 169–75.

P. 125   *The tribes took preemptive action.* Most accounts point to Enos, a Canadian Indian, as a main advocate for using force. See, e.g., ibid., pp. 173–74.

P. 125 *Ben Wright murdered.* Wright, seen by some as "champion" of the tribes (see, e.g., Carey, *General History of Oregon*, p. 597), has also received criticism for various actions during his career; see, e.g., Schwartz, *The Rogue River Indian War*, p. 71.

P. 125 *"terminating the Rogue river war."* See Walling, *History of Southern Oregon*, p. 276.

P. 125 *"I have said the white men have come."* Joel Palmer, "Notes on a Speech Made at Table Rock Treaty Negotiations," Joel Palmer Papers, AX 057, Doc. 33, *at* Special Collections and University Archives, University of Oregon Libraries, Eugene.

P. 125 *Indians were killed and taken prisoner.* See, e.g., Walling, *History of Southern Oregon*, pp. 279–82; Beckham, *Requiem*, pp. 181–82.

P. 125 *Buchanan decided not to mount his offensive.* See Beckham, *Requiem*, p. 181.

P. 125 *The weather was miserable.* Victor, *The Early Indian Wars*, p. 398.

P. 125 *General Lamerick had 535 troops.* Ibid., pp. 182–83; Walsh, *Indian Battles*, p.11, puts the figure at 545.

P. 126 *"Many Indians had not yet got out of their huts."* Ibid., p. 14 (quoting a report from Kelsay to Lamerick). See also Victor, *The Early Indian Wars*, pp. 401–2.

P. 127 *Fort Lamerick on Big Meadows.* See, e.g., Schwartz, *The Rogue River Indian War*, p. 132.

P. 127 *council at Oak Flat.* See, e.g., Victor, *The Early Indian Wars*, pp. 406–7; Walling, *History of Southern Oregon*, p. 279.

P. 127 *At first, the Indians refused.* See Victor, *The Early Indian Wars*, p. 407; Walling, *History of Southern Oregon*, p. 279; T. O'Donnell, *An Arrow in the Earth*, p. 271.

P. 127 *"You are a great chief. So am I."* Quoted in Victor, *The Early Indian Wars*, p. 407.

P. 128 *Smith was warned by Indian boys.* See Jeffery A. Applen, "Battle of Big Bend," p. 47 (M.A. thesis, Oregon State University, 1998) (quoting Captain A. Smith, "Report of Killed and Wounded, " May 30, 1856 [transcription of letter from the National Archives, *at* M689 Roll 567, Adjutant General's Office file 6839]).

P. 128 *The Battle of Big Bend.* We now know much more about the Battle of Big Bend as the result of a valuable 1998 thesis by Jeffery Applen, a retired Marine lieutenant colonel, for his master's degree at Oregon State University. See Applen, "Battle of Big Bend." He did the most thorough literature search to date, including transcribing handwritten reports, located in the National Archives, from the three commanders of the Battle of Big Bend. Most importantly, he conducted an extensive site survey that included using metal detectors, excavating soils, and digging ammunition out of trees, thus recovering items such as lead bullets, pistol balls, an American smoking pipe, buttons, metal eyelets, and nails. This allowed him to establish all the positions of federal and tribal forces, create detailed maps of the conflict, and reach a number of conclusions including the likelihood, since his survey turned up no evidence of bows and arrows and since no American deaths or injuries were caused by arrows, that the Indians relied primarily or exclusively on firearms. On the probable use of firearms rather than bows and arrows, see ibid., pp. 124–25.

P. 128 *John's warriors began arriving.* See, e.g., Applen, "Battle of Big Bend," p. 138 (quoting Captain Smith, "Report of Killed and Wounded"); Victor, *The Early Indian Wars*, p. 408.

P. 128 *"the iron chief."* Victor, *The Early Indian Wars*, p. 413.

P. 128 *As many as three or four hundred.* See T. O'Donnell, *An Arrow in the Earth*, p. 271 ("three to four hundred men"); Walsh, *Indian Battles*, p. 15 ("150 braves"); Walling, *History of Southern Oregon*, p. 281 (Captain Cram estimated "about 400," but Walling concluded that "two hundred would probably be nearer the mark.").

P. 128 *At about 11:00 in the morning the Indians opened fire.* See Applen, "Battle of Big Bend," p. 49 (quoting from Captain Smith, "Report of Killed and Wounded"). Applen's account of the battle is the most extensive. See ibid., pp. 44–57. See also Beckham, *Requiem*, pp. 186–87.

P. 128 *the Indians had the Americans nearly surrounded.* Applen, "Battle of Big Bend," p. 115.

P. 128 *Both sides take heavy losses.* Ibid., p. 53.

P. 128 *"we will catch and hang you."* T. O'Donnell, *An Arrow in the Earth*, p. 271.

P. 128 *"Hello, Captain Smith!"* LaFayette Grover, *Notable Things in a Public Life in Oregon*, pp. 48–49 (San Francisco, 1878), at Bancroft Collection, Bancroft Library, University of California, Berkeley.

P. 129 *"After 30 hours of fighting."* Applen, "Battle of Big Bend," p. 6.

P. 129 *leaving behind a pile of ropes.* Victor, *The Early Indian Wars*, pp. 410–11.

P. 129 *Indians assemble at Big Bend for surrender.* See chapter 8, pp. 155–56.

P. 130 *attack at Painted Rock Creek.* See Walling, *History of Southern Oregon*, p. 282; Beckham, *Requiem*, pp. 187–88; Hubert Howe Bancroft, vol. 2, *History of Oregon*, p. 419.

P. 130 *Tyee John's people.* See Beckham, *Requiem*, p. 189 ("near Port Orford"); Walsh, Indian Battles, p. 17 ("on Rinehart Creek").

P. 130 *Finally, Tyee John himself walked into the circle.* For the most detailed account of John's surrender, see Victor, *The Early Indian Wars*, p. 414.

7 *The Coast Reservation*

P. 131 *Lane's career after the Table Rock Treaty.* See generally James E. Hendrickson, *Joe Lane of Oregon: Machine Politics and the Sectional Crisis, 1849–1861*, pp. 80–181 (New Haven, CT: Yale University Press, 1967).

P. 132 *Cow Creek Band of Umpquas.* Treaty with the Umpqua–Cow Creek Band, art. 2, Sept. 19, 1853, 10 Stat. 1027 (1854), *in* Kappler, vol. 2, *Indian Affairs*, pp. 606–7.

P. 132 *Tualatin Band of Kalapuyas.* Treaty with the Tualatin Band of Kalapuyas, March 25, 1854 (unratified), *in* Vine Deloria Jr. and Raymond J. DeMallie, eds., vol. 2, *Documents of American Indian Diplomacy: Treaties, Agreements, and Conventions, 1775–1979*, pp. 1306–09 (Norman: University of Oklahoma Press, 1999).

P. 133 *Tualatin Band assured a reservation in the future.* This assurance was made in somewhat oblique terms: "The United States engage to provide and designate a suitable tract of country for the residence of said Band. . . ." Ibid., art. 4. That article, and the third, fifth, sixth, and ninth as well, reference the nature of the future reservation and the actions the United States was to take in creating it.

P. 133 *"Between the Si us Slaw and the Neachasna."* J. Palmer, superintendent of Indian Affairs for Oregon, transcript of report to G. Manypenny, commissioner of Indian Affairs (Sept. 11, 1854), M2 Roll 7, Doc. 9, pp. 6–7, *at* Archival Collection of the Siletz Tribe Cultural Department [hereinafter Siletz Archival Collection].

P. 133 *"An abundance of nutricious grasses."* Ibid., p. 7.

P. 133 *"suited to the colonization."* Ibid., pp. 7–8.

P. 133 *Palmer dispensed with the idea.* In April 1855, Palmer set aside the Coast Reservation temporarily for the coast and valley tribes. See J. Palmer transcript of letter to G. Manypenny (April 17, 1855), M2 Roll 5, Doc. 48 and attachments, *at* Siletz Archival

Collection, see below, p. 137. Then, in November 1855, he set aside the Grand Ronde area for the valley tribes as a temporary encampment that was made permanent in 1857. See J. Palmer transcript of letter to G. Manypenny (Nov. 12, 1855), M2 Roll 5, Doc. 107, *at* Siletz Archival Collection, see below, p. 147.

P. 134 *"It is of great importance."* G. Manypenny transcript of letter to J. Palmer (Aug. 15, 1854), M2 Roll 5, Doc. 7, p. 1, *at* Siletz Archival Collection.

P. 134 *confederation was more efficient.* See, e.g., Francis Paul Prucha, vol. 1, *The Great Father: The United States Government and the American Indians*, p. 401 (Lincoln: University of Nebraska Press, 1984) (stating that most of the Palmer treaties "were made with 'confederated tribes and bands,' an often more or less arbitrary grouping for convenience"). Manypenny also argued that reservations "immediately adjacent" to white settlements would lead to "disturbances of the Peace." G. Manypenny transcript of letter to J. Palmer (Aug. 15, 1854), M2 Roll 5, Doc. 7, p. 1, *at* Siletz Archival Collection. But this argument only supported the creation of remote reservations, not the confederation of tribes on fewer reservations. Palmer explicitly addressed another federal concern, that of financial expense, in his report to Manypenny about the November 15, 1854, treaty negotiations with the Rogue River tribes. J. Palmer transcript of letter to G. Manypenny (Dec. 28, 1854), M2 Roll 5, Doc. 22, p. 1, *at* Siletz Archival Collection.

P. 134 *Tyees Joe, Sam, and John balked.* See Palmer letter to Manypenny (Dec. 28, 1854), M2 Roll 5, Doc. 22, p. 1, *at* Siletz Archival Collection.

P. 134 *The Indian agent pressed on.* Ibid. On the benefits to be provided should the Indians of the Table Rock Reserve agree to allow other tribes to move to the reservation, see Treaty with the Rogue River, art. 2, Nov. 15, 1854, 10 Stat. 1119 (1855), *in* Charles J. Kappler, ed., vol. 2, *Indian Affairs: Laws and Treaties*, pp. 654–55 (Washington, D.C.: Government Printing Office, 1904) [hereinafter Treaty with the Rogue River of 1854].

P. 134 *unfettered federal authority.* Ibid., art. 1 (providing that new tribes may be added "as . . . the President of the United States shall direct").

P. 135 *Shasta, Scotons, and Grave Creek Band.* See Treaty with the Chasta, Etc., Nov. 18, 1854, 10 Stat. 1122 (1855), *in* Kappler, ed., vol. 2, *Indian Affairs*, pp. 655–57. The tribal names in this treaty are confused anthropologically. The treaty refers to the "Chasta tribe," and probably means the Upper Applegate Shasta bands since the treaty was signed by "Ko-ne-che-quot, or Bill," son of Shasta leader Tyee John. The Shasta Tribe had already ceded its land in Oregon, including the Applegate Valley, in the 1853 Table Rock Treaty. Palmer must have had reasons for wanting to reconfirm that cession.

The second grouping in the treaty is several "bands of Scotons." On the location of the village of Scoton described in the text, see Daythal L. Kendall, "Takelma," *in* Wayne Suttles, ed., vol. 7, *Handbook of North American Indians*, pp. 589–92 (Washington, D.C.: Smithsonian Institution, 1990) (designating village #2 on a map of Takelma territory as "skastan," which most likely signifies the village of Scoton). The treaty apparently was intended to cover other Takelma villages in that area.

The third grouping of the treaty is the "Grave Creek band of Umpquas," but the people in the Grave Creek area were Takelmas, not Umpquas. The cession in article 1 includes the Illinois River watershed, where there were several Athapaskan villages. See Dennis J. Gray, "The Takelma and Their Athapascan Neighbors: A New Ethnographic Synthesis for the Upper Rogue River Area of Southwestern Oregon," no. 37

University of Oregon Anthropological Papers, pp. 22–24 (1987) (containing a thorough discussion of the issue and concluding that the permanent settlements in the Illinois Valley were Athapaskan, not Takelman or Shasta). No treaty signers were from that area, although that omission was never challenged.

My thanks to Robert Kentta for his help in untangling these confused provisions. Robert Kentta, interview with author, Nov. 9, 2008, Lincoln City, Oregon; Robert Kentta, email to author, May 4, 2009.

P. 135 *Tribes strenuously objected to being amalgamated.* See J. Palmer transcript of letter to G. Manypenny (Dec. 29, 1854), M2 Roll 5, Doc. 23, p. 1, *at* Siletz Archival Collection.

P. 135 *Treaty with the bands of the middle Umpqua Valley.* Treaty with the Umpqua and Kalapuya, Nov. 29, 1854, 10 Stat. 1125 (1855), *in* Kappler, vol. 2, *Indian Affairs*, pp. 657–60. On federal authority to add more bands to the confederation and move them to the reservation, see ibid., art. 1.

P. 135 *"most difficult task."* J. Palmer transcript of letter to G. Manypenny (Jan. 23, 1855), M2 Roll 5, Doc. 27, p. 2, *at* Siletz Archival Collection.

P. 135 *Palmer had the force of empire on his side.* Treaty with the Kalapuya, Etc., Jan. 22, 1855, 10 Stat. 1143 (1855), *in* Kappler, vol. 2, *Indian Affairs*, pp. 665–69.

P. 136 *7.5 million acres at about 3 cents per acre.* J. Palmer transcript of letter to G. Manypenny (Jan. 23, 1855), M2 Roll 5, Doc. 27, p. 1, *at* Siletz Archival Collection.

P. 136 *largest removal of all, probably to the Coast.* Charles F. Coan, "The Adoption of the Reservation Policy in the Pacific Northwest, 1853–1855," vol. 23, no. 1 *Oregon Historical Quarterly*, p. 17 (March 1922), described the situation in early 1855: "It will be noticed in these treaties that the reservations were temporary. Palmer was instructed to make treaties first with the Indians in the vicinity of the settlements. It was necessary to make the above treaties, therefore, prior to treating with the Coast tribes, in whose cession the proposed Coast Reservation was to be located. The temporary reservations were to continue only until the superintendent was able to make the treaty with the Coast tribes."

P. 136 *American settlement along the Columbia.* See, e.g., William G. Loy et al., *Atlas of Oregon*, pp. 26, 42–43, 64–66, 126–27 (Eugene: University of Oregon Press, 1976).

P. 136 *Yakama Chief Kamiakin.* See Richard D. Scheuerman and Michael O. Finley, *Finding Chief Kamiakin: The Life and Legacy of a Northwest Patriot* (Pullman: Washington State University Press, 2008).

P. 136 *Stevens and Palmer negotiated.* See, e.g., Terrence O'Donnell, *An Arrow in the Earth: General Joel Palmer and the Indians of Oregon*, pp. 195–209 (Portland: Oregon Historical Society Press, 1991); Kent D. Richards, *Isaac I. Stevens: Young Man in a Hurry*, pp. 215–25 (Provo, UT: Brigham Young University Press, 1979).

P. 136 *mid-Columbia treaties.* See Treaty with the WallaWalla, Cayuse, Etc., June 9, 1855, 12 Stat. 945 (1859) (including the Umatilla); Treaty with the Yakima, June 9, 1855, 12 Stat. 951 (1859) (including the Palouse and twelve other tribes and bands); Treaty with the Nez Percés, June 11, 1855, 12 Stat. 957 (1859); Treaty with the Tribes of Middle Oregon, June 25, 1855, 12 Stat. 963 (1859) (including the Warm Springs and Wasco Tribes). All of these treaties are reprinted in Kappler, vol. 2, *Indian Affairs*, pp. 694–706, 714–19.

P. 137 *April 17, 1855, designation of an Indian reservation.* For the formal declaration and Palmer's report to the Department of the Interior in Washington, see J. Palmer transcript of letter to G. Manypenny (April 17, 1855), M2 Roll 5, Doc. 48 and attachments, *at* Siletz Archival Collection.

P. 137 *"I would be pleased."* J. Palmer transcript of letter to O. Waterman, Editor of the *Oregon Weekly Times* (April 17, 1855), M2 Roll 5, Doc. 48, p. 3, *at* Siletz Archival Collection. The *Oregon Weekly Times* printed Palmer's notice a month later. Joel Palmer, "Indian Reservation," *Oregon Weekly Times*, p. 3 (May 19, 1855). Palmer's announcement began, "Notice is hereby given that I have designated as an Indian Reservation, for the coast and Willamette Tribes, and such others as may hereafter be located thereon, the following described district of country." After giving the physical landmarks of the reservation, he went on to say: "The tract described presents few attractions to the white settler, while it is believed to be better adapted for the colonization of the Indians than any other portion of Territory west of the Cascade Mountains affording so few facilities of settlement to our citizens.

The object of this notice is to inform the public that this Reservation will not be subject to settlement by whites."

P. 137 *setting aside the coastal lands had caused little stir.* J. Palmer transcript of letter to G. Manypenny (July 10, 1855), M2 Roll 5, Doc. 68, p. 1, *at* Siletz Archival Collection.

P. 137 *Know Nothing allegation.* See T. O'Donnell, *An Arrow in the Earth*, pp. 187–92.

P. 138 *shipment of goods.* See J. Palmer transcript of letter to G. Manypenny (July 10, 1855), M2 Roll 5, Doc. 68, pp. 1–2, *at* Siletz Archival Collection; J. Palmer transcript of letter to E. Drew, Indian sub-agent (July 13, 1855), M2 Roll 5, Doc. 71, *at* Siletz Archival Collection; C. Taylor transcript of letter to S. Snow and Co. (July 20, 1855), M2 Roll 5, Doc. 76, *at* Siletz Archival Collection.

P. 138 *He would establish by treaty.* Treaty with the Indians along the Oregon Coast, Aug. 11, 17, 23, 30 and Sept. 8, 1855, art. 1 (unratified), *in* Deloria and DeMallie, vol. 2, *Documents of American Indian Diplomacy*, pp. 1320–28.

P. 138 *Palmer's cavalcade of three pack trains.* See transcription of John Flett Papers [hereinafter John Flett Papers], MS 120, Box 1, Folder 36 [1st stapled group folder], pp. 15–16, Washington Historical Society, Olympia, Washington, *at* Siletz Archival Collection.

P. 139 *council at Yaquina Bay.* See J. Palmer transcript of letter to G. Manypenny (July 10, 1855), M2 Roll 5, Doc. 68, p. 2, *at* Siletz Archival Collection.

P. 139 *Forty-one tyees.* In the treaty, Palmer identified two Tillamook bands, the Siletz and Salmon ("Ne-a-ches-na"). He wrongly identified the Alsea and Yaquina ("Yah-quo-na") as bands of Tillamooks. The Alseas and Yaquinas are from a separate language group, the Alsean.

P. 139 *"Some old Indians."* Beverly Ward, *White Moccasins*, p. 51 (Myrtle Point, OR: Myrtle Point Printing, 1986).

P. 139 *"If we have a bad man."* Joel Palmer, "Council Convened 3PM on the 23rd August," Joel Palmer Papers, AX 057, Doc. 32, *at* University of Oregon Special Collections.

P. 139 *Tututni and Chetco council.* Palmer's papers include a short document entitled "Myrtle Grove Council," which appears to be notes recounting brief statements and questions by tyees and Palmer's responses. In this account, most of the tyees expressed a willingness to go to the reservation. See Joel Palmer, "Myrtle Grove Council," Joel Palmer Papers, AX 057, Doc. 34, *at* University of Oregon Special Collections.

P. 139 *"The council ground."* R. Glisan, *Journal of Army Life*, p. 241 (San Francisco: A. L. Bancroft and Co., 1874).

P. 139 *Dr. Glisan reported 1,200 Indians in attendance.* Ibid., p. 245.

P. 140 *"You say you take us Willamette."* Lionel Youst and William Seaburg, *Coquelle*

Thompson: Athabaskan Witness, pp. 36–37 (Norman: University of Oklahoma Press, 2002) (quoting Coquelle Thompson in a 1935 interview with anthropologist Elizabeth Jacobs).

P. 141 *Confusion over establishing a reservation.* Manypenny forwarded Palmer's agreement with the Coast Indians and the map of the proposed reservation to the interior secretary on October 29, 1855. G. Manypenny transcript of letter to R. McClelland, secretary of the Interior (Oct. 29, 1855), M348 Roll 9, Doc. 3, *at* Siletz Archival Collection. The Interior secretary did not receive the signed treaty, however, until after the reservation had been established by executive order. See G. Manypenny transcript of letter to R. McClelland (Feb. 5, 1857), M348 Roll 10, Doc. 9, *at* Siletz Archival Collection. Most likely, because the reservation was in place and covered approximately the same land area, there may have been a sense that no further action was needed.

P. 141 *the Coast Treaty sat in the Interior department for 15 months.* Much later, in 1893, the Senate asked the interior secretary to look into the matter. The given reason for the delay in the Interior department was that the treaty was "accidentally overlooked." The treaty was formally sent to the Senate on February 11, 1857. F. Armstrong, acting commissioner of Indian Affairs, letter to H. Smith, secretary of the Interior (Oct. 5, 1893), *in* Senate Doc. No. 25, "Letter from the Secretary of the Interior, transmitting copies of treaties between the United States and certain Indians in Oregon, in response to Senate resolution of September 2, 1893," 53d Congress, 1st Session, p. 3 (Washington, D.C.: Government Printing Office, 1894).

P. 141 *treaty had been "overlooked."* See G. Manypenny transcript of letter to R. McClelland (Feb. 5, 1857), M348 Roll 10, Doc. 9, p. 2, *at* Siletz Archival Collection.

P. 141 *Palmer sent treaty and report.* See J. Palmer transcript of letter to G. Manypenny (Oct. 3, 1855), M2 Roll 5, Doc. 92, *at* Siletz Archival Collection.

P. 141 *The treaty package went by slow boat.* On mail service in early Oregon, see Charles H. Carey, vol. 2, *A General History of Oregon: Prior to 1891*, pp. 737–40 (Portland, OR: Metropolitan Press, 1936). In 1853 the Oregon Legislature received just one mail delivery in six weeks. Ibid., p. 738. See also Winther, *The Old Oregon Country*, pp. 141–45 (pronouncing that "throughout the entire prestatehood period the mail service remained abominable. Complaints were constant, bitter, and many"). Ibid., p. 141.

P. 141 *mail took between five weeks and three months..* Manypenny summarized the episodic and confused journey of the Coast Reservation papers in his letter to McClelland on October 29, 1855. See G. Manypenny transcript of letter to R. McClelland (Oct. 29, 1855), M348 Roll 9, Doc. 3, *at* Siletz Archival Collection. Palmer sent his letter delineating the Coast Reservation with the map on April 17. That letter arrived in Washington, D.C., on June 29, but the map did not arrive until July 27. In September, as Palmer was proceeding with the treaty signings along the Coast, the General Land Office had taken up Palmer's cause in Washington, D.C. With only one final accidental stopover in the Pension Office, Manypenny finally compiled the Coast Reservation proposal for Secretary McClelland on October 29, seven months after Palmer sent it.

P. 141 *Palmer's report on the April 17 declaration.* See J. Palmer transcript of letter to G. Manypenny (April 17, 1855), M2 Roll 5, Doc. 48, *at* Siletz Archival Collection.

P. 142 *the map had been delayed.* See C. Mix, Acting Commissioner of Indian Affairs, transcript of letter to J. Palmer (June 29, 1855), M2 Roll 5, Doc. 80, *at* Siletz Archival Collection.

P. 142 *the Interior department advised Palmer.* Ibid.

P. 142 *the Commissioner of the General Land Office recommended.* T. Hendricks, commissioner of the General Land Office, transcript of letter to J. Campbell, acting secretary of the Interior (Sept. 10, 1855), *at* Siletz Archival Collection.

P. 142 *Commissioner Manypenny's full report of October 29.* G. Manypenny transcript of letter to R. McClelland (Oct. 29, 1855), M348 Roll 9, Doc. 3, pp. 1–2, *at* Siletz Archival Collection.

P. 143 *Palmer's request for "a permanent Indian reserve."* J. Palmer transcript of letter to G. Manypenny (April 17, 1855), M2 Roll 5, Doc. 48, *at* Siletz Archival Collection.

P. 143 *Secretary McClelland's recommendation.* R. McClelland letter to President F. Pierce (Nov. 8, 1855), *in* Kappler, ed., vol. 1, *Indian Affairs*, p. 890.

P. 144 *two months before, Palmer and tribal leaders had executed the Coast treaty.* See E. Geary, clerk of superintendent of Indian Affairs for Oregon, transcript of letter to G. Manypenny (Oct. 3, 1855), M2 Roll 5, Doc. 92, *at* Siletz Archival Collection.

P. 144 *treaty arrived just five days after.* See G. Manypenny transcript of letter to R. McClelland (Feb. 5, 1857), M348 Roll 10, Doc. 9, *at* Siletz Archival Collection (treaty and Palmer's report received by Interior Department in Washington, D.C., on Nov. 14, 1855).

P. 144 *"The reservation of the land."* Exec. Order, Nov. 9, 1855, *in* Kappler, vol. 1, *Indian Affairs*, p. 891.

P. 144 *Treaty land is fully owned by the tribe.* While reservation land is held in trust by the Interior department for tribes, the tribes are the owners. See, e.g., United States v. Shoshone Tribe, 304 U.S. 111, 115–16 (1938). On treaty land generally, see Felix S. Cohen's Handbook of Federal Indian Law, *2005*, §15.04(3)(a) (Newark, NJ: LexisNexis, 2005).

P. 144 *Treaty land not subject to unilateral presidential action.* See, e.g., *Minnesota v. Mille Lacs Band of Chippewa Indians*, 526 U.S. 172, 189–90 (1999).

P. 144 *Congressional power to abrogate treaties.* See, e.g., *Lone Wolf v. Hitchcock*, 187 U.S. 553, 566 (1903).

P. 144 *tribe entitled to full compensation. Shoshone Tribe*, 304 U.S. at 115–16.

P. 144 *Stand-alone executive orders are different.* In general, the courts have treated tribal interests in executive order lands as lesser in stature than is the case with treaty lands. See *Sioux Tribe v. United States*, 316 U.S. 317, 326–30 (1942). Additionally, Congress, without affecting existing executive orders, prohibited future presidential executive order reservations in 1919. Ch. 4, §27, June 30, 1919, 41 Stat. 34 (codified at 43 U.S.C. § 150 [2006]). In more recent times, however, Congress has taken a number of actions that have had the effect of providing modern executive order reservations with most or all of the protections afforded treaty reservations. See generally Cohen, *Handbook of Federal Indian Law, 2005* §15.04(4); Prucha, vol. 2, *The Great Father*, pp. 887–88.

P. 144 *"subject to termination at the will of the executive or Congress." Sioux Tribe*, 316 U.S. at 331.

P. 144 *Land not subject to compensation under the Fifth Amendment.* See ibid., pp. 330–31. Cases brought by tribes under the Indian Claims Commission Act of 1946 did allow for compensation for federal takings of executive order land but, unlike treaty land, no interest could be awarded. See, e.g., Howard M. Friedman, "Interest on Indian Claims: Judicial Protection of the Fisc," vol. 5 Valparaiso University Law Review, pp. 26–47

(1970). Again, Congress and administrative practices in recent years have softened these rules. See, e.g., Cohen, Handbook of Federal Indian Law, *2005*, §15.09(1)(d)(iii).

P. 145 *McClelland's brief and seriously flawed letter.* See text and accompanying note, pp. 143–44 above.

P. 145 *McClelland misquoted Manypenny's letter.* See text and accompanying note, pp. 143–44 above.

P. 145 *Executive orders creating Indian reservations used only three times.* See Exec. Order, May 14, 1855, reprinted in Kappler, vol. 1, *Indian Affairs*, p. 847 (Isabella Reserve, Chippewa); Exec. Order, Aug. 9, 1855, *in* Kappler, vol. 1, *Indian Affairs*, p. 850 (Ottawa and Chippewa Reserves); Exec. Order, Sept. 25, 1855, *in* Kappler, vol. 1, *Indian Affairs*, p. 849 (Ontonagon Reserve). As a result of the new use of executive orders and the unique provisions of the ratified Oregon treaties, Secretary McClelland—and others then and later—may have been confounded by the new and unique junction of four lines of action that seem to have been available to the Interior department and the president: administrative ratification of Palmer's temporary withdrawal on April 17 of land for Indian purposes pending the creation of a permanent reservation; approval of Palmer's actual request, which was for a permanent reservation; use of the president's recently exercised power to create executive order reservations, which could be conditional; and exercise of the president's authority to establish only permanent reservations under the Oregon treaties.

P. 145 *Reservations can be altered or terminated.* See *Lone Wolf*, 187 U.S. at 566.

P. 146 *Table Rock Treaty of 1853.* Treaty with the Rogue River, art. 2, Sept. 10, 1853, 10 Stat. 1018 (1854), *in* Kappler, vol. 2, *Indian Affairs*, pp. 603–5.

P. 146 *Cow Creek Band of Umpqua Treaty.* Treaty with the Umpqua–Cow Creek Band, art. 2, Sept. 19, 1853, 10 Stat. 1027 (1854), *in* Kappler, vol. 2, *Indian Affairs*, pp. 606–7.

P. 146 *other five ratified treaties.* The Treaty with the Rogue River of 1854, which was made with the original Table Rock tribes, was not itself a land treaty but is important in the "permanent reservation" context. The Table Rock tribes agreed that other tribes could be removed to the Table Rock Reserve, stating in Article 1 that these additional tribes in the confederation "shall enjoy equal rights and privileges with the Rogue River Tribe." This certainly includes the right in the 1853 treaty, upon removal, to be assured of a "permanent residence." Under the Treaty with Chasta, Etc., Nov. 18, 1854, 10 Stat. 1122 (1855), negotiated just three days later, the Shasta, Scoton, and Grave Creek Umpqua had the right to a permanent residence under the 1853 treaty since these newly confederated tribes possessed "equal rights and privileges with the Rogue River tribe." The Treaty with the Umpqua and Kalapuya, Nov. 29, 1854, 10 Stat. 1125 (1855), does not use the "permanent residence" language, but Article 1 does provide for removal and the construction of "permanent improvements on the new reserve." Article 1 of the comprehensive treaty with the Willamette Valley tribes, Treaty with the Kalapuya, Etc., Jan. 22, 1855, 10 Stat. 1143 (1855), provided for a "permanent home" upon removal from the temporary reservation. Article 3 of the Treaty with the Molala, Dec. 21, 1855, 12 Stat. 981 (1859), provided for removal to the tract that would become the Grand Ronde Reservation in 1857 and then for removal "to said coast reservation, or such other point as may, by direction of the President of the United States, be designated as their permanent residence." All treaties listed can be found in Kappler, vol. 2, *Indian Affairs*, pp. 654–55 (Rogue River), 655–57 (Chasta), 657–60 (Umpqua and Kalapuya), 665–69 (Kalapuya), 740–42 (Molala).

P. 146 *Ambiguities interpreted in favor of the tribes.* On interpretation generally, see Cohen, Handbook of Federal Indian Law, *2005*, §2.02; United States v. Dion, 476 U.S. 734, 738–39 (1986) ("We have required that Congress' intention to abrogate Indian treaty rights be clear and plain. . . . Indian treaty rights are too fundamental to be easily cast aside."); Mille Lacs Band of Chippewa Indians, 526 U.S. at 196–97 (treaty's silence on hunting and fishing rights "likely not accidental" since negotiations and agreement were limited to the land); see, e.g., Arizona v. California, 373 U.S. 546, 598 (1963); Antoine v. Washington, 420 U.S. 194, 205–6 (1975).

P. 146 *"satisfied of the futility."* J. Palmer transcript of letter to G. Manypenny (Nov. 12, 1855), M2 Roll 5, Doc. 107, p. 1, *at* Siletz Archival Collection.

P. 147 *establishment of the Grand Ronde Reservation in 1857.* Palmer reported in November 1855 that he had obtained from settlers the land that would be used for the encampment. J. Palmer, transcript of letter to J. Astoria (Nov. 26, 1855), M2 Roll 5, Doc. 133, *at* Siletz Archival Collection. However, he never completed the job of submitting the papers to the Interior department in Washington, D.C., and having the area declared a reservation. As commissioner of Indian Affairs, Denver explained, "For want of a map, and specific boundaries, and probably the matter not having been specifically noticed thereafter, I find that this subject has never been presented for the consideration of the Secretary and the Executive." J. Denver, transcript of letter to J. Thompson, secretary of the Interior (May 1, 1857), M348 Roll 10, Doc. 13, *at* Siletz Archival Collection [hereinafter Commissioner Denver letter to Secretary Thompson]. As discussed in the text, President Buchanan then proclaimed the reservation.

P. 147 *"extension" of the Coast Reservation.* See, e.g., ibid.

P. 147 *"the key to the entrance."* J. Palmer transcript of letter to G. Manypenny (Nov. 12, 1855), M2 Roll 5, Doc. 107, p. 2, *at* Siletz Archival Collection.

P. 147 *"the treaty provisions with the Willamette tribes."* Commissioner Denver letter to Secretary Thompson.

P. 147 *"particularly for the Willamette tribes."* J. Thompson letter to President J. Buchanan (June 30, 1857), *in* Kappler, vol. 1, *Indian Affairs*, p. 886.

P. 147 *President Buchanan proclaimed.* Exec. Order, June 30, 1857, *in* Kappler, vol. 1, *Indian Affairs*, p. 886.

P. 148 *Knowledgeable figures treated the reservation as permanent.* See Commissioner Denver letter to Secretary Thompson; J. Nesmith, superintendent of Indian Affairs for Oregon and Washington Territories, report to C. Mix, commissioner of Indian Affairs (Aug. 20, 1858), *in* House Doc. No. 2, 1859 Commissioner Report, 35th Congress, 2d Session, p. 568 ("a permanent home for the Indians"). Additionally, Manypenny was prompted to finally forward the treaties to Secretary McClelland in early 1857, when the superintendent of the reservation requested that the government provide the funds and services the Coast tribes had agreed to in 1855. See G. Manypenny transcript of letter to R. McClelland (Feb. 5, 1857), M348 Roll 10, Doc. 9, *at* Siletz Archival Collection.

P. 148 *Joseph Lane developed a bill.* Lane's bill passed the Senate and was presented in the House on March 20, 1860. The *Congressional Globe*, April 4, 1860, 36th Congress, 1st Session, vol. 29, no. 94, p. 1491 (Washington, D.C.: John C. Rives, 1860) reported that the bill was ordered to be printed by the House on April 2, 1860. There is no explanation for why the bill stalled out just before being passed, though it may have been related to the imminent Civil War.

P. 148 *"the Indians inhabiting said tract."* On March 19, the full bill passed in the Senate (S. 142, 36th Congress, 1st Session, 1860). The text reads:

> Whereas, by a treaty entered into on tenth of September, eighteen hundred and fifty-three, between the government of the United States and the Rogue River tribe of Indians in Oregon, it was stipulated that said tribe of Indians should be allowed to occupy temporarily a certain tract or district of territory described in the second article of said treaty, said tract to be deemed and considered an Indian reserve until a suitable selection should be made, under the direction of the President of the United States, for their permanent residence; and whereas such selection was made in the year eighteen hundred and fifty-five, and the Indians inhabiting said tract temporarily set apart for their use were removed to the Grand Ronde and Siletz reserves, which had been selected for their permanent residence; and whereas certain individuals, citizens of the United States, have settled upon and improved a portion of the tract described in the second article of said treaty of tenth September, eighteen hundred and fifty-three, and still reside thereon, or who were compelled to abandon the same to the use of the Indians as part of their reserve:

> Therefore—

> Be it enacted by the Senate and the House of Representatives of the United States of America in Congress assembled, That every such settler upon said tract, who now resides, or has settled and resided upon and cultivated the same . . . in good faith . . . be allowed to purchase the same. . . .

In 1862, letters from the General Land Office to the Bureau of Indian Affairs confirmed that the former Table Rock Reserve was no longer needed for Indian purposes. See J. Edmunds, commissioner of the General Land Office, letter to W. Dole, commissioner of Indian Affairs (May 5, 1862), *at* Siletz Archival Collection ("in view of [the Table Rock Indian reserve] having been abandoned the lands comprised within the same will be merged into the public domain"); J. Edmunds letter to B. Pengra, surveyor general for Oregon (May 10, 1862), *at* Siletz Archival Collection. For Lane's reasons for introducing S. 142, see vol. 29, no. 190 *Congressional Globe*, June 16, 1860, 36th Congress, 1st Session, p. 3032 (Washington, D.C.: John C. Rives, 1860).

8 Trails of Tears

P. 149 *The uprooting of some 4,000 western Oregon Indians.* In September 1857, Superintendent of Indian Affairs for Oregon James Nesmith wrote in his annual report to the commissioner that there were 3,939 western Oregon Indians on reservations—2,049 at Siletz, 1,200 at Grand Ronde, and 690 at Fort Umpqua (at the mouth of the Umpqua River, near the southern boundary of the Siletz Reservation). Most of these people had been removed from distant points while others—some of those at Grand Ronde and most of those at Fort Umpqua—were within fifty miles of their aboriginal homes. All, however, had been displaced, moved to a new residence, and, as Nesmith put it in his report, "dependent on the government for their support." See J. Nesmith, superintendent of Indian Affairs for Oregon, letter to J. Denver, commissioner of

Indian Affairs (Sept. 1, 1857), *in* Senate Doc. No. 11, 1858 Commissioner Report, 35th Congress, 1st Session, p. 606.

P. 149   *"For my own part my heart is sick."* Statement of Tyee John, in U.S. Department of the Interior, "Report on the condition of the Indian reservations in the Territories of Oregon and Washington, from J. Ross Browne, special agent," in House Doc. No. 39, "Letter from the Secretary of the Interior, Transmitting, In compliance with the resolution of the House of Representatives of the 19th instant, the report of J. Browne, special agent, on the subject of Indian affairs in the Territories of Oregon and Washington," 35th Congress, 1st Session, p. 45 (Nov. 17, 1857) (Washington, D.C.: Government Printing Office, 1858) [hereinafter Browne Report].

P. 149   *"Let us go back to our homes."* Statement of Tyee George, *in* Browne Report, pp. 45–46.

P. 149   *"I think we have been here long enough."* Statement of Tyee Jim, *in* Browne Report, p. 46.

P. 150   *Ki-Ya-Na-Ha, "who lived in the beautiful Rogue River Valley."* Statement of Pauline Bell Ricks, *in* Hearings Before the Senate Committee on Interior and Insular Affairs, Subcommittee on Indian Affairs, "Siletz Restoration Act: On S. 2801," 94th Congress, 2d Session, pp. 123, 125 (March 30–31, 1976) (Washington D.C.: Government Printing Office, 1976) [hereinafter Siletz Restoration Hearings].

P. 151   *Palmer began planning for removal.* See, e.g., L. Lea, commissioner of Indian Affairs, report to A. Stuart, secretary of the Interior (Nov. 27, 1850), in Senate Doc. No. 1, 1853 Commissioner Report, 31st Congress, 2d Session, p. 36; J. Palmer, superintendent of Indian Affairs for Oregon, transcript of letter to G. Manypenny, commissioner of Indian Affairs (June 23, 1853), M2 Roll 11, Doc. 87, at Archival Collection of the Siletz Tribe Cultural Department [hereinafter Siletz Archival Collection] ("a home, remote from the settlements must be selected for them"). See also discussion of Palmer's reservation plan in chapter 5, pp. 95–96.

P. 152   *Little Butte Creek massacre.* See J. Palmer transcript of letter to J. Wool, major general commanding Pacific Division (Dec. 6, 1855), M2 Roll 5, Doc. 123, *at* Siletz Archival Collection; J. Palmer transcript of letter to G. Manypenny (Nov. 12, 1855), M2 Roll 5, Doc. 107, *at* Siletz Archival Collection.

P. 152   *"this war has been forced upon these Indians."* J. Palmer transcript of letter to J. Wool (Dec. 6, 1855), M2 Roll 5, Doc. 123, at Siletz Archival Collection.

P. 152   *Government purchase of homesteads from settlers.* J. Palmer transcript of letter to G. Manypenny (Nov. 12, 1855), M2 Roll 5, Doc. 107, at Siletz Archival Collection. See also p. 432, "establishment of a Grand Ronde Reservation in 1857."

P. 152   *Palmer also envisioned.* J. Palmer transcript of letter to G. Manypenny (Nov. 12, 1855), M2 Roll 5, Doc. 107, *at* Siletz Archival Collection. See chapter 7, pp. 146–47.

P. 153   *"Winter with all its severity."* G. Ambrose, Indian agent, transcript of letter to J. Palmer (Dec. 2, 1855), M2 Roll 5, Doc. 128, *at* Siletz Archival Collection (underline in original).

P. 153   *close to 400 Indians set out.* The sources of the Table Rock removal are few, consisting of Ambrose's journal and correspondences from Palmer and Ambrose. The journal, the most elucidating, is written in the clipped style of an administrative memorandum and has entries, many brief, for almost every day of the month-long trip (Feb. 22–March 25). G. Ambrose transcript of "Journal of the removal of the Rogue River Tribe of Indians, etc.," M2 Roll 14, Doc 15, at Siletz Archival Collection [hereinafter Ambrose Journal]. It has also been reprinted, with useful comments, in Stephen Dow

Beckham, "Trail of Tears: 1856 Diary of Indian Agent George Ambrose," vol. 2 Southern Oregon Heritage, p. 16 (Summer 1996).

P. 153 *the going was slow, sloggy, and fatiguing.* Ambrose Journal, pp. 1–2.

P. 153 *"Our teams now numbered eight."* Ibid., p. 1.

P. 153 *the number of sick people increased.* Ibid., p. 5.

P. 153 *Indians and Ambrose "in constant alarm."* See G. Ambrose transcript of letter to J. Palmer (Jan. 31, 1856), M2 Roll 14, Doc. 8, *at* Siletz Archival Collection (Indians "in constant alarm" over violence during the proposed removal); G. Ambrose transcript of letter to J. Palmer (Feb. 24, 1856), M2 Roll 14, Doc 12, *at* Siletz Archival Collection.

P. 153 *Timcolean Love killed an Indian man.* See G. Ambrose transcript of letter to J. Palmer (Feb. 27, 1856), M2 Roll 14, Doc. 13, *at* Siletz Archival Collection (giving a description of the shooting); Ambrose Journal, p. 1.

P. 154 *Smith ordered Love arrested.* Ambrose Journal, pp. 1–3. Ambrose's journal entry of March 10 shows that Love had been taken into custody. Ibid., pp. 3–4.

P. 154 *reached level, open space of the Willamette Valley.* See ibid., pp. 4–5.

P. 154 *Thirty-three days, 263 miles.* Ibid., p. 5.

P. 154 *The journey had taken eight lives..* Ibid. ("Eight deaths and Eight births, leaving the number the same as when started.").

P. 154 *"I will not be surprised."* N. Ford transcript of letter to G. Ambrose, Indian agent (Dec. 18, 1855), M2 Roll 14 Doc. 1, at Siletz Archival Collection. See also Terence O'Donnell, An Arrow in the Earth: General Joel Palmer and the Indians of Oregon, p. 235 (Portland: Oregon Historical Society Press, 1991).

P. 154 *Joel Palmer spent three days urging them to leave.* John Flett's papers include quite a detailed account of the Umpqua removal, describing weather conditions and local hostility among the whites. See Transcription of John Flett Papers [hereinafter John Flett Papers], MS 120, Box 1, Folder 35 [2nd stapled group folder], pp. 4–16, Washington Historical Society, Olympia, Washington, *at* Siletz Archival Collection.

P. 154 *"heavy storm of rain and snow."* Hubert Howe Bancroft, vol. 2, *History of Oregon*, p. 398n3 (San Francisco: The History Co., 1888).

P. 154 *The Umpquas' "ordeal lasted nearly a month."* See T. O'Donnell, *An Arrow in the Earth*, pp. 251–52 (citing a letter from Joseph Jeffers to Joel Palmer, dated Feb. 7, 1856).

P. 154 *"to the extent that it makes humanity shudder."* Ibid., p. 252 (quoting Joseph Jeffers's letter to Joel Palmer).

P. 155 *"owing to the nature of the Country."* J. Palmer transcript of letter to G. Manypenny (July 3, 1856), M2 Roll 6, Doc. 49, p. 5, *at* Siletz Archival Collection.

P. 155 *It took soldiers five difficult days.* Captain E. O. C. Ord took five days to march a group from Big Bend to the mouth of Rogue—June 10, 11, 13, 14, and 15, with a layover of one day at the mouth of the Illinois River on June 12. Captain Ord's granddaughter, Ellen Francis Ord, transcribed and notated his diary as part of her master's degree thesis. Ellen Francis Ord, "The Rogue River Indian expedition of 1856 (Diary by Capt. E.O.C. Ord, 3rd Art. U.S. Army, with Introduction and Editorial Notes)," pp. 60–63, M.A. thesis, University of California (1922) [hereinafter Ord Diary].

P. 155 *The Indian warriors retreated.* See discussion in chapter 6, pp. 128–29.

P. 155 *Captain E.O.C. Ord's account.* Ord Diary, pp. 22–83.

P. 155 *hundreds straggled into camp.* Ord did not systematically calculate the number of Indians but made references to incoming Indians on several days. See, e.g., Ord Diary, pp. 54–59.

P. 155   *"the never-ending melancholy wail."* Ibid., p. 58. On the night of June 12, Ord wrote
again of the women's wailing. Ibid., p. 62.

P. 156   *"4 men 9 squaws and some children."* Ibid., pp. 58–59.

P. 156   *Ord led 100 Indians down the river.* See ibid., p. 62.

P. 156   *600 Indians in a temporary camp at Oak Flat.* J. Palmer transcript of letter to G.
Manypenny (July 3, 1856), M2 Roll 6, Doc. 49, p. 5, *at* Siletz Archival Collection ("on
the morning of the 12th 421 Indians had joined Capt. Augur's Camp this with the 227
made an aggregate of 708 Souls"). Ord's group of 100 Indians was in the camp on the
12th, so apparently there were about 600 other Indians there.

P. 156   *encampment of about 165 at Gold Beach.* Ord Diary, p. 64.

P. 156   *"Indn women packing the mules."* Ibid., p. 67.

P. 156   *1,100 Indians were marched in.* R. Glisan, *Journal of an Army Doctor*, p. 345 (San
Francisco: A. L. Bancroft and Co., 1874).

P. 157   *Tensions ran high.* See, e.g., J. Palmer transcript of letter to G. Manypenny (July 3,
1856), M2 Roll 6, Doc. 49, pp. 4–5, *at* Siletz Archival Collection.

P. 157   *"What was the poor Indian to do but go?"* Marjorie H. Hays, *The Land That Kept Its
Promise: A History of South Lincoln County*, p. 34 (Newport, OR: Lincoln County
Historical Society, 1976) (quoting George Thompson, "The Story of Siletz," *Waldport
Record* [March 9, 1950]) [hereinafter George Thompson's account of Coquelle Thompson's stories, *in* Hays, *The Land That Kept Its Promise*]. In this excerpted newspaper
article, a sixth-grader George Thompson, the grandson of Coquelle Thompson,
transcribed his father's dictation of Coquelle's remembrances. Lionel Youst and William R. Seaburg, *Coquelle Thompson, Athabaskan Witness*, p. 58 (Norman: University
of Oklahoma Press, 2002). The George Thompson account is consistent with other
renditions given by Coquelle Thompson during his long life (ca. 1849–1946).

P. 157   *Ki-Ya-Na-Ha"began to cry."* Siletz Restoration Hearings, p. 124.

P. 157   *The steamship* Columbia. Glisan, *Journal of an Army Doctor*, p. 346.

P. 157   *The goliath was 200 feet long.* E. W. Wright, ed., *Lewis and Dryden's Marine History of
the Pacific Northwest*, pp. 35–36 (New York: Antiquarian Press, 1961) (describing the
Columbia); Youst and Seaburg, *Coquelle Thompson, Athabaskan Witness*, pp. 43–49
(Youst and Seaburg do a fine job of describing the *Columbia* and the journey north).
On early steamships generally, see Erik Heyl, *Early American Steamers*, 6 vols. (Buf-
falo, NY: Erik Heyl, 1953–1969).

P. 157   *Rumors spread.* See Youst and Seaburg, *Coquelle Thompson, Athabaskan Witness*, p.
44; George Thompson's account of Coquelle Thompson's stories, *in* Hays, *The Land
That Kept Its Promise*, p. 34.

P. 157   *Palmer promised to accompany them.* J. Palmer transcript of letter to G. Manypenny
(July 3, 1856), M2 Roll 6, Doc. 49, p. 7, *at* Siletz Archival Collection.

P. 157   *The boarding was rushed and chaotic.* "They were put on board in a hurry." Ibid., p. 6.

P. 158   *"they lost all their belongings."* Lillie Butler, interview with author, Siletz, Oregon,
Feb. 7, 2007.

P. 158   *"We left behind many fine canoes."* George Thompson's account of Coquelle Thompson's stories, *in* Hays, *The Land That Kept Its Promise*, p. 34.

P. 158   *the* Columbia *rumbled away from Port Orford.* Contrary to an earlier, lower estimate,
Palmer's final count was "seven hundred and ten souls (199 Men 266 Women 127 Boys,
118 Girls ninety five of the boys & girls are infants)." J. Palmer transcript of letter to G.
Manypenny (July 3, 1856), M2 Roll 6, Doc. 49, p. 6, *at* Siletz Archival Collection.

P. 158 *"many of the Indians got seasick."* George Thompson's account of Coquelle Thompson's stories, *in* Hays, *The Land That Kept Its Promise*, p. 34.

P. 158 Columbia's *average passenger load was 100.* Wright, ed., *Lewis and Dryden's Marine History*, p. 35n7. In its first five years the *Columbia* made 102 trips and carried 10,000 customers.

P. 158 *"It turned out to be a terrible voyage."* T. O'Donnell, *An Arrow in the Earth*, p. 274.

P. 160 *"Now everybody is glad."* Youst and Seaburg, *Coquelle Thompson*, p. 48 (quoting Thompson's interview with Elizabeth D. Jacobs in 1935).

P. 160 *Reaching Portland on June 23, passage to Dayton.* J. Palmer transcript of letter to G. Manypenny (June 23, 1856), M2 Roll 6, Doc. 45, *at* Siletz Archival Collection; J. Palmer transcript of letter to R. Buchanan (June 24, 1856), M2 Roll 6, Doc. 46, *at* Siletz Archival Collection; J. Palmer transcript of letter to G. Manypenny (July 3, 1856), M2 Roll 6, Doc 49, p. 6, *at* Siletz Archival Collection.

P. 160 *Courtney Walker led the procession.* On Palmer's instructions to Walker, see J. Palmer transcript of letter to C. Walker, Indian Agent (July 13, 1856), M2 Roll 6, Doc. 53, *at* Siletz Archival Collection. On Courtney Walker, see Howard McKinley Corning, ed., *Dictionary of Oregon History*, p. 256 (Portland, OR: Binford & Mort, 1989).

P. 160 *The group headed out on July 14.* J. Palmer transcript of letter to W. Raymond, Indian Agent (July, 13, 1856), M2 Roll 6, Doc. 54, *at* Siletz Archival Collection; J. Palmer transcript of letter to A. Smith, Captain (July 14, 1856), M2 Roll 6, Doc 56, *at* Siletz Archival Collection.

P. 160 *1,500 already camped at Grand Ronde.* J. Palmer transcript of letter to R. Buchanan (June 24, 1856), M2 Roll 6, Doc. 46, *at* Siletz Archival Collection.

P. 160 *Encampment the largest population center in Oregon.* See U.S. Department of the Interior, Superintendent of the Census, "Population of the United States in 1860; Compiled from the Original Returns of the Eighth Census," p. 403 (Washington, D.C.: Government Printing Office, 1864) (reporting that North Salem had a population of 625, and South Salem 902, so that the total Salem population in 1860 was 1,527). Oregon's population, however, was surging in the 1850s and Salem's size in 1856 would have been considerably lower than the figure for 1860. See also Leslie M. Scott, "Gold Brings Immigration, Civilization Soon Follows," vol. 2, no. 7 Historical Gazette, p. 1 (1993) (stating that the population of Portland in 1857 was 1,280 persons). Jacksonville was at about the same level. See chapter 4, pp. 80–81.

P. 160 *"this Indian boy received his first lesson."* Ben Maxwell, "Coquille Thompson of Old Siletz 'Remembers When,' " *The Oregon Sunday Journal* (Nov. 28, 1937).

P. 161 *Ki-Ya-Na-Ha and Coquelle Thompson.* Statement of Pauline Bell Ricks, Siletz Restoration Hearings, p. 125.

P. 161 *first arrivals to the Coast Reservation.* Youst and Seaburg, *Coquelle Thompson*, p. 51.

P. 161 *729 Indians on the second voyage.* J. Palmer transcript to G. Manypenny (July 18, 1856), M2 Roll 6, Doc. 59, *at* Siletz Archival Collection (reporting 729 Indians on second *Columbia* voyage—a higher figure than the initial estimate). This second group stayed only a few days at Dayton and departed on July 18, whereas the first group had lain over for more than two weeks—thus the short period of time between the arrivals at Salmon River of the first and second groups. Ibid.

P. 161 *Coquelle Thompson rejoiced in the mussels.* George Thompson's account of Coquelle Thompson's stories, *in* Hays, *The Land That Kept Its Promise*, p. 34; Youst and Seaburg, *Coquelle Thompson*, p. 51.

P. 161   *Palmer decided on the site for the new reservation's headquarters.* On July 18, Palmer left to inspect the Siletz Valley. J. Palmer transcript of letter to G. Manypenny (July 18, 1856), M2 Roll 6, Doc. 59, *at* Siletz Archival Collection. Palmer began exploring the "Celetz" River on July 23. See Transcript of Joel Palmer Diary for 1856, p. 13, *at* Oregon State Library, Salem. On July 25, his short entry explains a key reason for his choice of the reservation's location: "On the north side of [the Siletz] river is a brush prairie of about 1500 acres. Several prairies passed along the trail . . . prairies, surrounded by mountains, well adapted for settling. Here will doubtless be a military post." Ibid. Thus, he decided on the upper prairies, near the town of Siletz, as the best site "to settle an extensive Colony of Indians." J. Palmer transcript of letter to D. Jones, Captain (July 28, 1856), M2 Roll 6, Doc. 60, *at* Siletz Archival Collection.

P. 164   *Tyee John had been all the talk.* See, e.g., J. Palmer transcript of letter to G. Manypenny (June 23, 1856), M2 Roll 6, Doc. 45, at Siletz Archival Collection; J. Palmer transcript of letter to G. Manypenny (July 3, 1856), M2 Roll 6, Doc. 49, p. 1, at Siletz Archival Collection; J. Rinearson, Indian Agent, transcript of letter to J. Palmer (July 30, 1856), M2 Roll 14, Doc. 20, at Siletz Archival Collection; Ord Diary, pp. 72–73; Glisan, Journal of an Army Doctor, pp. 344–50 ("the famous Old John and his band, the terror of Southern Oregon.")

P. 164   *John and his men would not be prosecuted.* See, e.g., Frances Fuller Victor, *The Early Indian Wars of Oregon*, p. 414 (Salem, OR: Frank C. Baker, State Printer, 1894).

P. 164   *The steamship was cheaper and quicker.* See J. Palmer transcript of letter to G. Manypenny (July 3, 1856), M2 Roll 6, Doc. 49, pp. 6–7, *at* Siletz Archival Collection. Ibid., p. 7.

P. 164   *Chetco and Pistol River groups also forced to march.* See R. Buchanan transcript of letter to J. Palmer (July 4, 1856), M2 Roll 14, Doc. 19, *at* Siletz Archival Collection.

P. 164   *Thompson's father, an Upper Coquille tyee.* See William Ronald Seaburg, "Collecting Culture: The Practice and Ideology of Salvage Ethnography in Western Oregon, 1877–1942," p. 209, Ph.D. diss., University of Washington (1994) (citing Elizabeth D. Jacobs's 1935 recorded interview with Coquelle Thompson).

P. 164   *This throng set out on July 10, 1856.* Rodney Glisan, an army doctor, was in Port Orford at the time and reported in detail on the expedition. Glisan, *Journal of an Army Doctor,* pp. 349–50. Beckham, without citation, reports that 215 Indians were marched north. Stephen Beckham, *The Indians of Western Oregon: This Land Was Theirs,* p. 144 (Coos Bay, OR: Arago Books, 1977).

P. 165   *"people who came overland had to drive cattle."* Seaburg, "Collecting Culture," p. 209 (citing Elizabeth D. Jacobs's 1935 recorded interview with Coquelle Thompson).

P. 165   *"The number of Indians."* J. Palmer transcript of letter to G. Manypenny (Jan. 6, 1856), M2 Roll 6, Doc. 7, *at* Siletz Archival Collection.

P. 165   *an ordeal of about one month.* J. Palmer transcript of letter to G. Manypenny (July 3, 1856), M2 Roll 6, Doc. 49, p. 6, *at* Siletz Archival Collection.

P. 165   *No known journals or field notes by soldiers.* My research assistants and I went to great lengths to obtain military records of the Rogue River War, including the Trail of Tears march north, but uncovered very little. On October 28, 2009, Matt Samelson had a lengthy telephone discussion with Jeffrey Applen, military historian and author of the fine account, "Battle of Big Bend" (M.A. thesis, Oregon State University, 1998). In doing that research and searching for documents on the removal north as well as the battle itself, Applen faced the same frustrations that we did, although he did manage to retrieve from the Smithsonian some handwritten documents (which proved very useful to me) by officers detailing the action at Big Bend. But, like us, he never found any formal military records similar to the reports routinely prepared by federal Indian officials.

P. 165   *"The people had to swim the rivers."* Terry Russell, interview with Josh Tenneson, research assistant, Lincoln City, Oregon, June 21, 2006. Russell's great-grandfather was Tyee John (Tututni). Russell's mother, who was interviewed at the same time, said that she had heard the same accounts about removal.

P. 165   *"Our trail of tears began."* Statement of Pauline Bell Ricks, Siletz Restoration Hearings, pp. 124–25.

P. 165   *"The terrain was harsh."* Agnes Pilgrim, interview with author, Grants Pass, Oregon, June 16, 2005.

P. 166   *"No. Walk on, and don't look back."* Edward G. Olsen, ed., *Then Till Now in Brookings-Harbor: A Social History of the Chetco Community Area*, p. 7 (Brookings, OR: Coastal Printing Co. for the Brookings Rotary Club, 1979) (quoting the written account of Lucy Dick's great granddaughter, Jeannette Giddings), *at* Oregon Historical Society, Portland, Research Library.

P. 166   *Siletz ancestors reached Yaquina Bay.* See J. Rinearson transcript of letter to J. Palmer (July 30, 1856), M2 Roll 14, Doc. 20, *at* Siletz Archival Collection. Frances Fuller Victor wrote that this march, instead of staying on the Coast, went up the Coquille River Valley to Roseburg and then on to Siletz. Victor, *The Early Indian Wars*, pp. 414–15. No one else has reported this. While the route would have avoided the most difficult terrain on the Coast, it would have been much longer. Further, if that route had been taken, there would have been no reason to go to Siletz by way of Yaquina Bay.

P. 167   *Coast treaty in the summer of 1855.* See chapter 7, pp. 136–41.

P. 167   *the settlers viewed the Indians as good workers.* See Robert H. Ruby and John A. Brown, *The Chinook Indians, Traders of the Lower Columbia River*, pp. 226–27 (Norman: University of Oklahoma Press, 1976).

P. 167   *The combined population plummeted to just 431.* See Robert Boyd, *The Coming of the Spirit of Pestilence*, p. 264 (Seattle: University of Washington Press, 1999).

P. 167   *only 41 representatives came.* See chapter 7, p. 139.

P. 167   *members on the Quinault, Shoalwater Bay, and Chehalis reservations.* See Ruby and Brown, *The Chinook Indians*, p. 239 (Quinault); pp. 241–42 (Shoalwater Bay and Chehalis).

P. 168   *The final form of removal.* By far the largest removals involved Southeastern tribes, sometimes referred to as the Five Civilized Tribes. In all, some 46,000 Indians were removed from the Southeast to Indian Territory, now the state of Oklahoma. See generally Grant Foreman, *Indian Removal: The Emigration of the Five Civilized Tribes of Indians* (Norman: University of Oklahoma Press, 1972); Ronald N. Satz, *American Indian Policy in the Jacksonian Era*, pp. 78–83, 97–115 (Lincoln: University of Nebraska Press, 1975). After that, there were no large-scale removals until the uprooting of western Oregon Indians. Other major removals followed. See, e.g., Frank McNitt, *Navajo Wars: Military Campaigns, Slave Raids and Reprisals* (Albuquerque: University of New Mexico Press, 1972) (Navajo Long Walk); Lynn R. Bailey, *Bosque Redondo: An American Concentration Camp* (Pasadena, CA: Socio-Technical Books, 1970) (removal of Navajo and Apache); Peter Decker, *"The Utes Must Go!": American Expansion and the Removal of a People* (Golden, CO: Fulcrum Publishing,

2004) (removal of 1,500 Utes from western Colorado to northern Utah); Theodore
Stern, *The Klamath Tribe* (Seattle: University of Washington Press, 1966) (removal of
153 Modocs from Oregon to the Indian Territory by wagon and railroad).

P. 168   *federal agents sternly insisted that everyone relocate.* See J. Palmer transcript of letter
to J. Day (July 14, 1856), M2 Roll 6, Doc. 58, *at* Siletz Archival Collection.

P. 168   *Palmer's policies had offended just about every American..* See, e.g., T. O'Donnell, *An
Arrow in the Earth,* pp. 278–79.

P. 168   *reports came in that numbers of Indians still had not moved.* See, e.g., G. Davidson,
transcript of letter to A. Hedges (Jan. 15, 1857), M2 Roll 15, Doc. 3, *at* Siletz Archival
Collection (estimating about 37 Indians still in Jackson County); P. Ruffner, transcript of letter to J. Nesmith (March 21, 1858), M2 Roll 16, Doc. 4, *at* Siletz Archival
Collection (stating that Chetcoes had killed one man and intended to kill another).
See also A. G. Walling, *History of Southern Oregon,* pp. 284–85 (Portland: A. G. Walling, 1884).

P. 168   *a special agent to track down south Coast Indians.* See A. Hedges, transcript of letter
to W. Tichenor, captain and special agent (Sept. 25, 1856), M2 Roll 6, Doc. 78, *at* Siletz
Archival Collection; Beckham, *The Indians of Western Oregon,* p. 144 (describing
Tichenor as a "bounty hunter").

P. 168   *Dozens of Indians were killed and wounded at Battle Rock.* See chapter 4, pp. 75–77.
Tichenor was not there, having taken the ship out for supplies, but he authorized
the removal of the cannon from the ship and its positioning on Battle Rock. See
Orvil Dodge, ed., Pioneer History of Coos and Curry Counties, Or., p. 35 (Salem, OR:
Capital Printing Co., 1898) (recording the eye-witness narrative of J. M. Kirkpatrick, a
member of Tichenor's crew).

P. 168   *"the most desperate and murderous of all the Indians."* W. Tichenor, special agent,
report to E. Drew, Indian sub-agent (June 30, 1858), in Senate Doc. No. 1, 1858 Commissioner Report, 35th Congress, 2d Session, p. 611.

P. 169   *"Indians were killed in attempting to escape."* J. Nesmith transcript of letter to J.
Scott, major (July 16, 1858), M2 Roll 7, Doc 42, at Siletz Archival Collection.

P. 169   *Tichenor brought in several hundred Indians.* Nathan Douthit, *Uncertain Encounters: Indians and Whites at Peace and War in Southern Oregon, 1820s to 1860s,* p. 167
(Corvallis: Oregon State University Press, 2002).

P. 169   *He sent eighty-five north from Port Orford on the* **Columbia.** See A. Hedges transcript
of letter to G. Manypenny (Nov. 11, 1856), M2 Roll 6, Doc. 116, at Siletz Archival Collection ("The expense will be heavy but it is thought the object justifies it.").

P. 169   *"I . . . told them the consequences."* P. Sheridan, lieutenant, transcript of letter to C.
Augur, captain (April 13, 1857), M2 Roll 15, Doc. 11, *at* Siletz Archival Collection.

P. 169   *"She made up her mind."* Statement of Pauline Bell Ricks, Siletz Restoration Hearings, p. 125.

P. 169   *One woman hid in a flour barrel.* See Kenneth Liberman, "The Native Environment:
Contemporary Perspectives of Southwestern Oregon's Native Americans," *in* Nan
Hannon and Richard K. Olmo, eds., *Living with the Land: The Indians of Southwest
Oregon,* p. 85 (Medford: Southern Oregon Historical Society, 1990).

P. 169   *"The last time they came after Inds."* Elaine L. Mills, ed., vol. 1 *The Papers of John
Peabody Harrington in the Smithsonian Institution, 1907–1957,* C-153, Reel 027 (Mill-
wood, NY: Kraus International Publications, 1981) (containing a microfilm copy of
Harrington's handwritten notes detailing an interview with Wolverton Orton).

P. 170　*He "walked all the way to Siletz and all the way back."* Sally Engstrom, Siletz tribal member, letter to Kathleen Van Pelt Forster, Siletz tribal member (Aug. 2000) (on file with author).

9 *Survival in a New Land*

P. 173　*Bureau of Indian Affairs.* In this era, the official name of the agency was Office of Indian Affairs. It was often called "Bureau of Indian Affairs" and the name, long in common usage, was officially adopted in 1947.

P. 173　*Federal assimilation policy.* See Francis Paul Prucha, *The Great Father: The United States Government and the American Indians,* 2 vols. (Lincoln: University of Nebraska Press, 1984) (on Christianity and assimilation efforts generally, see pp. 501–33 and 611–30; on the Allotment policy, see pp. 659–86; on Indian schools, see pp. 687–715). See also Robert Berkhofer, *The White Man's Indian: Images of the American Indian from Columbus to the Present,* pp. 166–75 (New York: Knopf, 1978); Frederick E. Hoxie, *A Final Promise: The Campaign to Assimilate the Indians, 1880–1920,* pp. 1–39 (Lincoln: University of Nebraska Press, 2001). For a treatment of assimilation-ist attitudes generally, and among BIA agency superintendents and Edwin Chalcraft in particular, see Cary C. Collins, "Editor's Introduction," *in* Edwin L. Chalcraft, *Assimilation's Agent: My Life as a Superintendent in the Indian Boarding School System,* Cary C. Collins, ed., pp. ix–lxii (Lincoln: University of Nebraska Press, 2004). Chalcraft, who served as superintendent at Siletz from 1914 to 1925, was a staunch believer in the policy and, in addition to Collins's introduction, the book as a whole captures the flavor of the era.

P. 173　*"to tame—to put in a corral."* Frank Simmons, interview with the author, Lincoln City, Oregon, Nov. 10, 2008.

P. 174　*"How can our Indian tribes be civilized?"* Nathaniel Taylor, commissioner of Indian Affairs, "Annual Report of the Commissioner of Indian Affairs," Nov. 23, 1868, *in* Prucha, *Documents,* 3d ed., p. 122.

P. 175　*"There is no resistless clog."* Prucha, vol. 2, *The Great Father,* p. 697 (quoting Captain Richard Henry Pratt).

P. 176　*"All the Indian there is."* Scott Riney, *The Rapid City Indian School, 1898–1933,* p. 8 (Norman: University of Oklahoma Press, 1999).

P. 176　*Early population of 2,700 souls.* The population figures in the early days of the res-ervation kept changing with the advent of new arrivals. Tabulations taken during the first years in August and December 1856, showed 1,285 and 1,399, respectively. R. Metcalfe, "Census on the Coast Station" (Aug. 20, 1856), M234 Roll 609, Doc. 2, *at* Archival Collection of Siletz Tribe Cultural Department [hereinafter Siletz Archival Collection]; R. Metcalfe, "Census of Indians engaged in the late war; now under my charge" (Dec. 24, 1856), M2 Roll 14, Doc. 29, *at* Siletz Archival Collection. In 1857 a census at the Siletz agency showed a total of 2,049. R. Metcalfe, Indian Agent, "Census List of Indians, Coast Reservation, Selets Ind. Agency" (Sept. 22, 1857), M2 Roll 30, Doc. 1, *at* Siletz Archival Collection. But that number is misleadingly low since people were still being brought in from the south Coast, Grand Ronde, and the Salmon River. With an additional 690 Siuslaw, Lower Umpqua, and Coos people at the Umpqua (later Alsea) sub-agency, the official total in 1857 was 2,739. See E. Drew, Indian sub-agent, letter to J. Nesmith, superintendent of Indian Affairs for Oregon

(July 1, 1857), *in* Senate Doc. No. 11, 1857 Commissioner Report, 35th Congress, 1st Session, p. 647 (Washington, D.C.: William A. Harris, 1858). As Superintendent Nesmith mentioned in his 1857 report, there also were some 250 members of the Tillamook and other tribes living north of the reservation and also an estimated 250 Indians who had hid out and avoided removal (some of the latter group would later be captured and brought to the reservation). J. Nesmith letter to J. Denver, commissioner of Indian Affairs (Sept. 1, 1857), *in* Senate Doc. No. 11, 1857 Commissioner Report, 35th Congress, 1st Session, pp. 606–7.

P. 176   *1.1 million acres.* Estimates of the size of the reservation have ranged from 800,000 acres to 1.4 million acres. Both of those estimates are wrong, and I have used the correct figure of 1.1 million acres. Brady Smith, telephone interview with research assistant Daniel Cordalis; Smith is the Siletz tribal cartographer.

P. 176   *The spruce, fir, and cedar forests.* See, e.g., Elmo Richardson, *BLM's Billion-Dollar Checkerboard: Managing the O & C Lands*, p. vii (Santa Cruz, CA: Forest History Society, 1980). See also Ralph W. Hidy, Frank Ernest Hill, and Allan Nevins, *Timber and Men: The Weyerhaeuser Story*, p. 217 (New York: The Macmillan Co., 1963).

P. 177   *Pacific salmon.* Chad C. Meengs and Robert T. Lackey, "Estimating the Size of Historical Oregon Salmon Runs," vol. 13, no. 1 *Reviews in Fisheries Science*, pp. 51–66 (Feb. 2005). Table 2 displays the size of the runs, with the Siletz River having average historic runs of 122,000 coho and 30,000 chinook). See also Joseph E. Taylor III, *Making Salmon: An Environmental History of the Northwest Fisheries Crisis*, pp. 3–67 (Seattle: University of Washington Press, 1999).

P. 177   *habitat for deer, Roosevelt elk, bear, and small game.* See, e.g., A. Rogers and S. Mann, transcript of letter to E. Drew (July 12, 1856), M2 Roll 14, Doc. 23, *at* Siletz Archival Collection; *Tillamook Tribe of Indians v. United States*, Ind. Cl. Comm. No. 239 (1955), *in* vol. 4, *Indian Claims Commission Decisions*, p. 41 (Boulder, CO: Native American Rights Fund, 1973).

P. 177   *Large fires, including Yaquina Burn.* See "Appendix H: History of the Northwest Oregon State Forests," in *Northwest Oregon State Forests Management Plan*, p. H-5 (Jan. 2001), *at* http://www.odf.state.or.us/divisions/management/state_forests/sfplan/nwfmp01-final/29-H-History.prn.pdf (accessed May 21, 2009) ("Between 1846 and 1853, a series of large fires burned over 800,000 acres in the central Oregon Coast Range."); Oregon Department of Forestry, "Historic Fires in Oregon," *at* http://www.oregon.gov/ODF/FIRE/Historic_Fires_In_Oregon.shtml (accessed May 27, 2009) (the 1849 Siletz Fire burned 800,000 acres).

P. 177   *Traditional burning and excellent elk habitat.* See chapter 2, pp. 50–53.

P. 177   *farming could not thrive.* See, e.g., Samuel N. Dicken and Emily F. Dicken, *Oregon Divided: A Regional Geography*, pp. 12–13 (Portland: Oregon Historical Society, 1982) (with a map showing low percentages of cropland in Oregon coastal counties, and stating that rugged terrain, too much rain, and cool summers are factors).

P. 177   *Yaquina Bay could not receive larger vessels.* See, e.g., J. Nesmith report to C. Mix, commissioner of Indian Affairs (Aug. 20. 1858), *in* Senate Doc. No. 1, 1858 Commissioner Report, 35th Congress, 2d Session, pp. 568–69 (Washington, D.C.: William A. Harris, 1858). Later, the building and lengthening of the jetty at the entrance to the harbor allowed larger ships to use the harbor. See, e.g., Mike O'Donnell, *The First Hundred Years: Lincoln County, 1893–1993*, p. 31 (Newport, OR: News-Times, 1993).

P. 178   *No buildings or tents.* J. Browne, special agent of the Treasury Department, report to J. Denver (Nov. 17, 1857), *in* House Doc. No. 39, 35th Congress, 1st Session, p. 40 (Washington, D.C.: Government Printing Office, 1858) [hereinafter Browne Report]. Special Agent Browne also observed that "the whole country was deluged with water. The Indians, naturally averse to being taken away from their homes, not knowing what was going to be done with them, strangers to the arts of civilization, disappointed in the fulfillment of nearly all the treaty stipulations, and suffering from cold and partial starvation, were in a disaffected and dangerous condition."

P. 178   *"No means have been provided for their sustenance."* A. Hedges, superintendent of Indian Affairs for Oregon, transcript of letter to G. Manypenny, commissioner of Indian Affairs (Aug. 22, 1856), M2 Roll 6, Doc. 69, *at* Siletz Archival Collection.

P. 178   *That first winter wrought great suffering.* A. Hedges transcript of letter to G. Manypenny (March 17, 1857), M2 Roll 6, Doc. 102, p. 1, *at* Siletz Archival Collection ("The winter has however been most unpropitious, the worst we have had for fifteen years."). A. Hedges transcript of letter to G. Manypenny (Feb. 24, 1857), M2 Roll 6, Doc. 97, p. 1, *at* Siletz Archival Collection; R. Metcalfe report to J. Nesmith (July 15, 1857), *in* House Doc. No. 2, 1857 Commissioner Report, 35th Congress, 1st Session, p. 646 (It "commenced raining [in November 1856], and rained until the last day of March, with only eighteen days' intermission").

P. 178   *A schooner wrecked at the mouth of the Siletz.* Local Indians and then Agent Metcalfe tried to save the shipment, "but before they were ready to remove the flour [to a hastily constructed log cabin on the beach] there came a heavy blow from the west and destroyed the entire cargo with the exception of about one thousand pounds of flour." R. Metcalfe transcript of letter to A. Hedges (Dec. 13, 1856), M2 Roll 14, Doc. 29, p. 1, *at* Siletz Archival Collection. See also A. Hedges transcript of letter to G. Manypenny (Dec. 19, 1856), M2 Roll 6, Doc. 90, *at* Siletz Archival Collection.

P. 178   *"the Indians were in a state of starvation."* Browne Report, p. 41.

P. 178   *"only fit for cattle."* Ibid.

P. 178   *only twenty-seven houses for Indians.* Ibid., p. 43.

P. 178   *Hedges replaced by Nesmith.* Hedges's departure seemed to come unexpectedly, and his last letter to Commissioner Manypenny spoke not only of the challenges of the long, hard winter, but also expressed hopefulness about the rebuilding of the wrecked schooner and the plans for spring planting. A. Hedges transcript of letter to G. Manypenny (March 17, 1857), M2 Roll 6, Doc. 102, p. 1, *at* Siletz Archival Collection. Hedges turned over administration of the Oregon Superintendency to Nesmith on May 1, 1857, although Nesmith was "left without a single dollar to discharge soon the current expenses of the office, to say nothing of the large and daily increasing debts of the Indian Service." J. Nesmith transcript of letter to G. Manypenny (May 5, 1857), M2 Roll 6, Doc. 103, *at* Siletz Archival Collection.

P. 179   *"Almost daily we hear of the death."* R. Metcalfe report to J. Nesmith (Sept. 1, 1857), *in* House Doc. No. 2, 1857 Commissioner Report, 35th Congress, 1st Session, p. 605.

P. 179   *Loss of life at Grand Ronde.* Grand Ronde Agent Miller reported an estimated loss of 500 Indians, predominately from the southern tribes, due primarily to sickness resulting from removal, change of climate, and change of diet. J. Nesmith transcript of letter to J. Denver (May 5, 1857), M2 Roll 6, Doc. 103, pp. 1–2 *at* Siletz Archival Collection.

P. 179   *"Many . . . have died from a depression of spirits."* R. Metcalfe report to J. Nesmith (July 15, 1857), *in* House Doc. No. 2, 1857 Commissioner Report, 35th Congress, 1st

Session, pp. 645–46; statement of Pauline Bell Ricks, Siletz Tribal Council Member, *in* Hearings Before the Senate Committee on Interior and Insular Affairs, Subcommittee on Indian Affairs, "Siletz Restoration Act: On S. 2801," 94th Congress, 2d Session, p. 125 (March 30–31, 1976) (Washington, D.C.: Government Printing Office, 1976). (Pauline Ricks recounted that her grandmother, Ki-Ya-Na-Ha, "remembered a lot of people dying from many kinds of diseases unknown to her. Probably chicken pox, tuberculosis, she didn't know. For she always believed most of them died of depression, heartbreak, and mis-treatment.")

P. 179   *"It is your peace that is killing us."* J. Nesmith report to J. Denver (Sept. 1, 1857), *in* Senate Doc. No. 11, 1857 Commissioner Report, 35th Congress, 1st Session, p. 604.

P. 179   *Indian doctors caught in a bind.* Robert Kentta, "A Siletz History, Part IX: Early Days on the Siletz Reservation," *Siletz News*, p. 29 (July 2000), *at* http://www.ctsi.nsn.us/chinook-indian-tribe-siletz-heritage/our-history/part-ix#content (accessed May 22, 2009). See also J. Miller, Indian Agent, report to J. Nesmith (July 20, 1857), *in* Senate Doc. No. 11, 1857 Commissioner Report, 35th Congress, 1st Session, p. 649 ("upon the death of any of their number, the relatives of the deceased will immediately wreak vengeance upon some 'doctor'"); J. Ostrander, superintendent of Rogue River and Umpqua School, letter J. Miller (July 21, 1857), *in* Senate Doc. No. 11, 1857 Commissioner Report, 35th Congress, 1st Session, p. 657; R. Metcalfe report to E. Geary, superintendent of Indian Affairs (July 8, 1859), *in* Senate Doc. No. 2, 1859 Commissioner Report, 36th Congress, 1st Session, p. 793 ("In the last five years, I have known more than one hundred doctors and doctresses murdered").

P. 179   *"D" River conflict.* Robert Kentta, interview with author, Lincoln City, Oregon, Nov. 9, 2009.

P. 179   *"Captain Smith, U.S.A., Palmer, Metcalf, and others, promised."* Browne Report, p. 27.

P. 179   *"A long time ago we made a treaty with Palmer."* Ibid., p. 45.

P. 180   *The area gradually became more settled.* I benefited greatly from Robert Kentta's explanation of the geography and settlement of the reservation. Robert Kentta, interview with author, Siletz, Oregon, Feb. 24, 2005. See also Lionel Youst and William R. Seaburg, *Coquelle Thompson, Athabaskan Witness: A Cultural Biography*, pp. 54–56 (Norman: University of Oklahoma Press, 2002); M. Susan Van Laere, "The Grizzly Bear and the Deer: The History of Federal Indian Policy and Its Impact on the Coast Reservation Tribes of Oregon, 1856–1877," pp. 95–99, M.A. thesis, Oregon State University, 2000.

P. 181   *Alsea sub-agency at Yachats.* See ibid., pp. 123–25. The southernmost Umpqua sub-agency was closed in 1859—it had been plagued by funding problems and white settlers hostile to Sub-Agent Drew's policy out of necessity, of allowing the Siuslaw, Coos, Lower Umpqua, and others off the reservation to fish. The tribes were relocated north to the Alsea sub-agency on the Yachats River in 1860, so that they would be within the boundaries of the Coast Reservation. See also J. Sykes, Indian sub-agent, transcript of letter to E. Geary (Nov. 16, 1860), M234 Roll 612, Doc. 65.

P. 181   *Salmon River Station closed.* See F. Jones transcript of letter to A. Hedges (Aug. 2, 1856), M2 Roll 6, Doc. 65, *at* Siletz Archival Collection; A. Hedges transcript of letter to G. Manypenny (Nov. 7, 1856), M234 Roll 609, Doc. 8, p. 1, *at* Siletz Archival Collection. E. Geary transcript of letter to A. Greenwood, Commissioner of Indian Affairs (Oct. 10, 1859), M2 Roll 8, Doc. 7, *at* Siletz Archival Collection.

P. 181   *In the first few years at Siletz.* See, e.g., J. Nesmith transcript of letter to J. Denver

(Dec. 24, 1857), M2 Roll 7, Doc. 23, p. 1, *at* Siletz Archival Collection.

P. 181   *Comparison of Rogue and Siletz as salmon rivers.* Meengs and Lackey, "Estimating the Size of Historical Oregon Salmon Runs," Table 2, pp. 64–65, estimate that, in the late 1800s, the Rogue River had runs of 154,000 chinook and 114,000 coho; whereas the Siletz River had runs of 30,000 chinook and 122,000 coho. Chinook, the largest of the salmon, generally weigh in at about 40 pounds and have been reported up to 120 pounds. NOAA Fisheries, Office of Protected Resources, "Chinook Salmon," *at* http://www.nmfs.noaa.gov/pr/species/fish/chinooksalmon.htm (accessed May 22, 2009). fly02_Freeman (accessed May 22, 2009).

P. 182   *"[We would] net."* Hoxie Simmons, testimony before the Indian Claims Commission, *Tillamook Tribe of Indians v. United States*, Ind. Cl. Comm. No. 239 (1955), *at* Siletz Archival Collection.

P. 183   *directed to erase Indian religions, cultures.* See, e.g., Jane Marie Harger, "The History of the Siletz Reservation, 1856–1877," p. 44, M.A. thesis, University of Oregon, 1972.

P. 183   *Simpson employed whipping and the buck-and-gag.* See J. Fairchild report to E. Smith (Sept. 1, 1875), *in* House Doc. No. 1, Pt. 5, 1875 Commissioner Report, 44th Congress, 1st Session, p. 852 ("Knowing the character of the Indians, the earlier agents, perhaps wisely, adopted a policy of severity and compulsion. The whipping-post and the buck and gag were in constant requisition."). Joel Palmer ended the use of the buck and gag and other severe punishments when he succeeded Simpson as agent in 1871. W. Bagley report to E. Smith (Aug. 29, 1876), *in* House Doc. No. 1, Pt. 5, 1876 Commissioner Report, 44th Congress, 2d Session, p. 527.

P. 183   *"indomitable energy and will."* R. Lee Lyman, "Alexander W. Chase and the Nineteenth-Century Archaeology and Ethnography of the Southern Oregon and Northern California Coast," vol. 25, no. 2 *Northwest Anthropological Research Notes*, p. 164 (Fall 1991). Lyman described Alexander Chase, a self-taught, "non-professional" anthropologist in the early days of the discipline, as doing sound work. Ibid., p. 156.

P. 183   *"our brother's keeper."* See Edgar S. Cahn, ed., *Our Brother's Keeper: The Indian in White America*, pp. 5–13 (Washington, D.C.: New Community Press, 1969).

P. 183   *Ben Simpson insisted.* Lyman, "Alexander W. Chase," p. 166.

P. 183   *ratification of treaties.* See, e.g., D. Newcomb, Indian agent, transcript of letter to W. H. Rector, superintendent of Indian Affairs (Aug. 15, 1861), M2 Roll 19, Doc. 16, *at* Siletz Archival Collection ("Treaties were made with them, and they gave up their lands and came here to live, thus fulfilling their part of the stipulation, they are receiving nothing that was promised them on the part of our Gov't. I would respectfully and urgently suggest that some immediate action be taken for their relief"); W. Bagley, Indian agent, transcript of letter to J. I. Smith, commissioner of Indian Affairs (Oct. 30, 1876), M234 Roll 613, Doc. 4, *at* Siletz Archival Collection ("I again desire through you to call the attention of the Department to the necessity of confirming the treaties made with these Indians. They have waited anxiously for ten years for the fulfilling of the promises made to them when they surrendered their lands to the United States.").

P. 183   *Moving Alsea Indians to Siletz.* W. Bagley transcript of letter to J. Q. Smith, commissioner of Indian Affairs (April 8, 1876), M234 Roll 622, Doc. 3, *at* Siletz Archival Collection.

P. 183   *concerns about funding.* See J. B. Condon, agent, transcript of letter to W. H. Rector (Aug. 3, 1861), M2 Roll 19, Doc. 6 (needed more farmers and the services of a physician, carpenter and blacksmith); J. Miller, agent, transcript of letter to E. Geary, superintendent of Indian Affairs (Nov. 21, 1859), M2 Roll 17, Doc. 29, *at* Siletz Archival Collection (only received half the Grand Ronde's needed blankets and none of their portion of the Rogue River Annuity funds.); R. Metcalfe transcript of financial statement for Siletz Agency (June 30, 1858), M2 Roll 16, Doc. 15, *at* Siletz Archival Collection.

P. 184   *"I am informed that a short time before."* J. Condon, Indian agent, transcript of letter to W. H. Rector (Sept. 18, 1861), M2 Roll19, Doc. 8, *at* Siletz Archival Collection.

P. 185   *"generally unsuited to cultivation."* Stuart Allan, Aileen R. Buckley, and James E. Meacham, *Atlas of Oregon*, ed. William G. Loy, pp. 152–53 (Eugene: University of Oregon, 2001) (containing a map showing land capability classifications determined by the Oregon Agricultural Experiment Station and the U.S. Soil Conservation Service). The USDA Natural Resources Conservation Service maintains county-by-county climate data in Temperature and Precipitation Summary (TAPS) Tables, *at* http://www.wcc.nrcs.usda.gov/climate/foguide.html#taps (accessed May 22, 2009). According to Chad McGrath, USDA state soil scientist for Oregon, although pasturage crops can be grown in the Siletz climate, "many of the soils in the isometric zone have soil properties that are conducive for 'farming' but the cool summer soil and air temperatures restrict the maturation of crops that people associate with farming and/or are typically grown for food." Chad McGrath email to Carrie Covington, research assistant, Feb. 5, 2008 (on file with author). See also p. 177 and accompanying note, above.

P. 185   *Without the help of modern soil science.* J. Palmer, Indian agent, report to T. Odeneal, superintendent of Indian Affairs for Oregon (Sept. 28, 1872), *in* House Doc. No. 1, Pt. 5, 1872 Commissioner Report, 42d Congress, 3d Session, p. 753 (Washington, D.C.: Government Printing Office, 1872).

P. 186   *Cultivation of tobacco.* See chapter 2, p. 35.

P. 186   *Metcalfe was optimistic.* R. Metcalfe report to J. Nesmith (July 15, 1857), *in* House Doc. No. 2, 1857 Commissioner Report, 35th Congress, 1st Session, pp. 645–46 ("They are generally industrious, and manifest a disposition to imitate the whites. . . . Many of the Indians expressed a desire to engage in agriculture, and . . . it is confidently believed that they will be able to subsist themselves in that pursuit.").

P. 186   *some tribal members took to farming.* B. Simpson, Indian agent, report to J. Huntington, superintendent of Indian Affairs for Oregon (Aug. 20, 1863), *in* House Doc. No. 1, 1863 Commissioner Report, 38th Congress, 1st Session, p. 184.

P. 186   *the difficulties soon rose up.* M. Susan Van Laere, "The Grizzly and the Deer," pp. 91–101, offers a good analysis of the first generation on the Siletz Reservation and early reservation farming.

P. 186   *The wheat crops were disappointing.* See, e.g., B. Simpson report to J. Huntington (July 31, 1866), *in* House Doc. No. 1, 1866 Commissioner Report, 39th Congress, 2nd Session, p. 86.

P. 186   *corn and beans failed.* See, e.g., R. Metcalfe report to J. Nesmith (July 27, 1858), *in* Senate Doc. No. 1, 1858 Commissioner Report, 35th Congress, 2nd Session, p. 603.

P. 186   *weeds invaded farmland.* J. Willis, Siletz Agency farmer, report to B. Simpson (Aug. 1, 1863), *in* House Doc. No. 1, 1863 Commissioner Report, 38th Congress, 1st Session, p. 188.

P. 186   *"never grained 100 bushels."* Royal A. Bensell, *All Quiet on the Yamhill: The Civil War in Oregon*, ed. Gunter Barth, p. 138 (Eugene: University of Oregon Books, 1959).

P. 186 *The white employees hired to manage.* See Harger, "The History of Siletz Reservation," pp. 92–94.

P. 186 *"the hard labor which the women are obliged to perform."* J. Bayley, Siletz agency physician, report to B. Simpson (July 31, 1863), *in* House Doc. No. 1, 1863 Commissioner Report, 38th Congress, 1st Session, pp. 187–88.

P. 186 *Production tailed off in the 1890s.* See E. A. Schwartz, *The Rogue River Indian War and Its Aftermath, 1850–1980*, p. 224 (Norman: University of Oklahoma Press, 1997).

P. 187 *Schoolhouse promptly abandoned.* R. Metcalfe report to E. Geary (July 8, 1859), *in* Senate Doc. No. 2, Pt. 1, 1859 Commissioner Report, 36th Congress, 1st Session, p. 794.

P. 187 *School had no stove or fireplace.* J. Clarke, Siletz Agency teacher, report to B. Simpson (Aug. 1, 1863), *in* House Doc. No. 1, 1863 Commissioner Report, 38th Congress, 1st Session, pp. 191–192. When Clarke arrived to teach in August of 1863, he reported that he "found the building formerly used as a school-house in a dilapidated and filthy condition, destitute of doors and windows . . . it had become a place of refuge for stock of all kinds, thereby damaging the floors and walls, rendering it unfit for occupation." Ibid. Additionally, Clarke asked Simpson to purchase a cooking stove, as "in the school-house there is neither stove nor fireplace." Ibid.

P. 187 *"entirely separated from the noxious influences."* W. Shipley, Siletz Agency teacher, report to B. Simpson (Sept. 30, 1870), *in* House Doc. No. 1, Pt. 4, 1870 Commissioner Report, 41st Congress, 3d Session, p. 855.

P. 187 *"The parents are more interested."* M. Gaines, Siletz Agency teacher, report to B. Biddle, Indian agent (Aug. 10, 1862), *in* House Doc. No. 1, 1862 Commissioner Report, 37th Congress, 3d Session, p. 425.

P. 187 *President Grant's Peace Policy.* See generally Prucha, vol. 1, *The Great Father*, pp. 512–27; Robert H. Keller Jr., *American Protestantism and United States Indian Policy, 1869–82*, pp. 17–30 (Lincoln: University of Nebraska Press, 1983); Christine Bolt, *American Indian Policy and American Reform*, pp. 75–81 (London: Allen & Unwin, 1987).

P. 187 *"I determined to give all the [Indian] agencies."* President Ulysses S. Grant, Second Annual Message to Congress, Dec. 5, 1870, *in* James D. Richardson, compiler, vol. 9, *A Compilation of the Messages and Papers of the Presidents*, pp. 4063–64 (New York: Bureau of National Literature, Inc., 1897).

P. 188 *"Not, therefore, as a dernier resort."* E. Parker, commissioner of Indian Affairs, report to J. Cox, secretary of the Interior (Oct. 31, 1870), *in* House Doc. No. 1, Pt. 4, 1870 Commissioner Report, 41st Congress, 3d Session, p. 474.

P. 188 *The Peace Policy made its mark.* The force of the Peace Policy is well set out by Prucha in vol. 1, *The Great Father*, p. 519:

> What the government wanted from the churches was a total transformation of the agencies from political sinecures to missionary outposts. The religious societies were expected not only to nominate strong men as agents but to supply to a large extent the subordinate agency personnel. Teachers especially were desired, men and women with a religious dedication to the work that would make up for the low pay and often frightening conditions. The churches, too, it was assumed, would pursue more energetically and more effectively the strictly missionary activities already begun now that conflicts

between government agents and missionaries would no longer be an obstacle. The commissioner of Indian affairs, in fact, asserted in 1872 that "the importance of securing harmony of feeling and concert of action between the agents of the Government and the missionaries at the several agencies, in the matter of the moral and religious advancement of the Indians, was the single reason formally given for placing the nominations to Indian agencies in the hands of the denominational societies." Agency physicians, interpreters, and mechanics, if they were of solid moral worth, could all contribute to the goal of civilizing and Christianizing the Indians.

Utopia seemed to be within grasp. The reports of the secretaries of the interior, the commissioners of Indian affairs, the Board of Indian Commissioners, and Grant himself rang loud with praise for the new policy.

P. 188   *"The romantic ideal of depoliticizing."* Ibid., p. 520.

P. 188   *Methodist Church congregation of 100.* A Methodist presence was first established in 1873. J. Fairchild, Indian agent, report to E. Smith, commissioner of Indian Affairs (Sept. 13, 1873), *in* House Doc. No. 1, Pt. 5, 1873 Commissioner Report, 43d Congress, 1st Session, p. 690. In 1874, Fairchild reported that "the religious interest continues. Nearly one hundred have united with the church," J. Fairchild report to E. Smith (Sept. 8, 1874), *in* House Doc. No. 1, Pt. 5, 1874 Commissioner Report, 43d Congress, 2d Session, p. 629. But perhaps Fairchild's 1875 report best exemplifies the ebbs and flows of the "Christian civilizing" efforts of the Indian Agents:

> The change that has taken place—and this change is the foundation of all other change for good—is astonishing. . . . Not so much that a certain number have thrown off the yoke of their old superstitions and united with the church, but that the principles of the Christian religion have . . . penetrated to all ranks. . . . The number uniting with the church the past year has not been great. Probably twenty have in that time been received on probation. . . . The church here, though not numerous, is earnest and aggressive, and the circle of its influence is daily widening.

J. Fairchild report to E. Smith (Sept. 1, 1875), *in* House Doc. No. 1, Pt. 5, 1875 Commissioner Report, 44th Congress, 1st Session, p. 854. See also W. Bagley, Indian agent, report to E. Smith (Aug. 20, 1877), *in* House Doc. No. 1, Pt. 5, 1877 Commissioner Report, 45th Congress, 2d Session, p. 573.

Although the Methodists were the primary congregation on the Siletz Reservation, "Father Croquet has been resident priest [on the Grand Ronde Reservation] for twenty-two years, and during twenty-two years he visited Siletz agency frequently every year as missionary." P. Sinnott, Grand Ronde Indian agent, report to E. Smith (Aug. 11, 1883), *in* House Doc. No. 1, Pt. 5, 1883 Commissioner Report, 48th Congress, 1st Session, p. 185. Father Croquet made visits to the Siletz Reservation and coastal fishing spots throughout the 1860s. His visits were somewhat restricted under the Peace Policy, but a congregation was maintained in his absence and he returned to maintain the Siletz Catholic congregation into the 1890s. See Friar Martinus Cawley, *Father Crockett of Grand Ronde*, Story #25 (Oregon Archdiocese: Guadalupe Translations, 1996), *at* Lincoln County Historical Society, Newport, Oregon. The two congregations remained a significant part of the community throughout the late 1800s. See B. Gaither, Indian agent, report to Commissioner of Indian Affairs (Aug.

24, 1894), *in* House Doc. No. 1, Pt. 5, 1894 Commissioner Report, 53d Congress, 3d Session, p. 266.

P. 188   *Joel Palmer's return.* On Palmer's short, unsatisfying term as Siletz agent, see Terence O'Donnell, *An Arrow in the Earth: General Joel Palmer and the Indians of Oregon*, pp. 290–94 (Portland: Oregon Historical Society Press, 1991) (upon his return to Siletz in April of 1871, Palmer wrote, "If we judge of the future by the little progress among these people during the last sixteen years, the prospect is not hopeful. Still there is hope. But I would rather have taken these people precisely in the condition they were in when I sent them here nearly sixteen years ago, than now.").

P. 188   *"it is useless to preach."* Ibid., p. 293.

P. 188   *Palmer resigned.* Ibid., p. 294 (in a letter dated November 1872, Palmer admitted to being "disheartened and utterly discouraged in this work"). His frustrations are evident in his final report to the superintendent. See J. Palmer report to T. Odeneal (Sept. 28, 1872), *in* House Doc. No. 1, Pt. 5, 1872 Commissioner Report, 42d Congress, 3d Session, pp. 752–55.

P. 188   *"Christianity is the best civilizer."* J. Fairchild report to E. Smith (Sept. 1, 1875), *in* House Doc. No. 1, Pt. 5, 1875 Commissioner Report, 44th Congress, 1st Session, p. 853.

P. 189   *School enrollment between 60 and 90.* See, e.g., L. Hunt, superintendent of Siletz School, report to B. Gaither (July 10, 1894), *in* House Doc. No. 1, Pt. 5, 1894 Commissioner Report, 53d Congress, 3d Session, p. 267; G. Myers, superintendent of Siletz School, report to B. Gaither (Aug. 28, 1895), *in* House Doc. No. 5, 1895 Commissioner Report, 54th Congress, 1st Session, p. 272; B. Betz, superintendent of Siletz School, report (Aug. 6, 1900) *in* House Doc. No. 5, 1900 Commissioner Report, 56th Congress, 2d Session, p. 362; T. Buford, Indian agent, report to the Commissioner of Indian Affairs (Aug. 5, 1901), *in* House Doc. No. 5, 1901 Commissioner Report, 57th Congress, 1st Session, p. 350. For an article on this era, see K. Tsianina Lomawaima, "Estelle Reel, Superintendent of Indian Schools, 1898–1910: Politics, Curriculum, and Land," vol. 35, no. 3 *Journal of American Indian Education* (May 1996).

P. 189   *About ten students per year went to Chemawa.* See, e.g., D. McArthur, school superintendent in charge of Siletz Agency, report to the Commissioner of Indian Affairs (Aug. 4, 1902), *in* House Doc. No. 5, 1902 Commissioner Report, 57th Congress, 2d Session, p. 318.

P. 189   *A few went to Carlisle and Haskell.* William Eugene Kent, "The Siletz Indian Reservation 1855–1900," p. 29, M.S. thesis, Portland State University, 1973.

P. 189   *"The children, one and all, use the English language."* G. Myers report to B. Gaither (Aug. 28, 1895), *in* House Doc. No. 5, 1895 Commissioner Report, 54th Congress, 1st Session, p. 272.

P. 191   *"We are Slaves."* W. Rector, superintendent of Indian Affairs for Oregon, transcript of letter to W. Dole, commissioner of Indian Affairs (June 10, 1862), M234 Roll 613, Doc. 5, p. 3, *at* Siletz Archival Collection.

P. 191   *"I want a gun."* Ibid., p. 4.

P. 192   *"I think our people have improved."* Ibid., p. 2.

P. 192   *"He is a daring, restless man."* J. Nesmith transcript of letter to W. Machall, adjutant general (April 23, 1858), M2 Roll 7, Doc. 39, *at* Siletz Archival Collection.

P. 192   *Cultus Jim attacked an Indian doctor.* R. Glisan, *Journal of Army Life*, p. 391 (San Francisco: A. L. Bancroft and Co., 1874). On John's arrest and imprisonment, see Schwartz, *The Rogue River Indian War*, pp. 151–52.

P. 192 *Metcalfe's account of Cultus Jim's death.* R. Metcalfe letter to J. Nesmith (Oct. 13, 1857), M2 Roll 15, Doc. 24, *at* Siletz Archival Collection (quoted in full in Van Laere, "The Grizzly Bear and the Deer," pp. 115–16).

P. 192 *Coquelle Thompson heard a different version.* Ben Maxwell, "Coquille Thompson of Old Siletz 'Remembers When'—," *Portland Oregon Sunday Journal* (Nov. 28, 1937).

P. 192 *Arrest of Tyee John and Adam.* See J. Nesmith transcript of letter to R. Metcalfe (April 26, 1858), M2 Roll 7, Doc. 39, *at* Siletz Archival Collection ("Your Act with reference to the arrest of Old John and his son has my hearty approval.").

P. 192 *Tyee John and Adam tried to take over the steamer.* Lafayette Grover, *Notable Things in a Public Life in Oregon*, p. 39 (San Francisco, 1878), *at* Bancroft Collection, Bancroft Library, University of California, Berkeley.

P. 192 *"ear-piercing" scream.* See Schwartz, *The Rogue River Indian War*, p. 152 (citing "the newspaper report" but failing to give any further information); Van Laere, "The Grizzly Bear and the Deer," pp. 117–19. There are varying accounts of the incident. Perhaps John's "ear-piercing" scream was related to Adam's being shot in the leg, inflicting such damage that the lower half had to be amputated.

P. 192 *"A few days ago I was a great Chief."* Grover, *Notable Things*, p. 39.

P. 193 *"his daughters made a very strong appeal."* W. Rector, superintendent of Indian Affairs for Oregon, report to W. Dole (Sept. 2, 1862), *in* House Doc. No. 1, 1862 Commissioner Report, 37th Congress, 3d Session, p. 399.

P. 193 *"his indomitable spirit."* E. Geary transcript of letter to R. Metcalfe (Oct. 24, 1859), M2 Roll 8, Doc. 8, *at* Siletz Archival Collection.

P. 193 *"to return him to his family."* W. Rector transcript of letter to Brig. Gen. Wright, Pacific Department (May 7, 1862), M2 Roll 9, Doc. 22, *at* Siletz Archival Collection.

P. 193 *"souse every Soldier in the River."* Bensell, *All Quiet on the Yamhill*, p. 11 (journal entry of April 5, 1862).

P. 193 *Bensell's two poignant journal entries.* Ibid., pp. 21, 24.

P. 193 *"This is my country."* Frances Fuller Victor, *The Early Indian Wars of Oregon*, p. 407 (Salem, OR: Frank C. Baker, State Printer, 1894). See also chapter 6, p. 127 and accompanying note.

P. 193 *Tyee John passed away.* Oregonian, p. 2 (June 15, 1864). The account read:

> INDIAN NOTABLES DEAD—John, the War Chief of the Klamath and Rogue river Indians, known and dreaded for several years on account of his desperate hate of the whites, died of old age at Fort Yamhill on the 6th inst., within an hour or two of Stock Whitly, the head chief of the Nez Perces. Thus in one day the two most notable Indian warrior-chiefs of the Northern Pacific Coast, have gone to the great hunting grounds.

P. 194 *Biddle and Rector did relent.* Kent, "The Siletz Indian Reservation," p. 15. See also B. Biddle, Indian agent, report to W. Rector (Aug. 13, 1862), *in* House Doc. No. 1, 1862 Commissioner Report, 37th Congress, 3d Session, p. 420.

P. 194 *People who left without permission.* Schwartz, *The Rogue River Indian War*, p. 174.

P. 194 *"After being publicly whipped."* Maxwell, "Coquille Thompson of Old Siletz 'Remembers When'—" (relating his interview of Coquelle Thompson and Lucy Smith).

P. 194 *In 1864, Simpson conducted a grand sweep.* B. Simpson report to J. Huntington (Sept. 12, 1864), *in* House Doc. No. 1, 1864 Commissioner Report, 38th Congress, 2d Session, pp. 249–50.

P. 194 *Agency jobs being done by Indians.* See Kent, "The Siletz Indian Reservation," pp. 27, 30–31.

P. 194 *tribal members did other farm and ranch jobs in the valley.* See ibid., pp. 29, 31.

P. 198 *Gathering, preparing, and selling chittum bark.* T. Buford report to the Commissioner of Indian Affairs (Aug. 14, 1899), *in* House Doc. No. 5, 1899 Commissioner Report, 56th Congress, 1st Session, p. 318. Agent Buford reported that "the peeling, preparing, and sale of chittum bark (cascara sagrada) is growing into quite an industry among these people. It is found all over the reservation and the price, 3 cents per pound, makes the work of preparing it very profitable." Ibid.

P. 198 *The advent of modern canning technology.* The Hume brothers established the first Pacific coast cannery on the Sacramento River in 1864, but in 1867 they moved their operation to the Columbia River. See Arthur F. McEvoy, *The Fisherman's Problem: Ecology and Law in the California Fisheries, 1850–1980*, pp. 70–71 (Cambridge, UK: Cambridge University Press, 1986). The process quickly came into use in Oregon, with several canneries operating on the Coast by the 1870s and 1880s. See Glenn Cunningham, "Oregon's First Salmon Canner, 'Captain' John West," vol. 54, no. 3 *Oregon Historical Quarterly*, pp. 240–41 (Sept. 1953).

P. 198 *Salmon proceeds and hop-picking wages regularly exceeded.* See, e.g., T. Buford report to the Commissioner of Indian Affairs (Aug. 14, 1899), *in* House Doc. No. 5, 1899 Commissioner Report, 56th Congress, 1st Session, p. 318. Agent Buford's report, which contained a table listing the principal sources of earnings for the year, listed "Fish sold to cannery" as providing the most income at a total of $3,250. The next three highest wage-earning occupations, with their amounts, are as follows: "Sale of chittum bark: $2,500"; "Earned picking hops: $2,100"; "Sale of hay, grain, stock, and wool: $1,900." Ibid.

P. 198 *"demand of your agents to keep their Indians on their reservations."* Kent, "The Siletz Indian Reservation," p. 29 (quoting John Connor, who wrote to all of the Oregon Indian agents and to the commissioner of Indian Affairs).

P. 198 *the rise of the Warm House Dance.* See "Revival: The Thompson War House Dance," chapter 5 *in* Youst and Seaburg, *Coquelle Thompson, Athabascan Witness*, pp. 89–107.

P. 198 *A California Shasta named Bogus Tom.* See Michael E. Harkin, "Feeling and Thinking in Memory and Forgetting: Toward an Ethnohistory of the Emotions," vol. 50, no. 2 *Ethnohistory*, p. 272 (Spring 2003).

P. 198 *Ghost Dance promised the return of ancestors.* See Harkin, "Feeling and Thinking in Memory and Forgetting," p. 273.

P. 199 *Ghost Dance spread quickly.* See generally Alice Beck Kehoe, *The Ghost Dance: Ethnohistory and Revitalization* (New York: Holt, Rinehart and Winston, Inc., 1989); Shelley Anne Osterreich, *The American Indian Ghost Dance, 1870 and 1890: An Annotated Bibliography* (New York: Greenwood Press, 1991).

P. 199 *"I saw the first dance at Corvallis."* Cora Du Bois, "The 1870 Ghost Dance," vol. 3, no. 1 *Anthropological Records*, ed. A. L. Kroeber, R. H. Lowie, and R. L. Olson, p. 27 (Berkeley: University of California Press, 1939) (quoting Coquelle Thompson). In connection with this classic article on the Ghost Dance, anthropologist Cora Du Bois interviewed Coquelle Thompson, Hoxie Simmons, and several other Siletz tribal members involved in the Warm House Dance and described the dance in detail.

P. 199 *The dance houses were subterranean.* See ibid.

P. 199 *"When you went in."* Ibid., p. 28 (quoting Hoxie Simmons).

P. 199 *The songs were delivered in the Shasta language.* Ibid. Youst suggests that they may have been sung in Northern Paiute. Youst and Seaburg, *Coquelle Thompson, Athabascan Witness*, p. 92.

P. 199 *The dancers wore headbands.* Du Bois, "The 1870 Ghost Dance," p. 27. Bogus Tom introduced the headbands and feather capes that were worn by the dancers. Later, dancers would fashion regalia out of whatever materials were available to them, as Coquille Thompson explained: "[Chetco Charlie] made four or five capes out of chicken feathers and gunny sacks. They tied around the neck and under the arms and hung down to the shin bone. . . . Charlie didn't have yellowhammer feathers for headbands, so he made imitation ones out of paper and paint. He made whistles out of bird legbones for the cape dancers and a split-stick clapper for me as chief singer." Ibid., p. 32.

P. 199 *women were active participants.* Ibid., pp. 27–28. Coquille Thompson described to Du Bois how "women painted red and black spots on cheek bones. . . . Dancers blew whistles. Singers started new song; women joined in. . . . Caretaker 'went from woman to woman before the dance and straightened her hair down her back and saw that it looked nice.' After dance men bathed and returned to house; then women bathed." Ibid.

P. 200 *"When the dance house was finished."* Ibid., p. 27 (quoting Coquelle Thompson).

P. 200 *Thompson took the dance to several towns on the Coast.* See Youst and Seaburg, *Coquelle Thompson, Athabascan Witness*, pp. 101–6; Du Bois, "The 1870 Ghost Dance," pp. 32–34. Of the fees for attendance, Youst observed that "charging money for dances was nothing new. In this acquisitive, wealth-centered society [that Indian people had now entered] almost everything had its price." Youst and Seaburg, *Coquelle Thompson, Athabascan Witness*, p. 101.

P. 200 *burned all six dance houses.* Frank Simmons, interview with author, Siletz, Oregon, Feb. 8, 2007 (reporting on family accounts about Coquelle Thompson and Hoxie Simmons, who were his grandfathers). Robert Kentta also confirmed this, saying that he has been told by elders that the Bureau did burn down six dance houses in the 1870s. John Adams, Kentta's great-grandfather, was a BIA policeman who was ordered to do the burning. These statements by Adams were passed down to Kentta by his uncle, George Kentta, who received the information from Frances Johnson, married at one time to Adams; and by his mother, who was told the information by Adams's daughter, Mae Downey. Robert Kentta, interviews with author, Siletz, Oregon, May 23, 2005, and May 12, 2009. See also Du Bois, "The 1870 Ghost Dance," pp. 29–30.

P. 200 *"He thought the dead had started to come back."* Du Bois, "The 1870 Ghost Dance," p. 29 (quoting Hoxie Simmons). See also Youst and Seaburg, *Coquelle Thompson, Athabascan Witness*, pp. 100–101.

P. 200 *indications that Warm House Dances continued.* See Du Bois, "The 1870 Ghost Dance," p. 30.

10 Losing the Land

P. 201 *Yaquina's tricky, shifting channel.* Bruce Linn Engel, "Oregon Coast Indian Reserve: Establishment and Reduction, 1855–1875," p. 31, B.A. thesis, Reed College, 1961.

P. 201 *Oysters "thickly clustered."* B. Simpson, Indian agent, letter to J. Huntington, superintendent of Indian Affairs for Oregon (Aug. 20, 1863), *in* House Doc. No. 1, 1863 Commissioner Report, 38th Congress, 1st Session, p. 184.

P. 201 *paying quantities of beach gold.* See J. Huntington transcript of letter to W. Dole, commissioner of Indian Affairs (Nov. 21, 1863), M234 Roll 613, Doc. 7, *at* Archival Collection of Siletz Tribe Cultural Department [hereinafter Siletz Archival Collection].

P. 202 *Soldiers directed gold miners to leave.* See M. Susan Van Laere, "The Grizzly Bear and the Deer: The History of Federal Indian Policy and Its Impact on the Coast Reservation Tribes of Oregon, 1856–1877," p. 103, M.A. thesis, Oregon State University, 2000 (citing *The Corvallis Oregon Weekly Union* of Aug. 6, 1859).

P. 202 *reservation was closed to homesteading.* See J. Huntington transcript of notice to public (Nov. 20, 1864), M234 Roll 613, Doc. 8, *at* Siletz Archival Collection ("No settlement of persons not in the employ of the Indian Department can be permitted within the boundaries above named, and parties attempting such settlement will be required to remove forthwith.").

P. 202 *exclusive [oyster] harvesting permit.* B. Simpson transcript of letter to Winant & Co. (Dec. 1, 1863), M2 Roll 30, Doc. 25, *at* Siletz Archival Collection.

P. 202 *wagon road from Corvallis to Yaquina Bay.* See J. Huntington transcript of letter to W. Dole (Sept. 26, 1864), *in* House Doc. No. 1, 1864 Commissioner Report, 38th Congress, 2d Session, p. 227 ("The Aquina bay . . . is found to be a navigable and safe harbor, and a practicable route for a wagon road from the Willamette valley to the head of tide-water on the bay has been discovered and partially opened by citizens."). Congress formally authorized construction of the wagon road in 1866, with land patents subsequently awarded to the wagon road company that did the construction. See Senate Committee on Interior and Insular Affairs, Jerry A. O'Callaghan, "The Disposition of the Public Domain in Oregon," 86th Congress, 2d Session, p. 55 (Washington, D.C.: Government Printing Office, 1960). For a description of the construction of the road, including the seventy-five mule teams used, see Engel, "Oregon Coast Indian Reserve," p. 32.

P. 202 *By the summer of 1864.* See David D. Fagan, *History of Benton County, Oregon*, pp. 478–91 (Portland, OR: A. G. Walling, Printer, 1885); Jane Marie Harger, "The History of the Siletz Reservation, 1856–1877," pp. 86–87, M.A. thesis, University of Oregon, 1972.

P. 202 *Hillyer refused to stop harvesting oysters.* See Van Laere, "The Grizzly Bear and the Deer," p. 105; J. Huntington letter to W. Dole (Sept. 26, 1864), *in* House Doc. No. 1, 1864 Commissioner Report, 38th Congress, 2d Session, pp. 227–28.

P. 202 *Hillyer sued Agent Simpson.* See J. Huntington transcripts of letters to B. Alvord, brigadier general commanding the District of Oregon (March 18–Nov. 17, 1864), M2 Roll 9, Doc. 90 at Siletz Archival Collection. See also Transcript of A Ludlow & Co v. Benjamin Simpson, —Benslay and J. W. P. Huntington (Benton County Circuit Court, March 11, 1864), at Siletz Archival Collection. The case was filed in March 1864, dismissed for lack of subject matter jurisdiction and failure to state sufficient facts in November 1864, and appealed in February 1865. The Oregon Supreme Court rejected the appeal in September 1865, and ordered Hillyer, Ludlow, and Harris to pay the defendants' costs. Ibid.

P. 202 *Hillyer argued that the bay was "outside."* J. Huntington transcript of letter to B. Alvord (March 25, 1864), M2 Roll 9, Doc. 90, *at* Siletz Archival Collection.

P. 202 *"The reservation might as well be abandoned."* Ibid.

P. 202 *Hillyer protected by fifteen "roughs."* Royal A. Bensell, *All Quiet on the Yamhill: The Civil War in Oregon, The Journal of Corporal Royal A. Bensell*, Gunter Barth, ed., p. 176 (Eugene: University of Oregon Press, 2001). J. Huntington transcript of letter to W. Dole (Sept. 26, 1864), *in* House Doc. No. 1, 1864 Commissioner Report, 38th Congress, 2d Session, p. 228.

P. 202 *Judge Stratton rejected Hillyer's claim.* See Harger, "The History of the Siletz Reservation," p. 85; "Jurisdiction on Indian Reservations," *Oregon Statesman*, p. 1 (Nov. 28, 1864). See also Transcript of *A Ludlow & Co v. Benjamin Simpson, —Benslay and J. W. P. Huntington* (Benton County Circuit Court, March 11, 1864), *at* Siletz Archival Collection.

P. 203 *"cause the immediate ejection of all such persons."* J. Huntington transcript of letter to B. Simpson (Nov. 17, 1864), M2 Roll 9, Doc. 90, *at* Siletz Archival Collection.

P. 203 *a direct route to the ocean at Yaquina harbor.* See A. Barnard letter to J. Usher, secretary of the Interior (Dec. 22, 1864), *in* House Doc. No. 1, 1865 Commissioner Report, 39th Congress, 1st Session, p. 277 (the writer is incorrectly identified as "H. D." Barnard in the report):

> Heretofore the farmers of the Willamette valley have had to transport their grain and produce, generally at great expense to them of transportation, on the river, handling over four times, including a portage around the falls of the Willamette river, moving it in all some 225 miles from here and 275 miles from the upper end of this valley, to the sea-shore, at the mouth of the Columbia river, occupying in transit five to seven days. In contrast, we now do with a new road, not perfect, and in 45 miles' travel, with our own means of transportation, reach salt water.

P. 203 *Opening Yaquina Bay to non-Indian settlement.* W. Dole transcript of letter to W. Otto, assistant secretary of the Interior (Aug. 22, 1864), M348 Roll 14, *at* National Archives and Records Administration, Denver, Rocky Mountain Region.

P. 203 *Dole requested a full report.* W. Otto, acting secretary of the Interior, transcript of letter to J. Huntington (Aug. 31, 1864), M2 Roll 21, Doc. 15, *at* Siletz Archival Collection.

P. 203 *Barnard urged that a townsite be established at Yaquina Bay.* See A. Barnard letter to J. Usher (Dec. 22, 1864), *in* House Doc. No. 1, 1865 Commissioner Report, 39th Congress, 1st Session, pp. 276–77.

P. 203 *Yaquina Bay to benefit the counties.* J. Huntington letter to J. Usher (Dec. 12, 1864), *in* House Doc. No. 1, 1865 Commissioner Report, 39th Congress, 1st Session, p. 276.

P. 203 *boundary moved "somewhere between the Yaquina and Siletz."* Ibid., p. 275.

P. 203 *two-thirds of the reservation be eliminated!* Huntington wrote that his recommendation would remove "the whole southern half" of the reservation. Ibid. He was about right if measured by miles north-to-south. The southern part of the reservation, however, was much wider east-to-west so that the total loss in acres would have been larger than half, about two-thirds.

P. 204 *Nesmith quick to respond to his non-Indian constituents.* See J. Nesmith, U.S. senator for Oregon, transcript of letter to J. Huntington (Dec. 6, 1865), M2 Roll 22, Doc. 6, at Siletz Archival Collection ("Knowing the anxiety of our people to occupy the Yaquinna Bay . . .").

P. 204 *"no Indians on the strip proposed to be vacated."* J. Nesmith transcript of letter to J. Huntington (Dec. 27, 1865), M2 Roll 22, Doc. 9, *at* Siletz Archival Collection.

P. 204 *Yaquina Bay was "not occupied or desired by the Indians."* J. Harlan, secretary of the Interior, letter to President A. Johnson (Dec. 20, 1865), *in* Charles J. Kappler, ed., vol. 1, *Indian Affairs: Laws and Treaties*, p. 891 (Washington, D.C.: Government Printing Office, 1904). In his memorandum to President Johnson recommending the executive order, Secretary Harlan described the Siletz Reservation as "set apart conditionally." Ibid. Doubtless, Harlan had looked back to Secretary McClelland's use of the term "conditional" in his memorandum to President Pierce in 1855, which misquoted an earlier memorandum by the commissioner of Indian Affairs, violated the terms of the western Oregon treaties, and cannot be accepted if read to mean that later presidents could unilaterally take land from the Siletz reservation. See chapter 7, pp. 142–46 and accompanying notes.

P. 204 *The recommendation of the Secretary of the Interior.* Exec. Order, Dec. 21, 1865, reprinted in Kappler, ed., vol. 1, *Indian Affairs*, p. 891.

P. 204 *mapping out the separation of powers.* The Indian Commerce Clause is at U.S. Const. art. I, § 8, cl. 3. On Congress' "plenary and exclusive" authority over Indian affairs, see, e.g., *United States v. Lara*, 541 U.S. 193, 200 (2004). See also *Felix S. Cohen's Handbook of Federal Indian Law*, 2005, §5.02 (Newark, NJ: LexisNexis, 2005). On the power of Congress to abrogate treaties, see *Lone Wolf v. Hitchcock*, 187 U.S. 553, 566 (1903); *United States v. Dion*, 476 U.S. 734, 738–740 (1986). If treaty land is taken, a tribe must be fully compensated since treaty rights are vested under the Fifth Amendment. See, e.g., *United States v. Shoshone Tribe*, 304 U.S. 111 (1938); Cohen, *Handbook of Federal Indian Law*, 2005, §15.09(1)(d).

P. 205 *tribal lands can be sold . . . only with the approval of Congress.* In the Trade and Intercourse Acts passed between 1790 and 1834, Congress prohibited transfers of Indian land without congressional approval. See, e.g., Trade and Intercourse Act of 1790, ch. 33, July 22, 1790, 1 Stat. 137 (1790). This prohibition has remained in force for over two centuries and is codified at 25 U.S.C. § 177 (2006). See also *Johnson v. McIntosh*, 21 U.S. 543 (1823) (invalidating a grant of Indian land made to private individuals); *County of Oneida v. Oneida Indian Nation*, 470 U.S. 226 (1985) (invalidating a treaty between the tribe and the state conveying Indian land). See generally Cohen, *Handbook of Federal Indian Law*, 2005, §15.09(1).

P. 205 *cases invalidated executive actions.* See, e.g., *Cramer v. United States*, 261 U.S. 219 (1923); *Lane v. Pueblo of Santa Rosa*, 249 U.S. 110 (1919).

P. 205 Minnesota v. Mille Lacs Band of Chippewa Indians. 526 U.S. 172 (1999).

P. 205 *"The President's power."* Ibid., pp. 188–89.

P. 206 *"made by the direction of the President."* See chapter 7, pp. 104–5, 142–46 and accompanying notes.

P. 206 *Senator Nesmith's statement and Secretary Harlan's assurance.* J. Nesmith transcript of letter to J. Huntington (Dec. 27, 1865), M2 Roll 22, Doc. 9, *at* Siletz Archival Collection; J. Harlan letter to A. Johnson (Dec. 20, 1865), *in* Kappler, ed., vol. 1, *Indian Affairs*, p. 891.

P. 207 *"a large population lived full time at Yaquina Bay."* Robert Kentta, "1865 Executive Order Reducing the Coast Reservation and a Report of its Results" (1993), at Siletz Archival Collection.

P. 207 *Huntington recommended gaining tribal consent.* See J. Huntington letter to J. Usher

(Dec. 12, 1864), *in* House Doc. No. 1, 1865 Commissioner Report, 39th Congress, 1st Session, p. 275 ("In removing the Indians, [should that course be determined upon,] their consent must first be obtained, and provisions made for the expense which will be incurred.").

P. 207 *"Upon this tract were located some Indians."* J. Huntington report to Commissioner of Indian Affairs (Aug. 20, 1867), *in* House Doc. No. 1, 1867 Commissioner Report, 40th Congress, 2d Session, p. 65.

P. 208 *Indian people . . . never received any compensation.* See Harger, "The History of the Siletz Reservation," pp. 88–89; J. Huntington letter to D. Cooley, commissioner of Indian Affairs (Oct. 15, 1866), *in* House Doc. No. 1, 1866 Commissioner Report, 39th Congress, 2d Session, p. 74; J. Huntington report to Commissioner of Indian Affairs (Aug. 20, 1867), *in* House Doc. No. 1, 1867 Commissioner Report, 40th Congress, 2d Session, p. 65.

P. 208 *A petition to throw open the reservation.* See B. Simpson letter to A. Meacham, superintendent of Indian Affairs for Oregon (Sept. 30, 1870), *in* House Doc. No. 1, 1870 Commissioner Report, 41st Congress, 3d Session, p. 854. Schwartz does a good job of presenting the lead-up to the 1875 statute. See E. A. Schwartz, *The Rogue River Indian War and Its Aftermath, 1850–1980*, pp. 176–84, 191–98 (Norman: University of Oklahoma Press, 1997).

P. 208 *"it was useless for them to plant their crops."* B. Simpson letter to A. Meacham (Sept. 30, 1870), *in* House Doc. No. 1, 1870 Commissioner Report, 41st Congress, 3d Session, p. 854.

P. 208 *Some fled the reservation.* See ibid. ("Quite a number of the Indians ran away from the agency, while many others were very much discouraged, and it was with the greatest difficulty that I was enabled to keep them at work on their farms. . . . The Indians, as a general rule, are much opposed to giving up their homes, and, in fact, many of them will die before they will be removed.").

P. 209 *"it would be beneficial to both Indians and whites."* Senate Joint Memorial, concurred in by the House of Representatives, Legislative Assembly of the State of Oregon, "Praying That the Siletz Indian reservation in said State may be vacated and the Indians removed therefrom," 41st Congress, 3d Session, p. 1 (Jan. 9, 1871) (Washington, D.C.: Government Printing Office, 1871) (having been adopted by both houses of the Oregon Legislature on Oct. 7, 1870).

P. 209 *white settlers to the north circulated a petition.* T. Odeneal, superintendent of Indian Affairs for Oregon, transcript of letter to E. Smith, commissioner of Indian Affairs (May 30, 1873), M234 Roll 618, Doc. 2, *at* Siletz Archival Collection. The petition also called for the removal to Siletz of more than 200 Tillamook, Clatsop, and other Indians located in this area. Ibid.

P. 209 *Odeneal gave his support to the proposal.* Ibid. J. H. Fairchild, the agent at Siletz, originally did not support the proposal. See, e.g., J. Fairchild, Indian agent, transcript of letter to E. Smith (Sept. 29, 1873), M234 Roll 617, Doc. 4, *at* Siletz Archival Collection ("An act of grosser injustice and wrong was never contemplated"). But, as described in the text, the proposal for reduction and removal already was receiving attention in Washington, D.C.

P. 209 *"A long time ago the whites defeated the Indians."* Letter from the Acting Secretary of the Interior, "Accompanying . . . a Report of Inspector E. C. Kemble in relation to the condition of the Indians of the Siletz Agency in Oregon," Senate Doc. No. 65, 43d

Congress, 1st Session, p. 4 (Jan. 7, 1874) (Washington, D.C., 1874) (including Kemble's report and the minutes of the council held at Siletz Agency on Dec. 15, 1873) [hereinafter Kemble's Report]. The report is also found at E. Kemble transcript of letter to E. Smith (Jan. 7, 1874), M1070 Roll 33, Doc. 6, *at* Siletz Archival Collection. The quotation is from George Harney in the minutes of the council held at Siletz Agency on Dec. 15, 1873.

P. 209 *"You told us not to speak."* Ibid., p. 5 (quoting Depoe Charlie in the council minutes).

P. 210 *"I am proud and glad to see you."* Ibid., p. 6 (quoting William Strong in the council minutes).

P. 210 *"these Indians desirous, to a man."* The report is also found at Kemble's Report, p. 3. E. Kemble transcript of letter to E. Smith (Jan. 7, 1874), M1070 Roll 33, Doc. 6, at Siletz Archival Collection.

P. 210 *"The call for the removal of the Siletz."* Kemble's Report, p. 3.

P. 210 *Siletz made good workers.* Ibid.

P. 210 *"confirming their right to the lands they now occupy."* Ibid., pp. 3–4.

P. 211 *The center was gone.* Nathan Douthit admirably explores how, up through the mid-1850s, the Americans and the tribes at various times reached "middle-ground" accords and strategies. See Douthit, *Uncertain Encounters: Indians and Whites in Peace and War in Southern Oregon, 1820s to 1860s* (Corvallis: Oregon State University Press, 2002). It was that capability that had disappeared by the 1870s.

P. 211 *Senator John Mitchell.* There is no full biography of Mitchell. On his career, see e.g., William G. Robbins, "Mitchell, John Hipple," American National Biography Online (Feb. 2000), *at* http://www.anb.org/articles/05/05-00535-print.html (accessed July 30, 2007); Gordon B. Dodds, *Oregon: A Bicentennial History*, pp. 153–54 (New York: W. W. Norton & Co., 1977); "Mitchell, John Hipple," *in* Howard McKinley Corning, ed., *Dictionary of Oregon History*, pp. 167–68 (Portland, OR: Binford & Mort, 1956).

P. 211 *"The one constancy of Mitchell's . . . career."* Robbins, "Mitchell."

P. 211 *Mitchell was indicted in the Oregon land frauds.* See Jerry A. O'Callaghan, "Senator Mitchell and the Oregon Land Frauds, 1905," vol. 21, no. 3 *Pacific Historical Review*, pp. 255–61 (1952).

P. 211 *Simpson as Siletz agent.* See chapter 9, p. 183 and accompanying notes.

P. 211 *Simpson as surveyor general.* For a brief account of his career, see David Newsom, *David Newsom: The Western Observer, 1805–1882*, p. 284n173 (Portland: Oregon Historical Society, 1972).

P. 211 *Simpson opposed a break-up of the reservation.* See Schwartz, *The Rogue River Indian War*, p. 182 ("Agent Simpson, however, saw no advantage in removal. What would become of his job and patronage power that went with it if the reservation were abolished?").

P. 212 *Willamette Valley–Yaquina Bay railroad and public officials.* Engel, "Oregon Coast Indian Reserve," pp. 47–49.

P. 212 *Mitchell came out in favor of large-scale reduction.* See, e.g., J. Mitchell, U.S. senator for Oregon, transcript of letter to C. Delano, secretary of the Interior (Jan. 2, 1874), M234 Roll 619, Doc. 1, at Siletz Archival Collection. See also Schwartz, *The Rogue River Indian War*, p. 193; E. A. Schwartz, "Sick Hearts: Indian Removal on the Oregon Coast, 1875–1881," vol. 92 *Oregon Historical Quarterly*, pp. 233–34 (Fall 1991).

P. 213 *"will greatly accommodate the whites."* Schwartz, *The Rogue River Indian War*, p. 194 (quoting a June 1874 letter from Simpson to Mitchell).

P. 213 *"that all of them desired to remain."* J. Fairchild transcript of letter to E. Smith (Jan. 28, 1874), M234 Roll 619, Doc. 3, *at* Siletz Archival Collection.

P. 213 *"there would be no difficulty."* J. Fairchild transcript of letter to E. Smith (Dec. 4, 1874), M234 Roll 619, Doc. 9, *at* Siletz Archival Collection. On Fairchild's earlier opposition, see, e.g., J. Fairchild transcript of letter to E. Smith (Sept. 29, 1873), M234 Roll 617, Doc. 4, *at* Siletz Archival Collection; see also Schwartz, *The Rogue River Indian War*, p. 192.

P. 213 *Mitchell brought his proposal to the Senate.* See Address by Senator Mitchell of Jan. 26, 1875, vol. 3 *Congressional Record*, 43d Congress, 2d Session, pp. 729–30 (Washington, D.C.: Government Printing Office, 1875); address by Senator Mitchell of Feb. 20, 1875, vol. 3 *Congressional Record*, 43d Congress, 2d Session, pp. 1528–29 (Washington, D.C.: Government Printing Office, 1875).

P. 213 *"without their consent being first obtained."* Address by Senator Allison of Feb. 20, 1875, vol. 3 *Congressional Record*, 43d Congress, 2d Session, p. 1529 (Washington, D.C.: Government Printing Office, 1875). On Senator Allison's long career in Congress, see Leland L. Sage, *William Boyd Allison: A Study in Practical Politics* (Iowa City: State Historical Society of Iowa, 1956).

P. 213 *Senator John Sherman.* See Winfield S. Kerr, *John Sherman: His Life and Public Service* (Boston: Sherman, French & Co., 1907); George Mayer, *The Republican Party, 1854–1966*, pp. 276–77 (New York: Oxford University Press, 1967).

P. 213 *"It is manifestly the purpose to disturb this Indian reservation."* Address by Senator Sherman of Feb. 20, 1875, vol. 3 *Congressional Record*, 43d Congress, 2d Session, p. 1529 (Washington, D.C.: Government Printing Office, 1875).

P. 213 *"I desire to say in answer."* Ibid. The other inspection report, by William Vandever, was commissioned to look into a different issue—a dispute over the jurisdictions of the Grand Ronde and Siletz agencies. The report said only that "it may soon be thought advisable to abandon the whole of the Coast Reservation South of the Alsea River." W. Vandever, U.S. Indian inspector, transcript of letter to E. Smith (Aug. 21, 1874), M1070 Roll 33, Doc. 9, *at* Siletz Archival Collection.

P. 214 *"Provided, that these Indians shall not be removed."* Indian Appropriation Act, ch. 132, March 3, 1875, 18 Stat. 420 (1875) (not codified).

P. 214 *"such other inducements as will seem proper."* E. Smith transcript of letter to J. Fairchild (March 30, 1875), M21 Roll 134, Doc. 2, *at* Siletz Archival Collection. In a letter addressed the same day to G. Litchfield, agent at the Alsea sub-agency, Commissioner Smith failed to mention the consent provision when notifying Litchfield of his duty to assist in "the carrying out of this legislation by Congress, and the wishes of the Department in seeking what is deemed the best interests of all concerned by consolidating your Indians with those at Siletz." E. Smith transcript of letter to G. Litchfield, Indian agent (March 30, 1875), M21 Roll 134, Doc. 1, *at* Siletz Archival Collection.

P. 214 *"we all want to stay in our country."* The Tillamook tyee continued: "There are many old people at Tillamook, who all say they do not wish to leave. They want to die and be buried where their Fathers were before them." "Minutes of Council held with the Tillamook and other bands of Indians residing north of Siletz Reservation" (June 1, 1875), M234 Roll 621, Doc. 6, *at* Siletz Archival Collection.

P. 214 *"bad white men will debauch your women."* Fairchild also offered inducements, promising "as much land as [each head of family] can cultivate," along with supplies, a school, and a mill. Ibid.

P. 214 *The tyee of the Nestuccas.* J. Fairchild transcript of letter to E. Smith (June 4, 1875), M234 Roll 621, Doc. 7, *at* Siletz Archival Collection. Fairchild did hold "a consultation" with a chief of the Nestuccas a few days later, reporting in J. Fairchild transcript of letter to E. Smith (June 5, 1875), M234 Roll 621, Doc. 8, *at* Siletz Archival Collection: "It was evident however, that their minds were fully made up—they . . . were determined under no circumstances to leave their houses, unless forced to do so."

P. 214 *the council at Alsea.* See "Proceedings of a Council held June 27 1875 . . . with the tribes of Alsea, Coos, Umpqua and Siuslaw Indians residing on Alsea Indian Reservation" (June 17, 1875), M234 Roll 621, Doc. 12, *at* Siletz Archival Collection.

P. 214 *"to talk strait and true."* Ibid.

P. 214 *"As long as I live on my land."* Ibid.

P. 215 *"I have long had a sick heart.* Ibid.

P. 215 *"Yes it is like the whites had made us poor."* Ibid.

P. 215 *"I doubt the possibility of their peaceful removal."* J. Fairchild transcript of letter to E. Smith (June 21, 1875), M234 Roll 621, Doc. 10, *at* Siletz Archival Collection.

P. 216 Indians *"should not be coerced."* E. Smith transcript of letter to B. Simpson, surveyor general (July 17, 1875), M234 Roll 621, Doc. 13, *at* Siletz Archival Collection.

P. 216 *"the great importance of obeying."* B. Simpson, special agent, transcript of letter to E. Smith (Aug. 27, 1875), M234 Roll 621, Doc. 17, *at* Siletz Archival Collection.

P. 216 *"the necessity of complying."* M. Chafeman, clerk, transcript of letter to J. Fairchild (Sept. 8, 1875), M234 Roll 620, Doc. 3, *at* Siletz Archival Collection (styled as a report on the Aug. 24 and 25 Alsea Agency Council).

P. 216 *Simpson adjourned the council.* B. Simpson transcript of letter to E. Smith (Aug. 27, 1875), M234 Roll 621, Doc. 17, *at* Siletz Archival Collection.

P. 216 *the tyees continued to hold their ground."* Ibid.

P. 216 *"Quite a number of the Indians spoke."* M. Chafeman, clerk, transcript of letter to J. Fairchild (Sept. 8, 1875), M234 Roll 620, Doc. 3, *at* Siletz Archival Collection.

P. 216 *George Harney, Depoe Charlie, and William Strong attended.* B. Simpson transcript of letter to E. Smith (Aug, 27, 1875), M234 Roll 621, Doc. 17, *at* Siletz Archival Collection.

P. 216 *"they expected to move to Siletz."* J. Fairchild transcript of letter to E. Smith (Sept. 2, 1875), M234 Roll 621, Doc. 18, *at* Siletz Archival Collection.

P. 216 *"being of the same race."* Ibid.

P. 216 *Fairchild recommended that the government begin removing public property.* See B. Simpson transcript of letter to E. Smith (Aug. 27, 1875), M234 Roll 621, Doc. 17, *at* Siletz Archival Collection; J. Fairchild transcript of letter to E. Smith (Sept. 2, 1875), M234 Roll 621, Doc. 18, *at* Siletz Archival Collection. Simpson and Fairchild both believed that this course of action would induce (or coerce) the Alsea to remove to Siletz.

P. 217 *"it was a terrible mistake."* B. Simpson transcript of letter to J. Mitchell (Aug. 26, 1875), M234 Roll 621, Doc. 15. Fairchild was even more forceful in an angry, rambling letter of November 3, 1875, to Commissioner Smith, when he left no doubt that the Alseas had not consented at the August council and still had not done so by November: "I am fully persuaded of one thing—Agent Litchfield's *opposition alone has prevented the Alsea Indians removing to Siletz. At any time since this negotiation* for the removal of the Alseas has been going forward, if he had made the *slightest effort to induce* his Indians to *consent to removal* they would have done so. I once thought otherwise—now I feel sure of what I write. The Indians think if they hold firm they will have their Agency continued as it has been" (emphasis in original). J. Fairchild transcript of letter to E. Smith (Nov. 3, 1875), M234 Roll 621, Doc. 28, *at* Siletz Archival Collection.

P. 217   *"they consented to abandon their country."* B. Simpson transcript of letter to E. Smith (Oct. 28, 1875), M234 Roll 621, Doc. 26, *at* Siletz Archival Collection. See also J. Fairchild transcript of letter to E. Smith (Sept. 30, 1875), M234 Roll 621, Doc. 23, *at* Siletz Archival Collection (referring to the "treaty" negotiated by Simpson).

P. 217   *funds to provide assistance to the Tillamooks.* See J. Fairchild transcript of letter to J. Mitchell (Oct. 20, 1875), M234 Roll 621, Doc. 24, *at* Siletz Archival Collection.

P. 217   *the Tillamooks waited by the mouth of the Salmon River.* J. Fairchild transcript of letter to E. Smith (Nov. 3, 1875), M234 Roll 621, Doc. 28, *at* Siletz Archival Collection. By this point, Fairchild had submitted his resignation as Indian agent, and, in this, his final correspondence with Smith, predicted disaster for the Tillamook: "Bloodshed will probably result At all events *one thing is certain—if they return they will never go to Siletz Reservation again alive* I cannot blame them They have acted in good faith throughout—the Government has failed to perform a single promise" (emphasis in original).

P. 217   *"Consent reported by Special Agent Simpson."* Kappler, ed., vol. 1, *Indian Affairs*, p. 157.

P. 218   *California termination statutes.* See *Table Bluff Band of Indians v. Andrus*, 532 F. Supp. 255 (N.D. Cal. 1981); *Smith v. United States*, 515 F. Supp. 56 (N.D. Cal. 1978); *Duncan v. Andrus*, 517 F. Supp. 1 (N.D. Cal. 1977). See also Cohen, *Handbook of Federal Indian Law*, 2005, §§6.01-6.02 (2005).

P. 219   *Senator Henry Dawes and the allotment legislation.* See generally Frederick E. Hoxie, *A Final Promise: The Campaign to Assimilate the Indians, 1880–1920*, pp. 40–41, 70–73 (Lincoln: University of Nebraska Press, 1984); Francis Paul Prucha, vol. 2, *The Great Father: The United States Government and the American Indians*, pp. 660–71 (Lincoln: University of Nebraska Press, 1984).

P. 219   *Interest in bringing science into public policy.* See generally Samuel P. Hays, *Conservation and the Gospel of Efficiency: The Progressive Conservation Movement, 1890–1920* (New York: Atheneum, 1980).

P. 219   *Social scientists' theory of human advancement.* See Fred Eggan, *The American Indian: Perspectives for the Study of Social Change*, pp. 143–44 (Chicago: Aldine Publishing Co., 1966); Edwin L. Chalcraft, *Assimilation's Agent: My Life as a Superintendent in the Indian Boarding School System*, ed. Cary C. Collins, pp. xix–xx (Lincoln: University of Nebraska Press, 2004); Lewis H. Morgan, *Ancient Society* (London: MacMillan & Co., 1877).

P. 219   *Assimilationist policy with attention to land.* See Hoxie, *A Final Promise*, pp. 19–20.

P. 219   *"If I stand alone in the Senate."* Address by Senator Teller of Jan. 20, 1881, vol. 11, pt. 1 *Congressional Record,* 46th Congress, 2d Session, p. 783 (Washington, D.C.: Government Printing Office, 1881).

P. 219   *"we shall have a quarter of a million paupers."* Address by Senator Dolph of Jan. 25, 1887, vol. 18, pt. 1 *Congressional Record*, 49th Congress, 2d Session, p. 974 (Washington, D.C.: Government Printing Office, 1887).

P. 219   *John Wesley Powell.* On Powell's career, see Wallace Stegner, *Beyond the Hundredth*

Meridian (Boston: Houghton Mifflin, 1954); Donald Worster, *A River Running West* (New York: Oxford University Press, 2001); William deBuys, ed., *Seeing Things Whole* (Washington, D.C.: Island Press, 2001).

P. 220 *"The Indian religion is localized."* Worster, *A River Running West*, p. 270 (quoting Powell's Feb. 16, 1888, letter to Senator Teller).

P. 220 *"the first step to be taken in their civilization."* Ibid.

P. 220 *Friends of the Indian.* See generally Robert Winston Mardock, *The Reformers and the American Indian* (Columbia: University of Missouri Press, 1971); Francis Paul Prucha, *American Indian Policy in Crisis: Christian Reformers and the American Indian, 1865–1900*, pp. 143–68 (Norman: University of Oklahoma Press, 1976).

P. 220 *Allotment program never received scrutiny.* See Hoxie, *A Final Promise*, pp. 71–73.

P. 221 *No new land would be brought into Indian ownership.* Section 4 of the General Allotment Act did allow for public domain allotments—or "Section 4" allotments—in which Indians not residing on a reservation could obtain trust allotments from federal public domain lands, but not from reservation lands. See Section 4 of the General Allotment Act, ch. 119, Feb. 8, 1887, 24 Stat. 389 (1887) (codified as amended at 25. U.S.C. §334 [2006]).

P. 221 *Tribal land versus allotments.* On the progression from tribal land to individual trust allotments or fee patents, see Prucha, vol. 2, *The Great Father*, pp. 667–68; Cohen, *Handbook of Federal Indian Law, 2005*, §§16.03(2). For insights into the allotment process on one reservation, see E. Jane Gay, *With the Nez Perces: Alice Fletcher in the Field, 1889–92*, ed. Frederick E. Hoxie and Joan T. Mark (Lincoln: University of Nebraska Press, 1981).

P. 221 *"It was beautiful land."* Gladys Bolton, interview with María Aparicio, research assistant, Keizer, Oregon, March 26, 2007.

P. 221 *"the allotment was no longer there."* Eddie Collins, interview with María Aparicio, research assistant, Lincoln City, Oregon, May 20, 2007; Eddie Collins, interview with Josh Tenneson, research assistant, Lincoln City, Oregon, June 20, 2006.

P. 221 *"many Siletz people lost their allotments."* Frank Simmons, interview with María Aparicio, research assistant, Siletz, Oregon, March 26, 2007.

P. 222 *"We want to hold this land."* Kemble's Report, p. 6 (including the minutes of the council held at Siletz Agency on Dec. 15, 1873).

P. 222 *"I want the land divided."* Ibid.

P. 222 *Several other speakers wanted the land "divided."* See, e.g., ibid., pp. 5 (Sixes Mack and McAllen); 7 (Coquille Charlie).

P. 223 *tribal land holdings had plummeted.* See Alvin M. Josephy Jr., *Now that the Buffalo's Gone: A Study of Today's American Indians*, p. 132 (New York: Alfred A. Knopf, 1982); Frank Pommersheim, *Braid of Feathers: American Indian Law and Contemporary Tribal Life*, p. 20 (Berkeley: University of California Press, 1995).

P. 223 *"a mighty pulverizing machine."* Brian W. Dippie, *The Vanishing American: White Attitudes and U.S. Indian Policy*, p. 244 (Middletown, CT: Wesleyan University Press, 1982).

P. 223 *Congress delegated authority to issue allotments.* See General Allotment Act, ch. 119, Feb. 8, 1887, 24 Stat. 388 (1887) (codified as amended, *at* 25 U.S.C. §§331-58 (2006) (§§ 331-33 repealed 2007).

P. 223 *Surplus lands required agreements with the tribes.* Ibid., §5 ("it shall be lawful for the Secretary of the Interior to negotiate with such Indian tribe for the purchase and release . . . of such portions of its reservation not allotted as such tribe shall . . . consent to sell. . . ."); see also Indian Appropriation Act, ch. 543, March 3, 1891, 26 Stat. 989 (1891) (not codified) ("To enable the Secretary of the Interior in his discretion to negotiate with any Indians for the surrender of portions of their respective reservations").

P. 223   *Commissioners met with tribal members.* See "Full Reporting of Proceedings of a council held with the Indians of the Siletz Reservation" (Oct. 17 and 29, 1892), at Siletz Archival Collection [hereinafter Proceedings of 1892 Council]. For the reports and transmittal letters that were provided to the Senate, see letter from the Secretary of the Interior, "Transmitting an agreement made by the commission appointed to treat with the Indians of the Siletz Reservation for the cession of certain lands," Senate Doc. No. 39, 52d Congress, 2d Session (Feb. 1, 1893) (Washington, D.C.: Government Printing Office, 1893) [hereinafter 1893 Agreement with the Siletz].

P. 223   *"long explanation and discussion."* Proceedings of 1892 Council, p. 20.

P. 223   *tribal committee reached agreement.* Regarding the tribal members' high degree of civilization, see R. Boise, W. Odell, and H. Harding letter to J. Nobel, secretary of the Interior, and T. Morgan, commissioner of Indian Affairs (Nov. 9, 1892), *in* 1893 Agreement with the Siletz, p. 6 ("We find these Indians exceptionally intelligent—they having adopted the manner of life of the white people—living in frame houses, wearing ordinary citizens' dress, and houses having similar furniture to whites in similar circumstances, the younger Indians being educated and writing and speaking the English language, and are shrewd and provident in managing their business to a large extent."). For a list of the 118 signatories, many of whom gave their approval with "X" marks, see 1893 Agreement with the Siletz, pp. 11–12.

P. 224   *Tribal members elected the committee.* See Proceedings of 1892 Council, p. 19. The seven committee members were Scott Lane, Frank Carson, U. S. Grant, John Adams, Depoe Charlie, George Harney, and Sitely Morris. Ibid. 1893 Agreement with the Siletz, p. 11.

P. 224   *the committee was appointed by the agent.* See Hoxie Simmons's testimony before the Indian Claims Commission, *Tillamook Tribe of Indians v. United States,* Ind. Cl. Comm. No. 239 (1955), *at* Siletz Archival Collection.

P. 224   *"Our agent instructed them."* Ibid., p. 6.

P. 224   *"They wanted to keep for the next generation."* Ibid., p. 3.

P. 224   *"'Keep the land, don't sell it.'"* Ibid.

P. 225   *being "fair" and acting in "good faith."* See Proceedings of 1892 Council, pp. 2, 6, 10.

P. 225   *called Harney's statements "rash."* See ibid., p. 8.

P. 225   *"We want to know how much land is left."* Ibid., p. 13.

P. 225   *"The amount of land ceded is over 175,000 acres."* R. Boise, W. Odell, and H. Harding transcript of letter to J. Nobel and T. Morgan (Nov. 9, 1892), *in* 1893 Agreement with the Siletz, p. 6. In his report to the secretary, the commissioner of Indian Affairs set the figure at 178,840 acres. T. Morgan report to J. Noble (Dec. 14, 1892), *in* 1893 Agreement with the Siletz, p. 3.

P. 225   *"The Government does not think that these lands are of much value."* Proceedings of 1892 Council, p. 1.

P. 225   *"The government does not buy these lands because they want them."* Ibid., p. 5.

P. 225   *"They are of so little value."* Ibid., p. 8.

P. 225   *The surplus lands were "densely timbered."* R. Boise, W. Odell, and H. Harding letter to J. Nobel and T. Morgan (Nov. 9, 1892), *in* 1893 Agreement with the Siletz, pp. 5–6.

P. 225 *"lands . . . being generally valuable for the timber."* W. Stone, commissioner of the General Land Office, letter to J. Nobel (Jan. 26, 1893), *in* 1893 Agreement with the Siletz, p. 9.

P. 225 *80 cents per acre.* See T. Morgan report to J. Noble (Dec. 14, 1892), *in* 1893 Agreement with the Siletz, pp. 2 ("the United States will pay to the Indians the sum of $142,600"), 3 ("the commissioners state that the quantity of land ceded is over 175,000 acres").

P. 225 *Harney requested $1.25 per acre.* See Proceedings of 1892 Council, p. 7.

P. 226 *Fraud on the western federal lands.* On timber fraud, see generally Paul W. Gates, *History of Public Land Law Development*, pp. 463–94 (Washington, D.C.: Government Printing Office, 1968); Samuel T. Dana and Sally K. Fairfax, *Forest and Range Policy: Its Development in the United States*, 2d ed., pp. 50–69 (New York: McGraw-Hill Book Co., 1980).

P. 226 *former Siletz tribal forest lands became a prime target.* See A. W. Morgan, *Fifty Years in Siletz Timber*, pp. 1–2 (Portland, OR: A. W. Morgan, 1959) (describing the surplus land sale, the use of dummy homesteaders, and "the timber frauds that were current along the coast").

P. 226 Looters of the Public Domain. S. A. D. Puter, *Looters of the Public Domain* (New York: Arno Press, 1972). For the chapter on Siletz, see ibid., pp. 469–82. Puter certainly had the requisite expertise: he had participated in some of the schemes and wrote his book from prison.

P. 226 *Tens of thousands of acres to timber companies.* See Morgan, *Fifty Years in Siletz Timber*, pp. 33–39. On the prosecutions for land fraud, see ibid. pp. 7–11.

P. 226 *obtained the surplus lands agreement they had aimed for.* See 1893 Agreement with the Siletz, pp. 9–12.

P. 226 *43,000 acres for 551 individual allotments.* The original estimate was that 536 allotments would be issued but that number turned out to be a bit low, as some supplemental allotments were later awarded. In all, 551 tribal members received allotments totaling 44,459 acres. House Report No. 2492 to accompany S. 2746, "Termination of Federal Supervision over Property of Certain Indians in Western Oregon," 83d Congress, 2d Session, p. 9 (Washington, D.C.: Government Printing Office, 1954).

P. 226 *387 section 4 allotments from federal public lands.* On section 4 allotments, see Prucha, *Great Father*, p. 866; 25 U.S.C. §334 (2000). The total of 387 section 4 allottees is reported in U.S. Department of the Interior, "Report of the Commissioner of Indian Affairs, to the Secretary of the Interior for the Fiscal Year Ended June 30, 1920," p. 71 (Washington D.C.: Government Printing Office, 1920).

P. 227 *$42,000 fund would be exhausted in just a few years.* We do not have an exact figure for the number of adults at this time. If, however, there were 300 adults (a low estimate), the first year's payments of $75 would have totaled $22,500—more than half of the fund. On the terms of payment to the tribe, see 1893 Agreement with the Siletz, p. 10.

P. 227 *Congress approved the agreement in 1894.* Indian Appropriation Act of 1894, ch. 290, Aug. 15, 1894, 28 Stat. 286 (1894) (not codified).

P. 227 *aboriginal populations.* Alfred Kroeber's 1937 estimate of pre-Columbian aboriginal populations at 900,000 is universally considered as too low, and Henry Dobyns's 1982 figure of 18 million too high. See generally Russell Thornton, *American Indian Holo-*

caust and Survival: A Population History since 1492 (Norman: University of Oklahoma Press, 1987); Elizabeth A. Fenn, *Pox Americana: The Great Smallpox Epidemic of 1775–82* (New York: Hill and Wang, 2002); Jared Diamond, *Guns, Germs, and Steel: The Fates of Human Societies* (New York: W. W. Norton & Co., 1997); Henry F. Dobyns, *Their Number Become Thinned: Native American Population Dynamics in Eastern North America* (Knoxville: University of Tennessee Press, 1983).

P. 227 *Siletz population of 2,700 in 1857.* See J. Nesmith, superintendent of Indian Affairs for Oregon, letter to J. Denver, commissioner of Indian Affairs (Sept. 1, 1857), *in* House Doc. No. 2, 1857 Commissioner Report, 35th Congress, 1st Session, p. 606.

P. 227 *Siletz population of 500 in 1900.* The 1900 Commissioner Report estimated 482 but probably failed to account for some off-reservation tribal members. T. Buford, Indian agent, letter to W. Jones, commissioner of Indian Affairs (Aug. 10, 1900), *in* House Doc. No. 5, 1900 Commissioner Report, 56th Congress, 2d Session, p. 360.

11 Change and Perseverance

P. 231 *The General Allotment Act.* For the background and provisions of the 1887 Act, see chapter 10, pp. 218–21 and accompanying notes.

P. 231 *Siletz Inherited Lands Act of 1901.* See Section 9 of the Indian Appropriation Act, ch. 832, March 3, 1901, 31 Stat. 1085 (1901) (codified at 25 U.S.C. §348 [2006]).

P. 231 *"Many of these people would be benefited."* W. Jones, commissioner of Indian Affairs, report to E. Hitchcock, secretary of the Interior (Nov. 21, 1901), *in* Letter from the Secretary of the Interior, "Transmitting a Report from the Commissioner of Indian Affairs . . . Authorizing the Issuance of Patents to the Indians of the Siletz Reservation in Oregon," Senate Doc. No. 80, 57th Congress, 1st Session, p. 3 (Dec. 16, 1901) (Washington, D.C.: Government Printing Office, 1902).

P. 231 *the "Dead Indian Act."* Act of May 27, 1902, ch. 888, 32 Stat. 275 (1902) (codified at 25 U.S.C. §379 [2006]).

P. 231 *tribal agricultural production steadily declined.* See chapter 9, pp. 184–86

P. 232 *The Burke Act of 1906.* The Burke Act amended the General Allotment Act of 1887, giving the Secretary of the Interior discretion to deem an allottee "competent and capable of managing his or her affairs." Once designated competent, the allottee was issued a patent in fee simple. See ch. 2348, May 8, 1906, 34 Stat. 182 (1906) (codified at 25 U.S.C. §349 [2006]). The practical effect of the statute was to accelerate greatly the sale of allotments. See Francis Paul Prucha, vol. 2, *The Great Father: The United States Government and the American Indians*, pp. 875–77 (Lincoln: University of Nebraska Press, 1984).

P. 232 *"the beginning of the end of the Indian problem."* In a 1917 declaration of policy, Commissioner Sells set forth an administrative policy of "discontinuing guardianship of all competent Indians and giving even closer attention to the incompetent that they may more speedily achieve competency." C. Sells, commissioner of Indian Affairs, declaration of policy (Oct. 15, 1917), *in* House Doc. No. 915, vol. 2, 1917 Commissioner Report, 65th Congress, 2d Session, pp. 3–4.

P. 232 *"competency commissions."* See Prucha, *The Great Father*, pp. 880–83; Frederick E. Hoxie, *A Final Promise: The Campaign to Assimilate the Indians, 1880–1920*, pp. 175–87 (Lincoln: University of Nebraska Press, 1984).

P. 233 *"forced-fee" patents.* On these transactions, see, e.g., LeAnn Larson Lafave, "South

Dakota's Forced Fee land Claims: Will Landowners be Liable for Government's Wrongdoing?" vol. 30 *South Dakota Law Review*, p. 59 (1985). Several suits have been filed to set aside forced fee patents in modern times but have typically been barred by statutes of limitations. See, e.g., *United States v. Mottaz*, 476 U.S. 834 (1986).

P. 233   *27 million acres passed out of Indian hands.* Wilcomb E. Washburn, *Red Man's Land / White Man's Law*, p. 145 (Norman: University of Oklahoma Press, 1995). For more information on allotment and the loss of Indian trust land, see chapter 10, pp. 218–21 and accompanying notes.

P. 233   *unemployment surely reached 50 percent.* There are no hard figures for employment at Siletz in the early 1900s. Some government documents reported on employment, but they were sporadic and tended to be incomplete. Those reports indicated very low employment at Siletz (and other at reservations as well). For example, the employment table in the 1911 Commissioner of Indian Affairs Report shows a total of fifteen Siletz people employed by the BIA (six of which held "irregular" seasonal jobs) and reported no jobs in the private sector. "Table 17: Employment of Indians for fiscal year ended June 30, 1911," *in* House Doc. No. 120, vol. 2, 1911 Commissioner Report, 62d Congress, 2d Session, p. 144. We do know that unemployment across Indian country in the 1950s and 1960s, when economic conditions were much the same as in the early part of the century, was in the 50 percent range or higher. Charles Wilkinson, *Blood Struggle: The Rise of the Modern Indian Nations*, p. 22 (New York: W. W. Norton & Co., 2005). Of course, a form of income was obtained by Siletz tribal members through sources such as hunting, fishing, gathering, home gardens, odd jobs, and barter.

P. 233   *"we won't know where [the allotments] went."* Bob Tom, interview with María Aparicio, research assistant, Lincoln City, Oregon, Aug. 9, 2006.

P. 233   *The land loss was steady and substantial.* For an account of the loss of allotments, see E. A. Schwartz, *The Rogue River Indian War and Its Aftermath, 1850–1980*, pp. 224–38 (Norman: University of Oklahoma Press, 1997).

P. 233   *half of the allottees had passed away.* K. C. Egbert, superintendent of Siletz Agency, report to Commissioner of Indian Affairs (Aug. 18, 1905), *in* House Doc. No. 5, 1905 Commissioner Report, 59th Congress, 1st Session, pt. 1, p. 326.

P. 233   *"this land is in demand."* J. McKoin, superintendent of Siletz Agency, report to Commissioner of Indian Affairs (June 30, 1904), *in* House Doc. No. 5, 1904 Commissioner Report, 58th Congress, 3d Session, pt. 1, p. 317.

P. 233   *an average of just $7.12 per acre.* K. C. Egbert report to Commissioner of Indian Affairs (Aug. 6, 1906), *in* House Doc. No. 5, 1906 Commissioner Report, 59th Congress, 2d Session, pt. 1, p. 333. The value in current dollars was calculated using the Consumer Price Index through Measuringworth, *at* http://www.measuringworth.com (accessed May 28, 2009).

P. 235   *"white interests formed a ring about the Indian reservation."* D. S. Otis, *The Dawes Act and the Allotment of Indian Lands*, ed. Francis Paul Prucha, p. 141 (Norman: University of Oklahoma Press, 1973).

P. 235   *60 percent of allotments had gone out of trust.* Schwartz, *The Rogue River Indian War*, p. 234.

P. 235   *second largest source of annual reservation income.* See "Table 10: Incomes of Indians (by reservations), including tribal incomes, for fiscal year ended June 30, 1919," *in* House Doc. No. 409, vol. 2, 1919 Commissioner Report, 66th Congress, 2d Session, p.

120 (showing total Siletz income for the year at $42,815, with $22,000 from crops and $11,580 from land sales).

P. 235 *"should be required to assume their responsibilities."* Edwin L. Chalcraft, *Assimilation's Agent: My Life as a Superintendent in the Indian Boarding School System*, ed. Cary C. Collins, p. 291 (Lincoln: University of Nebraska Press, 2004).

P. 235 *"Many of the best farms on the Siletz."* Hearings Before a Subcommittee of the Senate Committee on Indian Affairs, "Survey of Conditions of the Indians in the United States: On S. Res. 79, 308, 263, and 416," 71st Congress, 3d Session, pt. 21, p. 11722 (Washington, D.C.: Government Printing Office, 1932) [hereinafter Survey of Conditions of the Indians]; see also William G. Robbins, *Oregon: This Storied Land*, p. 109 (Portland: Oregon Historical Society Press, 2005).

P. 236 *"the money derived from the sale."* Schwartz, *The Rogue River Indian War*, p. 225.

P. 236 *"the policy of this department."* F. Pierce, acting secretary of the Interior, report to M. Clapp, chairman, Senate Committee on Indian Affairs (Feb. 15, 1908), *in* Senate Report No. 305 to Accompany S. 4713, "Sale of Certain Lands on Siletz Reservation, Oregon," 60th Congress, 1st Session, pp. 1–2 (Feb. 27, 1908) (Washington, D.C.: Government Printing Office, 1908).

P. 236 *The bill passed in 1910.* See Act of May 13, 1910, ch. 233, 36 Stat. 367 (1910) (not codified).

P. 236 *"the land allotted to the Siletz Indians."* E. Reel, superintendent of Indian Schools, report to Commissioner of Indian Affairs (Sept. 25, 1908), *in* House Doc. No. 1046, vol. 2, 1907 Commissioner Report, 60th Congress, 2d Session, p. 131.

P. 237 *put up for sale to non-Indians.* House Report No. 1098 to Accompany S. 539, "Sale of Certain Lands on Siletz Indian Reservation," 61st Congress, 2d Session, p. 1 (April 22, 1910) (Washington, D.C.: Government Printing Office, 1910) (quoting the language of the Act of May 13, 1910, ch. 233, 36 Stat. 367).

P. 237 *Only 76 of the original 551 allotments remained in trust.* Senate Report No. 1325 to Accompany S. 2746, "Termination of Federal Supervision over Property of Certain Indians in Western Oregon," 83d Congress, 2d Session, p. 13 (Washington, D.C.: Government Printing Office, 1954) [hereinafter 1954 Senate Termination Report].

P. 237 *Siletz children attended Chemawa.* Early attendance records are incomplete. Graduation lists for most years show that, from 1888 through 1940, between one and four Siletz students graduated in a typical year. *Chemawa Alumni Class Lists*, Chemawa Indian School, *at* http://www.chemawa.bia.edu/classlists.htm (accessed May 27, 2009).

P. 237 *"No Indian Talk."* Patrick Michael McKeehan, "The History of Chemawa Indian School," p. 92, Ph.D. diss., University of Washington, 1981. See also James Allen Smith, "To Assimilate the Children: The Boarding School at Chemawa, Oregon, 1880–1930," M.A. thesis, Central Washington University, 1993. On Indian education and boarding schools, see generally Margaret Connell Szasz, *Education and the American Indian* (Albuquerque: University of New Mexico Press, 1974); Margaret L. Archuleta, Brenda J. Child, and K. Tsianina Lomawaima, eds., *Away from Home: American Indian Boarding School Experiences, 1879–2000* (Phoenix, AZ: Heard Museum, 2000); Jon Reyhner and Jeanne Eder, *American Indian Education* (Norman: University of Oklahoma Press, 2004).

P. 237 *severe punishment continued to be administered.* Cary C. Collins, "Through the Lens of Assimilation: Edwin L. Chalcraft and Chemawa Indian School," vol. 98 *Oregon*

Historical Quarterly, p. 414 (Winter 1997–1998). A major incident took place at Chemawa six years after the 1904 ban was instated. Edwin Chalcraft, the influential advocate for assimilation who served both as BIA superintendent at Siletz and as superintendent at Chemawa, was fired from his position at the boarding school for inflicting corporal punishment. In response, Chalcraft claimed that every BIA boarding school superintendent used corporal punishment in spite of the 1904 directive. Ibid., pp. 414–16. A nine-year-old Siletz/Coos girl who attended Chemawa from 1927 to 1932 reported that

> some of [the punishment] could be kind of severe. I remember one time going to breakfast and they had three boys. They had a bar, cross beam affair and they had ropes tied to it and they had these three boys tied by their wrists. Their feet were on the ground, just touching. They couldn't stand flat, but on their tippy toes. God I almost died because one of them was my brother. It seemed that what they had done was run away the night before. They were captured and brought back. That was their punishment, for embarrassment. They weren't flogged. I can remember seeing him yet.

Sonciray Bonnell, "Chemawa Indian Boarding School: The First One Hundred Years, 1880 to 1980," p. 50, M.A. thesis, Dartmouth College, 1997.

P. 238 *they "have been fitted for better things."* McKeehan, "History of Chemawa," p. 130.

P. 238 *"every such capable young man and woman."* A student was designated "competent" based upon his or her "degree of Indian blood, health condition, course of study pursued and how long, statement of how his personal funds have been handled, and a biographical sketch," along with recommendations addressing the student's "industry, reliability, apparent business qualifications, general character and habits." Ibid., p. 126.

P. 238 *"They beat us if anyone was caught talking Indian."* Terry and Emma Russell, interview with Josh Tenneson, research assistant, Lincoln City, Oregon, June 21, 2006. Aurilla Tom was Emma Russell's mother and Terry Russell's grandmother. Terry Russell explained that school officials told students like his grandmother that "if you want to be anything you have to talk in English." However, speaking English proved difficult for some students who struggled with the nuances of the language. Mr. Russell recalled the story of a girl at Chemawa who was punished for calling one of her teachers a witch. The girl was told to stand in the corner until she apologized. After standing there nearly all day, another student asked her why she had not apologized yet. The girl responded that she did not know what "apologize" meant, and the other student explained that it meant saying sorry. The girl then approached the teacher and said, "I'm sorry you're a witch." Ibid.

P. 238 *"in keeping with the tribes' cultural traditions." Chemawa Mission and Vision*, Chemawa Indian School, *at* http://www.chemawa.bia.edu/missionvision.htm (accessed May 28, 2009).

P. 239 *hold the school in "high regard."* Bonnell, "Chemawa," pp. 2, 5. Bonnell's thesis explores the history of Chemawa from the perspective of its Indian alumni. To assure anonymity for her interviewees, she does not use the students' actual names, only tribal affiliation, in the text of her thesis.

P. 239 *learned the trade of tailoring.* Kay Steele, interview with Carrie Covington, research assistant, Portland, Oregon, May 18, 2007.

P. 239 *"a whole new world with stores."* June Austin, interview with Carrie Covington, research assistant, Siletz, Oregon, May 17, 2007.

P. 239 *"Oh, we were white girls then."* Bonnell, "Chemawa," p. 57.

P. 239 *"we should not give up Chemawa."* Stephen Dow Beckham, ed., *Oregon Indians: Voices from Two Centuries*, p. 387 (Corvallis: Oregon State University Press, 2006).

P. 239 *"I didn't know why they were strapping me."* Confidential communication with author, 2008. The tribal member remembered being rounded up with all of the kids who did not speak English and whipped with a 2½-foot-long leather strap. He would run away, but then the agents would "bring me back and strap me for running away." The tribal member summed up his early experience at Chemawa: they "down-grade you, make you ashamed of being an Indian, to talk their language."

P. 240 *an impromptu pow-wow.* Gilbert Towner, interview with Carrie Covington, research assistant, Siletz, Oregon, Sept. 10, 2007.

P. 240 *Poverty during the Great Depression.* The unemployment rate in Indian country was at least 50 percent or higher for generations, see p. 233, while national unemployment in the 1930s never went above 25 percent, and stayed at that level for only a brief time. See, e.g., Frederick E. Hosen, *The Great Depression and the New Deal*, p. 257 (Jefferson, NC: McFarland & Co., Inc., 1992).

P. 241 *After the BIA closed the Siletz agency.* The detailed and often candid testimony during the 1931 Senate Subcommittee on Indian Affairs hearings on the "Conditions of Indians in the United States" provide valuable insight into the economic and social conditions at Siletz, and the government's response to them, during this era. See Survey of Conditions of the Indians, pp. 11713–47. Regarding the clerk at Chemawa functioning as sole BIA employee for Siletz and Grand Ronde, see ibid., p. 11718. C. F. Larsen, who was employed as the clerk at the Siletz agency before its closure, expressed to the Subcommittee his dismay with the lack of services. Ibid., pp. 11713, 11716. Regarding the discontinuation of rations, see ibid., p. 11717, and of health care, p. 11719.

The extent of Lincoln County welfare payments is unclear from the hearing. Mr. Larsen testified that the county asked for reimbursement from the federal government for about $1,300 in welfare payments made to Indians during 1930 and that the county refused to make welfare payments to Indians who have "inherited Indian lands" because "it is an imposition upon the county to support these Indians while they have property in their own right." Ibid., pp. 11716–17. J. E. Cooter, the county representative, testified that the county has "been contributing this [welfare] support to the indigent Indians that need it regardless of whether they are wards or non-wards" and gave an example of a Siletz woman receiving "$12 or $15 a month." Ibid., pp. 11723–24. Regarding the poor condition of the frame houses built forty or fifty years ago, see ibid., p. 11715. The testimony of Mr. Cooter reveals that the condition of the old doctor providing medical care on the reservation was at least partly to blame for the terrible health conditions at Siletz. The doctor did his work for the "love of the Indians," but apparently was "unable to even take care of himself" and denied the severity of the tuberculosis epidemic on the reservation. Ibid., p. 11725.

P. 241 *"You turn an old horse loose."* Ibid., p. 11729.

P. 241 *second-largest producer of hops.* Otis W. Freeman, "Hop Industry of the Pacific Coast States," vol. 12, no. 2 *Economic Geography*, p. 161 (April 1936). Today Oregon ranks second in hops production nationally, behind Washington. See *Hops: National Sta-*

tistics, Ranking of Top States (2008), USDA National Agricultural Statistics Service, *at* http://www.nass.usda.gov/QuickStats/index2.jsp (accessed May 28, 2009).

P. 244 *$1.25 to $1.50 per hundred pounds.* Freeman, "Hop Industry," pp. 157–58.

P. 244 *The early fall expeditions to the fields.* See, e.g., Emma Russell, interview with Josh Tenneson, research assistant, June 21, 2006; Frank Simmons, interview with author, Siletz, Oregon, Feb. 8, 2007; June Austin, interview, May 17, 2007; Lionel Youst and William R. Seaburg, *Coquelle Thompson, Athabaskan Witness*, pp. 176–77 (Norman: University of Oklahoma Press, 2002).

P. 244 *estimated 3,000 Indians picked hops.* Freeman, "Hop Industry," p. 157.

P. 244 *"The hop harvest fit perfectly."* Youst and Seaburg, *Coquelle Thompson, Athabaskan Witness*, p. 177.

P. 244 *Florists coveted.* Lillie Butler, interview with author, Siletz, Oregon, Feb. 7, 2007.

P. 244 *Commercial logging on the Oregon Coast.* On the early commercial logging industry in Oregon, see, e.g., Gordon B. Dodds, *Oregon: A Bicentennial History*, pp. 78–79 (New York: W. W. Norton & Co., Inc., 1977); William G. Robbins, *Hard Times in Paradise: Coos Bay, Oregon, 1850–1986*, p. 13 (Seattle: University of Washington Press, 1988); Oregon Department of Forestry, "Oregon's Timber Harvests: 1849–2004," pp. 1, 3 (2005). On the use of horse and oxen teams, supplanted by "steam donkeys," see, e.g., Joseph H. Pierre, *When Timber Stood Tall*, pp. 9–24 (Seattle: Superior Publishing Co., 1979).

P. 244 *rampant fraudulent claims.* See generally Paul W. Gates, *History of Federal Public Land Law Development*, pp. 463–93 (Washington, D.C.: Government Printing Office, 1968). For more information on fraudulent land claims, see chapter 10, p. 226 and accompanying notes.

P. 244 *"I sometimes feel thankful."* A. W. Morgan, *Fifty Years in Siletz Timber*, p. 10 (Portland, OR: A. W. Morgan, 1959).

P. 246 *light Sitka spruce.* See generally A.S. Harris, "Sitka Spruce," *in* U.S. Forest Service, Agriculture Handbook 654, *Silvics of North America*, vol. 1, *at* http://www.na.fs.fed.us/Spfo/pubs/silvics_manual/Volume_1/picea/sitchensis.htm (accessed May 28, 2009). On the discovery of Lincoln County Sitka spruce as a valuable commodity during World War I, see Bolling Arthur Johnson, ed., "Pacific Spruce Corporation and Subsidiaries," reprinted from *Lumber World Review*, pp. 32–33 (Newport, OR: Lincoln County Historical Society, 1924) (*Lumber World Review* was published in Chicago). On Oregon Coast ecology, see generally E. William Anderson, Michael M. Borman, and William C. Krueger, "The Ecological Provinces of Oregon: A Treatise on the Basic Ecological Geography of the State," pp. 21–27 (Oregon Agricultural Experiment Station, Oregon State University, 1998) (discussing the Coast Ecological Province).

P. 246 *Spruce Production Corporation.* For a detailed account of the formation of the Spruce Production Corporation and the logging industry in Lincoln County, see Johnson, "Pacific Spruce Corporation." See also Robbins, *Oregon*, pp. 105–6 (regarding the corporation's harvest of 54 million board feet); Youst and Seaburg, *Coquelle Thompson, Athabaskan Witness*, pp. 193–94. For a description and excellent photographs of logging in Lincoln County, see also Ray T. Moe, ed., *The First One Hundred Years in Lincoln County Oregon, 1893 to 1993*, pp. 70–75 (Newport, OR: Lincoln County Centennial Committee, 1993); Mike O'Donnell, *The First Hundred Years: Lincoln County, 1893–1993*, pp. 85–121 (Newport, OR: News-Times, 1993).

P. 246 *"generous terms."* Robbins, *Oregon*, p. 106.

P. 246 *vast amounts of timber land.* On the corporation's acquisition of valuable timber land, see Johnson, "Pacific Spruce Corporation," p. 32. The Blodgett Tract held approximately 12,700 acres and 800 million board feet of timber, while the corporation's stands in the Siletz watershed totaled approximately 14,600 acres and 835 million board feet. Ibid.

P. 246 *Oregon became the top timber-producing state.* See, e.g., Robbins, *Oregon: This Storied Land,* pp. 144–45.

P. 246 *sixty-eight mills operated in the Toledo area.* M. O'Donnell, *The First Hundred Years,* p. 87.

P. 247 *discriminatory practices kept them from higher-paying jobs.* See Ed Ben, interview with Josh Tenneson, research assistant, Salem, Oregon, June 21, 2006. Ben recounted that "Siletz Indians were damn good loggers" but that "you never saw Indians running any of the mechanical equipment, unless an Indian owned the company."

P. 247 *logging was dangerous.* Robert Kentta, interview with author, near Agness, Oregon, Sept. 15, 2007. The loggers who lost their lives were Klamath Billy, Randy Strickler, Calvin Bell, and Hawley Catfish.

P. 247 *$225–$250 a month.* Bureau of Indian Affairs, Salem Agency, "Ten-Year Program, 1946–1955, Siletz, Oregon," p. 10 (March 1944), RG 75, Grand Ronde-Siletz Indian Agency Holdings 77, Box 161, 10 Year Program 1944 Folder, *at* National Archives Records Administration, Seattle, Pacific Northwest Region [hereinafter BIA Ten-Year Program].

P. 247 *$17 per hour.* Reggie Butler, interview with author, Siletz, Oregon, Feb. 7, 2007.

P. 248 *"My boys will be loggers."* Lillie Butler, interview, Feb. 7, 2007 (Lillie Butler is Eleanor Logan's daughter).

P. 248 *"there were always eels and salmon."* Gladys Bolton, interview with María Aparicio, research assistant, Keizer, Oregon, March 26, 2008.

P. 248 *Clayburn Arden.* Jessie Davis, interview with María Aparicio, research assistant, Salem, Oregon, May 22, 2007; Jessie Davis, interview with the author, Salem, Oregon, Sept. 12, 2007.

P. 248 *the state had no right to control fishing and hunting on trust land.* See I. H. Van Winkle, attorney general for Oregon, opinion to M. T. Hoy, master fish warden, Fish Commission of Oregon, "In re status of Siletz Indians and other Indians residing on or in the vicinity of the Siletz Indian Reservation, to take or catch fish with certain fishing gear either within or without such reservation" (March 31, 1938), *in* "Biennial Report and Opinions of Attorney-General of the State of Oregon," pp. 602–5 (Salem, OR: The Attorney General, 1908–1968). See also 1954 Senate Termination Report, p. 19 ("the Indians are under jurisdiction of the Federal Government in taking game or fish on their lands"); BIA Ten-Year Program, p. 4 ("Some disagreement has existed in past years between the State, County, and the Indians as to the Indian's right to fish, but these rights are quite generally conceded now by law-enforcing officials.").

P. 248 *The BIA issued tags to tribal fishermen.* 1954 Senate Termination Report, p. 19. The tags were placed on fishing nets to alert state officers that such nets belonged to tribal members fishing on trust property.

P. 248 *"I didn't grow up thinking hunting was against state law."* Reggie Butler, interview, Feb. 7, 2007.

P. 248 *Eels.* On the hooking, cleaning, cooking, and eating of eels, see, e.g., Gladys Bolton, interview with María Aparicio, research assistant, March 26, 2008; Lillie Butler, interview with author, Feb. 7, 2007. For a detailed report on the declining population of lampreys, including a compilation of nearly twenty oral histories on eeling, see Tom Downey et al., "Skwakol: The Decline of the Siletz Lamprey Eel Population During the 20th Century" (Corvallis: Oregon State University, 1996). The report concludes that a dramatic decline in lamprey population between 1981 and 1991 likely was due to a combination of climatic conditions, poisoning from chemical runoff, and mismanagement of watershed uplands. Ibid., p. v. "Skwakol" is the Chinook Jargon used by the Siletz to refer to the eels.

P. 249 *People came together to help neighbors.* Bob Tom, interview with Carrie Covington, research assistant, Grand Ronde, Oregon, Aug. 12, 2007. Tom recounted that "a lot of times people didn't have to ask for help because people could just see" that it was needed and so would help without being asked. Ibid.

P. 249 *Trading and exchanging cans and jars.* Terry and Emma Russell, interview, June 21, 2006.

P. 249 *"If we wanted to eat, we'd have to help."* LaVera Simmons, interview with Carrie Covington, research assistant, Siletz, Oregon, May 17, 2007.

P. 249 *"We didn't know we were poor."* June Austin, interview, May 17, 2007.

P. 249 *James Collins.* Room 211, Memorial Union Building, Oregon State University, visit by the author, Corvallis, Oregon, January 31, 2008. Professor Kurt Peters showed the author Collins's photograph, which is displayed in a formal university conference room.

P. 249 *Coquelle Thompson Jr.* Youst and Seaburg, *Coquelle Thompson, Athabaskan Witness,* pp. 205–7.

P. 249 *Reuben Saunders.* "Hall of Fame Inductees, 1972," American Indian Athletic Hall of Fame, *at* http://americanindianathletichalloffame.com/inductees.php (accessed May 28, 2009).

P. 249 *Art Bensell and Mary Alice Bensell Munsee.* Joan Bensell Fisher, interview with Carrie Covington, research assistant, Siletz, Oregon, Aug. 10, 2007 (Art Bensell is Joan's father); *Arthur S. Bensell Memorial Scholarship*, Confederated Tribes of Siletz Indians' Web site, *at* http://www.ctsi.nsn.us (under the Tribal Services tab, click on Education, then Scholarships) (accessed May 28, 2009).

P. 249 *Elwood A. Towner.* Gilbert Towner, telephone interview with María Aparicio, research assistant, Oct. 4, 2007 (Elwood Towner was Gilbert Towner's paternal uncle).

P. 250 *Oregon miscegenation statute.* Act to Prohibit Amalgamation and the Intermarriage of Races, Or. L. §2163 (1866) (codified at Or. Laws §23-1010). The Oregon Supreme Court rejected a constitutional challenge to the law and held that a Clatsop woman was "not the lawful wife" of a deceased white man and therefore not entitled to administer his estate. *In Re Paquet's Estate,* pp. 911, 914 (Or. 1921). The law was repealed in 1951. House Bill No. 664, An Act Relating to Marriages, Or. Laws 1951, ch. 455, §2 (repealing section 23-1010). The United States Supreme Court struck down such statutes as violating the Constitution's guarantee of equal protection of the laws. *Loving v. Virginia,* 388 U.S. 1, 12 (1967). For a useful chronology of Oregon's miscegenation laws, see Alex Davis, "History of mixed-race marriages shifts with time," *Salem Statesman Journal* (Jan. 3, 2003).

P. 250 *some employees refused to work for Art Bensell.* Kathryn Harrison, interview with Carrie Covington, research assistant, Grand Ronde, Oregon, Aug. 12, 2007.

P. 253 *Origins of the Shaker Church.* A comprehensive book on the church is Robert H. Ruby and John A. Brown, *John Slocum and the Indian Shaker Church* (Norman: University of Oklahoma Press, 1996). For an account of Slocum's 1881 and 1882 revivals and the beginnings of the Indian Shaker Church, see ibid., pp. 3–10. An earlier work, H. G. Barnett, *Indian Shakers: A Messianic Cult of the Pacific Northwest* (Carbondale: Southern Illinois University Press, 1957), is near-encyclopedic but has received some criticism because of its heavy dependence on the primary observations of non-Indian missionary Myron Eells. See George P. Castile, "The 'Half-Catholic' Movement," *Pacific Northwest Quarterly*, p. 165 (Oct. 1982). For a useful summary of Shakerism, see Pamela T. Amoss, "The Indian Shaker Church," *in* Wayne Suttles, ed., vol. 7, *Handbook of North American Indians*, pp. 633–39 (Washington, D.C.: Smithsonian Institution, 1990).

P. 253 *Slocum taken for dead.* Amoss, "Indian Shaker Church," p. 633.

P. 253 *Attempts to suppress the Shaker Church.* See, e.g., Castile, "'Half-Catholic' Movement," p. 166. Of missionary Myron Eells and his Indian agent brother Edwin Eells, who were both active during the birth of the Shaker Church, Castile wrote: "I find that at the time when Edwin was crushing traditional Indian practices, Myron was preaching Christianity, yet denying entrance to the church." Ibid. See also Amoss, "Indian Shaker Church," p. 633 ("Most Indian agents and missionaries to Southern Coast Salish tried to suppress Shakerism when they became aware of it."). However, these attitudes may have lessened over time: "Indian agents were initially suspicious of Shakerism but eventually grew tolerant toward it, since it called for temperance and restrained behavior." Cesare Marino, "History of Western Washington Since 1846," *in* Wayne Suttles, ed., vol. 7, *Handbook of North American Indians*, p. 174 (Washington, D.C.: Smithsonian Institution, 1990).

P. 253 *A syncretic religion.* See, e.g., Thomas Buckley, "The Shaker Church and the Indian Way in Native Northwestern California," vol. 21, no. 1 *American Indian Quarterly*, pp. 4–8 (Winter 1997). Buckley describes how the Shaker Church identified with both the "old Indian Way" and the Protestant and Catholic missions in the Puget Sound area. Not surprisingly, the Church's syncretic nature was a source of controversy, especially with respect to issues of Indian identity. Ibid., p. 7.

P. 253 *"Whoever believes this thing."* Stephen Dow Beckham, Kathryn Anne Toepel, and Rick Minor, "Native American Religious Practices and Uses in Western Oregon," no. 31 *University of Oregon Anthropological Papers*, p. 105 (1984) (quoting Elizabeth D. Jacobs's Notebook 113 from 1934).

P. 253 *"The [Shaker] approach to worship."* Leone Letson Kasner, *Siletz: Survival for an Artifact*, p. 27 (Dallas, OR: Itemizer-Observer, 1976). In 1928, Reverend Charles Raymond was appointed to undertake a preaching mission to address "the deplorable fact that the Catholic Siletz Indians have joined the Shakers and the Four Square [Pentecostal] churches." Barnett, *Indian Shakers*, p. 75.

P. 254 *"the egalitarian nature of the Shaker church."* Lee Sackett, "The Siletz Indian Shaker Church," *Pacific Northwest Quarterly*, p. 124 (July 1973).

P. 254 *"God gave Indian people something."* Lillie Butler, daughter of Eleanor Logan, interview with author, Siletz, Oregon, Feb. 7, 2007.

P. 254 *The first Siletz Shaker services.* Sackett reports that the Indian Shakers initially "met in the homes and barns of members, for they had no church building." Sackett, "Siletz Indian Shaker Church," p. 122.

P. 254 *Church building in Siletz.* Ibid.

P. 254 *California effort.* Ruby and Brown, *John Slocum*, p. 151; Sackett, "Siletz Indian Shaker Church," p. 122–23.

P. 254 *Church at Smith River.* See Amoss, "Indian Shaker Church," p. 634; Sackett, "Siletz Indian Shaker Church," p. 123.

P. 254 *built a larger church.* Ibid.

P. 254 *the church was held in near-universal high regard.* See ibid.

P. 254 *"dancing as a means of expression."* Department of the Interior, Siletz Agency, "1927 Annual Report, Narrative Section," RG 75, Grand Ronde-Siletz Indian Agency Holdings 16, Box 48, Annual Status Reports Folder, *at* National Archives Records Administration, Seattle, Pacific Northwest Region.

P. 255 *Shakers—all dressed in white.* Woody Muschamp, interview with Daniel Cordalis, research assistant, Siletz, Oregon, July 2, 2009, and confidential communications. On Shaker ceremony, worship, and ritual, see generally Ruby and Brown, *John Slocum*, pp. 83–108; Barnett, *Indian Shakers*, pp. 243–84.

P. 255 *Shaker Church started to lose momentum.* Two sources have ascribed the decline to a dispute over the use of the Bible. See Sackett, "Siletz Indian Shaker Church," pp. 123–24; Ruby and Brown, *John Slocum*, pp. 151–53. However, several tribal members, whose family members were shakers, do not recall mention of such a dispute.

P. 255 *dinners at the church.* Geneva Johnson, telephone interview with María Aparicio, research assistant, Sept. 14, 2007.

P. 256 *Gladys Muschamp.* Woody Muschamp, interview with María Aparicio, research assistant, Logsden, Oregon, Jan. 2, 2008; Woody Muschamp, telephone interview with María Aparicio, Sept. 2, 2008. Mr. Muschamp is Gladys Muschamp's son and believes his mother was one of the first to attend the Shaker Church in Siletz.

12 Struggles to Make the White Man's Laws Fit

P. 257 *Wasson initiated the first claims case.* These developments involve "claim cases"— litigation to recover money for the value of tribal land taken by the United States. Congress can also authorize and make direct payments for taken land, and in the early 1900s, Tillamooks and Clatsops did receive congressional compensation for such takings. Later, Tillamooks sued and received additional amounts in 1955 on the grounds that the congressional payment did not reflect the full value of the taken land.

P. 257 *His spirited grandmother.* George Bundy Wasson Jr., "Growing Up Indian: An Emic Perspective," pp. 217–19, Ph.D. diss., University of Oregon, 2001.

P. 257 *"All this land."* Laura Berg, ed., *The First Oregonians*, p. 94 (Portland: Oregon Council for the Humanities, 1991). See also Stephen Dow Beckham, ed., *Oregon Indians: Voices from Two Centuries*, p. 425 (Corvallis: Oregon State University Press, 2006). Both of these sources provide useful summaries of George Wasson's work and the western Oregon Indian claims process. For somewhat more detailed accounts of the claims, see Stephen Dow Beckham, *The Indians of Western Oregon*, pp. 180–82, 185–87 (Coos Bay, OR: Arago Books, 1977); E. A. Schwartz, *The Rogue River Indian War and Its Aftermath, 1850–1980*, pp. 245–51 (Norman: University of Oklahoma Press, 1997).

P. 257 *"I was the fourth son."* Wasson, "Growing Up Indian," p. 187 (quoting from his father's papers).

P. 258 *"raring to go."* Beckham, ed., *Oregon Indians*, p. 427.

P. 258 *doctrine of sovereign immunity.* Edwin M. Borchard, "Government Liability in Tort," vol. 34, *Yale Law Journal*, pp. 1, 4 (1924), provides an excellent account of British and early American sovereign immunity law.

P. 258 *"The law supposes it impossible."* Joseph Chitty, *A Treatise on the Law of the Prerogatives of the Crown*, p. 5 (London: Joseph Butterworth and Son, 1820).

P. 258 *Suits by tribes in the Court of Claims.* Section 9 of the 1863 Act, which amended the 1855 Act that had established the Court of Claims, declared that the Court lacks jurisdiction over claims "growing out of or dependent on any treaty stipulation entered into with foreign nations or with Indian tribes." Ch. 92, §9, March 3, 1863, 12. Stat. 765 (1863). On suits by tribes in the Court of Claims, see generally, *Felix S. Cohen's Handbook of Federal Indian Law*, 2005, §5.06(2) (Newark, NJ: LexisNexis, 2005); David H. Getches, Charles F. Wilkinson, and Robert A. Williams Jr., *Cases and Materials on Federal Indian Law*, 5th ed., pp. 281–88 (St. Paul, MN: Thompson West, 2005).

P. 259 *The tribes continued to own their aboriginal lands.* For additional discussion and authorities, see chapter 3, p. 64 and accompanying notes; chapter 4, pp. 79–80 and accompanying notes.

P. 259 *Monetary compensation and getting back land.* Although the tribes' case—and cases of other tribes throughout Oregon and elsewhere—for monetary compensation was straightforward, a related matter was not: if the 1855 treaty was unratified and the tribes continued to own the land, could they sue to recover the land rather than money damages? Decades later, several eastern tribes successfully sued to recover aboriginal land ceded in invalid treaties, despite the fact that the transactions at issue often were centuries old. See, e.g., *County of Oneida v. Oneida Indian Nation*, 470 U.S. 226 (1985); *Joint Tribal Council of Passamaquoddy Tribe v. Morton*, 528 F.2d 370 (1st Cir. 1975); *Cramer v. United States*, 261 U.S. 219 (1923). Although these claims were settled in different ways (award of money damages in *Oneida*; in *Passamaquoddy*, award of federal funds, pursuant to the subsequent passage of the Maine Indian Claims Settlement Act, with which to purchase lands back; and cancellation of a federal patent that had deeded aboriginal lands to non-Indians in *Cramer*), the underlying claim always was to establish title to aboriginal lands. See also chapter 10, p. 205 and accompanying notes. The Maine Indian Claims Settlement Act can be found at Pub. L. No. 96-420, §2, Oct. 10, 1980, 94 Stat. 1785 (1980) (codified at 25 U.S.C. §§1721–1735 [2006]).

The courts also have ruled, however, that a final judgment for money damages in a tribal claims case closes the matter and bars any future attempts to recover land. See *United States v. Dann*, 470 U.S. 39, 44 (1985). Of the many failings of the system for litigating tribal land claims, this may be the most egregious. Undoubtedly, most tribes would have chosen a return of land over a money payment, especially when technical rules greatly reduced dollar awards.

Why did tribes not bring land-recovery cases before the late 1960s? Some attorneys did not realize the potential of that approach, which is part of an exceptionally complex body of law. Other lawyers may have understood the approach but rejected it as overly theoretical and unrealistic. Still others may have chosen not to raise the issue with their tribal clients because the contingency fees available in the money damage awards were substantial and more certain. This problem, along with Congress's insistence on money damages and unwillingness to consider any program for land return, made the claims process an enterprise of limited benefit to tribes from the beginning. The delays, procedural barriers, and questionable judicial decisions, as exemplified by the experience of the western Oregon tribes, only made it worse. But in the early and mid-twentieth century, claims litigation for money damages was the only option known to the tribes.

P. 260 *assimilationist policies raged.* Francis Paul Prucha, vol. 2, *The Great Father: The United States Government and the American Indians*, pp. 801–5 (Lincoln: University of Nebraska Press, 1984).

P. 260 *Hubert Work personally wrote to Congress.* See H. Work, Secretary of the Interior, letter to S. Leavitt, chairman, House Committee on Indian Affairs (May 24, 1928), *in* House Report No. 2209, "Authorizing Adjudication of Claims of the Coos Bay, Lower Umpqua, and Siuslaw Tribes of Indians of Oregon," 70th Congress, 2d Session, p. 3 (Washington, D.C.: Government Printing Office, 1929).

P. 260 *Court of Claims to hear* Coos *case.* Special Act of Congress to confer jurisdiction on the Court of Claims to hear Coos, Lower Umpqua, and Siuslaw Claims against the United States, Feb. 23, 1929, 45 Stat. 1256 (1929) (not codified) (amended by Act of June 14, 1932, 47 Stat. 307 [1932]).

P. 260 *five dollars a month.* Beckham, *The Indians of Western Oregon*, p. 181.

P. 260 *court-administered testimony.* James Buchanan's testimony before the United States Court of Claims, *Coos Bay, Lower Umpqua, and Siuslaw Indians v. United States*, 87 Ct. Cl. 143 (Ct. Cl. 1938), *at* Siletz Archival Collection (testimony of tribal members was taken on November 10–13, 1931 in North Bend, Oregon).

P. 261 *"There is no doubt."* See *Coos Bay, Lower Umpqua, and Siuslaw Indians v. United States*, 87 Ct. Cl. 143, 1938 WL 4076, p. 6 (Ct. Cl. 1938).

P. 262 *distrust of the tribal witnesses.* The court distinguished the tribal witnesses—who "have a direct interest in the outcome of this case"—from "reliable sources of information" such as Bureau of Ethnology's *Handbook of American Indians*. See ibid., pp. 6–7.

P. 262 *dismissed the case outright.* Ibid., p. 8. Epitomizing the frustration a reader has with the court's reasoning, the decisive passage in the court's opinion reads: "To establish Indian title to a vast acreage of lands by oral testimony, irrespective of the obstacles of establishing it by any other method, [requires] a degree of proof sufficient to overcome contemporaneous documentary and historical evidence to the contrary." Ibid., p. 7. But this reasoning does not explain this case. The court found no "contemporaneous documentary and historical evidence" contrary to the tribal testimony.

P. 262 *Supreme Court declined to review.* See *Coos Bay, Lower Umpqua, and Siuslaw Indian Tribes v. United States*, 306 U.S. 653 (1939).

P. 262 *President Hoover and Charles Rhoads.* See Prucha, vol. 2, *The Great Father*, pp. 921–24. For the Meriam Report, see Lewis Meriam et al., Institute for Government Research, "The Problem of Indian Administration" (Baltimore, MD: Johns Hopkins University Press, 1928) [hereinafter Meriam Report].

P. 262 *Rhoads fought the claims.* Although the Hoover Administration was attempting to develop an Indian Claims Commission to better accommodate tribal land claims (see Prucha, vol. 2, *The Great Father*, pp. 925–26), Commissioner Rhoads repeatedly opposed on technical grounds a bill that would have conferred jurisdiction on the Court of Claims to hear the Tillamook, Coquille, Tututni, and Chetco claim. See C.

Rhoads, Commissioner of Indian Affairs, memorandum to R. Wilbur, Secretary of the Interior (Feb. 24, 1930), *in* Senate Report No. 1361, "Conferring Jurisdiction upon Court of Claims to Hear Claims of Certain Oregon Indians," 71st Congress, 3d Session, pp. 2–3 (Washington, D.C.: Government Printing Office, 1931); C. Rhoads memorandum to R. Wilbur (Feb. 24, 1930), *in* House Report No. 2758, "Court of Claims to Adjudicate Claims of Certain Bands of Indians in Oregon," 71st Congress, 3d Session, pp. 2–3 (Washington D.C.: Government Printing Office, 1931); C. Rhoads memorandum to R. Wilbur (Jan. 26, 1932), *in* Senate Report No. 430, "Court of Claims to Hear and Determine Claims of Certain Bands, Nations, or Tribes of Indians Residing in the State of Oregon," 72d Congress, 1st Session, p. 2 (Washington, D.C.: Government Printing Office, 1932).

P. 263 *"I want full justice."* H. Hoover, president of the United States, "Veto of a Bill Relating to Indian Claims" (April 25, 1932), in *Public Papers of the Presidents of the United States: Herbert Hoover, 1932–33*, p. 179 (Washington D.C.: Government Printing Office, 1977).

P. 263 *"I am further constrained."* Ibid.

P. 263 *President Roosevelt and John Collier.* See below, pp. 270–71 and accompanying notes.

P. 263 *the Alceas are a separate tribe.* Alceas had close ties to the neighboring Tillamooks and had been incorrectly classified as Tillamooks before. See generally Henry R. Zenk, "Alseans," *in* Wayne Suttles, ed., vol. 7, *Handbook of North American Indians*, pp. 568–71 (Washington, D.C.: Smithsonian Institution, 1990).

P. 263 *"much stronger evidence."* See *Alcea Band of Tillamooks v. United States*, 59 F. Supp. 934, 965 (Ct. Cl. 1945).

P. 263 *"beyond any shadow of a doubt."* Ibid., p. 967.

P. 264 *The Supreme Court affirmed.* 329 U.S. 40 (1946). The Court held that the tribes had "satisfactorily proved their claim of original Indian title and an involuntary taking thereof" and were entitled to compensation. The Court further elaborated that "the power of Congress over Indian affairs may be of a plenary nature; but it is not absolute. It does not enable the United States to give the tribal lands to others, or to appropriate them to its own purposes, without rendering . . . just compensation for them." Ibid., p. 54.

P. 264 *"INDIANS WIN LAND CLAIM."* "Oregon Indians Win Land Claim of $16,515,614," *Oregonian* (Jan. 4, 1950).

P. 264 *far greater amount accrued from interest.* See *Alcea Band of Tillamooks v. United States*, 87 F. Supp. 938 (Ct. Cl. 1950). For the total value as of 1855, see ibid., p. 952. For the court's analysis of the interest issue, see ibid., pp. 954–55.

P. 264 *government took the case to the Supreme Court.* See *United States v. Alcea Band of Tillamooks*, 341 U.S. 48 (1951).

P. 264 *"It is hardly likely that Congress."* Brief of Petitioner at 20, *United States v. Alcea Band of Tillamooks*, 341 U.S. 48 (1951) (No. 281).

P. 264 *"INDIANS TO LOSE INTEREST."* "Indians to Lose Interest on Claims Dating to 1855," *Oregonian*, p. 1 (April 10, 1951).

P. 264 *the Supreme Court denied interest.* See *Alcea Band of Tillamooks*, 341 U.S. at 49.

P. 264 *Payments for individual tribes.* See *Alcea Band of Tillamooks v. United States*, 119 Ct. Cl. 835 (Ct. Cl. 1951).

P. 265 *Amounts for individual tribal members.* Bureau of Indian Affairs, "Payments Made to Western Oregon Indians," RG 75, Portland Area Office Holdings 07, Box 33, Western Oregon Judgment Fund Folder, *at* National Archives Records Administration, Seattle, Pacific Northwest Region (n.d.).

P. 265 *payments a "windfall."* "Millions Due For Indians," *Oregonian* (April 27, 1951).

P. 265 *celebratory salmon bakes.* Frank Simmons, interview with Carrie Covington, research assistant, Siletz, Oregon, May 22, 2007.

P. 266 *the* Rogue River *case.* See *Rogue River Tribe of Indians v. United States*, 64 F. Supp. 339 (Ct. Cl. 1946); 89 F. Supp. 798 (Ct. Cl. 1950), cert. denied 341 U.S. 902 (1951). Like the *Alcea* claim, this case also involved ethnological confusion. There was no "Rogue River Tribe"—the name Americans gave to the Takelmas, Shastas, and Applegate Athapaskan bands in the Upper Rogue River watershed—but the Table Rock Treaty of 1853 referred to the Rogues and so the lawsuit was brought in that name.

P. 266 *"in 1855 this reservation."* See *Rogue River Tribe of Indians*, 89 F. Supp. at 807.

P. 266 *Court of Claims award.* Ibid.

P. 266 *Molala Tribe.* See *Rogue River Tribe of Indians*, 64 F. Supp. at 341.

P. 266 *Molala award.* See *Rogue River Tribe of Indians*, 89 F. Supp. at 808.

P. 266 *No award at all was made.* Ibid., pp. 807–8.

P. 267 *reservations were permanent.* See chapter 5, pp. 94–95, 104–5 and accompanying notes; chapter 7, pp. 132–36, 146 and accompanying notes.

P. 267 *"The Coast or Siletz Reservation."* See *Rogue River Tribe of Indians*, 64 F. Supp. at 342. Judge Jones then held that "the Executive order, under the facts of this case did not amount to the establishment of a permanent reservation." Ibid.

P. 267 *"the rightful occupants of the soil."* See *Johnson v. McIntosh*, 21 U.S. 543, 574 (1823).

P. 268 *"gratuitous offsets."* These offsets are described in John R. White, "Barmecide Revisited: The Gratuitous Offset in Indian Claims Cases," vol. 25, no. 2 *Ethnohistory*, pp. 179–81 (Spring 1978) (concluding that the courts failed to define consistently what constitutes an allowable offset expenditure, often leading to highly inequitable and sometimes outrageous results). See also Cohen, *Handbook of Federal Indian Law*, 2005, §5.06(6)(c); Getches, Wilkinson, and Williams, Cases and Materials, p. 284. Under the Indian Claims Commission Act of 1946, gratuitous offsets were much more limited: "the Commission may . . . consider all money or property given to or funds expended gratuitously for the benefit of the claimant and if it finds that the nature of the claim and the entire course of dealings . . . between the United States and the claimant in good conscience warrants such action, may set off all or part of such expenditures against any award. . . ." Indian Claims Commission Act, Pub. L. 79-726, Aug. 13, 1946, 60 Stat. 1049 (1946) (codified at 25 U.S.C. §70a [2006]).

P. 268 *subtracting from the tribal awards.* See *Rogue River Tribe of Indians*, 89 F. Supp. at 808. The court listed the total gratuities for each tribe in its findings of fact. *Rogue River Tribe of Indians v. United States*, 116 Ct. Cl. 454, 473 (Ct. Cl. 1950).

P. 268 *by nearly 60 percent.* Getches, Wilkinson, and Williams, *Cases and Materials*, p. 284.

P. 268 *"there is no balance due."* See *Rogue River Tribe of Indians*, 89 F. Supp. at 808.

P. 268 *The Supreme Court denied review.* See *United States v. Rogue River Tribe of Indians*, 341 U.S. 902 (1951).

P. 268 *Indian Claims Commission Act.* See generally Sandra C. Danforth, "Repaying Historical Debts: The Indian Claims Commission," vol. 49 *North Dakota Law Review*, p. 359 (1973); Nell Jessup Newton, "Compensation, Reparations, & Restitution: Indian Property Claims in the United States," vol. 28 *Georgia Law Review*, p. 453 (Winter 1994).

P. 269 *"claims based upon fair and honorable dealings."* Indian Claims Commission Act, Pub. L. No. 726, ch. 959, Aug. 13, 1946, 60 Stat. 1049 (1946) (codified at 25 U.S.C. §70a; now repealed).

P. 269 *"a new era for our Indian citizens."* Prucha, vol. 2, *The Great Father*, p. 1019 (quoting President Truman's statement upon signing the ICC Act into law on August 13, 1946).

P. 269 *laid the moral foundation for termination.* See ibid., pp. 1018, 1023. Professor of anthropology and former associate commissioner of Indian Affairs James Officer elaborates on this ulterior motive for establishing the Claims Commission: "The record of hearings on the various Indian claims bills considered in the seventy-ninth Congress makes clear that some powerful legislators believed that resolution of Indian claims would remove a major barrier to federal withdrawal and, where awards were made to tribes, would help to launch them on the way to economic self-sufficiency. Certain attorneys who later would become wealthy from fees earned in claims cases did little to discourage this thesis, and some openly espoused it." Kenneth R. Philp, ed., *Indian Self-Rule: First-Hand Accounts of Indian-White Relations from Roosevelt to Reagan*, p. 118 (Salt Lake City, UT: Howe Brothers, 1986).

P. 269 *Tillamook and Nehalem Bands of Tillamooks.* The Commission's Findings of Fact in *Tillamook Band of Tillamooks v. United States*, Ind. Cl. Comm. No. 240 (1955) can be found at vol. 3, *Indian Claims Commission Decisions*, pp. 526–32 (Boulder, CO: Native American Rights Fund, 1973). The Opinion of the Commission, maintaining that the bands did hold aboriginal title and were entitled to recover the value of their land, is at ibid., pp. 533–39. In 1962, the commission made additional findings of fact to determine the appropriate award, less offsets. *Tillamook Band of Tillamooks v. United States*, Ind. Cl. Comm. No. 240 (1962), *in* vol. 11, *Indian Claims Commission Decisions*, pp. 52(a)–52(b) (Boulder, CO: Native American Rights Fund, 1973). All of the Indian Claims Commission decisions are also maintained online by the Oklahoma State University Library Electronic Publishing Center, available at http://digital.library.okstate.edu/icc/index.html.

P. 269 *The ICC awarded $72,000.* See *Tillamook Band of Tillamooks v. United States*, Ind. Cl. Comm. No. 240 (1962), *in* vol. 11, *Indian Claims Commission Decisions*, pp. 51–52 (Boulder, CO: Native American Rights Fund, 1973).

P. 269 *Claim by Confederated Tribes of Siletz Indians.* See *Tillamook Tribe of Indians v. United States*, Ind. Cl. Comm. No. 239 (1955), *in* vol. 4, *Indian Claims Commission Decisions*, pp. 31–65 (Boulder, CO: Native American Rights Fund, 1973). This case was titled Tillamook Tribe of Indians, but the Siletz Confederated Tribes was co-plaintiff.

P. 269 *amount "unconscionable."* Ibid., p. 56.

P. 269 *the award came to $432,800.* Ibid., p. 65. Regarding the later reduction due to allowance of attorneys' and witness' fees, see *Tillamook Tribe of Indians v. United States*, Ind. Cl. Comm. No. 239 (1959), *in* vol. 7, *Indian Claims Commission Decisions*, pp. 92–97, 97(a) –97(b) (Boulder, CO: Native American Rights Fund, 1973).

P. 269 *Tribal members received checks for $400.* Bureau of Indian Affairs, "Payments Made to Western Oregon Indians," RG 75, Portland Area Office Holdings 07, Box 33, Western Oregon Judgment Fund Folder, *at* National Archives Records Administration, Seattle, Pacific Northwest Region (n.d.).

P. 270 *"My father spent much of his life."* Ed Ben, interview with Josh Tenneson, research assistant, Salem, Oregon, June 21, 2006.

P. 270 *Meriam Commission.* See Meriam Report.

P. 270 *recommended reforms.* The Report did not envision Indian reservations as permanent; rather, "the national government can expedite the transition and hasten the day when there will no longer be a distinctive Indian problem." Ibid., p. 22.

P. 270 *The Hoover Administration.* See Prucha, vol. 2, *The Great Father*, pp. 921–39.

P. 270 *John Collier.* On Collier's career, see Kenneth R. Philp, *John Collier's Crusade for Indian Reform, 1920–1954* (Tucson: University of Arizona Press, 1977); Lawrence Kelly, *The Assault on Assimilation: John Collier and the Origins of Indian Policy Reform* (Albuquerque: University of New Mexico Press, 1983). See also John Collier, *The Indians of the Americas* (New York: W. W. Norton & Co., 1947).

P. 271 *proposed Indian Reorganization Act.* For the most thorough account of the development of the bill and its prelude, see Elmer R. Rusco, *A Fateful Time: The Background and Legislative History of the Indian Reorganization Act*, pp. 137–219 (Reno: University of Nevada Press, 2000). While the ideas were Collier's, Associate Solicitor for Indian Affairs Felix Cohen took responsibility for much of the drafting. Ibid., pp. 192–207.

P. 271 *controversial provisions.* See Vine Deloria Jr. and Clifford M. Lytle, *The Nations Within: The Past and Future of American Indian Sovereignty*, pp. 74–75 (New York: Pantheon Books, 1984); Prucha, vol. 2, *The Great Father*, p. 958; Rusco, *A Fateful Time*, pp. 197–98, 228–29.

P. 271 *bill met with congressional objections.* See Rusco, *A Fateful Time*, pp. 242–45 (objections of Senator Wheeler), 245–49 (Indian concerns).

P. 271 *Indian congresses.* For in-depth coverage of these gatherings, see Deloria and Lytle, *The Nations Within*, pp. 101–21, describing Collier's decision as "a radical step" because it "broke with the established pattern of simply telling Indians after the fact how laws would apply to them." Ibid., p. 102. See also Rusco, *A Fateful Time*, pp. 245–49.

P. 271 *some 500 Indians.* Beckham, ed., *Oregon Indians*, p. 379 (referencing an account from the *Salem Capital Journal*).

P. 271 *split about equally.* Deloria and Lytle, *The Nations Within*, pp. 117–18.

P. 271 *"What I have heard from you gentlemen."* Bureau of Indian Affairs, p. 60, "Minutes of the Northwest Indian Congress at Chemawa, Oregon to Discuss with the Howard-Wheeler Bill, March 8–9, 1934," RG 75, Portland Area Office Holdings 43, Siletz–Grand Ronde–Chemawa 1931–1955 Box, Proceedings of the Conference at Chemawa . . . Wheeler-Howard Bill Folder, *at* National Archives Records Administration, Seattle, Pacific Northwest Region (the title page erroneously cites the congress dates as April 8–9, 1934) (transcribing Abe Logan's statement as given by his interpreter, Hoxie Simmons).

P. 271 *Coquelle ("Tom") Thompson Jr. and Elwood Towner.* Ibid., p. 74 (Thompson), pp. 79–80 (Towner).

P. 272 *"Will another commissioner come out?"* Ibid., pp. 62–63.

P. 272 *The Indian Reorganization Act of 1934.* For a summary of the statute as enacted, see Cohen, *Handbook of Federal Indian Law, 2005*, §1.05; Prucha, vol. 2, *The Great Father*, pp. 957–63 (also describing passage of the Act). The IRA is codified at 25 U.S.C. §§461–79 (2006).

P. 272 *"I've noticed in these meetings."* Beckham, ed., *Oregon Indians*, p. 384 (quoting Coquelle Thompson Jr.). This meeting took place on Feb. 10, 1934, four months before final passage of the IRA, but its purpose was to fully discuss the issues raised in the pending bill, including tribal self-government.

P. 272 *"In time, when we are ready to be turned loose."* Ibid., p. 385.

P. 272 *"Uncle Sam has to fulfill his promise."* Ibid., pp. 389–90 (Bensell Orton). Abe Logan voiced similar sentiments at the same meeting. See ibid., pp. 385–86.

P. 272 *Siletz allotment holders opposed provisions.* See, e.g., ibid., pp. 386 (Alfred Lane), 387 (Wilbur Martin), 388 (Abraham Tom), 390 (Agnes Isaacson).

P. 272 *Towner "talked against the Bill."* Department of Interior, Siletz Agency, p. 4, "1935 Annual Report, Narrative Section," RG 75, Grand Ronde–Siletz Indian Agency Holdings 16, Box 50, Annual Status Reports Folder, *at* National Archives Records Administration, Seattle, Pacific Northwest Region [hereinafter 1935 Annual Statistical Report].

P. 273 *"the Siletz people were afraid" of the IRA.* Robert Kentta, "The Confederated Tribes of Siletz Indians: Diverse Peoples Brought Together on the Siletz Reservation," *in* Berg, ed., *The First Oregonians*, p. 167.

P. 273 *tribal members voted against organizing under the IRA.* 1935 Annual Statistical Report, p. 4.

P. 273 *The Siletz vote was of little consequence.* See, e.g., Kentta, "The Confederated Tribes of Siletz Indians," p. 167: "Votes taken to incorporate under the Indian Reorganization Act failed at Siletz. It is impossible to say how much things would have changed had the Siletz people accepted the act, but it is likely that the reservation was already so close to being abolished thanks to the massive reductions in its land and resource base that little would have changed."

P. 274 *"the Siletz people are not properly organized."* Bureau of Indian Affairs, Grand Ronde–Siletz Agency, pp. 7–8, "Minutes of the Conference Held in Siletz on Feb. 18, 1940," RG 75, Portland Area Office Holdings 56, Box 1501, George Lavatta Folder, Minutes of Meetings-Oregon (Siletz 1940), *at* National Archives Records Administration, Seattle, Pacific Northwest Region [hereinafter Minutes of 1940 Conference].

P. 274 *selected seven representatives.* C. Thompson Jr. letter to J. Collier, commissioner of Indian Affairs (Jan. 25, 1940), *in* Minutes of 1940 Conference, pp. 31–32.

P. 274 *"you may be assured."* Ibid., p. 32.

P. 274 *"an approved [by the BIA] constitution."* F. H. Daiker, assistant commissioner of Indian Affairs letter to C. Thompson Jr. (Jan. 6, 1940), *in* Minutes of 1940 Conference, p. 12.

P. 274 *"The Indians here as a tribe are all together."* Minutes of 1940 Conference, p. 19.

P. 274 *"I don't think that mine or Mrs. Fitzpatrick's question."* Ibid., p. 22.

P. 275 *"please raise your right hand."* Ibid., p. 47. Seventeen voted for and thirty-eight against "expressing themselves" regarding the proposed projects.

P. 275 *Federal officials kept funding levels fairly constant.* A comprehensive 1944 BIA report showed approximately $8,400 in CCC expenditures in 1940, up from $4,400 in 1939. Bureau of Indian Affairs, Salem Agency, p. 18, "Ten-Year Program, 1946–1955, Siletz, Oregon," (March 1944) RG 75, Grand Ronde–Siletz Indian Agency Holdings 77, Box 161, 10 Year Program 1944 Folder, *at* National Archives Records Administration, Seattle, Pacific Northwest Region [hereinafter BIA Ten-Year Program]. These funds for 1940 may have been programmed before the February 18, 1940 meeting at which tribal members refused to vote on the proposed resolutions. CCC funding declined to $4,500 in 1941 and was not reported after that. Ibid. But this may well have been due to the phasing out of the CCC, which began in 1941 as a wartime measure and was completed by 1942. See John A. Salmond, *The Civilian Conservation Corps,*

1933–1942: A New Deal Case Study, pp. 200–17 (Durham, NC: Duke University Press, 1967). Other BIA programs at Siletz, including forestry, roads, and rehabilitation assistance, continued on. See BIA Ten-Year Program, pp. 17–19.

P. 275 *The tribe voted down another proposed constitution.* H. R. Cloud, regional representative, letter to Commissioner of Indian Affairs (Feb. 25, 1949), RG 75, Portland Area Office Holdings 07, Box 37, Siletz Tribes Constitution and Bylaws Folder, *at* National Archives Records Administration, Seattle, Pacific Northwest Region. However, in 1950, the tribe did agree to adopt a constitution as part of the build-up to termination. See chapter 13, p. 290–91 and accompanying notes.

P. 275 *BIA suppression had gone on so long.* In the 1920s and 1930s, the Siletz had no formal tribal council. The BIA did convene a "Business Committee" even though "the Indians, under this jurisdiction, ha[d] no tribal funds to their credit." Department of Interior, Siletz Agency, p. 6, "1929 Annual Report, Narrative Section," RG 75, Grand Ronde–Siletz Indian Agency Holdings 16, Box 48, Annual Status Reports Folder, *at* National Archives Records Administration, Seattle, Pacific Northwest Region. The committee was BIA-controlled: "This committee does not meet unless called upon, and there is no interference with the official duties of the superintendent." Ibid.

P. 276 *Senate Committee criticized Collier's emphasis on tribalism.* From the beginning, Collier faced charges of "communism." See, e.g., Deloria and Lytle, The Nations Within, p. 132. The 1939 Committee Report asserted, among other things, that the IRA "force[d]" Indians "back into a primitive state" and required a communal form of government. Senate Report No. 1047 to Accompany S. 2103, "Repeal of the So-Called Wheeler-Howard Act," 76th Congress, 1st Session, pp. 3–4 (Washington, D.C.: Government Printing Office, 1939). For a discussion of the Report, see also Prucha, vol. 2, *The Great Father*, p. 999.

P. 276 *subcommittee advocated the end of the reservation system.* See Senate Report No. 310, "Survey of Conditions among the Indians of the United States: Analysis of the Statement of the Commissioner of Indian Affairs in Justification of Appropriations for 1944, and the Liquidation of the Indian Bureau," 78th Congress, 1st Session (Washington, D.C.: Government Printing Office, 1943). The report is summarized in Prucha, vol. 2, *The Great Father*, pp. 1000–1001.

P. 276 *"final termination of such help."* BIA Ten-Year Program, p. 23.

P. 276 *Collier resigned in 1945.* For an account of the circumstances surrounding Collier's resignation, see Philp, *John Collier's Crusade for Indian Reform*, pp. 210–13.

P. 276 *World War II brought economic benefits.* For economic conditions in 1944, see BIA Ten-Year Program, pp. 8–11.

P. 276 *Lincoln County timber production.* Oregon Department of Forestry, "Oregon's Timber Harvests: 1849–2004," p. 90 (2005). Production in Lincoln County more than tripled between 1938 (100.3 million board feet) and 1943 (360.6 million board feet). For figures on production statewide, see ibid., p. 4.

P. 276 *employment in the mammoth shipyards.* See BIA Ten-Year Program, p. 4; Robert Kentta email to María Aparicio, research assistant, July 31, 2008; William G. Robbins, *Oregon: This Storied Land*, p. 125 (Portland: Oregon Historical Society Press, 2005).

P. 276 *lookout tower in Siletz.* June Austin and LaVera Simmons, interview with Carrie Covington, research assistant, Siletz, Oregon, May 17, 2007.

P. 276 *income for these war years.* See BIA Ten-Year Program, p. 8 ("families . . . except the old age group, are now enjoying earnings never before received").

P. 276 *Indians served at a rate three times higher.* Mary B. Davis, ed., *Native America in the Twentieth Century: An Encyclopedia*, p. 341 (New York: Garland Publishing, Inc., 1996). Approximately 10 percent of living American Indians are veterans. Ibid. See also Jere' Bishop Franco, *Crossing the Pond: The Native American Effort in World War II* (Denton: University of North Texas Press, 1999); Kenneth William Townsend, *World War II and the American Indian* (Albuquerque: University of New Mexico Press, 2000); Alison R. Bernstein, *American Indians and World War II* (Norman: University of Oklahoma Press, 1991).

P. 276 *"the Indian's fame is world wide."* Townsend, *World War II and the American Indian*, p. 134.

P. 276 *"best damn soldier in the Army."* Ibid.

P. 276 *more than one-third of adult males served.* In 1944, the tribal population was 518, of which 257 were male. BIA Ten-Year Program, p. 2. Estimating from the BIA's age data, it appears that at least 115 males were over- or under-age (42 over-age and 73 school-age), leaving about 142 eligible males. Ibid. Thus the conclusion that more than one-third of the adult males served.

P. 276 *Houses were dilapidated.* Ibid., p. 12.

P. 277 *"a basic purpose of Congress."* Arthur V. Watkins, "Termination of Federal Supervision: The Removal of Restrictions Over Indian Property and Person," vol. 311 *The Annals of the American Academy of Political and Social Science*, p. 50 (May 1957).

13 Termination

P. 279 *Fourteen termination laws.* For a listing of the termination laws and summary of the individuals and lands affected, see Charles F. Wilkinson and Eric R. Biggs, "The Evolution of the Termination Policy," vol. 5 *American Indian Law Review*, p. 151 (1977).

P. 279 *"You're not Indian any more."* Doug Foster, "Landless Tribes: Termination of the Klamath Reservation," vol. 1, no. 2 *Oregon Heritage*, p. 7 (1994) (quoting Lynn Schonchin of the Klamath Tribe).

P. 280 *termination in everything but name.* See Harold E. Fey and D'Arcy McNickle, *Indians and Other Americans: Two Ways of Life Meet*, pp. 148–49 (New York: Harper & Row, 1970) (members of a special Senate committee subsequently claimed that they had never authorized the contents of the termination-style report, but the document was never recalled); Kenneth R. Philp, *Termination Revisited: American Indians on the Trail to Self-Determination*, 1933–1953, pp. 1–2 (Lincoln: University of Nebraska Press, 1999). The committee's report can be found at Senate Report No. 310 "Survey of Conditions Among the Indians of the United States: Analysis of the Statement of the Commissioner of Indian Affairs in Justification of Appropriations for 1944, and the Liquidation of the Indian Bureau," 78th Congress, 1st Session (June 11, 1943) (Washington, D.C.: Government Printing Office, 1943). On calls for "emancipation," see Wilkinson and Biggs, "Evolution of the Termination Policy," pp. 146–47.

P. 280 *Zimmerman testimony.* Hearings Before the Senate Committee on Civil Service, "S. Res. 41: A Resolution to Investigate Certain Matters Relating to Officers and Employees of the Federal Government," 80th Congress, 1st Session, pt. 3, p. 546 (Feb. 8, 1947) (Washington, D.C.: Government Printing Office, 1947). See also Fey and

McNickle, *Indians and Other Americans*, pp. 161–62; Francis Paul Prucha, vol. 2, *The Great Father: The United States Government and the American Indians*, pp. 1026–27 (Lincoln: University of Nebraska Press, 1984); Donald L. Fixico, *Termination and Relocation: Federal Indian Policy, 1945–1960*, p. 33 (Albuquerque: University of New Mexico Press, 1986); S. Lyman Tyler, *A History of Indian Policy*, pp. 163–64 (Washington, D.C.: Government Printing Office, 1973); Philp, *Termination Revisited*, p. 75. The Grand Ronde Tribe was included on Zimmerman's list. Perhaps out of inadvertence—the list was put together hurriedly—the Siletz Tribe was not. In 1944, John Collier had been required by a congressional committee to produce a similar list, which included the Siletz. Philp, *Termination Revisited*, p. 72.

P. 280   *Termination advocates used Zimmerman's "plan."* Prucha, vol. 2, *The Great Father*, p. 1027; Fixico, *Termination and Relocation*, p. 33.

P. 280   *"Decreasing government assistance."* Bureau of Indian Affairs, Salem Agency, "Ten-Year Program, 1946–1955, Siletz, Oregon," p. 23 (March 1944), RG 75, Grand Ronde–Siletz Indian Agency Holdings 77, Box 161, 10 Year Program 1944 Folder, *at* National Archives Records Administration, Seattle, Pacific Northwest Region [hereinafter BIA Ten-Year Program].

P. 280   *Senator Guy Cordon and Governor Douglas McKay.* On Cordon, see W. Gardner, acting secretary of Interior letter to G. Cordon, U.S. senator for Oregon (May 29, 1947), at Archival Collection of the Siletz Tribe Cultural Department [hereinafter Siletz Archival Collection]; G. Cordon, letter to H. Simmons, tribal representative (June 3, 1947), at Siletz Archival Collection. On McKay, see D. McKay, governor, letter to E. M. Pryse, Department of Interior regional director (Aug. 21, 1951), in Hearing Before the Senate Committee on Interior and Insular Affairs, "S. 3005 and S. 3004," 82d Congress, 2d Session, vol. 2, pp. 87–88 (May 21, 1952) (Washington, D.C.: Ward & Paul, 1952), at Siletz Archival Collection.

P. 280   *Closing the Grand Ronde–Siletz agency.* See E. M. Pryse memorandum to Commissioner of Indian Affairs (Nov. 29, 1946), RG 75, Portland Area Office Holdings 01, Box 1, Monthly Narrative Reports for 1948 Folder, at National Archives Records Administration, Seattle, Pacific Northwest Region (proposing elimination of the agency); Senate Report No. 1325 to Accompany S. 2746, "Termination of Federal Supervision over Property of Certain Indians in Western Oregon," 83d Congress, 2d Session, p. 11 (Washington, D.C.: Government Printing Office, 1954) [hereinafter 1954 Senate Termination Report].

P. 280   *Major 1948 initiative.* E. M. Pryse memorandum to Commissioner of Indian Affairs (Sept. 1, 1948), RG 75, Portland Area Office Holdings 01, Box 1, Monthly Narrative Reports for 1948 Folder, *at* National Archives Records Administration, Seattle, Pacific Northwest Region.

P. 280   *"spent much of his own time."* E. M. Pryse letter to Commissioner of Indian Affairs (Dec. 7, 1953) in Joint Hearings Before the Subcommittees of the Committees on Interior and Insular Affairs, "On S. 2746 and H.R. 7317: Termination of Federal Supervision over Certain Tribes of Indians," 83d Congress, 2d Session, pt. 3 (Western Oregon), p. 139 (Feb. 17, 1954) (Washington, D.C.: Government Printing Office, 1954) [hereinafter Western Oregon Joint Hearings].

P. 280   *"Morgan Pryse who has never been in our Indian homes."* D. Orton, vice chairman, Siletz Tribal Council, letter to G. Cordon (Feb. 11, 1949), *at* Siletz Archival Collection (informing Senator Cordon that "our people are in bad shape and are in dire need of assistance" and urging that the senator not be misled by the "deceit and deception" of Pryse).

P. 281 *"the basis for historic Indian culture."* Commission on Organization of the Executive Branch of the Government Special Task Force Report, "Social Security and Education—Indian Affairs: A Report to Congress," pp. 54–55 (Washington, D.C.: Government Printing Office, 1948) (quoted in Prucha, vol. 2, *The Great Father*, p. 1029).

P. 282 *The Interior department was of two minds.* See generally Prucha, vol. 2, *The Great Father*, pp. 1017, 1023–30. Prucha describes this period as "vacillating" between self-determination and termination (ibid., p. 1017), and characterizes the department's approach as " a moderate form of terminationism" (ibid., p. 1027).

P. 282 *Dillon S. Myer.* See generally Richard Drinnon, *Keeper of Concentration Camps: Dillon S. Myer and American Racism* (Berkeley: University of California Press, 1987).

P. 282 *WRA years.* See ibid., pp. 76–116.

P. 282 *terminate tribes "as fast as possible."* Dean Frank T. Wilson, "Interview with Dillon S. Meyer, commissioner of Indian Affairs," vol. 7, no. 2 *The Journal of Religious Thought*, p. 99 (Spring/Summer 1950).

P. 282 *Myer cleaned house in the BIA.* On the purge of Collier adherents, see Kenneth R. Philp, *John Collier's Crusade for Indian Reform, 1920–1954*, p. 225 (Tucson: University of Arizona Press, 1977); Fixico, *Termination and Relocation*, pp. 65–66.

P. 282 *deep changes to facilitate termination.* The activist Myer Administration is discussed in Prucha, vol. 2, *The Great Father*, pp. 1030–36; Fixico, *Termination and Relocation*, pp. 63–77; Philp, *Termination Revisited*, pp. 87–124; Philp, *John Collier's Crusade*, p. 225; Wilkinson and Biggs, "Evolution of The Termination Policy," pp. 147–48. Myer justified the Bureau's controlling regulations over the hiring of tribal attorneys as a way to prevent disreputable lawyers from exploiting vulnerable tribes. See, e.g., Fixico, *Termination and Relocation*, pp. 67–68. For a detailed discussion on tribes' right to employ legal counsel, see Philp, *Termination Revisited*, pp. 108–24. Myer's relocation program was meant to "break the cycle of poverty, paternalism, and despair on Indian reservations" by moving employable Indians to urban areas where "they would become self-reliant and civic-minded people." According to Philp, the purpose of Myer's "boarding-home placement program for Indian children" was for Indian students "to better appreciate Christian civilization." Philp, *Termination Revisited*, pp. 97–99.

P. 282 *"By effectively reducing the division directors."* Prucha, vol. 2, *The Great Father*, p. 1038.

P. 283 *"museum specimens."* Philp, *Termination Revisited*, p. 90 (quoting Myer).

P. 283 *"the sunlight of independence."* Ibid., p. 94 (quoting Myer).

P. 283 *"THESE PEOPLE SHALL BE FREE!"* Arthur V. Watkins, "Termination of Federal Supervision: The Removal of Restrictions over Indian Property and Person," vol. 311 *The Annals of the American Academy of Political and Social Science*, p. 55 (1957).

P. 284 *"social genocide"* Philp, *John Collier's Crusade*, p. 227 (quoting Collier's letter to President Eisenhower).

P. 284 *"Hitler and Mussolini rolled into one."* Prucha, vol. 2, *The Great Father*, p. 1030.

P. 284 *"makes mandatory our close attention."* Bureau of Indian Affairs, Portland Area Office, "Program for the Early Termination of Selected Activities and Withdrawing Federal Supervision over the Indians at Grand Ronde–Siletz and Southwestern Oregon," p. 6 (Dec. 1950), RG 75, Grand Ronde–Siletz Indian Agency Holdings 77,

Box 161, 10 Year Program 1944 Folder, *at* National Archives Records Administration, Seattle, Pacific Northwest Region [hereinafter 1950 Program].

P. 284 *"Program for the Early Termination."* See generally ibid. Pryse's enthusiasm was evident: "If the Bureau of Indian Affairs should initiate new plans and encourage certain Indian tribes to travel along this new road to the future, it seems feasible that Indians under the Grand Ronde–Siletz Administration should be included in the program." Ibid., p. 6.

P. 285 *The "Ten-Year Program."* See generally BIA Ten-Year Program.

P. 285 *"This picture, however, will change materially."* Ibid., p. 8.

P. 285 *"quite a number of indigent Indians."* E. M. Pryse memorandum to Commissioner of Indian Affairs, p. 6 (Sept. 1, 1950), RG 75, Portland Area Office Holdings 01, Box 1, Monthly Narrative Reports for 1950 Folder, *at* National Archives Records Administration, Seattle, Pacific Northwest Region.

P. 285 *"gradual closing down of the mills and logging camps."* E. M. Pryse, area director, memorandum to Commissioner of Indian Affairs (Dec. 1, 1949), RG 75, Portland Area Office Holdings 01, Box 1, Monthly Narrative Reports for 1948–1949 Folder, *at* National Archives Records Administration, Seattle, Pacific Northwest Region.

P. 285 *"old and weather-beaten."* BIA Ten-Year Program, p. 12.

P. 285 *"more than 80 families without houses."* Ibid.

P. 286 *"only one resident family."* Ibid., p. 10

P. 286 *Siletz tribal resolution.* 1950 Program, pp. 20–21. According to the resolution—which declared that the Siletz were "willing and should assume the duties and responsibilities of full American citizenship" and that "Federal supervision has ceased to be necessary"—"there were no dissenting votes cast."

P. 286 *"many Siletz people have long expressed."* Ibid., p. 6.

P. 286 *Agnes and Coquelle Thompson incident.* Lionel Youst and William R. Seaburg, *Coquelle Thompson, Athabaskan Witness,* pp. 238–50 (Norman: University of Oklahoma Press, 2002). For Agnes's initial letter to the agent concerning the IIM account and his response, see ibid., p. 239.

P. 287 *Agnes Thompson letter.* Ibid., pp. 240–41.

P. 287 *Steady decline in federal services.* The BIA discontinued some programs in the late 1930s and early 1940s. See chapter 12, p. 274 and accompanying notes. By the late 1940s, national BIA appropriations had been reduced and the Portland area office felt the effects. See, e.g., Fixico, *Termination and Relocation,* pp. 34–35; E. M. Pryse, area director, memorandum to Commissioner of Indian Affairs, p. 4 (May 2, 1947), RG 75, Portland Area Office Holdings 01, Box 1, Monthly Narrative Reports for 1948–1949 Folder, *at* National Archives Records Administration, Seattle, Pacific Northwest Region (abolishing the medical program at Grand Ronde–Siletz "owing to lack of funds"). In 1952, Commissioner Myer testified that, except for financial matters involving land, "we [a]re providing very little of the other social services to [the Grand Ronde–Siletz] Indians at this stage of the game." Hearing Before the House Committee on Interior and Insular Affairs, "H.R. 7489," 82d Congress, 2d Session (May 21, 1952) (Washington, D.C.: Columbia Reporting Co., 1952), *at* Siletz Archival Collection.

P. 287 *area office allowed only the most minimal health care.* In 1947, Pryse reported that the medical program for Siletz and Grand Ronde had been abolished, but, apparently, in some years a doctor was available a few hours a week in Siletz for minor ailments and a hospital in Tacoma, a day's drive, would take some serious cases. E. M. Pryse memorandum to Commissioner of Indian Affairs, p. 4 (May 2, 1947), RG 75, Portland Area Office Holdings 01, Box 1, Monthly Narrative Reports for 1948–1949 Folder, *at* National Archives Records Administration, Seattle, Pacific Northwest Region. In 1950, Pryse reported that the Siletz-Tacoma hospital arrangement was in force. 1950 Program, p. 16.

P. 287 *"the word 'termination' was not used."* Statement of Joseph Lane, former chairman, Siletz Tribal Council, *in* Hearings Before the Senate Committee on Interior and Insular Affairs, Subcommittee on Indian Affairs, "Siletz Restoration Act: On S. 2801," 94th Congress, 2d Session, p. 43 (March 30–31, 1976) (Washington, D.C.: Government Printing Office, 1976) [hereinafter Siletz Restoration Hearings].

P. 288 *"permission for the tribe."* W. Gardner letter to G. Cordon (May 29, 1947), *at* Siletz Archival Collection (describing Simmons's letter).

P. 288 *"our tribes want immediate liquidation."* E. Logan, tribal chairman, letter to D. Myer, commissioner of Indian Affairs (Aug. 29, 1950), RG 75, Portland Area Office Holdings 56, Box 1508, Grand Ronde–Siletz General 1947–1951 Folder, *at* National Archives Records Administration, Seattle, Pacific Northwest Region. This is a rare instance in which the tribe's use of the term "liquidation" referred to removing allotments, as well as the tribe's timber sections, from trust status.

P. 288 *tribe requested that the four timber sections be sold.* Confederated Tribes of Siletz Indians Special Meeting Minutes, Siletz, Oregon, Oct. 7, 1951, *at* Siletz Archival Collection; E. M. Pryse memorandum to Commissioner of Indian Affairs, p. 9 (Nov. 1, 1951), RG 75, Portland Area Office Holdings 01, Box 1, Monthly Narrative Reports for 1951 Folder, *at* National Archives Records Administration, Seattle, Pacific Northwest Region.

P. 288 *Per capita payments from the tribe's trust account.* See, e.g., H. R. Cloud, regional representative, letter to Commissioner of Indian Affairs (June 7, 1949), RG 75, Portland Area Office Holdings 56, Box 1508, Grand Ronde–Siletz General 1947–1951 Folder, *at* National Archives Records Administration, Seattle, Pacific Northwest Region (referring to attached May 29, 1949 Tribal Business Committee resolution requesting per capita payments); E.M. Pryse, letter to Commissioner of Indian Affairs (Aug. 7, 1950), RG 75, Portland Area Office Holdings 56, Box 1508, Grand Ronde–Siletz General 1947–1951 Folder, *at* National Archives Records Administration, Seattle, Pacific Northwest Region (enclosing a June 25, 1950 tribal council resolution requesting a $150 per capita payment to each of the 685 eligible members).

P. 288 *"You will recall."* D. Orton letter to G. Cordon (Feb. 11, 1949), *at* Siletz Archival Collection.

P. 288 *Oregon's law prohibiting interracial marriages.* Termination did not address that matter, although the Oregon legislature repealed the statute in 1951. See chapter 11, p. 250 and accompanying note.

P. 289 *"The Bureau of Indian Affairs officials had told us."* Roberta Ulrich, *A Lot of Funerals: The Failed Termination Experiment, 1953–2006*, p. 6 (chap. 4) (Lincoln: University of Nebraska Press, 2010) (quoting Wilfred Wasson).

P. 289 *Senator Watkins withheld claims payments.* See, e.g., Vine Deloria Jr., *Custer Died for Your Sins: An Indian Manifesto*, pp. 69, 71–73 (New York: Avon Books, 1969) (on the Klamath and Menominee, respectively). See also American Indian Policy Review Commission, Final Report, "Task Force Ten: Terminated and Nonfederally Recognized Indians," p. 42 (Oct. 1976) [hereinafter Task Force Ten]; Prucha, vol. 2, *The Great Father*, p. 1050; Fixico, *Termination and Relocation*, p. 96.

P. 289 *The Alcea claims case.* See chapter 12, pp. 263–65 and accompanying notes.

P. 289 *Widespread belief of BIA coercion.* See, e.g., M. Thompson, commissioner of Indian Affairs, letter to J. Abourezk, U.S. senator for South Dakota (April 6, 1976), in Siletz Restoration Hearings, p. 325.

P. 289 *Review of the coercion issue.* Ibid., pp. 323–26.

P. 289 *Pryse testified there was no such pressure.* Ibid., p. 325. The Pryse testimony can be found in the Western Oregon Joint Hearings, p. 187. In response to the inquiry whether the termination legislation "had to be passed before [the Indians] could get their distribution of their funds," Pryse answered "oh, no," and pointed out that "the tribes have never withdrawn their resolutions" consenting to termination.

P. 289 *tantalizing piece of circumstantial evidence.* M. Thompson letter to J. Abourezk (April 6, 1976), *in* Siletz Restoration Hearings, p. 325 (the Termination Act was dated Aug. 13, 1954; the Alcea Judgment Per Capita Act was dated Aug. 30, 1954).

P. 290 *1935 push for an IRA constitution.* See chapter 12, pp. 272–75 and accompanying notes.

P. 290 *In 1940, the agency urged a constitution.* See chapter 12, pp. 273–75 and accompanying notes.

P. 290 *BIA motive to pave the way for termination.* H. R. Cloud letter to Commissioner of Indian Affairs (Feb. 25, 1949), RG 75, Portland Area Office Holdings 07, Box 37, Siletz Tribe—Constitution and By-Laws 1948–1950 Folder, *at* National Archives Records Administration, Seattle, Pacific Northwest Region. The vote against the 1949 proposed constitution was 77 to 4. Ibid.

P. 290 *Adoption of a constitution in September 1950.* Pryse reported the adoption in a report to Commissioner Myer, calling the vote "unanimous." E. M. Pryse memorandum to Commissioner of Indian Affairs, p. 7 (Oct. 1, 1950), RG 75, Portland Area Office Holdings 01, Box 1, Monthly Narrative Reports for 1950 Folder, *at* National Archives Records Administration, Seattle, Pacific Northwest Region. See also E. M. Pryse letter to Commissioner of Indian Affairs (Oct. 18, 1950), RG 75, Portland Area Office Holdings 7, Box 37, Siletz Tribe—Constitution and By-Laws 1948–1950 Folder, *at* National Archives Records Administration, Seattle, Pacific Northwest Region. Although there do not seem to be existing tribal council minutes for the September 10, 1950, tribal council meeting, a later council resolution refers to the adoption of the constitution on that date. See Tribal Council, Confederated Tribes of Siletz Indians, Resolution of Oct. 7, 1951, *at* Siletz Archival Collection.

P. 290 *"were especially busy in drafting."* H. R. Cloud letter to Commissioner of Indian Affairs (Feb. 25, 1949), RG 75, Portland Area Office Holdings 7, Box 37, Siletz Tribe—Constitution and By-Laws 1948–1950 Folder, *at* National Archives Records Administration, Seattle, Pacific Northwest Region. Later in the same letter, Roe Cloud noted that Elwood Towner and Dan Orton, whom Roe Cloud asserted were instrumental in drafting the constitution, strongly opposed adoption in a public meeting on the day of the election. Ibid.

P. 291 *boilerplate charters drafted by the BIA.* Although the 1950 constitution was not technically an IRA constitution because the tribe had voted down an IRA constitution in 1935, the document was of the same style and substance as the IRA versions. For a collection of the IRA constitutions, see *Indian Reorganization Act Era Constitutions and Charters*, University of Oklahoma Law Center, *at* http://thorpe.ou.edu/IRA.html (accessed Feb. 6, 2009). See also, e.g., Robert L. Bennett et al., "Implementing the IRA," *in* Kenneth R. Philp, ed., *Indian Self-Rule: First-Hand Accounts of Indian-White Relations from Roosevelt to Reagan*, p. 83 (Salt Lake City, UT: Howe Brothers, 1986) ("most of the IRA constitutions were quite similar").

P. 291   *"very little understanding of what termination was all about."* Hiroto Zakoji, telephone interview with Carrie Covington, research assistant, July 27, 2007.

P. 291   *"I don't think there was more than a handful."* Statement of Hardy Simmons (March 14, 1976), *in* Siletz Restoration Hearings, p. 140.

P. 292   *"The vote came very quickly."* Statement of Archie Ben (March 14, 1976), *in* Siletz Restoration Hearings, p. 141.

P. 292   *"termination was inevitable."* Task Force Ten, p. 46.

P. 292   *"people in the amounts of 25 or 30."* Statement of Joseph Lane, *in* Siletz Restoration Hearings, p. 43.

P. 292   *"the Bureau pushed hard."* Dolly Fisher, interview with author, Siletz, Oregon, May 23, 2005.

P. 292   *"I just figured it was going to happen."* Jo Anne Miller, interview with author, Siletz, Oregon, May 24, 2005.

P. 292   *many of the 786 tribal members.* The "final" tribal roles, approved on August 7, 1954, counted 786 tribal members. Western Oregon Joint Hearings, p. 141.

P. 292   *Few tribal meetings exceeded 40 members.* See, e.g. Confederated Tribes of Siletz Indians Special Meeting Minutes, Siletz, Oregon, June 24, 1951, *at* Siletz Archival Collection (29 members present); Confederated Tribes of Siletz Indians Special Meeting Minutes, Siletz, Oregon, Oct. 7, 1951, *at* Siletz Archival Collection (34 members present); Confederated Tribes of Siletz Indians Regular Meeting Minutes, Siletz, Oregon, Nov. 3, 1951, *at* Siletz Archival Collection (15 members present).

P. 292   *"able, willing, and should assume the duties and responsibilities."* Tribal Council, Confederated Tribes of Siletz Indians, Resolution of Nov. 12, 1950, *in* Western Oregon Joint Hearings, pp. 159–60.

P. 292   *"an enthusiastic meeting."* E. M. Pryse memorandum to Commissioner of Indian Affairs, p. 5 (Dec. 1, 1951), RG 75, Portland Area Office Holdings 01, Box 1, Monthly Narrative Reports for 1950 Folder, *at* National Archives Records Administration, Seattle, Pacific Northwest Region.

P. 293   *Bill telegraphed on August 10, 1951.* H. Lee, acting commissioner of Indian Affairs, telegram of draft bill to E. M. Pryse (Aug. 10, 1951), *at* Siletz Archival Collection.

P. 293   *"I believe the Commissioner would be justified."* E. M. Pryse letter to Commissioner of Indian Affairs (Sept. 11, 1951), RG 75, Portland Area Office Holdings 01, Box 12, Grand Ronde–Siletz 1952–1954 Folder, *at* National Archives Records Administration, Seattle, Pacific Northwest Region.

P. 293   *"it was not possible to get affirmative action."* E. M. Pryse memorandum to Commissioner of Indian Affairs (Sept. 1, 1951), RG 75, Portland Area Office Holdings 01, Box 1, Monthly Narrative Reports for 1951 Folder, *at* National Archives Records Administration, Seattle, Pacific Northwest Region.

P. 293   *Action was tabled for a week.* Confederated Tribes of Siletz Indians Regular Meeting Minutes, Siletz, Oregon, Sept. 30, 1951, *at* Siletz Archival Collection.

P. 293   *October 7 special general council meeting.* Confederated Tribes of Siletz Indians Special Meeting Minutes, Siletz, Oregon, Oct. 7, 1951, *at* Siletz Archival Collection.

P. 293 *Resolution to transfer lands to tribal corporation.* Confederated Tribes of Siletz Indians Regular Meeting Minutes, Siletz, Oregon, Nov. 3, 1951, *at* Siletz Archival Collection.

P. 293 *Request not added to the bill.* Neither the 1952 nor 1954 bill, as originally introduced, included the provision requested by the tribe. As finally enacted, the Siletz Termination Act did address the issue but in a different fashion: the secretary was authorized to transfer these lands to "any tribe or any member or group of members" or to "a public or nonprofit body." Pub. L. No. 588, ch. 733, §8, Aug. 13, 1954, 88 Stat. 724, 726 (1954). The land eventually went to the City of Siletz. See p. 293 and accompanying note.

P. 293 *Grand Ronde–Siletz termination bills.* See Hearing Before the Senate Committee on Interior and Insular Affairs, "S. 3005 and S. 3004," 82d Congress, 2d Session, vol. 2, pp. 87–88 (May 21, 1952) (Washington, D.C.: Ward & Paul, 1952), *at* Siletz Archival Collection; Hearing Before the House Committee on Interior and Insular Affairs, "H.R. 7489," 82d Congress, 2d Session (May 21, 1952) (Washington, D.C.: Columbia Reporting Co., 1952), *at* Siletz Archival Collection.

P. 294 *Eisenhower decided not to keep Myer.* See, e.g., Charles Wilkinson, *Blood Struggle: The Rise of Modern Indian Nations*, p. 65 (New York: W. W. Norton & Co., 2005).

P. 294 *Arthur V. Watkins.* See, e.g., ibid. pp. 66–69; Fixico, *Termination and Relocation*, pp. 93–96; Prucha, vol. 2, *The Great Father*, pp. 1015–16.

P. 295 *A tough, aggressive chairman.* On Watkins's tactics and the political tone of Congress during the termination years, see the in-depth study by Gary Orfield, *Professor of Education at the Harvard Graduate School of Education.* See generally Gary Orfield, "A Study of the Termination Policy," pp. 14–15 (Denver, CO: National Congress of American Indians, 1966). Orfield's study also can be found as a congressional reprint in Senate Committee on Labor and Public Welfare, "The Education of American Indians," 91st Congress, 1st Session, vol. 4, pp. 673–816 (Washington, D.C.: Government Printing Office, 1970). See also Wilkinson and Biggs, "Evolution of the Termination Policy," pp. 155–56.

P. 295 *"Why can [Indians] not do the same?"* Fixico, *Termination and Relocation*, pp. 92–93 (quoting Watkins).

P. 295 *"agree now to grow up."* Ibid., p. 96 (quoting Watkins).

P. 295 *Indians "want all the benefits."* Orfield, "A Study of the Termination Policy," p. 690 (quoting Watkins).

P. 295 *"Whereas it is the policy of Congress."* For the full text of the Resolution, see H. Con. Res. 108, Aug. 1, 1953, 67 Stat. B132 (1953) (not codified). See also House Report No. 841 to Accompany House Concurrent Resolution 108, "Expressing the Sense of Congress that Certain Tribes of Indians Should be Freed from Federal Supervision," 83d Congress, 1st Session (Washington, D.C., 1953); Senate Report No. 794 to Accompany House Concurrent Resolution 108, "Expressing the Sense of Congress that Certain Tribes of Indians Should be Freed from Federal Supervision," 83d Congress, 1st Session (Washington, D.C., 1953).

P. 296 *Subcommittee hearings for the Utah and Texas tribes.* See Joint Hearings Before the Subcommittees of the Committees on Interior and Insular Affairs, "On S. 2760 and H.R. 7674: Termination of Federal Supervision over Certain Tribes of Indians," 83d Congress, 2d Session, pt. 1 (Utah) (Feb. 15, 1954) (Washington, D.C.: Government Printing Office, 1954) [hereinafter Southern Paiute Joint Hearings]; Joint Hearings

Before the Subcommittees of the Committees on Interior and Insular Affairs, "On S. 2744, H.R. 6282, and H.R. 6547: Termination of Federal Supervision over Certain Tribes of Indians," 83d Congress, 2d Session, pt. 2 (Texas) (Feb. 16, 1954) (Washington, D.C.: Government Printing Office, 1954) [hereinafter Alabama-Coushatta Joint Hearings].

P. 296 *The Southern Paiutes had received an inquiry.* Southern Paiute Joint Hearings, p. 60. The "usual procedure" referred to was that leases of Indian lands go through a competitive bidding procedure. Ibid.

P. 296 *The Alabama-Coushatta had 4,000 acres.* Alabama-Coushatta Joint Hearings, pp. 102–3.

P. 296 *Bill for Siletz termination.* See Western Oregon Joint Hearings.

P. 297 *"Almost every employable male person."* Ibid., p. 143.

P. 297 *Ability to handle own affairs.* Ibid., p. 150.

P. 297 *"these Indians have made great progress."* Ibid., pp. 185–86.

P. 298 *November 12, 1950 resolution.* See ibid., pp. 159–60. Regarding the October 7, 1951 resolution, see Confederated Tribes of Siletz Indians Special Meeting Minutes, Siletz, Oregon, Oct. 7, 1951, *at* Siletz Archival Collection.

P. 299 *"we think it would be less disrupting."* Western Oregon Joint Hearings, p. 189.

P. 299 *"is being used 100 percent by the tribe."* Ibid., p. 190.

P. 299 *The lands were conveyed to the City of Siletz.* Regarding the bill's treatment of the tribe's request, see above, p. 293 and accompanying notes. The Interior department ultimately transferred the lands to the City of Siletz. See Bureau of Indian Affairs, Siletz Agency, "Report on Status of Government Reserves, Siletz, Oregon" (May 31, 1979), *at* Siletz Archival Collection.

P. 299 *"a lot of Indians didn't want to admit they were Indians."* Ulrich, *A Lot of Funerals*, p. 8 (chap. 4) (quoting Jim Metcalf).

P. 300 *Indian unemployment and college education in the 1950s.* See Wilkinson, *Blood Struggle*, pp. 22–25 and accompanying notes.

P. 300 *Siletz unemployment was estimated at 44 percent.* On Siletz unemployment, see Siletz Restoration Hearings, p. 201; on Siletz income, see ibid., pp. 204–5.

P. 300 *Nearly half of Siletz young people did not finish high school.* Ibid., p. 203.

P. 300 *Pryse had the courage to tell Senator Watkins.* When asked what he thought would happen to Klamath land transferred out of trust and into the hands of individual Indians, Pryse responded, "I am afraid it would pass out of Indian ownership, a great portion of it, in a matter of a few years." Pryse's rationale for this prediction was that the Indians "haven't had the experience of making a living and providing for taxes and also withstanding the pressure of people to buy their property." Wilkinson, *Blood Struggle*, pp. 78–79.

P. 301 *seventy-six family allotments totaling 5,390 acres.* See Western Oregon Joint Hearings, p. 144.

P. 301 *$792.50 could be paid to each tribal member.* The $792.50 was paid out in two distributions: $250 in 1954 and $542.50 in 1956. Siletz Restoration Hearings, p. 340.

14 Restoration

P. 305 *The socioeconomic statistics were dismal.* The statistics in the text are drawn from the only comprehensive study of Siletz socioeconomic status in the early and mid-1970s.

Jerome Sayers and John M. Volkman, Center for Urban Education, "A Statistical Profile of the Confederated Tribes of Siletz Indians" (Portland, OR: Center for Urban Education, 1976), *in* Hearings Before the Senate Committee on Interior and Insular Affairs, Subcommittee on Indian Affairs, "Siletz Restoration Act: On S. 2801," 94th Congress, 2d Session, pp. 190–261 (March 30–31, 1976) (Washington, D.C.: Government Printing Office, 1976) [hereinafter Siletz Restoration Hearings]. For data regarding Siletz population estimates and migration, see ibid., pp. 196–201; unemployment rates, pp. 201–2; education, pp. 203–4; income, pp. 204–5; and health and alcoholism, pp. 205–6. The Bureau of Indian Affairs also completed a study in 1978, relying heavily on Sayers and Volkman's report. See U.S. Department of Interior, Bureau of Indian Affairs, "A Profile of the Confederation Tribes of Siletz Indians of Oregon," Report No. 264 (Feb. 1978).

P. 306   *The Lincoln County timber harvest dropped.* In 1968, the county's timber harvest was over 450 million board feet; in 1970, it had plummeted to 226 million board feet, with an average throughout the early 1970s hovering around 275 million board feet. "Oregon's Timber Harvests: 1849–2004," pp. 90–93 (Salem: Oregon Department of Forestry, 2005).

P. 306   *Diaspora of two-thirds of the Siletz people living in Lincoln County.* In 1954, approximately 73 percent of the tribal members lived on or near the reservation; by 1975 this figure had dropped to 27 percent. Sayers and Volkman, "A Statistical Profile of the Confederated Tribes of Siletz Indians," pp. 8–9.

P. 306   *"after termination we would go to pow-wows."* Ed Ben, interview with Josh Tenneson, research assistant, Salem, Oregon, June 21, 2006.

P. 306   *"It made me feel vulnerable."* Agnes Pilgrim, interview with author, Grants Pass, Oregon, June 16, 2005.

P. 306   *Government programs for Indians improved.* The modern tribal resurgence, often referred to as the "self-determination era," has received a significant amount of attention in the literature. For works attempting to synthesize the modern era, see Charles Wilkinson, *Blood Struggle: The Rise of Modern Indian Nations* (New York: W. W. Norton & Co., 2005); Stephen Cornell, *The Return of the Native: American Indian Political Resurgence* (New York: Oxford University Press, 1988); Harvard Project on American Indians, *The State of Native Nations: Conditions under U.S. Policies of Self-Determination* (New York: Oxford University Press, 2008). For an earlier work, but perhaps the most influential one, see Vine Deloria Jr., *Custer Died for Your Sins: An Indian Manifesto* (New York: Avon Books, 1969).

P. 306   *Health care for Native people improved.* Brenneman et al., "Health Status and Clinical Indicators," in Everett R. Rhoades, ed., *American Indian Health: Innovations in Health Care, Promotion, and Policy*, p. 103 (Baltimore, MD: Johns Hopkins University Press, 2000).

P. 308   *Paul Washington Cemetery Association.* The organization incorporated as a nonprofit under Oregon law in February, 1975. The initial directors were Arthur Bensell, Stanley Strong, Archie Ben, Mary Alice Muncey, Joe Lane, and Wolverton Orton. State of Oregon Department of Commerce, Corporation Division, "Certificate of Incorporation of Paul Washington Cemetery Association" (Feb. 10, 1975), Archival Collection of the Siletz Tribe Cultural Department [hereinafter Siletz Archival Collection].

P. 308   *Siletz Alcohol and Drug Program.* See Statement of Robert Tom, Siletz Tribal Council Member, *in* Siletz Restoration Hearings, pp. 154–58.

P. 308   *Portland Urban Indian Center.* See Cynthia Viles, interview with María Aparicio, research assistant, Portland, Oregon, Dec. 30, 2007.

P. 308   *September 1973 meeting to form a tribal government.* See Statement of Joseph Lane, Siletz Tribal Council chairman, *in* Siletz Restoration Hearings, pp. 166–69; "Siletz Tribes Pick Ex-Salem Resident" (undated article from unidentified newspaper; clipped and given to the author by Ed Ben); Ed Ben, letter to author (Oct. 1, 2005), *at* Siletz Archival Collection (explaining that Pauline Ricks and Lindsey John were initial tribal council members in addition to the seven listed in the newspaper).

P. 308   *It was a frenetic time.* L. Merrill, letter to author, "Pre Restoration & Restoration, 1973/1974" (undated), *at* Siletz Archival Collection.

P. 308   *CETA-Manpower program.* See Statement of Robert Rilatos, Siletz Tribal Council vice-chairman, *in* Siletz Restoration Hearings, pp. 145–46. Rilatos was selected by the tribal council to coordinate the CETA-Manpower program. In addition to the contract with Warm Springs, the tribe received an additional CETA-Manpower grant from the Urban Indian Center in Portland, which also was eligible for grants under CETA.

P. 309   *Tribal drop-in center.* Ibid., p. 146.

P. 309   *"those signs are wooden books."* Tribal Council of the Confederated Tribes of Siletz Indians, letter to Tom McCall, governor of Oregon, "Re: Proclamation of the Confederated Tribes of Siletz Indians" (July 1, 1974), *at* Siletz Archival Collection. The letter prompted media attention. See, e.g., Paul Jacobs, "Indians Protest Bias in State Historical Markers," *Salem Capital Journal*, p. 16 (July 19, 1974).

P. 309   *Senator Hatfield spoke at tribal meeting.* "Siletz Tribes Pick Ex-Salem Resident."

P. 309   *"Sis, what do you think?"* Gladys Bolton, interview with María Aparicio, research assistant, Keizer, Oregon, March 26, 2007.

P. 310   *"We want to be restored."* John Volkman, interview with Carrie Covington, research assistant, Portland, Oregon, Aug. 8, 2007 (recalling his first meeting with Joe Lane).

P. 310   *the Menominee were a special case.* On Menominee restoration, see Stephen J. Hertzberg, "The Menominee Indians: Termination to Restoration," vol. 6, no.1 *American Indian Law Review*, pp. 143–86 (1978); Nicholas C. Peroff, *Menominee Drums: Tribal Termination and Restoration, 1954–1974* (Norman: University of Oklahoma Press, 1982).

P. 310   *the Boldt Decision.* See generally Fay G. Cohen, *Treaties on Trial: The Continuing Controversy over Northwest Indian Fishing Rights*, pp. 3–17, 83–106 (Seattle: University of Washington Press, 1986); American Friends Service Committee, *Uncommon Controversy: Fishing Rights of the Muckleshoot, Puyallup, and Nisqually Indians* (Seattle: University of Washington Press, 1986); Charles Wilkinson, *Messages from Frank's Landing: A Story of Salmon, Treaties, and the Indian Way* (Seattle: University of Washington Press, 2000).

P. 310   *Congressman Wyatt introduced a restoration bill.* H.R. 15604, 93d Congress, 2d Session (1974).

P. 311   *Statistical Profile of tribal members [1976].* See Siletz Restoration Hearings, pp. 190–206.

P. 311   *The People Are Dancing Again (film).* *The People Are Dancing Again: The Siletz Indians' Dramatic Struggle to Restore their Tribal Identity*, VHS (Portland, OR: Siletz Films, 1976) (produced by Harry Dawson Jr. and John Volkman); John Volkman, interview, Aug. 8, 2007 (Northwest Film Festival award).

P. 315 *The influential Fish and Wildlife Commission.* John McKean, director of Oregon Department of Fish and Wildlife, letter to Mark Hatfield, U.S. senator for Oregon (Nov. 17, 1975), *at* Siletz Archival Collection.

P. 315 *The* **Sunday Oregonian** *editorialized against the tribe.* Editorial Board, "'Aboriginal' Rights?" *Sunday Oregonian*, p. C2 (Nov. 9, 1975) ("In supporting such legislation, however, *The Oregonian* is impelled to urge [that the bill be amended] to make it clear that restoration of tribal rights will not lead to Siletz Indian claims to exclusive or unusual hunting and fishing rights").

P. 315 *"Nets in the Alsea all fall and winter."* Pete Cornacchia, "Poor Who?" *Eugene Register-Guard*, p. D1 (Nov. 25, 1975) (quoting State Wildlife Director John McKean for the "Circle the wagons" statement). After meeting Tribal Chairman Art Bensell a week later, Cornacchia described Bensell as "a seemingly gentle and sincere man" and wrote a column entitled "Siletz Side," which did fairly explain the Siletz position. *Eugene Register-Guard*, p. C1 (Dec. 2, 1975). Cornacchia did not change his mind on the bill, but the second column departed from the inflammatory tone of the first. See ibid.

P. 317 *Co-sponsors of restoration bill.* In the House, AuCoin had signed up two co-sponsors from the Oregon delegation, Bob Duncan from the Portland area and Jim Weaver, whose district included Eugene. In the Senate, Bob Packwood of Oregon, Dewey Bartlett of Oklahoma, and Jim Abourezk of South Dakota joined with Hatfield on the bill. Packwood, himself well-regarded, had already given his support but this put both Oregon senators on record. Bartlett, also a Republican, served on the Interior Committee, as did the Democrat Abourezk, a strong Indian advocate.

P. 317 *Governor Robert Straub supported the bill.* See Robert Straub, governor of Oregon, letter to Mark Hatfield (Dec. 4, 1975), *in* Siletz Restoration Hearings, pp. 65–66; Editorial Board, "Indians Deserve Support," *Salem Capital Journal* (Nov. 18, 1975), *in* Siletz Restoration Hearings, p. 368 ("Gov. Robert Straub is right in sticking with his support of the proposed Siletz Indian Restoration Bill.").

P. 317 *Attorney General Lee Johnson supported restoration.* See Lee Johnson, attorney general for Oregon, letter to Mark Hatfield (Dec. 24, 1975), *in* Siletz Restoration Hearings, pp. 370–72.

P. 317 *local municipalities.* Lincoln City, Oregon, "City Council Resolution 461" (March 23, 1976), *in* Siletz Restoration Hearings, p. 369.

P. 318 *"We were like kids."* Kathryn Harrison, interview with Carrie Covington, research assistant, Grand Ronde, Oregon, Aug. 12, 2007.

P. 318 *All Coast Fishermen's Marketing Association.* Statement of Arthur Bensell, Siletz Tribal Council chairman, *in* Siletz Restoration Hearings, p. 56 (Bensell reading supporting telegram from ACFMA).

P. 318 *Pauline Bell Ricks presented nineteenth-century history.* Statement of Pauline Bell Ricks, Siletz Tribal Council member, *in* Siletz Restoration Hearings, pp. 120–29.

P. 318 *Joe Lane recounted the tribe's reorganization.* Statement of Joseph Lane, former chairman, Siletz Tribal Council, *in* Siletz Restoration Hearings, pp. 43–45.

P. 318 *Others addressed health, alcoholism.* See Siletz Restoration Hearings, pp. 52–53 (statement of Alta Courville, Siletz Tribal Council member, addressing health); pp. 50–51 (statement of Robert Tom, Siletz Tribal Council member, addressing alcoholism); pp. 47–50 (statement of Sister Francella Griggs, Siletz Tribal Council member, addressing education); pp. 45–47 (statement of Robert Rilatos, vice chairman, Siletz

Tribal Council, addressing economic conditions); pp. 51–52 (statement of Delores Pigsley, Siletz Tribal Council member, addressing current tribal membership); pp. 54–55 (statement of Kathryn Harrison, secretary, Siletz Tribal Council, addressing tribal administration).

P. 318 *Art Bensell gave an overarching account.* Statement of Arthur Bensell, *in* Siletz Restoration Hearings, pp. 55–57.

P. 319 *"Mr. Chairman, as indicated in testimony."* Statement of Ted Kennedy, U.S. senator for Massachussets, *in* Siletz Restoration Hearings, p. 65.

P. 320 *"Senator Hatfield. Now, Mr. Chambers."* Statement of Mark Hatfield, U.S. senator for Oregon, *in* Siletz Restoration Hearings, p. 28.

P. 320 *Hall was unwilling to submit corrective language.* Senator Hatfield was plainly struggling to understand what Hall's (and the Oregon Fish and Wildlife Commission's) objections were to the language he had worked hard to make neutral. The senator invited the witnesses to offer language that would make the bill clearer. Hall declined and responded with semantic distinctions that seemed to make no difference. Her tone was often dismissive and sarcastic, and would have drawn rebukes from senators less forbearing than Hatfield. On the refusal to offer alternative language on neutrality, see, e.g., Siletz Restoration Hearings, p. 76: Senator Hatfield: "Now, would you please specify what procedural advantages that this act will create?" Hall: "I can't do that because of the interference of the U.S. Government in the case of *Kimball v. Callahan* [the Klamath hunting and fishing case], which will determine whether this bill creates any procedural advantages." If that case raised any fears, language could have been drafted to address them. After Hatfield had explained his efforts to make the bill neutral and his willingness to make further changes, he implored the witness to offer constructive language changes: "Now, you come here to testify and indicate that you have questions in your mind, you have doubts, what I am seeking is some way to allay and perhaps resolve those differences. I would very much like to have the Fish and Wildlife Commission giving—[;]" Hall interrupted the Senator and, rather than directly responding, challenged him to hold "local hearings" in Oregon. Ibid., p. 78.

P. 321 *The McKean Amendment.* See Siletz Restoration Hearings, p. 66.

P. 321 *"we might as well kiss the bill goodbye."* Statement of Mark Hatfield, *in* Siletz Restoration Hearings, p. 81.

P. 321 *"It is unconscionable for the Congress."* Statement of Beverly Hall, assistant attorney general for Oregon, *in* Siletz Restoration Hearings, p. 69.

P. 321 *John McKean's "Siletz Health and Welfare Act."* See J. McKean, director, Oregon Department of Fish and Wildlife, letter to A. Bensell (May 12, 1976), *at* Siletz Archival Collection (including enclosures of the department's draft bill and an explanatory memorandum).

P. 321 *In the summer of 1977 the issue reignited in the press.* See, e.g., "State Aides, Siletz Indians Still at Odds over Rights Bill," *Salem Capital Journal*, p. 2B (June 7, 1977); Editorial Board, "Tribal Rights for Siletz," *Salem Capital Journal*, p. 4A (June 9, 1977); "Wildlife Commission Holds Closed Session on Siletz Bill," *Newport News-Times* (June 15, 1977); Associated Press, "AuCoin: Hunting, Fishing Issue Stalling Siletz Bill," *Salem Capital Journal* (Aug. 25, 1977); Associated Press, "AuCoin to Review Bill in Light of AG Opinion," *Daily Astorian* (Aug. 25, 1977).

P. 321 *Attorney General James Redden circulated a memorandum.* James Redden, Oregon attorney general, letter to Mark Hatfield and Les AuCoin, congressman for Oregon (Aug. 8, 1977), *at* Siletz Archival Collection (including the memorandum prepared by Beverly Hall).

P. 322 *"would not have the territorial ramifications."* Richard Ehlke, legislative attorney, Congressional Research Service, Library of Congress, letter to Les AuCoin (Aug. 17, 1977), *at* Siletz Archival Collection.

P. 322 *With one exception, the bill received only technical amendments.* For the two 1977 committee reports, see Senate Report No. 95-386, "Siletz Indian Tribe Restoration Act," 95th Congress, 1st Session (Washington, D.C.: Government Printing Office, 1977); House Report No. 95-623, "Restoring the Confederated Tribes of Siletz Indian of Oregon as a Federally Recognized Sovereign Indian Tribe," 95th Congress, 1st Session (Washington, D.C.: Government Printing Office, 1977).

P. 322 *The statute called for a more elaborate study.* Siletz Indian Tribe Restoration Act, Pub. L. No. 95-195, Nov. 18, 1977, 91 Stat. 1415 (1977) (codified at 25 U.S.C. §711e(b) [2006]).

P. 324 *"I thought the first restoration bill was hard."* Delores Pigsley, interview with Carrie Covington, research assistant, Lincoln City, Oregon, May 22, 2007.

P. 324 *The restoration act gave few specifics.* See 25 U.S.C. §711.

P. 324 *The tribe retained CH2M Hill.* Steve Graham, "Siletz Tribe Hires CH2M Hill for Planning," *Salem Capital Journal,* p. 1C (Dec. 18, 1979).

P. 325 *the tribe would require about $600,000 annually.* The tribal goals are set forth in the U.S. Department of Interior, Bureau of Indian Affairs, "Siletz Indian Reservation Plan," pp. 57–59 (Nov. 1979), *at* Siletz Archival Collection [hereinafter Siletz Reservation Plan]. Projected financial needs for tribal government are found at ibid., pp. 92–95.

P. 325 *national forest lands would not be available.* See Meeting with R. E. Worthington, regional forester for Region 6, Forest Service, U.S. Department of Agriculture, Portland, Oregon, March 23, 1979, *in* Siletz Reservation Plan, p. 137.

P. 325 *The tribe made a formal proposal to Georgia-Pacific.* Meeting with Robert Floweree, CEO of Georgia-Pacific, Portland, Oregon, June 21, 1979, *in* Siletz Reservation Plan, p. 137.

P. 325 *CH2M Hill located 3,630 acres of BLM land.* The Siletz Reservation Plan discusses the general physical characteristics of the land at pp. 61–70; the timber resources are analyzed at pp. 70–76; and the estimated annual timber revenues of $598,500 are computed at p. 96.

P. 326 *value of the land was estimated at $26 million.* See ibid.

P. 326 *"OK. I'll keep my pistol under the table if you will."* Meeting with Murl Storms, Oregon State director, Bureau of Land Management, U.S. Department of the Interior, Portland, Oregon, March 7, 1979 (personal recollection of the author, who was in attendance at the meeting).

P. 328 *"we're not going to give those people city land."* Ronald J. Schleyer, "Siletz Indians Attempting to Regain Former Reservation Land," *Oregonian,* p. B8 (Aug. 21, 1979) (quoting sixty-five-year-old Leonard Whitlow, who owned a tavern in Siletz).

P. 328 *City officials believed that the turnout was the largest.* See, e.g., Grace Castle, "Siletz Voters Approve Poll to Give City Land to Tribe," *Salem Capital Journal* (Nov. 2, 1979). On the election, see also Dave Peden, "Siletz Voters OK Transfer of City Land to Tribe," *Oregonian,* p. A17 (Nov. 3, 1979).

P. 329 *the Council voted 3 to 1.* See, e.g., Dave Sitterson, "Siletz Council Okays Indian Land Transfer," *Newport News Times*, p. 1 (Nov. 14, 1979). The opponents later alleged election fraud but the Lincoln County District Attorney found the charge unsubstantiated and closed the investigation. Dave Sitterson, "Election 'Investigation' Ends," *Lincoln County Leader* (Jan. 2, 1979).

P. 329 *"the Siletz Indian Tribe must have a reservation on the central Oregon Coast."* Editorial Board, "Siletz Need a Home," *Oregonian* (Aug. 28, 1979). See also Editorial Board, "The Siletz Reservation Issue," *Lincoln County Leader* (Sept. 5, 1979); Editorial Board, "Siletz Should Get Back Part of Their Homeland," *Oregon Journal* (Sept. 5, 1979); Calvin Henry, "Restoration of Siletz Reservation Is Long Overdue," *Salem Statesman Journal*, p. 3F (Oct. 28, 1979); Editorial Board, "Restoration Eue," *Eugene Register-Guard* (Nov. 7, 1977). Leonard Whitlow and other Siletz locals, along with some fishing interests, continued their opposition. See, e.g., Ronald J. Schleyer, "Siletz Restoration Sparks Hostility," *Corvallis Gazette-Times*, p. 17 (Aug. 10, 1979).

P. 329 *"I think it is fair to state that the members . . . approve."* J. Redden, letter to V. Atiyeh, governor of Oregon (Dec. 5. 1979), *at* Siletz Archival Collection.

P. 330 *AuCoin raised a scattershot of concerns.* See Press Release, Congressman Les AuCoin, "AuCoin Statement on Proposed Siletz Reservation Bill" (Nov. 29, 1979), *at* Siletz Archival Collection; Bill Monroe, "AuCoin Balks at Backing Siletz Tribe," *Corvallis Gazette-Times* (Nov. 30, 1979); "AuCoin Still Not Supporting Siletz Reservation Plan," *Lincoln County Leader* (Jan. 30, 1980); Dave Sitterson, "AuCoin Hedges on Support of Siletz Indians' Reservation Bill," *Newport News-Times*, p. 8 (March 12, 1980).

P. 330 *"Will it or will it not enhance prospects for superior hunting and fishing rights?"* AuCoin press release (Nov. 29, 1979).

P. 330 *final settlement of the rights issue was "fundamental."* Sitterson, "AuCoin Hedges On Support of Siletz Indians' Reservation Bill," p. 8 (quoting Congressman Les AuCoin).

P. 330 *no new rights would be created.* Jim Redden, letter to Vic Atiyeh (Dec. 5. 1979), *at* Siletz Archival Collection.

P. 330 *"that position is not tenable any more."* Don Holm, "Siletz Submit Plan for Tribal Hunting, Fishing Rights on Coast Lands," *Oregonian*, p. C8 (Dec. 15, 1979) (quoting Herb Lundy).

P. 330 *An agreement was signed on April 22, 1980.* For the text of the agreement, see "Agreement among the state of Oregon, the United States of America and the Confederated Tribes of Siletz Indians of Oregon to permanently define tribal hunting, fishing, trapping, and gathering rights of the Siletz Tribe and its members" (April 22, 1980), *at* Siletz Archival Collection. For congressional discussion about the agreement, see Statement by Congressman Les AuCoin of Aug. 18, 1980, vol. 126 *Congressional Record*, 96th Congress, 2d Session, p. 21764 (Washington, D.C.: Government Printing Office, 1980). For media reaction to the agreement, see Jim Kadera, "Settlement Spells Out Tribe Rights," *Oregonian* (April 22, 1980); Tom McAllister, "Oregon, Siletz Tribe Reach Agreement on Fish, Game Rights," *Oregon Journal*, p. 28 (April 22, 1980); Pete Cornacchia, "State, Siletz Agree on Hunting, Fishing," *Eugene Register-Guard*, p. 2E (April 27, 1980).

P. 331 *Three Siletz tribal members filed a statement of objection.* See Dave Sitterson, "AuCoin Introduces Bill for Siletz Reservation," *Newport News-Times*, p. 1 (May 7, 1980).

P. 331 *Judge Burns signed the consent decree.* "Final Decree & Order," *Confederated Tribes of Siletz Indians v. Oregon*, Civ. No. 80-433 (D. Or. May 2, 1980), *at* Siletz Archival Collection. See also Statement by Congressman Les AuCoin of Aug. 18, 1980, vol. 126 *Congressional Record*, 96th Congress, 2d Session, p. 21764 (Washington, D.C.: Government Printing Office, 1980).

P. 331   *AuCoin introduced a bill endorsing the reservation plan.* The bill to establish a reservation for the Confederated Tribes of Siletz Indians of Oregon was introduced by Congressman AuCoin on May 5, 1980, and referred to the House Committee on Interior and Insular Affairs. H.R. 7267, 96th Congress, 2d Session (1980). See also Sitterson, "AuCoin Introduces Bill for Siletz Reservation," p. 1.

P. 332   *The bill received President Carter's signature on September 3, 1980.* An Act to Establish a Reservation for the Confederated Tribes of Siletz Indians of Oregon, Pub. L. No. 96-340, Sept. 4, 1980, 94 Stat. 1072 (1981) (not codified, but set out at 25 U.S.C. §711e [2006]). See also United Press International, "Carter Signs Bill Establishing Reservation for Siletz," *Eugene Register-Guard*, p. 6A (Sept. 6, 1980); Associated Press, "Carter Signs Measure for Siletz Reservation," *Oregonian* (Sept. 6, 1980); Associated Press, "Carter Signs Bill for Reservation for Siletz Tribe," *Albany Democrat Herald* (Sept. 6, 1980); Editorial Board, "Siletz Solution Corrects Injustice," *Oregonian* (Sept. 10, 1980).

P. 332   *More than a thousand celebrants flowed in.* See Dan Wyant, "A Reservation Reborn: Siletz Are Home Again," *Eugene Register-Guard*, p. 1B (Sept. 22, 1980); Sue McCracken, "Siletz Celebrate Return of Forefathers' Land," *Oregonian* (Sept. 21, 1980); Dan Wyant, "Siletz Reservation Reborn," *Eugene Register-Guard* (Sept. 21, 1980); Editorial Board, "Siletz Get a Reservation," *Newport News-Times* (Sept. 17, 1980).

15 *Rebuilding Sovereignty*

P. 334   *The highest calling of the Siletz Tribe.* Siletz Const., purposes 1–4. The constitution and all tribal ordinances are available on the tribe's Web site, *at* http://www.ctsi.nsn. us (under Government Listings, click on Tribal Ordinances) (accessed May 14, 2009).

P. 336   *"Sexiest Casino in the Country."* "Chinook Winds Casino Resort: NAC's 2008 Sexiest Casino," vol. 8, no. 5 *Native American Casino Magazine*, pp. 20–21 (May 2008).

P. 336   *high-stakes gambling operations.* On modern Indian gaming, see generally W. Dale Mason, *Indian Gaming: Tribal Sovereignty and American Politics* (Norman: University of Oklahoma Press, 2000); Kathryn R. L. Rand and Steven Andrew Light, *Indian Gaming Law and Policy* (Durham, NC: Carolina Academic Press, 2006).

P. 336   *"Tribal sovereignty," the Court held.* See *California v. Cabazon Band of Mission Indians*, 480 U.S. 202, 207 (1987) (quoting *Washington v. Confederated Tribes of Colville Indian Reservation*, 447 U.S. 134, 154 [1980]).

P. 337   *"Self-determination and economic development."* Ibid., pp. 218–19.

P. 337   *Indian Gaming Regulatory Act of 1988.* On IGRA, Pub. L. No. 100-497, Oct. 17, 1988, 102 Stat. 2467 (1988) (codified at 25 U.S.C. §§2701-2721 [2006]), see generally Mason, *Indian Gaming*, pp. 64–69; David H. Getches, Charles F. Wilkinson, and Richard A. Williams Jr., *Cases and Materials on Federal Indian Law*, 5th ed., pp. 722–37 (St. Paul, MN: West Group, 2005). See also Kevin K. Washburn, "Federal Law, State Policy, and Indian Gaming," vol. 4 *Nevada Law Journal*, pp. 289–93 (Winter 2003/2004); Stephen Cornell, "The Political Economy of American Indian Gaming," vol. 4 *Annual*

Review of Law and Social Science, pp. 65–69 (2008). IGRA grants tribes "the exclusive right to regulate gaming activity on Indian lands if the gaming activity is not specifically prohibited by Federal law and is conducted within a State which does not, as a matter of criminal law and public policy, prohibit such gaming activity." 25 U.S.C. §2701(5). Utah and Hawaii are the only states that have not legalized some form of gaming. See Fox Butterfield, "As Gambling Grows, States Depend on Their Cut," *New York Times* (March 31, 2005), at http://www.nytimes.com (National Archive) (accessed May 15, 2009).

P. 337   *Gross 2008 tribal revenues of about $27 billion nationally.* National Indian Gaming Commission press release, "NIGC Announces 2008 Indian Gaming Revenues" (June 3, 2009), *at* http://www.nigc.gov (under Reading Room, click on Press Releases, then 2009 Press Releases) (accessed November 5, 2009).

P. 337   *Tribal yield 30 percent of national total.* American Gaming Association, "Industry Information Fact Sheet: Gaming Revenue: Current-Year Data," *at* http://www.americangaming.org/Industry/factsheets/index.cfm (click on Gaming Revenue: Current-Year Data) (accessed May 28, 2009) (listing $92.3 billion in total national gaming revenue for 2007).

P. 337   *Casino gambling and state lotteries.* See generally American Gaming Association, "Industry Information Fact Sheet: States with Gaming," *at* http://www.americangaming.org/Industry/factsheets/index.cfm (click on States with Gaming) (accessed May 14, 2009) (listing twelve states that allow commercial casinos and forty-two states and the District of Columbia that have lotteries).

P. 337   *The 225 gaming tribes fall into three groups.* See Kevin K. Washburn, "Recurring Problems in Indian Gaming," vol. 1 *Wyoming Law Review*, pp. 434–35 (2001); Charles Wilkinson, *Blood Struggle: The Rise of Modern Indian Nations*, pp. 336–37 (New York: W. W. Norton & Co., 2005) (current figures are slightly higher than in this analysis). On the relatively small number of tribes responsible for a large percentage of Indian gaming revenue, see, e.g., National Indian Gaming Commission, "NIGC Tribal Gaming Revenues," *at* http://www.nigc.gov/ (under Reading Room, click on Reports, then Gaming Revenue Reports, then Gaming Revenues 2007–2003) (accessed May 28, 2009) (In 2007, twenty-two gaming operations each raised over $250 million in revenue, constituting 42.3 percent of total Indian gaming revenues.).

P. 338   *"I was afraid the tribe would go bankrupt."* Delores Pigsley, interview with author, Siletz, Oregon, June 17, 2005.

P. 338   *"a few trailer houses" into "mega-casinos."* Jessie Davis, interview with María Aparicio, research assistant, Salem, Oregon, May 22, 2007.

P. 338   *The first Siletz effort was full of promise.* The basic facts and legal principles are set forth in the two court opinions ruling against the tribe. See *Confederated Tribes of Siletz Indians v. United States*, 841 F. Supp. 1479 (D. Or. 1994); *Confederated Tribes of Siletz Indians v. United States*, 110 F.3d 688 (9th Cir. 1997). Most tribal land is held in trust by the Interior department, and trust lands cannot be sold, taxed, zoned, or otherwise regulated by state laws. It is on trust land that tribal sovereign rights are the strongest; a number of federal Indian statutes, such as IGRA, apply only on trust land.

P. 339   *"fear of competition."* See Cheryl Martinis, "BIA Office Clears Siletz Indians' Plan for Casino in Salem," *Oregonian*, p. B4 (Aug. 26, 1992) (quoting a report by BIA representative David Bartele).

P. 339   *Governor Roberts announced her opposition.* See Carmel Finley and Cheryl Martinis, "Roberts' Opposition to Casino Setback at Least to Siletz Plan," *Oregonian*, p. C2 (April 22, 1992); Carmel Finley, "Siletz Tell Governor of Casinos," *Oregonian*, p. B5 (Nov. 18, 1992).

P. 339   *Senator Hatfield declined to co-sponsor the bill but supported it.* See Davis, interview, May 22, 2007.

P. 339   *The legislation was signed into law on November 2, 1994.* Pub L. No. 103-435, Nov. 2, 1994, 108 Stat. 4566 (1994) (amending 25 U.S.C. §711 to include the land taken into trust).

P. 339   *The tribe negotiated a compact with the state.* "Tribal-State Compact for Regulation of Class III Gaming Between the Confederated Tribes of Siletz Indians of Oregon and the State of Oregon," Nov. 10, 1994, *at* Siletz Archival Collection. The compact gained the requisite federal approval on March 14, 1995. A. Deer, assistant secretary of Indian Affairs, letter to D. Pigsley, Chairman, Siletz Tribal Council (March 14, 1995), *at* Siletz Archival Collection. See also U.S. Department of the Interior, Bureau of Indian Affairs, "Notice of approval for Tribal-State compact," vol. 60, no. 55 *Federal Register*, p. 15194 (March 22, 1995). The tribal negotiation team for the compact included Chairman Delores Pigsley, Council member Jessie Davis, and tribal attorney Craig Dorsay. The state was represented by the governor's attorney, the captain of the State Police, and a representative from the Attorney General's Office. Jessie Davis, email to author, Jan. 6, 2009, *at* Siletz Archival Collection.

P. 339   *Some local citizens and city officials objected.* One objection was that the tribe had not formally consulted with the city in advance of the tribal-state compact and land-into-trust legislation. *The Oregonian* editorialized that Lincoln City complainants were "protesting too much." Editorial Board, "Help Siletz Tribe Succeed," *Oregonian*, p. B8 (Nov. 22, 1994).

P. 339   *"money isn't everything."* Steve Duin, "At Our Latest Gambling Resort, Tempers Are Shorter than the D River," *Oregonian*, p. C1 (May 18, 1995) (quoting Robert Portwood).

P. 340   *Indian art and historical Siletz photographs are abundant.* The ambiance of the casino and the notable presence of Siletz culture are due in part to the hands-on approach by the tribal council. The council appointed a Construction Committee—composed of council members, tribal employees, representatives of the construction and architectural firms, the owner of a Nevada casino, and Hiroto Zakoji, a prominent retired BIA officer—but the council took an active role and made decisions on all phases, down to the colors of the walls and carpet design. The council also sought advice from the Cultural Department. See Davis, email to author, Jan. 6, 2009.

P. 340   Newport News–Times *six-part retrospective.* Barton Grover Howe wrote all six articles in the series, entitled "Winds of Change," which ran in the *Newport News-Times* in April of 2006. See "Part I: Ready or Not, Casino Brings Change to the Coast," p. A1 (April 12, 2006); "Part II: Dispelling Myths," p. A1 (April 14, 2006); "Part III: The 800-Pound Gorilla," p. A1 (April 19, 2006); "Part IV: Oregon Laws Complicate City Budget," p. A1 (April 21, 2006); "Part V: Back in Time," p. A1 (April 26, 2006); "Part VI: Here to Stay," p. A1 (April 28, 2006).

P. 340   *"Casino Town."* Howe, "Part II: Dispelling Myths," p. A1.

P. 340   *tribe has paid Lincoln City $170,000 each year."* See "Agreement Between the City of Lincoln City, Oregon, and The Confederated Tribes of Siletz Indians of Oregon

Regarding the Provision of City Services and Other Matters Related to Reservation Lands Within the City of Lincoln City," p. 15, signed August 1, 1995, *at* Siletz Archival Collection. In addition, the tribe also contributes to the fire department and the water district, and pays $85,000 annually to offset the impact of all trust lands. Craig Dorsay, Siletz tribal attorney, email to the author, May 26, 2009.

P. 341   *"Clearly, people who come to the casino."* Howe, "Dispelling Myths," p. A3.

P. 341   *Workforce of over 800.* ECONorthwest, "The Economic Impacts and Benefits of Chinook Winds Casino Resort on the Local Economy," p. 6 (Portland, OR: ECONorthwest, 2005) (presenting the results of a study by an independent consulting firm hired by the tribe to analyze the casino's impacts).

P. 341   *Chinook Winds as "Large Business of the Year."* See Howe, "Part V: Back in Time," p. A1 (photo caption).

P. 341   *casino glitz is "untraditional."* Delores Pigsley, interview with María Aparicio, research assistant, Lincoln City, Oregon, Sept. 1, 2006.

P. 341   *"the only way we can get to where we want to go."* Delores Pigsley, interview with Carrie Covington, research assistant, Siletz, Oregon, May 22, 2006.

P. 341   *"a stepping stone, not an end in itself."* Ibid.

P. 341   *Tribal ordinance allocating Chinook Winds revenues.* Tribal ordinances are available on the tribe's Web site, *at* http://www.ctsi.nsn.us (under Government Listings, click on Tribal Ordinances) (accessed May 14, 2009).

P. 341   *Desktop and laptop computers.* Tina Retasket, interview with author, Siletz, Oregon, Dec. 9, 2008; Delores Pigsley, interview with author, Siletz, Oregon, May 12, 2009.

P. 343   *three sources of sovereignty in the United States.* See, e.g., *Felix S. Cohen's Handbook of Federal Indian Law, 2005,* §4.01 (Newark, NJ: LexisNexis, 2005); Charles F. Wilkinson, *American Indians, Time, and the Law: Native Societies in a Modern Constitutional Democracy,* pp. 53–63 (New Haven, CT: Yale University Press, 1988).

P. 343   *United States and tribes as separate sovereigns.* See *Talton v. Mayes,* 163 U.S. 376, 384 (1896) (right to grand jury proceeding, a protection afforded by the Bill of Rights, inapplicable in tribal courts because "the powers of local self-government enjoyed by the Cherokee Nation existed prior to the constitution"); *United States v. Wheeler,* 435 U.S. 313 (1978).

P. 343   *Congress has sweeping authority under the Commerce Clause.* U.S. Const. art. I, §8, cl. 3. On the clause's application to Indian law, see, e.g., *McClanahan v. Arizona State Tax Commission,* 411 U.S. 164 (1973); *United States v. Lara,* 541 U.S. 193 (2004).

P. 344   *A matter of citizenship, not racial discrimination.* See *Morton v. Mancari,* 417 U.S. 535 (1974).

P. 344   *Establishment Clause does not apply to tribes.* U.S. Const. amend. I. See *Santa Clara Pueblo v. Martinez,* 436 U.S. 49 (1978) (constitutional Bill of Rights guarantees do not apply to tribes; most of those guarantees, but not the Establishment Clause, have been applied to tribes through the Indian Civil Rights Act of 1968, 25 U.S.C §§1301-1341 [2006]). See also Cohen, *Handbook of Federal Indian Law, 2005,* §14.03(2)(c).

P. 345   *"an idea belonging to the other side of the Atlantic."* Wilkinson, *American Indians, Time, and the Law,* p. 54 (quoting Thomas Jefferson).

P. 346   *1975 Indian Self-Determination Act and Education Assistance Act.* Indian Self-Determination Act, Pub. L. No. 93-638, Jan. 4, 1975, 88 Stat. 2203 (1975) (codified at 25 U.S.C. §§450-458bbb-2 [2006]). The Office of Self-Governance Communication & Education has an informative website that includes both discussion and links to relevant statutes and sources, *at* http://www.tribalselfgov.org (accessed May 29, 2009).

P. 346 *The tribe signed a compact with the BIA.* Siletz Tribe, "1992 Annual Report," pp. 9, 16, *at* Siletz Archival Collection (containing the text of the compact). The annual report asserts that the compact was "the next logical step to self-determination. Ibid., p. 3.

P. 346 *Chinook Winds and BIA and IHS contributions to tribal budget.* See Siletz Tribe, "2003–2007 Annual Reports," *at* Siletz Archival Collection. During this five-year period, total Siletz governmental revenue averaged $44.5 million per year. On average, $16.5 million came from the casino and $13 million from the IHS and BIA. See also Sharon Edenfield, administrative manager of the Siletz Tribe, memorandum to author, Jan. 16, 2009.

P. 346 *"We thought we could make better decisions."* Brenda Bremner, interview with author, Lincoln City, Oregon, Dec. 12, 2008.

P. 347 *Siletz Community Health Clinic.* See Confederated Tribes of Siletz Indians' Web site, *at* http://www.ctsi.nsn.us (under Tribal Services, click on Healthcare) (accessed May 14, 2009); Siletz Tribe, "2005–2007 Annual Reports," *at* Siletz Archival Collection.

P. 347 *Funding from the state and IHS.* Tina Retasket, Tribal Council member and former assistant general manager of the Siletz Tribe, interview with author, Lincoln City, Oregon, Nov. 9, 2008.

P. 347 *over 40,000 physical visits.* See Siletz Tribe, "2007 Annual Report," p. 17, *at* Siletz Archival Collection.

P. 347 *Tillicum Fitness Center and neighboring gymnasium.* See Siletz Tribe, "2007 Annual Report," p. 16, *at* Siletz Archival Collection. The annual report sets a hopeful note: "There will be no excuses in 2008—everyone will be challenged to improve their health." Ibid.

P. 348 *"for pretty much all people I see."* George Nagel, telephone interview with María Aparicio, research assistant, Nov. 26, 2008.

P. 349 *"People are experiencing anger."* Janet Wicklund, telephone interview with María Aparicio, research assistant, July 3, 2008.

P. 349 *The early research on generational trauma.* See, e.g., John J. Sigal and Morton Weinfeld, *Trauma and Rebirth: Intergenerational Effects of the Holocaust* (New York: Praeger Publishers, 1989).

P. 349 *other examples of psychological wounding.* Maria Yellow Horse Brave Heart, on the faculty at the Columbia University School of Social Work, has been a leader in the scholarship in this area. See, e.g., Maria Yellow Horse Brave Heart, "The Impact of Historical Trauma: The Example of the Native Community," *in* M. Bussey & J. Wise, eds., *Transforming Trauma: Empowerment Responses* (New York: Columbia University Press, forthcoming); Maria Yellow Horse Brave Heart, "The Historical Trauma Response among Natives and Its Relationship with Substance Abuse: A Lakota Illustration," vol. 35 *Journal of Psychoactive Drugs*, pp. 7–13 (Jan.–March 2003); Maria Yellow Horse Brave Heart and Lemyra M. DeBruyn, "The American Indian Holocaust: Healing Historical Unresolved Grief," vol. 8, no. 2 *American Indian and Alaska Native Mental Health Research*, pp. 60–82 (1998). See also Teresa Evans-Campbell, "Historical Trauma in American Indian/Native Alaska Communities: A Multilevel Framework for Exploring Impacts on Individuals, Families, and Communities," vol. 23 *Journal of Interpersonal Violence*, pp. 316–38 (March 2008) (including a comprehensive bibliography); Eduardo Duran and Bonnie Duran, *Native American Postcolonial Psychology* (Albany: State University of New York Press, 1995); Ashley Quinn,

"Reflections on Intergenerational Trauma: Healing as a Critical Intervention," vol. 3, no. 4 *First Peoples Child & Family Review*, pp. 72–82 (2007); Michael G. Kenny, "A Place for Memory: The Interface between Individual and Collective History," vol. 41, no. 3 *Comparative Studies in Society and History*, pp. 420–437 (July 1999).

P. 349 *"The lifeworld as had been known for centuries."* Duran and Duran, *Native American Postcolonial Psychology*, p. 32.

P. 350 *"The events are usually perpetrated by outsiders."* Evans-Campbell, "Historical Trauma in American Indian/Native Alaska Communities," p. 321.

P. 350 culture *"has to be part of treatment."* George Nagel, telephone interview, Nov. 26, 2008.

P. 351 *Siletz Education Program.* See, e.g., Siletz Tribe, "2007 Annual Report," pp. 12–13, *at* Siletz Archival Collection.

P. 351 *Funding of students beyond high school.* Tina Retasket, interview with author, Dec. 9, 2008; Alissa Lane, education specialist for the Siletz Tribe, email to María Aparicio, research assistant, Dec. 17, 2008.

P. 351 *number of students in higher education has increased.* Ibid.

P. 351 *petitioning for a charter school.* This episode was covered quite widely in the local press. See, e.g., the following *Newport News-Times* articles, *at* http://www.newportnewstimes.com (under Search tab, use Search Web Archives) (accessed May 29, 2009): "Confederated Tribes of Siletz to Pursue Charter School" (Oct. 11, 2002); "Siletz Tribe Envisions Native Culture for Charter School" (Feb. 7, 2003); "Siletz Tribal Charter School Plans in Limbo" (April 2, 2003); "School Board OKs Siletz Charter School Application" (July 11, 2003); "State Approves Siletz Charter School Grant" (July 30, 2003); "Siletz Charter School Set to Open Sept. 8" (Aug. 6, 2003); Terry Dillman, "Siletz Valley School Winds Up 'Pretty Successful' First Year" (July 2, 2004).

P. 351 *"early college academy."* See Oregon State University press release, "OSU Aids Siletz Valley Early College Academy" (Feb. 15, 2006). See also the following articles by Terry Dillman for the *Newport News-Times*, *at* http://www.newportnewstimes.com (under Search tab, use Search Web Archives) (accessed May 29, 2009): "Siletz school officials sign pact with Oregon State" (Feb. 15, 2006); "Proposed Siletz Charter High School Gets Unanimous Approval" (March 3, 2006); "Siletz Dual School Begins New Era; Students Enrolled in Grades 9–12 for First Time since 1982" (Sept. 6, 2006). Although grades K–12, which are all in the same building, are commonly referred to as the Siletz Valley School, after the creation of the Academy there are now two separate charter schools—the K–8 school and the 9–12 Academy. In its first review by the county school district, the charter was renewed with the school board chair stating that the Siletz Valley School was "an extremely successful school operating below their cap." Dillman, "Proposed Siletz Charter High School Gets Unanimous Approval" (quoting School Board Chair Ron Beck).

P. 352 *The school "couldn't operate without."* Kyle Odegard, "School's Return Boosts Tribal Pride," *Corvallis Gazette-Times*, p. A1 (May 3, 2007) (quoting Van Peters). From 2004–2009, the tribe contributed a total of $1.7 million to the charter school. See Kelley Ellis, administrative assistant in Siletz Tribe's Natural Resources Department, memorandum to author, Jan. 13, 2009.

P. 352 *2007 high school graduation.* Terry Dillman, "Siletz Celebrates First High School Graduation since 1982," *Newport News-Times* (June 13, 2007) (quoting valedictorian Monica Serna).

P. 353   *major oil spill.* See U.S. Fish and Wildlife Service press release, "Agencies, Tribes Release Final Restoration Plan For Damages Caused By New Carissa Oil Spill" (Jan. 31, 2006), *at* http://www.fws.gov/pacific/news/2006/Restoration.Plan.news.release. pdf (accessed May 13, 2009); Oregon Department of Fish and Wildlife press release, "Coastal Forest Goes to Siletz Tribe for Management to Restore Marbled Murrelet Populations Lost to New Carissa Oil Spill" (July 31, 2007), *at* http://www.dfw.state. or.us/news/2007/july/073107b.asp (accessed May 13, 2009); The Conservation Fund press release, "Out of Tragedy, a New Tomorrow in the Oregon Coast Range Forest: Roughly 3,900 Acres Protected" (July 31, 2007), *at* http://www.conservationfund.org/ node/669 (accessed May 13, 2009); Terry Dillman, "Siletz Tribe Given Coastal Forest Management Responsibilities," *Newport News-Times* (Aug. 1, 2007), *at* http://www. newportnewstimes.com (under Search tab, use Search Web Archives) (accessed May 29, 2009).

P. 353   *Management "in perpetuity" as murrelet habitat.* Chairman Delores Pigsley signed the "Marbled Murrelet Conservation Easement" between the Confederated Tribes of Siletz Indians, the Department of the Interior, and the State of Oregon, Department of Fish and Wildlife, on December 29, 2008. The easement grants the tribe the property in return for the tribe "provid[ing] for the benefit and conservation of the marbled murrelet by protection of Marbled Murrelet Habitat." The easement also allows for limited commercial timber harvest "to protect and promote . . . mature forest conditions, native fish and wildlife." "M/V New Carissa Conservation Easement," Dec. 29, 2008 (Confederated Tribes of Siletz Indians, U.S. Department of the Interior, and State of Oregon, Department of Fish and Wildlife, signatories), *at* Siletz Archival Collection.

P. 354   *"From what . . . I've seen, they do a good job."* Jeff Classen, telephone interview with Alison Flint, research assistant, Feb. 6, 2009.

P. 354   *"long history of forest management."* Oregon Department of Fish and Wildlife press release (July 31, 2007).

P. 354   *"a perfect match for this program."* Dillman, "Siletz Tribe Given Coastal Forest Management Responsibilities."

P. 355   *"Lhuuke Illahee."* See Stan van de Wetering, telephone interview with Alison Flint, research assistant, Feb. 19, 2009; Bennett Hall, "Hatchery Tries Out Natural Habitat," *Corvallis Gazette-Times* (June 22, 2008), *at* http://www.democratherald.com/ articles/2008/06/22/news/local/1aaa02_coho.txt (accessed May 11, 2009); "Natural Resources," Confederated Tribes of Siletz Indians' Web site, *at* http://www.ctsi.nsn. us (under Tribal Services, click on Other Departments, then Natural Resources) (accessed April 10, 2009) [hereinafter Siletz Natural Resources Web page].

P. 355   *"'hatchery' is really a misnomer."* Stan van de Wetering, interview, Feb. 19, 2009.

P. 355   *Hatcheries have been controversial.* See, e.g., James Lichatowich, *Salmon without Rivers: A History of the Pacific Salmon Crisis*, pp. 111–50 (Washington, D.C.: Island Press, 1999).

P. 356   *Oyster restoration project.* See National Oceanic and Atmospheric Administration, "Hands on Habitat: Celebrating 10 Years of Coastal Restoration," p. 64 (March 2006); National Oceanic and Atmospheric Administration press release, "NOAA Awards $47,000 for Native Oyster Restoration" (July 18, 2005), *at* http://www.nmfs.noaa.gov/ docs/05-R953%20Oregon%20Yaquina%20oyster%20habitat%20grantCLEARED.pdf (accessed May 12, 2009); Siletz Natural Resources Web page. On the Native Olympic Oyster, see generally Oregon Department of Fish and Wildlife, "Native Oysters, *Ostrea conchaphila*," *at* http://www.dfw.state.or.us/mrp/shellfish/bayclams/oysters. asp (accessed May 12, 2009).

P. 356 *"We want oysters here."* NOAA, "Hands on Habitat," p. 64 (quoting Frank Simmons).

P. 357 *Lamprey restoration effort.* See, e.g., Joyce Campbell, "Saving the Ancient Pacific Lamprey," *Methow Valley News* (Nov. 13, 2008), *at* http://www.methowvalleynews. com/story.php?id=378 (accessed May 11, 2009); Northwest Indian Fisheries Commission, "Lamprey Study Part of Elwha River Restoration," (Oct. 4, 2007), *at* http://www. nwifc.org/2007/10/lamprey-study-part-of-elwha-river-restoration (accessed May 11, 2009); Columbia River Basin Lamprey Technical Workgroup, *at* http://www.fws. gov/columbiariver/lamprey.htm (accessed May 11, 2009); Western Oregon Lamprey Workshop, Feb. 26–27, 2008, Canyonville, Oregon, *at* http://www.fws.gov/pacific/ fisheries/sp_habcon/lamprey/pdf/Western%20Oregon%20Lamprey%20Workshop%20 2_2008.pdf (accessed May 29, 2009) (hereinafter Western Oregon Lamprey Workshop). Lampreys are often referred to as "lamprey eels" although they are not eels to the scientific community—they possess no backbone, instead having a flexible, cartilage skeleton. Siletz people call them "eels," and I will mostly refer to them as eels.

P. 357 *Skwakol.* See Tom Downey et al., " 'Skwakol': The Decline of the Siletz Lamprey Eel Population during the 20th Century" (Corvallis: Oregon State University, 1996).

P. 358 *the primary cause for the drop in eel numbers.* Several of the elders, who had long lived in the watershed, believed that timber harvesting was the main cause of the eel decline. When asked why he thought there has been a decline in the eel population, Everett Butler responded, "Because of this 2-4-5 T, and Silvex Defoliation that the property owners sprayed around on their property. And also the big corporations who sprayed to get rid of the broadleaf trees and replace it with fir trees for pulpwood and mowed down everything to the ocean." Ibid., p. 41. Frank Simmons responded to the same question: "The logging that is going on in the areas and the logging practices of dragging logs and debris across natural habitats and spawning areas for salmon and eels and that damages their spawning areas." Ibid., p. 72. Tribal Aquatic Programs Leader Stan van de Wetering also is satisfied that logging is the major cause: "The timber industry has negatively affected eels. When timber is harvested, the waterways are left with big sediment loads." Stan van de Wetering interview with María Aparicio, research assistant, Siletz, Oregon, March 23, 2007. See also Stan van de Wetering, "Past, present and future activities of the Siletz Tribe regarding lamprey harvests, lamprey research and habitat restoration directed at lamprey populations," *in* Western Oregon Lamprey Workshop, p. 6 (Siletz tribal members "saw a significant population decline in the 1970s and are asking what was going on. Primarily it was aggressive timber harvest, which included cutting riparian zones, sediment in the river in winter, cleaning streams with bull dozers, and applying chemicals"); Kelly C. Palacios, "The Potential of Dynamic Segmentation for Aquatic Ecosystem Management: Pacific Lamprey Decline in the Native Lands of the Confederated Tribes of Siletz Indians," p. 27, Oregon State University (2007), *at* http://dusk2.geo.orst.edu/djl/ theses/palacios_thesis.pdf (accessed May 11, 2009).

P. 358 *"We are using eels as an indicator of watershed health."* U.S. Forest Service, Economic Action Programs, "Lamprey Eel Decline Study" (quoting Mike Kennedy).

P. 358 *"They had strong leadership at restoration."* Stanley Speaks, telephone interview with author, Dec. 19, 2008.

P. 358 *The Siletz constitution and tribal council elections.* Siletz Const., art. IV, §1 (number of members and terms; election of president by tribal council members); art. VI, §3 (Siletz Tribal Council elections).

P. 359 *Chinook Winds administration controversial.* See, e.g., Siletz General Council Meeting Minutes, Siletz, Oregon, Aug. 2, 1997, pp. 1–3, *at* Siletz Archival Collection; Siletz Tribal Council Meeting Minutes, Siletz, Oregon, Aug. 16–17, 1997, pp. 11–12, 14, *at* Siletz Archival Collection.

P. 359 *talk of a recall.* See, e.g., Siletz Tribal Council Meeting Minutes, Siletz, Oregon, July 19–20, 1997, p. 13, *at* Siletz Archival Collection.

P. 359 *the council passed over two tribal-member candidates.* See Siletz Special Tribal Council Meeting Minutes, Lincoln, Oregon, Aug. 29, 1997, pp. 1, 3, *at* Siletz Archival Collection.

P. 359 *In late August, the council filled the position.* Ibid., p. 3.

P. 359 *The administrator took heavy criticism.* The motion to terminate the administrator for just cause was initially approved 5 to 4, but then the motion was rescinded by a vote of 7 to 2. The tribal council then voted 9 to 0 to terminate the administrator because false information was provided on the employment application. Siletz Special Tribal Council Meeting Minutes, Siletz, Oregon, Feb. 7, 1998, pp. 1–2, *at* Siletz Archival Collection.

P. 359 *The Siletz constitution provides for a general council.* Siletz Const., art. II, §2. While the tribal council has broad legislative authority and the general council does not, the idea of a general council made up of all eligible voters has great intangible significance. As a reminder of this, the general council is presented ahead of the tribal council in Article IV entitled "Branches of Government."

P. 359 *Siletz constitution's recall requirements.* Siletz Const., art. VII, §3.

P. 359 *Judge Viles's opinion. Duncan v. Siletz Election Board*, T.C. 98-02 (Siletz Tribal Ct. March 23, 1998).

P. 360 *The Appellate Court promptly issued an emergency order.* See *Duncan v. Siletz Election Board*, T.C. 98-02AP, p. 1 (Siletz Tribal App. Ct. Sept. 15, 1998). (This final opinion on the merits refers to the earlier emergency order.)

P. 360 *The Siletz Tribe now has its own Appellate Court.* See Siletz Tribal Code §3.064.

P. 360 *the court found that there still were enough valid signatures. Duncan*, T.C. 98-02AP, pp. 8–11. The required number of signatures was 667 and, after removing invalid signatures, the lowest number on any petition was 688. Ibid., p. 9. The Appellate Court also rejected several arguments based on technical procedural deficiencies. See ibid., pp. 11–18.

P. 360 *the four council members were recalled by margins of 70 percent.* The recall results were announced in "Tribal Council Members Recalled," vol. 26, no. 8 *Siletz News*, p. 1 (Aug. 1998). The closest of the four recalls was 446 in favor, 188 against. Ibid.

P. 360 *Filling council vacancies.* Siletz Const., art. VI, §6.

P. 360 *Chairman refused to call a tribal council meeting.* Siletz General Council Meeting Minutes, Siletz, Oregon, Aug. 1, 1998, pp. 3, 21, *at* Siletz Archival Collection [hereinafter August General Council Minutes].

P. 360 *The tribal council has a steady stream of responsibilities.* See Delores Pigsley, "Chairman's Report," vol. 26, no. 8 *Siletz News*, p. 1 (Aug. 1998).

P. 360 *"we are in turmoil."* August General Council Minutes, p. 3.

P. 360 *"political unrest for many, many years to come."* Ibid., p. 4.

P. 360 *"comments continued from the attendees."* Ibid., p. 9.

P. 360 *"after carefully weighing all the options."* Ibid., p. 21.

P. 360 *five-member quorum.* Siletz Const., art. V, §2(D) ("five members of the Tribal Council shall constitute a quorum").

P. 360 *"force the Bureau of Indian Affairs."* August General Council Minutes, p. 21.

P. 361 *"continue forever" the Tribe's identity.* See *In the Matter of Delores Pigsley*, T.C. 98-11, *at* Petition for Declaratory Action (Siletz Tribal Ct. Aug. 1, 1998) (quoting Siletz Const., purposes 1-2).

P. 361 *Judge Roe ruled that such a course was "fair." In the Matter of Delores Pigsley*, T.C. 98-11, *at* Order (Siletz Tribal Ct. Aug. 3, 1998).

P. 361 *The council held a special meeting.* Siletz Emergency Tribal Council Meeting Minutes, Siletz, Oregon, Aug. 3, 1998, pp. 1–2, *at* Siletz Archival Collection (appointing Jesse Davis as the fifth member of the tribal council to establish a quorum); Siletz Special Tribal Council Meeting Minutes, Siletz, Oregon, Aug. 3, 1998, pp. 1–4, *at* Siletz Archival Collection (council meeting held directly after the emergency meeting in order to fill the remaining seats).

P. 362 *We* will *survive.* Delores Pigsley, interview, June 17, 2005.

16 Cultural Revival

P. 363 *Kentta and Rilatos at the NMAI.* Robert Kentta, interview with author, Siletz, Oregon, Feb. 25, 2005; Robert Kentta, telephone interview with Carrie Covington, research assistant, Jan. 29, 2009.

P. 363 *Outrage over way Indian burials were treated.* See generally Roger C. Echo-Hawk and Walter R. Echo-Hawk, *Battlefields and Burial Grounds: The Indian Struggle to Protect Ancestral Graves in the United States* (Minneapolis, MN: Lerner Publications Co., 1994); Jack F. Trope and Walter R. Echo-Hawk, "The Native American Graves Protection and Repatriation Act: Background and Legislative History," vol. 24 *Arizona State Law Journal*, p. 35 (Spring 1992).

P. 363 *Initially, the archaeology community was indignant.* See, e.g., Echo-Hawk and Echo-Hawk, *Battlefields and Burial Grounds*, pp. 34–35. The profession continues to adjust to the NAGPRA. Prominent archaeologist Larry J. Zimmerman addressed the broad currents and the nuances of the profession's academic objectives and its obligations to contemporary tribes, *in* Thomas Biolsi, ed., *A Companion to the Anthropology of American Indians*, p. 539 (Malden, MA: Blackwell Publishing, 2004).

P. 363 *National Museum of the American Indian Act.* See National Museum of the American Indian Act of 1989, Pub. L. No. 101–185, Nov. 28, 1989, 103 Stat. 1336 (1989) (codified as amended at 20 U.S.C. §§80q – 8q-15 [2006]). Sections 80q-9–80q-9a deal specifically with repatriation of Indian human remains, funerary objects, sacred objects, and cultural patrimony.

P. 364 *NAGPRA.* See Native American Graves Protection and Repatriation Act of 1990, Pub. L. No. 101-601, Nov. 16, 1990, 104 Stat. 3048 (1990) (codified at 25 U.S.C. §§3001-3013 [2006]). For a comprehensive symposium on NAGPRA, see Julie A. Pace, ed. "Symposium: The Native American Graves Protection and Repatriation Act of 1990 and State Repatriation-related Legislation," vol. 24 *Arizona State Law Journal* (Spring 1992). The National Park Service also has a useful Web site on NAGPRA. See *National NAGPRA*, National Park Service, *at* http://www.nps.gov/history/nagpra/ (accessed May 12, 2009).

P. 364　*Repatriation of sacred and cultural objects.* While NAGPRA did not apply to the Smithsonian, 25 U.S.C. §§3001(4) (8), it led to a change in NMAI requirements for cultural objects: in 1996 the NMAI Act was amended to provide for repatriation by the Smithsonian with respect to sacred and cultural objects not related to gravesites. See 20 U.S.C. §80q-9a.

P. 364　*The agent at Siletz ordered all six dance houses torched.* See Marian A. Kaminitz, Robert Kentta, and David Moses Bridges, "First Person Voice: Native Communities and Conservation Consultations at the National Museum of the American Indian," vol. 1 *Ethnographic Collections*, p. 3 (2005); Frank Simmons, interview with author, Siletz, Oregon, Feb. 8, 2007; Robert Kentta, interview with author, Siletz, Oregon, May 23, 2005. On the suppression of dances at Siletz, see also chapter 9, p. 200 and accompanying notes. The suppression continued until the 1930s, when John Collier ordered that there would be "no interference" with traditional dances and other cultural activities. See, e.g., Francis Paul Prucha, vol. 2, *The Great Father: The United States Government and the American Indians*, p. 951 (Lincoln, University of Nebraska Press, 1984).

P. 364　*Nee Dosh held in peoples' homes.* See Bud Lane, interview with María Aparicio, research assistant, Siletz, Oregon, Aug. 10, 2006; Gladys Bolton, interview with María Aparicio, Keizer, Oregon, March 26, 2007.

P. 366　*"There wasn't really any opposition."* Robert Kentta, telephone interview, Jan. 29, 2009.

P. 367　*"It was really exciting."* Ibid.

P. 370　*I went to my first Nee Dosh in 2005.* This description is based on my visits to Nee Dosh and those of my research assistants, Josh Tenneson and María Aparicio, who attended and wrote full reports. I confirmed details of the dance through discussions with numerous tribal members.

P. 370　*revival of Nee Dosh grew stronger after restoration.* See Bud Lane, interview with María Aparicio, research assistant, Siletz, Oregon, Dec. 29, 2007; Bud Lane, telephone interview with author, Feb. 27, 2009. Lane recalls the initial concern of some elders that, "there's a fine line between good and evil" and that the dances were too powerful, too evil, to be used for anything other than as curing ceremonies.

P. 370　*"It's a loss for me, but now it's completely natural for my kids."* Margot Hudson, interview with author, Siletz, Oregon, June 16, 2008.

P. 373　*The tribes have worked closely on modern cultural issues.* Many people at Siletz and Smith River have commented on this. See, e.g., Loren Bommelyn and Joseph Hostler, interviews with María Aparicio, research assistant, Smith River, California, Aug. 4–5, 2006.

P. 375　*half of the world's languages have gone extinct.* See, e.g., David Nettle and Suzanne Romaine, *Vanishing Voices: The Extinction of the World's Languages*, p. 2 (New York: Oxford University Press, 2000); John Noble Wilford, "World's Languages Dying Off Rapidly," *New York Times* (Sept. 18, 2007), *at* http://www.nytimes.com (International Archive) (accessed May 11, 2009); David Crystal, *Language Death*, p. 19 (Cambridge, UK: Cambridge University Press, 2000). Leanne Hinton and Ken Hale, eds., *The Green Book of Language Revitalization in Practice* (San Diego, CA: Academic Press, 2001) is an excellent, comprehensive source.

P. 375　*"politically dominant languages."* Ken Hale et al., "Endangered Languages," vol. 68 *Language*, p. 1 (March 1992).

P. 375 *"Language death does not happen in privileged communities."* James Crawford, "Endangered Native American Languages: What Is to Be Done, and Why?" vol. 19 *Bilingual Research Journal*, p. 35 (Winter 1995).

P. 375 *language loss diminishes the world's intellectual and cultural diversity.* See ibid., pp. 21–22. Anthropologist Russell Bernard has argued that: "We know that the reduction of biodiversity today threatens all of us. I think we are conducting an experiment to see what will happen to humanity if we eliminate 'cultural species' in the world. This is a reckless experiment. If we don't like the way it turns out, there's no going back." Russell H. Bernard, "Preserving Language Diversity," vol. 51, no. 1 *Human Organization*, p. 82 (1992) (quoted in Jon Reyhner, "Rationale and Needs for Stabilizing Indigenous Languages," *in* Gina Cantoni, ed., *Stabilizing Indigenous Languages*, p. 4 [Flagstaff: Center for Excellence in Education, Northern Arizona University, 2007]).

P. 375 *"Language is part of us."* Quoted in Orna Feldman, "Inspired by a Dream: Linguistics Grad Works to Revive the Wampanoag Language," *MIT Spectrum* (Spring 2001), *at* http://spectrum.mit.edu/issue/2001-spring/inspired-by-a-dream/ (accessed Nov. 9, 2009).

P. 375 *"Same reason you don't burn down your libraries."* Pete Fromm, "Raising Minipokaiax," *Big Sky Journal* (Fall 2003), *at* http://www.pieganinstitute.org/raisingminipokaiax.pdf (accessed Nov. 9, 2009).

P. 375 *Maori language revival.* See generally Jeanette King, "Te Kōhanga Reo: Māori Language Revitalization," *in* Hinton and Hale, eds., *The Green Book*, pp. 119–31.

P. 375 *Native Hawaiian language revival.* See generally Sam L. No'eau Warner, "The Movement to Revitalize Hawaiian Language and Culture," *in* Hinton and Hale, eds., *The Green Book*, pp. 133–44.

P. 375 *Hawaiian one of the two official state languages.* Haw. Const. art. XV, §4 ("English and Hawaiian shall be the official languages of Hawaii").

P. 376 *Native American Languages Act.* Native American Languages Act of 1990, Pub. L. No. 101-477, Oct. 30, 1990, 104 Stat. 1153 (1990) (codified as amended at 25 U.S.C. §§2901-2906 [2006]).

P. 376 *There are now hundreds of tribal language programs.* The most recent Congressional acknowledgement of the importance of language survival is the Esther Martinez Native American Languages Preservation Act of 2006, funding native language educational programs. P.L. 109-394, 120 Stat. 2705 (codified at 42 U.S.C §2991).

P. 376 *Mainland tribes and Alaska Natives face an uphill battle.* On language loss and revival in the United States, see generally Cantoni, ed., *Stabilizing Indigenous Languages*; Crawford, "Endangered Native American Languages"; Allison M. Dussias, "Waging War with Words: Native Americans' Continuing Struggle against Suppression of Their Languages," vol. 60 *Ohio State Law Journal*, pp. 901–93 (1999); Michael Krauss, "Status of Native American Language Endangerment," *in* Cantoni, ed., *Stabilizing Indigenous Languages*, pp. 15–20; Stephen May, *Language and Minority Rights* (New York: Routledge, 2008). For a list of indigenous languages still spoken in the United States and the number of speakers, see *Languages of USA*, Ethnologue.com, *at* http://www.ethnologue.com/show_country.asp?name=US (accessed May 11, 2009). The list is not limited to indigenous languages. On language recovery for several individual tribes, see Hinton and Hale, eds., *The Green Book*.

P. 376 *"The work is much too difficult to be a fad."* Marjane Ambler, "Native Languages: A

Question of Life or Death," vol. 15 *Tribal College Journal*, p. 9 (Spring 2004) (quoting Dr. Janine Pease).

P. 376 *Grande Ronde Tribe and Chinuk WaWa*. See, e.g., Nancy Bartley, "Once-Dying Chinook Language Finds Future in Voices of Children," *Seattle Times* (June 8, 2004), *at* http://community.seattletimes.nwsource.com/archive/?date=20040608&slug=chinoo ko8m (accessed May 12, 2009).

P. 376 *"nvn-nvst-'an."* Bud Lane, email to author, Feb. 18, 2009; Bud Lane, telephone interview with author, Feb. 25, 2009; Bud Lane, interview with author, Lincoln City, Oregon, May 12, 2009.

P. 377 *Bud Lane and learning Athapaskan*. Bud Lane, interview with author, Siletz, Oregon, May 24, 2005; Nikole Hannah-Jones, "Last of the Siletz Speakers," *Oregonian*, pp. O10–O11 (Nov. 25, 2007).

P. 377 *Lane's teaching and research*. In an email to María Aparicio, research assistant, Jan. 9, 2009, Lane described his teaching method as follows:

> My teaching method is very simple. I first have my students learn simple nouns and at the same time teach them to learn to use our practical alphabet. The practical alphabet is a single sound alphabet. It uses all of the letters in the English alphabet, but assigns each letter only one sound. By teaching nouns like family members, foods, animals, counting, my students learn a basic noun vocabulary. Next I introduce them to simple verbs to make the nouns do something, first in the present tense and then in the past tense and the rules of Athabaskan syntax. Just simple phrases. Eventually I teach them verb prefixes and suffixes, personifiers, aspects of time, etc. At the same time I interject as much history and cultural things as possible to show how our language directly evolved from how our people view themselves and view the world that the Creator put together for us to live on.

P. 377 *Athapaskan-English dictionary, Nuu-Wee-Ya'*. In working on expanding this dictionary, Lane expresses heavy gratitude to Loren Bommelyn of the Smith River Rancheria for creating *Xush Wee-Ya*, a Tolowa-English dictionary. Lane transliterated that work and expanded it by including many words and phrases from other Oregon coastal Athapaskan dialects and varieties.

Before he passed away in 2009, Gilbert Towner, a tribal elder, also instructed students in the Athapaskan language of Tututni. Towner met with young people once a year and created a DVD that students could use at home. Working from a 1953 tape of an interview by anthropologist Morris Swedesh with Tututni speaker Miller Collins, Towner developed course materials consisting of 400 words and sentences. He also provided students with a shorter laminated list that they were encouraged to carry around with them. Gilbert Towner, telephone interview with María Aparicio, research assistant, Jan. 15, 2009; Gilbert Towner, interview with Carrie Covington, research assistant, Siletz, Oregon, Aug. 10, 2007; Gilbert Towner, interview with author, May 8, 2008.

P. 377 *"Siletz Talking Dictionary."* See "Siletz Dee-Ni Talking Online Dictionary Project," Living Tongues Institute for Endangered Languages, *at* http://www.livingtongues. org/siletz.html (accessed May 12, 2009).

P. 377 *"Athabaskan is the last indigenous language."* Bud Lane, email to María Aparicio, research assistant, Jan. 6, 2009.

P. 378 *Students are studying native languages in college.* For example, Carson Viles, a Siletz tribal member and linguistics major, is taking a course in Sahaptin at the University of Oregon. He and his father are also studying Athapaskan. Carson's brother is in the Sahaptin course and is also studying Chinuk WaWa. See Shelby Martin, "Rare Yakama Language Now Taught at University of Oregon," *Associated Press* (Feb. 13, 2009), *at* http://www.indiancountrynews.net/index.php?option=com_content&task=view&id=5762&Itemid=1 (accessed May 12, 2009).

P. 378 *"a language spoken by less than 100."* Crystal, *Language Death*, p. 12.

P. 378 *Only Hawaiian has shown a net gain.* See Ron Staton, "Language Revival: Hawaiian Rates as the Nation's Only Growing Indigenous Tongue," *Honolulu Star-Bulletin* (March 14, 2005), *at* http://archives.starbulletin.com/2005/03/14/news/story7.html (accessed May 11, 2009).

P. 378 *Baskets were pervasive in Siletz traditional life.* This section on Siletz basketmaking draws on several sources: Bud Lane and Robert Kentta, interview with author, Siletz, Oregon, May 24, 2005; Bud Lane and Cheryl Lane, tribal member, interview with author, Logsden, Oregon, May 25, 2005; Woody Muschamp, interview with María Aparicio, research assistant, Logsden, Oregon, Jan. 2, 2008; Woody Muschamp, telephone interview with María Aparicio, Sept. 2, 2008; Northwest Native American Basketweavers Association, "The Basket is a Song" (2005), *at* http://www.nnaba.org/documents/2005_Gathering_Newsletter.pdf (accessed May 11, 2009); Jack McNeel, "Siletz Basketmaker Keeps the Art Alive," *Indian Country Today* (Aug. 30, 2006), *at* http://www.indiancountrytoday.com/archive/28155539.html (accessed May 11, 2009); Lawrence Kreisman and Glenn Mason, *The Arts and Crafts Movement in the Pacific Northwest*, pp. 27–31, 278–80 (Portland, OR: Timber Press, 2007). The unpublished manuscript by Leone Letson Kasner, "Siletz: Survival for an Artifact" (1976), is a comprehensive, knowledgeable treatment of Siletz basketry. It deserves to be formally published. Also noteworthy is vol. 4, no. 2 *American Indian Basketry and Other Native Arts* (issue no. 14), entitled "Traditional Arts of the Indians of Western Oregon" (1984).

On the plant communities relevant to Siletz basketmaking, see generally Dana Lepofsky, "Paleoethnobotany in the Northwest," *in* Paul E. Minnis, ed., *People and Plants in Ancient Western North America*, pp. 378–84 (Washington, D.C.: Smithsonian Books, 2004).

P. 382 *"the basket is a song."* In 2005, when the Siletz Tribe hosted the annual gathering of the Northwest Native American Basketweavers Association, the title of the gathering was "The Basket Is a Song." See Northwest Native American Basketweavers Association, "The Basket Is a Song," *at* http://www.nnaba.org/documents/2005_Gathering_Newsletter.pdf (accessed May 11, 2009).

P. 382 *"A northern California basket maker."* W. Richard West, "A Song Made Visible," vol. 83, no. 5 *Museum News*, pp. 35–36 (Sept./Oct. 2004).

P. 382 *Run to the Rogue.* See "Run to the Rogue," Confederated Tribes of Siletz Indians' Web site, *at* http://www.ctsi.nsn.us (under Tribal Services, click Education, then Culture and Language) (accessed May 29, 2009).

BIBLIOGRAPHY

Siletz History

FOR THOSE WISHING TO DO FURTHER READING, A NUMBER OF readily available books are especially useful in addressing different aspects of Siletz history.

The Rogue River War of 1850–1856 has received the most attention. The standard account is Stephen Dow Beckham's *Requiem for a People: The Rogue Indians and the Frontiersmen.* Nathan Douthit's *Uncertain Encounters: Indians and Whites at Peace and War in Southern Oregon, 1820s to 1860s* is a fine treatment of that era with an emphasis on attempts by both sides to find a middle ground. The dominant figure on the American side during those tempestuous years, Joel Palmer, is portrayed well in Terence O'Donnell's biography, *An Arrow in the Earth: General Joel Palmer and the Indians of Oregon.* E. A. Schwartz's *The Rogue River Indian War and Its Aftermath, 1850–1980* focuses primarily on the war but covers later eras as well; his research on how the government carried out allotment in the early 1900s is particularly useful.

Stephen Dow Beckham has made many other contributions to Oregon Indian history. *The Indians of Western Oregon: This Land Was Theirs* is an engaging short history. *Oregon Indians: Voices from Two Centuries* presents edited texts of important historical documents along with excellent commentary. The Oregon Council for the Humanities also produced a useful historical summary, *The First Oregonians,* edited by Laura Berg.

The literature has been enriched by biographies, authored by anthropologists, of two prominent, long-lived Siletz people, *She's Tricky Like Coyote: Annie Miner Peterson, an Oregon Coast Indian Woman,* by Lionel Youst, and *Coquelle Thompson, Athabascan Witness: A Cultural Biography,* by Youst and

William R. Seaburg. Both books shed much light on Siletz history. Biographies of this sort are all too rare and we can hope that this genre will grow in years to come. Siletz, with its forced mixings of so many tribes, produced quite a large amount of anthropological research based on interviews with Siletz people who lived in their ancestral homelands before removal to the reservation in the mid-1850s or who were born shortly afterward and heard firsthand accounts. The anthropologists included J. Owen Dorsey, Franz Boas, Livingston Farrand, Edward Sapir, Leo Frachtenberg, John Harrington, Philip Drucker, Cora DuBois, Melville Jacobs, Elizabeth Jacobs, Morris Swadesh, and Dennis Gray. Their work is nicely analyzed in William Seaburg's excellent introduction to Elizabeth Jacobs's *The Nehalem Tillamook: An Ethnography*. A standard anthropological source is *Indians of the Northwest Coast* (Anthropological Handbook No. 10), compiled by the American Museum of Natural History.

Robert Boyd has written two important books that bear upon the Siletz tribes. *The Coming of the Spirit of Pestilence: Introduced Infectious Diseases and Population Decline among Northwest Coast Indians, 1774–1874* is a careful, comprehensive, and powerful examination of the impacts of epidemics caused by European diseases on the tribes of the Pacific Northwest. *Indians, Fire, and the Land in the Pacific Northwest* is a collection, capably edited by Boyd, of essays by Boyd and others on the extensive use of fire by the tribes before the arrival of Europeans; among other things, the book is one of the best sources disproving the "pristine myth," holding that Indians left the land untouched, and showing that Native people managed the landscape in various ways. Another worthy volume on the relationship between Indian people and the natural world is *The Pacific Raincoast: Environment and Culture in an American Eden, 1778–1900*, by Robert Bunting.

Siletz history, of course, is entwined with both Oregon history and American history. William Robbins was one of the first historians of the American West to integrate Indian history seamlessly into state and regional history. This craftsmanship is evident in *Oregon: This Storied Land*, his history of Oregon, and *Landscapes of Conflict: The Oregon Story, 1940–2000*, an environmental history of the state in modern times. Richard White accomplishes this meshing of Indian history with the history of the American West in *"It's Your Misfortune and None of My Own": A New History of the American West*, as does Patricia Nelson Limerick in *The Legacy of Conquest: The Unbroken Past of the American West*. Nationally, we are blessed with Father Francis Paul Prucha's great two-volume history of federal-tribal policy, *The Great Father:*

The United States Government and the American Indians. The Great Father is also published in an abridged paperback edition.

Vine Deloria Jr., Standing Rock Sioux, left some thirty books. Deloria's belief in the values of history and comprehensive understanding of the American Indian experience, salted with occasional humor and outrageousness, had an impact beyond the counting. While his work never squarely dealt with the Siletz, his influence on policy benefited all Indians and his work inspired Siletz people. Leading examples include *Custer Died for Your Sins: An Indian Manifesto*, a bestseller that put wind beneath the wings of Indian reform efforts in modern times, including Siletz restoration; *God Is Red: A Native View of Religion*, which explored the profundity of Native spirituality; and *The Nations Within: The Past and Future of American Indian Sovereignty*, a stout and persuasive defense of the tribal sovereignty that is so dear to all tribes, certainly including the Siletz.

Books

Allan, Stuart, Aileen R. Buckley, and James E. Meacham. *Atlas of Oregon*, edited by William G. Loy. Eugene: University of Oregon, 2001.

American Friends Service Committee. *Uncommon Controversy: Fishing Rights of the Muckleshoot, Puyallup, and Nisqually Indians.* Seattle: University of Washington Press, 1986.

Archuleta, Margaret L., Brenda J. Child, and K. Tsianina Lomawaima, eds. *Away from Home: American Indian Boarding School Experiences, 1879–2000.* Phoenix, AZ: Heard Museum, 2000.

Bailey, Lynn R. *Bosque Redondo: An American Concentration Camp.* Pasadena, CA: Socio-Technical Books, 1970.

Bancroft, Hubert Howe. *History of Oregon, 1848–1888.* Vol. 2. San Francisco: The History Co., 1888.

Barker, Dr. Burt Brown. *Letters of Dr. John McLoughlin: Written at Fort Vancouver, 1829–1832.* Portland, OR: Binfords & Mort, 1948.

Barnett, H. G. *Indian Shakers: A Messianic Cult of the Pacific Northwest.* Carbondale: Southern Illinois University Press, 1957.

Beckham, Stephen Dow. *Requiem for a People: The Rogue Indians and the Frontiersmen.* Norman: University of Oklahoma Press, 1971.

———. *The Indians of Western Oregon: This Land Was Theirs.* Coos Bay, OR: Arago Books, 1977.

Beckham, Stephen Dow, ed. *Oregon Indians: Voices from Two Centuries.* Corvallis: Oregon State University Press, 2006.

Beeson, John. *John Beeson's Plea for the Indians: His Lone Cry in the Wilderness for Indian Rights: Oregon's First Civil-Rights Advocate.* Medford, OR: Webb Research Group, 1994.

Benke, Arthur C., and Colbert E. Cushing, eds. *Rivers of North America.* Boston: Elsevier Academic Press, 2005.

Bensell, Royal A. *All Quiet on the Yamhill: The Civil War in Oregon*, edited by Gunter Barth. Eugene: University of Oregon Books, 1959.

Berg, Laura, ed. *The First Oregonians.* Revised 2d ed. Portland: Oregon Council for the Humanities, 2007. (Original edition by Carolyn Baun and Richard Lewis was published in 1991.)

Berkhofer, Robert. *The White Man's Indian: Images of the American Indian from Columbus to the Present.* New York: Knopf, 1978.

Bernstein, Alison R. *American Indians and World War II: Toward a New Era in Indian Affairs.* Norman: University of Oklahoma Press, 1991.

Berreman, Joel V. *Chetco Archaeology: A Report on the Lone Ranch Creek Shell Mound on the Coast of Southern Oregon.* Menasha, WI: George Banta Publishing Co., 1944.

Biolsi, Thomas, ed. *A Companion to the Anthropology of American Indians.* Malden, MA: Blackwell Publishing, 2004.

Bolt, Christine. *American Indian Policy and American Reform: Case Studies of the Campaign to Assimilate the American Indians.* London: Allen & Unwin, 1987.

Bommelyn, Loren. *Now You're Speaking—Tolowa.* Arcata, CA: Center for Indian Community Development, Humboldt State University, 1995.

Bowden, Henry Warner. *American Indians and Christian Missions: Studies in Cultural Conflict.* Chicago: University of Chicago Press, 1981.

Boyd, Robert. *The Coming of the Spirit of Pestilence: Introduced Infectious Diseases and Population Decline Among Northwest Coast Indians, 1774–1874.* Seattle: University of Washington Press, 1999.

Boyd, Robert, ed. *Indians, Fire, and the Land in the Pacific Northwest.* Corvallis: Oregon State University Press, 1999.

Bradley, Glenn D. *The Story of the Pony Express*, edited by Waddell F. Smith. San Francisco: Hesperian House, 1960.

Brooks, Howard C., and Len Ramp. *Gold and Silver in Oregon.* Portland: State of Oregon Department of Geology and Mineral Industries, 1968.

Brown, Richard Maxwell. *Strain of Violence: Historical Studies of American Violence and Vigilantism.* New York: Oxford University Press, 1975.

Buckley, Thomas. *Standing Ground: Yurok Indian Spirituality, 1850–1990.* Berkeley: University of California Press, 2002.

Bunting, Robert. *The Pacific Raincoast: Environment and Culture in an American Eden, 1778–1900.* Lawrence: University Press of Kansas, 1997.

Bussey, M., and J. Wise, eds. *Transforming Trauma: Empowerment Responses.* New York: Columbia University Press, forthcoming.

Cahn, Edgar S., ed. *Our Brother's Keeper: The Indian in White America.* Washington, D.C.: New Community Press, 1969.

Cantoni, Gina, ed. *Stabilizing Indigenous Languages.* Flagstaff: Center for Excellence in Education, Northern Arizona University, 2007.

Carey, Charles H. *A General History of Oregon: Prior to 1861.* Vol. 2. Portland, OR: Metropolitan Press, 1936.

———. *General History of Oregon: Through Early Statehood.* Portland, OR: Binford & Mort, for the Peter Binford Foundation, 1971.

Chalcraft, Edwin L. *Assimilation's Agent: My Life as a Superintendent in the Indian Boarding School System*, edited and with an introduction by Cary C. Collins. Lincoln: University of Nebraska Press, 2004.

Chittenden, Hiram Martin. *The American Fur Trade of the Far West.* Vol. 1. New York: Barnes and Noble, Inc., 1935.

Chitty, Joseph. *A Treatise on the Law of the Prerogatives of the Crown; and the Relative Duties and Rights of the Subject.* London: Joseph Butterworth and Son, 1820.

Clark, Malcolm, Jr., ed. *Pharisee among Philistines: The Diary of Judge Matthew P. Deady, 1871–1892.* Portland: Oregon Historical Society, 1975.

Clodfelter, Michael. *Warfare and Armed Conflicts: A Statistical Reference to Casualty and Other Figures, 1618–1991.* Jefferson, NC: McFarland & Co., 1992.

Cohen, Fay G. *Treaties on Trial: The Continuing Controversy over Northwest Indian Fishing Rights.* Seattle: University of Washington Press, 1986.

Cohen, Felix S. See *Felix Cohen's Handbook of Federal Indian Law.*

Collier, John. *The Indians of the Americas.* New York: W. W. Norton & Co., 1947.

Collins, Cary C. *See* Chalcraft, Edwin L.

Cornell, Stephen. *The Return of the Native: American Indian Political Resurgence.* New York: Oxford University Press, 1988.

Corning, Howard McKinley, ed. *Dictionary of Oregon History.* 2d ed. Portland, OR: Binford & Mort, 1989.

Cressman, L. S. *Prehistory of the Far West: Homes of Vanished Peoples.* Salt Lake City: University of Utah Press, 1977.

Crystal, David. *Language Death.* Cambridge, UK: Cambridge University Press, 2000.

Curtis, Edward S. *The North American Indian.* Vol. 13, edited by Frederick Webb Hodge. Norwood, MA: Plimpton Press, 1924.

Dale, Harrison Clifford, ed. *The Explorations of William H. Ashley and Jedediah Smith, 1822–1829.* Lincoln: University of Nebraska Press, 1991.

Dana, Samuel T., and Sally K. Fairfax. *Forest and Range Policy: Its Development in the United States.* 2d ed. New York: McGraw-Hill Book Co., 1980.

Davies, K. G. *Peter Skene Ogden's Snake Country Journal, 1826–27.* London: The Hudson's Bay Record Society, 1961.

Davis, Mary B., ed. *Native America in the Twentieth Century: An Encyclopedia.* New York: Garland Publishing, Inc., 1996.

D'Azevedo, Warren L., ed. *Handbook of North American Indians.* Vol. 11: *Great Basin.* Washington, D.C.: Smithsonian Institution, 1986.

Debo, Angie. *A History of the Indians of the United States.* Norman: University of Oklahoma Press, 1970.

———. *And Still the Waters Run: The Betrayal of the Five Civilized Tribes.* Princeton, NJ: Princeton University Press, 1972.

deBuys, William, ed. *Seeing Things Whole: The Essential John Wesley Powell.* Washington, D.C.: Island Press, 2001.

Decker, Peter. *"The Utes Must Go!": American Expansion and the Removal of a People.* Golden, CO: Fulcrum Publishing, 2004.

Deloria, Vine, Jr. *Custer Died for Your Sins: An Indian Manifesto.* New York: Avon Books, 1969.

———. *God Is Red: A Native View of Religion.* New York: Grosset & Dunlap, 1973.

Deloria, Vine, Jr., and Clifford M. Lytle. *The Nations Within: The Past and Future of American Indian Sovereignty.* New York: Pantheon Books, 1984.

Deloria, Vine, Jr., and Raymond J. DeMallie, eds. *Documents of American Indian Diplomacy: Treaties, Agreements, and Conventions, 1775–1979.* Vol. 2. Norman: University of Oklahoma Press, 1999.

DeVoto, Bernard. *The Year of Decision, 1846.* Boston: Little, Brown and Co. 1943.

Diamond, Jared. *Guns, Germs, and Steel: The Fates of Human Societies.* New York: W. W. Norton & Co., 1997.

Dicken, Samuel N., and Emily F. Dicken. *The Making of Oregon: A Study in Historical Geography.* Portland: Oregon Historical Society, 1979.

———. *Oregon Divided: A Regional Geography.* Portland: Oregon Historical Society, 1982.

Dictionary of Indian Tribes of the Americas. Vol. 2. Newport Beach, CA: American Indian Publishers, Inc., 1980.

Dippie, Brian W. *The Vanishing American: White Attitudes and U.S. Indian Policy.* Middletown, CT: Wesleyan University Press, 1982.

Dobyns, Henry F. *Their Numbers Become Thinned: Native American Population Dynamics in Eastern North America.* Knoxville: University of Tennessee Press, 1983.

Dodds, Gordon B. *Oregon: A Bicentennial History.* New York: W. W. Norton and Co., 1977.

Dodge, Orvil, ed. *Pioneer History of Coos and Curry Counties, Or.* Salem, OR: Capital Printing Co., 1898.

Douthit, Nathan. *Uncertain Encounters: Indians and Whites at Peace and War in Southern Oregon, 1820s to 1860s.* Corvallis: Oregon State University Press, 2002.

Drinnon, Richard. *Keeper of Concentration Camps: Dillon S. Myer and American Racism.* Berkeley: University of California Press, 1987.

Drucker, Philip. *Indians of the Northwest Coast.* Anthropological Handbook No. 10. New York: McGraw Hill Book Co., for the American Museum of Natural History, 1955.

———. *Cultures of the North Pacific Coast.* San Francisco: Chandler Publishing Co., 1965.

Duran, Eduardo, and Bonnie Duran. *Native American Postcolonial Psychology.* Albany: SUNY Press, 1995.

Echo-Hawk, Roger C., and Walter R. Echo-Hawk. *Battlefields and Burial Grounds: The Indian Struggle to Protect Ancestral Graves in the United States.* Minneapolis, MN: Lerner Publications Co., 1994.

Edwards, G. Thomas, and Carlos A. Schwantes, eds. *Experiences in a Promised Land: Essays in Pacific Northwest History.* Seattle: University of Washington Press, 1986.

Eggan, Fred. *The American Indian: Perspectives for the Study of Social Change.* Chicago: Aldine Publishing Co., 1966.

Engerman, Stanley, Seymour Drescher, and Robert Paquette, eds. *Slavery.* New York: Oxford University Press, 2001.

Fagan, David D. *History of Benton County, Oregon.* Portland, OR: A. G. Walling Printer, 1885.

Felix Cohen's Handbook of Federal Indian Law. Charlottesville, VA: Michie Bobbs-Merrill, 1982; Newark, NJ: Lexis/Nexis, 2005.

Fenn, Elizabeth A. *Pox Americana: The Great Smallpox Epidemic of 1775–82.* New York: Hill and Wang, 2001.

Fey, Harold E., and D'Arcy McNickle. *Indians and Other Americans: Two Ways of Life Meet.* New York: Harper & Row, 1970.

Finkelman, Paul, and Joseph C. Miller. *Macmillan Encyclopedia of World Slavery.* New York: Simon & Schuster Macmillan, 1998.

Foreman, Grant. *Indian Removal: The Emigration of the Five Civilized Tribes of Indians.* Norman: University of Oklahoma Press, 1972.

Franco, Jere' Bishop. *Crossing the Pond: The Native American Effort in World War II.* Denton: University of North Texas Press, 1999.

Gates, Paul W. *History of Public Land Law Development.* Washington, D.C.: Government

Printing Office, 1968.

Gay, E. Jane. *With the Nez Perces: Alice Fletcher in the Field, 1889–92*, edited by Frederick E. Hoxie and Joan T. Mark. Lincoln: University of Nebraska Press, 1981.

Getches, David H., Charles F. Wilkinson, and Robert A. Williams Jr. *Cases and Materials on Federal Indian Law.* 5th ed. St. Paul, MN: Thompson West, 2005.

Gibbs, George. *Dictionary of the Chinook Jargon, or, Trade Language of Oregon.* New York: Cramoisy Press, 1863.

Glisan, R. *Journal of Army Life.* San Francisco: A. L. Bancroft and Co., 1874.

Gould, Richard A. *Archaeology of the Point St. George Site, and Tolowa Prehistory.* Berkeley: University of California Press, 1966.

Grover, Lafayette. *Notable Things in a Public Life in Oregon.* San Francisco, 1878, *at* Bancroft Library, University of California, Berkeley.

Hafen, LeRoy R., ed. *The Mountain Men and the Fur Trade of the Far West.* Vol. 1. Glendale, CA: Arthur H. Clark Co., 1965.

Hale, Horatio. *An International Idiom: A Manual of the Oregon Trade Language or "Chinook Jargon."* London: Whittaker and Co., 1890.

———. *Ethnography and Philology.* Ridgewood, NJ: Gregg Press, 1968.

Harvard Project on American Indians. *The State of Native Nations: Conditions under U.S. Policies of Self-Determination.* New York: Oxford University Press, 2008.

Hays, Marjorie H. *The Land That Kept Its Promise: A History of South Lincoln County.* Newport, OR: Lincoln County Historical Society, 1976.

Hays, Samuel P. *Conservation and the Gospel of Efficiency: The Progressive Conservation Movement, 1890–1920.* New York: Atheneum, 1980.

Heizer, Robert F., ed. *Handbook of North American Indians.* Vol. 8: *California.* Washington, D.C.: Smithsonian Institution, 1978.

Hendrickson, James E. *Joe Lane of Oregon: Machine Politics and the Sectional Crisis, 1849–1861.* New Haven, CT: Yale University Press, 1967.

Heyl, Erik. *Early American Steamers.* 6 vols. Buffalo, NY: Erik Heyl, 1953–69.

Hidy, Ralph W., Frank Ernest Hill, and Allan Nevins. *Timber and Men: The Weyerhaeuser Story.* New York: Macmillan, 1963.

Hinton, Leanne, and Ken Hale, eds. *The Green Book of Language Revitalization in Practice.* San Diego, CA: Academic Press, 2001.

Hodge, Frederick Webb. *See* Curtis, Edward S.

Hoebel, E. Adamson. *The Law of Primitive Man: A Study in Comparative Legal Dynamics.* Cambridge, MA: Harvard University Press, 1954.

Holliday, J. S. *The World Rushed In: The California Gold Rush Experience.* New York: Simon & Shuster, 1981.

Holmes, Kenneth L. *Ewing Young: Master Trapper.* Portland, OR: Binford & Mort, for the Peter Binford Foundation, 1967.

Holton, Jim. *Chinook Jargon: The Hidden Language of the Pacific Northwest.* San Leandro, CA: Wawa Press, 2004.

Hoopes, Alban W. *Indian Affairs and Their Administration: With Special Reference to the Far West, 1849–1860.* Philadelphia: University of Pennsylvania Press, 1932.

Hosen, Frederick E. *The Great Depression and the New Deal.* Jefferson, NC: McFarland & Co., Inc., 1992.

Howay, Frederic W. *Voyages of the "Columbia" to the Northwest Coast: 1787–1790 and 1790–1793.* New York: Da Capo Press, 1969.

Hoxie, Frederick E. *A Final Promise: The Campaign to Assimilate the Indians, 1880–1920.* Lincoln: University of Nebraska Press, 2001.

Irving, Washington. *Astoria, or Anecdotes of an Enterprise beyond the Rocky Mountains.* Norman: University of Oklahoma Press, 1964.

Jacobs, Elizabeth D. *The Nehalem Tillamook: An Ethnology.* Corvallis: Oregon State University Press, 2003.

Jacobs, Melville. *Coos Myth Texts.* Seattle: University of Washington Press, 1940.

———. *Kalapuya Texts.* University of Washington Publications in Anthropology, vol. 11. Seattle: University of Washington Press, 1945.

Josephy, Alvin M., Jr. *The Nez Perce Indians and the Opening of the Northwest.* Boston: Houghton Mifflin Co., 1965.

———. *Now That the Buffalo's Gone: A Study of Today's American Indians.* New York: Alfred A. Knopf, 1982.

Judson, Katharine Berry. *Myths and Legends of the Pacific Northwest: Especially of Washington and Oregon.* Chicago: A. C. McClurg & Co., 1912.

Juntunen, Judy Rycraft, May D. Dasch, and Ann Bennett Rogers. *The World of the Kalapuya: A Native People of Western Oregon.* Philomath, OR: Benton County Historical Society and Museum, 2005.

Kappler, Charles J., ed. *Indian Affairs: Laws and Treaties.* 2 vols. Washington, D.C.: Government Printing Office, 1904.

Kasner, Leone Letson. *Siletz: Survival for an Artifact.* Dallas, OR: Itemizer-Observer, 1976.

Keenan Jerry. *Encyclopedia of American Indian Wars, 1492–1890.* Santa Barbara, CA: ABC-CLIO, 1997.

Kehoe, Alice Beck. *The Ghost Dance: Ethnohistory and Revitalization.* New York: Holt, Rinehart and Winston, Inc., 1989.

Keller, Robert H., Jr. *American Protestantism and United States Indian Policy, 1869–82.* Lincoln: University of Nebraska Press, 1983.

Kelly, Lawrence. *The Assault on Assimilation: John Collier and the Origins of Indian Policy Reform.* Albuquerque: University of New Mexico Press, 1983.

Kerr, Winfield S. *John Sherman: His Life and Public Service.* Boston: Sherman, French & Co., 1907.

Kessel, William B., and Robert Wooster, eds. *Encyclopedia of Native American Wars and Warfare.* New York: Facts on File, Book Builders, 2005.

Krech, Shepard, III. *The Ecological Indian: Myth and History.* New York: W. W. Norton & Co., 1999.

Kreisman, Lawrence, and Glenn Mason. *The Arts and Crafts Movement in the Pacific Northwest.* Portland, OR: Timber Press, 2007.

Kroeber, A. L. *Handbook of the Indians of California.* Washington, D.C.: Bureau of American Ethnology, 1923.

Lane, Joseph. *Autobiography.* Portland, OR, 1878, *at* Bancroft Library, University of California, Berkeley.

Lang, George. *Making Wawa: The Genesis of Chinook Jargon.* Vancouver: UBC Press, 2008.

Lichatowich, James. *Salmon without Rivers: A History of the Pacific Salmon Crisis.* Washington, D.C.: Island Press, 1999.

Limerick, Patricia Nelson. *The Legacy of Conquest: The Unbroken Past of the American West.* New York: W. W. Norton & Co, 1987.

Llewellyn, K. N., and E. Adamson Hoebel. *The Cheyenne Way: Conflict and Case Law in*

Primitive Jurisprudence. Norman: University of Oklahoma Press, 1941.

Loy, William G., Stuart Allan, Clyde P. Patton, and Robert D. Plank. *Atlas of Oregon.* Eugene: University of Oregon, 1976.

Lyman, R. Lee. *Prehistory of the Oregon Coast: The Effects of Excavation Strategies and Assemblage Size on Archaeological Inquiry.* San Diego: Academic Press, 1991.

Mackie, Richard Somerset. *Trading Beyond the Mountains: The British Fur Trade on the Pacific, 1793–1843.* Vancouver: UBC Press, 1997.

Mardock, Robert Winston. *The Reformers and the American Indian.* Columbia: University of Missouri Press, 1971.

Mason, W. Dale. *Indian Gaming: Tribal Sovereignty and American Politics.* Norman: University of Oklahoma Press, 2000.

May, Stephen. *Language and Minority Rights: Ethnicity, Nationalism and the Politics of Language.* New York: Routledge, 2008.

Mayer, George. *The Republican Party, 1854–1966.* New York: Oxford University Press, 1967.

McCoy, Charles A. *Polk and the Presidency.* Austin: University of Texas Press, 1960.

McEvoy, Arthur F. *The Fisherman's Problem: Ecology and Law in the California Fisheries 1850–1980.* Cambridge, UK: Cambridge University Press, 1986.

McFeat, Tom, ed. *Indians of the North Pacific Coast.* Seattle: University of Washington Press, 1966.

McNitt, Frank. *Navajo Wars: Military Campaigns, Slave Raids and Reprisals.* Albuquerque: University of New Mexico Press, 1972.

Michno, Gregory. *Encyclopedia of Indian Wars: Western Battles and Skirmishes, 1850–1890.* Missoula, MT: Mountain Press Publishing Co., 2003.

Mills, Elaine L., ed. *The Papers of John Peabody Harrington in the Smithsonian Institution, 1907–1957.* Vol. 1. Millwood, NY: Kraus International Publications, 1981.

Milner, Clyde A., II, Carol O'Connor, and Martha A. Sandweiss, eds. *The Oxford History of the American West.* New York: Oxford University Press, 1994.

Minnis, Paul E., ed. *People and Plants in Ancient Western North America.* Washington, D.C.: Smithsonian Books, 2004.

Moe, Ray T., ed. *The First One Hundred Years in Lincoln County Oregon, 1893 to 1993.* Newport, OR: Lincoln County Centennial Committee, 1993.

Morgan, A. W. *Fifty Years in Siletz Timber.* Portland, OR: A. W. Morgan, 1959.

Morgan, Dale. *Jedediah Smith and the Opening of the West.* Lincoln: University of Nebraska Press, 1953.

Morgan, Lewis H. *Ancient Society, or, Researches in the Lines of Human Progress from Savagery through Barbarism to Civilization.* London: MacMillan & Co., 1877.

Native American Rights Fund. *Indian Claims Commission Decisions.* Vols. 3, 4, 7, and 11. Boulder, CO: Native American Rights Fund, 1973.

Neel, David. *The Great Canoes: Reviving a Northwest Coast Tradition.* Seattle: University of Washington Press, 1995.

Neils, Selma. *The Klickitat Indians.* Portland, OR: Binford & Mort, 1985.

Nettle, David, and Suzanne Romaine. *Vanishing Voices: The Extinction of the World's Languages.* New York: Oxford University Press, 2000.

Newsom, David. *David Newsom: The Western Observer, 1805–1882.* Portland: Oregon Historical Society, 1972.

Nunis, Docye B., Jr. *The Golden Frontier: The Recollections of Herman Francis Reinhart, 1851–1869.* Austin: University of Texas Press, 1962.

O'Donnell, Mike. *The First Hundred Years: Lincoln County, 1893–1993*. Newport, OR: News-Times, 1993.

O'Donnell, Terence. *An Arrow in the Earth: General Joel Palmer and the Indians of Oregon.* Portland: Oregon Historical Society, 1991.

Olsen, Edward G. *Then Til Now in Brookings-Harbor: A Social History of the Chetco Community Area.* Brookings, OR: Coast Printing Co., for the Brookings Rotary Club, 1979.

Osterreich, Shelley Anne. *The American Indian Ghost Dance, 1870 and 1890: An Annotated Bibliography.* New York: Greenwood Press, 1991.

Otis, D. S. *The Dawes Act and the Allotment of Indian Lands*, edited by Francis Paul Prucha. Norman: University of Oklahoma Press, 1973.

Parkman, Francis. *The Oregon Trail.* Garden City, NY: Doubleday, Doran and Co., 1946.

Paul, Rodman W. *California Gold: The Beginning of Mining in the Far West.* Lincoln: University of Nebraska Press, 1947.

Peroff, Nicholas C. *Menominee Drums: Tribal Termination and Restoration, 1954–1974.* Norman: University of Oklahoma Press, 1982.

Phillips, W. S. *The Chinook Book: A Descriptive Analysis of the Chinook Jargon in Plain Words, Giving Instructions for Pronunciation, Construction, Expression and Proper Speaking of Chinook with All the Various Shaded Meanings of the Words.* Seattle: R. L. Davis Printing Co., 1913.

Philp, Kenneth R. *John Collier's Crusade for Indian Reform, 1920–1954.* Tucson: University of Arizona Press, 1977.

Philp, Kenneth R., ed. *Indian Self-Rule: First-Hand Accounts of Indian-White Relations from Roosevelt to Reagan.* Salt Lake City, UT: Howe Brothers, 1986.

Pierre, Joseph H. *When Timber Stood Tall.* Seattle: Superior Publishing Co., 1979.

Pinkerton, Robert E. *Hudson's Bay Company.* New York: Henry Holt and Company, 1931.

Pommersheim, Frank. *Braid of Feathers: American Indian Law and Contemporary Tribal Life.* Berkeley: University of California Press, 1995.

Prucha, Francis Paul. *American Indian Policy in Crisis: Christian Reformers and the American Indian, 1865–1900.* Norman: University of Oklahoma Press, 1976.

———. *The Great Father: The United States Government and the American Indians.* 2 vols. Lincoln: University of Nebraska Press, 1984.

———. *Documents of United States Indian Policy.* 3d ed. Lincoln: University of Nebraska Press, 2000.

Puter, S. A. D. *Looters of the Public Domain.* New York: Arno Press, 1972.

Rajtar, Steve. *Indian War Sites: A Guidebook to Battlefields, Monuments, and Memorials, State by State with Canada and Mexico.* Jefferson, NC: McFarland & Co., 1999.

Rand, Kathryn R. L., and Steven Andrew Light. *Indian Gaming Law and Policy.* Durham, NC: Carolina Academic Press, 2006.

Reyhner, Jon, and Jeanne Eder. *American Indian Education: A History.* Norman: University of Oklahoma Press, 2004.

Richards, Kent D. *Isaac I. Stevens: Young Man in a Hurry.* Provo, UT: Brigham Young University Press, 1979.

Richardson, Elmo. *BLM's Billion-Dollar Checkerboard: Managing the O & C Lands.* Santa Cruz, CA: Forest History Society, 1980.

Richardson, James D., comp. *A Compilation of the Messages and Papers of the Presidents.* Vol. 9. New York: Bureau of National Literature, Inc., 1897.

Riddle, George W. *Early Days in Oregon: A History of the Riddle Valley.* Riddle, OR: Riddle

Parent Teachers Association, 1953.

Riney, Scott. *The Rapid City Indian School, 1898–1933*. Norman: University of Oklahoma Press, 1999.

Robbins, William G. *Hard Times in Paradise: Coos Bay, Oregon, 1850–1986*. Seattle: University of Washington Press, 1988.

——. *Oregon: This Storied Land*. Portland: Oregon Historical Society Press, 2005.

——. *Landscapes of Conflict: The Oregon Story, 1940–2000*. Seattle: University of Washington Press, 2004.

Rogin, Michael Paul. *Fathers and Children: Andrew Jackson and the Subjugation of the American Indian*. New York: Vintage Books, 1975.

Ruby, Robert H., and John A. Brown. *The Chinook Indians: Traders of the Lower Columbia River*. Norman: Oklahoma University Press, 1976.

——. *A Guide to the Indian Tribes of the Pacific Northwest*. Norman: University of Oklahoma Press, 1992.

——. *John Slocum and the Indian Shaker Church*. Norman: University of Oklahoma Press, 1996.

Rusco, Elmer R. *A Fateful Time: The Background and Legislative History of the Indian Reorganization Act*. Reno: University of Nevada Press, 2000.

Sage, Leland L. *William Boyd Allison: A Study in Practical Politics*. Iowa City: State Historical Society of Iowa, 1956.

Salmond, John A. *The Civilian Conservation Corps, 1933–1942: A New Deal Case Study*. Durham, NC: Duke University Press, 1967.

Satz, Ronald D. *American Indian Policy in the Jacksonian Era*. Lincoln: University of Nebraska Press, 1975.

Sauter, John, and Bruce Johnson. *Tillamook Indians of the Oregon Coast*. Portland, OR: Binford & Mort, 1974.

Scheuerman, Richard D., and Michael O. Finley. *Finding Chief Kamiakin: The Life and Legacy of a Northwest Patriot*. Pullman: Washington State University Press, 2008.

Schwartz, E. A. *The Rogue River Indian War and Its Aftermath, 1850–1980*. Norman: University of Oklahoma Press, 1997.

Seaburg, William R., ed. *Pitch Woman and Other Stories: The Oral Traditions of Coquelle Thompson, Upper Coquille Athabaskan Indian*. Lincoln: University of Nebraska Press, 2007.

Seaburg, William R., and Pamela T. Amoss, eds. *Badger and Coyote Were Neighbors: Melville Jacobs on Northwest Indian Myths and Tales*. Corvallis: Oregon State University Press, 2000.

Shaw, George C. *The Chinook Jargon and How to Use It: A Complete and Exhaustive Lexicon of the Oldest Trade Language of the American Continent*. Seattle: Rainier Printing Co., 1909.

Sigal, John J., and Morton Weinfeld. *Trauma and Rebirth: Intergenerational Effects of the Holocaust*. New York: Praeger Publishers, 1989.

Starr, Kevin. *Americans and the California Dream, 1850–1915*. New York: Oxford University Press, 1973.

Stegner, Wallace. *Beyond the Hundredth Meridian: John Wesley Powell and the Second Opening of the West*. Boston: Houghton Mifflin, 1954.

Stein, Julia K. *Deciphering a Shell Midden*. San Diego: Academic Press, Inc., 1992.

Stern, Theodore. *The Klamath Tribe: A People and Their Reservation*. Seattle: University of Washington Press, 1966.

Sullivan, Maurice S. *The Travels of Jedediah Smith*. Santa Ana, CA: Fine Arts Press, 1934.

Suttles, Wayne, ed. *Handbook of North American Indians*. Vol. 7: *Northwest Coast*. Washington, D.C.: Smithsonian Institution, 1990.

Swan, James G. *The Northwest Coast, or, Three Years' Residence in Washington Territory*. Seattle: University of Washington Press, 1969.

Szasz, Margaret Connell. *Education and the American Indian: The Road to Self-Determination since 1928*. Albuquerque: University of New Mexico Press, 1974.

Taylor, Joseph E., III. *Making Salmon: An Environmental History of the Northwest Fisheries Crisis*. Seattle: University of Washington Press, 1999.

Thomas, Edward Harper. *Chinook: A History and Dictionary of the Northwest Coast Trade Jargon*. 2d ed. Portland, OR: Binford & Mort, 1970.

Thornton, Russell, *American Indian Holocaust and Survival: A Population History since 1492*. Norman: University of Oklahoma Press, 1987.

Thwaites, Reuben Gold, ed. *Original Journals of the Lewis and Clark Expedition, 1804–1806*. Vol. 4. New York: Dodd, Mead and Co., 1905.

Toledano, Ehud R. *Slavery and Abolition in the Ottoman Middle East*. Seattle: University of Washington Press, 1998.

Townsend, Kenneth William. *World War II and the American Indian*. Albuquerque: University of New Mexico Press, 2000.

Transactions of the Eleventh Annual Re-Union of the Oregon Pioneer Association for 1883. Salem, OR: E. M. Waite, Steam Printer and Bookbinder, 1884.

Trennert, Robert A., Jr. *Alternative to Extinction: Federal Indian Policy and the Beginnings of the Reservation System, 1846–51*. Philadelphia: Temple University Press, 1975.

Tucker, William. *Vigilante: The Backlash against Crime in America*. New York: Stein and Day, 1985.

Twain, Mark. *Roughing It*. New York: Airmont Publishing Co., 1967.

Ulrich, Roberta. *A Lot of Funerals: The Failed Termination Experiment, 1953–2006*. Lincoln: University of Nebraska Press, forthcoming.

Utley, Robert M. *The Indian Frontier of the American West, 1846–1890*. Albuquerque: University of New Mexico Press, 1984.

Victor, Frances Fuller. *The Early Indian Wars of Oregon*. Salem, OR: Frank C. Baker, State Printer, 1894.

Vorenbery, Michael. *Final Freedom: The Civil War, the Abolition of Slavery, and the Thirteenth Amendment*. New York: Cambridge University Press, 2001.

Walker, Deward E. *Mutual Cross-Utilization of Economic Resources in the Plateau: An Example from Aboriginal Nez Perce Fishing Practices*. Pullman: Laboratory of Anthropology, Washington State University, 1967.

Walker, Deward E., Jr., ed. *Handbook of North American Indians*. Vol. 12: *Plateau*. Washington, D.C.: Smithsonian Institution, 1998.

Wallace, David Rains. *The Klamath Knot: Exploration of Myth and Evolution*. San Francisco: Sierra Club Books, 1983.

Walling, A. G. *History of Southern Oregon*. Portland, OR: A. G. Walling, Printer, 1884.

Walsh, Frank K. *Indian Battles along the Rogue River, 1855–56: One of America's Wild and Scenic Rivers*. North Bend, OR: Te-Cum-Tom Publications, 1996.

Ward, Beverly. *White Moccasins*. Myrtle Point, OR: Myrtle Point Printing, 1986.

Washburn, Wilcomb E. *Red Man's Land/White Man's Law: The Past and Present Status of the American Indian*. Norman: University of Oklahoma Press, 1995.

Wheat, Carl I., ed. *The Shirley Letters from the California Mines, 1851–1852.* New York: Alfred A. Knopf, 1970.

White, Richard. *"It's Your Misfortune and None of My Own": A New History of the American West.* Norman: University of Oklahoma Press, 1991.

———. *The Middle Ground: Indians, Empires, and Republics in the Lakes Region, 1650–1815.* Cambridge, UK: Cambridge University Press, 1991.

Whitesitt, Shiela, and Richard E. Moore, eds. *A Memoir of the Indian War: The Reminiscences of Ezra M. Hamilton.* Ashland, OR: Tree Stump Press, 1987.

Wilkinson, Charles. *American Indians, Time, and the Law: Native Societies in a Modern Constitutional Democracy.* New Haven, CT: Yale University Press, 1988.

———. *Messages from Frank's Landing: A Story of Salmon, Treaties, and the Indian Way.* Seattle: University of Washington Press, 2000.

———. *Blood Struggle: The Rise of Modern Indian Nations.* New York: W. W. Norton and Co., 2005.

Williams, Robert A., Jr. *The American Indian in Western Legal Thought: The Discourse of Conquest.* New York: Oxford University Press, 1990.

Winther, Oscar Osburn. *The Old Oregon Country: A History of Frontier Trade, Transportation, and Travel.* Bloomington: Indiana University Press, 1950.

Wolle, Muriel Sibell. *The Bonanza Trail: Ghost Towns and Mining Camps of the West.* Bloomington: Indiana University Press, 1958.

Woodcock, George. *Peoples of the Coast: The Indians of the Pacific Northwest.* Bloomington: Indiana University Press, 1977.

Worster, Donald. *A River Running West: The Life of John Wesley Powell.* New York: Oxford University Press, 2001.

Wright, E. W., ed. *Lewis and Dryden's Marine History of the Pacific Northwest.* New York: Antiquarian Press, 1961.

Youst, Lionel. *She's Tricky Like Coyote: Annie Miner Peterson, an Oregon Coast Indian Woman.* Norman: University of Oklahoma Press, 1997.

Youst, Lionel, and William R. Seaburg. *Coquelle Thompson, Athabascan Witness: A Cultural Biography.* Norman, University of Oklahoma Press, 2002.

Articles

Ambler, Marjane. "Native Languages: A Question of Life or Death," vol. 15 *Tribal College Journal* (Spring 2004).

Ames, Kenneth M. "Household Archaeology of Southern Northwest Coast Plank House," vol. 19, no. 3 *Journal of Field Archaeology* (Autumn 1992).

Applegate, Lindsay. "Notes and Reminiscences of Laying Out and Establishing the Old Emigrant Road into Southern Oregon in the Year 1846," vol. 22 *Oregon Historical Quarterly* (March–Dec. 1921).

Arneson, James. "Property Concepts of 19th-Century Oregon Indians," vol. 81 *Oregon Historical Quarterly* (Winter 1980).

Beckham, Stephen Dow, ed. "Trail of Tears: 1856 Diary of Indian Agent George Ambrose," vol. 10 *Southern Oregon Heritage* (Summer 1996).

Beckham, Stephen Dow, Kathryn Anne Toepel, and Rick Minor. "Native American Religious Practices and Uses in Western Oregon," no. 31 *University of Oregon Anthropological Papers* (1984).

Bernard, Russell H. "Preserving Language Diversity," vol. 51, no. 1 *Human Organization* (1992).

Bernholtz, Charles D. "The 'Other' Treaties: Comments on Deloria and DeMaillie's Documents of American Indian Diplomacy," vol. 24 *Legal Reference Services Quarterly* (2005).

Berreman, Joel V. "Tribal Distributions in Oregon," no. 47 *Memoirs of the American Anthropological Association* (1937).

Borchard, Edwin M. "Government Liability in Tort," vol. 34 *Yale Law Journal* (1924).

Braithwaite, John. "Restorative Justice: Assessing Optimistic and Pessimistic Accounts," vol. 25 *Crime and Justice* (1999).

Brave Heart, Maria Yellow Horse. "The Historical Trauma Response among Natives and Its Relationship with Substance Abuse: A Lakota Illustration," vol. 35 *Journal of Psychoactive Drugs* (January–March 2003).

Brave Heart, Maria Yellow Horse, and Lemyra M. DeBruyn. "The American Indian Holocaust: Healing Historical Unresolved Grief," vol. 8, no. 2 *American Indian and Alaska Native Mental Health Research* (1998).

Buckley, Thomas. "The Shaker Church and the Indian Way in Native Northwestern California," vol. 21, no. 1 *American Indian Quarterly* (Winter 1997).

Byram, R. Scott. "Colonial Power and Indigenous Justice: Fur Trade Violence and Its Aftermath in Yaquina Narrative," vol. 109, no. 3 *Oregon Historical Quarterly* (Fall 2008).

Castile, George P. "The 'Half-Catholic' Movement," *Pacific Northwest Quarterly* (October 1982).

Clark, Malcolm, Jr., ed. "My Dear Judge: Excerpts from the Letters of Justice Stephen J. Field to Judge Matthew P. Deady," vol. 1 *Western Legal History* (Winter/Spring 1988).

Clinton, Robert N., and Margaret Tobey Hotopp. "Judicial Enforcement of the Federal Restraints on Alienation of Indian Land: The Origins of the Eastern Land Claims," vol. 31 *Maine Law Review* (1979).

Coan, C. F. "The First Stage of the Federal Indian Policy in the Pacific Northwest, 1849–1852," vol. 22 *Oregon Historical Quarterly* (March 1921).

———. "The Adoption of the Reservation Policy in Pacific Northwest, 1853–1855," vol. 23 *Oregon Historical Quarterly* (March 1922).

Collins, Cary C. "Through the Lens of Assimilation: Edwin L. Chalcraft and Chemawa Indian School," vol. 98 *Oregon Historical Quarterly* (Winter 1997–98).

Cornell, Stephen. "The Political Economy of American Indian Gaming," vol. 4 *Annual Review of Law and Social Science* (2008).

Crawford, James. "Endangered Native American Languages: What Is to Be Done, and Why?" vol. 19 *Bilingual Research Journal* (Winter 1995).

Cunningham, Glenn. "Oregon's First Salmon Canner, 'Captain' John West," vol. 54, no. 3 *Oregon Historical Quarterly* (September 1953).

Danforth, Sandra C. "Repaying Historical Debts: The Indian Claims Commission," vol. 49 *North Dakota Law Review* (1973).

Denevan, William M. "The Pristine Myth: The Landscape of the Americas in 1492," vol. 82, no. 3 *Annals of the Association of American Geographers* (September 1992).

Dixon, Roland B. "The Shasta," vol. 17, no. 5 *Bulletin of the American Museum of Natural History* (July 1907).

Dorsey, J. Owen. "Indians of Siletz Reservation, Oregon," vol. 2, no. 1 *American Anthropologist* (January 1889).

———. "The Gentile System of the Siletz Tribes," vol. 3, no. 10 *Journal of American Folklore*

(July–September 1890).

Drucker, Philip. "The Tolowa and Their Southwest Oregon Kin," vol. 34, no. 4 *University of California Publications in American Ethnology* (1937).

DuBois, Cora. "Tolowa Notes," vol. 34, no. 2 *American Anthropologist* (April–June 1932).

———. "The Wealth Concept as an Integrative Factor in Tolowa-Tututni Culture," *in Essays in Anthropology Presented to A. L. Kroeber*, edited by Robert H. Lowie. Berkeley: University of California Press, 1936.

———. "The 1870 Ghost Dance," vol. 3, no. 1 *Anthropological Records* (1939).

Dussias, Allison M. "Waging War with Words: Native Americans' Continuing Struggle against Suppression of Their Languages," vol. 60 *Ohio State Law Journal* (1999).

Evans-Campbell, Teresa. "Historical Trauma in American Indian/Native Alaska Communities: A Multilevel Framework for Exploring Impacts on Individuals, Families, and Communities," vol. 23 *Journal of Interpersonal Violence* (March 2008).

Farrand, Livingston. "Notes on the Alsea Indians of Oregon," vol. 3, no. 2 *American Anthropologist* (April–June 1901).

Farrand, Livingston, and Leo J. Frachtenberg. "Shasta and Athapascan Myths from Oregon," vol. 29, no. 109 *Journal of American Folklore* (July–September 1915).

Feldman, Orna. "Inspired by a Dream: Linguistics Grad Works to Revive the Wampanoag Language," *MIT Spectrum* (Spring 2001).

Foster, Doug. "Landless Tribes: Termination of the Klamath Reservation," vol. 1, no. 2 *Oregon Heritage* (1994).

Frazar, Thomas. "Pioneers from New England," vol. 83, no. 1 *Oregon Historical Quarterly* (Spring 1982).

Freeman, Otis W. "Hop Industry of the Pacific Coast States," vol. 12, no. 2 *Economic Geography* (April 1936).

Friedman, Howard M. "Interest on Indian Claims: Judicial Protection of the Fisc," vol. 5 *Valparaiso University Law Review* (1970).

Fromm, Pete. "Raising Minipokaiax," *Big Sky Journal* (Fall 2003).

Goodrich, Chauncey Shafter. "The Legal Status of California Indians," vol. 14 *California Law Review* (1925–1926).

Gray, Dennis J. "The Takelma and Their Athapascan Neighbors: A New Ethnographic Synthesis for the Upper Rogue River Area of Southwestern Oregon," no. 37 *University of Oregon Anthropological Papers* (1987).

Gunther, Erna. "An Analysis of the First Salmon Ceremony," vol. 28, no. 4 *American Anthropologist* (October–December 1926).

Harkin, Michael E. "Feeling and Thinking in Memory and Forgetting: Toward an Ethnohistory of the Emotions," vol. 50, no. 2 *Ethnohistory* (Spring 2003).

Harring, Sidney L. "Crow Dog's Case [*Ex parte Crow Dog*, 109 U.S. 556 (1883)]: A Chapter in the Legal History of Tribal Sovereignty," vol. 14 *American Indian Law Review* (1989).

Harris, Barbara, P. "Chinook Jargon: Arguments for a Pre-Contact Origin," vol. 29, no. 1 *Pacific Coast Philology* (September 1994).

Hermann, Binger. "Early History of Southern Oregon," vol. 19, no. 1 *Oregon Historical Society Quarterly* (March 1918).

Hertzberg, Stephen J. "The Menominee Indians: Termination to Restoration," vol. 6, no. 1 *American Indian Law Review* (1978).

Holt, Catharine. "Shasta Ethnography," vol. 3, no. 4 *University of California Anthropological Records* (1946).

Jacobs, Elizabeth D. "A Chetco Athabaskan Myth Text from Southwest Oregon," vol. 34, no. 3 *International Journal of American Linguistics* (July 1968).

Kaminitz, Marian A., Robert Kentta, and David Moses Bridges. "First Person Voice: Native Communities and Conservation Consultations at the National Museum of the American Indian," vol. 1 *Ethnographic Collections* (2005).

Kenny, Michael G. "A Place for Memory: The Interface between Individual and Collective History," vol. 41, no. 3 *Comparative Studies in Society and History* (July 1999).

Kessler, Friedrich. "Contract of Adhesion—Some Thoughts about Freedom of Contract," vol. 43 *Columbia Law Review* (1962).

Kroeber, A. L. "Games of the California Indians," vol. 22, no. 3 *American Anthropologist* (July–September 1920).

Kroeber, A. L., and E. W. Gifford. "World Renewal: A Cult System of Native Northwest California," vol. 13, no. 1 *Anthropological Records* (1949).

Kurki, Leena. "Restorative and Community Justice in the United States," vol. 27 *Crime and Justice* (2000).

LaLande, Jeffrey M. "The Indians of Southwestern Oregon: An Ethnohistorical Review," no. 6 *Anthropology Northwest* (1991).

Lomawaima, K. Tsianina. "Estelle Reel, Superintendent of Indian Schools, 1898–1910: Politics, Curriculum, and Land," vol. 35, no. 3 *Journal of American Indian Education* (May 1996).

Losey, Robert J. "Native American Vulnerability and Resiliency to Great Cascadia Earthquakes," vol. 108, no. 2 *Oregon Historical Quarterly* (Summer 2007).

Meengs, Chad C., and Robert T. Lackey. "Estimating the Size of Historical Oregon Salmon Runs," vol. 13, no. 1 *Reviews in Fisheries Science* (2005).

Meier, Bernd-Dieter. "Alternative to Imprisonment in the German Criminal Justice System" vol. 16, no. 3 *Federal Sentencing Reporter* (February 2004).

Mooney, Ralph James. "Matthew Deady and the Federal Judicial Response to Racism in the Early West," vol. 63 *Oregon Law Review* (1984).

Moss, Madonna L., and Jon M. Erlandson. "Reflections on North American Pacific Coast Prehistory," vol. 9, no. 1 *Journal of World Prehistory* (1995).

Nesmith, James W. "Reminiscences of Table Rock by Senators James W. Nesmith and General Joseph Lane," vol. 7, no. 2 *Oregon Historical Quarterly* (June 1906).

Newton, Nell Jessup. "Compensation, Reparations, and Restitution: Indian Property Claims in the United States," vol. 28 *Georgia Law Review* (Winter 1994).

Niedermeyer, Deborah. "'The True Interests of a White Population': The Alaska Indian Country Decisions of Judge Matthew P. Deady," vol. 21, no. 1 *New York University Journal of International Law and Politics* (Fall 1988).

O'Callaghan, Jerry A. "Senator Mitchell and the Oregon Land Frauds, 1905," vol. 21, no. 3 *Pacific Historical Review* (1952).

Pace, Julie A., ed. "Symposium: The Native American Graves Protection and Repatriation Act of 1990 and State Repatriation-related Legislation," vol. 24 *Arizona State Law Journal* (Spring 1992).

Peters, Robert N. "The 'First' Oregon Code: Another Look at Deady's Role," vol. 82, no. 4 *Oregon Historical Quarterly* (Winter 1981).

Quinn, Ashley. "Reflections on Intergenerational Trauma: Healing as a Critical Intervention," vol. 3, no. 4 *First Peoples Child & Family Review* (2007).

Reese, Jo, and John L. Fagan. "An Early-Holocene Archaeological Site in Oregon's Willamette

Valley," vol. 14 *Current Research in the Pleistocene* (1997).

Reid, John Philip. "Principles of Vengeance: Fur Trappers, Indians, and Retaliation for Homicide in the Transboundary North American West," vol. 24, no. 1 *Western Historical Quarterly* (February 1993).

Sackett, Lee. "The Siletz Indian Shaker Church," *Pacific Northwest Quarterly* (July 1973).

Sapir, Edward. "Notes on the Takelma Indians of Southwestern Oregon," vol. 9, no. 2 *American Anthropologist* (April–June 1907).

———. "Takelma Texts," vol. 2, no. 1 *Anthropological Publications of the University Museum* (1909).

Sargent, Alice Applegate. "A Sketch of the Rogue River Valley and the Southern Oregon History," vol. 22, no. 1 *Oregon Historical Quarterly* (March 1921).

Schumacher, Paul. "Researches in the Kjökkenmöddings and Graves of a Former Population of the Coast of Oregon," vol. 3, no. 1 *Bulletin of the U.S. Geological and Geographical Survey of the Territories* (January 1877).

Schwartz, E. A. "Sick Hearts: Indian Removal on the Oregon Coast, 1875–1881," vol. 92 *Oregon Historical Quarterly* (Fall 1991).

Scott, Leslie M. "Gold Brings Immigration, Civilization Soon Follows," vol. 2, no. 7 *Historical Gazette* (1993).

Spaid, Stanley S. "The Later Life and Activities of General Joel Palmer," vol. 55, no. 4 *Oregon Historical Quarterly* (December 1954).

Thornton, Russell. "Social Organization and the Demographic Survival of the Tolowa," vol. 31, no. 3 *Ethnohistory* (Summer 1984).

Trope, Jack F., and Walter R. Echo-Hawk. "The Native American Graves Protection and Repatriation Act: Background and Legislative History," vol. 24 *Arizona State Law Journal* (Spring 1992).

Van Dyke, Walter. "Early Days in Klamath," vol. 18, no. 104 *Overland Monthly and Out West Magazine* (August 1891).

Washburn, Kevin K. "Recurring Problems in Indian Gaming," vol. 1 *Wyoming Law Review* (2001).

———. "Federal Law, State Policy, and Indian Gaming," vol. 4 *Nevada Law Journal* (Winter 2003/2004).

Waterman, T. T. "The Village Site in Tolowa and Neighboring Areas in Northwestern California," vol. 17, no. 4 *American Anthropologist* (October–December 1925).

Watkins, Arthur V. "Termination of Federal Supervision: The Removal of Restrictions Over Indian Property and Person," vol. 311 *Annals of the American Academy of Political and Social Science* (May 1957).

West, W. Richard. "A Song Made Visible," vol. 83, no. 5 *Museum News* (September/October 2004).

White, John R. "Barmecide Revisited: The Gratuitous Offset in Indian Claims Cases," vol. 25, no. 2 *Ethnohistory* (Spring 1978).

Wilkinson, Charles F., and Eric R. Biggs. "The Evolution of the Termination Policy," vol. 5 *American Indian Law Review* (1977).

Wilson, Dean Frank T. "Interview with Dillon S. Meyer, Commissioner of Indian Affairs," vol. 7, no. 2 *Journal of Religious Thought* (Spring/Summer 1950).

Interviews

Jeffery Applen, June Austin, Ed Ben, Loren Bommelyn, Brenda Bremner, Gladys Bolton, Dino Butler, Jennifer Butler, Lillie Butler, Reggie Butler, Henry Cagey, Lou Carey, Jeff Classen, Eva Clayton, Eddie Collins, Jessie Davis, William "Bill" DePoe, Rebecca Dobkins, Pete Downey, Art Fisher, Dolly Fisher, Joan Bensell Fisher, Judge Calvin Gantenbein, Sister Francella Griggs, Kathryn Harrison, Joseph Hostler, Margot Hudson, Don Ivy, Jane John, Geneva Johnson, Lori Johnson, Katy Kaady, Robert Kentta, Jim Kikumoto, Walt Klamath, Kelly LaChance, Louis LaChance, Bud Lane, Cheryl Lane, Wanda Melton, Jo Anne Miller, Tami Miner, Woody Muschamp, George Nagel, Bonnie Petersen, Tom Picciano, Delores Pigsley, Agnes Pilgrim, Angela Ramirez, Selene Relatos, Tina Retasket, Joyce Retherford, Kathy Kentta Robinson, Emma Russell, Terry Russell, Frank Simmons, LaVera Simmons, Stanley Speaks, Kay Steele, Bob Tom, Gilbert Towner, Shirley Walker, Sylvia Walker, Stan van de Wetering, Rebecca Williams, Janne Underinner, Kathleen Van Pelt, Cynthia Viles, John Volkman, Janet Wickland, and Hiroto Zakoji.

Government Documents

Treaty with Great Britain ("in regard to limits westward of the Rocky Mountains"), June 15, 1846, 8 Stat. 869 (1846).

Treaty with the Navaho, September 9, 1849, 9 Stat. 974 (1850).

Treaty with the Utah, December 30, 1849, 9 Stat. 984 (1850).

Treaty with the Apache, July 1, 1852, 10 Stat. 979 (1853).

Treaty with the Rogue River, articles 2–6, September 10, 1853, 10 Stat. 1018 (1854).

Treaty with the Umpqua—Cow Creek Band, article 2, September 19, 1853, 10 Stat. 1027 (1854).

Treaty with the Rogue River, article 2, November 15, 1854, 10 Stat. 1119 (1855).

Treaty with the Chasta, Etc., November 18, 1854, 10 Stat. 1122 (1855).

Treaty with the Umpqua and Kalapuya, November 29, 1854, 10 Stat. 1125 (1855).

Treaty with the Kalapuya, Etc., January 22, 1855, 10 Stat. 1143 (1855).

Treaty with the Walla Walla, Cayuse, Etc., June 9, 1855, 12 Stat. 945 (1859).

Treaty with the Yakima, June 9, 1855, 12 Stat. 951 (1859).

Treaty with the Nez Percé, June 11, 1855, 12 Stat. 957 (1859).

Treaty with the Tribes of Middle Oregon, June 25, 1855, 12 Stat. 963 (1859).

Treaty of Fort Laramie with Sioux and Other Tribes, September 17, 1851, 11 Stat. 749 (1859).

Treaty with the Molala, December 21, 1855, 12 Stat. 981 (1859).

FEDERAL STATUTES

Trade and Intercourse Act of 1790, ch. 33, July 22, 1790, 1 Stat. 137 (1790).

Trade and Intercourse Act, ch. 13, March 30, 1802, 2 Stat. 139 (1802).

Indian Removal Act of 1830, ch. 148, May 28, 1830, 4 Stat. 411 (1830) (not codified).

Trade and Intercourse Act, ch. 161, June 30, 1834, 4 Stat. 729 (1834) (codified as amended at 25 U.S.C. §177 [2006]).

Law of July 5, 1843, art. 12, Oregon Territory Laws (codified in Statutes of Oregon, ch. 4, title 1, §6 [3] [Oregon: Asahel Bush, Public Printer, 1853]).

Act to Establish the Territorial Government of Oregon, ch. 177, August 14, 1848, 9 Stat. 323 (1848) (not codified).

Donation Land Act, ch. 76, September 27, 1850, 9 Stat. 496 (1850) (not codified).

BIBLIOGRAPHY

Indian Treaty Act, ch. 16, June 5, 1850, 9 Stat. 437 (1850) (not codified).

Oregon Indian Act, ch. 16, June 5, 1850, 9 Stat. 437 (1850) (not codified).

S. 142, 36th Congress, 1st Session (1860).

Act of March 3 1863, ch. 92, §9, 12 Stat. 765 (1863)

Indian Appropriation Act, ch. 132, March 3, 1875, 18 Stat. 420 (1875) (not codified).

General Allotment Act, ch. 119, February 8, 1887, 24 Stat. 388 (1887) (codified as amended at 25 U.S.C. §§331-358 [2000]).

Indian Appropriation Act of 1894, ch. 290, August 15, 1894, 28 Stat. 286 (1894) (not codified).

Act of May 27, 1902, ch. 888, 32 Stat. 275 (1902) (codified at 25 U.S.C. §379 [2000]).

The Burke Act, ch. 2348, May 8, 1906, 34 Stat. 182 (1906) (codified at 25 U.S.C. § 349 [2000]).

Act of May 13, 1910, ch. 233, 36 Stat. 367 (1910) (not codified).

Act of June 30, 1919, ch. 4, §27, 41 Stat. 34 (codified at 43 U.S.C. §150 [2000]).

Special Act of Congress to confer jurisdiction on the Court of Claims to hear Coos, Lower Umpqua, and Siuslaw Claims against the United States, February 23, 1929, 45 Stat. 1256 (1929) (not codified) (amended by Act of June 14, 1932, 47 Stat. 307 [1932]).

Indian Reorganization Act, Pub. L. No. 73-383, June 18, 1934, 48 Stat. 984-988 (1934) (codified at 25 U.S.C. §§461-479 [2000]).

Indian Claims Commission Act, Pub. L. No. 79-726, August 13, 1946, 60 Stat. 1049 (1946) (codified at 25 U.S.C. §70a [2000]).

H. Con. Res. 108, August 1, 1953, 67 Stat. B132 (1953) (not codified).

Pub. L. No. 588, ch. 733, §8, August 13, 1954, 88 Stat. 724, 726 (1954) (Siletz Termination Act).

H.R. 15604, 93d Congress, 2d Session (1974) (Siletz Restoration Bill).

Indian Self-Determination Act, Pub. L. No. 93-638, January 4, 1975, 88 Stat. 2203 (1975) (codified at 25 U.S.C. §§450-458bbb-2 [2000]).

Siletz Indian Tribe Restoration Act, Pub. L. No. 95-195, November 18, 1977, 91 Stat. 1415 (1977) (codified at 25 U.S.C. §711e(b) [2001]).

H.R. 7267, 96th Congress, 2d Session (1980) (bill to establish reservation, AuCoin).

An Act to Establish a Reservation for the Confederated Tribes of Siletz Indians of Oregon, Pub. L. No. 96-340, September 4, 1980, 94 Stat. 1072 (1981) (not codified, but set out at 25 U.S.C. §711e [2000]).

The Maine Indian Claims Settlement Act, Pub. L. No. 96-420, § 2, October 10, 1980, 94 Stat. 1785 (1980) (codified at 25 U.S.C. §§1721-1735 [2000]).

Indian Gaming Regulatory Act, Pub. L. No. 100-497, October 17, 1988 (codified at 25 U.S.C. §2701[5]).

National Museum of the American Indian Act of 1989, Pub. L. No. 101-185, November 28, 1989, 103 Stat. 1336 (1989) (codified as amended at 20 U.S.C. §§80q–8q-15 [2000]).

Native American Languages Act of 1990, Pub. L. No. 101-477, October 30, 1990, 104 Stat. 1156 (1990) (codified as amended at 25 U.S.C. §§2901-2906 [2000]).

Native American Graves Protection and Repatriation Act of 1990, Pub. L. No. 101-601, November 16, 1990, 104 Stat. 3048 (1990) (codified at 25 U.S.C. §§3001-3013 [2000]).

Pub. L. No. 103-435, November 2, 1994, 108 Stat. 4566 (1994) (to take land into trust for Siletz).

Esther Martinez Native American Languages Preservation Act of 2006. P.L. 109-394, December 14, 2006, 120 Stat. 2705.

Federal Court Cases

U.S. SUPREME COURT

Alcea Band of Tillamooks v. United States, 329 U.S. 40 (1946); 59 F. Supp. 934 (Ct. Cl. 1945).

Antoine v. Washington, 420 U.S. 194 (1975).

Arizona v. California, 373 U.S. 546 (1963).

Cherokee Nation v. Georgia, 30 U.S. (5 Pet.) 1, 15, 19 (1831).

City of Sherrill v. Oneida Indian Nation, 544 U.S. 197 (2005).

Coos Bay, Lower Umpqua, and Siuslaw Indian Tribes v. United States, 306 U.S. 653 (1939).

County of Oneida v. Oneida Indian Nation, 470 U.S. 226 (1985).

Cramer v. United States, 261 U.S. 219 (1923).

Johnson v. McIntosh, 21 U.S. 543 (1823).

Lane v. Pueblo of Santa Rosa, 249 U.S. 110 (1919).

Lone Wolf v. Hitchcock, 187 U.S. 553 (1903).

Loving v. Virginia, 388 U.S. 1 (1967).

McClanahan v. Arizona State Tax Commission, 411 U.S. 164 (1973).

Minnesota v. Mille Lacs Band of Chippewa Indians, 526 U.S. 172 (1999).

Morton v. Mancari, 417 U.S. 535 (1974).

Santa Clara Pueblo v. Martinez, 436 U.S. 49 (1978).

Sioux Tribe v. United States, 316 U.S. 317 (1942).

Talton v. Mayes, 163 U.S. 376 (1896).

Tee-Hit-Ton Indians v. United States, 348 U.S. 272 (1955).

United States v. Alcea Band of Tillamooks, 341 U.S. 48 (1951).

United States v. Dann, 470 U.S. 39 (1985).

United States v. Dion, 476 U.S. 734 (1986).

United States v. Lara, 541 U.S. 193 (2004).

United States v. Shoshone Tribe, 304 U.S. 111 (1938).

United States v. Wheeler, 435 U.S. 313 (1978).

Washington v. Washington State Commercial Passenger Fishing Vessel Assoc., 443 U.S. 658 (1979).

Worcester v. Georgia, 31 U.S. 515 (1832).

U.S. COURT OF APPEALS

Confederated Tribes of Siletz Indians v. United States, 110 F.3d 688 (9th Cir. 1997).

Joint Tribal Council of the Passamaquoddy Tribe v. Morton, 528 F.2d 370 (1st Cir. 1975).

United States v. Dann, 865 F.2d 1528 (9th Cir. 1989).

United States v. Washington, 520 F.2d 676 (9th Cir. 1975).

U.S. COURT OF CLAIMS

Alcea Band of Tillamooks v. United States, 119 Ct. Cl. 835 (Ct. Cl. 1951).

Coos Bay, Lower Umpqua, and Siuslaw Indians v. United States, 87 Ct. Cl. 143 (Ct. Cl. 1938).

Rogue River Tribe of Indians v. United States, 64 F. Supp. 339 (Ct. Cl. 1946); 89 F. Supp. 798 (Ct. Cl. 1950), cert. denied 341 U.S. 902 (1951).

U.S. DISTRICT COURTS

Confederated Tribes of Siletz Indians v. Oregon, Civ. No. 80-433 (D. Or. 1980).

Confederated Tribes of Siletz Indians v. United States, 841 F. Supp. 1479 (D. Or. 1994)

Duncan v. Andrus, 517 F. Supp. 1 (N.D. Cal. 1977).

Smith v. United States, 515 F. Supp. 56 (N.D. Cal. 1978).
Table Bluff Band of Indians v. Andrus, 532 F. Supp. 255 (N.D. Cal. 1981).
United States v. Washington, 384 F. Supp. 312 (W.D. Wash. 1974).

Congressional Documents

JOINT CONGRESSIONAL REPORTS

Senate Joint Memorial, concurred in by House of Representatives, of the Legislative Assembly of the State of Oregon, "Praying that the Siletz Indian reservation in said State may be vacated and the Indians removed therefrom," 41st Congress, 3d Session, p. 1 (January 9, 1871) (Washington, D.C.: Government Printing Office, 1871).

JOINT HEARINGS OF THE SENATE AND HOUSE

Joint Hearings before the Senate and House Committees on Interior and Insular Affairs, Subcommittees on Indian Affairs, "On S. 2760 and H.R. 7674: Termination of Federal Supervision over Certain Tribes of Indians," 83d Congress, 2d Session, pt. 1 (Utah) (February 15, 1954) (Washington, D.C.: Government Printing Office, 1954).

Joint Hearings before the Senate and House Committees on Interior and Insular Affairs, Subcommittees on Indian Affairs, "On S. 2744, H.R. 6282, and H.R. 6547: Termination of Federal Supervision over Certain Tribes of Indians," 83d Congress, 2d Session, pt. 2 (Texas) (February 16, 1954) (Washington, D.C.: Government Printing Office, 1954).

Joint Hearings before the Senate and House Committees on Interior and Insular Affairs, Subcommittees on Indian Affairs, "On S. 2746 and H.R. 7317: Termination of Federal Supervision over Certain Tribes of Indians," 83d Congress, 2d Session, pt. 3 (Western Oregon), p. 139 (February 17, 1954) (Washington, D.C.: Government Printing Office, 1954).

SENATE REPORTS

S.R. No. 305 to Accompany S. 4713, "Sale of Certain Lands on Siletz Reservation, Oregon," 60th Congress, 1st Session, pp. 1–2 (February 27, 1908) (Washington, D.C.: Government Printing Office, 1908).

S.R. No. 1361, "Conferring Jurisdiction upon Court of Claims to Hear Claims of Certain Oregon Indians," 71st Congress, 3d Session, pp. 2–3 (Washington, D.C.: Government Printing Office, 1931).

S.R. No. 430, "Court of Claims to Hear and Determine Claims of Certain Bands, Nations, or Tribes of Indians Residing in the State of Oregon," 72d Congress, 1st Session, p. 2 (Washington, D.C.: Government Printing Office, 1932).

S.R. No. 310, Senate Committee on Indian Affairs, "Survey of Conditions Among the Indians of the United States: Analysis of the Statement of the Commissioner of Indian Affairs in Justification of Appropriations for 1944, and the Liquidation of the Indian Bureau," 78th Congress, 1st Session (June 11, 1943) (Washington, D.C.: Government Printing Office, 1943).

S.R. No. 794 to Accompany House Concurrent Resolution 108, "Expressing the Sense of Congress that Certain Tribes of Indians Should be Freed from Federal Supervision," 83d Congress, 1st Session (Washington, D.C.: Government Printing Office, 1953).

S.R. No. 1325 to Accompany S. 2746, "Termination of Federal Supervision over Property of Certain Indians in Western Oregon," 83d Congress, 2d Session, p. 13 (Washington, D.C.: Government Printing Office, 1954).

Senate Committee on Labor and Public Welfare, "The Education of American Indians," 91st Congress, 1st Session, vol. 4, pp. 673–816 (Washington, D.C.: Government Printing Office, 1970).

S.R. No. 95-386, "Siletz Indian Tribe Restoration Act," 95th Congress, 1st Session (Washington, D.C.: Government Printing Office, 1977).

SENATE DOCUMENTS

S.D. No. 1, 1850 Commissioner Report, 31st Congress, 2d Session, p. 36.

S.D. No. 1, 1853 Commissioner Report, 31st Congress, 2d Session, p. 36.

S.D. No. 1, "Report of the Commissioner of Indian Affairs," 32d Congress, 2d Session, vol. 1, p. 293 (Washington, D.C.: Government Printing Office, 1851).

S.D. No. 1, 33d Congress, 1st Session, vol. 1, part 1, p. 449 (Washington: Robert Armstrong, Printer, 1853).

S.D. No. 66, Report of the Secretary of War, 34th Congress, 1st Session, pp. 37–39 (1856).

S.D. No. 11, 1857 Commissioner Report, 35th Congress, 1st Session (Washington, D.C.: William A. Harris, 1858).

S.D. No. 11, 1858 Commissioner Report, 35th Congress, 1st Session.

S.D. No. 1, 1858 Commissioner Report, 35th Congress, 2d Session (Washington, D.C.: William A. Harris, 1858).

S.D. No. 2, 1859 Commissioner Report, 36th Congress, 1st Session.

Congressional Globe, vol. 29, no. 94, April 4, 1860, 36th Congress, 1st Session, p. 1491 (Washington, D.C.: John C. Rives, 1860).

S.D. No. 59, "Communication from C.S. Drew ... giving an account of the origin and early prosecution of the Indian war in Oregon," 36th Congress, 1st Session, pp. 3–8 (May 9, 1860) (Washington, D.C.: Government Printing Office, 1860).

S.D. No. 39, 52d Congress, 2d Session (February 1, 1893) (Washington, D.C.: Government Printing Office, 1893).

S.D. No. 25, "Letter from the Secretary of the Interior, transmitting copies of treaties between the United States and certain Indians in Oregon, in response to Senate resolution of September 2, 1893," 53d Congress, 1st Session, p. 3 (Washington, D.C.: Government Printing Office, 1894).

Senate Committee on Labor and Public Welfare, "The Education of American Indians," 91st Congress, 1st Session, vol. 4, pp. 673–816 (Washington, D.C.: Government Printing Office, 1970).

SENATE HEARINGS

Hearings before a Subcommittee of the Senate Committee on Indian Affairs, "Survey of Conditions of the Indians in the United States: On S. Res. 79, 308, 263, and 416," 71st Congress, 3d Session, pt. 21, p. 11722 (Washington, D.C.: Government Printing Office, 1932).

Senate Committee on Indian Affairs, "Repeal of the So-Called Wheeler-Howard Act," S. Report No. 1047, 76th Congress, 1st Session, pp. 3–4 (Washington, D.C.: Government Printing Office, 1939).

Hearings before the Senate Committee on Civil Service, "S. Res. 41: A Resolution to Investigate Certain Matters Relating to Officers and Employees of the Federal Government," 80th Congress, 1st Session, pt. 3, p. 546 (February 8, 1947) (Washington, D.C.: Government Printing Office, 1947).

Senate Committee on Interior and Insular Affairs, Jerry A. O'Callaghan, "The Disposition of the Public Domain in Oregon," 86th Congress, 2d Session, p. 4 (Washington, D.C.: Government Printing Office, 1960).

Hearings before the Senate Committee on Interior and Insular Affairs, Subcommittee on Indian Affairs, "Siletz Restoration Act: On S. 2801," 94th Congress, 2d Session, March 30–31, 1976 (Washington, D.C.: Government Printing Office, 1976).

HOUSE REPORTS

H.R. No. 1098 to Accompany S. 539, "Sale of Certain Lands on Siletz Indian Reservation," 61st Congress, 2d Session, p. 1 (April 22, 1910) (Washington, D.C.: Government Printing Office, 1910).

H.R. No. 2209, "Authorizing Adjudication of Claims of the Coos Bay, Lower Umpqua, and Siuslaw Tribes of Indians of Oregon," 70th Congress, 2d Session, p. 3 (Washington, D.C.: Government Printing Office, 1929).

H.R. No. 2758, "Court of Claims to Adjudicate Claims of Certain Bands of Indians in Oregon," 71st Congress, 3d Session, pp. 2–3 (Washington, D.C.: Government Printing Office, 1931).

H.R. No. 841 to Accompany House Concurrent Resolution 108, "Expressing the Sense of Congress that Certain Tribes of Indians Should be Freed from Federal Supervision," 83d Congress, 1st Session (Washington, D.C.: Government Printing Office, 1953).

H.R. No. 2492 to Accompany S. 2746, "Termination of Federal Supervision over Property of Certain Indians in Western Oregon," 83d Congress, 2d Session, p. 9 (Washington, D.C.: Government Printing Office, 1954).

H.R. No. 95-623, "Restoring the Confederated Tribes of Siletz Indian of Oregon as a Federally Recognized Sovereign Indian Tribe," 95th Congress, 1st Session (Washington, D.C.: Government Printing Office, 1977).

HOUSE DOCUMENTS

H.D. No. 2, "Message from the President of the United States to the Two Houses of Congress," 32d Congress, 1st Session, pp. 145–46 (Washington, D.C.: A. Boyd Hamilton, 1851).

H.D. No. 1, 1852 Commissioner Report, 32d Congress, 2d Session, pp. 455–58.

H.D. No. 1, 1854 Commissioner Report, 33d Congress, 2d Session, pt. 1, p. 477 (Washington, D.C.: Government Printing Office, 1854).

H.D. No. 93, "Indian Hostilities in Oregon and Washington," 34th Congress, 1st Session, pp. 23–24 (1856).

H.D. No. 2, 1857 Commissioner Report, 35th Congress, 1st Session.

H.D. No. 39, 35th Congress, 1st Session (Nov. 17, 1857) (U.S. Department of the Interior, "Report on the condition of the Indian reservations in the Territories of Oregon and Washington, from J. Ross Browne, special agent") (Washington, D.C.: Government Printing Office, 1858).

H.D. No. 2, 1859 Commissioner Report, 35th Congress, 2d Session, p. 568.

H.D. No. 1, 1862 Commissioner Report, 37th Congress, 3d Session.

H.D. No. 1, 1863 Commissioner Report, 38th Congress, 1st Session.

H.D. No. 1, 1864 Commissioner Report, 38th Congress, 2d Session.

H.D. No. 1, 1865 Commissioner Report, 39th Congress, 1st Session.

H.D. No. 1, 1866 Commissioner Report, 39th Congress, 2nd Session.

H.D. No. 1, 1867 Commissioner Report, 40th Congress, 2d Session.

H.D. No. 1, Pt. 4, 1870 Commissioner Report, 41st Congress, 3d Session.

H.D. No. 1, Pt. 5, 1872 Commissioner Report, 42d Congress, 3d Session, p. 753 (Washington, D.C.: Government Printing Office, 1872).

H.D. No. 1, Pt. 5, 1873 Commissioner Report, 43d Congress, 1st Session.

H.D. No. 1, Pt. 5, 1874 Commissioner Report, 43d Congress, 2d Session.

H.D. No. 1, Pt. 5, 1875 Commissioner Report, 44th Congress, 1st Session.

H.D. No. 1, Pt. 5, 1876 Commissioner Report, 44th Congress, 2d Session.

H.D. No. 1, Pt. 5, 1877 Commissioner Report, 45th Congress, 2d Session.

H.D. No. 1, Pt. 5, 1883 Commissioner Report, 48th Congress, 1st Session.

H.D. No. 1, Pt. 5, 1894 Commissioner Report, 53d Congress, 3d Session.

H.D. No. 5, 1895 Commissioner Report, 54th Congress, 1st Session.

H.D. No. 5, 1899 Commissioner Report, 56th Congress, 1st Session.

H.D. No. 5, 1900 Commissioner Report, 56th Congress, 2d Session.

H.D. No. 5, 1901 Commissioner Report, 57th Congress, 1st Session.

H.D. No. 5, 1902 Commissioner Report, 57th Congress, 2d Session.

H.D. No. 5, 1904 Commissioner Report, 58th Congress, 3d Session,

H.D. No. 5, 1905 Commissioner Report, 59th Congress, 1st Session.

H.D. No. 5, 1906 Commissioner Report, 59th Congress, 2d Session.

H.D. No. 1046, vol. 2, 1907 Commissioner Report, 60th Congress, 2d Session.

H.D. No. 120, vol. 2, 1911 Commissioner Report, 62d Congress, 2d Session.

H.D. No. 915, vol. 2, 1917 Commissioner Report, 65th Congress, 2d Session.

H.D. No. 409, vol. 2, 1919 Commissioner Report, 66th Congress, 2d Session.

HOUSE HEARINGS

Hearings before the Senate Committee on Interior and Insular Affairs, Subcommittee on Indian Affairs, "Siletz Restoration Act: On S. 2801," 94th Congress, 2d Session (March 30–31, 1976) (Washington, D.C.: Government Printing Office, 1976).

AGENCY REPORTS

Annual Report of Superintendent Joel Palmer, Oct. 8, 1853.

Pullen, Reg, "Overview of the Environment of Native Inhabitants of Southwestern Oregon, Late Prehistoric Era" (Bandon, OR: Report for USDA Forest Service, 1996).

U.S. Department of the Interior, Superintendent of the Census, "Population of the United States in 1860; Compiled from the Original Returns of the Eighth Census" (Washington, D.C.: Government Printing Office, 1864).

U.S. Department of the Interior, Bureau of Indian Affairs, "A Profile of the Confederated Tribes of Siletz Indians of Oregon," Report No. 264 (February 1978).

U.S. Department of the Interior, Bureau of Indian Affairs, "Siletz Indian Reservation Plan" (November 1979).

U.S. Department of the Interior, Bureau of Indian Affairs, "Notice of approval for Tribal-State compact," vol. 60, no. 55 *Federal Register*, p. 15194 (March 22, 1995).

MISCELLANEOUS

Letter from the Acting Secretary of the Interior, "Accompanying . . . a Report of Inspector E.C. Kemble in relation to the condition of the Indians of the Siletz Agency in Oregon," Senate Doc. No. 65, 43d Congress, 1st Session, p. 3 (January 7, 1874) (Washington, D.C.: Government Printing Office, 1874).

Address by Joseph Lane of March 31, 1856, *Congressional Globe*, 34th Congress, 1st Session, p. 776 (Washington, D.C.: John C. Rives, 1856).

Address by Senator Mitchell of Jan. 26, 1875, vol. 3 *Congressional Record*, 43d Congress, 2d Session, pp. 729–30 (Washington, D.C.: Government Printing Office, 1875)

Address by Senator Mitchell of Feb. 20, 1875, vol. 3 *Congressional Record*, 43d Congress, 2d Session, pp. 1528–29 (Washington, D.C.: Government Printing Office, 1875).

Address by Senator Allison of Feb. 20, 1875, vol. 3 *Congressional Record*, 43d Congress, 2d Session, p. 1529 (Washington, D.C.: Government Printing Office, 1875).

Address by Senator Sherman of Feb. 20, 1875, vol. 3 *Congressional Record*, 43d Congress, 2d Session, p. 1529 (Washington, D.C.: Government Printing Office, 1875).

Address by Senator Teller of Jan. 20, 1881, vol. 11, pt. 1 *Congressional Record*, 46th Congress, 2d Session, p. 783 (Washington, D.C.: Government Printing Office, 1881).

Address by Senator Dolph of Jan. 25, 1887, vol. 18, pt. 1 *Congressional Record*, 49th Congress, 2d Session, p. 974 (Washington, D.C.: Government Printing Office, 1887).

Letter from the Secretary of the Interior, "Transmitting a Report from the Commissioner of Indian Affairs . . . Authorizing the Issuance of Patents to the Indians of the Siletz Reservation in Oregon," Senate Doc. No. 80, 57th Congress, 1st Session, p. 3 (December 16, 1901) (Washington, D.C.: Government Printing Office, 1902).

Commission on Organization of the Executive Branch of the Government Special Task Force Report, "Social Security and Education—Indian Affairs: A Report to Congress," pp. 54–55 (Washington, D.C.: Government Printing Office, 1948).

Gates, Paul W., *History of Federal Public Land Law Development* (Washington, D.C.: Government Printing Office, 1968).

Tyler, S. Lyman, *A History of Indian Policy*, pp. 163–64 (Washington, D.C.: Government Printing Office, 1973).

Public Papers of the Presidents of the United States: Herbert Hoover, 1932–1933, p. 179 (Washington, D.C.: Government Printing Office, 1977).

Statement by Congressman Les AuCoin of August 18, 1980, vol. 126, *Congressional Record*, 96th Congress, 2d Session, p. 21764 (Washington, D.C.: Government Printing Office, 1980).

Siletz Government Documents

Constitution of the Confederated Tribes of Siletz Indians of Oregon.

Siletz Tribal Code.

COURT CASES
Duncan v. Siletz Election Board, T.C. 98-02 (Siletz Tribal Ct. March 23, 1998).

In the Matter of Delores Pigsley, T.C. 98-11 at Petition for Declaratory Action (Siletz Tribal Ct. August 1, 1998).

Duncan v. Siletz Election Board, T.C. 98-02AP (Siletz Tribal App. Ct. September 15, 1998).

SILETZ TRIBAL COUNCIL DOCUMENTS
Tribal Council, Confederated Tribes of Siletz Indians, Resolution of October 7, 1951.

Tribal Council Special Meeting Minutes, Siletz, Oregon, June 24, 1951.

Tribal Council Regular Meeting Minutes, Siletz, Oregon, September 30, 1951.

Tribal Council Special Meeting Minutes, Siletz, Oregon, October 7, 1951.

Tribal Council Regular Meeting Minutes, Siletz, Oregon, November 3, 1951.

Tribal Council Meeting Minutes, Siletz, Oregon, July 19–20, 1997.
Tribal Council Meeting Minutes, Siletz, Oregon, August 16–17, 1997.
Special Tribal Council Meeting Minutes, Lincoln City, Oregon, August 29, 1997.
Special Tribal Council Meeting Minutes, Siletz, Oregon, February 7, 1998.
Emergency Tribal Council Meeting Minutes, Siletz, Oregon, August 3, 1998.
Special Tribal Council Meeting Minutes, Siletz, Oregon, August 3, 1998.

SILETZ GENERAL COUNCIL DOCUMENTS
General Council Meeting Minutes, Siletz, Oregon, August, 2, 1997.
General Council Meeting Minutes, Siletz, Oregon, August 1, 1998.

SILETZ TRIBE REPORTS
Annual Reports, 1992, 2003–2007.

State Government Documents

STATUTES
House Bill No. 664, An Act Relating to Marriages, Or. Laws 1951, ch. 455, § 2 (repealing 23-1010).

STATE SUPREME COURT CASE
In Re Paquet's Estate, 200 P. 911 (Or. 1921).

STATE AGENCY REPORTS
Anderson, E. William, Micahel M. Borman, and William C. Krueger. "The Ecological Provinces of Oregon: A Treatise on the Basic Ecological Geography of the State." Oregon Agricultural Experiment Station, Oregon State University, 1998.
"Biennial Report and Opinions of Attorney-General of the State of Oregon." Salem, OR: The Attorney General, 1908–68.
Northwest Power Planning Council, "Compilation of Information on Salmon and Steelhead Losses in the Columbia River Basin," pp. 66–76, March 1986.
Oregon Department of Forestry, "Northwest Oregon State Forests Management Plan," January 2001.
Oregon Department of Forestry, "Oregon's Timber Harvests: 1849–2004." 2005.

MISCELLANEOUS
Meriam, Lewis, et al. *The Problem of Indian Administration*. Baltimore, MD: Johns Hopkins University, Institute for Government Research, 1928.

Siletz Archives

TRANSCRIPTS OF NARA LETTERS
J. Palmer letter to G. Manypenny (October 8, 1853).
S. Culver, Indian agent, letter to J. Palmer (June 1, 1854), M2 Roll 4, Doc. 44.
G. Manypenny letter to J. Palmer (Aug. 15, 1854), M2 Roll 5, Doc. 7.
J. Palmer letter to G. Manypenny (Dec. 28, 1854), M2 Roll 5, Doc. 22.
J. Palmer letter to G. Manypenny (Dec. 29, 1854), M2 Roll 5, Doc. 23.
J. Palmer letter to G. Manypenny (Jan. 23, 1855), M2 Roll 5, Doc. 27.

J. Palmer letter to G. Manypenny (April 17, 1855), M2 Roll 5, Doc. 48 and attachments.

J. Palmer letter to O. Waterman, editor of the *Oregon Weekly Times* (April 17, 1855), M2 Roll 5, Doc. 48.

J. Palmer letter to G. Ambrose, Indian agent (July 6, 1855), M2 Roll 5, Doc. 65.

J. Palmer letter to G. Manypenny (July 10, 1855), M2 Roll 5, Doc. 68.

J. Palmer letter to E. Drew, Indian agent (July 13, 1855), M2 Roll 5, Doc. 71.

C. Taylor letter to S. Snow and Co. (July 20, 1855), M2 Roll 5, Doc. 76.

J. Palmer letter to G. Manypenny (Oct. 3, 1855), M2 Roll 5, Doc. 92.

J. Palmer, Order (Oct. 13, 1855), M2 Roll 5, Doc. 97.

G. Ambrose, Indian agent, letter to J. Palmer (Oct. 20, 1855), M2 Roll 5, Doc. 104.

J. Palmer letter to G. Manypenny (Nov. 12, 1855), M2 Roll 5, Doc. 107.

J. Palmer, superintendent of Indian Affairs for Oregon, letter to J. Wool, major general of the Pacific Division (Dec. 6, 1855), M2 Roll 5, Doc. 123.

G. Ambrose, Indian agent, letter to J. Palmer (Dec. 2, 1855), M2 Roll 5, Doc. 128.

J. Palmer letter to G. Manypenny (Jan. 6, 1856), M2 Roll 6, Doc. 7.

J. Palmer letter to G. Manypenny (June 23, 1856), M2 Roll 6, Doc. 45.

J. Palmer letter to R. Buchanan (June 24, 1856), M2 Roll 6, Doc. 46.

J. Palmer letter to G. Manypenny (July 3, 1856), M2 Roll 6, Doc. 49.

J. Palmer letter to C. Walker, Indian agent (July 13, 1856), M2 Roll 6, Doc. 53.

J. Palmer letter to W. Raymond, Indian agent (July, 13, 1856), M2 Roll 6, Doc. 54.

J. Palmer letter to A. Smith, captain (July 14, 1856), M2 Roll 6, Doc 56.

J. Palmer letter to J. Day (July 14, 1856), M2 Roll 6, Doc. 58.

J. Palmer transcript to G. Manypenny (July 18, 1856), M2 Roll 6, Doc. 59.

J. Palmer letter to D. Jones, captain (July 28, 1856), M2 Roll 6, Doc. 60.

F. Jones letter to A. Hedges (Aug. 2, 1856), M2 Roll 6, Doc. 65.

A. Hedges, superintendent of Indian Affairs for Oregon, letter to G. Manypenny, commissioner of Indian Affairs (Aug. 22, 1856), M2 Roll 6, Doc. 69.

A. Hedges letter to W. Tichenor, captain and special agent (Sept. 25, 1856), M2 Roll 6, Doc. 78.

A. Hedges letter to G. Manypenny (Dec. 19, 1856), M2 Roll 6, Doc. 90.

A. Hedges letter to G. Manypenny (Feb. 24, 1857), M2 Roll 6, Doc. 97.

A. Hedges letter to G. Manypenny (March 17, 1857), M2 Roll 6, Doc. 102.

J. Nesmith letter to G. Manypenny (May 5, 1857), M2 Roll 6, Doc. 103.

J. Nesmith letter to J. Denver (May 5, 1857), M2 Roll 6, Doc. 103.

A. Hedges letter to G. Manypenny (Nov. 11, 1857), M2 Roll 6, Doc. 116.

J. Palmer letter to G. Manypenny, commissioner of Indian Affairs (Sept. 11, 1854), M2 Roll 7, Doc. 9.

J. Nesmith letter to W. Machall, U.S. adjutant general (April 23, 1858), M2 Roll 7, Doc. 39.

J. Nesmith letter to R. Metcalfe (April 26, 1858), M2 Roll 7, Doc. 39.

J. Nesmith letter to J. Scott, Major (July 16, 1858), M2 Roll 7, Doc 42.

E. Geary letter to A. Greenwood, Commissioner of Indian Affairs (Oct. 10, 1859), M2 Roll 8, Doc. 7.

E. Geary letter to R. Metcalfe (Oct. 24, 1859), M2 Roll 8, Doc. 8

W. Rector letter to Brig. Gen. Wright, Pacific Department (May 7, 1862), M2 Roll 9, Doc. 22.

J. Huntington letter to B. Alvord (March 25, 1864), M2 Roll 9, Doc. 90.

J. Huntington letter to B. Simpson (Nov. 17, 1864), M2 Roll 9, Doc. 90.

J. Palmer, superintendent of Indian Affairs for Oregon, letter to G. Manypenny, commissioner of Indian Affairs (June 23, 1853), M2 Roll 11, Doc. 87.

N. Ford letter to G. Ambrose, Indian agent (Dec. 18, 1855), M2 Roll14, Doc. 1.

G. Ambrose letter to J. Palmer (Jan. 31, 1856), M2 Roll 14, Doc. 8.

G. Ambrose letter to J. Palmer (Feb. 24, 1856), M2 Roll 14, Doc 12.

G. Ambrose letter to J. Palmer (Feb. 27, 1856), M2 Roll 14, Doc. 13.

G. Ambrose, "Journal of the removal of the Rogue River Tribe of Indians, etc.," M2 Roll 14, Doc 15.

R. Buchanan letter to J. Palmer (July 4, 1856), M2 Roll 14, Doc. 19.

J. Rinearson, Indian agent, letter to J. Palmer (July 30, 1856), M2 Roll 14, Doc. 20.

A. Rogers and S. Mann letter to E. Drew (July 12, 1856), M2 Roll 14, Doc. 23.

R. Metcalfe letter to A. Hedges (Dec. 13, 1856), M2 Roll 14, Doc. 29.

R. Metcalfe, "Census of Indians engaged in the late war; now under my charge" (Dec. 24, 1856), M2 Roll 14, Doc. 29.

G. Davidson letter to A. Hedges (Jan. 15, 1857), M2 Roll 15, Doc. 3.

P. Sheridan, lieutenant, letter to C. Augur, captain (April 13, 1857), M2 Roll 15, Doc. 11.

R. Metcalfe letter to J. Nesmith (Oct. 13, 1857), M2 Roll 15, Doc. 24.

P. Ruffner letter to J. Nesmith (March 21, 1858), M2 Roll 16, Doc. 4.

W. Otto, acting secretary of the Interior, letter to J. Huntington (Aug. 31, 1864), M2 Roll 21, Doc. 15.

J. Nesmith, U.S. senator, letter to J. Huntington (Dec. 6, 1865), M2 Roll 22, Doc. 6.

J. Nesmith letter to J. Huntington (Dec. 27, 1865), M2 Roll 22, Doc. 9.

R. Metcalfe, Indian agent, "Census List of Indians, Coast Reservation, Selets Ind. Agency" (Sept. 22, 1857), M2 Roll 30, Doc. 1.

B. Simpson letter to Winant & Co. (Dec. 1, 1863), M2 Roll 30, Doc. 25.

E. Smith letter to G. Litchfield, Indian agent (March 30, 1875), M21 Roll 134, Doc. 1.

E. Smith letter to J. Fairchild (March 30, 1875), M21 Roll 134, Doc. 2.

R. Metcalfe, "Census on the Coast Station" (Aug. 20, 1856), M234 Roll 609, Doc. 2.

A. Hedges letter to G. Manypenny (Nov. 7, 1856), M234 Roll 609, Doc. 8.

W. Rector, superintendent of Indian Affairs for Oregon, letter to W. Dole, commissioner of Indian Affairs (June 10, 1862), M234 Roll 613, Doc. 5, p. 3.

J. Huntington letter to W. Dole, commissioner of Indian Affairs (Nov. 21, 1863), M234 Roll 613, Doc. 7.

J. Huntington notice to public (Nov. 20, 1864), M234 Roll 613, Doc. 8.

J. Fairchild, Indian agent, letter to E. Smith (Sept. 29, 1873), M234 Roll 617, Doc. 4.

T. Odeneal, superintendent of Indian Affairs for Oregon, letter to E. Smith, commissioner of Indian Affairs (May 30, 1873), M234 Roll 618, Doc. 2.

J. Mitchell, senator, letter to C. Delano, secretary of the Interior (Jan. 2, 1874), M234 Roll 619, Doc. 1.

J. Fairchild letter to E. Smith (Jan. 28, 1874), M234 Roll 619, Doc. 3.

J. Fairchild letter to E. Smith (Dec. 4, 1874), M234 Roll 619, Doc. 9.

M. Chafeman, clerk, letter to J. Fairchild (Sept. 8, 1875), M234 Roll 620, Doc. 3.

J. Fairchild letter to E. Smith (June 4, 1875), M234 Roll 621, Doc. 7.

J. Fairchild letter to E. Smith (June 5, 1875), M234 Roll 621, Doc. 8.

J. Fairchild letter to E. Smith (June 21, 1875), M234 Roll 621, Doc. 10.

"Proceedings of a Council held June 27th 1875 . . . with the tribes of Alsea, Coos, Umpqua and Siuslaw Indians residing on Alsea Indian Reservation" (June 17, 1875), M234 Roll 621, Doc. 12.

E. Smith letter to B. Simpson, surveyor general (July 17, 1875), M234 Roll 621, Doc. 13.

B. Simpson letter to J. Mitchell (Aug. 26, 1875), M234 Roll 621, Doc. 15.

B. Simpson, special agent, letter to E. Smith (Aug. 27, 1875), M234 Roll 621, Doc. 17.

J. Fairchild letter to E. Smith (Sept., 2, 1875), M234 Roll 621, Doc. 18.

J. Fairchild letter to E. Smith (Sept. 30, 1875), M234 Roll 621, Doc. 23.

J. Fairchild letter to J. Mitchell (Oct. 20, 1875), M234 Roll 621, Doc. 24.

B. Simpson letter to E. Smith (Oct. 28, 1875), M234 Roll 621, Doc. 26.

J. Fairchild letter to E. Smith (Nov. 3, 1875), M234 Roll 621, Doc. 28.

B. Simpson letter to E. Smith (Aug. 27, 1875), M234 Roll 621, Doc. 17.

G. Manypenny letter to R. McClelland, secretary of the Interior (Oct. 29, 1855), M348 Roll 9, Doc. 3.

G. Manypenny letter to R. McClelland (Feb. 5, 1857), M348 Roll 10, Doc. 9.

J. Denver, commissioner of Indian Affairs, letter to J. Thompson, secretary of the Interior (May 1, 1857), M348 Roll 10, Doc. 13.

E. Kemble letter to E. Smith (Jan. 7, 1874), M1070 Roll 33, Doc. 6.

W. Vandever, U.S. Indian inspector, letter to E. Smith (Aug. 21, 1874), M1070 Roll 33, Doc. 9.

TRANSCRIPTS OF LETTERS

J. Palmer, superintendent of Indian Affairs for Oregon, letter to G. Manypenny, commissioner of Indian Affairs (Oct. 8, 1853).

T. Hendricks, commissioner of the General Land Office, letter to J. Campbell, acting secretary of the Interior (Sept. 10, 1855).

I. Stevens, governor and superintendent of Indian Affairs for Washington, letter to J. Lane, general (Sept. 19, 1857).

GENERAL CORRESPONDENCE

J. Edmunds, commissioner of the General Land Office, letter to W. Dole, commissioner of Indian Affairs (May 5, 1862).

J. Edmunds letter to B. Pengra, surveyor general for Oregon (May 10, 1862).

W. Gardner, acting Interior secretary, letter to G. Cordon, U.S. senator (May 29, 1947).

G. Cordon, U.S. senator, letter to H. Simmons, tribal representative (June 3, 1947).

D. Orton, vice chairman, Tribal Council, letter to G. Cordon (Feb. 11, 1949).

H. Lee, acting commissioner of Indian Affairs, telegram of draft bill to E. M. Pryse (Aug. 10, 1951).

Tribal Council of the Confederated Tribes of Siletz Indians, letter to T. McCall, governor of Oregon, "Re: Proclamation of the Confederated Tribes of Siletz Indians" (July 1, 1974).

J. McKean, director of Oregon Department of Fish and Wildlife, letter to M. Hatfield, U.S. senator for Oregon (Nov. 17, 1975).

J. McKean, director, Oregon Department of Fish and Wildlife, letter to A. Bensell (May 12, 1976).

J. Redden, Oregon attorney general, letter to M. Hatfield and L. AuCoin, congressman for Oregon (Aug. 8, 1977).

R. Ehlke, legislative attorney, Congressional Research Service, Library of Congress, letter to L. AuCoin (Aug. 17, 1977).

J. Redden, letter to V. Atiyeh, governor of Oregon (Dec. 5. 1979).

L. Merrill letter to author, "Pre Restoration & Restoration, 1973/1974" (undated).

A. Deer, assistant secretary of Indian Affairs, letter to D. Pigsley, chairman, Siletz Tribal Council (March 14, 1995).

TESTIMONY

Hoxie Simmons, testimony before the Indian Claims Commission, *Tillamook Tribe of Indians v. United States*, Ind. Cl. Comm. No. 239 (1955).

A Ludlow & Co v. Benjamin Simpson,—Benslay and J. W. P. Huntington (Benton County Circuit Court, March 11, 1864).

"Full Reporting of Proceedings of a council held with the Indians of the Siletz Reservation" (Oct. 17 and 29, 1892).

REPORTS

Bureau of Indian Affairs, Siletz Agency, "Report on Status of Government Reserves, Siletz, Oregon" (May 31, 1979).

U.S. Department of the Interior, Bureau of Indian Affairs, "Siletz Indian Reservation Plan" (Nov. 1979).

MISCELLANEOUS

"Minutes of Council held with the Tillamook and other bands of Indians residing north of Siletz Reservation" (June 1, 1875), M234 Roll 621, Doc. 6.

Hearing Before the Senate Committee on Interior and Insular Affairs, "S. 3005 and S. 3004," 82d Congress, 2d Session, vol. 2, pp. 87–88 (May 21, 1952). Washington, D.C.: Ward & Paul, 1952.

Hearing Before the House Committee on Interior and Insular Affairs, "H.R. 7489," 82d Congress, 2d Session (May 21, 1952). Washington, D.C.: Columbia Reporting Co., 1952.

State of Oregon Department of Commerce, Corporation Division, "Certificate of Incorporation of Paul Washington Cemetery Association" (Feb. 10, 1975).

"Siletz Tribes Pick Ex-Salem Resident" (undated article from unidentified newspaper; clipped and given to the author by Ed Ben).

Press Release, Congressman Les AuCoin, "AuCoin Statement on Proposed Siletz Reservation Bill" (Nov. 29, 1979).

"Agreement among the state of Oregon, the United States of America and the Confederated Tribes of Siletz Indians of Oregon to permanently define tribal hunting, fishing, trapping, and gathering rights of the Siletz Tribe and its members" (April 22, 1980).

"Tribal-State Compact for Regulation of Class III Gaming Between the Confederated Tribes of Siletz Indians of Oregon and the State of Oregon" (Nov. 10, 1994).

Kentta, Robert, "1865 Executive Order Reducing the Coast Reservation and a Report of its Results" (1993).

"M/V New Carissa Conservation Easement," Dec. 29, 2008 (Confederated Tribes of Siletz Indians, U.S. Department of the Interior, and State of Oregon, Department of Fish and Wildlife, signatories).

National Archives

WASHINGTON, D.C.

Letters received by superintendency of Indian Affairs, Microfilm, M2 Series, Roll 14.

PACIFIC ALASKA AND SEATTLE

Department of the Interior, Siletz Agency, "1927 Annual Report, Narrative Section," RG 75, Grand Ronde–Siletz Indian Agency Holdings 16, Box 48, Annual Status Reports Folder.

Department of the Interior, Siletz Agency, p. 6, "1929 Annual Report, Narrative Section," RG 75, Grand Ronde–Siletz Indian Agency Holdings 16, Box 48, Annual Status Reports Folder.

Department of the Interior, Siletz Agency, p. 4, "1935 Annual Report, Narrative Section," RG 75, Grand Ronde–Siletz Indian Agency Holdings 16, Box 50, Annual Status Reports Folder.

Bureau of Indian Affairs, "Payments Made to Western Oregon Indians," RG 75, Portland Area Office Holdings 07, Box 33, Western Oregon Judgment Fund Folder.

Bureau of Indian Affairs, "Minutes of the Northwest Indian Congress at Chemawa, Oregon to Discuss with the Howard-Wheeler Bill, March 8–9, 1934," RG 75, Portland Area Office Holdings 43, Siletz–Grand Ronde–Chemawa 1931–1955 Box, Proceedings of the Conference at Chemawa . . . Wheeler-Howard Bill Folder.

Bureau of Indian Affairs, Portland Area Office, "Program for the Early Termination of Selected Activities and Withdrawing Federal Supervision over the Indians at Grand Ronde–Siletz and Southwestern Oregon," p. 6 (Dec. 1950), RG 75, Grand Ronde–Siletz Indian Agency Holdings 77, Box 161, 10 Year Program 1944 Folder.

Bureau of Indian Affairs, Grand Ronde–Siletz Agency, pp. 7–8, "Minutes of the Conference Held in Siletz on Feb. 18, 1940," RG 75, Portland Area Office Holdings 56, Box 1501, Oregon (1940 . . . Siletz) Folder.

Bureau of Indian Affairs, Salem Agency, p. 18, "Ten-Year Program, 1946–1955, Siletz, Oregon," (March 1944) RG 75, Grand Ronde–Siletz Indian Agency Holdings 77, Box 161, 10 Year Program 1944 Folder.

E. M. Pryse memorandum to Commissioner of Indian Affairs (Nov. 29, 1946), RG 75, Portland Area Office Holdings 01, Box 1, Monthly Narrative Reports for 1948 Folder.

E. M. Pryse memorandum to Commissioner of Indian Affairs, p. 4 (May 2, 1947), RG 75, Portland Area Office Holdings 01, Box 1, Monthly Narrative Reports for 1948–1949 Folder.

H. R. Cloud letter to Commissioner of Indian Affairs (Feb. 25, 1949), RG 75, Portland Area Office Holdings 07, Box 37, Siletz Tribes Constitution and Bylaws Folder.

H. R. Cloud letter to Commissioner of Indian Affairs (June 7, 1949), RG 75, Portland Area Office Holdings 56, Box 1508, Grand Ronde–Siletz General 1947–1951 Folder.

E. M. Pryse memorandum to Commissioner of Indian Affairs (Dec. 1, 1949), RG 75, Portland Area Office Holdings 01, Box 1, Monthly Narrative Reports for 1948–1949 Folder.

E. M. Pryse letter to Commissioner of Indian Affairs (Aug. 7, 1950), RG 75, Portland Area Office Holdings 56, Box 1508, Grand Ronde–Siletz General 1947–1951 Folder.

E. Logan, tribal chairman, letter to D. Myer, Commissioner of Indian Affairs (Aug. 29, 1950), RG 75, Portland Area Office Holdings 56, Box 1508, Grand Ronde–Siletz General 1947–1951 Folder.

E. M. Pryse memorandum to Commissioner of Indian Affairs, p. 6 (Sept. 1, 1950), RG 75, Portland Area Office Holdings 01, Box 1, Monthly Narrative Reports for 1950 Folder.

E. M. Pryse letter to Commissioner of Indian Affairs (Oct. 18, 1950), RG 75, Portland Area Office Holdings 7, Box 37, Siletz Tribe—Constitution and By-Laws, 1948–1950 Folder.

E. M. Pryse memorandum to Commissioner of Indian Affairs (Sept. 1, 1951), RG 75, Portland Area Office Holdings 01, Box 1, Monthly Narrative Reports for 1951 Folder.

E. M. Pryse letter to Commissioner of Indian Affairs (Sept. 11, 1951), RG 75, Portland Area Office Holdings 01, Box 12, Grand Ronde–Siletz 1952–1954 Folder.

E. M. Pryse memorandum to Commissioner of Indian Affairs, p. 7 (Oct. 1, 1950), RG 75, Portland Area Office Holdings 01, Box 1, Monthly Narrative Reports for 1950 Folder.

E. M. Pryse memorandum to Commissioner of Indian Affairs, p. 5 (Dec. 1, 1950), RG 75, Portland Area Office Holdings 01, Box 1, Monthly Narrative Reports for 1950 Folder.

E. M. Pryse memorandum to Commissioner of Indian Affairs, p. 9 (Nov. 1, 1951), RG 75, Portland Area Office Holdings 01, Box 1, Monthly Narrative Reports for 1951 Folder.

ROCKY MOUNTAIN, DENVER

W. Dole letter to W. Otto, assistant secretary of the Interior (Aug. 22, 1864), M348 Roll 14.

LINCOLN COUNTY HISTORICAL SOCIETY, NEWPORT, OR

Johnson, Bolling Arthur, ed. "Pacific Spruce Corporation and Subsidiaries," reprinted from *Lumber World Review.* Newport, OR: Lincoln County Historical Society, 1924.

Cawley, Friar Martinus. *Father Crockett of Grand Ronde: Oregon Missionary, 1860–1898.* Story #25. Oregon ArcH.D. iocese: Guadalupe Translations, 1996.

OTHER ARCHIVAL COLLECTIONS

California State University, San Marcos

J. Sykes, Indian sub agent, letter to E. Geary, superintendent of Indian Affairs for Oregon (Nov. 16, 1860), M234 Roll 612, Doc. 65, Native American Documents Project.

University of California, Berkeley, Bancroft Library, Berkeley

Cardwell journal from 1850 to 1852, pp. 9–10.

DuBois, Cora. "Tututni (Rogue River Athapaskan) Field Notes: Typescript, 1934," p. 29.

Grover, Lafayette. *Notable Things in a Public Life in Oregon*, p. 39, Bancroft Collection (1878).

Oglesby, W. W. "The Calapooyas Indians: a dictation made Aug. 28, 1884," p. 5.

University of Oregon, Eugene, Special Collections, University Libraries

Palmer, Joel. "Council Convened 3PM on the 23rd August," Joel Palmer Papers, AX 057, Doc. 32.

———. "Myrtle Grove Council," Joel Palmer Papers, AX 057, Doc. 34.

———. "Notes on a Speech Made at Table Rock Treaty Negotiations 1853," Joel Palmer Papers, AX 057, Doc. 33.

Dissertations, Theses

Applen, Jeffrey A. "Battle of Big Bend," M.A.thesis, Oregon State University, 1998.

Engel, Bruce Linn. ""Oregon Coast Indian Reserve: Establishment and Reduction, 1855–1875," B.A. thesis, Reed College, 1961.

Harger, Jane Marie. "The History of the Siletz Reservation, 1856–1877," M.A. thesis, University of Oregon, 1972.

Kent, William Eugene. "The Siletz Indian Reservation, 1855–1900," M.A. thesis, Portland State University, 1973.

Ord, Ellen Francis. "The Rogue River Indian expedition of 1856 (Diary by Capt. E. O. C. Ord 3rd Art. U.S. Army, with Introduction and Editorial Notes)," M.A. thesis, University of California, 1922.

Palacios, Kelly C. "The Potential of Dynamic Segmentation for Aquatic Ecosystem Management: Pacific Lamprey Decline in the Native Lands of the Confederated Tribes of Siletz Indians, Oregon USA," M.S. thesis, Oregon State University, 2001.

Seaburg, William Ronald. "Collecting Culture: The Practice and Ideology of Salvage Ethnography in Western Oregon, 1877–1942," Ph.D. diss., University of Washington, 1994.

Spaid, Stanley Sheldon. "Joel Palmer and Indian Affairs in Oregon," Ph.D. diss., University of Oregon, 1950.

Taylor, Joseph E. "Steelhead's Mother Was His Father, Salmon: Development and Declension of Aboriginal Conservation in the Oregon Country Salmon Fishery," M.A. thesis, University of Oregon, 1992.

Van Laere, M. Susan. "The Grizzly Bear and the Deer: The History of Federal Indian Policy and Its Impact on the Coast Reservation Tribes of Oregon, 1856–1877," M.A. thesis, Oregon State University, 2000.

Zybach, Bob. "The Great Fires: Indians Burning and Catastrophic Forest Fire Patterns of the Oregon Coast Range, 1491–1951," Ph.D. diss., Oregon State University, 2003.

Newspaper Publications

Kentta, Robert. "A Piece of Siletz History, Part I," *Siletz News* p. 27, November 1999.

———. "A Siletz History, Part III: Fur Trade & Early Exploration," *Siletz News* p. 27, November 1999.

———. "A Siletz History, Part V: The Early Treaty Making Period of 1851," *Siletz News*, p. 31, March 2000.

———. A Siletz History, Part VI: The Western Oregon Treaties of 1853–1855," *Siletz News*, p. 2, April 2000.

Albany Democrat Herald, Associated Press, Corvallis Gazette-Times, Daily Astorian, Eugene Register-Guard, Indian Country Today, Lincoln County Leader, Methow Valley News, Native American Casino Magazine, Newport News Times, New York Times, Oregonian, Oregon Journal, Oregon Statesman, Oregon Weekly Times, Portland Oregon Sunday Journal, Salem Capital Journal, Salem Oregon Argus, Salem Statesman Journal, Seattle Times, United Press International, and *Washington, D.C., Daily National Intelligencer*

PRESS RELEASES

National Oceanic and Atmospheric Administration, "NOAA Awards $47,000 for Native Oyster Restoration," (July 18, 2005), *at* http://www.nmfs.noaa.gov/docs/05-R953%20 Oregon%20Yaquina%20oyster%20habitat%20grantCLEARED.pdf.

U.S. Fish and Wildlife Service, "Agencies, Tribes Release Final Restoration Plan for Damages Caused by New Carissa Oil Spill" (Jan. 31, 2006) (at fws.gov).

Oregon State University, "OSU Aids Siletz Valley Early College Academy" (Feb. 15, 2006).

The Conservation Fund, "Out of Tragedy, a New Tomorrow in the Oregon Coast Range Forest: Roughly 3,900 Acres Protected" (July 31, 2007), *at* http:www.conservationfund.org/ node/669.

Oregon Department of Fish and Wildlife, "Coastal Forest Goes to Siletz Tribe for Management to Restore Marbled Murrelet Populations Lost to New Carissa Oil Spill" (July 31, 2007), *at* http://www.dfw.state.or.us/news/2007/july/073107b.asp.

Multimedia

VIDEO

The People Are Dancing Again: The Siletz Indians' Dramatic Struggle to Restore their Tribal Identity. VHS. Portland, OR: Siletz Films, 1976.

WEB SITES

American Indian Athletic Hall of Fame, http://americanindianathletichalloffame.com/inductees.php.

American National Biography Online, http://www.anb.org/articles/05/05-00535-print.html.

American National Biography Online, http://www.anb.org/articles/05/05-00704-print.html.

American Gaming Association, http://www.americangaming.org.

Brookings Curry Coastal Pilot, http://www.currypilot.com/Community/Community/History-of-Brookings.

Chemawa Indian School, http://www.chemawa.bia.edu/classlists.htm.

Confederated Tribes of Siletz Indians Web site, http://www.ctsi.nsn.us.

ESPN, http://www.espn.com.

Languages of USA, http://www.ethnologue.com.

Indian Reorganization Act Era Constitutions and Charters, University of Oklahoma Law Center, http://thorpe.ou.edu/IRA.html.

Measuringworth, http://www.measuringworth.com.

National Indian Gaming Commission, http://www.nigc.gov.

National Park Service, http://www.nps.gov.

NOAA Fisheries, http://www.nmfs.noaa.gov/pr/species/fish/chinooksalmon.htm.

Northwest Indian Fisheries Commission, "Lamprey Study Part of Elwha River Restoration," (Oct. 4, 2007), http://www.nwifc.org/2007/10/lamprey-study-part-of-elwha-river-restoration.

Northwest Native American Basketweavers Association, "The Basket is a Song," (2005), http://www.nnaba.org/documents/2005_Gathering_Newsletter.pdf.

Office of Self-Governance Communication, http://www.tribalselfgov.org.

Oregon Department of Fish and Wildlife, "Native Oysters, *Ostrea conchaphila*," http://www.dfw.state.or.us/mrp/shellfish/bayclams/oysters.asp.

Oregon Department of Forestry, http://www.oregon.gov/ODF/FIRE/Historic_Fires_In_Oregon.shtml.

Oregon Interpretative Corporation, http://www.oregon.com.

Pacific Fishery Management Council and National Marine Fisheries Service, http://www.pcouncil.org/salmon/salsafe08/salsafe08.html.

Rogue River Country – Oregon, http://www.roguerivertrips.info/locations/Wild_Scenic_Rivers.asp.

Siletz Dee-Ni Talking Online Dictionary Project, Living Tongues Institute for Endangered Languages, http://www.livingtongues.org/siletz.html.

USDA National Agricultural Statistics Service, http://www.nass.usda.gov.

USDA Natural Resources Conservation Service, http://www.wcc.nrcs.usda.gov.

U.S. Forest Service, Agriculture Handbook 654, *Silvics of North America*, vol. 1, http://www.na.fs.fed.us/Spfo/pubs/silvics_manual.

United States Geological Survey, National Water Information System, http://waterdata.usgs.gov/or/nwis/monthly.

Western Oregon Lamprey Workshop, Feb. 26–27, 2008, Canyonville, Oregon, http://www.fws.gov/pacific/fisheries/sp_habcon/lamprey/pdf/Western%20Oregon%20Lamprey%20Workshop%202_2008.pdf.

Miscellaneous

American Indian Policy Review Commission, Final Report, "Task Force Ten: Terminated and Nonfederally Recognized Indians" (Oct. 1976).

Connolly, Thomas J. "Anthropological and Archaeological Perspectives on Native Fire Management of the Willamette Valley," paper presented to the American Association for the Advancement of Science, Pacific Division, June 11–14, 2000.

Downey, Tom, et al., *Skwakol: The Decline of the Siletz Lamprey Eel Population during the 20th Century*. Corvallis: Oregon State University, 1996.

ECONorthwest, "The Economic Impacts and Benefits of Chinook Winds Casino Resort on the Local Economy," p. 6. Portland, OR: ECONorthwest, 2005.

Kasner, Leone Letson, "Siletz: Survival for an Artifact." Manuscript, 1976, *at* Siletz Archival Collection.

National Oceanic and Atmospheric Administration, "Hands on Habitat: Celebrating 10 Years of Coastal Restoration," March 2006.

"Traditional Arts of the Indians of Western Oregon," vol. 4, no. 2 *American Indian Basketry and Other Native Arts* (1984).

Xush Wee-Ya, a Tolowa-English dictionary.

ACKNOWLEDGMENTS

THIS HAS BEEN A LONG JOURNEY, FIVE AND A HALF YEARS, BUT it has been a commitment of more than time and energy. For many people, doing this work and getting it right has been a sacred task. If, finally, we—that is the necessary pronoun—have got it right, it is because so many have brought ideas, sources, words, images, maps, support, and inspiration to these pages.

Without doubt my first thanks go to the Siletz Tribe. Of their many gifts, the greatest has been freedom. I have been given the room to move in whatever directions the historical facts and patterns took me; I am now finished with this book and, while I have received countless facts and views, never once was I constrained by any direction, request, or suggestion on what to write. Although I live a thousand miles away, the tribe financially supported as many trips as I needed for the interviews and explorations of the landscape that are the bloodstream of this book. I had needs—at times they must have seemed endless to people at Siletz—for documents, phone conversations, manuscript reviews, and face-to-face meetings, and my every request was met.

Delores Pigsley, tribal chairman and one of the most able people I have known, took a keen interest in the book and made many valuable suggestions. Bud Lane, Jessie Davis, Tina Retasket, Lillie Butler, Loraine Butler, Reggie Butler, Robert Kentta, Phil Rilatos, Frank Simmons, and Sharon Edenfield served as tribal council members during this project. They were active participants and I thank them for all they have given to this book. Along with Chairman Pigsley, they approved the project at the beginning, authorized financial support, gave me extended interviews, and encouraged tribal members to give interviews and provide documents. The council also engaged in the extraordinarily useful retreats described in the Introduction by reading the full draft manuscript and then participating in the page-by-page discussion of the manuscript that resulted in many corrections and new perspectives. As mentioned in the book, a strength of the Siletz Tribe is the stability and quality at the council level, and that strength is manifested throughout these pages.

This book owes a great debt to the many tribal members and others who gave the interviews that have proven to be of such value to an understanding of Siletz history. In many cases, people gave two, three, or more interviews in order to cover additional topics. I give my gratitude to Jeffery Applen, June Austin, Ed Ben, Loren Bommelyn, Brenda Bremner, Gladys Bolton, Dino Butler, Jennifer Butler, Lillie Butler, Reggie Butler, Henry Cagey, Lou Carey, Jeff Classen, Eva Clayton, Eddie Collins, Jessie Davis, William "Bill" DePoe, Rebecca Dobkins, Pete Downey, Art Fisher, Dolly Fisher, Joan Bensell Fisher, Judge Calvin Gantenbein, Sister Francella Griggs, Kathryn Harrison, Joseph Hostler, Margot Hudson, Don Ivy, Jane John, Geneva Johnson, Lori Johnson, Katy Kaady, Robert Kentta, Jim Kikumoto, Walt Klamath, Kelly LaChance, Louis LaChance, Bud Lane, Cheryl Lane, Wanda Melton, Jo Anne Miller, Tami Miner, Woody Muschamp, George Nagel, Bonnie Petersen, Tom Picciano, Delores Pigsley, Agnes Pilgrim, Angela Ramirez, Selene Relatos, Tina Retasket, Joyce Retherford, Kathy Kentta Robinson, Emma Russell, Terry Russell, Frank Simmons, LaVera Simmons, Stanley Speaks, Kay Steele, Bob Tom, Gilbert Towner, Janne Underinner, Kathleen Van Pelt, Cynthia Viles, John Volkman, Shirley Walker, Sylvia Walker, Stan van de Wetering, Janet Wickland, Rebecca Williams, and Hiroto Zakoji.

The tribal council requested the staff to cooperate with this venture and I give my appreciation to Brenda Bremner, Sharon Edenfield, Kelley Ellis, Natasha Kavanaugh, Jim Kikumoto, Celesta Lee, Tami Miner, Bonnie Petersen, Selene Rilatos, and Diane Rodriquez, all busy employees who were always quick to provide me and my assistants with interviews, documents, and statistical compilations. Mary Dederick of the Cultural Department gave my work an enormous boost through her painstaking accomplishment, over the course of several years, of faithfully transcribing nineteenth-century handwritten government documents and thus making accessible thousands of pages of crucial primary materials. Buddy Lane, finishing up his studies at Oregon State University and serving an internship with the Cultural Department, did yeoman's work as computer expert, photographer, and essential "go-to guy."

ACKNOWLEDGMENTS

Another tribal staff member deserves special mention. Chairman Pigsley and the council assigned the tribal cartographer, Brady Smith, to bring his expertise to the task of producing the maps for this book. Working with Brady has been one of the joys of my life. All of these maps were created specifically for this book and they presented Brady with many challenges. One of the challenges was me. I believe in the worth of maps in my writing and always have high hopes for them, but I got especially ambitious when I saw what Brady could do. Still, despite his other demands, despite how detailed my requests, and how short the deadlines, Brady knew only one answer: "Yeah, I think I can do that." Thank you, my friend. Your rigor and mastery are now part of Siletz history.

In the Introduction, I tried to articulate my debt to Robert Kentta and Bud Lane, staff of the Cultural Department as well as tribal council members, and to explain their eminence as tribal historians. I'll never, though, actually find the words. What giants. What a lifetime privilege to walk this trail with them.

I have been blessed by the first-rate work and spirited collegiality of a group of law students who served as research assistants for this book. Students at Colorado Law normally don't have jobs during their first year, so usually I have them for their second and third years, including summers. They are Greg De Bie (Spring 2005), Joshua Tenneson (Summer 2005–Spring 2007), Maria Aparicio (Fall 2006–Fall 2008), Carrie Covington Doyle (Summer 2007–Spring 2009), Alison Flint (Fall 2008–Spring 2009), Matt Samelson (Spring 2009–Fall 2010), and Daniel Cordalis (Spring 2009–Fall 2010). They have been full partners in this work. They do extensive archival and Web research and put all note sources in final form, but their involvement goes far beyond that. With the exception of Greg, who came on at the end of his third year, they all made interview trips out to the Northwest and, like their book research, the results of their interviews are found from one end of this volume to the other. Joshua, Maria, Carrie, and Alison also participated in the retreats with tribal council members in Oregon, and Daniel and Matt attended a day-long meeting in Seattle with staff of the University of Washington Press to go over the distinctive issues attendant to publishing this complex volume.

And I depended on my research assistants' wisdom and commitment. I regularly bounced ideas off them and ran draft passages and chapters past them. Because of their interviewing trips and telephone interviews with Siletz people, they witnessed—and felt—the Siletz experience and became imbued with the intangible tone and tenor that is so central to any history, certainly this one. Like their research and interviews, their informed observations and recommendations, based on particularized, real-world knowledge and respect for tribal culture, were immense assets to me as I put words on paper. As each of them has explained to me in their own ways, their time on this book will be of special importance to them throughout their lives. My debt to them, and affection and respect for them, will stay with me forever.

The same is true with Cynthia Carter, a faculty assistant and general professional at the law school. We have worked together for nearly two decades now, and trying to do what I do without Cynthia is unimaginable. She is my right hand and lifetime friend. For this book, she did conceptual and copy edits of the manuscript at every stage; made recommendations on and organized and obtained permissions for all the many photographs; conducted telephone interviews; carried on continuous correspondence and telephone conversations with people at Siletz; and generally had complete involvement in this book from beginning to end. Her contributions, both subtle and bold, enriched these pages beyond the saying.

As has always been the case, my law school has been supportive in every way. Dean David Getches, who also teaches and writes on Indian law and policy, has taken an interest in this project from the beginning and I thank him for his advice and encouragement as well as for his institutional support. In addition to providing funds for my assistants, the school awarded me the Goldstein Fellowship, made possible through the generosity of MDC-Richmond Homes Foundation and President Larry Mizel, in honor of Colorado Law alumnus Gilbert Goldstein. This fellowship supports a research semester for a senior faculty member and, along with a sabbatical semester, allowed me to devote the entire 2008-2009 academic year to this book, exactly when I needed it the most.

The People Are Dancing Again necessarily involves a number of disciplines, and I have benefited from comments of colleagues in various fields: historian Tim Garrison; legal historian Rennard Strickland; attorney Craig Dorsay; Frank Walsh, author of histories of the Rogue River War; military historian Jeffery Applen; linguist Janne Underriner; and attorney Richard Trudell. One of the most significant contributors to this book was Professor Rebecca Dobkins of Willamette University. An anthropologist, Rebecca was ever available despite her own heavy load, including service as department chair. Deeply knowledgeable about Northwest tribes and American Indian culture, history, and policy generally, she participated in all of the retreats with the tribal council and her penetrating observations and advice there and on many other occasions were invaluable. Rebecca is truly a Renaissance Woman, and nothing short of it.

Many libraries and historical societies were essential. At the University of Colorado's Wise Law Library, Jane Thompson handled many inquiries and Matt Zafiratos was always willing to scour the stacks and Internet for sources. Norlin Library here at the University provided hundreds of books. Numerous others provided routine services but also (even in a time when their budgets were short) went the extra mile to track down hard-to-find books, documents, and images: University of Washington Libraries Special Collections (Nicolette Bromberg, Christina Burtner, Nancy Hines, and Kris Kinsey), University of Oregon Libraries Special Collections, Lincoln County Historical Society (Jodi Weeber), North Lincoln County Historical Society (Anne Hall), Southern Oregon Historical Society (Allison Weiss, Kathy Enright, and Jean Taylor), Curry County Historical Society (Meryl Boice), University of California-Berkeley Bancroft Library, National Archives and Record Administration Pacific Alaska Region (Seattle) (Patty McNamee and Charliann Becker), the National Archives in Washington, D.C., and Denver, and *The Oregonian* (Drew Vattiat).

The Oregon Historical Society played a special role. Articles in the *Oregon Historical Quarterly*, founded in 1898, provide a wealth of information on Oregon history. The Society's photographic collection is the most extensive on Oregon history; Scott Rook and Scott Daniels were most helpful in corralling the many OHS photos used here. In 2009, the Society invited me to present one of the lectures at the annual Mark O. Hatfield Distinguished Historians Forum. I delivered two different lectures on successive nights in Portland and at Willamette University in Salem, both based on material from the manuscript for this book. Many thanks to OHS Executive Director George Vogt and members of his staff, Eliza Canty-Jones, Sue Metzler, and Rachel Schoening, as well as Willamette University President Lee Pelton and Professor Rebecca Dobkins for making both of those evenings such fine occasions.

One of my best learning experiences for this book came in July 2008 on a blue-sky day on the Oregon Coast, when Delores Pigsley, Bud Lane, Robert Kentta, three of my research assistants, Rebecca Dobkins, Marianne Keddington-Lang, and I spent an intensive day going over the material on aboriginal culture in chapters 1 and 2, the true cornerstones of the book. We met at the perfect place—the interpretive center at the Bureau of Land Management's Yaquina Head Outstanding Natural Area, a splendid facility made possible by Senator Mark Hatfield, such a towering figure in Siletz history. Many, many thanks to Manager Joe Ashor and his staff for making the interpretive center available.

Finally, I want to acknowledge the role of the University of Washington Press, which made it possible for *The People Are Dancing Again* to realize its full possibilities. Scholarly work on the Indians of the Pacific Northwest is at the center of the Press's mission and from my earliest discussions with Director Pat Soden, it was clear that the Press would enthusiastically respond to our requests on a whole range of matters, including page length, number of photographs and maps, and compelling design.

Soden, whom I knew from our earlier book together, *Messages from Frank's Landing—A Story of Salmon, Treaties, and the Indian Way*, took this Siletz history under his wing and shepherded it through editing, production, and marketing. My sponsoring editor, Marianne Keddington-Lang, has a great eye for words and added much substance to the book since she is an expert on Northwest Indian history and policy. Marianne also evidenced her extraordinary commitment to the project by participating in all of the lengthy retreats with the tribal council; this caused her to do two full edits—one before the retreats and one after. I had the good luck to have, as my copy editor, Marilyn Trueblood, formerly a copy editor and now managing editor. My thanks to Marilyn for taking on this editing project in addition to her day job and applying her precise mind and great judgment to these pages. As anyone who picks up this volume can see, Tom Eykemans is a multitalented designer whose artistry helps portray the color and dignified traditions of the Siletz Tribe's history. I also thank Alice Herbig, Beth DeWeese, Phoebe Daniels, and Rachael Levay. *The People Are Dancing Again* demonstrates what a committed, excellent publishing house can do.

My family has been with me all the way. I'm honored by the way they take an interest in my work and come along with me on trips for my books. My heart will always be with my wife, Ann, and my boys, Seth, Philip, David, and Ben. And now I look forward to including my two young grandchildren, Khalil and Meera in my ventures, and dare to trust that their numbers will increase.

ACKNOWLEDGMENTS

INDEX

Page numbers for maps and photographs are in boldface type.

A

B

P

The Pacific Raincoast: Environment and Culture in an American Eden, 1778–1900 (Bunting), 512

Palmer, Joel, 83, 89, **90**, 95–96, 127, 132–34, 138, 157; and move to Coast Reservation, 150–55, 160–62, 165, 167, 168; removal policy of, 92–95, 131–32; and Rogue River War, 108, 129. *See also* Coast (or Siletz) Reservation: Coast Treaty of 1855; Table Rock Treaty

Parker, Ely, 187–88

Paul Washington Cemetery, 308, 327, 332

peace policy, 188–89, 447–48; and Ulysses S. Grant, 187

Pearson, Clara, 46

The People Are Dancing Again (film), 311

Petersen, Frank, **384**

Peterson, Annie Miner, 41–42, **42**, 52–53

Pierce, Franklin, 141, 142, 144–47

Pigsley, Delores, xii, 313, **319**, 324, 338, 341, **347**, 359, 362

Pilgrim, Agnes, 4, 165–66, 306

A Plea for the Indians (Beeson), 110, 111, 112–13, 118

Pond, Alfred, 277

Pond, Clayton, 277

Portland Urban Indian Center, 308

Powell, John Wesley, 219–20

Pow-wow, 367–68; Chinook Wind, 238; and Ricks Memorial Pow-Wow Grounds, 368

Pratt, Richard Henry, 175–76

Prucha, Francis Paul, 188, 282–83, 447–48, 512–13

Pryse, E. Morgan, 279–82, **281**, 284–86, 289–93, 296–301

R

Rector, William, 191, 193, 194

Redden, James, 321, 329, 330

Reed, Albert (Tootsel), 277

Reed, Elmer, 277

Reed, Tony, 277

removal policy, 92–95, 134–36, 168, 439; and James Nesmith, 168; and Joel Palmer, 92–95, 131–32; Oregon Indian Treaty Act and, 92–93

removal to the Coast Reservation, 146–70, **163**; from Big Bend of Rogue River, 155–74; and California-Oregon Trail, 153, 154; and Coquelle Thompson Sr., 157, 158, 160, 161, 165; and Grand Ronde encampment, 152, 154, 160, 433–34; illness associated with, 153; overland march and, **164**, 165–66, **166**; roundup of holdouts, 167–70; routes taken, **151**; and Salmon River camp, 161–62; from Table Rock reserve, 143–54; "voluntary," 167

Requiem for a People: The Rogue Indians and the Frontiersmen (Beckham), 511

reservation policy, announcement of, 94. *See also* Coast (or Siletz) Reservation

restoration. *See* Siletz Restoration Act

Rhoan, Arlissa, **367**

Richardson, Bill, 339

Ricks, Pauline Bell, 308, 313, **315**, 318, **319**, 323; accounts of Ki-Ya-Na-Ha, 150, 157, 165, 169

Rilatos, Edward (Ochie), 277

Rilatos, Manuel, 277

Rilatos, Robert, 308, **309**, 312, **312**, 313, **319**

Rilatos, Selene, 363

Robbins, William, 211, 246, 512

Roberts, Barbara, 338–39

Roe, John, 361

Rogue River, 19, 21, **22**, 121, 397–98

Rogue River battles: Battle Bar, 125–26; Battle Rock, 75–77; Big Bend, 125–30; Grave Creek Massacre, 91–92; Humbug Creek incident, 116; Hungry Hill, 121–23; Little Butte Creek, 118–19

The Rogue River Indian War and Its Aftermath, 1850–1980 (Schwartz), 511

Rogue River Jenny, **197**

Rogue River Tribe of Indians v. United States, 265–68, 269

Rogue River War, 106–30 passim; and Andrew Smith, 112, 118–20, 122, 128, 129; events leading to, 114–16, 119; human lives lost, 107; and Joel Palmer, 108, 129; and John Adams, 107–8; and

Rogue River War (cont.)
John Beeson, 109–12, 113, 118–19; major events of, **122**; and Matthew Deady, 96–97, 108, 117; and Robert Buchanan, 125, 127, 129, 384; and Tipsu Tyee, 115, 117, 421; and Tyee John, 112–13, 119–21, 124–25, 127–30, 156, 422. *See also* Rogue River battles

Roosevelt, Franklin, 263, 270
Roosevelt, Theodore, 236
Russell, Emma, 467
Russell, Terry, 165, 467

S

Sackett, Lee, 253–54
Salmon River camp, 161–62, **162**
Sapir, Edward, 36, 38–39, 185, 512
Saunders, Reuben, **252**
Sayer, Jonathan, 311
Schwartz, E. A., 511
Seaburg, William, 511–12
Shaker Church, 253–56, 472
Shastas, 178–79, 180, 182, 267; village life, 39
shellfish restoration, 356
Sherman, John, 213
She's Tricky Like Coyote: Annie Miner Peterson (Youst), 42, 511
Siletz, town of, **343**; City Council, 327–29; Planning Commission, 327
Siletz Agency, **181**
Siletz Boat Works, 276
Siletz Indian agents, generally, 183–84
Siletz Inherited Lands Act (1901), 231, 233
Siletz Reservation. *See* Coast (or Siletz) Reservation
Siletz Restoration Act: building consensus for, 310–14; celebration of, 322–24; early stirrings, 307; introduction, 317; lands restored in *1980*, **326**; reservation planning, 324–29; Senate hearings, 317–21
Siletz Termination Act, 237, 292–301. *See also* termination
Siletz Tribal Council, 308–9, 358–61
Siletz Tribe (modern confederation): composition of, 182; and Cultural Department, 363–64, 365–67; and education, 249,

351–52, 502; and health care, 346–51; and land reacquisition, 342; and mental health, 348–50; and Natural Resources Department, 352–58, 503; and Run to the Rogue, 382–87, **383**, **384**, **385**; and self-governance, 358–62; and Treaty Day, 383
Siletz Tribes (individual tribes and bands), 12–31 passim; creation stories, 394; oral traditions, xiv, 389
—Alseas, 181, 182, 183, 201, 385
—Chetcoes, 34–35, 180, 182, 194, 262–65, 289
—Chinooks, 44–46, 48, 182
—Clatsops, 44–46, 48, 182
—Coos, 40–42, 181, 182, 198, 216, 218, 257–62, 264
—Coquilles, 289
—Galice/Applegate Athapaskans, 179, 180, 182
—Kalapuyas, 48, 50–53, 182, 266, 335
—Klickitats, 48–50, 182
—Lower Umpquas, 181, 182, 218, 258–62, 264, 385
—Molalas, 48, 49, 182, 266
—Shastas, 39, 178–79, 180, 182, 267
—Siletz (historical), 175
—Siuslaws, 182, 218, 258–62, 264, 385
—Takelmas, 36–39, 178–79, 180, 182
—Tillamooks, 179, 182, 214, 217–18, 262–65, 269, 289
—Tolowas, 34, 182, 254
—Tututnis, 17–32, 180–81, 262–65, 289
—Upper Umpquas, 182, 266
Siletz Valley School, 351–52, 502
Simmons, Frank, 221, **354**, 356, 386
Simmons, Frederick, 277
Simmons, Hardy, 277, 292
Simmons, Hoxie, 200, 221, 224, 241, **243**, **252**; request for self-determination, 288
Simmons, LaVera, 249
Simpson, Ben, 183, 211–13, **212**, 215–18; punishment, 194
Simpson, George, 63, 66, 67
Simpson, Jane, **197**
Siuslaws, 182, 218, 258–62, 264, 385
Slocum, John, 253
Slocum, Mary, 253

Tyee Jeff, 215

Tyee Jim, 81, 87–88, 98, 104, 149

Tyee Joe (Apserkahar), 74, 75, 82, 84, 86, **86**, 88, 408; and Indian Mary, 84

Tyee Joe Scott, 215

Tyee John (Siuslaw), 214–15

Tyee John (Tecumtum) (Shasta), 85, 88, 106, 112–13, **124**, 351, 384, 386, 387; homesick for Rogue River, 179–80; imprisonment at the Presidio, 192; last days on the reservation, 193; obituary, 450; and "Princess" Mary (daughter), **86;** speech, 127. *See also* Rogue River War

Tyee Joseph Duncan, 214, 458

Tyee Lympy, 88, 104, 119, 126, 127, 155, 209

Tyee Sam, 75, 82, 84, 88; homesick for Rogue River, 179

Tyee William, 191

U

Udall, Morris, 337

Uncertain Encounters: Indians and Whites at Peace and War in Southern Oregon, 1820s to 1860s (Douthit), 511

Upper Umpquas, 182, 266

V

van de Wetering, Stan, 355

Van Pelt, Amelia, 170

Van Pelt, Sam, 23, 35

Victor, Frances Fuller, 120, 128

Viles, Andrew, 359–61

Volkman, John, 309–12

W

Walling, Albert G., 74, 84, 115–16, 120, 122

Wanamaker, Rodman, **240**

Warm House Dance. *See* dances

wars, Indian, 106–7. *See also* Rogue River War

Washington, Andrew (Gippy), 277

Washington, Mary, **291**

Washington, Paul, 277

Wasson, George Bundy, Sr., 257–65, **259**, 271–72

Wasson, Wilfred, 288–89

Watkins, Arthur V., 277, **283**, 297–300; and termination, 283, 294–95; withholds claims payments, 289

Watts, Darvin, 277

Watts-Umatata, Ruth, 380

West, W. Richard, 382

Wicklund, Janet, 348-349

White, Richard, 512

Whitehead, Craig, **384**

Williams, Aggie, **291**

Williams, Edgar, 277

Williams, Joseph (Sharp), 277

Williams, Willie, 277

Wool, John E., 108–9, 113, 116, 125

World War I, 246, 307; Siletz servicemen in, 276–77

World War II, 247, 282, 357; Siletz servicemen in, 276–77

Wyatt, Wendell, 310

Y

Yachats, 385

Yanna, Jane, **251**

Yaquina, 385

Yaquina Bay, 42–43, 167, 201–3

Yaquina Strip, 1865 taking of, **205**

Youst, Lionel, 511–12

Z

Zakoji, Hiroto, 291, 499

Zimmerman, William, 280, 282

ABOUT THE AUTHOR

CHARLES WILKINSON IS THE MOSES LASKY PROFESSOR OF LAW at the University of Colorado School of Law. The University has named him Distinguished Professor, one of twenty-five on the Boulder campus. His fourteen books on law, history, and society in the American West and Indian Country include the standard law texts on American Indian Law and Federal Public Land Law: *Felix S. Cohen's Handbook of Federal Indian Law* (managing editor) (Michie-Bobbs Merrill, 1982); *American Indians, Time and the Law: Native Societies in a Modern Constitutional Democracy* (Yale, 1987); *The American West: A Narrative Bibliography and a Study in Regionalism* (Colorado, 1989); *The Eagle Bird: Mapping a New West* (Pantheon, 1992); *Crossing the Next Meridian: Land, Water, and the Future of the West* (Island, 1992); *Messages from Frank's Landing: Salmon, Treaties, and the Indian Way* (Washington, 1999); and *Blood Struggle: The Rise of Modern Indian Nations* (W. W. Norton, 2005).

Wilkinson has received campus-wide teaching awards at the University of Oregon and University of Colorado and student teaching awards at the Oregon, Michigan, and Colorado law schools. The National Wildlife Federation honored him with its National Conservation Award. In its ten-year anniversary issue, *Outside* magazine named him one of fifteen "People to Watch" in the American West. In 2004, the University of Oregon presented him with its Distinguished Service Award, and in the same year the High Desert Museum in Bend, Oregon, named him the recipient of the Earle A. Chiles Award, which honors thoughtful management of natural and cultural resources of the High Desert.

Federal, state, and tribal governments have called on Wilkinson to help resolve difficult public issues. He has taken on many special assignments for the U.S Departments of Agriculture, Interior, and Justice, including service as special counsel to the Department of the Interior solicitor for the drafting of the Presidential Proclamation, signed by President Clinton in September 1996, establishing the Grand Staircase–Escalante National Monument in Utah. His work as mediator includes negotiations between the National Park Service and the Timbisha Shoshone Tribe, concerning a tribal land base in Death Valley National Park (2000 congressional legislation ratified the resulting agreement); and successful negotiations between the City of Seattle and the Muckleshoot Indian Tribe that involved city water rights and threatened salmon runs in the Cedar River.

Wilkinson has four sons, Ben, Dave, Philip, and Seth, two grandchildren, Kahlil and Meera, and lives with his wife, Ann, in Boulder, Colorado, where he enjoys daily hikes with his faithful companion, Brittany spaniel Isabella.

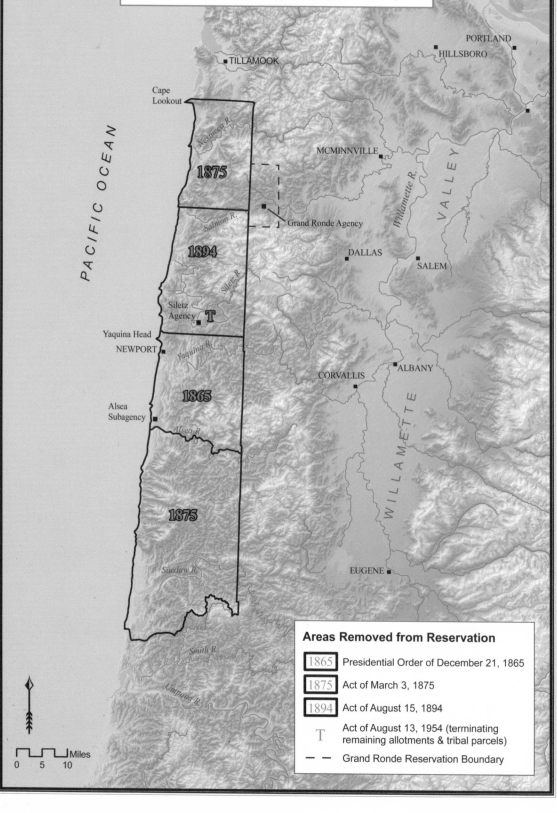

SILETZ TREATY RESERVATION REDUCTIONS

PACIFIC OCEAN

TILLAMOOK

Cape Lookout

Nestucca R.

1875

MCMINNVILLE

PORTLAND

HILLSBORO

Salmon R.

Grand Ronde Agency

1894

Siletz R.

Siletz Agency **T**

Yaquina Head
NEWPORT

Yaquina R.

1865

DALLAS

SALEM

Willamette R.

VALLEY

CORVALLIS

ALBANY

Alsea
Subagency

Alsea R.

1875

Siuslaw R.

WILLAMETTE

EUGENE

Smith R.

Umpqua R.

Areas Removed from Reservation

1865   Presidential Order of December 21, 1865

1875   Act of March 3, 1875

1894   Act of August 15, 1894

T   Act of August 13, 1954 (terminating remaining allotments & tribal parcels)

– – –   Grand Ronde Reservation Boundary

Miles
0   5   10